Labouring Lives:
Work and Workers in
Nineteenth-Century Ontario

EDITED BY PAUL CRAVEN

Labouring Lives:
Work and Workers in
Nineteenth-Century Ontario

A publication of the
Ontario Historical Studies Series
for the Government of Ontario
Published by University of Toronto Press
Toronto Buffalo London

Printed in Canada

ISBN 0-8020-0641-8 (cloth)
ISBN 0-8020-7594-0 (paper)

Printed on acid-free paper

Canadian Cataloguing in Publication Data

Main entry under title:

Labouring lives : work and workers in nineteenth-
century Ontario

(Ontario historical studies series)
Includes index.
ISBN 0-8020-0641-8 (bound) ISBN 0-8020-7594-0 (pbk.)

1. Working class – Ontario – History – 19th century.
2. Ontario – Social life and customs. I. Craven,
Paul, 1950–   . II. Series.

HD8109.052L3 1995   305.5′62′09713   C95-930586-6

This book has been published with the assistance of funds provided by the Government
of Ontario through the Ministry of Culture, Tourism and Recreation.

Contents

vi   Contents

The Ontario Historical Studies Series

For many years the principal theme in English-Canadian historical writing has been the emergence and the consolidation of the Canadian nation. This theme has been developed in uneasy awareness of the persistence and importance of regional interests and identities, but because of the central role of Ontario in the growth of Canada, Ontario has not been seen as a region. Almost unconsciously, historians have equated the history of the province with that of the nation and have often depicted the interests of other regions as obstacles to the unity and welfare of Canada.

The creation of the province of Ontario in 1867 was the visible embodiment of a formidable reality, the existence at the core of the new nation of a powerful if disjointed society whose traditions and characteristics differed in many respects from those of the other British North American colonies. The intervening century has not witnessed the assimilation of Ontario to the other regions in Canada; on the contrary, it has become a more clearly articulated entity. Within the formal geographical and institutional framework defined so assiduously by Ontario's political leaders, an increasingly intricate web of economic and social interests has been woven and shaped by the dynamic interplay between Toronto and its hinterland. The character of this regional community has been formed in the tension between a rapid adaptation to the processes of modernization and industrialization in modern Western society and a reluctance to modify or discard traditional attitudes and values. Not surprisingly, the Ontario outlook has been, and in some measure still is, a compound of aggressiveness, conservatism, and the conviction that its values should be the model for the rest of Canada.

From the outset the objective of the Series' Board of Trustees was to describe and analyse the historical development of Ontario as a distinct region within Canada. The Series includes biographies of several premiers, and thematic studies on the growth of the provincial economy, educational institutions, labour, welfare, the Franco-Ontarians, the Native Peoples, and the arts.

Since the 1960s much scholarly attention has been devoted to labour and working-class history in Ontario. In practice, however, historians have focused largely on the relations between urban craft workers and the emerging factory system in the post-Confederation period. In this volume, Professor Craven and his colleagues have incorporated detailed studies of working people's experiences in nineteenth-century Ontario in areas hitherto neglected or requiring reconsideration, such as farm labour, housework, lumbering, and industrial labour in factories or on the railways. They have sought to present 'a more capacious and nuanced account of the diversity of working people's experience than has been available,' hitherto. In so doing, they have illustrated the process of class formation, the nature and meaning of work, labour relations, and the unresolved contrast between the evidence of economic growth and the evident persistence of hardship and deprivation in late nineteenth-century Ontario.

Professor Craven and his contributors have written a well-integrated, scholarly, and judicious account of the working lives of many, perhaps the majority of, nineteenth-century Ontarians. They have indeed broken new ground. We hope that their example will encourage others to produce additional critical studies of unexplored areas in Ontario labour history.

The editors and the Board of Trustees are grateful to Paul Craven and his colleagues for undertaking this task.

GOLDWIN FRENCH
PETER OLIVER
JEANNE BECK
J.M.S. CARELESS, Chairman of the Board of Trustees

Toronto
August 1993

The corporation known as the Ontario Historical Studies Series ceased to exist on 31 August 1993. This volume was completed and approved for publication before 31 August 1993.

Acknowledgments

When I was approached to undertake this book, the editors of the Ontario Historical Studies Series had in mind a survey of the province's labour history in the nineteenth century. After consulting friends and colleagues, some of whom were later to find themselves recruited to the cause, I proposed that it commission instead 'an integrated collection of studies that break new ground and represent new approaches to the field. This would be a forward-looking project that would help establish an intellectual agenda for the rediscovery of the nineteenth century by exploring crucial though neglected aspects of the labour history.' This volume is the product of five years in which this undertaking consumed the lives and labours of a remarkably cooperative and forbearing group of authors. Acknowledgments are due to Lykke de la Cour, Barbra Lee, and Darryl Newbury, who compiled newspaper inventories of Barrie, London, and Ottawa for the general use of contributors to this volume; to Goldwin French, Jeanne Beck, and Peter Oliver of the Ontario Historical Studies Series editorial board for their encouragement and assistance; to the anonymous reviewers of the manuscript for their useful suggestions and the speed with which they delivered them; and to copy editor Freya Godard for her efforts to tame our prose. The rest is up to you. If this volume encourages you to imagine the past in unfamiliar ways, to further our explorations, challenge our assumptions, or disprove our conclusions, we will have achieved our goal.

PAUL CRAVEN

Contributors

Paul Craven teaches labour studies in the Social Science Division, York University. His publications include *'An Impartial Umpire': Industrial Relations and the Canadian State 1900–11* as well as articles and chapters on Canadian labour, business, and legal history.

Terry Crowley, a former agricultural labourer, teaches in the Department of History at the University of Guelph. His most recent publications include *Louisbourg: Atlantic Fortress and Seaport* and *Agnes Macphail and the Politics of Equality*.

Jeremy Webber is a member of the Institute of Comparative Law, in the Faculty of Law at McGill University. He has written extensively on the history of Canadian labour law and, more recently, on constitutional law.

Ian Radforth, a member of the Department of History at the University of Toronto, is the author of *Bushworkers and Bosses: Logging in Northern Ontario, 1900–1980*. He is now researching the social and cultural history of mid-nineteenth-century Ontario.

Lynne Marks teaches history at the University of Victoria. She has published articles on the history of women and education, social welfare, and the social history of religion.

Bettina Bradbury teaches history and women's studies at York University. She is the author of numerous articles and the editor of *Canadian Family History: Selected Readings*. She won the Sir John A. Macdonald

Prize and the Harold Adams Innis Prize for her book *Working Families: Age, Gender and Daily Survival in Industrializing Montreal.*

Craig Heron teaches social science and history at York University. He is co-editor (with Robert Storey) of *On the Job: Confronting the Labour Process in Canada* and author of *Working in Steel: The Early Years in Canada, 1883–1935* and *The Canadian Labour Movement: A Brief History.*

Labouring Lives:
Work and Workers in
Nineteenth-Century Ontario

Introduction

PAUL CRAVEN

The attempt to force upon a community like this the universal relation of master and servant, of capitalist and hired labourer, must be vain; it may be successful in a new country, from where the poor man cannot escape; – the trial is in vain here.

R.B. Sullivan and A. Baldwin
Executive Councillors, 1840

This is a book about working people in nineteenth-century Ontario.[1] Throughout the century the majority of people lived on farms or in small rural communities. Although they worked hard, most did not spend their lives working for others, or at least for others outside their own families. But waged work was not uncommon in nineteenth-century Ontario; in fact most working people probably earned wages at one time or another. Throughout much of the century, waged work was what they or other members of their families did to earn enough to start a farm or a business, or to help out in tough times, or to supplement family incomes during seasons when there was less to do about the farm, or when short term wages were exceptionally high. Waged labour was a necessary and familiar part of most working people's experience, but for many, at least until the last decades of the century, it was not the pivot of their social or economic lives.

The first problem that arises in writing about working people in nineteenth-century Ontario, therefore, is deciding whom to include. For the most part, writers of 'labour history' and 'working-class history' have barely mentioned the majority of the province's workers.

Labour history, though on its face the broader term, has nevertheless acquired by use a close focus on the collective economic and political institutions of the organized working-class movement, on trade unions, and on left-wing political parties.[2] For most working people in Ontario throughout most of the nineteenth century, these institutions would hardly have existed but for an occasional glimpse in the columns of a newspaper. While the emergence of the trade union movement and working-class politics are important chapters, they are by no means the whole story. If we limit our focus to workers in unions, the overwhelming majority of working people in nineteenth-century Ontario must remain in the shadows of history.

'Working-class history' emerged in the 1960s and 1970s out of a debate between institutional labour historians and the New Left.[3] It was profoundly influenced by E.P. Thompson's brilliant study of 'lived experience' in *The Making of the English Working Class* (1963). In its Canadian incarnation, this approach promised to open windows onto a hitherto neglected and even unsuspected past. It aimed to 'constitute a new distinctive synthesis' in which the history of labour 'becomes part of the history of society,' and in which class relations are understood to encompass not only the 'relationship of exploitation that exists between capitalist and wage labourer,' but also 'the beliefs, values, ideas and traditions that people carry with them in their lives and work.'[4] Despite the breadth of the program, however, most of the writing about nineteenth-century Ontario has concerned itself with the confrontation between male urban craft workers and the factory system in the last third of the century. While there are some exceptions, most of these studies have concentrated on a handful of trades in Hamilton and Toronto since Confederation.[5]

So circumscribed an account of nineteenth-century Ontario was not a necessary consequence of the working-class history project. To some extent it may be explained by the relative unpopularity of Ontario subjects and the growing interest in twentieth-century research topics in the last two decades. To some extent, working-class history was overtaken by other 'new social histories' that have so far been only imperfectly integrated with it: women's history, ethnic history, the history of migration. But the narrow focus of working-class history in practice was also due to some assumptions about the character of economic and social change in industrializing Ontario that drew attention away from the lived experience of significant numbers of working people in the province.

Working-class history, and the political economy that underpinned it, assumed a clutch of dichotomies that shaped its image of the nineteenth-century experience: the forced separation of town and country, of home and workplace, of property and labour power, by the process of industrialization. The result was the urban proletariat, a new social class defined by its dependence on waged work and its alienation from the means of production. It is well established that in the last third of the nineteenth century such a working class emerged in Ontario's factory cities, with significant consequences for politics and social organization. Nevertheless, to focus almost exclusively on this urban working class is to misunderstand the experience of working people in nineteenth-century Ontario as a whole.

This is so on at least two levels. First, as I have already suggested, for most people throughout most of the century wage labour was but one aspect of their strategy for making a living. In his contribution to this volume, Terry Crowley shows how working for others could be a routine step on the road to farm ownership that was the life goal of most nineteenth-century immigrants. Jeremy Webber stresses intermittent employment and multiple occupations in explaining why employment law in Ontario diverged from English models. Ian Radforth reminds us that lumbering, the province's leading industry after agriculture, depended mightily on a labour force that was employed elsewhere in the off season. To recapitulate, the experience of most working people throughout most of the century was largely rural. Wage labour was crucial to them, but they were not permanently or exclusively bound to it either in expectation or reality. To limit labour history to the urban working class of the last third of the century is to ignore the experience of this majority.

On another level, to view the working class through the bifocals of the traditional dichotomies is to risk distorting its experience. The separation of town and country has led to a concentration on the main cities, Toronto and Hamilton. Yet, as Craig Heron argues here, the factory system took root in the very different social environment of small towns throughout the province.[6] The separation of home and workplace has led to an emphasis on work process and shop-floor control. Yet, as Bettina Bradbury insists, the household remained at the centre of working-class survival strategies; and as Lynne Marks reminds us, working people staked out their identities as much by their religion and leisure as by their work. The separation of property and labour power, with its emphasis on the wage nexus and wage dependency, has not only diverted attention from the frequent success of a wage-based strategy for the acquisition of property through much of the century, but has also led to the neglect of non-waged forms of labour, in particular the work of women and children in the home. Of course, none of this is to say that there is nothing more to be learned from or about the workplace experience of skilled urban males: in my own contribution to this volume I try to explain the trajectory of labour-management relations on Hamilton's Great Western Railway by analysing its workers' experience and action in the light of the history of the business.

In the opening and closing chapters of this volume, Terry Crowley and Craig Heron argue (from different perspectives) that the 'universal' English and American models that informed much of the 'new working-class history' in the 1970s and 1980s are not perfectly applicable to understanding industrial transformation and the making of a working class in nineteenth-century Ontario. Those models alerted historians to certain important themes: the 'crisis of the craftsman,' the struggle for control of the shop floor, the emergence of an urban working-class culture. At the same time, they masked other themes that were at least as central to the experience of working people in nineteenth-century Ontario: the seasonal and transitory character of much paid employment; migration to and from the province, and within it; the persistence and reinvigoration of older forms of work relations alongside the new; the continuing significance of religion and ethnicity in working-class life; the crucial importance of the unpaid work of women and children in the industrial economy; the rural and small-town settings in which most economic activity took place – in short, the diversity of working people's lives. The point is not that Ontario is exceptional: it is rather that those models have been unable to account for much that is of interest about the complex interplay of economic development, class formation, and social change, even in the societies for which they were devised.

We have not tried in this volume to provide a comprehensive survey of work and workers in nineteenth-century Ontario. Such an overview will be truly useful only when more light has been cast into the shadows of the past and more work has been done to assimilate the various new approaches to nineteenth-century social history. Instead, we have tried to lay out some exploratory trails in a series of detailed studies of particular aspects of working people's experience that have been neglected or need to be reconsidered. These include the more populous occupations – farm labour, housework, lumbering – and the more pervasive institutions – the churches, the law, the family – as well as industrial labour in the factories and on the railways. We have not been able, even in this large volume, to complete the whole task we set ourselves. John Bullen's untimely death has meant that we still lack a thorough investigation of the paid and unpaid labour of children, although the topic is addressed in several of the studies published here. We had also hoped to include a study of construction labour in nineteenth-century Ontario.

All histories are political, but labour and working-class histories especially reveal the stamp of their times. In Canada, labour history emerged out of the struggle between communism and social democracy to shape the political left in the postwar years. The new working-class history was shaped by the shifting intellectual and ideological currents of the 1960s and 1970s, above all by a deep conviction about the liberating power of class consciousness and its potential for social transformation. The studies in this volume are inevitably influenced by the economic, social, and political context of the 1990s, including the world-wide collapse of communism and the brutal recurrence of ethnic, religious, and national conflict abroad, but also, in Ontario, the experience of the province's first social-democratic government, in a deindustrialized and recession-plagued economy. This volume does not offer a single grand theory of the lives of labouring people in nineteenth-century Ontario. The task of the historian is to make the past intelligible to the present, not to explain it away. Our goal has been to present a more capacious and nuanced account of the diversity of working people's experience than has been available before. The spirit of this volume is close to W.H. Sewell's recent call for a new labour history, 'more multiple in its theoretical strategies, more ironic in its rhetorical stance, and more open in its search for understanding.'[7] Despite the diversity of approaches, common themes emerge.

Class formation is necessarily a central theme. The working-class history of the 1960s and 1970s embraced what has become known as the proletarianization thesis, which in its crudest form proposed that the crucible of the modern working class was the struggle between skilled craftsmen and factory owners over control of the work process. In varying degrees, the chapters in this volume challenge many of the assumptions implicit in the proletarianization thesis. The factory was not the only or even the most important setting in which people forged their identities as workers. The hay field, the shanty, the back kitchen, and the locomotive shed were only a few of the many arenas in which working people constructed their worlds as they earned their livelihoods. Nor should it be assumed that their particular occupations and employments were inevitably more important to how working people saw themselves and understood their society than their sex, ethnicity, religion, or other affiliations. Moreover, whatever the terrain of social relations, struggle and opposition were no more frequent than accommodation and consent. None of this meant that working people, however diverse their identities, could not sometimes see themselves as a class with common interests. Their experience was no less authentic when they did not. A new understanding of nineteenth-century class formation will have to take much fuller account of the wide range of experience that shaped working people's consciousness and identity. It will have to assimilate and build upon recent work in women's history and the social history of immigration, and incorporate a sophisticated understanding of the geographic, occupational, and social mobility that played so prominent a part in many labouring lives.

A second pervasive theme is the nature and meaning of work itself.[8] The wage nexus no longer determines our understanding of work. Work performed within families and households is now as much a part of labour history as paid work outside the home. In her contribution to this volume, Bettina Bradbury argues that the emergence of wage labour involved a re-articulation of the links between households and the larger economy rather than the separation of home and workplace. At the same time, it is self-evident that different valuations were attached to different forms of work and to similar activities performed in different settings, so that the processes of constructing and revising the many meanings of work require investigation.

Perhaps no idea is more complex and deceptive in this connection than the notion of skill, whether in 'skilled worker' or 'skilled work.' Skill's claim to privilege was the subject of continuous redefinition and contention throughout the nineteenth century, as indeed it remains in the debate about training today. (For the nineteenth century, substitute the term 'apprenticeship' for 'training,' and see Jeremy Webber's and Craig Heron's discussions in this volume.) But skill, as a characterization of the meaning of work and the social situation of the worker, was bound up as well with other equally pervasive factors, notably gender, religion, and ethnicity. In combination their social meaning extended far beyond the locus of work into ideas about respectability, property, and citizenship, and into the seamless, subtly shaded web of culture. Similarly, working people constructed their identities out of the entirety of their experience. The working class made itself – in all its variety – in chapels, taverns, and neighbourhoods as well as at the point of (re)production. In her study of religion and leisure, Lynne Marks shows the complicated interweaving of these largely voluntary aspects of working-class life with the more mundane necessities of making a living.

A third broad theme is labour relations. Although working-class and labour historians have written at length about trade unionism and related state policy, it is only recently that historians have begun to explore in depth the individual employment contract, the relation of master and servant that permeated labour relations through most of the nineteenth century.[9] It is one of the ironies of the new labour history that as we learn more about the terms of employment, we become more sceptical about the importance and persistence of a 'feudal' personal labour relationship in early nineteenth-century Ontario and more persuaded of the significance of paternalism as a strategy of large employers after mid-century. Terry Crowley and Jeremy Webber argue persuasively that long-term engagements were the exception rather than the norm in most rural occupations. Paternalism was a more important labour-relations strategy in larger-scale employments where there was a premium on recruiting and retaining a skilled or experienced workforce. Loyalty to the company was mediated by personal relations with supervisors in lumbering, where foremen hand-picked the work gangs, often recruiting their relatives and neighbours, and on the Great Western Railway, where the client-patron relation and shared national and career backgrounds were important ingredients in the glue of paternalism. Paternalism became more common in factory industry after mid-century, where its form and importance also varied with changes in the labour market. The deep recession of the later 1870s shattered paternalism in the factories and on the railways. It was only rebuilt, albeit in a more impersonal and authoritarian guise, after the 'great upheaval' of the 1880s had run its course.

Questions of labour supply, recruitment, and retention are central to several of the chapters in this volume. Much work remains to be done as a wider range of jobs and work settings is investigated. Payment systems also receive new attention in these studies. Wage rates interacted with land prices to determine how long a new entrant might have to work for others before achieving a tenuous independence. When, where, and how wages were paid were important links between the household economy and the industrial workplace. While we are still far from a comprehensive account of wage rates, hours of labour, duration of employment, occupational and geographic mobility, and patterns of retention and re-employment through the whole period, these studies show the importance of a detailed understanding of labour markets for nineteenth-century labour history.

Before the 1880s, trade unionism was to be found only in the largest cities, and even there in only a handful of trades. Collective labour relations could take other forms, of course, ranging from bloody riot – a not uncommon method of allocating work and protesting pay cuts in canal and railway construction around mid-century – to the 'binding supplication'[10] implicit in petitions for improved wages and benefits. An angry and determined group of irreplaceable workers could wage a successful strike without a union, as the Great Western shop crafts proved in 1856.

As they went on to show in 1872, still greater successes were possible when there was a union, even without a strike. The brutal recession of the later 1870s dealt a serious blow to the craft-union movement centred in Toronto and Hamilton, so that its legislative gains were not accompanied by organizational ones. In this volume, Jeremy Webber assesses the legislative changes, I re-examine the nine-hours movement among railway workers and describe the impact of the recession, and Craig Heron recounts the limits of craft organization. It was only in the 1880s with the emergence of the Knights of Labor that trade unionism reached far into industrial Ontario. Craig Heron views the Knights' success as a response to the breakdown of industrial paternalism, while Lynne Marks analyses the order's appeal in the context of such cultural phenomena as the Salvation Army, the temperance movement, and the fraternal lodges. Nevertheless, most of the Knights' organizational gains proved short-lived in the economic turmoil of the late 1880s.

This raises another recurring theme and another open debate. The evidence of the labour history – the evidence of wages and working conditions, strikes and unemployment, the persistence of labour protest, and the fragility of labour organization – points to prolonged periods of economic hardship in the last third of the century. This inference is not new, but it stands in stark contrast to the current view among economic historians, boldly stated elsewhere in this series, that 'it is absolutely certain that the province's industrial economy did not stagnate or retrogress for any extended period' from 1870 on.[11] There are remarkable discrepancies between the stories told by aggregate statistics of economic growth and those told by the experience of working people in the last third of the century. They will be resolved only by much more detailed research to uncover conditions in a wide range of industries and locations. Craig Heron maps out the debate in the final chapter of this volume.

NOTES

1 The province was officially known as Upper Canada until the Act of Union, Canada West from 1841 to Confederation, and Ontario from 1867 on. For simplicity I use its modern name here.

2 See, for example, H.A. Logan, *Trade Unions in Canada: Their Development and Functioning* (Toronto: Macmillan 1948); Charles Lipton, *The Trade Union Movement of Canada, 1827–1959* (Montreal: Canadian Social Publications 1967); Martin Robin, *Radical Politics and Canadian Labour, 1880–1930* (Kingston: Industrial

Relations Centre, Queen's University 1968); and Eugene Forsey, *Trade Unions in Canada 1812–1902* (Toronto: University of Toronto Press 1982).

3 Although I have emphasized here the objectives of the latter group, organized as the Committee on Canadian Labour History, it must not be imagined that the debate was one-sided. See, for example, D.J. Bercuson, 'Through the Looking Glass of Culture: An Essay on the New Labour History and Working Class Culture in Recent Canadian Historical Writing,' *Labour/Le Travailleur* 7 (Spring 1981), 95–112; and K. McNaught, 'E.P. Thompson vs Harold Logan: Writing about Labour and the Left in the 1970's,' *Canadian Historical Review* 62, no. 2 (June 1981), 141–68.

4 G.S. Kealey and Peter Warrian, eds, *Essays in Canadian Working Class* History (Toronto: McClelland & Stewart 1976), 7f.

5 See Bryan Palmer, *A Culture in Conflict: Skilled Workers and Industrial Capitalism in Hamilton, Ontario, 1860–1914* (Montreal: McGill-Queen's University Press 1979); and Gregory Kealey, *Toronto Workers Respond to Industrial Capitalism 1867–1892* (Toronto: University of Toronto Press 1980). In G.S. Kealey and B.D. Palmer, *Dreaming of What Might Be: The Knights of Labor in Ontario, 1880–1900* (Cambridge: Cambridge University Press 1982; Toronto: New Hogtown Press 1987), these authors recognized 'the necessity of pursuing the Kings of Labor into their eastern and western Ontario lairs, extending our collective work beyond the confines of Toronto and Hamilton' (xiii). Few of the articles about nineteenth-century Ontario published in the journal *Labour/Le Travailleur* (from 1984 on, *Labour/Le Travail*) have ventured beyond the big-city working class. Apart from theoretical articles and studies of law and policy the main exceptions have been studies of canal labour and of the feminization of certain occupations. Interestingly enough, *Labour/Le Travail* has presented a more diverse treatment of Atlantic Canada and the West than of Ontario. Although *Labour/Le Travail* remains the leading journal of Canadian labour and working-class history, important contributions have also appeared in *Historical Papers* (now the *Journal of the Canadian Historical Association*), the *Canadian Historical Review*, *Acadiensis*, *Histoire Sociale/Social History*, and other places.

6 See also Joy Parr, *The Gender of Breadwinners: Women, Men, and Change in Two Industrial Towns, 1880–1950* (Toronto: University of Toronto Press 1990).

7 William H. Sewell, Jr, 'Toward a Post-materialist Rhetoric for Labor History,' in L.R. Berlanstein, ed., *Rethinking Labor History: Essays on Discourse and Class Analysis* (Urbana, Ill.: University of Illinois Press 1993), 35.

8 The best recent overview is the introductory essay in Patrick Joyce, ed., *The Historical Meanings of Work* (Cambridge: Cambridge University Press 1987), 1–30.

9 For a brief overview of the international significance of master and servant legislation, see Douglas Hay and Paul Craven, 'Master and Servant in England and the Empire: A Comparative Study,' *Labour/Le Travail* 31 (spring 1993), 175–84.

10 I am indebted for this phrase to Ken Swan and the collective bargaining committee of the Canadian Association of University Teachers, c. 1980.

11 Ian M. Drummond, *Progress without Planning: The Economic History of Ontario from Confederation to the Second World War* (Toronto: University of Toronto Press 1987), 106.

Rural Labour

TERRY CROWLEY

One winter morning in the late 1880s George Arthur Disbrowe headed for his accustomed job cutting wood in a cedar swamp near Aylmer in southern Ontario. Unusually pensive, he reflected on his lot in life since his father, an Anglican clergyman, had sent him and three of his brothers to Canada to farm. They had arrived in 1873 just before the onset of a depression that was to last until 1879. After the farm enterprise collapsed within twelve months, George Disbrowe tried to open a school to teach other immigrants how to avoid his fate, but it also failed and he became a farm labourer. Anxious to be his own boss, Disbrowe rented a farm near the shores of Lake Erie with another young Englishman named Frank Ingram. Both of them married, Disbrowe in 1878 choosing Melissa Monteith, the daughter of poor northern Irish who had settled on a hundred-acre tract during the high immigration of the 1840s. When the house proved too small to accommodate two expanding families, Ingram bought out Disbrowe, and the latter became a day labourer in Aylmer. Wages were so low that the young family only managed to survive by keeping a cow, a few chickens, and a vegetable garden. The children got odd jobs when they were old enough, and a little cash was set aside. By 1887 George Disbrowe had acquired a team of horses and secured a job hauling milk to the local condenser factory. As dairy production was highly seasonal, he continued to pick up other work when he could and sawed wood during the cold months for a dollar each twelve-hour day. So many years in Ontario had produced so little. A grim shadow of doubt engulfed him as he entered the swamp woodlot that day. George Disbrowe lay down in the snow and cried.[1]

The plight of a despondent man no longer able to contain his despair contrasts sharply with the buoyant optimism of a young woman his own age hurt by the slighting of her amorous intentions. Born in 1859, Elizabeth Smith belonged to a Winona farm family that employed a half dozen field hands in spring, a domestic servant, and a governess. Their privileged economic position, which later saw her brother, E.D. Smith, become the largest fruit grower and nursery owner in the Niagara district, allowed the determined young woman to train initially as a rural school teacher. At twenty years of age she was attracted to a neighbouring youth who lived in less fortunate circumstances. Elizabeth Smith wanted to capture his attentions totally, but he was struggling, thin and depressed, to support a family where the father was unemployed. A 'shame, a heartless shame,' she reflected with a typically young, middle-class petulance. 'A boy [is] kept on supporting his people when rather the father should have helped him.' In ascribing suitable roles to men living in different economic circumstances, Smith's remarks reveal as much about differing class points of view as they do about gender. Other diary entries were equally conventional in expressing some of the most cherished middle-class beliefs of her era. 'Sunday I was over the farm, in the vineyard, over the house,' Elizabeth Smith recorded in her diary. 'The place looks so well & all the farm so thriving – looks like the 19th century.'[2]

CONFIGURING RURAL LABOUR HISTORY

In their thoughts and actions, George Disbrowe and Elizabeth Smith gave expression to two radically different versions of Ontario's rural history that have been reflected in its historiography. On the one hand, highly quantified statistical soundings of local areas have portrayed the province's rural social development as a series of crises resulting from overpopulation and lack of land in southern Ontario by the 1850s, shrinking economic opportunities among both anglophone and francophone farmers that produced impoverishment in the Ottawa Valley by 1881, and a lack of employment that drove people to move to the United States and elsewhere in the decades preceding the First World War.[3] In contrast to this portrait of the unsettling of the Ontario countryside by a half century of recurring trauma, economic historians have found an environment open to technical change and characterized by expanding production and increased productivity. They conclude that the development of the province in the nineteenth century was a 'success story.'[4]

Perhaps more than any other approach, it is the quantitative studies that have most fully influenced our understanding of rural history. While immensely useful, these studies have sometimes produced a seemingly lifeless world that accords too little place to human agency or individual experience. Since statistics, like nature, do not give up their secrets readily, in historical quantitative studies much depends on the nature of the available data, the opening and concluding dates chosen, and the assumptions made. Most of all, the conclusions may be based on scientific theories, formulated in other times and places, that are inappropriate historically. Moreover, as quantitative investigations must go where the data lie, the number of questions that can be asked about the past is narrowed. As geographical mobility remained high in Ontario, it has also been difficult to follow people between manuscript censuses. Only a quarter of the rural population in Peel County in 1861 had remained ten years in one location, and the largest census linkage study, covering a section of south-central Ontario between 1861 and 1871, cannot trace 45 per cent of the people in its sample.[5]

The study of rural labour in nineteenth-century North America must move beyond these bounds while not ignoring their import. The manner in which farmers and rural labourers spoke in letters, diaries, account books, surveys, newspapers, and journals is an important way of augmenting our knowledge. These sources are particularly valuable for Ontario, which, unlike Quebec, did not develop a rural anthropological tradition. Such records need to be approached cautiously in view of the position in society of those who created them. The agricultural press that made its appearance early in the century served as the mouthpiece primarily for improving farmers, but increasingly its pages were open to all. After the provincial Bureau of Agriculture was begun in 1852, the government was concerned almost exclusively with commercial farmers who would feed the cities and produce exports. This same middle- and upper-class outlook also pervaded the extensive travel literature and information guides that influenced historical writing profoundly in subsequent generations. Numerous collections of family papers not intended for publication allow historians to transcend this viewpoint if they are trained to see the economic condition of their creators. But other means must be sought to glimpse the lives of illiterates and the largely destitute, who left few records of their own.

The history of rural labour has seldom been studied in Canada as a subject in its own right. The wide diffusion of property ownership in the Ontario countryside from the beginnings of its settlement blurred the social, but not the economic, distinctions within rural society. The distinctive patterns of rural social stratification in the province paralleled those in the United States rather than in Britain or western Europe. Labouring in return for wages was often a waystation on the road to achieving proprietorship. As ownership, which was often accompanied by indebtedness, did not end manual work, there was no great gulf separating farmers from labourers and from labourers who aspired to become farmers until cheap land became scarce towards the end of the century's third quarter. Consequently, the history of rural labour in Ontario begins with immigration and settlement, but evolves into an examination of the factors that prompted differentiation and the divisions that came to characterize the countryside.

Rural areas are most often characterized by physical, though not necessarily social, isolation, rudimentary or small-scale organizations, seasonal labour, unremitting work, and an element of resolution in the face of adversity.[6] In many rural environments, such as Ontario's, agriculture predominated. Farm populations interacted regularly with towns and villages, but on the fringes of agricultural settlement agrarian life also intertwined with resource industries such as lumbering. While rural areas include villages and small towns, those are not the primary subject of this section.[7] Working relations and conditions in rural environments were usually paternalistic and were not always based on strictly economic criteria. While paternalism implied a mutuality that was often expressed in cooperative and close working relations, its inherent inequality came increasingly under fire when alternatives presented themselves.[8] Work, as social production, assumed many forms in rural settings. Farms, in particular, were economic units where all family members contributed to productive activity, although this also occurred among lower-income earners elsewhere. While the tasks accorded to each sex varied with age, ethnicity, race, and economic circumstances, greater gender specificity in work developed as the nineteenth century advanced.

The transition from feudalism to capitalism – or from societies based on orders to ones predicated on classes – has figured heavily in the historiography of the United States, Europe, and Quebec, but Ontario's rural history cannot be described in these terms.[9] The province was largely newborn, apart from its small and scattered aboriginal population, its tiny French settlements, and the diverse customs, values, and institutions that nineteenth-century immigrants brought with them. At first the availability of land inhibited the formation of the sizeable body of destitute labourers seen in so many other parts of the world. The value of labour was enhanced, while the forest-clearing experience and physically hard farm life forged a commonality of experience. When the best acreages had become fully occupied by the third quarter of the century, agrarian expression assumed a collective form, but in a manner that differed substantially from the political conflicts that had led to the Rebellion of 1837.[10] Farmers who saw themselves as being engaged in a business activity organized to advance their interests as a distinct sector in society, while improved material standards permitted some redefinitions in the nature of women's and men's work in agriculture.

At the same time immigration slowed and the focus for new agricultural settlements shifted northward to less desirable lands in the Canadian Shield that attracted fewer people. Rising prosperity and better communications in southern and eastern Ontario brought many rural dwellers more fully into a money economy. Farm families, which had traditionally functioned as producers, became consumers. Rural society solidified as it aged, and new opportunities lured youth in increasing numbers to other parts. A highly fragmented and stratified rural Ontario emerged, although agriculture remained the foremost sector in the economy of the province. The dividing point in this transformation was marked by the founding in the 1870s of the Grange – the first significant provincial voluntary organization of farmers by and for themselves. Thereafter many women and men in the Ontario farm community saw themselves as a distinct social entity. Labourers also came to view their position as separate from that of their employers, but they lacked the means to develop effective counter-organizations.

From its inception, rural Ontario was characterized by economic differentiation. The varying amounts of capital that immigrants brought with them, their differing social outlooks, the lack of scientific advice about which land was best suited to agriculture, the uneven penetration of market mechanisms, and the inequalities inherent in commercial exchanges served to stratify rural society. The general rise, until 1880, of land values, and the expansion of commercial agriculture after mid-century eventually marginalized small producers and rural dwellers dependent on casual labour. Those who had engaged in agriculture mainly for domestic purposes and who had often laboured for others left the rural areas in increasing numbers. Mechanization, which was both a cause and a consequence of the new consumerism, served to depress wages. No longer was wage labour the principal means of gaining proprietorship, partially because land could be obtained more cheaply in the Canadian or American west. Higher incomes and better working conditions could also be found in the cities. Governments responded by channelling new arrivals into the farm sector, but as the sources of immigration had changed, fewer wanted to work in the countryside and more were attracted to cities.

THE EARLY NINETEENTH CENTURY

The traditions inherited by the province presupposed a civil society separate from government, and market economies based on commercial exchange. Under the model town concept of Governor John Graves Simcoe, Toronto was to be sustained by a ring of farms hacked out of the surrounding forests. And when the colony's first newspaper appeared in 1793, it contained a notice forecasting a brewery in Niagara with the inducement that 'whoever will sow Barley and cultivate their Land so that it will produce grain of good quality, they may be certain of a Market in the fall at one DOLLAR on delivery.'[11] By the 1820s merchants at shipment points in the countryside were well aware of wheat prices over 150 kilometres away and were sharply attuned to what their competition was offering. Henry Nelles, a Grimsby wholesaler, constantly adjusted his prices for pork and wheat by as little as a quarter penny a bushel to keep his old customers and to induce farmers 'to sell at the market price.'[12] The separation of state and civil society, and reliance on the market expressed the pluralistic traditions of British and American democracies. Land, labour, and commodities were bought and sold, but the mercantilist traditions of close market regulation by local governments in order to protect the consumer were especially strong in Ontario during its earliest years.[13] On the other hand, the older traditions of wage fixing by municipalities do not appear to have been transposed, nor do the British poor board and settlement system.[14] Ethnic, racial, and religious diversity flourished within this environment, as did occupational pluralism. In order to survive, many people worked at a variety of jobs in their lifetimes, as they had in their country of origin.

Rural Ontarians lived in perpetual motion. The population of the province, which had stood at about 60,000 before the War of 1812, nearly doubled between 1828 and 1833, reached 427,000 by 1840, and again mushroomed to 952,000 a decade later.[15] As the border to the United States was open, there were no boundaries to limit immigration. 'No immigrants reach us,' wrote a gentleman farmer near Belleville, bemoaning the high cost of help in 1852 when the number of new arrivals was reaching its apogee, 'they are swallowed up in the vortex of this vast continent.'[16] Having already come so far, immigrants were prepared to move again in search of better economic opportunities. A close eye was trained on developments in the United States, and some ethno-religious groups such as the Mennonites frequently visited their parent communities in Pennsylvania to assess the economic opportunities.[17] Within the province, notable population movements occurred, beginning in the 1820s, away from the St Lawrence and Great Lakes waterfront and from east to west.

Wherever cheap land or jobs beckoned, people moved, with significant effects on family relationships. 'I shall say nothing of my feelings of parting with him,' a Brockville area mother wrote as her son moved to take up better land in southwestern Ontario. 'I may never see him more on earth. None can tell what a mother feels when obliged to part with her children.'[18] But laments were less common than an acceptance of physical separation, although sentiments of affection remained. 'Nothing strange or important has happened since you left,' wrote an Irish woman to her husband in Ontario, where he was ascertaining the prospects for his family to follow. 'James Phillips was in Quebec and home again; he is out of a situation at present ... Johnston Gregory is in a good situation in New York and his Mistress is going out again in March. Since you left we have had a letter from Isabella. She is in a town called new London Canada West. My brother-in-law is in the township of Adelaide, Canada West. Has got a farm of land; 100 acres in it.'[19] The migratory fever was increased by the California gold rush of 1849.

Labour was costly in early Ontario. Recently arrived from the United States, Hannah Jarvis discovered that the wages of artisans and servants were higher here, noting that she doubted some carpentry would go ahead, 'labour being so immensely dear, a dollar and a half the usual price for a man, or if you have him by the month, eight dollars and find them with victuals.'[20] Most people worked freely, but the Loyalists had brought African-American slaves with them and there was some enslavement of Indians. In 1793 Ontario became the first and only British North American colony to legislate against slavery. Chattel servitude was not abolished, but provisions for the emancipation of slaves at the age of twenty-five were enacted in legislation prefaced 'Whereas it is unjust that a people who enjoy freedom by law should encourage the introduction of slaves ...'[21] Society was divided by more than the division between free and unfree; it was also stratified into those who worked for others, a middle section that farmed for themselves (with the help of their children), and a few that lived off the labour of those they hired. In one Loyalist township, the grasp of the top 10 per cent of the taxpayers on a third of the wealth remained secure from 1784 to 1820, although the bottom half increased its share from 10 to 17 per cent.[22] But as land prices remained low, the key difference among farm families in the early nineteenth century was less the size of their holdings than the amount of land that was cleared. A graph of arable acreage per farm in selected townships reveals that there was little change in the pattern before 1842 (See figure 1). Farms with fewer than twenty arable acres varied between 31 and 43 per cent of the total; the highpoint was due to post-Napoleonic immigration. Those in the intermediate range of twenty to forty-nine cleared acres stood between 36 and 43 per cent. Large farms with more than eighty arable acres never constituted more than 7 to 8 per cent.[23]

IMMIGRATION AND RURAL SETTLEMENT

Studies of immigrant adjustment to the land and occupational mobility,

FIGURE 1 Percentage Distribution of Farm Size, Ontario, 1812–42

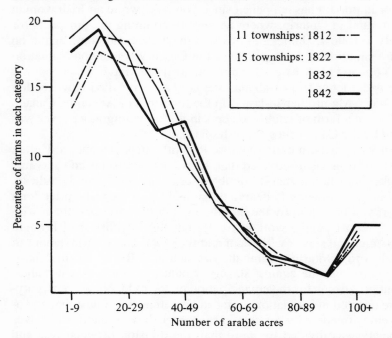

SOURCE: Peter A. Russell, 'Attitudes to Social Structure and Social Mobility in Upper Canada (1815–1840) (PhD thesis, Carleton University 1981), 74.

particularly among the Irish, the largest ethnic group to arrive in the province up to 1857, have reinforced the view that before 1871 neither religion nor ethnicity was a barrier to settlement or becoming a farmer in rural Ontario.[24] It is clear, however, that the massive influx of nearly half a million immigrants from the end of the Napoleonic Wars to mid-century increased the disparities in wealth. In comparison to the United States, central Canada attracted relatively larger numbers of people with lower incomes because fares for steerage passage in timber ships returning to Quebec were relatively cheap. As this unprecedented human flow gathered momentum before declining after 1857, the number of poorer immigrants increased further. In 1846, for example, 98 per cent of people landing at Quebec were steerage passengers. Labourers constituted 54 per cent of the arrivals, while 39 per cent were farmers and agricultural workers. Occupational breakdowns for subsequent years showed that most people came from these ranks, augmented by skilled craftspeople and domestic servants.[25] About the movement of people from the United States or through the United States to Canadian soil we know less, although it has been estimated that about 12,000 Germans had entered Ontario via New York by 1848 and that 10,000–12,000 Germans, mostly poor, settled in Canada between 1850 and 1857.[26] Americans of African descent also arrived in small numbers until the passing of the 1850 Fugitive Slave Law in the United States. By the time of the Civil War, some 20,000–40,000 African Americans had become residents.

Even if immigrants were the more prosperous or resolute elements within their home societies, as were the escaped slaves or the Scottish Highlanders who settled Glengarry County in eastern Ontario, their resources were frequently unequal to their expenditures upon arrival, especially if they chose the arduous route to acquiring land for farming. Few records provide information about the cash that immigrants carried with them. But evidence for the Irish during the second high water mark of post-Napoleonic immigration in the 1830s does show that the vast majority failed to reach the $250 to $300 necessary to secure a passage and see a farm through the first winter.[27] Consequently, many required assistance when they arrived. One writer from London in 1832 observed that the Irish in the area 'generally come in poor' and that they 'labour under many disadvantages.'[28] The famine emigration of 1847, which drew two and a half times as many people as the previous year, worsened the situation further by attracting immigrants from more remote parts of Ireland that had less connection with the country's commercial economy. Many had less money and fewer skills; and more were Roman Catholics. Similarly, whereas the German Americans that settled in the Niagara, Waterloo, and Toronto regions were considered to be generally prosperous by the 1820s, many of those that came directly from Europe during a migration that peaked in the 1850s were East Elbian peasants freed by land reforms, or refugees from Hanover, Saxony, Silesia, and Alsace-Lorraine fleeing conscription, coal mining, or the factory system. A quarter of the Germans landing at Quebec required official assistance and lack of financial resources was probably one of their reasons for settling in Ontario rather than proceeding on to the United States.[29] African Americans, some 60 per cent of whom seem to have been ex-slaves, suffered even greater handicaps. Many arrived as destitute as their white counterparts, although the vast majority established themselves without the help of the voluntary organizations working on their behalf. So unfamiliar were they with commercial accords that some lost their lands because they did not understand that annual payments in lease-purchase agreements were applied against interest rather than principal.[30]

The settlement of the southern and eastern Ontario countryside often afforded immigrants the opportunity to reverse the detrimental effects that industrialization and change in their home societies had wrought in their lives. The decision to move long distances represented an adaptive strategy designed to ensure the family's survival through greater material security. The purchase of a farm, or even simple squatting, afforded the best prospect of supporting oneself throughout the year rather than being totally reliant on the highly seasonal demand for labour. Land provided economic and social security. In Ontario, a Scots woman wrote, 'a man can make independent of the world & have something for old age & to leave to his family.'[31] Another, the granddaughter of a former groom in Germany, said that her grandfather 'felt that he'd like to own a house of his own, and he had in mind that he would like to own a farm.'[32] Farming was 'not a business that fortunes can be hastily made,' wrote one immigrant in Huron County after six years of experience, 'but it is a very shure system. There is no risk of losing,' he suggested, 'and a good opportunity of improving property and making more of it. All the necessities and even the luxeries of life is in abundance.'[33] Most Ontario farms were so rough and limited in output as not to be comparable to their European counterparts.

That the countryside attracted people from diverse backgrounds accounted for the great variation in agricultural practices. The degree to which new farmers engaged primarily in subsistence or commercial agriculture depended on their background, their location in relation to outlets for crops, the state of transportation, and the vitality of the market economy nearest them. Prior experience with commercial agriculture was frequently a determining element. 'I only wish you were all in Canada'; an immigrant in the London area wrote to his family in 1855, 'if you had been here a dozen years ago, your fortune would have been made, and you in early and comfortable circumstances, your own landlord, as hundreds of Scottish farmers are here. There are great numbers of agriculturalists from Perth, Banf, and Aberdeenshire ... They are all papists of course, but nice folks.'[34] Many people possessed no such skills. 'I likewise think there is no farmer here who has been bred to it at home,' a former agriculturalist in the Kingston area in the 1830s concluded.[35] Another near Toronto had written in 1825: 'Farming is very little attended to here with any propriety. Ploughing is most wretchedly performed, seldom any manure is used, and, owing to the very favourable climate, if the seed be thrown into the ground any way, it gives up a crop. Owing to high wages, low prices for grain, almost everyone has his own land. Few raise more than their own consumption.'[36] Even when there were products to sell and a means to get them to outlets, markets were sometimes unavailable. 'No *cash* for it,' a gentleman farmer noted of his pork in 1848, 'nor for any kind of produce except wheat.'[37]

Although relative security of tenure, low taxes on land, and the absence of a tithe enhanced the social status of property owners in Upper

Canada, some people consciously rejected the class divisions and deferential modes of conduct in the societies they had abandoned. One immigrant who resented such practices recounted how 'she and her people' were no longer required 'to curtsy when she met the gentry on the street' as they had been before leaving Cornwall in England.[38] 'The poor are made of the same materials as the rich,' it was observed of the Perth area in eastern Ontario in 1824, 'and imitate their conduct when it is in their power. Our half-pay officers and other gentry in the village having a ball at the commencement of the year, the mechanics, farmers, and others aping the conduct of their superiors got up two balls to which most of the servants in the village were invited.'[39]

The mental and material transition to a new environment was neither easy nor uniform. For people with little money, the first concern during a move was for basic food and clothing. 'I saw more want and privation of the people coming to settle the new township,' one woman recalled of the 1820s, 'than I could describe. It appeared to me, if it had not been for the potash that they made from clearing the land, they would have starved. But they boiled and made potash, and sold it in Belleville, and it kept them alive.'[40] Referring to a family that had moved from Perth to Huron County to take up the new lands being cleared in the western part of the province, one farmer wrote: 'I wanted to know how they were geting along. He says they have planty to eate and something to war, but says nothing about what crops they raise nor what stalk they have.'[41] Wages and prices were naturally prominent concerns. A husband who had preceded his wife and children from Ireland in 1848, working as an agricultural labourer and then as a school teacher for a short time, related that there was 'no question, my Dearest Jane, which of the two countryes is best for parties suited as we are. Here every kind of living is four times cheaper and at the same time work of every kind is trebly paid. A family of children has infinitely better prospects of being provided for and receiving excellent education.'[42] Asked by his brother what he thought of southwestern Ontario, one carpenter-turned-farmer replied: 'It is a land of Hard labour both summer and winter. Summer is the worst, but wages is good and so is the Board and a steady man will make money.'[43]

FARMING AND WAGE LABOUR

Immigrants with limited means, whatever their racial or ethnic background, were forced to practise their craft or to hire out either before acquiring a farm or while they were in the process of settlement. The demand for trades, such as stone masonry, carpentry, and cooperage, that required apprenticeship training was high until the effects of continuing immigration were felt and the panic of 1837 arrived, although the call for skills that were picked up less formally (e.g., shoemaking and weaving) was considerably more variable as early as the 1820s.[44] Trades were hierarchical in status and remuneration. Wages varied further according to region, skill, season, and demand, and women domestics earned one-half, or less, as much as male agricultural labourers. 'A blacksmith and a shoemaker are excellent trades here,' a farmer commented in 1827. 'The wages of labourers has been on the rise from 12 to 14 doll. the month ... a servant girl from 4 to 6 dollars.'[45] A German immigrant to New York City in 1831 recounted not only how he ended up in Waterloo County but also why he remained:

In Buffalo we stayed eight days. We found no employment there and continued on to Canada. Here we found work. Wilhelm Beilstein now works at an inn in Schippenwege; he earns nine dollars a month there. I was working for a farmer. He paid me 8 dollars a month. When one month was up we walked to Waterloo Township. Here I am working for a cooper. In winter months I earn 9 dollars a month, but more in the summer. This is when a cabinet maker earns a dollar a day, that is two and a half guilders. A blacksmith earns fifteen to sixteen dollars a month. A tailor gets 5 dollars for a formal suit, cartwrights and shoemakers-cobblers are also well paid. A farmhand earns 110–120 dollars a year. A woman earns 4–5 dollars a month.'[46]

Wherever new land opened up, remuneration was high owing to competing demands. The 'wedges here is better than at home,' wrote a farm labourer trying to acquire a stake in 1845, 'i wrought 1 mounth with a man at three dollars which is twelve of your shillings and had bed and board. The like of it is not in Bequham house.'[47] Even after buying a farm, a man often continued to hire out while other members of his family did the farm work; or he might provide services such as mechanized threshing, which brought 'good wedges for men that is no mackanacks.'[48]

Because attempts to collect consistent data on farm wage labour did not begin until the twentieth century, only rough measures can be employed, especially for men. Prices were quoted by the hour, day, month, season, and year. Male rates for more than a month generally included room, board, and washing, but they might also include sewing, or the farmer might provide a cow and garden plot for the labourer's family. Semi-skilled occupations such as grain cutting at harvest paid the highest, with seasonal workers earning more per month than year-round employees, although some farmers paid a lower monthly rate in winter. Wages also varied by region; in areas just opening to agriculture, they were higher because of the lack of labourers.

Farm labour wages for men rose in the 1820s, when they were competing with such projects as the building of the Erie and Welland canals, edging up slowly from ten to twelve dollars a month in the 1830s to between ten and eighteen in the 1850s – a rate comparable with what Ottawa Valley shantymen received in 1853.[49] In contrast, the majority of wage-earning women, for whom domestic service constituted the principal employment, saw their wages eroded over the period from 1820 to 1840 to such an extent that domestic service is best viewed as a chronic form of underemployment. Comparisons between men and women are extremely difficult, particularly as many female servants were young, but women farm domestics started employment at one-third the male agricultural wage rate and might only reach one-half that earned by men, even though their work often included dairying and poultry labour in addition to housework. Women made as little as two and a half dollars a month in 1845, and those with experience as much as five dollars by 1855.

As a wide variety of menial jobs were available to those who were mobile, labouring often acted as a spur to other occupations or the hiring of others. Such was the case with Joseph Elson, born in 1804 in Markham. His German parents were so poor that their family dressed in tattered deer skins, as did many of those eking out a bare subsistence in early Ontario. As a boy, he was engaged as a farm labourer with the proviso that he be sent to school for six months of the year. Later he was apprenticed to a miller and worked as a store clerk. Then he became a wood chopper and a pedlar selling hazelnuts and small items. Later he went to New York in search of employment, but, arriving too late to work on the construction of the Erie Canal, he walked some five hundred kilometres back home with many of those returning once the project had been completed in 1825. He took up chopping again and earned enough money to pay a man to teach him pottery making, the skill that finally led to a series of less physically demanding occupations that included farming and part ownership in a small distillery. Though he hired men to work with him in both enterprises, Elson never made the transition from employee to employer. 'I was forever perplexed,' he wrote, 'if I hiered men to work on the farm. The work was sure to go wrong there and if I was out of the [pottery] shop, it was sure to go wrong there.'[50]

Farmers often earned additional income by hiring themselves out unless, like settlers in north Wellington County from the Isle of Uist in the Outer Hebrides, they came from non-commercial cultures and continued to live on the margins of subsistence. The main sources of work were forest clearing, agriculture, domestic or farm service, and public works (when there were any). In the pre-mechanization era farms with more than twelve to fifteen acres under cultivation required labour beyond what could be supplied by a farm family.[51] Although all labour was seasonal, agriculture and lumbering were complementary in their demands. Because of the climate and the limited development of agricultural techniques, there was little work for men on farms during the winter other than in the woods once such jobs as threshing had been completed. Joseph Elson explained that as a young man with few opportunities, 'there was no chance for me but to go chopping for a living, that being the principal kind of work in the country.' Other Germans and African Canadians were frequently noted among woodsmen, but the demand for forest clearing was such that French-Canadian migrant workers left their farms in the lower St Lawrence Valley during the fall to work in the southern Ontario bush before returning home in the spring. 'I will venture to say that if Ned Griffiths will come here,' a British immigrant advised light-heartedly in 1835, 'he will cash 7/6 [seven shillings and sixpence] a day and get drunk four times for sixpence. The most suitable man for this country would be Tom Price. No one would send him to gaol for stealing timber, but [would] thank him for taking it.'[52]

As currency was in short supply, labour was often bartered for commodities, other services, or even land. Output was sometimes calculated by the hour and no payments were made for sickness or inclement weather. Wages were paid irregularly. Few payments were made after the beginning of the year, and most were jammed into the fall and early winter, when the farm's output was sold. Work agreements were generally not written, but in one that has survived from 1825 a farmer named Robert Comfort engaged 'Jonithan Lane to work six Monts for Sixty dolers & to do good and lawfull days work, & if he shood have any black dais, he is to make it up, even [if] the time is out. This on his peart.'[53] Payment was to be made in cash and kind: thirty-two dollars, a yoke of oxen, and the remainder in goods. Lane was also allowed to rent a garden and cow from Comfort for a dollar a month.

Because of the relative scarcity of labour, work contracts in Ontario were for periods varying from one to eight months, or occasionally for the year, whereas in England many agricultural labourers had been reduced to hiring by the week or day.[54] Nor were annual hiring fairs imported from Britain. As servants and waged labourers were hard to secure and to keep, they demanded and received greater respect in a number of ways. One immigrant from Sussex in the 1830s told his correspondent to inform his former employer that Ontario was 'a good place for farmers, but they must not think to do here what they do at home, telling men if they do not like it, they may go, for the masters must humble more to the men, than the men to the master.'[55] In highly personal work situations, fair consideration by employers was a major concern. The operation of the small mills and tanneries that dotted the countryside was sometimes halted when owners refused conditions set by their employees or when walkouts occurred over inadequate food or accommodation. 'They behave well with me,' wrote a young immigrant of his employers in 1835 while working six months as a farm labourer in order to acquire a hundred-acre farm.

I always go to my meals with them excepting when there be a great number and they always look to me as well as their visitor, having tea twice a day, pork three times a day, and often buckwheat cakes, made little like pancakes, which I do very much admire. My master is a framer; he can make an excellent frame house. My work is to milk, take care of his cattle, and horses; he has got three of them. They are all mares, two of them in foal, and I dare say a third; to thrash, and chop down trees, and sometimes go to mill with his goods.'[56]

A woman servant noted that where 'the farmers get their penny out of them [servants] in hard work, they should pay for it, but isn't it better [to] be with a mistress that's [e]asy and good humoured and good, and won't work one to the stumps? But without any matter of doubt, the servants are great plagues; they think of nothing but bettering themselves.'[57]

Large public or private projects drew workers away from agriculture, despite the demanding conditions, because the work was less intermittent and wages were paid in cash. As early as 1819 the timber industry was luring the earliest Scottish highlanders in Glengarry County to more gainful employment.[58] Some seven hundred men were noted working on the Grenville Canal in 1822. 'Teams were drawing stones on sleds,' an observer noted of the Rideau Canal nine years later, 'over seas of mud and water, and the men in boots wading almost to their knees. Those employed in excavation were no better off, digging clay, by the heavy rains, turned to mud.'[59] When the Canada Company began to build settlement roads in the southwest during the late 1820s, it was reported from the Galt area that it employed 'all the hands. They have about a hundred and thirty men to work about fourteen miles from here and is giving from 6 shillings to 8 York currency ... so that a farmer is not able to hire a man to work at this time.'[60] Seasonal employment created a drift of underemployed persons to the province's villages and small towns during the winter. Since most of these places consisted of little more than a tavern, a tannery, a blacksmith shop, and one or more grist, saw, carding, or fulling mills, they offered fewer opportunities for survival than agriculture.[61] But the greater conviviality afforded by these centres was an attractive alternative to being snow-bound or isolated on a farm without transportation.

INTERMEDIATE ADJUSTMENTS: TENANCY AND SHARECROPPING

As it was estimated to take only two to four years for a family to earn enough to begin a farm during the first half of the century, skilled and non-skilled wage work was frequently transitory and the number of people so engaged was small. In 1848 only 5.3 per cent of men aged twenty-one to sixty were farm hands and another 3 per cent servants, while among women, servants accounted for 7.2 per cent of those aged fourteen to forty-five.[62] Other entries to farm life for those with less capital were offered by squatting, lease-purchase agreements, tenancy, and sharecropping. Renting a farm served as a means for some settlers to adjust to their new environment and make a better assessment of soil conditions before buying. In some instances, tenancy also provided a temporary conveyancing of inheritance before the parents died, while in others it was connected with land speculation. By 1848 there were 43,199 tenants in rural Ontario (42.7 per cent of the total population) and 57,882 proprietors (57.3 per cent of the total). Those proportions are consistent with male property holding in the United States at that time.[63] Renting continued to grow while immigration increased, but it declined steadily after 1858, when large-scale immigration ended. Because of the mounting concern for the maintenance of soil fertility and the preservation of woodlands as well as the dependency inherent in tenancy, renting was never favoured as highly as ownership in rural Ontario.

Rental properties were readily available, and standard farm leases later in the century contained clauses requiring lessees to follow conservationist land husbandry, but rental practices were sometimes contested.[64] The Canada Company, which provided sales as well as lease-purchase agreements, became a prime target owing to the size of its holdings. Patrick Bell, who visited recently arrived settlers in their Huron tract in 1833, recorded that some had been on the verge of starvation by the end of winter and were near rebellion against 'their cruel seducers.'[65] Little more than two decades later another author attacked the company's lease-purchase agreements, charging that not one in twenty settlers could pay their annual rent and save enough to pay for their land at the end of the ten-year contracts.[66] While the difficulties encountered by new arrivals were real, most of this antagonism stemmed from the company's size and its high annual leasing charge of 6 per cent of the purchase price.[67] Most people wanted to own, but the road was often arduous.

The practice of letting work on shares had been brought to the province by the first American settlers in the late eighteenth century. As both parties assumed risks as well as potential benefits, sharecropping sometimes functioned like today's futures market, although in a more decentralized way that was attuned to the inequalities of life and scarcity of capital. Whole farms, fields, and specific agricultural operations such as sheep grazing and sugaring were let on shares. Although such relationships were not governed by any uniform formula, most often there was a lease in which produce or livestock was divided on an equal or one-third/two-thirds basis depending on what each party contributed. By the third quarter of the century sharecropping agreements were sometimes referred to as rentals; they also served as a model for contractual arrangements in small rural establishments that manufactured such items as wheels.[68]

Despite the opportunities, many people failed. Migration is always characterized by adjustment problems and a rate of return that varies with the distance travelled and the state of transportation. 'Some immigrants who indulged the hope of wealth in this country,' a Presbyterian minister in Perth wrote in 1825, 'have found in the end nothing but disappointment.'[69] Women travelling alone with their children to meet relatives preceding them were especially prone to temporary destitution. They often required the assistance provided by the immigrant aid societies that had been formed in various parts of the province after 1819, when the first such organization began. For twenty years following 1847, women consistently outnumbered men in the Kingston House of Industry, a county poorhouse located in this port town through which many immigrants flowed.[70]

The successful immigrants denied altogether the existence of social problems other than those associated with adjusting to the land. 'Here their is no objects of human misery claiming from the hand of charity, no person in tattered rags appearing as a lamentable evidence of the wants and poverty of the people,' wrote one farmer in 1827.[71] 'Every individual appears to exhibit the appearance of a comfortable independence,' he continued in words repeated by others many times in succeeding years. Such laudatory assessments were repeated in travel books and settlers' guides, but they were false. The number of destitute and those incapable of supporting themselves grew with the dramatic rise in population after 1815, although it paled in comparison to the situation in Britain. 'There is no doubt cases of poverty and suffering in this county,' noted a Scots baker turned agriculturalist in 1845, 'but I can safely say that so far as I have seen the great mass of people are much better off than in Scotland.'[72]

PRIVATION AND FAMINE

Like all pre-industrial Western societies heavily dependent on agriculture, life and death on the edge of subsistence sometimes hung on the success of crops. Farming seldom produced large enough surpluses, particularly among new settlers, to be a cushion against the adverse effects of crop failures. Cows and pigs were regularly turned out to the woods to forage in winter, while squirrels, pigeons, rabbits, and deer provided protein to those recently established on the land.[73] The first widespread famine occurred in the Niagara region after an infestation of black squirrels that ravaged the maize crop in 1796. The following year the crops failed. People ate their seed potatoes and other plantings before turning to eating frogs and forest greens. In some instances starvation was averted only by government handouts.[74] In 1819 and 1820 the wheat harvests failed in Glengarry owing to intense heat and the spread of blight, but Bishop Alexander Macdonell attributed part of the distress to Highland men who preferred lumbering to farming.[75] In the spring of 1837 livestock feed was so scarce in some parts of the province that cattle starved to death, although the farmers tried to keep them alive by feeding them dandelion roots. When wheat did not do well in 1839 and prices rose, a Quaker farmer noted that it 'coms tof on poor people who have their bread to purchas.'[76]

The culmination of several years of hardship, the great famine of 1859 affected more lives than any other. It struck at least the area from Guelph to Goderich, southwestern Ontario's bread basket, but its extent may have been greater. The difficulties started with the wheat midge that entered the province in 1855 and spread to the northern shores of Lakes Ontario and Erie in the next year.[77] When a severe international depression struck in 1857 a country merchant reported that money could 'not be had in Canada. Farmers willing to give their farms in security cannot get it to borrow and have to see their cattle and horses sold to pay debts.'[78] Large numbers of people took to the roads in search of work. The summer of 1858 was so hot and dry that in the area around Goderich artisans and labourers, who also depended on casual farm labour for income, were desperate. After paying their leases to the Canada Company, many Huron County settlers found themselves without cash.[79] The following year one woman wrote that the Highland Scottish settlers in the southern part of neighbouring Bruce County who 'depended on the cultivation of the new farms, are subsisting on roots gathered in the bush.' They 'could hardly be worse at home than this,' she concluded.[80] In the countryside north of Guelph a small retailer wrote to his aunt in Scotland that few 'of the most squalid in your city are in a worse position than many of the settlers within forty miles back from this ... Cases of severe suffering from want and a few of the extreme Finale are reported.'[81] In the village of Elora in that area, farmers with their oxen gathered at the mill begging for handouts of flour, but a local merchant estimated that the miller had already extended over twenty thousand dollars in credit. On one farm a husband left his wife and children to search for food, but when he did not return, she set out with her baby and toddler for the home of two bachelors. They refused to help her. Departing, she collapsed and died; the village arrested the two men.

Creating farms subjected all but a very few to difficult physical exertions. 'You have no idea of the suffering of new settlers in this country,' wrote a middle-class farmer south of Guelph about to hire himself and his wife out as servants after a bad winter. 'No negroes work harder in the West Indies.'[82] In eastern Ontario, William Bell noted in 1825 that the 'settlers are poorer than a stranger can well imagine. They have little to sell, or even that little brings them nothing. The only people likely to prosper are the storekeepers and lawyers. Their risks are no doubt considerable, but their profits are enormous.'[83] Brinton Paine Brown, whose family had immigrated from New York state, said that clearing a farm 'will wear out one life to clear these pines, then another life to get rid of the stumps and, when done, the deed will not hold the sand from blowing away.'[84] He and his wife returned to her parents' farm to sharecrop. The father of the farm leader J.J. Morrison, who had emigrated from Ireland in 1845, confided to his son that he would never have tackled a bush farm if he had known all the trials that it was to entail.[85]

Changes in language in nineteenth-century Ontario reflected the gradual formation of a new society. At first the British term 'yeoman' was used to describe a rural property owner. During an election in Perth in 1830, one Tory candidate retorted to the accusation that his supporters were ruffians by saying that he 'did not think it right to call the yeomanry of the country, who were his supporters, Banditti.'[86] While the concept of the yeomanry continued to be invoked for political purposes until the third quarter of the century, 'farmer' was early accepted in common discourse. In Britain, a farmer was a member of the gentry, but in Ontario the term often implied no more than an agricultural vocation, whether or not the person owned a property. The language of law remained archaic throughout the century, and British appellations were legislated in the Master and Servant Act of 1847, but they were quickly overridden in common parlance by American terms. 'Hired help' superseded the British term 'farm servant.' Similarly, women servants were generally called 'girls,' a non-demeaning designation that implied the temporary nature of most such employment before marriage.[87]

FARM WOMEN AND WORK IN THE EARLY NINETEENTH CENTURY

The work of women and children was vital to the economy of the rural household.[88] Sexuality was viewed as a mixed blessing and matrimony as the natural state for most people. 'And for the wound you have received from cupid's dart,' one farm couple wrote their brother in 1840, '[it] may be the best means of procuring to you the comfort of this world & hapiness in the world to come, so that to some he is a Devil to torment and to others he is a god to adore.'[89] Common wisdom viewed farming as entailing too many different jobs and being too solitary a life for one sex alone. Consequently, when James Thompson had secured his farm in the eastern part of the province after ten years of practising his craft, his father advised him that the 'next thing you have to do is to look out for a good wife to help you manage the farm.'[90] An English immigrant of peasant stock who had initially migrated in 1843 to New Jersey, where he had found work labouring for low wages, said that he decided to look for a farm because 'I thought I would try and be a man for myself; that is what I left my Native land for.' This decision required that he marry, he maintained, in order to secure a 'helpmate to share my pleasures and sorrows in the work.'[91]

For immigrant women, farming created a triple burden. The amount of work was greater than what they had done in the old country, and additional tasks had to be assumed. As in other regions of recent settlement, labour in the forest and fields was added to the traditional domestic and maternal duties.[92] Women chopped trees, ploughed the land, threshed grain with flails, butchered livestock and fowl, planted, hoed, weeded, raked, and bound field crops during harvesting, pulled flax, hauled manure and mangels (large turnips used for animal feed), picked stones from fields, washed and sheared sheep, and drove farm machinery. One English immigrant claimed that his mother and sister were such excellent threshers that there was 'hardly a man in the township that can thrash as much as them two.'[93] Sometimes women felled the trees along with the men or cut down the underbrush before chopping and helped make potash. Even at the age of sixty-one, Margaret Somerville, who lived with a daughter married to a former farm labourer, cleaned barley all day, dug mangels, and bound wheat. She also did all the farm tasks that might have been expected of a younger woman, but she did not undertake ploughing, manure spreading, or cradling wheat. Her family could not afford to hire help other than the neighbours' children while their own were very young, and they were paying for the farm.[94]

Such was the weight of women's work that not only were children expected to lighten it, but the men often helped by crossing gender lines to milk, churn butter, clean the stove pipes each spring, help with interior decoration, work in the vegetable garden, and sometimes even cook.[95] In poorer farm families such as the Morrisons, the burden of harvesting fell principally on the women and children. The men, who hired out in August, often travelled up to 150 kilometres from their homes, and continued threshing into the dead of winter, barely returning to their families in time for spring ploughing. One woman farmer recounted how 'her husband, being a stone mason, always worked at his trade in summer, and Mrs Borthwick always had the responsibility about the farm, which she bought from the Crown. They had a family of sons and daughters who grew up in time and were able to make home happy.'[96] The only kinds of work that women did not generally do were cradling and ditch digging, the latter a task necessary for field drainage that farm labourers also refused and that came increasingly to be a specialized operation done by hired labourers. Among some immigrants, such as the Germans, English, and Irish, women wielded the sickle – a dangerous instrument because it cut towards the body. The 'hoe was our plough and the sickle was our reaper,' one German woman recounted about her earliest experiences on their farm. With the adoption of the much heavier but more efficient cradle, with its scythe blade and wooden prongs that were often too heavy even for a man, the women were relegated to raking and stooking.[97]

In an economy characterized by poor transportation and few markets, domestic production for home consumption grew. In confronting the Ontario wilderness, many settlers stepped back in time to produce for themselves the goods and services they had once purchased. 'This country is much like about the time our grandfather was a boy,' an English immigrant observed in 1835. 'We have good fires in the hearth and the farmer and his family clothing is homemade. The[y] keep sheep for the wool and geese for the feathers.'[98] Despite these conditions, individual human lives were valued highly, especially at their beginning and end. One woman exclaimed, 'It is the custom of this country to have 7 or eight folks take care of one baby – instead of one woman taking care of seven or eight babies as your mother and mine used to do.'[99] Another new arrival, relating the funeral of his daughter, thought his correspondent would find it 'strange when I tell you the custom of this place that they need no invitation. One neighbour tells the other the day of the interment and there was thirty-nine waggons loaded with people, seventeen riders, and a great number walking.'[100] The importance that was attached to the individual worked particularly in favour of women. One farm woman who noted that she and her sisters 'have plenty of work in the summer burning wood and racking leaves,' also pointed out to her

Scottish relatives it was thought 'a very mean thing for a school girl to go out to hire hear.'[101]

Women's work was constant and laborious. Natural products had first to be grown or gathered and then subjected to an intricate series of processes by which they were rendered fit for human consumption. Canning remained limited to sweet preserves and large crocks until after 1900, when cheap glass became increasingly available. Farm daughters spent part of the year spinning wool and weaving cloth from seven in the morning until five at night. Rural women made maple sugar and preserved fruit as well as looking after the traditional domains: the vegetable garden, the dairy, and the poultry. Straw was made into hats and mats. Linen and woollen manufacture involved many steps, with shearing and weaving purchased when they could be afforded. In order to gain money to buy essential household commodities such as tea, women carried their butter or maple sugar on their backs or heads to local markets. 'Sugar making was all the rage,' a farm woman related, 'and many days and nights were worked in the woods gathering sap and boiling maple syrup and sugar. My sisters used to carry baskets of eggs and maple sugar on their heads eight miles to store. We used to go forty miles for apples.'[102] A woman's independent income was frequently applied to household purchases, a man's earnings to the farm. Outside the money economy, doctoring and nursing the sick also fell to women, a service that was generally returned in kind.

In some ethno-religious communities medical practice evolved into a specialized function performed by a few select individuals. 'There is only my auntie and myself for this particular sect of Mennonites that devote their time to nursing,' one young woman wrote. 'I'll get lots of work but, oh, they feel they own you. I know what that did to me some years ago, and I'm scared, oh, I'm scared.'[103] As living standards became higher, women's work changed, as did their deportment. 'They all dress as high ranking people in Germany,' a newly arrived immigrant to Waterloo County wrote in 1831. 'The women are lucky. They do not have to work in the fields. They do not have to cook food for the livestock, either, only for the farmworkers.'[104] Icelandic women settling in Ontario later in the century also found some of their work shifted to men.[105]

For most women there was little concept of domesticity, only an annual round of tasks more demanding than men's work. Even simple household chores such as hauling water might be rendered difficult if the well was located over a kilometre from the house and the water had to be carried with a baby in hand. One mother of four children, but in reasonable financial circumstances, noted, 'No servant I ever had at home or here ever went through the work I have to do when I am without one.'[106] A man observed: 'I have known women, in addition to raising a large family, to do the work of the house; attend to the dairy; to all the gardening that was done; to work up all the wool, commencing with clipping it from the sheep, and ending with making it up into wearing apparel, from the socks to the overcoat. The greater part of the work had to be done after baby was put to bed for the night, and while her "lord and master" was snoozing away the evening in the chimney corner, notwithstanding each had shared alike during the day logging, hoeing or harvesting as the case might be.'[107]

The extent of the labour required of rural women outside the house depended on the wealth and aspirations of their families as well as on the productivity of other immediate family members. While domestic production was essential to the satisfaction of material needs, field production remained the vital core for all who hoped that farming would lead to material betterment. When money was scarce, assistance with the household tasks as well as milking, churning butter, and tending poultry was more likely to be dispensed with than the hired man. These family priorities combined with the endless nature of work in the farm operation to overburden women. 'We think that in this country,' the editor of the *Farmer's Advocate* wrote, 'that the work of women is more wearing, unremitting, and unrelieved than that of men, and the old distich is too often true, "Men's work is from sun to sun / Women's work is never done."'[108]

Just as farms required the work of all household members, so their material benefits might accrue to every member despite discriminatory inheritance laws in cases of intestacy. As wills allowed such provisions to be circumvented, historical attention has been drawn in that direction, although many families also made use of dowries, dower rights, marriage settlements, and maintenance agreements.[109] The first study of rural Ontario inheritance practices led some to conclude that women had been severely disadvantaged. Families were non-egalitarian, it was maintained, and 'ownership of the means of production both in law and in practice was in the hands of the male head of the household.'[110]

Families have never been egalitarian, but wills need to be interpreted within this larger context. For centuries English peasants had adhered to the idea that 'family land belonged to the whole family; every member had a claim to support from it, generation after generation.'[111] Research on Tipperary Protestants in the Ottawa Valley has revealed that in half the wills where men predeceased their wives, the widows retained control of the homestead for life. In another fifth of the cases, the widow was provided with the house or control over a specific room. In a further

10 per cent, they received cash or an annuity enabling them to live independently.[112] That there was no significant shift in this pattern from 1820 to 1890 may be due to particular ethnic tradition. Inheritance practices varied with particular ethnic groups, but among farmers in upper New York State, the percentage of wills leaving the entire estate to wives increased from 37 per cent in the period 1798–1824 to 56 per cent by 1845–65.[113] Such findings lead one to question whether ownership of the means of production can actually be attributed to men other than in a strictly legal sense. Daughters were nevertheless treated less generously than sons owing to patrilineal inheritance and the belief that most women would marry. There was more equality between rural men and women in social reality than in legal theory, but further studies of inheritance practices are needed to clarify the issue.

CHILDREN AND ADOLESCENTS

Children from most backgrounds were expected to contribute to the family economy by working with their mothers at an early age and helping with harvesting. The jobs assigned to them, which were more repetitive than dexterous, included such things as raking field crops, helping to spin wool, feeding animals, stooking grain sheaves at harvest, hauling wood and water, and even collecting fares on toll roads. 'It is no use coming here,' one settler advised his brother, 'unless he has a family to assist. If he is obliged to hire, his work wages is so high that it will not pay him.'[114] At puberty, children's work divided more fully along gender lines. For adolescent boys driving the team and ploughing signified the onset of manhood. One of the reasons for the high birth rate in early Ontario was that children were 'considered a blessing and a source of wealth, instead of bringing with them, as in the old country, an increase of care.'[115] Children of poorer families hired out locally from the age of seven or eight to help their families financially, and their father often collected the children's wages from their employer. Although child immigration schemes brought destitute children from Britain to Ontario as early as the 1820s and continued to do so for a century, only 5 per cent of enumerated households in Peel County in the mid-Victorian era counted children from outside the family within the household, while the proportion of nuclear-family households increased from 56 per cent in 1851 to 73 per cent twenty years later.[116]

Children were sometimes indentured at an early age, a practice called 'adopting out' during the second half of the century when it became less formal. The terms of indentures adhered to a formula that outlined the responsibilities of both parties, placed proscriptions on the young person's activities, and provided for payment at the end of the work period. In 1797, when Barbara Carr contracted with farmers Jacob and Caty Miller 'of her free, voluntary will & Consent, by and with the consent of her mother Elizabeth Shelton,' her indenture stated that she was to 'be taught all kinds of women's work.'[117] Whereas Carr was to be instructed in Bible reading, the indenture for John Green three years previously had also provided that he be taught the 'Trade, Science, Occupation' of wheelwrighting and given three months of day schooling. An additional provision required Green to keep his master's secrets, something not found when seven-year-old Elias Tanner was contracted to a Niagara farmer in 1806 for fourteen years. Like most indentured children Elias Tanner was bound to obey his master's orders, not to embezzle or waste his goods, and not to gamble or frequent public entertainments. 'Fornication,' one clause read, 'he shall not commit, nor matrimony contract during said term.'[118] In return, the boy received clothes (including washing), room, and board, but these meagre rewards were insufficient to keep him from later running away. Similar but more rigid terms were included when five-year-old Catharine Aiken was apprenticed by her mother as a domestic to a farmer outside Toronto in 1855. Until she was twenty-one, her indenture prohibited her from haunting taverns or playhouses, or 'absent[ing] herself from her said Master's service day or night unlawfully.'[119] Catharine Aiken was to receive two years of schooling and, upon the termination of her indenture, two cows, a feather bed, and linens. Such apprenticeships were too constricting for too long a period in a young person's life, and they were also legally enforceable, for failure to follow a master's order might bring sentences of up to a month, although the courts were sometimes lenient.[120] By mid-century indentures were in decline, and by the 1880s they had virtually disappeared altogether, despite the security offered both parties by a written contract. Indenture fell victim to rising expectations and a quickened pace of change.

Not only country children, early inured to the rigours of work, grew up quickly in mid-nineteenth century Ontario. The very nature of a polyglot rural society composed of transplanted people from a variety of ethnic and religious backgrounds seems to have encouraged exogamous marriages in which children acted against their parents' wishes. One Scots immigrant, whose family farm lay in southern Huron County, described those around him as a 'mixty moxty Quire hotch potch of high and low country scotch, English, welch, irish, dutch [German], french, Yankies of the states, new brunswick, and novacosea with native born canadians.'[121] The opportunities afforded by the availability of land and hopes for an unbridled future made young people less deferential. 'The children of the settlers, both boys and girls,' one woman farmer wrote, 'know well that on attaining the age of eighteen, they can each claim and take up from Government a free grant of one hundred acres. They naturally feel their incipient independence and their individual interest in the country, and this makes them less inclined to submit to the few restrictions of servitude still sanctioned by common sense and general observance.'[122] One immigrant in the 1830s explained his family's attempt at farming: 'My brothers did not erect suitable buildings to put the crop in, but the fact is that neither of them was any help to my father. My brother Rowland who had a farm of his own was always at work for himself, cleaning his lands and building his house to receive a young Irish wife ... My brother Brisbain did not like farming, so he took off to the lakes, and that was the last we saw of him for some years.'[123]

Parents sometimes sought to retain their children by indulging them, within clearly defined limits, in preparation for a life that might be more difficult as they aged. 'I have invited Mrs Lucas here for a visit as it pleases the children,' Catherine Van Norman noted in her diary in 1850. 'I am willing they should enjoy themselves all they can,' wrote this farm woman who had almost died in childbirth and suffered incessantly from boils, 'for they will soon have to bear hardships and trials as the older ones.'[124] Children sometimes disagreed with their parents' desire to mould them after their own ideas. 'You can't change a thorn into a lily,' wrote a young woman objecting to her father's plans a little later in the century, 'nor cultivate a spruce in a hothouse, but give it time and air, and not even the English oak will surpass it. I am sorry that I cannot be what you would wish me, a good, quiet, domestic character, but I would prefer being an evergreen to an English rose.'[125] Mothers and fathers were often crestfallen at such responses. 'I feel that I have done all I am called on to do,' lamented one farmer about his son in regard to a small woollen business, 'in giving him an interest in the "work" as he calls it, which means on his part an acknowledgement, on mine that I cannot get on without him, but must fight my own way or surrender myself to his management. As I have always told him that he is at liberty to please himself, so I retain the same right, & will continue to be boss while I live. It is my intention that my children should respect my memory and not despise me while living & dead.'[126]

Worked too hard, more adventuresome youths took off, sometimes getting help from relatives in distant locations. When a young Thomas Good found he could not get along with his father on the farm, his aunt counselled forbearance. 'There is no use in impatience,' she wrote. 'Poor people like we are have to work long and hard for their money.' Wanderlust led Tom Good to the United States in 1866. 'If you like the city best by all means remain in it; you may do well and gain a competence, or scratch for a living all your life,' Anne Good advised.[127] Farming had its material rewards, she thought, 'but then it is hard work and farmers have rough hands and rough clothes.' By 1870 the drift of farm youth to the cities had become an important cause of the unease that began to infest rural Ontario.[128]

The 1869 diary of Albert Smith, living on a farm near the village of Mount Forest in north Wellington County, reveals both the social life enjoyed by rural young people and some of the ways in which they decided what paths they intended to pursue. In most respects it was a typical year in the life of a nineteen-year-old son of a middling farmer, except that diphtheria afflicted the area, fodder was so short that livestock died of starvation, and Albert Smith encountered death for the first time when a lathe malfunctioned and disembowelled a man. The youth did not leave farm work to return to school until late January. His social life consisted of skating, croquet, carpet bowling, lacrosse, cricket, and summer picnics. He attended a local debate on the question of whisky, saw a touring theatrical company perform a play entitled *Pissaro*, and attended two fall agricultural fairs later in the year. After autumn harvesting, Albert Smith left home to work in a local hotel.

Being alone on his own for the first time gave him pause for reflection on his future. His brother had moved to Florida two years previously, a friend had departed to join him, and a third confided that he also might leave for there 'or some other place where he can learn more than by staying in this old place.' The young man thought about his phrenological reading that advised him to be a teacher or preacher, and although he considered phrenology a true science, he rejected its findings. Smith decided that he would complete one final stint of education at an academy over the winter and attempt to secure an apprenticeship at the local pharmacy. The farm never entered his plans. Once Albert Smith had determined that he would be a druggist, he ended his diary.[129]

ETHNICITY AND PEOPLE OF COLOUR

Despite chain migration and cluster settlement, the preponderance of the British and Irish in Ontario's population promoted assimilation, but not without initial discord and occasional violence, especially among the young. Language created difficulties, even among Scots and Irish who both spoke forms of Gaelic. When a servant named Julie in the Lizars family in Goderich fell ill in 1859 and refused to take medicine, the family called for a priest, 'a french man who can scarce speak English, so between his broken English and Julie's Irish, they must not have understood a great deal of each other's conversation.'[130] Violence predicated on ethnic or religious rivalries was random and sporadic, but in periods of high immigration, confrontations assumed larger proportions, particularly when inflamed for political ends as seen during the Shiners' War that involved French Canadians and Irish in the Ottawa Valley.[131] Religious communalism among Christian sects such as the Amish or Mennonites afforded greater protection against ethnic seepage, as did the increasing concentration of French Canadians in the eastern counties of Stormont, Glengarry, and Russell later in the century.

But colour mixed with cultural factors was a more formidable barrier to toleration and integration. The labour of Indians and people of colour was readily accepted on farms throughout the province, although they often lived in isolation from the mainstream of white rural society. Indians traded game and handiwork for the use of rifles or for foods they had grown accustomed to. Almost always they were viewed by whites as benign peoples, experts at hunting and gentle with their children. That they were a distinct culture living separately in the midst of an invading horde created a immense gulf that was easily transformed into fears among the farming population, as witnessed in the Penetanguishene area in 1849. When the government failed to pay the Indians their annuity, the farmers became apprehensive. The Indians were 'threatening to wipe out all the whites,' Sarah Drinkwater exclaimed. The soldiers in the area provided some reassurance: 'How glad I am we live near the barracks,' she wrote.[132] Nevertheless, Indians often served as labourers. On the Good family farm in Brant County, twenty-two of them worked on the thirty-six-man harvest crew in 1847. As late as the beginning of the twentieth century Indians were still moving into north Wellington County, where they pitched their tents and worked with the whites in the annual flax pulling, a harvest activity that remained unmechanized when the crop was intended for linen making. Indigenous people also constituted a principal element in the seasonal labour required by the Niagara fruit-growing industry, where they were noted for their workplace solidarity. If their collective demands in regard to payment were not met, they decamped, throwing the growers back on their own resources.[133] Though the Indians in southern Ontario existed precariously on the edges of the money economy, they remained a people living apart in their own ways.

Some African Canadians preferred to settle in clusters for self-protection against American fugitive slave hunters and, like various other groups, to recreate their social and religious institutions in a new environment. Having little money upon their arrival, many sought any employment available, including work on the railways, in order to meet the payments on their properties. The country's protection of escaped slaves stood in marked contrast to the personal and institutional prejudices that they encountered in Ontario. The debating society in the tiny village of Elora chose as its subject in 1853 'whether ... the Indian or the Negro suffered most from the aggression of the white man,' while in other quarters the absence of slavery allowed some Ontarians to indulge in traditional anti-Americanism.[134] Although African-Canadian leaders applauded the efforts of the British and Canadian governments to protect them from the long arm of the United States, people of colour were more likely than whites to encounter individual discrimination and to be the objects of criminal violence. A charivari in St Catharines intent on harassing a man of African descent recently married to a white woman set on the wrong person and stoned him to death. In court, one of the participants expressed no remorse, admitting only that his fellows had 'run down a Damned nigger, but he was not the right one.'[135] African Canadians also received stiffer sentences when convicted of crimes. The province gave in to bigotry further by allowing the creation of racially segregated schools after 1850.[136]

MID-CENTURY TRANSITION

Mid-century is generally viewed as the critical juncture in the history of rural Ontario. This transition was identified by Marxist and Marxist-influenced historiography with the transformation of Canadian capitalism and the emergence of proletarianization, defined as the separation of workers from the means of production and as a growing reliance on waged labour. While some in this school have argued that the creation of a Canadian working class dated from extensive immigration during the 1820s, others have seen it manifested in the experience of Irish immigrant navvies during the canalization of the St Lawrence River in the 1840s.[137] Conceptual confusion has surrounded these interpretations. Capitalism early in the nineteenth century has been defined as commerce, as small-scale manufacturing, and as mercantilism, although mercantilism consisted of ideas that governed the state's regulation of the economy. The lines dividing artisans and other small producers from those working purely with their hands have never been clarified satisfactorily. In other contexts, particularly later in the century, the emerging industrial and financial sectors are assumed to have been the foremost expressions of capitalism, and little heed is paid to capitalistic activity by petty producers, such as farmers, who engaged in independent commodity production. Outside this historiography, two more intensive statistical investigations, of townships in Peel and Prescott counties, argued that rural society was afflicted by crises at mid-century and again by 1880. For these localities, migration beyond the immediate district was considered a primary characteristic of deep-rooted problems that were deduced primarily from demographic data. Both studies were constrained by their methodology.[138] Neither adduced evidence from those involved to substantiate its conclusions; nor could they show what happened to people who disappeared from serial records, because longitudinal investigations were not conducted. Rural 'crises' were deduced from out-migration within limited local confines.

One of the crucial issues related to the proletarianization thesis has been the availability of land. The ideas of the British colonial reformer Gibbon Wakefield, for creating a labour force by restricting access to land were said to have influenced the Canadian government during the 1840s, but this contention has been discredited. The government had a policy of free grants even before the land act of 1840 that enshrined it in law. Speculators such as the Canada Emigration Association, which had profited from the Upper Canadian land bonanza, worked with governments to promote immigration and settlement rather than to restrict access to cheap land, in order to gain financially from their investments.[139] Most historians have nevertheless accepted mid-century anxieties that resulted when the last large chunks of arable public lands in southern Ontario were put on the auction block in 1852. As land prices rose, there was a chorus of consternation about the country's comparative advantage in regard to the United States. Various elite groups that have been called the Canadian 'expansionist movement' sought to influence the government to annex Rupert's Land, the vast northwestern region owned by the Hudson's Bay Company, to ensure the country's future prosperity.

While these developments influenced Canada irrevocably by helping to bring about Confederation in 1867, the acquisition of the Northwest, and the Dominion Lands Act of 1872, they did not create a crisis of rural society. The decline in the size of Ontario's rural households and the increase in family limitation practices that have underpinned the 'crisis' thesis have only recently come under closer scrutiny. In Ontario during the first half of the nineteenth century, more women had married, and at a younger age, than in most European countries. After 1850 families became smaller throughout the Western world, but this happened earlier in Ontario than in any other place except France.[140] Marital fertility declined 20 per cent by 1891, but the strong correlations between counties that were more recently settled and large families point to the importance of children during the simultaneous processes of land clearing and agricultural development. Rising prosperity among farm families in settled areas, the enhanced status of women, and the opportunities for geographical mobility partially explain why families became smaller.

There was no land shortage at mid-century that forced families to reduce the number of children. As much of the unspoiled land bought in 1852 went to speculators intent on selling to realize profits, land continued to reach the market. In 1855 some two million acres were reputed to be in private hands but ready for sale.[141] Speculation, together with the great demand for Canadian farm products stemming from the Crimean War and the optimism generated through the Reciprocity Treaty of 1854, created a boom in the rural economy that ended momentarily in the panic of 1857. Land prices, which had surged as patenting became frantic in both eastern and southern Ontario, dropped dramatically in 1858, the year that arrivals at the port of Quebec decreased 60 per cent from the previous year. After this momentary faltering, land values, abetted as speculators abandoned failing projects in the hope of realizing gains across the American border, rebounded in 1863 and rose at 7 per cent a year until the end of the 1870s.[142] Rising prices in largely settled counties such as Kent and Wellington and active land patenting in Addington County until 1880 reveal that people were gaining access to rural properties. In a long-established county such as Brant, where forest clearing continued into the 1870s, 11 per cent of the arable land had still not been claimed by 1861 and farms were available to rent cheaply.[143] As late as 1871, 24 per cent of the land in Essex County remained unoccupied.[144] The rising price of land rather than its unavailability was central to the transition the province experienced at mid-century.

As people sought better prospects and cheaper land, population movements remained constant. In 1865 the *Canada Farmer* commented that there was 'an internal emigration always going on from the front cleared lands, back into the forest, and the old cultivated lands may be bought at such prices as will form capital investments.'[145] Provincial mortgage companies extended their services into rural areas, where personal lending remained strong, and from the 1860s banks permitted loans to farmers on the basis of expected crop sales.[146] Farming was no longer primarily a stab at security; it was emerging more fully as a business requiring more capital than previously and with more lucrative returns. This mid-century transition did not represent a crisis for the province except in terms of its comparative advantage within North America because vast tracts of good land were available free in the United States. The adjustment to rising land values and to the money economy was difficult for those with few financial resources and little expectation of altering their condition. Many chose to leave. Why pay for something that could be obtained free, or more cheaply, elsewhere?

The settlement process continued into the third quarter of the century, not only as clearing progressed in many of the counties that had long had some population, but also as people sought out new wild lands in places such as Huron County and the former Queen's Bush, an extensive area south of Georgian Bay and east of Lake Huron that included Dufferin, north Wellington, Grey, and Bruce counties. 'There is no chance of a poor man getting a farm in this neighbourhood,' a London area farmer wrote in 1853. 'He will have to go back to some of the new townships where he can get it from 2 to 5 doullars an acre.'[147] As only 53 per cent of the province's farm land had been improved by 1870, the mammoth assault on the forests continued.[148] Its ecological effects were apparent late in the summer of 1881. As farmers also burned their fields to clear them of weeds, the smoke around Owen Sound was intense by the end of August. The first Monday in September was so intensely hot and densely dark with smoke in southwestern Ontario that black rain fell briefly and people sought refuge in their homes, lit candles, and prayed in fear that the apocalypse had arrived.[149]

RURAL LABOUR AT MID-CENTURY

The young native-born became most prone to migration by 1871.[150] As well, the conclusion of the Civil War in 1865 made land available that had been occupied by African Americans who chose to return to the United States. These trends served to facilitate a massive movement towards farm ownership in south-central Ontario during the 1860s, when the population of the province grew from 952,000 to 1,620,000. Farm small-holding and property ownership among artisans and labourers expanded significantly between 1861 and 1871. Labourers as a proportion of the paid male workforce had declined over the former decade from 27 per cent to 19 per cent, while the proportion of farmers had increased from 32 per cent to 38 per cent. Sixty per cent of labourers who can be traced between the two censuses became farmers, although this change may have been influenced by the manner in which information was collected.[151] The movement into farming remained the predominant occupational trend in Ontario during the third quarter of the nineteenth century and persistence in agriculture over ten years was extremely high.

The experience of John Jeffrey reveals how the practice of labouring in order to secure capital with which to purchase a farm continued, even though it took longer. Arriving in Ontario from Stirling, Scotland, in 1856 at the age of eighteen, Jeffrey became an agricultural labourer in south Wellington County. Of his first years in Canada we know little except what he wrote much later: that he had initially farmed for two years before hiring out. At first he worked as a labourer for a widow, Mary Todd, who had five children aged thirteen to twenty-two. The eldest son, Peter, often worked with John Jeffrey at the daily farm chores. At harvest, the younger man cradled while Mary Todd, Jeffrey, and the other children bound the wheat into sheaves and stooked them to dry. Totally accepted by the family, Jeffrey attended church with them and they visited friends and relatives together, but the ambitious man hired out to other farmers as well. While his annual income stood initially at $100, within seven years it rose to $156. Then John Jeffrey purchased a farm at a rock-bottom price of four dollars an acre. 'Fences need repairing,' he noted. 'Stable want repairing, and the old barn and the cow stable want repair.'[152] Despite the work on his own property, Jeffrey continued to labour for others within a fifty-kilometre radius until 1869, when he married and went to work the hundred-acre farm of his wife's aunt. Even then he augmented his income by blacksmithing.

Markets outside the province and the continuing growth of towns within served as outlets for Ontario's agricultural products. The number of people engaged in farming and Ontario's rural population continued to grow continuously until 1881.[153] By 1871 only 16 per cent of farm operators were tenants, a dramatic decline from 1848. Although the transition to commercial agriculture had begun well before mid-century, by 1861 some 84 per cent of Ontario farms were producing marketable surpluses.[154] While the distinction between subsistence and commercial agriculture no longer had any validity for the majority, the degree of involvement in the cash economy remained highly variable. The rising tide of prosperity was reflected in the abandonment of log buildings for those constructed of frame, brick, and stone, as well as in the acquisition of an assortment of farm equipment.[155] The dynamism of agriculture allowed profits to flow from farming to industry. Still, the remaining 16 per cent of farmers producing for domestic consumption – a figure which bears a close resemblance to the 20 per cent of Peel County households that showed no signs of improvement between 1851 and 1860 – constituted a new source of rural labour along with those struggling to pay mortgages or provide for families in other ways.[156]

While the third quarter of the nineteenth century represented neither the end of land availability nor a crisis in rural society, after 1857 immigration did not return to its previous levels for nearly fifty years, although migration into the province, especially by French Canadians into eastern Ontario, continued. Few Ontario farm labourers worked the entire year, but some short-term harvest workers were able to earn twice the rates paid those working on annual agreements. As there were few farms as large as that owned by the journalist and politician George Brown outside Brantford, or the stock-raising operation of F.W. Stone near Guelph, seasonal employment continued to predominate. The number of neighbouring children and young people hired by the day, the job, and the season – which varied from four to eight months – rose, but it cannot be ascertained whether there was any proportional change. Most contracts on Ontario farms were oral bargains among two or three people reached at the kitchen table or in the blacksmith's shop, the general store, or the local tavern.

Farmers complained about the rising cost of wages because by the 1870s on the average hundred-acre farm of a middling farmer, without children, hired help might represent 20 to 30 per cent of the annual cash outlay for an operation.[157] Consequently, when wages rose too high in relation to commodity prices, some farmers chose to employ less labour and risk having to plough under the crop. Wages for male hired hands rose at mid-century with increases in prices and the costs of land, but from 1856 to 1859 everything slumped with bad harvests and financial crises. During the Civil War, male wages were dampened by the arrival of Americans escaping the strife. The provision of room and board generally provided some hedge against inflation. In 1863 women earned between $2.50 and $3.50 a month, while agricultural labourers received $7.00 to $9.00. By 1870 male farm labourers averaged a monthly income of $13.50.[158] An annual migration of people from the towns to the countryside at harvest time began, but this movement proved inadequate to meet the need for workers to get in the harvest of 1878 in southern Ontario. Between 1863 and 1880 the price of typical eight-month farm labour rose by two-thirds for a Prince Edward County farmer, Stephen Dorland.

The unorganized nature of the labour market caused apprehension for farmers when hands could not be found. In the springs of 1870 and 1871, for instance, Thomas Good frequently rode home from marketing trips to Brantford troubled by the lack of workers for hire. As voluntary attempts to place immigrants on farms, seen in such ventures as the Emigration Settlement Society formed in Toronto in 1847, had proven ephemeral, the need for government employment offices that would work with municipal authorities was raised in the farm press. The province responded in 1870 with a survey of land availability and employment opportunities that established the need for 23,000 people: 15,125 agricultural labourers, 1,448 mechanics, and 6,576 women servants. A Peterborough County Immigration Society was created in that year to facilitate farm placements. From 1874 Ontario maintained an immigration section separate from the federal immigration department, and its local offices served as distribution centres for rural labour.[159]

ECONOMIC, TECHNOLOGICAL, AND SOCIAL CHANGE

After 1850 rural Ontario society began to be altered by economic growth and technological change. Improved communications, particularly in the form of the telegraph and the railway, allowed more farmers to sell greater amounts of produce. Slowly the mental world of rural Ontario also began to alter. The farm press expanded rapidly with the largest newspaper, the *Farmer's Advocate*, attaining a circulation of seventeen thousand by 1881. Newspapers extolled the virtues of 'scientific agriculture,' a term that implied the application of reason and experience to farm operations through practices such as manuring, crop rotation, and the use of improved varieties of livestock and seed. As what was no longer virgin soil lost its initial fertility, this new emphasis was useful to the aspirations of those farmers who wished to make their farms profitable businesses.[160] The efficiency of the scientific farm enterprise became the credo of the provincial Bureau of Agriculture. Government policies were directed towards influencing the farm communities through subsidies to agricultural societies – which numbered 60 at the county level and some 260 in the townships by 1867 – and later through grants to specialty producers' groups. The former sponsored ploughing matches and fairs where prizes were given for the best domestic manufactures, crops, and livestock. 'The Provincial Show took place in London last week,' a Huron County farmer noted in 1854. 'It was the greatest sight I have ever seen. All the productions of the Country Both of nature and not was exhibited. It lasted three days.'[161] While specialty operations in areas such as stock raising had taken root as early as the 1840s, producers' organizations appeared later, always dominated by men. A Fruit Growers' Association of Ontario was formed in 1857, the Ontario Poultry Society in 1866, the Canadian Dairymen's Association in 1867, and the Ayrshire Breeders' Association in 1870.[162] Through its assistance to the most prosperous farmers, the government contributed to productivity, but at the expense of many small farmers who were placed less advantageously and whose situation would become increasingly untenable.

More rural men and women were transformed into consumers of implements and machinery, manufactured furniture, lighting, cloth, and culture. In response to increasing production during the 1860s, monthly marketing fairs grew rapidly but declined in the following decade as railways enhanced the importance of towns over villages. Peddling, commonly viewed as little more than legitimized begging, was increasingly superseded by sales agents for a variety of business concerns filtering through the countryside. Items frequently made on the farm came more often to be purchased from outside the household, but the adjustment was gradual and did not affect everyone. Wood stoves, candles, coal oil lamps, fabrics for clothes, construction materials for new buildings, and especially farm tools and machines were among the goods purchased. The activities where women contributed most to production were among the last for which purchases were made outside the home. Weaving was not a full-fledged industry in most areas until 1881, and homemade cloth did not decline to insignificance until the following census.[163] With these changes the agricultural fairs that had once been so popular appeared less attractive. In 1888 the South Wellington Agricultural Society decided to reverse the decline in attendance by the addition of horse racing, pipers, and dancing women, but the first was denounced as cruelty to animals and the last as a threat to the morals of children.[164]

NORTHERN MIGRATION AND IMMIGRATION

Thousands of rural inhabitants who were unable or unwilling to participate in southern Ontario's rising land market moved north to obtain free land. In attempting to replicate the prior experience of the province's farmers, they found greater personal and collective privation than their counterparts had during the first half of the century. Ontario's free-land policies after 1840 applied only to marginal acreages in the mid-northern region stretching from the Ottawa River to Georgian Bay and, later, in the districts of Nipissing, Sault Ste. Marie, Manitoulin, Algoma, Rainy River, and Thunder Bay. Although some surveyors had reported that the thin soils of the Canadian Shield could not sustain viable agriculture, pressure from lumbering interests and the knowledge that the American Midwest had become the preferred destination for immigrants, as well as for many Canadians, led the province to continue building colonization roads and to pass the Homestead and Free Grants Act in 1868. The small but rapid influx into these areas brought the rural co-operative tradition of bees to fulfil a myriad of tasks, but as many of the settlers were very poor, extreme privation was common.

'We have had a terrable time of it out here in the bush,' wrote a farmer from the Haliburton area in 1864, a year of bad crops, 'many times on the border of starvation, leaving out the immence labour required to make a farm in what might be called a wilderness.'[165] In 1870, drought created a famine in Muskoka, and around 1873 crops were ravaged by grasshoppers. One settler noted how the climate so conspired against their winter wheat that in 1874 they 'suffered at intervals this year more severely than we had ever done.' Her son was forced to hire out logging and she to sell her writing. The family endured 'long spells of hunger and want which I trust have prepared us to feel a more full and perfect sympathy with our destitute fellow-creatures.'[166] When a late summer hailstorm and early frost destroyed crops in 1879, the result was starvation and death in the Muskoka and Parry Sound districts. During Ontario's last regional famine in the winter of 1880, the immense suffering was alleviated partially by government assistance in the form of food, seeds, and work on colonization roads.[167]

As only 12 per cent of the occupied land in Muskoka was cultivated by 1881, governments were forced to realize that the surveyors' reports they had previously believed were false and that only small areas of the 'near north' were suited to agriculture. The number of new settlers peaked in the 1870s, but the residual effects of these ill-conceived policies in the back townships of Peterborough, Hastings, Victoria, and Haliburton were not exposed until social science and judicial inquiries uncovered abject rural poverty early in the twentieth century.[168] So relentless was the desire for property that the land-hungry were easily duped by countless other ventures, such as the luckless Burriss settlement, involving Americans primarily, in the Rainy River district north of Lake Superior in 1898.[169] Though supported by the government and those who sought to profit from the sale of new lands, the colonization movement never assumed the proportions or importance that it did in Quebec.[170]

With the eyes of the world on the vast arable lands of the American Midwest made accessible through their Homestead Act in 1862, Ontario lost not only the competition for immigrants, but also increasing numbers of its own people who were lured to the United States by free and cheap land.[171] In response, after Confederation the new federal government undertook a series of immigration measures that included an invitation to Joseph Arch, head of the recently formed National Agricultural Labourers' Union in England, and his associate Arthur Clayden to visit Quebec and Ontario in 1873. Aghast at the stark contrast between the austere physical beauty of Muskoka and the deprivations experienced by its settlers, Clayden filed highly critical reports with a newspaper in Birmingham. 'The truth is,' he wrote, 'that the voluntary hardships of these Canadian settlers are far greater that any of the involuntary ones which are imposed on English labourers.'[172] Southern Ontario presented an entirely different picture, especially when the union leaders encountered former school chums near Brantford who, having emigrated decades before, had prospered to the extent that they owned property and had become creditors.

The agreements that Joseph Arch reached with the federal and provincial governments were designed to facilitate emigration while averting the exploitation of immigrant labourers. Thereafter Ontario's immigration officials worked with municipalities to gauge labour demand and assist with placing new arrivals on farms around the province. While the province became one destination for the 40,000 to 50,000 people whose emigration was assisted by the National Agricultural Labourers' Union, the depression from 1873 to 1879 conspired with a revival of pauper exodus from the British Isles to elicit protests from organized labour in Canada.[173] Government policies were aimed at providing financial assistance only to agricultural labourers and women domestics, but as no controls could be placed on people once they arrived in the province, organized labour viewed immigrants as competition in the fierce fight for scarce jobs. Objections raised against government policies by the Canadian Labour Union in 1875 marked the beginning of a controversy that drove a wedge between the farm and labour movements that continued well into the twentieth century.

THE BEGINNINGS OF COLLECTIVE FARM CONSCIOUSNESS

The Patrons of Husbandry, or Grange, forged a collective consciousness among Ontario's most prosperous farmers when they swept through the province during the depression of 1873 to 1879. At a time when the economy was becoming more complex and increasingly integrated vertically, they asserted the distinctiveness of agriculturalists as a social and economic group. By 1879, when the Ontario movement crested, there were 650 lodges and a membership of twenty-six thousand, a figure that represented some 20 per cent of farmers owning more than fifty acres in the province.[174] As the Grangers recognized that farmers had become consumers as well as producers, they sought a place for farmers in an expanding but momentarily distressed economy. They feared economic marginalization:

> A bold yeomanry their country's pride
> When once destroyed can never be supplied.[175]

Patrons' co-operative associations were formed at the local and regional levels, the subscribers being required to provide share capital for making bulk purchases at reduced prices. Though the Grange was open to all members of farm families, it consciously drove a wedge between different parts of rural communities. At its founding meeting in the village of Knock in Innisfil Township in 1875, the assembled agreed to accept all men and women farmers as well as their offspring, but 'moved not to take in as members any labourers or labourers' wives.'[176] The advent of the Patrons of Husbandry marked the critical juncture at which large numbers of farm men and women acknowledged the ways in which agriculture had changed during the past quarter century. No longer did farm survival rest primarily on sheer physical exertion, as it had for so many in times past. To members of the Grange, successful farms were business enterprises requiring mental as well as physical agility to produce surpluses. The Grange forged an integration by the province's most advanced farmers into a money economy from which they hoped to profit, although a recurring litany of frauds and deceptions well into the 1880s revealed how difficult were the adjustments to new economic realities for farmers who allowed themselves to be duped in the expectation of instant wealth.[177] The Grange nevertheless opened a chasm between farmers and rural labourers that reflected changing economic realities.

While the Grange furthered fragmentation in rural Ontario along occupational lines, it also deepened gender differentiation. The organization boasted of its enlightenment in providing a place for women. No unit could be formed without their participation, but women were segregated into separate ranks and could only hold offices created specifically for them. The movement fostered the ascription of specific attributes to females in a manner that reflected the social attitudes accompanying greater prosperity. 'Among other objects we admit women to membership,' a supporter wrote in 1876. 'In the dark ages uneducated women were treated as beasts of burden, and were compelled to do the work of slaves; but in our day educated women are in many things man's equal, if not superior, especially in modesty, intelligence, usefulness and love.'[178] Women were still too heavily engaged in farm work outside the house to speak against field labour, but there was a tendency within the Grange towards delimiting women's sphere by reference to the supposed characteristics of the sexes. 'While man is employed in the sterner duties of life,' Grand Master S.W. Hill informed the annual assemblage in 1876, 'it remains for woman, with her appreciation of refinement, to build up the social element in our rural districts to a higher standard than it has yet attained, and in directing the plan of adornment for her home.'[179] While such sentiments continued to resonate in the farm press, the Grange declined rapidly after the end of the depression. By 1886 two-thirds of its locals were inactive.

MECHANIZATION

Throughout the nineteenth century various elements of the Ontario farm community had been receptive to the replacement of human toil by both animal power and machines. As early as 1811 one immigrant noted to his correspondent in England how he might 'think it strange to see a man threshing with 6 or 8 horses, but it ans[wers] verey well.'[180] By the 1840s fanning mills were in use to separate wheat from chaff, hay mowers were noted, reapers had made their appearance on farms, and threshing crews circulated in established agricultural districts during the latter part of each year; only the application of steam power to this operation made this practice seem new four decades later. James Reid, a farmer in the Etobicoke area outside Toronto who had condemned agricultural practices in the province after immigrating from Scotland in the 1820s, commented on these changes in a letter to his brother in 1847: 'I think their is little difference of the mode of farming here by what is with you. We have got the reaping machine introduced and it seems to take place instead of cradling and we have travailing threshing machines that goes from farm to farm.'[181]

The spread of agricultural machinery around the province was highly uneven. In 1849 a correspondent from East Hawkesbury in the Ottawa Valley noted that farms in that area 'might be ameliorated by labour-saving devices, a great desideratum here.'[182] The more sophisticated the technology, the higher the price, and the greater likelihood that the task would be jobbed out or that neighbours would make joint purchases. Shares were sometimes purchased in pieces of equipment.[183] While few farms owned threshing machines, reapers increasingly came within the reach of individual farmers, but attempts to gauge their diffusion have been hampered by lack of statistics. In their absence, econometric models have been constructed, but their reliability has been undermined by the assumption that farmers purchased reapers individually.[184] The mutuality that was seen frequently in material transactions also governed labour exchanges, sometimes in the manner of financial transactions. One farmer told another close by 'of the day's plowing he owed me and, he seemed to look on the matter kindly, saying that if he owed me for that, he was only too glad to pay for it, and agreed to let the one account stand against the other.'[185] Neighbouring farm women and men assisted each other individually with specific tasks and collectively through innumerable bees. Hired help were expected to represent the employer in work parties or fulfil the obligations of statute labour on the days set aside for road maintenance. As well, employees frequently lent a hand on neighbouring farms once the demands of their employer had been satisfied.[186]

In 1857 the *Canadian Agriculturalist* calculated that in 1848 the use of the sickle in grain harvesting had required eighteen workers, the scythe ten, and the reaper seven, but this was a partial analysis that

TABLE 1
Grain Harvesting, 1848

	Women reaping, gathering	Men cutting	Men binding	Men at machine	Children at rake
Sickle	15		3		
Scythe	3	3	3		1
Hainault scythe	9		3		
Reaping machine	3		3	1	

SOURCE: *Canadian Agriculturalist* 9 (Dec. 1857)

excluded the cradle and did not take into account that women and children often bound the grain (see Table 1).

While the dependability of machines and the quality of their output in contrast to manual methods were debated, the chief deterrent to their dissemination was cost. Consequently, by 1871 the mechanization of farm work in Ontario was not extensive in most operations. Only 9 per cent of farms owned threshing machines, 24 per cent reapers and mowers, and 30 per cent horse rakes. On the other hand, most farmers possessed fanning mills for separating the wheat from the chaff.[187] The depression of the 1870s forestalled many purchases, although the growth in factory output of agricultural implements in Ontario during the decade far outstripped that in Quebec. As late as 1881 students at the Ontario Agricultural College were still being instructed in the use of the cradle rather than the reaper.[188]

With the return of relative prosperity after 1879 and increased emigration to Manitoba and the United States, harvest wages reached new highs. But the shortage of harvest labour and the high wages for skilled hands were insufficient to promote further mechanization without the added incentive of tumbling prices.[189] The price of a binder (a reaper that also bound the wheat into sheaves that were then set up by hand to dry in the fields) dropped from $300 in 1881 to between $135 and $150 six years later. Even a farmer working only fifty acres, it was claimed by a manufacturer, could purchase this piece of equipment. Factory output of farm machinery surged in 1884 and 1885 and continued in succeeding years.[190] The value of farm implements sold in Ontario by Harris and Company more than tripled between 1882 and 1889, when it reached $870,125. Agents lit upon the countryside offering ready discounts. They gave easy credit terms that involved no payments for more than a year and three-year lay-aways, but the degree of mechanization continued to vary according to region. The Ontario Agricultural Commission found in 1881 that 84 per cent of farmers in Middlesex County employed various horse-drawn implements despite the fact that only two-thirds of fields were free of stumps, but in Frontenac County, where rock outcroppings were common, only a third did so. Six years later half the farmers in Peel County outside Toronto were reported to have purchased binders, but they were not yet in general use in the Hawkesbury-Ottawa area, where oats and peas were the principal grains.[191] Cradling the pea harvest remained one of the most dreadfully dirty of all harvesting jobs because in hot, humid weather mud clung to the leaves of the plant and caked the cradler.

Mechanization was not restricted to grain harvesting. It extended to many other field operations through implements such as hay loaders, hay forks and slings, seed drills, two- and three-furrow ploughs, discs, cultivators, improved harrows, and potato diggers. Stump pullers, pile drivers for fence building, and horse-driven saws reduced the work done in other farm activities, although ditch-digging equipment was so defective that throughout the century most fields were tiled by manual digging and ploughing. Many farm activities continued to be relatively untouched, especially dairy production and market gardening, two areas that grew increasingly important as the province withdrew from competition with the west in wheat. In the dairy, the advent of mechanical cream separators in the 1890s slowly began to end the laborious process that had contributed to making butter so bad that it was massively rejected on the British market and frequently used only as axle grease.[192] Farm women and men no longer had to haul the milk into their cellars to wait for the cream to rise while flies and other contaminants invaded the product.

SOCIAL AND ECONOMIC EFFECTS OF MECHANIZATION

Despite the long cyclical trough in international farm prices during the last quarter of the nineteenth century, the period up to the depression of 1893–7 was dominated in rural Ontario by contradictory tendencies. During the 1880s a large surplus population developed that subsisted on small rural lots, but during the following decade a massive redistribution occurred. In most parts of the province the shift in production from dependence on wheat as the principal cash crop to mixed farming and greater specialty operations, apparent before 1861, was completed during the last quarter of the nineteenth century. The output of field crops in the province compared favourably with that of various American states, although Ontario agriculture remained considerably less productive in terms of output per acre than its European counterpart.[193] At the same time prosperous farmers made more capital-intensive investments through improved farm buildings and increased mechanization. The inefficient system of multiple barns and stables that British immigrants had originally imported was slowly superseded by Pennsylvania-style bank barns that were much more efficient on mixed farms. By the end of the century, windmills dotted the countryside and silos were being constructed as farmers began supplementing the diet of their animals in winter with ensilage rather than root crops.

The increasing use of machinery altered many facets of rural life. Farms became more capital-intensive and per acre investment grew steadily after 1881.[194] By 1887 it was estimated that the average hundred-acre Niagara area farm possessed machinery and transport vehicles worth five hundred dollars.[195] Mechanization increased the capacity of individual farm families to do more work themselves. Changes in the Franchise Act in 1874 recognized the family basis of agriculture by allowing farmers' sons to vote where the father possessed one hundred dollars in assessment for each son. Widespread mechanization of agricultural activities also radically reduced the available work, although studies pinpointing the labour savings from major farm implements were not conducted as they were in France.[196] As the rural population continued to increase, the disposable income derived from occasional labour was reduced. Farms came to rely less on hired hands, and the demand for labour at harvesting declined significantly. The results for labourers, tenants, and small proprietors were traumatic. High summer wages had been essential to survival because, as one rural labourer explained, 'all the rest of the year is spent in search of work, as the case may be, one day here, and two days there, and so forth. He is counted a lucky bird who finds constant employment for six months in one place.'[197] Fruit grower E.D. Smith described crassly the effects of mechanization from the farmer's viewpoint in 1885: 'One farmer buys a machine and cuts for his neighbour at $1 per acre, the neighbour finding the twine. The farmer follows the machine and sets up the wheat. Hired men don't ask $2 per day any more.'[198] Harvest wages, reported at the opening of the decade to have risen to two dollars and sometimes up to three a day for top jobs such as cradling, plummeted to between a dollar and a dollar and a quarter (see table 2). Small farmers rejoiced at the reduced costs and their freedom from dependence on an unstable seasonal labour market. 'So the Harvest of 1881 is in the barn,' reflected a nineteen-year-old immigrant running a farm near Owen Sound for his father and family. 'Seedtime and harvest shall not cease. We had a very pleasant harvest, dry weather, and the labour rendered lighter by the reaper. We have succeeded well without a hired man.'[199]

With machinery, some farmers expanded their holdings, and the aver-

TABLE 2
Agricultural Labour Rates, Ontario, 1885

	District	Low	Average	High
Men				
Farm labourers,	Amherstburg		$30.00	
per month[a] from	Belleville	16.00		20.00
April to Sept.	Chatham	16.66		20.83
	Hamilton	12.00		15.00
	Port Hope	10.00		20.00
	Sarnia	18.00		30.00
	Toronto	15.00		30.00
	Windsor	15.00		20.00
By the year[a]	Chatham	150.00		250.00
	Stratford	100.00		200.00
	Toronto		200.00	(1st class)
			150.00	(ordinary)
Without board			25.50	
Harvest hands	Belleville	1.00		1.25
per day	Chatham	1.25		2.50
	Stratford	1.25		2.25
Per month[a]	Hamilton	25.00		35.00
Women				
Household	Amherstburg		$12.00	
servants	Belleville	5.00		6.52
per month[a]	Chatham	4.00		8.00
	Hamilton	6.00		10.00
	Port Hope	5.00		8.00
	Sarnia	5.00		8.00
	Stratford	3.00		6.00
	Windsor	4.00		8.00

SOURCE: United States, Bureau of Foreign Commerce, Consular Reports, *Labor, Continent of North America,*, vol. 1 (Washington, 1885), no. 3, 1–79
[a]With board at $3.00 per week.

age size of Ontario farms grew from 93.8 acres in 1871 to 104.6 in 1901.[200] Rather than reduce work, as the manufacturers of 'labour-saving machines' always claimed, mechanization and the shift to mixed agriculture made many Ontario farms more labour-intensive in a way that was generally ignored by census takers. Productivity increased, but production depended increasingly on the contributions of women and children at critical times of the year as well as during the annual round of daily chores. 'Family farm' assumed a new meaning in rural Ontario during the last quarter of the nineteenth century.

The centrality of women and children to farm production heightened the anxiety about keeping young people on the farm. Advertisements for farm machinery often showed children operating machines, and for three decades Massey Manufacturing's promotion for its leading horse rake carried the testimonial of a ten-year-old girl about its ease of use. On many Ontario farms the work of one's own children was considered to be free, given in remuneration for parental care, with the only expectation of reward to come by eventually inheriting the property. Even though children were more important economically, farm families chose to have fewer children for reasons not yet fully understood. The province moved from having the highest birth rate in the country at mid-century to the lowest by 1900.[201] As a result, immigrant children were eagerly sought as additional hands and their numbers increased dramatically.

The rapid spread of mechanization at a time of declining commodity prices proved calamitous for rural residents who had depended on selling their small surpluses or their own seasonal labour to provide their families with some cash. Small farmers in the Ottawa Valley and Muskoka were hit particularly hard by the loss of markets as the lumber industry moved north and attracted men with higher wages. Seething resentment against machinery, low wages, and the arrogant attitudes of farmers were noted in the 1880s, but there were no known incidents of Luddism. Instead, many people followed the former practice of moving – to expanding towns and villages, cities, the prairies, and the United States. Both internal and external migration occurred simultaneously, and followed the twenty- to twenty-five-year lag between the arrival of immigrants and a new generation's reaching adulthood. Between 1871 and 1901 the number of Ontario's small towns and villages nearly doubled, a development that continued into the early years of the twentieth century.[202] Though massive numbers abandoned the land in the hope of better opportunities elsewhere, these flows of population did not represent rural depopulation as much as large-scale redistribution. Between 1871 and 1901 the rural population dropped by only 17,885 people, but the percentage of the population living in rural areas declined from 78 to 57 (see Table 3).[203]

During the 1870s, Ontario's rural population increased by 7 per cent; in the following decade the Canadian-born offspring of immigrants swelled the ranks of impoverished small property owners, tenants, and labourers – people who lived partially from the sale of their labour. The number of occupiers of rural land crested dramatically in 1891, standing at 224,034 owners and 60,483 tenants, but the number of households occupying ten acres or less swelled enormously, from 36,221 in 1881 to 108,724 ten years later. The completion of the Canadian Pacific Railway

TABLE 3
Rural/Urban Population of Ontario

	1871	1881	1891	1901	1911
Rural[a]	1,264,854	1,351,074	1,295,323	1,246,969	1,198,803
Urban	355,997	575,848	818,998	935,978	1,328,489
% rural	78.0	70.1	61.3	57.1	47.4

SOURCE: *Census of Canada* 1941, vol. 8, Agriculture, table 1.
[a]Rural population is defined as the population living outside the boundaries of incorporated cities, towns, and villages. The 1931 census was the first to collect statistics on the Ontario farm population.

in 1886, the continuing attraction of American lands, and the prospect of urban employment combined with the economic depression from 1893 to 1897 to shrink the numbers occupying small rural lots or renting by 1901 almost as dramatically as they had mushroomed in the previous decade (see Table 4). Those occupying from 51 to 100 acres of land held their own throughout the period from 1871 to 1911, although there was some increase in those owning larger farms. At the same time the number of female servants in the province increased by 65 per cent to 35,781 by 1891. As women subsequently found higher-paying wage labour that they liked better, domestic service declined (see Table 5).

More research into the material circumstances of these rural people, where they went, and how their circumstances altered is warranted. Longitudinal or life-history studies will allow historians to answer many of the questions raised by the snapshots emerging from the decennial censuses.[204]

What had been subsistence production emerged as poverty, most often hidden on the back concession roads but powerfully symbolized in the dreaded county poorhouse. Some people eked out their living by scavenging. In a Wellington County family so poor that they did not own a gun, the children in winter drove deer into snowdrifts and then clubbed them before the father slit their throats. The less ingenious survived by snaring rabbits.[205] For those who fell into destitution, relief remained decentralized, administered grudgingly by municipal governments or through voluntary efforts. In order to reduce welfare costs, ten Ontario counties had created houses of industry by 1890, when the province began to provide financial aid. Pauperism was no respecter of ethnic group or religious affiliation, but it was most likely to strike those in the lowest socioeconomic positions. Among the 326 men admitted to the Wellington County House of Industry and Refuge between 1877 and 1910, 223 were labourers and 73 were tradespeople. Whereas in earlier periods women and children were more likely than men to receive relief, the pattern

TABLE 4
Occupiers of Rural Property in Ontario, 1871 to 1911

	1852	1871	1881	1891	1901	1911
Owners		144,212	169,140	224,034	179,791	186,696
%		83.7	81.7	78.4	80.2	82.1
Tenants		27,340	36,690	60,483	32,360	31,201
%		15.9	17.7	21.2	14.4	13.8
Managers		706	1,159	1,091	–	–
Part owner/part tenant		–	–	–	11,976	8,904
%					5.3	3.9
Total occupying	99,860	172,258	206,989	285,608	224,127	226,801
Number occupying						
Under 1 acre				69,413[a]	20,073	14,693
Under 5 acres					18,639	18,827
5–10 acres					7,474	8,944
Under 10 acres	9,976	19,954	36,221	108,724	48,186	42,464
%	10.0	11.6	17.5	38.1	20.6	18.7
11–50 acres	20,356	38,882	41,497	38,283	34,912	36,249
%	20.4	22.6	20.0	13.4	15.6	16.0
51–100 acres	48,027	71,884	75,282	75,307	76,164	78,335
%	48.1	41.7	36.4	26.4	34.0	34.5
101–200 acres	18,421	33,984	42,476	49,358	52,534	54,908
%	18.4	19.7	20.5	17.3	23.4	24.2
Above 200 acres	3,080	7,574	11,513	13,936	14,331	14,845
%	3.1	4.4	5.6	4.7	6.4	6.5
Numbers of farmers						
Females			2,822	5,245		
Males			226,090	174,337		
Farmers' sons			71,642	113,188		
Agricultural class			304,630			
Farm labourers				39,803[b]		

SOURCES: A. Lillie, *Canada: Physical, Economic, and Social* (Toronto 1855), 141. *Census of Canada*, 1871, vol. 3, 48–9; 1881, vol. 2. 307–8, vol. 3, 110–11; 1891, vol. 2, 163, vol. 4, 470; 1901, vol. 3, 156; 1911, vol. 3, 7, 56.
[a]*Census of Canada* 1941, vol. 8: Agriculture, table 1.
[b]Some enumerators treated the eldest sons of farmers as farm labourers and eldest daughters as servants.

changed in the last quarter of the century.[206] Men were admitted much more frequently than women and children, perhaps because the latter secured social assistance locally or they enjoyed greater personal support in their lives. In Wellington, 58 per cent of admissions were men, 25 per cent women, and 17 per cent children. The most common situations prompting admission were old age and destitution. Sickness was cited

TABLE 5
Servants, Ontario, 1881–1911

	1881	1891	1911
Female	21,635	35,781	30,962
Male	5,424	7,262	2,254

SOURCE: *Census of Canada*, 1881, vol. 2, 313; 1891, vol. 2, 164; 1911, vol. 6, 164.

much more frequently among men than women. Mental illness and blindness were other reasons. Whereas the creation of a local Children's Aid Society removed children from the institution after 1900, the percentage of elderly increased steadily in this and other poorhouses.

The labour unrest that surged during the 1880s was not without reverberations in rural Ontario. By 1885 the rapid spread of the Knights of Labor reached into tiny communities such as Clinton, Amherstburg, Port Dalhousie, Carleton Place, Gananoque, and Perth.[207] Edward Amey, a self-styled journalist and farmer from Lennox and Addington County, published a pamphlet that year in which he severely criticized farm labour practices and called for a union of agricultural labourers. Whereas worker control of the shop floor was what animated those in the forefront of the Knights of Labor, Amey's appeal was predicated on human rights and fundamental justice. At a time when organized labour was pushing for an eight-hour day, Edward Amey proposed twelve hours for agricultural labour with overtime pay and regular holidays. His union was to provide collections to defray work-related and burial expenses; a contributory health plan was also outlined. Rural waged women were not neglected. 'It is not surprising that intelligent girls prefer working in factories for two or three dollars a week to being cooks, housemaids, and general servants, for ten dollars a month and board,' Amey wrote, 'because servants' duties are so heavy that none but those who have strong constitutions are able to stay many weeks in a situation ... No wonder intelligent girls consider service both monotonous and degrading. Going into service nowadays is simply going into slavery. Life is a blank to those who do nothing but eat, drink, work, and sleep.'[208]

Although Edward Amey's proposal failed to provide rural labourers with a counterpart to the Grange, farmers were unsettled by the agitation. In 1886 the Agricultural and Arts Association of Ontario invited labour leader and civil servant Daniel O'Donoghue to its annual meeting, where three addresses on the subject were presented. O'Donoghue forthrightly condemned farm work as so demanding and draining that most labourers preferred any other form of employment. Others, however, invoked a nostalgic past where 'the owner of the land was as much a labourer as the man he employed to help him clear it, and the latter was equally looking forward to the purchase of land himself.'[209] When the Trades and Labor Congress of Canada met with the Grange, the two groups differed over immigration policies and the eight-hour day. Although labour journalist Phillips Thompson proclaimed in *The Politics of Labor* (1887) that farmers were labourers united in the struggle against monopolies, most farmers were more concerned about the National Policy tariffs that had begun in 1879.[210]

The lives of Catherine and William Brown illustrate the adaptability required from small agrarian proprietors and their growing reliance on waged work. Like his father, who had joined the exodus from Peel County to Peel Township in Wellington County in search of cheap land, William Brown was proud of his Methodist and Liberal connections, although, unlike his father he did not rise to local prominence as township councillor and school trustee. The son followed his father in becoming a farmer; so too did one of his sisters when she married, but another took to dressmaking and a fourth to tinsmithing. After William married Catherine Trask, whose grandfather had been a watchmaker, the Browns purchased a small farm of fifty-six acres in Peel Township in 1887. The couple planned bigger things than farming. They envisioned making more money than they could earn by growing peas, oats, and wheat and raising three cows and seven calves.

The Browns wanted to engage in the threshing business, a part-time activity carried on in the fall and the beginning of winter. The traditional manner of separating grain from husks and straw involved the use of hand flails. The residue was then thrown into the air using a winnowing basket to allow the wind to separate the heavier grain from the lighter chaff. The spread of mechanical separators earlier in the century had eased this process, but larger threshing machines had been noted in the province during the 1840s. As few farmers could afford to purchase them, threshing was often hired out to crews travelling around the countryside, but their range was limited because the machines were bulky and difficult to transport.

In a few districts custom threshing came to be done by small businesses. Small farmers like William Brown purchased the equipment and hired young men.[211] As threshing provided income for young men from poorer families, it was disdained as an activity for the middle class. 'I don't favour threshing,' wrote a Brantford merchant. 'It is a very rough business & the men are coarse, rough people & not good.'[212] The crews were smaller than in Britain and did not include women and children.[213] Farmers were expected to use their own team and perhaps one belonging to a neighbour, bringing the number of horses up to eight. Most often the farmer's family, hired help, and farmers close by combined to augment the labour of the crews. The assemblage of so many people on the farm marked the occasion as one of the highlights of the year. The meal prepared by women served as an inducement for all to pitch in.

At the point of the Browns' entry into the threshing business in the 1880s, the spread of portable steam engines extended the hope for larger profits through greater efficiency, but a larger investment was required for the equipment. Catherine and William therefore sought the advice of a village lawyer about how to proceed. Title and mortgage were registered in Catherine's name, a legal device that the couple would use during their married life to lessen their liability and protect themselves against creditors. When they bought a twelve-horsepower Champion steam engine in 1888 from the Waterous Engine Works in Brantford, they needed more cash than they had. William Brown's chattels were sold to his wife and partially mortgaged to John McGowan, a local flax miller destined to become a source of credit on more than one occasion, but four acres surrounding their house were exempted.

Steam threshing was innovative, but as it was dangerous work, the couple bought life insurance in 1890 for William through the Canadian Order of Foresters. The profits they made from threshing and their mixed farming operation were sufficient to build a kitchen on their typical frame, storey-and-a-half farmhouse to accommodate an expanding family. Eventually they were able to acquire a hundred-acre farm with a larger house nearby and to buy some new equipment. In their entry in the county's historical atlas, the couple boasted about William's 'reputation of being one of the best threshers in his section.'[214] Seven children had been born to Catherine and William, but only four had survived. The two oldest sons sought new opportunities by moving to the Prairies. As Catherine Brown was averse to farm work and her remaining son disdained it, most agricultural chores (including ploughing) fell to the youngest child, a daughter. Because their farm was not far from a railway station, William Brown was able to supplement the family's income at other times by working for the Waterloo Manufacturing Company and the Sawyer Massey Manufacturing Company in Hamilton. With one eye lost in a work accident and looking forward to a less strenuous pace, William Brown applied for a job as janitor in the county courthouse in Guelph; he produced a large number of testimonials from politicians, former employers, creditors, and local residents.[215]

MODIFICATIONS IN THE GENDERED DIVISION OF LABOUR

Lives like those of Catherine and William Brown suggest much about gender relations and the resiliency needed at a time when there was little support outside the immediate family. For many women, farm work as social production entailed a multiplicity of tasks centring on housework, child-rearing, education, field crops, livestock and poultry raising, marketing, and domestic consumption. The new ideas gaining ground in other quarters that the man's income should constitute the 'family wage' did not penetrate the countryside to any degree. Work was partitioned efficaciously, but within bounds influenced by social values and views about the proper role of each sex. The changes that occurred in the economic basis of farming and technological advances in the second half of the nineteenth century led to readjustments in the gendered division of work among segments of the rural population. Some of the activities once performed in the home were transferred elsewhere with increasing numbers of rural women as the net beneficiaries. Domestic spinning and weaving declined, cheese production was moved increasingly to small local factories, where women often worked for wages, and other dairying functions followed with the later spread of creameries and refrigeration in the 1890s. The effects on work varied with the products produced. Home-made cheese production was halved during the 1870s and declined to the point of insignificance by 1910, but Ontario domestic butter production plateaued for three decades after 1881. In the country as a whole, home-made butter outpaced creamery butter by a ratio of three to one in 1900, but because of its variable quality, it fetched a much lower price.[216]

The transition to mixed farming and the growing reliance on urban outlets increased the work that was usually done by women. The sale of dairy products, poultry, eggs, and vegetables became more and more important to the incomes of an expanding number of farm families. Clothing, which was most often made at home, became more elaborate. Greater domestic comfort and better hygiene expanded women's work and made them more fully the managers of their family's consumption. The earliest historian of the province's agriculture was emphatic in this regard. 'Whatever qualifications a farmer should have, mental or physical, all are agreed on this point, that *a good wife* is indispensable,' James Croil had written in 1861. 'What it is the aim of the husband to accumulate, it becomes the province of the wife to manage,' he continued, 'and wherever we hear of a managing wife, we are sure to find a money-making farmer.'[217] Farm labourers also found that 'there are always two bosses on every farm (one too many), the farmer and his wife. The wife does not always give direct orders, but it amounts to the same thing.'[218] Rising standards of living also brought a closer proximity between rural and urban values that was reflected in the language. As early as 1869 one astute rural resident writing to a newspaper objected to the displacement of the traditional word 'women' by 'ladies' and 'females.'[219] The term 'lady' implied a leisured status that farm women did not enjoy.

With the adoption of machinery for crop production, the disparity between field labour and housework became the source for increasingly bitter comment among women farmers. 'Not near so much progress has been made in labour-saving machines for in-door as for outdoor work,' one woman had noted in 1869. 'One reason for this may be, that the inventors being principally men are rather selfish, easing their own labours before thinking of the opposite sex.'[220] Among the few additions to prosperous households that eased women's work were the sewing machine, improved butter churns, the washing mangle, and the mechanical cream separator, but men were frequently reluctant to invest in them. This was noticed by the instructors attached to the government's travelling dairies that were sent around the province to improve production after the country's wretched butter was rejected massively on the British market in 1891. 'If a farmer wants a new mower or a reaper or a plow, he gets it,' they reported. 'But let the women folk ask for a new churn or something of that kind to make the work easier and improve the product, and at once there is grumbling and the question is asked, "Can't you get along with what you have?"'[221]

By 1900 hand- or treadle-powered cream separators were well established around the province, but many farms still had no equipment designed for women's work. 'We have taken the spinning and weaving and soap and candlemaking out of the home,' a farm speaker observed in 1902, 'but still women are overworked.'[222] Another commented: 'But what woman in a farm house and with the average amount of help can ever say that her work is done? It is new every morning – and yet most exasperatingly old. It goes on with the ceaseless regularity of a treadmill, often with about the same effect on the worker.'[223] Farm women were portrayed as so beleaguered by constant drudgery that a common misconception, expounded by prominent people like Letitia Youmans and Adelaide Hoodless, portrayed them as suffering higher rates of mental illness than other women.[224] The stress of work showed in the life of Mary Ann King, a farmer in Chippewa who regularly suffered from severe migraines after a heavy bout of churning butter. Some women were indignant about their plight. 'Coming in after spending the day in the potato field and doing the milking and the rest of the evening work is bad enough,' one woman commented, 'but to discover that those plums just have to be canned, when every bone in your body is crying out a protest against every movement, is like adding insult to injury.'[225]

Rising prosperity led Ontario farm women in better economic circumstances to demand and secure a release from some of the labour that had been borne by their predecessors. In response to changing gender relations, an animated debate on women's farm work erupted in the press during the labour upheavals of the 1880s and continued periodically until the First World War. 'By what right does a farmer expect so much more from his wife than from any other man?' asked one woman. 'By what right has a husband to look for companionship and a home from a wife more heavily weighted than a beast of burden?'[226] Another correspondent placed the blame for the inequitable division of labour on child-rearing practices that taught men to command from birth. 'We read of the Chinese and their low estimate of baby girls. Are we, with our vaunted civilization,' she asked, 'any better in that respect?'[227] Some women refused to do work outside the home, while others demanded greater reciprocity from their husbands. 'If a man asks his wife to coil hay, build stooks and loads, etc., he, in his turn, should be willing to help her with the heavier part of her work,' it was noted. 'When a man can't manage his own work without making his wife and daughters help,' another woman asserted, 'then I say he'd better sell out, or get a smaller farm where he can manage the work.'[228] Unjust inheritance laws and practices that favoured male heirs were also denounced.

This desire for less work for women combined with evolving middle-class social values to make the organized dairy and poultry industries male-centred. In 1869, the first year that it had been active, the Canadian Dairymen's Association had only one woman among its 156 members.[229] Similarly, the farm press that served specialty producers was dominated by men. There was no hint of female influence in the first issue of the *Canadian Fancier and Farm Poultry Journal*, which appeared in Windsor in 1898. Male exclusivity was at play, but it was predicated on the middle-class conceptions shared by both sexes in prospering farm families. With greater productivity, larger numbers of such women had more options in their lives, although most did not withdraw completely from agricultural operations. Their labour was still frequently called upon at critical points in the farming season. Thus a son remembered that his mother, who had been born in 1859, was able to 'cook, sew, mend, spin, weave, care for children and nurse the sick,' and '*if need be* she could, with equal proficiency, make a garden, milk cows, drive a team, shear the sheep, or perform any other farm task' (italics mine).[230] A woman noted in 1884, 'I know a family of farmers' daughters who can harness their horses, and while one drives the reaper, others bind up the grain, draw it in etc., attend the pigs, calves, bees, vegetable garden, spin and manufacture the wool, and these are no ignorant rustics either. They are high school graduates ... These are not exceptions.'[231]

Economic historians working within the staples paradigm (that is, concerned with exports), or basing their conclusions primarily on census data, have viewed these modifications in the gendered division of labour as indicative of a decline of women's importance in dairying and a lowering of their productivity.[232] What is forgotten is that rural men and women, like farmers in upper New York state or working-class people in Ontario's small factory towns, shared their work in a flexible manner.[233] Gender roles were constantly renegotiated, but as such decisions fell outside the market, their effects on production for profit, and for women's work specifically, cannot be measured. Successful attempts by wealthier farm women, or even those like Catherine Brown, to remove themselves from heavy physical labour represented not loss of importance, but a reciprocity between the sexes that acknowledged changing economic conditions.

For a significant segment of the farm population, modifications in the gendered division of labour worked in favour of women who were favourably placed in the economic hierarchy. This development represented a decrease in productivity only if productivity is construed in the economist's narrow sense. That the census alone is an unreliable guide to women's farm work is shown in the contradictions that result from over-reliance on this source. If, as it has been argued, the 1851 census shows that Ontario farm women engaged primarily in housework, how can it then be maintained that up to 1891 'Ontario agriculture was becoming less dependent on female farm labour?'[234] The census is an inadequate guide to women's farm work because its framers were middle-class men intent on measuring work in middle-class male terms. Some Ontario rural census takers in 1881, for instance, arbitrarily classified all eldest sons as farm labourers while denoting the eldest daughters as domestic servants.[235] The census contains important information, but it is insufficient on its own to provide the exact picture of the period that is the historian's quest. The dynamism in gender relations that allowed some farm couples to readjust their work roles over the century is lost. Gender roles were fluid, but their viscosity depended on economic circumstances in ways that cannot be measured specifically.

Nor was farm income an exclusive male prerogative any more than the labour contributing to its production. In 1903 a questionnaire was circulated to Ontario farm women by the National Council of Women of Canada. The responses showed that the sexual division of labour in dairying varied greatly around the province. Asked about how economic developments such as cheese factories had affected their personal finances, most farm women said they saw little difference in their lives.[236] Twentieth-century rural sociologists have been much better able to disentangle the participation of the sexes in farm decision making, but historical evidence from earlier periods precludes hasty generalization.[237] All that can be said is that unpublished diaries and account books show farm men and women discussing or working together in deciding on such major purchases as horses or cream separators, but they seldom mention women's involvement in decisions about what crops to plant or other aspects of economic management.[238]

For less prosperous families, debates about the nature of women's involvement in farm life were far removed from daily existence. When economic studies were begun early in the twentieth century, it was found that Ontario's farms were the most labour-intensive in the country and had the highest input by women in dairying operations; the contribution of children, however, declined after 1900.[239] Nor did women's field work end. In 1912, for instance, a Waterloo County farmer noted in his diary that 'two Arabian [Syrian] women, Mrs Schultz, her daughter Gerty, and Mrs Brondeau all helped at the potatoes at Erdmans. Got them finished up, about sixty bags today.'[240] Rural women and children also constituted the primary labour force in the rurally based canning industry after it began to expand in the 1880s, although they tended to be drawn more from strictly labouring than farming families. Wages often varied in a ratio of 4/2/1 for men, women, and children, although in fruit picking the ratio was 4/3/2.[241] Women were also seasonal labourers in the tobacco-growing industry, which expanded after 1900, and in the Niagara fruit district, where their pay of seventy-five cents a day stood at three-quarters of what was paid to men. The work was gruelling and living conditions were bad. The eleven-hour work days began with breakfast at six-thirty and ended in the return from the fields at six in the evening. As female workers in Niagara lived in shacks, private employment agencies developed to provide placements and accommodations in hostels in exchange for a fee, but since pickers were so hard to secure, some farmers began to lease their orchards to intermediaries who employed gangs for harvesting.[242]

FARMERS AND LABOURERS IN THE LATE NINETEENTH CENTURY

Despite the upsurge in the 1890s of a second popular farm organization, the Patrons of Industry, Ontario farmers remained divided. Some stressed the manual nature of their occcupation while others linked the success of their operations to business acumen and increased efficiency. Nevertheless, the very qualities that had laid the basis for material success frequently made farmers inconsiderate employers, as we have seen already with Joseph Elson earlier in the century. Many Ontario farmers had struggled so hard to achieve prosperity that they drove their hired help with the same maniacal rigour that they displayed in their own work habits. 'Ploughing, ploughing, ploughing, all day, all day,' a young farmer noted in his diary in 1881. 'From morn till night with the wee intervals of eating time.'[243] Even during the biggest annual celebration in his life, New Year's Day, he reflected that it 'only comes once a year and the cows have to be fed all the same.' When asked to define a good agricultural labourer before the Royal Commission on the Relations of Labour and Capital, a Chatham area farmer responded: 'One who is willing to get up at five in the morning, attend to the team, and see to everything till eight o'clock at night.'[244] Fifteen-hour days, wretched working conditions, and condescending attitudes made farm labour abhorrent to many – the most lowly, demanding, and demeaning of all occupations after domestic service, and the least rewarding. 'Some farmers treat their hands much as they do their teams,' an essayist observed in 1886. 'They feed them and work them, without even noticing them or speaking to them, except to give them their orders and see that they work about fifteen hours per day. Others, we are sorry to say, actually despise their hired men, and when meal time comes, place them in a corner to eat by themselves, or make them wait till the family have finished, and then eat the fragments that remain.'[245] The same criticism pervaded the discussion of rural women's waged work. 'Why will female servants not stay on the farm?' a newspaper asked. 'We answer, without hesitation, because they are worked too hard. One girl has to work four or five cows twice a day, to feed the same amount of calves, to wash for the house, to prepare three meals a day for a lot of hungry workingmen, and to do all the other work about the house. She is up when the cock crows, and working all day; she must, in order to rise, go straight from the washing of the supper dishes to her bed ... Is it any wonder they crowd into factories, some to the prejudice of their health?'[246]

The growth of viable alternatives in the form of more attractive and remunerative jobs in cities, or homesteading one's own property in the Canadian or American west, worked to the detriment of agriculture in Ontario. After the price of land began to rise at the end of the century, it was estimated that it would take ten years of labour to acquire the capital necessary to begin a farm.[247] Farm life was frequently lonely and desolate; opportunities for social intercourse and companionship were strictly limited for someone stuck in one place without a horse. This often made it difficult for hired hands to avail themselves of the social amenities of nearby villages and towns. 'The most disagreeable feature of my first experience as a hired man,' one labourer observed, 'was having to work so much alone.'[248] Another declared himself 'heartily sick, not of farming but of the arrogant and supercilious manner in which the average farmer and his family treat the hired man ... Some farmers would be more at home with a white coat on, bossing a gang of slaves with a long whip, as they seem to think that, in hiring a man for a length of time, they have bought him body and soul, instead of just hiring his physical strength, and that their sole duty is to keep their face on the grinding stone fourteen hours a day, six days a week.'[249]

Ontario's farms were also unsafe and unhealthy workplaces. An analysis of farm well water by the Dominion Experimental Farm in Ottawa, published in 1897, showed that a large majority of the samples were unfit for human consumption and many absolutely dangerous to human health.[250] Working with animals, especially horses, is always dangerous, but farm machinery contained many unprotected moving parts and blades. Vehicles as well as machines were easily overturned on rough terrain. Local newspapers reported numerous dismemberments and deaths in farm accidents. The only legislation, passed in 1874, made the owners of threshing and other machines responsible for ensuring that moving parts were fitted with guards. But such was the political influence of farmers that Premier Oliver Mowat excluded farm workers from coverage under worker's compensation in 1893, an exemption that remained in effect until 1966.[251] Nor were farm workers included in the legislation of 1887 that created arbitration boards to settle labour disputes. Although Mowat's Liberal government did institute universal manhood suffrage in the following year, labourers and servants still could not vote in municipal elections or participate in annual school meetings because often they owned no land. Such ostracism made everyone in the rural communities aware of its property-based hierarchy.

More than the low wages, the absence of substantial year-round employment and poor living conditions made agricultural labour unappealing. Time had passed by the paternalistic work relations on which it was predicated. Yet farmers clung tenaciously to total control over employment on their farms, as a manifestation of the independence they had achieved, unable to understand why their hired help objected to such restrictions. As few farm workers in the province were provided with separate housing, the closeness in living circumstances made farm work seem like domestic service, another occupation from which people fled for similar reasons. Petty jealousies over treatment easily arose on such minor issues as why the help were given homemade soap while the family enjoyed the superior manufactured product.[252] As few employers would be pinned down to a written contract, disputes arose quickly, firings were immediate, and nothing resulted in getting the sack faster than contesting the hours of work.[253] The lack of work in winter was not simply the result of the Canadian climate, but part of a structural rigidity in Ontario agriculture resulting from the popularity of the hundred-acre farm. For dairy production, farms with sixty-one to seventy-five tillable acres – the size that many were – were too large to be worked by just one man but too small to need two throughout the year.[254]

Farm youth abandoned agriculture in droves, driven by a desire for the personal freedom attending an income that would support them. After 1900 domestic service and farming were both disdained to such an extent that two-thirds of 150 students surveyed at the Ontario Agricultural College found farm work distasteful.[255] It became increasingly common for the most talented young people to depart, while families kept 'at home the boy who will "only make a farmer."'[256] One farmer noted in 1894 that young women 'would rather live in a village, town, or city, working on the needle at one meal a day than work in a farm house and be well fed and receive good wages. All the same, a great cry will be raised about the sweating system.'[257] Beginning in the 1890s, the exodus was intensified by the harvest excursions to western Canada that were promoted by the Canadian Pacific Railway.

The slack was taken up by immigrants, principally from Britain, where, by the beginning of the twentieth century, at least twenty-eight charitable and philanthropic organizations were promoting emigration.[258] Not all associations were as reputable as the Barnardo Homes, the best-known of several major child-placement groups. The International Emigration Association in London, England, developed a scam called the farm-pupil scheme that placed 150 boys on North American farms in 1894, some through an agent in Bowmanville. Though the children were supposed to be taught farming, the principal motive in this traffic in young bodies was a financial cut for each boy for whom employment was found. The head of the association was wanted in Kansas City for alleged infractions of American alien labour laws. No care was taken in either the selection or the placement of the boys. Some were small and unaccustomed to farm work. Some reacted badly to the alien environment in which they found themselves. One, annoyed when a cow he was forced to milk whisked its tail, severed it near the animal's spine. Others were found in Carleton Place selling their meagre possessions to buy a railway ticket in order to escape.[259]

The Toronto Trades and Labour Council protested the activities of companies such as the International Association and called for an end to government subsidies to immigrants who were farm labourers or domestic servants. When the Dominion Police and immigration officials investigated, they found their hands tied by a group with headquarters overseas that operated in the shadow of the law. One boy took his employer to court for non-payment of wages and won his case in November of 1895, just before the ghastly revelations surrounding the tragic death of George Everitt Green on the farm of Helen Findlay near Owen Sound.[260] The physical abuse and malnutrition that contributed to the end of that young life finally provoked public indignation and an official response. In 1897 the Canadian government began to scrutinize the activities of child emigration societies in Britain more closely, and Ontario passed the Juvenile Immigration Act that required child immigrants to be screened and their situations to be inspected annually.

Immigrants remained a prime source of agricultural labourers, but fewer new arrivals wanted to work in the countryside. In the 1860s, with the advent of cheaper steamship fares to North America and changes in British society, more single people had begun to leave Britain and fewer came from rural backgrounds, while after 1900 the number of Europeans entering the province increased dramatically.[261] In 1902 the Ontario government created the Farm Labour Bureau in Toronto to promote the movement of immigrants into agriculture. Those who were persuaded often viewed their situation as a temporary means to earn some money before better prospects arrived. 'I have settled with this farmer for 1 year and I am perfectly happy and comfortable,' wrote one who had previously been unemployed in England, 'and could not be treated any better if I was at home. I have a nice bed, plenty to eat and drink, and I am contented. I find the work out here rough, but it's healthy, that's one blessing, and you are all on the go from morn till night, but there's one consolation in knowing that it is better than walking about London looking for work and nothin in your insides.'[262]

For many the dream turned rapidly sour with the first firings before the onset of winter. About one hundred families in Chatham in 1907, mostly immigrants who had been previously employed in farm labour, were reduced to destitution and required municipal assistance.[263] Some immigrants noticed immediately the different attitudes to work on this side of the Atlantic. A young English working-class woman was pleased to be receiving nutritious food but commented in 1891, 'The work is hard, in drawing up water from the cistern and carrying water to and fro and milk from the barn.'[264] A man who found himself labouring twelve hours a day, seven days a week, commented that work in Ontario 'is quite different from what work is in England, being longer hours and much harder.'[265] In fact there were so many conflicts between immigrant labourers and Ontario farmers that officials of the Farm Labour Bureau said that they devoted 90 per cent of their time to mediating disputes over terms and conditions of work. Some farmers called for immigration from Asia because Asians were thought to be more docile and willing to work for lower wages.

CONCLUSION

Although the settlement of rural Ontario had initially attracted all and sundry, the disappearance of cheap land in the province and the commercialization of farming during the third quarter of the nineteenth century intensified the social divisions in the countryside between property owners, who enjoyed the full benefits of Canadian life, and those who laboured for others. As agriculture generated profits to fuel the province's economy, the greater prosperity allowed some to renegotiate the gendered division of work in the countryside. The Grange and an expanding agricultural press provided farm men and women with a common forum, but the attempt to unionize rural workers failed. Unlike their later counterparts on the Prairies, who forged greater solidarity during the Depression of the 1930s, rural labourers in Ontario remained an amorphous group consisting primarily of young people, immigrants, and a few for whom it was a career.[266] Workers in rural areas were notoriously difficult to organize, as the short-lived National Agricultural Labourer's Union in Britain found. The freedom of movement enjoyed by civil society in Ontario also created conditions encouraging people to seek new opportunities in other places. After 1881 they did so in large numbers. As the new century opened, the fertile soils of the Little Clay Belt beckoned those who still hoped to find security through farming. Among the first to acquire homesteads there were Russian Jews, most of whom had been farmers, blacksmiths, and carpenters in their native country and had taken to tailoring in Toronto. Many of the women remained at their sewing machines in the city in order to support their new family venture at its onset.[267]

Although the history of rural labour needs to be studied in its own right, our knowledge of conditions in the countryside challenges the assumptions that have underpinned most accounts of industrialization. Without an understanding of labour and gender relations in rural areas, historians have lacked a measure against which to assess the effects of the industrial transformation. While this chapter has concentrated on agriculture, which sustained larger numbers than any other economic sector well into the twentieth century, the reciprocity between farm and non-farm life needs to be explored more fully. So, too, do the dynamics of rural/urban relationships, the nature of work in small towns, and the impact of new manufacturing processes in rural areas. We also need to know more about social and economic divisions in the countryside. While the extent of geographical mobility has become increasingly apparent, future studies will need to clarify who moved, why they moved, and whether their socio-economic status changed in new environments. The development of a rich diversity of institutional life in rural Ontario beckons as well. How did rural Ontarians spend their leisure time and what role did religion play in their lives? What influence did gender have? Regional variations within the province and in contrast to Quebec and the northern United States will help to increase our understanding, as will inter-ethnic comparisons. Only when such questions have been answered will historians be able to present a more rounded interpretation of the history of labouring lives in this province.

But what of George Disbrowe, who was left crying in the cedar swamp? By 1892 his family's labour had created enough capital for him to return to agriculture for a third time. The soil on the fifty-acre farm was sandy, but eventually the mortgage was cleared by all pitching in. George and Melissa Disbrowe then moved to a dairy farm twice its size that they worked on shares for three years. The property owner supplied the land and equipment, the family contributed its labour, and profits were divided equally. When this contract was concluded, they entered a second share agreement in 1906 for a property with 225 acres. Four years later they finally bought a farm for $8,300. One of the Disbrowe sons, who attended the Ontario Agricultural College and became a high school principal in the largely Mennonite community of Elmira, north of Kitchener, found the travail of his mother and father so singular that he committed it to paper. In one respect the son was right, but in another he was wrong. Their travail had been extraordinary, but it was far from uncommon.

NOTES

I would like to thank Terri Meilke, Mark Cortiula, and Paul Dickson, who served as research assistants. My colleagues Richard Reid and Kris Inwood drew my attention to valuable sources, while the comments of Catherine Wilson, Gordon Darroch, and Donald Davies on earlier versions of the manuscript were greatly appreciated. Archivists and librarians in Ontario's rich regional collections were unfailingly helpful. A special note of thanks is due to Gloria Troyer of the University of Guelph Library Archival and Special Collections, who put her vast knowledge of those records at my disposal over an extended period. Financial assistance towards research costs from the Social Science and Humanities Research Council of Canada is gratefully acknowledged.

1 H.B. Disbrowe, 'A Vignette of Yesterday' [ca. 1960], Disbrowe Papers, University of Guelph Library Archival and Special Collections (UG). See also G.A. Disbrowe, 'Help Wanted,' *Farmer's Advocate*, 8 January 1912.

2 Elizabeth Smith, *A Woman with a Purpose: The Diaries of Elizabeth Smith 1872–1884*, ed. Veronica Strong-Boag (Toronto 1980), 10, 99, 114–15, 246.

3 David Gagan, *Hopeful Travellers: Families, Land, and Social Change in Mid-Victorian Peel County* (Toronto 1981); Chad Gaffield, *Language, Schooling, and Cultural Conflict: The Origins of the French-Language Controversy in Ontario* (Montreal 1987); and Randy W. Widdis, 'Tracing Eastern Ontario Emigrants to New York State, 1880–1910,' *Ontario History* 81 (1989), 201–22.

4 Douglas McCalla and Peter George, 'Measurement, Myth and Reality: Reflections on the Economic History of Nineteenth-Century Ontario,' *Journal of Canadian Studies* 21 (1986), 71–86. See also Ian M. Drummond, *Progress without Planning: The Economic History of Ontario from Confederation to the Second World War* (Toronto 1987).

5 Gagan, *Hopeful Travellers*, 56; Gordon Darroch and Michael Ornstein, 'Ethnicity and Class: Transitions over a Decade, 1861–1871,' *Historical Papers 1984*, Canadian Historical Association, 111–37; and Gordon Darroch, 'Class in Nineteenth-Century Central Ontario: A Reassessment of the Crisis and Demise of Small Producers during Early Industrialization,' in Gregory S. Kealey, ed., *Class, Gender, and Region: Essays in Canadian Historical Sociology* (St John's 1988), 49–71. This last study estimated that 17–20 per cent of the untraced 45 per cent of the population moved from the large study area designated as 'south-central Ontario.' Though this approximates the American experience, no valid comparison can be drawn with the European experience before 1800 because studies there have concentrated on villages (where an annual exodus of 10 per cent has been estimated). See Charles Tilly, 'Demographic Origins of the European Proletariat,' in David Levine, ed., *Proletarianization and the Family* (New York 1984).

6 Robert P. Swierenga, 'Theoretical Perspectives on the New Rural History,' *Agricultural History* 56 (1982), 495–502. See also Steven Hahn and Jonathan Prude, eds., *The Countryside in the Age of Capitalist Formation: Essays in the Social History of Rural America* (Chapel Hill, N.C. 1985).

7 On the dividing lines between rural and urban in Britain and the United States, see Dudley Baines, *Migration in a Mature Economy: Emigration and Internal Migration in England and Wales, 1861–1900* (Cambridge 1985), 144–6; and Hahn and Prude, Introduction to *The Countryside in the Age of Capitalistic Transformation.* Canadian town planner Thomas Adams assumed a population of fifteen hundred as the threshold in *Rural Planning and Development: A Study of Rural Conditions and Problems in Canada* (Ottawa 1917), 20. George V. Haythorne and Leonard C. Marsh, *Land and Labour* ([Toronto] 1941), 40, took a population of 1,000 as separating the two.

8 On paternalism see Janice Potter, 'Patriarchy and Paternalism: The Case of Eastern Ontario Loyalist Women,' *Ontario History* 81 (1989), 4–5, and I.A. Newby, *Plainfolk in the New South: Social Change and Cultural Persistence, 1880–1915* (Baton Rouge 1989), chap. 9.

9 The best summary of the debate in the United States is Allan Kulikoff, 'The Transition to Capitalism in Rural America,' *William and Mary Quarterly* 3d ser., 46 (1989), 120–44. For Britain and Europe see T.S. Ashton and C.H.E. Philpin, eds, *The Brenner Debate: Agrarian Class Structure and Economic Development in Pre-Industrial Europe* (Cambridge 1987). Jerome Blum, *The Decline of the Old Order in Rural Europe* (Princeton 1978), and Eugen Weber, *Peasants into Frenchmen: The Modernization of Rural France 1870–1914* (Stanford 1976), adopt a non-Marxist approach. For Quebec see Fernand Ouellet, 'Ruralization, Regional Development and Industrial Growth before 1850,' in *Economy, Class and Nation in Quebec: Interpretive Essays*, trans. Jacques A. Barbier (Toronto 1991) and Bruno Ramirez, *On the Move: French-Canadian and Italian Migrants in the North Atlantic Economy, 1860–1914* (Toronto 1990).

10 See Colin F. Read and Ronald Stagg, eds, *The Rebellion of 1837 in Upper Canada: A Collection of Documents* (Ottawa 1985).

11 *Upper Canada Gazette*, 18 April 1793. The debate on the issue of commercial agriculture, and consequently whether rural dwellers were farmers or peasants, has been extensive in both Canada and the United States. For the United States see James Henrietta, 'Families and Farms: *Mentalité* in Pre-Industrial America,' *William and Mary Quarterly*, 3d ser., 35 (1978), 3–32; and James T. Lemon, 'The Weakness of Place and Community in Early Pennsylvania,' in James R. Gibson, ed., *European Settlement and Development in North America: Essays on Geographical Change in Honour and Memory of Andrew Hill Clark* (Toronto 1978).

For early Ontario, Leo Johnson emphasized the importance of domestic (or subsistence) agriculture in 'Land Policy, Population Change and Social Structure in the Home District, 1793–1851,' *Ontario History* 63 (1971), 41–60; *A History of the County of Ontario, 1615–1875* (Whitby 1973); and 'Independent Commodity Production: Mode of Production or Capitalist Class Formation?' *Studies in Political Economy: A Socialist Review* 6 (1981), 93–113.

Taking an opposing view that stressed the acquisitive, individualistic nature of early Ontarians are R. Cole Harris, Pauline Roulston, and Chris De Freitas, 'The Settlement of Mono Township,' *Canadian Geographer* 19 (1975), 1–17; and Donald H. Akenson, *The Irish in Ontario: A Study in Rural History* (Montreal 1984), which is an examination of Leeds and Lansdowne Township in eastern Ontario. Douglas McCalla bolsters this position in several articles: 'The Loyalist Economy of Upper Canada, 1784–1806,' *Histoire sociale/Social History* 16 (1983), 299–303; 'The Internal Economy of Upper Canada: New Evidence on Agricultural Marketing Before 1850,' in J.K. Johnson and Bruce G. Wilson, eds, *Historical Essays on Upper Canada* (Ottawa 1989), 237–60; and 'Rural Credit and Rural Development in Upper Canada, 1790–1850,' in Roger Hall, William Westfall, and Laurel S. MacDowell eds, *Patterns of the Past: Interpreting Ontario's History* (Toronto 1988), 37–54.

In a study of Nova Scotia, Debra McNabb, 'The Role of Land in the Development of Horton Township, 1760–1775,' in Margaret Conrad, ed., *They Planted Well* (Fredericton 1988), reveals that 80 per cent of grantees engaged in land trading for immediate profit.

12 Henry Nelles Letterbook, 1831–2, Robert Hamilton Papers, UG, John MacIntosh Duff Collection. See also George to John Brown, 9 September 1830, John Brown Letters, 12, Weldon Library Regional Collection, University of Western Ontario (UWO). `

13 W. Thomas Matthews, 'Local Government and the Regulation of the Public Market in Upper Canada, 1800–1860: The Moral Economy of the Poor?' *Ontario History* 79 (1987), 297–326. In contrast to mercantilist regulation in the towns, the town meetings of the early American settlers sought to ensure social harmony within a context of individual property rights in a manner seen elsewhere in the preceding two centuries. Fence adjudication, straying animals, and rights of way on roads were addressed in meetings in Niagara. See Niagara Township records, 1793–1803, Niagara Historical Research Centre, Reel 001; and William Canniff, *History of the Settlement of Upper Canada (Ontario) with Special Reference to the Bay of Quinte* (Toronto 1872).

14 See Winifred B. Rothenberg, 'The Emergence of Farm Labor Markets and the Transformation of the Rural Economy: Massachusetts, 1750–1855,' *Journal of Economic History* 48 (1988), 537–66.

15 Douglas McCalla, *Planting the Province: The Economic History of Upper Canada* (Toronto 1993), 31.

16 Gerald E. Boyce, *Hutton of Hastings: The Life and Letters of William Hutton, 1801–1864* (Belleville 1972), 181.

17 Miriam H. Snyder, *Hannes Schneider and His Wife Catharine Haus Schneider* (privately printed, Kitchener 1937), Kitchener Public Library, refers to a variety of primary sources and documents these visits even after mid-century. William Bell diary, Queen's University Archives (QU), includes references to people coming and going to the United States in the 1820s, as do James Alves to his brother and sister [1842], Alves Family Papers, QU, and R.A. Preston, ed., *For Friends at Home: A Scottish Emigrant's Letters from Canada, California, and the Cariboo* (Montreal 1974). J.T. Townsend to Lisa, 5 November 1863, Townsend Letters, UG, notes the demand for operators in Buffalo, the cost of living there, and the high wages being offered, 'but they be up top sound operators.'

Angus J. Winchester, ed., '"Scratching amongst the Stumps": Letters from Thomas Priestman, a Settler in the Niagara Peninsula, 1811–1839,' *Ontario History* 81 (1989), 41–58, reveals how a liberal English Quaker followed economic developments in the United States that would influence his farm; and Charles Julius Mickle to Charles Mickle, 28 July 1838, and Alexander Mickle to William Mickle, June 1838, Mickle Family Papers, UG, show that the sons of an English immigrant to a Guelph area farm in 1832 were off in Michigan six years later, scouting for cheaper land in the wake of disgruntlement created by the suppression of the 1837 rebellion.

Gregory S. Rose, 'The Origins of Canadian Settlers in Southern Michigan, 1820–1850,' *Ontario History* 79 (1987), 31–52, traces this movement geographically. Bernard Bailyn, *Voyages to the West* (London 1986); and T.M. Devine, 'The Paradox of Scottish Emigration,' in T.M. Devine, ed., *Scottish Emigration and Scottish Society* (Edinburgh 1992), 1–15, reach similar conclusions about geographic mobility in colonial America and in Scotland.

18 Anna Bellamy diary, 10 September 1855, Archives of Ontario (AO). James Reid to Thomas Reid, 8 January 1849, James Reid letters, AO, notes the sale of a farm during a period of economic uncertainty by someone 'going to look for better land and nearer a good market.'

19 Jane Johnson to Hugh Johnson, 9 January 1849, McConnell·Family Letters, UWO.

20 Hannah Jarvis to Samuel Peters, 25 October 1792, in Kenneth W. Cameron, ed., *The Papers of Loyalist Samuel Peters* (Hartford 1978), 178. Jarvis noted that domestic servants were paid from $2.50 to $12.00 a month and that she employed two at $7.00.

21 Quoted in William Canniff, *History of the Province of Ontario* (Toronto 1872), 73. Robin Winks, *The Blacks in Canada: A History* (Montreal 1971), 96–9, discusses the legislation.

22 Shirley C. Spragge, 'Organizing the Wilderness: A Study of a Loyalist Settlement, Augusta Township, Grenville County, 1784–1820' (PhD thesis, Queen's University 1986), 54. Although the assessment rolls did not include the poorest people with nothing to tax, the economic divisions in early Augusta Township were comparable to those in Pennsylvania in 1793 where the top 10 per cent of the population held 24 per cent of the wealth. See James T. Lemon, *The Best Poor Man's Country: A Geographical Study of Early Southeastern Pennsylvania* (Baltimore 1972); and Jackson Turner Main, *The Social Structure of Revolutionary America* (Princeton 1965). Rusty Bitterman, 'The Hierarchy of the Soil: Land and Labour in 19th-Century Cape Breton,' *Acadiensis* 18 (Fall 1988) examined the sources and development of such inequality within a predominantly Highland Scottish population.

23 Calculated from Peter A. Russell, 'Attitudes to Social Structure and Social Mobility in Upper Canada (1815–1840)' (PhD thesis, Carleton University 1981), 74.

24 Gordon Darroch and Michael D. Ornstein, 'Ethnicity and Occupational Structure in Canada in 1871: The Vertical Mosaic in Historical Perspective,' *Canadian Historical Review* 61 (1980), 305–33, showed that in Ontario by 1871 the proportion of farmers within various ethnic groups were: Irish Catholics, 48 per cent; Irish Protestants, 59 per cent; English, 47 per cent; Scots, 61 per cent; Germans, 63 per cent. Irish Catholics and Germans were overrepresented among labourers (21 per cent and 15 per cent respectively against a provincial average of 13 per cent) and underrepresented among artisans (15 per cent and 11 per cent against an average of 18 per cent). The French-Canadian element in the sample was too small to convey an accurate picture. See also Akenson, *The Irish in Ontario*; Darroch, 'Class in Nineteenth-Century, Central Ontario'; Bruce S. Elliott, *Irish Migrants in the*

Canadas: A New Approach (Montreal 1988); and Cecil J. Houston and William J. Smyth, *Irish Emigration and Canadian Settlement: Patterns, Links and Letters* (Toronto 1990).

25 Helen Cowan, *British Emigration to North America* (Toronto 1961), 304, provides an occupational breakdown of immigrants arriving at Quebec and Montreal for 1846 and 1853–9.

26 Heinz Lehmann, *The German Canadians, 1750–1937: Immigration, Settlement and Culture*, trans. Gerhard P. Bassler (St John's 1986), 22.

27 Cowan, *British Emigration*, 189, estimated that a poor person could cross the Atlantic, travel inland, and acquire fifty acres of land with £50. The Canada Company in the 1830s advised prospective settlers to plan on £100, the amount suggested in Robert Craig to his brother, 8 May 1834, Robert Craig Letters, QU. Houston and Smyth, *Irish Emigration*, 59, show that 97 per cent of 378 emigrants from County Antrim between 1835–9 carried less than £60 and that 13 per cent had no money at all. It should be remembered that £10 in Ireland represented the gross wage of a labourer for nine months' work. Elliott, *Irish Migrants*, 76, contrasts the greater wealth brought by the Tipperary Protestants he traces with the poverty of the Irish-Catholic settlers brought by Peter Robinson to the Peterborough area. Glengarry's Highland Scottish settlers, though relatively well off compared to others in their country of origin, frequently had no money by the time they arrived in the eastern part of the province. See Marianne McLean, 'Peopling Glengarry County: The Scottish Origins of a Canadian Community,' in Johnson and Wilson, *Historical Essays on Upper Canada*, 151–74.

28 J. Tuke to George, 23 June 1832, UWO. Thomas Fowler, *The Journal of a Tour through British America ...* (Aberdeen 1832), 144, noted that forty-four of the fifty-seven women cared for by the Female Benevolent Society of Kingston were Irish.

29 Lehmann, *The German Canadians*, 22.

30 James Walker, *The Blacks in Canada* (Ottawa 1980), 51, 59; and Benjamin Drew, *The Refugee: A North-Side View of Slavery* (1856; repr. New York 1969), 376. See also Donald G. Simpson, 'Negroes in Ontario from Early Times to 1870' (PhD thesis, University of Western Ontario 1971). The *Provincial Freeman* (6 May 1854) carried a notice from the Canada Company about some people losing their land.

31 Margaret Dougall addendum to James Dougall to his brother, 1845, Dougall Family Papers, UG. The desire for independence is also reflected in Nathaniel Carrothers to William Carrothers, 25 December, 1839, in Houston and Smyth, *Irish Emigration*; and in articles appearing in the *Journals and Transactions of the Board of Agriculture of Upper Canada*: William Hutton, 'Agriculture and Its Advantages as a Pursuit,' 1 (1852), 191; Thomas Mickling, 'The Dignity of Agricultural Labour,' 1 (1853), 331; and Henry Y. Hind, 'Agricultural Report on York, Peel, and Ontario Counties,' 1 (1853), 381–4. For evidence that such desires were not limited to those engaged in farming but also extended to those in commerce, see George Brown to John Brown, 9 September 1830, John Brown Letters. See also Michael Vance, 'The

Politics of Emigration: Scotland and Assisted Emigration to Upper Canada, 1815–26,' in Devine, *Scottish Emigration*, 37–60.

32 Alvin Koop and Sheila Koop, *Older Voices among Us* (Erin 1981), 19.

33 Andrew Dougall to his brother, 17 May 1850, Dougall Family Papers. See also Andrew Dougall to his brother, 1845 (this is 'the Finest counterey in the world'); Andrew Dougall to John Dougall, 9 June 1858; Robert Craig to his father, 8 May 1834, Robert Craig Letters, QU. John Lynch, 'Agriculture and Its Advantages as a Pursuit,' *Journals and Transactions of the Board of Agriculture of Upper Canada*, 1 (1852), 203.

34 John Rankin to his parents, 19 May 1855, UWO.

35 Robert Craig to his father, 2 September 1833, Robert Craig Letters. Similar views are expressed in a letter to the editor, *Newcastle Farmer*, 1 March 1847.

36 James Reid to Thomas Reid, 10 February 1825, James Reid Letters, AO. Mary O'Brien is often quoted by historians contending that early Ontario farmers were peasants engaged in subsistence agriculture: 'The fact is that the farmers here [north of Toronto] do not try to produce more than they consume' (A.S. Miller, ed., *The Journals of Mary O'Brien* [Toronto 1968], 20). O'Brien's comment referred to her family's attempt to haul potatoes some twenty-five kilometres to market over bad roads in winter – which some might have considered a foolhardy enterprise with a product readily spoiled by freezing.

37 Quoted in Boyce, *Hutton of Hastings*, 166.

38 J.B. Reynolds autobiography, UG. The family arrived in Canada in 1850.

39 William Bell diary, 1824, 68. At his first meeting with his Presbyterian parishioners in the local schoolhouse on 9 July 1817, Bell 'observed with regret that some came barefooted, and very poorly clad. The poverty of the people prevented anything being done at this meeting, beyond appointing a committee to manage the affairs of the congregation.' See also Edward J. Cowan, 'From the Southern Uplands to Southern Ontario: Nineteenth-Century Emigration from the Scottish Borders,' in Devine, *Scottish Emigration*, 61–83.

40 Mrs Richard Lazier Reminiscences, 1893, QU.

41 John Cameron to Hugh Cameron, 21 April 1852, Cameron Family Letters, UWO.

42 Hugh Johnson to Jane Johnson, 3 March 1849, McConnell Family Letters. Robert Craig expressed similar views to his parents, 20 July 1832, Robert Craig Letters.

43 Joseph Carrothers to William Carrothers, 10 October 1862, in Houston and Smyth, *Irish Emigration*, 283.

44 Letters in Boyce, *Hutton of Hastings*, 27, 38, 63, 75, 145, chronicle the demand for labour and wages in the Belleville area, noting that with the prosperity of the early 1840s they rebounded.

45 James Reid to Thomas Reid, September, 1827, James Reid Letters.

46 Philip Lautenschlager to his parents, 20 November 1831, in Gottlieb Liebbrandt, *Little Paradise: The Saga of the German Canadians of Waterloo County, Ontario, 1800–1975*, trans. G.K. Weissenborn (Kitchener 1980), 30–2.

47   James Dougall to his brother, 1845, Dougall Family Papers.

48   David Dougall to John Dougall, 4 October 1854, Dougall Family Papers; the same to the same, 13 April 1853. Itinerant threshing crews were noted in the Etobicoke area in the 1840s.

49   Though wages were always mentioned by immigrants in their correspondence home, Peter Russell, 'Wage Rates in Upper Canada, 1818–1840,' *Histoire sociale/Social History* 16 (1983), 61–80, referred only to published accounts. Sources for wages that I have also used include: Benjamin Fowler diary, 1802, AO; Archibald McLean record book, 5 April 1813, 20 September 1808 (and labour accounting in 1833 and 1834), Robert Craig to his brother, 24 [no month] 1833, Robert Craig Letters, QU; Andrew Dougall to his brother, 12 November 1846, and Dougall Family Papers; Duckworth-Shields account book, 1867; account book, 1840s–50s, Jarvis Collection, Ontario Agricultural Museum. (These accounts note both men's and women's wages.) Miller, *The Journals of Mary O'Brien*, 245, cites an instance of a labourer receiving fifty acres of land in exchange for farm work rendered.

50   Joseph Elson autobiography, 8, UWO. Elson figured that he had chopped 100 acres for others and 120 acres on his own land. Jardine diaries (1860s to 1890s), UG, give detailed daily accounts of a shoemaker who hired out as a farm labourer, acquired a farm where he continued to practise his craft, and later hired labour on his own farm.

51   Graeme Wynn, *Timber Colony: An Historical Geography of Early Nineteenth-Century New Brunswick* (Toronto 1981), 21.

52   Thomas Paddock to his brother, 31 June 1835, Thomas Paddock Letters, QU.

53   Comfort account book, 12 April 1825, UWO. Comfort duly noted each of Lane's 'black dais.' On 4 December 1822, he had made an agreement with Allen Lane to work for one year in return for 80 bushels of wheat or the price that they would bring, and on 25 May 1825 for him to work for a year in return for $100 in land and 80 bushels. On 28 October 1828 Comfort made a similar agreement with Daniel Lane, but the pay once again was only 80 bushels of wheat.

54   See Anne Kussmaul, *Servants in Husbandry in Early Modern England* (Cambridge 1981); Keith Snell, *Annals of the Labouring Poor* (Cambridge 1985); and Alan Armstrong, *Farm Workers in England and Wales: A Social and Economic History, 1770–1980* (Ames, Iowa 1988). As much labour might be hired from neighbours on Ontario farms, piece work and day labour were also common.

55   *Letters from Sussex Emigrants* (Chichester, England 1837), 7. See also Miller, *Journals of Mary O'Brien*, 17–22.

56   George to John Simpson, 15 February 1835, Simpson Family Letters, UWO. See also Miller, *Journals of Mary O'Brien*, 199.

57   Thomas Radcliffe, ed., *Authentic Letters from Upper Canada* (Dublin 1833; repr. Toronto 1953), 134.

58   Alexander Macdonell to Lt. Col. Chisholm, 24 October 1819, Bishop Alexander Macdonell Collection, UG.

59 William Bell diary, 6 October 1822 and September 1831. See also James Reid to
    Thomas Reid, 10 February 1825, James Reid Letters. Canal work had raised labour-
    ers' wages in the Toronto area to three pounds a month or 2/6 a day.
60 John Telfer to John Abbott, 17 May 1829, Niagara Historical Research Centre, Reel
    005.
61 John Newton to the *Leinster Express*, November 1843, John Newton Letters and
    Diaries, UWO.
62 *Census of Canada 1870–71*, vol. 4, Ontario, 1848, tables 4 and 6.
63 Ibid., table 5. See also James Reid to Thomas Reid, 1 March 1847, James Reid Let-
    ters, AO. John Clarke, 'Geographical Aspects of Land Speculation in Essex County
    to 1825: The Strategy of Particular Individuals,' in Johnson and Wilson, *Historical
    Essays on Upper Canada*, 81–130; and Gagan, *Hopeful Travellers*, 99.
64 See, for example, farm rental agreement (James Parrot and John Vanseckler), 1
    March 1807, Parrot Family Papers, QU, a very detailed document according to
    which Parrot was to provide a house and to give room and board to a hired man; and
    rental agreement, 22 August 1823, Burleigh Papers, vol. 43, file 14 (no. 50), QU.
    Neither the 1807 nor the 1823 lease contained a soil conservation clause. Legal doc-
    uments from the Village of Wellington in the Talbot District, QU, 1840 concern a
    tenant without a lease. A farm lease, 22 October 1864, in the Jarvis Collection is the
    earliest printed form containing soil conservation clauses (requirements to manure,
    preserve orchards, and rotate crops), and more are found in farm lease, 1 November
    1878. Allan Higinbotham Papers, Box 11D, UG. Gonder Family Papers, Niagara
    Historical Research Society Centre, Reel 017, contain a farm lease from 1809. The
    types of disputes that arose in renting are described in Boyce, *Hutton of Hastings*,
    212–13.
        The availability of rental properties can be seen in [Government of Ontario],
    Emigration to Canada: The Province of Ontario (Toronto 1869, 1871), and
    [Ontario Immigration Office], *Emigration: The British Farmer's and Farm
    Labourer's Guide to Ontario* ... (Toronto 1880; repr. Owen Sound 1974). Farm
    papers contained frequent notices for farm rentals and discussed various aspects in
    Canada Farmer, 15 February, 1 March, and 15 March 1865, 15 April 1867, and 15
    August 1872. The Ontario Bureau of Industries reported on farm rentals in the
    1880s.
65 Quoted in Marjorie Harper, *Emigration from North-East Scotland*, 2 vols. (Aber-
    deen 1988), 1:199.
66 Thomas McQueen, 'Report on the County of Huron,' *Journals and Transactions of
    the Board of Agriculture of Upper Canada*, 2 (1856), 172–6.
67 Rentals of Ontario farms from 1901 to 1966 stood at 5 to 6 per cent of value with
    profits of 3 to 4 per cent. See Edward C. Gray and Barry E. Prentice, 'Trends in the
    Price of Real Estate in Central Wellington County (Ontario) since 1836,' University
    of Guelph Agricultural Economic and Extension Education paper 82/1, 23.
68 On sharecropping, see Canniff, *History of the Settlement of Upper Canada*, 458. For

examples, see agreement between Mary Baker and John Allan (which contains a
soil conservation clause), 7 June 1832, Mary and Rebecca Baker Legal Records,
William Grant Papers, Goodwin-Haines Collection, Legal Documents series, UG;
(Lincoln and Grimsby) farm rental agreements, 1873, 1879 and Gainsborough
Township wheel manufacturing agreement, F.W. Macdonald Legal Papers, UG;
notice of sale, 12 November 1840, Lizars Papers, UG; a sharecropping indenture,
(between James Prentice and Kirby Zimmerman, witnessed by Levi Myers), 10
November 1874, Goodwin-Haines Collection; Isaac Simpson to John Simpson, 9
October 1843, Simpson Family Letters; J.H. Allan Daybook, 1866–75 (Allan
reached 18 sharecropping agreements in 1866; he supplied the seed and other items
and agreed to purchase back the crops at a set price), QU; and Anne Good to Thomas Good, 5 March 1868, Good Family Papers, 26:1, National Archives of Canada
(NAC). NAC RG17, no. 2325, provides the responses of successful farmers to a
questionnaire about how they got started in agriculture. See also *Canada Farmer*,
30 July 1873 and 15 May 1876; Boyce, *Hutton of Hastings*, 105. Beth Good Latzer,
Myrtleville: A Canadian Farm and Farm Family, 1837–1937 (Carbondale, Ill.
1976), 200, provides an instance from the 1890s. The beef rings that developed in
the 1890s were an application of the shares system to purchases of part of an animal
for consumption. Each member of the ring bought part of a slaughtered animal in
succession.

69 William Bell diary, 5 January 1825. Baines, *Migration in a Mature Economy*, notes
a return of a quarter to a third of emigrants from Europe up to 1914 (except for Jews
and Irish) and estimated that about 40 per cent of English emigrants returned to
Britain between 1860 and 1914 (28, 140). Likewise, Paul Voisey, *Vulcan: The
Making of a Prairie Community* (Toronto 1988), 44, notes that in the later settlement of Western Canada, 40 per cent of homestead entries were cancelled.

70 Kerry Abel of Carleton University kindly provided statistics based on Kingston
House of Industry, admission books, 1847–75, QU.

71 James Reid to John Reid, 22 September 1827, James Reid Letters. See also Macdonell to Chisholm, 15 August 1820, Macdonell Collection, despite the differing
position taken in other letters in this correspondence. William Hutton held similar
views in the 1830s, but the high immigration and unsettled economy of the 1840s
and fifties changed his tune. See Boyce, *Hutton of Hastings*, 23, 105, and 209.

72 Preston, *For Friends at Home*, 92–3. The way in which the Court of Quarter Sessions handled cases of destitution is analysed in David Murray, 'The Cold Hand of
Charity: The Court of Quarter Sessions and Poor Relief in the Niagara District,
1828–1841,' in W. Wesley Pue and Barry Wright, eds, *Canadian Perspectives on
Law and Society: Issues in Legal History* (Ottawa 1985), 179–206.

73 David Wardrope, Fragmentary Family Records (XR1 MSA255), 15, UG. Most
common accounts of settlement stress the abundance of wildlife, particularly the
threats posed by wolves and bears.

74 See letter 95, 1 January 1797, Jarvis Family Papers (1782–1901), 100, NAC; Elson

autobiography, UWO, 1; testimonies of Catherine White and John Clark, *Ontario History* 7 (1906); William Canniff, *Settlement of Upper Canada* (Toronto 1869), 196–200.

75 Alexander Macdonell to Chisholm, 23 May, 15 August 1820, Macdonell Collection.

76 Winchester, '"Scratching amongst the Stumps."' David Wardrope, Fragmentary Family Records, 19.

77 H.Y. Hind et al., *The Dominion of Canada* (Toronto 1868), 55–7.

78 Thomas Connon to his aunt, 9 October 1858, Thomas Connon Papers, UG.

79 Thomas McQueen, 'Report on the County of Huron.'

80 Houston and Smyth, *Irish Emigration*, 292, 296, 300.

81 Thomas Connon to his aunt, 1 July 1859 (for this and the incident that follows), Thomas Connon Papers.

82 Thomas Saunders to Joshua Saunders, 26 March 1836; Thomas Saunders to Joshua Saunders, 6 January 1835, Saunders Family Papers, Metropolitan Toronto Public Library.

83 William Bell diary, 1825, 88. Bell thought merchants' profits to be 33 per cent. David Wardrope, Fragmentary Family Records, provides an instance of a settler's family trying to retail but failing.

84 *Short Sketch of the Life of Brinton Paine Brown* (1904), 2, UWO.

85 J.J. Morrison Memoirs, NAC.

86 William Bell diary, October 1830. The concept of 'yeomanry' in public discourse is examined in David Mills, *The Idea of Loyalty in Upper Canada 1784–1850* (Toronto 1988), 28–9, 47, 76–7, 83. See also Charlotte Erickson, 'Agrarian Myths of English Immigrants,' in O. Fritiof Ander, ed., *In the Trek of the Immigrants* (Rock Island, Ill. 1964); and J.P. Cooper, 'In Search of Agrarian Capitalism,' in Ashton and Philpin, *The Brenner Debate*, 138–91.

87 Miller, *Journals of Mary O'Brien*, 17–22. J.B. Reynolds, in his 'autobiography,' describes how his mother, an English immigrant in the 1850s, was glad to have left behind the artificial deference shown to gentry and aristocrats.

88 The types of work described in [United Kingdom, Parliament], *Reports of Special Assistant Poor Law Commissioners on the Employment of Women and Children in Agriculture* (London 1843) are analysed by Snell, *Annals of the Labouring Poor*, largely on the basis of settlements available in that country. For Scotland see T.M. Devine, 'Women Workers, 1850–1914,' in T.M. Devine ed., *Servants and Labour in Lowland Scotland 1770–1914* (Edinburgh 1984), 98–123. On the subject of cultural transfer as applied to the Irish see John J. Mannion, *Irish Settlement in Eastern Canada: A Study of Cultural Transfer and Adjustment* (Toronto 1974).

89 Janet and Alex Alves to brother, 3 May 1840, Alves Family Papers.

90 Preston, *For Friends at Home*, 212. This subject is interpreted differently, largely on the basis of the polemical literature, by Rosemary Ball, '"A Perfect Farmer's

Wife": Women in 19th Century Rural Ontario,' *Canada: A Historical Magazine* 3 (1975), 2–21.

91 William Whetstone memoirs, AO.

92 See Alan Watson, 'Women in Colonial North Carolina,' *North Carolina Historical Review* 58 (1981), 1–22.

93 *Letters from Sussex Emigrants* (London 1830), 10.

94 John Jeffrey diaries, Wellington County Museum and Archives. See the years from 1860 to 1875 in particular. In Scotland women carried out virtually every farm task except the management of horses, a tradition they carried to the British colonies in the eighteenth century. See David H. Fischer, *Albion's Ways: Four British Folkways in America* (New York 1989), 678–80.

Women often noted their work and that of men. See *Letters from Sussex Emigrants*, 10. See also Polly to George and Amy Alves, 3 May 1889, Alves Family Papers; Mrs Richard Lazier Reminiscences; Mrs J. Booth diary, 1897–8, QU; Laura Robinson diary, 2 September 1901, Burleigh Papers, QU; Mary and Rebecca Baker Legal Records; Dougall Family Papers [Puslinch Historical Society], UG; McPhatter Letters, U.G. Diary of Mary Ann King, Chippewa, 1893–1910, Niagara Historical Research Centre; Good Family Papers; Snyder, *Hannes Schneider and His Wife*; Mary O'Brien journals, AO; Frances Milne diary (which is particularly good in recounting the daily seasonal round in 1867–8), AO; and Beth Light and Alison Prentice eds, *Pioneer and Gentlewomen of British North America 1713–1867* (Toronto 1988).

95 See Thomas Dick diary, 21 May 1867, AO. See also Walter Beatty journal, 5 April 1852, QU; James Alves to his brother and sister, 19 January 1845, Alves Family Papers; Walter Atkinson journal, 6 September 1881, QU; William Sunter diary, 5, 7, and 9 June 1893, UG; George Holmwood diary, 12 November 1912, UG; and J. Edward Shuh, ed., *Wavertree Chronicles: The Diary of Clayton H. Shuh, 1899–1935* (Truro, N.S. 1986), 7. James M. Nyce, ed., *The Gordon C. Eby Diaries, 1911–1913: Chronicle of a Mennonite Farmer* (Toronto 1982), reveal how gender roles in farm work continued to be flexible into the twentieth century.

96 Borthwick, McPhatter Letters.

97 Callfas, McPhatter Letters; David Wardrope, Fragmentary Family Records, 13–14. J.B. Reynolds autobiography relates how the cradle so blistered the hands of a carpenter that he quickly abandoned the assistance he had offered.

98 Thomas Paddock to his brother, 31 June 1835, Thomas Paddock Letters. James Alves to his brother and sister, 19 January 1845, Alves Family Letters, reveals the effect of this shift on the work of an older woman. See also Margaret Dougall to her brother and sister, 9 April 1847, Dougall Family Papers.

99 Calisha Baker to a Young Friend, 1835, Baker Family Papers, QU.

100 James Reid to Thomas Reid, 25 July 1851, James Reid Letters. See also William Bell diary, 1825; 62; James Fowlie to his uncle, 25 March 1863, Dougall Family

Papers; Ethel V. Gudgeon, ed., *Catherine Bell Van Norman, Her Diary, 1850* (Burlington, Ont.: Burlington Historical Society 1981), 27.

101 Margaret Dougall to her brother, 1845 and 12 March 1846, Dougall Family Papers.

102 Callfas, McPhatter Letters. Although Callfas was German, the experience of some Scots such as the grandparents of Agnes Macphail, first woman member of Parliament, was similar: see Terry Crowley, *Agnes Macphail and the Politics of Equality* (Toronto 1990), 10.

103 Lena Kraemer to friends, 6 October 1932 (letter in the possession of Leone Haggerty, Alma, Ontario). For comments on this function in the 1830s, see Peter Alison diary, 12, UWO.

104 Quoted in Liebbrandt, *Little Paradise*, 30–2. As Waterloo County had been settled first by German Americans in the late eighteenth century whereas this observer had arrived recently from Germany, some of the habits he observed were probably imported via the United States.

105 *The Muskokan*, 12, 19, 26 July and 23 August 1990, published translations of ten letters written in 1892–3 by an Icelandic settler in that region to a correspondent in his homeland.

106 Eliza Good to Miss Carroll, 5 October 1840, Good Family Papers.

107 Letter, *Canada Farmer* 1 May 1867, 131. See also the work of Fanny Hutton in Boyce, *Hutton of Hastings*, 61–3.

108 *Farmer's Advocate*, 15 June 1869. See also *Canada Farmer*, 15 December 1870.

109 See James G. Snell, 'Maintenance Agreements for the Elderly: Canada, 1900–1951,' *Journal of the Canadian Historical Association*, 3d ser. (1992), 197–216.

110 Marjorie Cohen, *Women's Work, Markets, and Economic Development in Nineteenth-Century Ontario* (Toronto 1988), 7, 43–4. The first study of rural inheritance was David Gagan, *Hopeful Travellers*.

111 Cicely Howell, 'Peasant Inheritance Customs in the Midlands, 1280–1700,' in J. Goody et al. eds, *Family Inheritance: Rural Society in Western Europe, 1200–1800* (Cambridge 1976), 200–7.

112 Elliott, *Irish Migrants in the Canadas*, 198–9.

113 Mary Ryan, *Cradle of the Middle Class: The Family in Oneida County, New York, 1790–1865* (Cambridge 1981), 27–8, 49, and 251. Ryan studied 378 wills.

114 Thomas Paddock to his brother, 31 June 1835, Thomas Paddock Letters. See also Thomas Saunders to Joshua Saunders, 6 January 1835, Saunders Family Papers; and Boyce, *Hutton of Hastings*, 102.

115 Samuel Strickland, *Twenty-Seven Years in Canada West* (repr. Edmonton 1970), 80.

116 Gagan, *Hopeful Travellers*, 64. This development conformed to the longer-term trends in England from Tudor to Victorian times. See Snell, *Annals of the Labouring Poor*, 321. On working-class children at a later time, see Jane Synge, 'The Transition from School to Work; Growing Up Working Class in Early Twentieth-

Century Hamilton,' in K. Ishwaran ed., *Childhood and Adolescence in Canada* (Toronto 1979), 249–69.

117   Indenture, Ernesttown (Addington), 12 December 1797, 43:16; and Indenture, 19 December 1794, 14:19, Burleigh Papers.

118   Indenture, 1806, Gonder Family Papers. See also *Ontario History* 40 (1949), 217–18, for a shoemaker's indenture from 1824; and Peter Moogk, 'Apprenticeship of Edward Davis, An Abandoned Child, by the Town Wardens of Waterloo Township to Christian Schwartzentruber, A Farmer of Wilmot Township, 1 June 1839,' *Waterloo County Historical Society Annual* 57 (1969), 80–1.

119   Indenture, 10 September 1855, Stoddard Family Papers, AO. James Croil, *Dundas, or a Sketch of Canadian History* (Montreal 1861; repr. Belleville 1972), 195, noted farm apprentices in eastern Ontario with similar terms of employment, but he claimed that they worked 'for free' – a sign of changing attitudes to indentures.

120   Wellington County Justice of the Peace Convictions, Allan versus Neil, 20 June 1865, Connon Collection.

121   Andrew Dougall to John Dougall, 12 March 1846, Dougall Family Papers. See also Winchester, 'Scratching amongst the Stumps,' letter dated 7 September 1823.

122   [Harriet B. King], *Letters from Muskoka by an Emigrant Lady* (London 1878), 130.

123   Peter John Alison Diary, 11.

124   Gudgeon, *Catherine Bell Van Norman*, 19.

125   Mary Leslie (Guelph) to her father, 17 October 1872, Mary Leslie Papers, Box 5, AO.

126   John Newton journal, 5 November 1871, John Newton Letters and Diaries, UWO.

127   Anne Good to Thomas Good, 17 February 1868, 3 January 1867, and 30 March 1868, Good Family Papers.

128   See *Ontario Farmer*, April, 1869, 103; May, 1869, 131; January, 1870, 121; and May, 1871, 159; *Canada Farmer*, 15 January 1875; *Farmer's Advocate*, December, 1875; *The Granger*, January, 1876.

129   Albert Smith diary, The Smith Family of Mount Forest Photographs and Diaries, UG. Unfortunately, his sister's diary for 1874 is not so revealing. Other informative writing by young people is found in Thomas Dick diary (1867) and William Dellow autobiography, AO; Thomas Connon Papers; Bremner Diary (1881), UG; and J.B. Reynolds autobiography; the letters between Thomas Good and his aunt (1867–8) after he had moved to urban life in the United States, Good Family Papers, box 26; Snyder, *Hannes Schneider and His Wife*, David B. Schneider diary (1858–61); Peter Macdonald Autobiography, Peter Macdonald Papers, UWO; Charles Edward Stewart diary, Harry Cummings Collection, QU; W.D. Gregory autobiography, QU; and A.W. Currie, 'Growing Up in Rural Ontario, 1908–1926,' QU. Shuh, *Wavertree Chronicles*, describes a graduate of the Ontario Agricultural College who was a harvest excursionist to the West in 1911. See also Nyce, *Eby Diaries*.

130   Queenie Lizars to Nanny, 27 February 1859, Lizars Family Papers.

131   Richard Reid, ed., *The Upper Ottawa Valley to 1855* (Toronto 1990), xxxv–xlii,

revises traditional interpretations of the Shiners' War and collective violence in the Ottawa Valley. Thomas Connon to his aunt, 8 September 1857, Thomas Connon Papers, and the McPhatter Letters relate instances of fighting between Scots and Irish. Jean Burnet, *Ethnic Groups in Upper Canada* (Toronto 1972), 105, notes Protestant/Catholic antagonisms among the Irish in Adjala, Mono, and Cavan townships.

132 Sarah Drinkwater diary, 19 May 1849, AO.

133 Latzer, *Myrtleville*, 43; and M.S. Nelles and W.B. Cody, 'Planning and Managing a Fifty-Acre Fruit Farm' (BScAgr thesis, University of Toronto 1922), 13. Fred McGrogan to John Haggerty, 20 December 1965 (letter in the possession of Leone Haggerty, Alma, Ontario), describes the flax-pulling bees at the turn of the twentieth century, the competitions among the harvesters, and the dances that followed in the evenings. The harvesting of flax for seed had been mechanized much earlier, but that for linen manufacture still had to be harvested manually. A.N.A. Jamieson, 'A Study of the Advancement Made by the Southern Ontario Indians in Agricultural Life during the Past Twenty-Five Years' (BScAgr thesis, University of Toronto 1930), reviewed agricultural developments on reserves.

134 Thomas Connon to his aunt, 7 September 1853, and the same to the same, 21 August 1851, Thomas Connon Papers. See also Boyce, *Hutton of Hastings*, 199: 'I observe that you call Canada "America." We dislike the name. We have *no slavery* here. We like to be distinguished from that odious country by our own *not dishonoured* appellation. It is true we "cannot touch pitch without being defiled," but we rejoice to be "come out here and be separate." We prefer our individual cognomen "Canada." She stands in every way higher than her neighbour – morally, politically, and socially.' The letter is from 1855.

135 Quoted in Ann A. McEwan, 'Crime in the Niagara District, 1827–1850' (MA thesis, University of Guelph 1991), 39–40. William Bell diary (1824), 167, provides two excellent descriptions of less destructive charivaris. The custom continued in a milder form into the twentieth century. See Shuh, *Wavertree Chronicles*, 5.

136 Alison Prentice and Susan Houston, *Schooling and Scholars in Nineteenth-Century Ontario* (Toronto 1988), 296–302. While Winks, *The Blacks in Canada*, 251, affirmed a high level of personal prejudice, he also argued that blacks remained equal in the eyes of Ontario law. Patrick Brode, *The Odyssey of John Anderson* (Toronto 1989), examines the legal and political intricacies involved in the extradition hearings concerning one celebrated fugitive slave.

137 Gary Teeple, 'Land, Labour and Capital in Pre-Confederation Canada,' in Gary Teeple, ed., *Capitalism and the National Question in Canada* (Toronto 1972), 45; Leo Johnson, 'Land Policy, Population Change and Social Structure,' and S. Langdon, 'The Emergence of the Canadian Working Class Movement, 1845–75,' *Journal of Canadian Studies*, May and Aug. 1973; H. Clare Pentland, *Labour and Capital in Canada 1650–1850* (Toronto 1981); Allan Greer, 'Wage Labour and the Transition to Capitalism: A Critique of Pentland,' *Labour/Le Travail* 15 (1985),

7–22; R.T. Naylor, *Canada in the European Age, 1453–1919* (Vancouver 1987); and Bryan D. Palmer, *Working-Class Experience: The Rise and Reconstitution of Canadian Labour, 1800–1980* (Toronto 1983).

138 Gagan, *Hopeful Travellers*; Gaffield, *Language, Schooling, and Cultural Conflict.*

139 J.K. Johnson, 'Land Policy and the Upper Canadian Elite Reconsidered: The Canada Emigration Association, 1840–41,' in David Keane and Colin Read, eds, *Old Ontario: Essays in Honour of J.M.S. Careless* (Toronto 1990), 217–33.

140 See R. M. McInnis, 'Childbearing and Land Availability: Some Evidence from Individual Household Data,' in R.D. Lee, ed., *Population Patterns in the Past* (New York 1977); 'Women, Work and Childbearing: Ontario in the Second Half of the Nineteenth Century,' *Histoire sociale/Social History* 24 (1991), 237–62. See also Glenn J. Lockwood, 'Irish Immigrants and the "Critical Years" in Eastern Ontario: The Case of Montague Township, 1821–1881,' in Johnson and Wilson, *Historical Essays on Upper Canada*, 203–36.

141 John S. Hogan, *Canada: An Essay* (Montreal 1855), 67. Hogan also reveals how land values varied by county.

142 Edward C. Gray and Barry E. Prentice, 'Exploring the Price of Farmland in Two Ontario Localities since Letters Patenting,' *Canadian Papers in Rural History* 4 (1984), 226–39; and Brian S. Osborne, 'Frontier Settlement in Eastern Ontario in the Nineteenth Century: A Study of Changing Perceptions of Land and Opportunity,' in David H. Miller and Jerome O. Steffen, eds., *The Frontier, Comparative Studies* (Norman, Okla. 1977), 201–25.

143 Anne Good to Thomas Good, 30 March 1868, Good Family Papers; and David Burley, 'The Businessmen of Brantford' (PhD thesis, McMaster University 1984).

144 *Ontario Farmer*, June, 1869, 180–82; and C. Herninan, 'The Development of Artificial Drainage Systems in Kent and Essex Counties, Ontario,' *Ontario Geography* 2 (1968), 13–24.

145 *Canada Farmer*, 15 April 1865. Canada Land and Emigration Company Books, 1862–1885, Harley Cummings Collection, QU, show that when these land developers established their company, they anticipated this internal movement as well as the entry of Americans from across the border during the Civil War. The Canada Land and Emigration Company initially secured inferior lands in more northerly areas.

146 Land values varied too greatly to be considered equity by banks. W.H. Graham, *Greenbank, Country Matters in 19th-Century Ontario* (Peterborough 1988), 115–16; Drummond, *Progress without Planning*, 41. The importance of private banks remains to be established.

147 Nathaniel Carrothers to William Carrothers, 5 December 1853, in Houston and Smyth, *Irish Emigration*, 259. See also Thomas J. Rorke to a friend, 1857, Stephen Dorland account book, 1857–1885, NAC. Rorke reported that land in the Collingwood area was selling for $4 to $12 an acre unimproved and $10 to $30 with various improvements. Good farmlands for sale and wild lands in Wellington and

Waterloo counties were also noted in 'Sketch of Waterloo,' 17 March 1851, William Grant Papers.

148 For rates of land improvement, see Kris Inwood, 'Comparative Perspectives on Nineteenth-Century Growth: Ontario in the Great Lakes Region,' *Canadian Papers in Business History* 2 (1993), 71–100.

149 John Elliot autobiography, 28, UWO; Joseph Gibbs diary, 5 September 1881, Gibbs Family Papers, UWO; Bremner diary, 31 August 1881.

150 Iain C. Taylor, 'Components of Population Change, Ontario: 1850–1940' (MA thesis, University of Toronto 1967), 36–8.

151 Darroch, 'Class in Nineteenth-Century, Central Ontario'; and Gordon Darroch and Lee Soltow, 'Inequality in Landed Wealth in Nineteenth-Century Ontario: Structure and Access,' *Canadian Review of Sociology and Anthropology* 29 (1992), 167-90.
      In 1861 census enumerators were instructed to list the occupation of farmers' sons as 'labourer' and some continued to do so at least until the 1881 census.

152 John Jeffrey diaries, ledger, and blacksmithing ledger. See also *1906 Atlas of Wellington County* (Toronto 1906), 37. A life course in the same era with distinct parallels to those of Jeffrey can be found in George Holmwood diary. Anne Good to Thomas Good, 30 March 1868, Good Family Papers, box 26:1, indicated that land was readily available and farms renting cheaply in Brant County if Thomas decided to leave the city work he had chosen and begin farming again. See also 'What an English Immigrant Thinks of Canada,' *Ontario Farmer* (April 1870), 121.

153 For the period up to 1870, see John McCallum, *Unequal Beginnings, Agriculture and Economic Development in Quebec and Ontario until 1870* (Toronto 1980).

154 Marvin McInnis, 'Marketable Surpluses in Ontario Farming, 1860,' *Social Science History* 8 (1984), 395–424, found that the marketable surpluses on many farms by 1861 were slight. That they were lower than for comparable samples in the United States is perhaps because the land clearing continued in southern Ontario throughout the century.

155 H.Y. Hind, 'Agricultural Report on York, Peel, and Ontario Counties, 1853'; H.Y. Hind, 'Agricultural report on Simcoe County, *Journals and Transactions of the Board of Agriculture of Upper Canada* 2(1855), 52; and Janine Grant, 'A Reinterpretation of Vernacular Architecture: Eramosa Township, Ontario' (MA thesis, University of Waterloo 1987), 41. Drummond, *Progress without Planning*, 375, provides the statistics from the 1871 census on farm vehicles and equipment. Will Carlton, *Farm Ballads* (Toronto 1887), 41–2, presents this transition in verse.

156 Darroch, 'Class in Nineteenth-Century, Central Ontario,' 55–64; and Gagan, *Hopeful Travellers*, 100–2. Note the letter in the *Canada Farmer*, 15 April 1865, from a disgruntled settler in Dawn township who failed in the transition to farming.

157 Calculated from Duckworth-Shields account book for the years from 1874 to 1876. This is the only farm ledger I have found that sets its labour costs within the context of other farm outlays. With income of $551 and expenditures of $183 in 1874, the farm was above average but not exceptional. Stephen Dorland account book, 1857–

1885, and David Smith cashbook, 1874–92, David Smith Papers, vol. 1, AO, also mention wages. The Frank Wooley diary, AO, contains a description of work done by hired hands, as does the John Jardine diary, John Jardine Collection, UG.

158 J.F. Snell, 'The Cost of Living in Canada in 1870,' *Histoire sociale/Social History* 12 (1979), 189–93. *Letters from Canada* (London: F. Algar 1863), 51–2 and 66, shows that rural wages were higher in Ontario than Quebec. Sources for wage information in this period include John Jeffrey Ledger; Williams Account Book, 1866–68, Wessler Papers, UG; NAC, RG17, vol. 2325, 1853; Anne Good to Thomas Good, 30 March 1868, Good Family Papers; *Ontario Farmer*, March 1870; *Canada Farmer*, 15 April and 15 July 1869; and *Farmer's Advocate*, August 1872. Regional differences within Ontario and in comparison to other provinces can be followed in United States, Bureau of Foreign Commerce, Consular Reports, *Labor, Continent of North America* (Washington 1885), 3:1–155.

159 Thomas A. Good diary, 1870–1, Good Family Papers; *Canada Farmer*, 20 April 1847, 1 December 1868, 15 February 1870, and 15 July 1870; *Farmer's Advocate*, June 1870; *Ontario Farmer*, January 1869, March 1869 and April 1871; Ontario, Commissioner of Agriculture and Public Works, *Annual Report* (Toronto 1870), iv; and Marilyn Barber, 'The Women Ontario Welcomed: Immigrant Domestics for Ontario Homes, 1870–1930,' in Alison Prentice and Susan M. Trofimenkoff, eds, *The Neglected Majority, Essays in Canadian Women's History*, vol. 2 (Toronto 1985), 102–21.

The farms of George Brown, F.W. Stone, and William Gooderham are described in *Canada Farmer*, 1 May 1865, 15 November 1869, and 15 January 1876; and in *Ontario Farmer*, June 1869, and August 1870. For the agricultural activities of eastern Ontario farmer D.L. Macpherson, see Macpherson Family Papers, UG. Information on other large-scale operations, including what had evolved from the grant south of Guelph to the family of Thomas Saunders, can be found in Ontario, Department of Agriculture, *Annual Report*, 1886, 29–66.

160 Most Ontario farm diaries were not diaries in the conventional sense, but narratives of daily business dealings, weather, sales, and contracts. A form was proposed by the *Canada Farmer* to its readers on 15 February 1869. On 16 January 1871 the same newspaper proffered a means for keeping farm accounts which many farmers also followed, although it provided no way of calculating profit. This can be contrasted with the more sophisticated business practices prescribed a quarter century later by J.L. Nichols, *The Farmer's Manual and Complete Accountant ...* (Toronto: J.L. Nichols & Co. 1895). The period after 1900 is discussed with special reference to Western Canada by Ian MacPherson and John H. Thompson, 'The Business of Agriculture: Farmers and the Adoption of "Business Methods," 1880–1950,' Baskerville, ed., *Canadian Papers in Business History* 1 (1989), 245–69.

161 Andrew Dougall to John Dougall, 4 October 1854, Dougall Family Papers. The same to the same, 9 June 1858, estimated attendance at the London fair that year at

40,000. See also Nathaniel Carrothers to William Carrothers, 29 January 1866, Houston and Smyth, *Irish Emigration*, 262.

Local societies such as the one in St Thomas in 1848 offered prizes for the best wheat, livestock, wool, butter, cheese, maple sugar, and fulled cloth. The provincial exhibition the following year offered competitions in a ladies department that included socks, mittens, gloves, straw hats, netting, embroidery, worsted work, and wax flowers as well as categories for fine art and textiles (blankets, flannel, fulled cloth, winter tweed, and linen). *Newcastle Farmer*, 1 October 1849. *General Rules of Order of the St Thomas Branch of the London District Agricultural Society* (St Thomas, 1848), UWO.

162 On organizational and legislative activity, see Jean M. MacLeod, 'Agriculture and Politics in Ontario since 1867' (PhD thesis, University of London 1961), and G. Elmore Reaman, *A History of Agriculture in Ontario*, 2 vols. (Toronto 1970).

163 The visible changes in farm clothing were noted in the Toronto *Weekly Globe*, 23 September 1881. See also Graham, *Greenbank*, 243–6; Janine Roelens and Kris Inwood, 'Labouring at the Loom: A Case Study in Rural Manufacturing in Leeds County, Ontario, 1870,' *Canadian Papers in Rural History* 7 (1990), 215–36; Janine Grant and Kris Inwood, 'Gender and Organization in the Canadian Cloth Industry, 1870,' in Peter Baskerville, ed., *Canadian Papers in Business History* 1 (1989), 17–31. On the decline of marketing fairs and peddling, see Brian S. Osborne, 'Trading on a Frontier: The Function of Peddlers, Markets, and Fairs in Nineteenth-Century Ontario,' *Canadian Papers in Rural History* 2 (1980), 59–82.

Unfortunately, historians are hampered by a lack of data on farm operating costs and the dynamics of the family economy throughout the nineteenth century, principally because farmers did not keep records or refused to divulge information. While farmers' jottings about their revenues and expenditures are fairly common, only Thomas Wheatly account books, 1872–1921, UWO, provide detailed yearly credits and debits for both home and farm. After 1910 agricultural economists, although relying only on samples, threw more light on farm operating costs.

164 Minutebook of the South Wellington Agricultural Society, 20 August 1888, Wellington Museum and Archives.

165 Quoted in Leopolda Z.L. Dobrzensky, *Fragments of a Dream, Pioneering in Dysart Township and Haliburton Village* (Peterborough 1985), 50. See also Charles Edward Stewart diary, 10 November 1870, Harley Cummings Collection; *Ontario Agricultural Commission*, vol. 5, appendix R (Toronto 1881), 16, 29; Robert Mayes diary, 1874–6, UG (recounting the experience of the Mayes family in settling near Bracebridge); Orm Overland, ed. and trans., *Johan Schroder's Travels in Canada 1863* (Montreal 1989); and Geoffrey Wall, 'Nineteenth-Century Land Use and Settlement on the Canadian Shield Frontier,' Miller and Steffen, *The Frontier*, 227–41.

Reports in the press that the first settlers to take up lands in Muskoka under the new legislation came from Illinois were probably fictitious, reflecting previous bitter quarrels over the relative merits of Ontario lands versus those in that state.

Adverse comment on the agricultural suitability of Muskoka can be found in 'Emigrant Letters on Canada,' *Ontario Farmer*, November 1869, 346–7.

Contrast the increasing tone of caution and reticence in literature promoting settlement in [Ontario] *Emigration to Canada: The Province of Ontario* (Toronto 1869, 1871) and [Ontario Immigration Office], *Emigration: The British Farmer's and Farm Labourer's Guide to Ontario* ... (Toronto 1880; repr. Owen Sound, 1974). The value of the free grants in the mid-north was questioned in the British and Canadian press from the inception of the 1868 Homestead Act. See 'What an English Emigrant Thinks of Canada,' *Ontario Farmer*, November 1869; and 'Emigrant Letters on Canada,' *Ontario Farmer*, April 1870. [Ontario], *Circular from the Department of Crown Lands Shewing How to Obtain Title to Public Lands Under the 'Free Grants and Homestead Act'* (Toronto 1883), provides the geographical locations in which grants were made available.

166 King, *Letters from Muskoka*, 165. King also noted that women in Muskoka worked as hard as men in logging, burning, planting, and digging.

167 John J. LePine, 'The Famine of 1880,' *East Georgian Bay Historical Journal* 3 (1983), 1–15.

168 See Thomas Adams, *Rural Planning and Development, A Study of Rural Conditions and Problems in Canada* (Ottawa 1917), 23–6, for the conclusions of a survey of these areas in 1913.

169 See NAC, C7322, file 47195, for the Burriss settlement.

170 See Normand Séguin, ed., *Agriculture et colonisation au Québec, Aspects historiques* (Montreal 1980); and J.I. Little, *Nationalism, Capitalism, and Colonization in Nineteenth-Century Quebec: The Upper St Francis District* (Montreal 1989).

171 The movement of Ontario people to the United States in the second half of the nineteenth century remains little studied, with the only major work being Marcus Lee Hansen, *The Mingling of the Canadian and American Peoples* (1940; repr. New York 1970). As early as the 1850s real estate agents migrated between southern Ontario and the states of New York and Michigan. Following the conclusion of the American Civil War, American land developers promoted western lands more aggressively within the province. Widdis, 'Tracing Eastern-Ontario Emigrants to New York State,' and Alan Brookes, 'Family, Youth and Leaving Home in Late-Nineteenth-Century Rural Nova Scotia: Canning and the Exodus, 1868–1893,' both in Joy Parr, ed., *Childhood and Family in Canadian Society* (Toronto 1982), 93–108, provide insight into this process.

172 Arthur Clayden, *The Revolt of the Field* (London 1874), 218. See also John O'Leary, ed., *The Autobiography of Joseph Arch* (London 1896; repr. 1966), 80; and Norman Macdonald, *Canada, Immigration and Colonization: 1841–1903* (Toronto 1966), 103.

173 Pamela Horn, 'Agricultural Trade Unionism and Emigration, 1872–1881,' *Historical Journal* 15 (1972), 97; Clayden, *Revolt of the Field*, 225–7, 230; Harper, *Emigration from North-East Scotland*, 1:129; and Paul Craven and Tom Traves, 'The

Class Politics of the National Policy, 1872–1933,' *Journal of Canadian Studies* 14 (1979), 14–38. Agreements negotiated by Arch allowed for union certification in order to qualify for low-cost passages to Canada rather than attestations by a priest or minister or a municipal government in England. Though the registry of labour needs was initially maintained only in Toronto, by 1891 Ontario immigration agents in Kingston, Ottawa, Hamilton, and London were performing the same function.

174 Louis A. Wood, *Farmers' Movements in Canada: The Origins and Development of Agrarian Protest, 1872–1924* (Toronto 1924; repr. 1975), 60. H. Michell, *The Grange in Canada* (Kingston 1914), 8. Russell Hann, *Farmers Confront Industrialism* (Toronto 1975), attempts to portray early farm movements as a counterculture.

175 *The Granger*, March 1875.

176 Janet Arnott, *The Grange Knock: An Account of the Patrons of Husbandry in the Village of Knock, Innisfil Township, Ontario, 1875–1900* (Stroud, Ont.: Innisfil Historical Society 1984), 28.

177 The growth in the availability of consumer goods can be seen by comparing the ledger of a general store in John Burch Ledger, 1818–27, QU, with W.P. Wright and Son Ltd. Records, QU. In 1889, Wright and Son, a Gananoque dry goods store had over eighty items in its inventory.

The existence of frauds and swindles is revealed in the *Farmer's Advocate*, November 1870; Canada, House of Commons, *Report of the Select Committee to Enquire into the Fraudulent Practices Perpetuated Upon the Farmers of the Dominion* (Ottawa 1888); and Ontario, Department of Agriculture, *Annual Report*, 1889, Appendix, 147–56.

178 *The Granger*, April 1876.

179 Ibid., September 1876. See also the account by provincial officer Christina Moffat, *Flora, Ceres and Pomona* (Cannington, Ont. 1886).

180 Thomas Priestman to John Thompson, 13 January 1811, in Winchester, 'Scratching amongst the Stumps.'

181 James Reid to Thomas Reid, 1 March 1847, James Reid Letters. See also George Simpson to John Simpson, 4 May 1840, Simpson Family Letters; E.B. Brown, *Short Sketch* (1842), 15–16, UWO; Harvest Journal, 17 July 1845, William Grant Papers; Margaret Dougall to her brother, 18 February 1848, Dougall Family Papers; Nathaniel Carrothers to William Carrothers, 5 December 1853, in Houston and Smyth, *Irish Emigration*, 256–7; Latzer, *Myrtleville*, 43; and Mannion, *Irish Settlement in Eastern Canada*, 93–101.

182 C.M. Everett to Charles P. Treadwell, *Journals and Transactions of the Board of Agriculture of Upper Canada* 1 (1849), 151. The following pages indicate that farmers in this area were achieving wheat yields of 17 to 20 bushels an acre.

183 Margaret Dougall to her brother, 18 February 1848, Dougall Family Papers; Decker, McPhatter Letters (concerning a joint purchase of a yoke of oxen with the future livestock breeder F.W. Stone before he was able to purchase one on his own); *Canada Farmer*, 15 May 1876; *Farmer's Advocate*, 19 (May 1884), 134; Ontario,

Department of Agriculture, *Annual Report*, 1898, 2:96. As late as 1913 the Commission of Conservation noted in its agricultural survey (vol. 5, 146ff) that the majority of Ontario farmers rented steam engines and separators for threshing grain. The same co-operative practices were used by women for the purchase of equipment such as vacuum cleaners. See Huron County, 1913, Tweedsmuir History Collection, UG; and Ontario, Department of Agriculture, *Agriculture: Rural Women's Institutes* (1913), 39. Such practices were also used in western Canada. See Lyle Dick, *Farmers 'Making Good': The Development of Abernethy District, Saskatchewan, 1880–1920* (Ottawa 1989), 64–5.

184 This assumption underlies the study by Richard Pomfret, 'The Mechanization of Reaping in Nineteenth-Century Ontario: A Case Study of the Pace and Causes of the Diffusion of Embodied Technical Change,' in Douglas McCalla, ed., *Perspectives on Canadian Economic History* (Toronto 1987), 81–95.

185 William Sunter Diary, 2 May 1893. The Dougall Family Papers and Thomas Paddock Letters reveal instances of neighbours from differing ethnic backgrounds helping families to harvest when illness struck, in the former case over three years.

186 Daniel Fowler diary, 30 [no month] 1802, AO; David Smith, cashbook, 1874–92, David Smith Papers, Box 1; Frank Wooley diary, April-September 1879 (Wooley employed three hands but also hired himself and his hands out); Walter Beatty Journal, 1838–1892; Duckworth-Shields account book, 1864–5; John Jardine Diary, 18 July and 24, 27, 29, and 31 August 1887, 10 May 1888, John Jardine Collection; and Ontario, Legislative Assembly, *Sessional Papers*, 28 (1908), 20. Latzer, *Myrtleville*, 109. A prosperous farm such as that owned by the parents of Elizabeth Smith was taxed ten days of statute labour in 1875. The commutation of statute labour into money payments of between 50 and 75 cents a day began late in the nineteenth century and was encouraged by new time study methods applied to work. In 1901, 10 per cent of Ontario's some 500 townships had admitted the practice. See the *Farming World*, 18 (28 May 1901), 1008–9, and 20 (17 June 1902), 655. After the First World War the tradition of bees in rural Ontario was transformed into collective work on communal projects such as churches and schools. See Shuh, *Wavertree Chronicles*, 54.

187 These proportions were calculated from Drummond, *Progress without Planning*, 375. They exclude occupiers of land under ten acres.

188 W.A. Latta manuscript, 'Trip to the Ontario Agricultural College' (1881), UG. For Quebec, see Claude Blouin, 'La méchanisation de l'agriculture entre 1830 et 1890,' in Séguin, *Agriculture et colonisation au Québec*, 107.

189 Canada, *Report of the Royal Commission on the Relations of Labour and Capital in Canada: Evidence – Ontario* (Ottawa 1889), 675. In 1882 the Toronto *Globe* (9 September) claimed that farm labour wages stood at $25 to $30 a month, twice the 1870 rate. See also 'Labourers versus Machinery,' *Farmer's Advocate* 20 (June 1885), 163. See also *White and Gold Herald* (a magazine for Massey Manufacturing sales agents), 22 January, 11 May, and 16 June 1887 and 5 January 1888. The

Massey company tripled the size of its Toronto works in the 1880s and claimed in 1888 that it was prepared to manufacture 4,000 binders, 4,500 mowers, 3,000 rakes, and 1,000 harvesters that year. See also Merrill Denison, *Harvest Triumphant: The Story of Massey-Harris* (Toronto 1948), 113, 135. For the view from the side of the farmer, see James Bremner diary, 11, 28, 30 July and 3 and 4 September 1881. Note also the deliberations between mother and son that went into the purchase of an electric cream separator in Nyce, *Eby Diaries*, 128.

190 A. Harris and Company Shareholders Minutebook, 1882–91, Massey Ferguson Collection, Ontario Agricultural Museum. In 1882 the Harris company expanded its factories in both Ontario and Manitoba.

191 Ontario Agricultural Commission, vol. 2, 340, 108; Ontario, Department of Agriculture, *Annual Report*, 1887, 173.

192 Graham, *Greenbank*, 284.

193 See Ontario, Legislative Assembly, *Sessional Papers* 28 (1910), 60–1. Earlier comparisons with Ohio based on the 1851 census can be found in A. Lillie, *Canada, Physical, Economic and Social* (Toronto 1855), 149–54.

194 The proportion of investment per acre devoted to implements increased on average from 4.5 per cent in 1881 to 5.9 per cent by 1900. See M.C. Urquhart and K.A. Buckley, eds, *Historical Statistics of Canada* (Toronto 1965), 354. Wage data (beginning in 1882) for Ontario farm labour in this work must be used cautiously. They were collected by the Ontario Bureau of Industries from its regular correspondents – always prosperous farmers – around the province. Not until the years before the First World War did the government of the United States attempt to calculate farm wages in a manner that allowed for the great variations in practices discussed in this chapter. See 'Wages of Farm Labor in the United States,' *Farmer's Advocate*, 21 November 1912.

The argument that the rapid spread of harvest mechanization did not take off until the 1880s in Ontario conforms to recent findings that as late as 1892 the majority of farms in Britain managed without reapers or binders. See Armstrong, *Farmworkers in England and Wales*, 112.

195 *Royal Commission on the Relations of Labour and Capital*, 676, 845. The value of farm machines on the average 100-acre farm without transport vehicles included was estimated at $300 to $350.

196 See Weber, *Peasants into Frenchmen*, 135.

197 Letter to the editor, *Ontario Farmer*, November 1869, 346. See also 'The Labor Problem – Valuable Suggestions by a Hired Hand,' *Farm and Dairy*, 20 April 1919.

198 Ontario, Department of Agriculture, *Annual Report*, 1885, cxviii.

199 James Bremner Diary, 9 September 1881. *Royal Commission on the Relations of Labour and Capital*, 563, 939.

200 Urquhart and Buckley, *Historical Statistics*, 351–2. These early effects of mechanization differed from those affecting dairying in eastern Ontario after the Second World War, when the main impact was that farmers could work shorter

hours. See J.A. Dawson, *The Dairy Business in Eastern Ontario* (Ottawa 1951), 27–8.

201 Cohen, *Women's Work, Markets, and Economic Development*, 121; Ontario, Legislative Assembly, Bureau of Industries *Annual Report*, Bulletin 53 (June 1895), 4; Bulletin 82 (May 1903). See Joy Parr, *Labouring Children: British Immigrant Apprentices to Canada, 1869–1924* (Montreal 1980), and Gillian Wagner, *Children of the Empire* (London 1982). For the effects of rural children working on school attendance, a component of what would be seen as the 'rural school problem' after the beginning of the twentieth century, see Robert Stamp, *The Schools of Ontario, 1876–1976* (Toronto 1982). Earlier patterns remained, and the unpublished memoirs of people like J. Reynolds, Agnes Macphail, and A.W. Currie describe a struggle to obtain the education they desired.

202 See the statistics for urban growth provided in Elizabeth Bloomfield, *Urban-Industrial Growth Processes in Southern Ontario, 1870–1930* (University of Winnipeg Institute of Urban Studies, Research and Working Paper no. 24, 1986), 4. Small centres refer to towns with populations in the ranges of 1,000 to 2,499 and 2,500 to 4,999.

203 Contrast these statistics with the estimates of farm population in Ontario and Quebec and regional changes within the two provinces found in Haythorne and Marsh, *Land and Labour*, 24. Haythorne and Marsh reveal the Ontario farm population remaining steady during the 1880s, declining slightly in the next decade, and again levelling off between 1901 and 1911. Between 1871 and 1901, the decline of the farm population was greatest in the Toronto, Lake Ontario, and Huron-Simcoe regions, but slight in Erie-Niagara. The farm population of Ottawa-St Lawrence increased marginally.

204 See Taylor, 'Components of Population Change,' and David M. Ray, 'Settlement and Rural Out-Migration in Easternmost Ontario, 1783 to 1956' (MA thesis, University of Ottawa 1961).

Elliott, *Irish Migrants in the Canadas*, provides a longitudinal study of one ethnic group, while Randy W. Widdis, 'Generations, Mobility and Persistence: A View from Genealogies,' *Histoire sociale/Social History* 25 (1992), 125–50, advocates a more general life-history approach in an attempt to combine the insights of demography and social history. Elizabeth Buchanan, 'In Search of Security: Kinship and the Family Farm on the North Shore of Lake Huron, 1879–1939' (PhD thesis, McMaster University 1989), is the finest study of the rural to rural migratory process undertaken so far.

205 Koop and Koop, *Older Voices among Us*, 25.

206 Murray, 'The Cold Hand of Charity,' shows that in the Niagara district from 1828 to 1840, 60 per cent of relief petitions came from women, 28 per cent from men, and 12 per cent from children. In the Kingston House of Industry for the years 1847, 1850, 1863, 1866, 1871–3, and 1875, female admissions outnumbered males in the early years with men predominating after 1866. The figures for Wellington County

are based on Wellington County House of Industry and Refuge, Admission Books, 1877–1910, Wellington County Museum and Archives. *Journal of the County Council, County of Wellington*, 1887, Connon Collection, suggests conditions were poor within the House of Industry, especially in regard to heating in winter. See also Joe Gabriel, 'What Ever Happened to the Poor in 19th Century Ontario: A Comparative Analysis of Public and Private Relief Mechanisms' (MA major paper, University of Guelph 1987), which examined institutions in Wellington and Waterloo counties. Sharon Cook, 'A Quiet Place ... to Die: Ottawa's First Protestant Old Age Home for Women and Men,' *Ontario History* 81 (1989), 25–40, emphasizes gender differences in care within a context of social control. For the formation of a Relief Society in the village of Rockwood, Wellington County, at the onset of the depression in 1893, see William Sunter diary, 25 March 1893.

207 Gregory S. Kealey and Bryan D. Palmer, *Dreaming of What Might Be: The Knights of Labor in Ontario, 1880–1900* (Cambridge 1982; repr. Toronto 1987), 76–7. The activities of the Knights in Gananoque are analysed in George de Zwaan, 'A Little Birmingham on the St Lawrence: An Industrial and Labour History of Gananoque, Ontario, 1871–1921' (PhD thesis, Queen's University 1987). See also Desmond Morton, 'The *Globe* and the Labour Question: Ontario Liberalism in the "Great Upheaval," May 1886,' *Ontario History* 73 (1981), 19–39.

208 Edward Amey, *Farm Life As It Should Be* (Toronto [1885?]), 37–9. This polemic is an amalgam that borrows from, but distorts, Arthur Clayden's *Revolt of the Field*. It relies on such evidence as letters to the editor of the Toronto *Globe*, 9 September, 11 October 1882.

209 Ontario, Department of Agriculture, *Annual Report* 1886, 63–7.

210 *Commercial Union*, 2:83 Peter Macdonald Papers, notes that 25 of 27 Farmers' Institutes approved the Liberals' counterproposal of unrestricted reciprocity in 1887.

211 Other information on threshing businesses, showing that they originated with small farmers, can be found in Dougall Family Papers; Gagan, *Hopeful Travellers*, 79; and Dobrzensky, *Fragments of a Dream*, 29. By 1911 the costs of a threshing outfit had increased to between $2,700 and $3,000. See *The Thresherman's Review of Canada*, 1, no. 4 (April 1911) no. 6 (June 1911), Ontario Agricultural Museum.

212 Ignatius Cockshutt Letterbooks, Ignatius Cockshutt to Charles Wallbridge, 18 July 1893, in the possession of W. Cockshutt, Grand Bend, Ontario.

213 In Britain, where the agricultural gang represented the most extreme form of casual work, heavily involving women and children, these workers have been cast as proletarians by Alun Hawkins, *Poor Labouring Men: Rural Radicalism in Norfolk 1870–1923* (London, 1985), 8–9.

214 *Historical Atlas of Wellington County*, 16.

215 Parts of the Browns' life course have been brought together from the Brown File, Henry Wessler Papers, vol. 1(D); University of Guelph Library; Wellington County

Land Registry Office; Peel Township Land Registry Copy Books, 1887–1930; the Census Manuscript of 1881 and 1891, NAC; Elora Public Cemetery Records; and an interview by the author with the Browns' daughter Dinah Cripps (born 1896), Kitchener, 15 March 1993.

216 Urquhart and Buckley, *Historical Statistics*, L253-60, L261-64. Butter prices also slid with advancing warm weather. Frances Milne diary showed prices dropping from 20 cents a pound in April to 12.5 cents in June in a year in which Milne made $16.20 from butter sales. Mrs J. Booth accounts records the following sales: butter, October–December 1897, $21.99; January–29 November 1898; $82.57; eggs and fowl, November, 1897–28 June 1898, $42.10.

217 Croil, *Dundas*, 211.

218 'Why Men Go to the City to Work,' by Another Hired Man, *Farm and Dairy*, 26 March 1914, 386. The *Farming World*, September 1904, 643, reported on the survey by the National Council of Women. Note, for example, how on the Laura Robinson farm her mother accompanied her father when a horse was to be purchased (Laura Robinson diary, 19 April 1901, Burleigh Papers). For other evidence on this subject, see also Ontario, Department of Agriculture, *Annual Report* 1902, 128; Alex Hyde, 'The Farmer's Wife,' *Farmer's Advocate*, 15 July 1880; 'The Woman on the Farm,' by A Farmer's Daughter, *Farmer's Advocate*, 3 June 1909; 'Nemo Too Easily Satisfied,' *Farmer's Advocate*, 19 March 1910; 'Husband Holds Purse Strings,' *Farmer's Advocate*, 5 May 1910; and 'How Should Income Be Apportioned?' *Farm and Dairy*, 9 October 1913.

Helen C. Abel, Lois Chipsham, and Phyllis D. Ferris, *Farm Families Today* (Toronto; Ontario, Department of Agriculture 1966), 27 reported surveys conducted after the Second World War that showed 40 per cent of farm women kept the accounts for the family business. N. Cebotarev, W.M. Blacklock, and L. McIssac, 'Farm Women's Work Patterns,' *Atlantis* 11, no. 2 (Spring, 1986), 1–21, discusses the variety of ways in which farm women and men continue to engage in joint decision making.

219 *Canadian Farmer*, 15 January 1869.

220 Letter to the editor, *Farmer's Advocate*, 15 June 1869.

221 Quoted in Graham, *Greenbank*, 284. The stagnation of wholesale butter prices throughout the later part of the nineteenth century was due to poor production and handling methods. The product was so frequently putrid that it was common for travellers to ask, 'How's the butter today?' before hotel meals. Farm practices were only partially responsible for the wretched quality. Pork packer William Davies placed greater blame on the manner in which rural merchants handled it. Exports – largely to Britain – surged in 1881 but collapsed in 1891. The travelling dairies, emanating from the Ontario Agricultural College, were one of the first large-scale, non-formal adult educational initiatives in Ontario. See *Canadian Farmer*, 1 June 1867, 15 April 1870, and 15 April 1872; Fred Dean, 'Visiting Farms and How to Take Care of the Cream at the Farm,' in Ontario, Legislative Assembly, Sessional

Papers, 1905, 178–82; and F.A. Leacy, ed., *Historical Statistics of Canada*, 2d ed. (Ottawa 1983), M228–238, M417–427.

222 Bessie Livingston, 'Domestic Science,' Ontario, Department of Agriculture, *Annual Report*, 1902, 128.

223 Miss J.D. Thomson, 'What Outdoor Work Should Farmers' Wives and Daughters Perform?' *Farmer's Advocate* June, 1886.

224 This view took hold and was spread by journalists because published statistics of admissions to provincial mental hospitals provided occupational categories for men but lumped women amorphously under the designation 'housewife.' A check of the admissions registers for the London Psychiatric Hospital from 1867 to 1906 at the Archives of Ontario showed that farmers' wives and daughters were not overrepresented, although any analysis of these records is problematic.

Joann Vanek, 'Work, Leisure and Family Roles: Farm Households in the United States, 1920–1955,' *Journal of Family History* 5 (1980), 422–31, found that as late as the 1920s women on American farms worked 11.7 hours daily, seven days a week. See also the results of a survey of farm women in Manitoba in the same period: Mary Kinnear, 'Do You Want Your Daughter to Marry a Farmer?: Women's Work on the Farm, 1922,' *Canadian Papers on Rural History* 6 (1988), 137–53.

225 Adeline, 'Another Experience of Farm Life,' *Farmer's Advocate*, 31 October, 1912. See also Diary of Mary Ann King, but contrast that with the help afforded with the churning by a husband in Mrs J. Booth diary.

226 Letter to the editor, from A Farmer's Daughter, 'Kitchen Economy,' *Farmer's Advocate*, June, 1886; July 1886.

227 Mrs W.E. Hopkins, 'Why Boys and Girls Leave the Farm,' *Farmer's Advocate*, 24 February 1910.

228 'Women's Work on the Farm: Extracts from Contributors,' *Farmer's Advocate*, 26 December 1912; and 'Is Marriage a Failure? Work on the Farm,' *Farmer's Advocate*, 14 November 1912. For criticism of inheritance practices, see *Farmer's Advocate*, 1 June 1899, December 1900, 2, 16, and 30 April, 21 May, and 23 July, 1908, 23 January 1909, and 16 January 1913; and *Farming World*, 15 January 1904. Legal inequities are examined in Annalee Golz, 'If a Man's Wife Will Not Obey Him, What Can He Do?: Reflections on the Family and the State in Nineteenth-Century Ontario' (paper presented to the Canadian Historical Association, 1991).

229 The Canadian Dairymen's Association, *Reports*, 1867–73, Dairymen's Association of Western Ontario, UG.

230 Disbrowe, 'A Vignette of Yesterday.'

231 Mrs Robert Warwick, 'Women as Farmers,' *Farmer's Advocate*, 19 (November 1884), 332. For an example of the trials experienced by a young couple beginning farming, see Latzer, *Myrtleville*, 162.

232 Marjorie G. Cohen, 'The Decline of Women in Canadian Dairying,' in Prentice and Trofimenkoff, *The Neglected Majority*, 61–83; Cohen, *Women's Work, Markets,*

and Economic Development, 59–92; and. R.M. McInnis, 'Women, Work and Child-bearing: Ontario in the Second Half of the Nineteenth Century,' *Histoire sociale/ Social History* 24 (1991), 237–62.

233 On the mutability of gender roles, see Nancy Grey Osterud, *Bonds of Community: The Lives of Farm Women in Nineteenth-Century New York* (Ithaca 1991), and Joy Parr, *The Gender of Breadwinners: Women, Men, and Change in Two Industrial Towns, 1880–1950* (Toronto 1990).

234 McInnis, 'Women, Work and Childbearing,' 249–50.

235 See Census of Canada, manuscript for Peel township, Wellington County. 1881, NAC. For the 1861 census, see Akenson, *The Irish in Ontario,* 306, n. 29. The *Report of the Ontario Commission on Unemployment* (Toronto 1916), 59, demonstrated the grave difficulties in arriving at statistics to reflect women's paid work.

236 *Farming World and Canada Farm and Home,* September 1904, 265.

237 See Abel, Chipsham, and Ferris, *Farm Families Today,* 27; and Cebotarev, Blacklock, and McIssac, 'Farm Women's Work Patterns.'

238 Laura Robinson diary, Burleigh Collection, 19 April 1901; Alex Hyde, 'The Farmer's Wife,' *Farmer's Advocate,* 15 July 1880; Ontario, Department of Agriculture, *Annual Report,* 1902, 128; 'The Woman on the Farm,' by A Farmer's Daughter, *Farmer's Advocate,* 3 June 1909; 'Nemo Too Easily Statisfied,' *Farmer's Advocate,* 19 March 1910; 'Husband Holds Purse Strings,' *Farmer's Advocate,* 5 May 1910; *Farm and Dairy,* 5 October 1911; 'How Should Income Be Apportioned?' *Farm and Dairy,* 9 October 1913; and Nyce, *Eby Diary,* 128.

   Graham, *Greenbank,* 282, provides the example of Margaret Blair (1870–1940) whose father and brother depended on her to make and execute all the financial decisions in relation to farm operations.

239 Canada, Commission on Conservation, *Report,* 5 (1914), 146, also showed Ontario's agriculture as the most labour-intensive in the country. This study also revealed that the vast majority of farms hauled water to the house from over 15 metres away and that only 10 per cent had indoor plumbing or a toilet – fewer than owned windmills. Most used their own weed-infested seed for sowing, while little top dressing of land occurred before planting. See also Ontario Agricultural College Bulletin No. 284, *Milk Production Costs* (1921).

240 Nyce, *Eby Diary,* 10 October 1912, 102.

241 *Royal Commission on the Relations of Labour and Capital,* 2:87 and *Evidence – Ontario,* 848, 891.

242 Mrs L.A. Hamilton, 'Help in Fruit Picking Time,' Ontario, Legislative Assembly, Sessional Papers, 44, 1914, 39–41; *The Canadian Woman's Annual and Social Service Directory* (Toronto 1915), 232–3; Ontario, Legislative Assembly, Sessional Papers, 33 1911, 10–12; and W.J. Kerr, 'Co-operation in the Purchase of Supplies and Sale of Products,' Ontario, Legislative Assembly, Sessional Papers, 34, 1914, 47–9.

   Women's industrial work outside agriculture in 1871, much of it in small rural locations, is examined in Elizabeth Bloomfield and G.T. Bloomfield, *Canadian Women in Workshops, Mills, and Factories: The Evidence of the 1871 Census Manuscript* (University of Guelph Department of Geography, Canadian Industry in 1871 Research Report 11, 1991).

243 James Bremner Diary, 23 April 1881.

244 *Royal Commission on the Relations of Labour and Capital: Evidence – Ontario*, 445. See also 'Might Court the Farmer's Daughter,' *Farmer's Advocate*, 46 (31 August 1911), 1435. Similar attitudes are displayed by farm women in 'Fanny Fern on Farmer's Wives,' *Farmer's Advocate*, 3 (1868), 19; *Farming World*, 15 (12 April 1898), 259; and *Farming World*, 16 (27 June 1898), 835.

245 'How Should the Farmer Treat His Hired Men ...?' *Farmer's Advocate*, 21 (May 1886), 136.

246 'Labour on the Farm,' *Canadian Farmer*, 4 (15 July 1872). See also Ontario, Department of Agriculture, *Annual Report*, 1887, 176.

247 'The City, the West or the Ontario Farm,' by A Hired Man, *Farmer's Advocate*, 49 (19 February 1914), 322.

248 'Reminiscences of an Ex-Hired Man,' *Farmer's Advocate*, 48 (22 May 1913), 950–1. See also Thomas Dick Diary, 2 June 1867; 'A Preachment to Hired Men,' by A Hired Man, *Farm and Dairy*, 26 February 1914, 235; and 'Why Men Go to the City to Work,' by Another Hired Man, *Farm and Dairy*, 26 March 1914, 386.

249 'The Hired Man's Side,' *Farmer's Advocate*, 46 (7 September 1911), 1483. See also 'Hours, Holidays and Privileges,' *Farmer's Advocate*, 46 (12 October 1911), 1677–8; 'The Hired Man in the Home,' *Farming World*, 18 (21 May 1901), 982; 'An Elaborate Toilet,' *Farmer's Advocate*, 46 (9 November 1911), 1822–3; and 'The Labor Problem,' *Farm and Dairy*, 20 April 1919.

250 Frank Shutt, 'The Farm Well and Its Contents,' Ontario, Department of Agriculture, *Annual Report*, 1897, 1:131–4. Ontario, Legislative Assembly, Sessional Papers, 25, 1905, 66–7, and 25, 1906, 25. Many farms had situated their buildings on ground above the area where they drew well water, and manure seepage contaminated the drinking supply.

251 A. Margaret Evans, 'Oliver Mowat and Ontario, 1874–1896: A Study in Political Success' (PhD dissertation, University of Toronto 1967), 97, 101 and 104–5.

252 Marilyn Barber, 'In Search of a Better Life: A Scottish Domestic in Rural Ontario,' *Polyphony*, 8, no. 1–2 (1986), 13–16.

253 'Inconsiderate Employers,' *Farmer's Advocate*, 46 (17 August 1911), 1352–3; 'Rube's Position Restated,' *Farmer's Advocate*, 46 (12 October 1911), 1680. 'From Another Hired Man,' *Farmer's Advocate*, 47 (29 February 1912), 374B.

254 Ontario Agricultural College, 'The Dairy Farming Business in Western Ontario, Second Survey,' *Farm Management – Part I*, 1919.

255 J.B. Reynolds, 'Present Day Agriculture,' Ontario, Legislative Assembly, Sessional Papers, 37, 1915, 61–4. Reynolds presented the same findings in 'Agricul-

tural Introspection,' *Farmer's Magazine*, 15 December 1920, 23. The reasons given
for disliking farming were, in order of importance, long hours, too much grind, too
few opportunities for recreation or amusement, poor returns, lack of capital, lack of
labour, lack of conveniences, and Sunday work.

256 A. Leitch, 'The Farm Labour Problem,' *O.A.C. Review*, 19, no. 2 (1906), 47–51.

257 Ontario, Department of Agriculture, *Annual Report*, 1894, 2:111.

258 Statistics about immigration into Ontario by principal ethnic groups for the years
from 1878–1905 are given in Ontario, Legislative Assembly, *Sessional Papers*,
32 (1905), 13, but as they were compiled by immigration agents and based on
the people with whom they came into contact, they can only be interpreted as a
rough guide. Attention to Americans settling in Ontario was sporadic, with no
coverage at all in the early years. Baines, *Migration in a Mature Economy*, traces
the increasing percentages of British emigrants from urban areas in England and
Wales during the second half of the nineteenth century.

259 NAC, RG 76, C4769, file 17921; C4782, file 22877.

260 Joy Parr, 'George Everitt Green,' *Dictionary of Canadian Biography*, 12 (Toronto
1990), 387–8.

261 Although these points are substantiated quantitatively in Baines, *Migration in a
Mature Economy*, the effects on Ontario immigration can be seen in Province of
Ontario, Destination Register, Quebec Agency, 1872–3, RG 11, series M, AO.

262 Letter of Alfred Scott, [1907], NAC, C10303, file 604526.

263 Fred Johnston to T. Southworth, 9 December 1907, NAC, C10303, file 604526.

264 Beth Light and Joy Parr, eds, *Canadian Women on the Move 1867–1920* (Toronto
1983), 62–4.

265 Letter of G. Blackburn, 5 March 1907, in Light and Parr, *Canadian Women on the
Move*.

266 For the twentieth century see Joy Parr, 'Hired Men: Ontario Agricultural Wage
Labour in Comparative Perspective,' *Labour/Le Travail* 15 (1985), 91–103; Charles
Johnston, 'A Motley Crowd: Diversity in the Ontario Countryside in the Early
Twentieth Century,' Canadian Papers in Rural History 7 (1990), 237–55. For the
West see Cecilia Dansyk, 'Showing Those Slaves Their Class Position: Barriers to
Organizing Farm Workers,' and W.J.C. Cherwinski, 'In Search of Jake Trumper:
The Farm Hand and the Prairie Farmer,' both in David C. Jones and Ian MacPher-
son, eds, *Building beyond the Homestead: Rural History in the Prairies* (Calgary
1985), 163–78 and 111–34; and David McGinnis, 'Farm Labour in Transition ...
Alberta 1921–51,' in *The Settlement of the West* (Calgary 1977). J.H. Thompson
and Allen Seager, 'The Labour Problem in the Alberta Beet Sugar Industry,'
Labour/Le Travail 3 (1978), 153–74.

267 Ontario, Legislative Assembly, Sessional Papers, 32, 1905, 11. See also Morris
Zaslow, *The Opening of the Canadian North 1870–1914* (Toronto 1971).

Native workers pulling flax in southern Ontario c. 1900–10

Back-breaking labour: planting potatoes

Sharpening the cradle for grain-cutting

Alex Sangster and sons Thomas (l.) and James (r.) with their new Harris binder: Howick Township, north Wellington County, c. 1890

Labour and the Law

JEREMY WEBBER

Throughout the North Atlantic world, the nineteenth century brought profound change in the nature of work, the relations between workers and those who benefited from their labour, and the ordering of those relations through law. Existing legal forms were squeezed, deformed, and reformed to address unprecedented situations, especially the rise of industrial employment and the increasing mobility of labour. A multitude of ways of organizing work was compressed into a few categories, increasingly marked by principles of contract rather than status. Relationships presupposing a complex web of personal duty and obligation were eroded and replaced by contracts tied more tightly to the execution of particular tasks. At the same time, industrialization threw up a host of new problems (or old problems in new guises) – child labour, unsanitary working conditions, industrial accidents, unemployment, and urban destitution – which generated new responses. And of course, the century saw the expansion of trade unions, representing for some a problem of social order, for others a problem of industrial justice.

In all of this, and in all societies, the law was pushed and pulled by specific conditions – the structure of the economy, the nature of economic opportunity, the balance of economic might. It was also shaped by various countries' institutions and traditions – their political structures, the organization of their courts, their distinctive languages of argument and justification, and the accumulated baggage of past practice. Thus, while the period was a time of change in the labour relations of all industrializing societies, the process assumed a unique character in each society in which it occurred.

In recent years, historians have turned their attention to the role of law in this process. There now exist good overviews of nineteenth-century labour law in the countries that were most influential in the development of Canadian law: England and the United States.[1] As yet, however, there have not been the same overviews of labour law in any of the British North American colonies. Instead, the studies have focused on prominent forms of legislative or judicial intervention: master and servant legislation, prosecutions for criminal conspiracy, compensation for industrial accidents, or factory regulation.[2] This has produced some very fine studies, but it has left us with little idea how the whole fits together, especially how the specialized regimes relate to the general structure of productive relations.

This chapter constitutes a first attempt to furnish an overview in the context of Upper Canada, later the province of Ontario. Its aspirations are modest. It is not a definitive history of the period. There remains a great deal of work to be done. Not only is the historian of labour law faced with the normal challenges of labour history – the lack of records produced by the principal subjects of the research – but even distinctively legal institutions have left only dispersed and sporadic records of themselves. Written contracts of employment were, with a few notable exceptions, rare in Ontario. Furthermore, the most important judicial actors in labour matters were the magistrates, whose sittings were not courts of record and whose practice varied from locality to locality, particularly in the early part of the century. Nevertheless, there is now enough material that a sense of the whole can be conveyed. This chapter therefore seeks to provide a preliminary map of nineteenth-century Ontario labour law, describing its main landmarks, showing their relationship to each other, and identifying areas that are still terra incognita.

Here and throughout this chapter, I speak of 'labour law' and 'employment,' but in fact the terms are misleading, especially with respect to the beginning of the century. At that time there was not a single, stable contract of employment with its own specific character. Instead, labour was performed under a number of forms, some of which lacked features now considered essential to employment (such as the subordination of employee to employer or, in the case of slavery, a contract); yet these often evolved into or were quickly replaced by modern employment relations. This chapter therefore deals with a variety of employment and near-employment structures in order to allow for the process of consolidation and standardization of legal forms.

It does not discuss all the ways in which labour was marshalled. One notable omission is the division of labour and allocation of property within the family. Family labour was extremely important to the economic development of nineteenth-century Ontario, but a discussion of its legal framework would lead us deep into the unique concerns of family law.[3] Nor does it address the employment conditions of soldiers or public servants (including teachers employed under statute), shaped as they

were by conceptions of sovereignty or public office far removed from
the law governing other forms of labour. Finally, it ignores compulsory
work such as prison or statute labour (the duties imposed on landowners
to build and maintain neighbouring roads). These too involve special
considerations only tangentially related to full-time labour under contract. In short, the focus of this chapter is not on the law governing all
work relations, but on those areas of law that approximate the domain of
labour law today.

The Institutions of Labour Law in Nineteenth-Century Ontario

Labour law in nineteenth-century Ontario was very much the product of
its institutional context. There was no single, unambiguous, integrated
body of employment law, but rather an interlocking set of largely auton-
omous forums and approaches.

The most prominent forums – and the institutions on which legal historians generally concentrate – were the superior courts. In Ontario these
were between 1794 and 1881 the Court of King's (or Queen's) Bench,
from 1788 to 1794 and from 1849 to 1881 the Court of Common Pleas,
and from 1837 to 1881 the Court of Chancery. In 1881 Queen's Bench,
Common Pleas, and Chancery were united as the High Court of Justice.[4]
These courts are often considered to be, collectively, the oracle of nineteenth-century Ontario law, imposing uniformity and consistency. In one
sense this was true, for if a superior court ruled on a question, the lower
courts were in principle bound to follow. In labour matters, however,
this controlling function was severely attenuated. Labour law was in
great measure the preserve of magistrates (usually justices of the peace,
often called simply 'justices'). The superior courts intervened rarely, and
then only on very specific matters.

This was true for the simple reason that with some notable exceptions
disputes between masters and servants simply did not fall within superior-
court jurisdiction. Throughout the period, most employment disputes
(absconding, disobedience, neglect of work, wage disputes, and even
minor criminal offences) came before magistrates, sitting alone or in
pairs. In those cases an appeal lay to the Court of General Quarter
Sessions of the Peace (which until 1841 was itself staffed by magistrates)
or, for master and servant disputes after 1880, to the Division Courts.[5] The
superior courts themselves exercised no appellate jurisdiction over these
subjects. When imprisonment was imposed, the superior courts could
become seised of the matter through applications for *habeas corpus* or
actions against the magistrates for false imprisonment, but these recourses

were uncommon.[6] Small civil actions could also be tried before Courts of Requests or Division Courts, from which (until 1880) there was no appeal, or if the amount was somewhat greater, before District (later County) Courts, from which there was a right of appeal, although this was rarely exercised.[7]

Thus, superior courts had little to do with the core of employment or near-employment relationships. Rather, their involvement was limited to peripheral matters. They had jurisdiction over the most serious criminal offences, which sometimes arose out of employment. They tried actions brought against an employer for enticing away another's servant. Other civil actions affecting employment might also come before the superior courts: an action against a surety for the misconduct of an apprentice, a claim against an employer for a work-related accident, or an action in damages for assault and battery. In all these cases, the trial would occur before a superior-court judge and jury during the assizes, with the jury deciding all issues of fact. After the trial, the losing party could move to have the verdict set aside, in which case questions of law would be considered by the full court. In addition, the jurisdiction of superior courts was relevant to the special remedies of the separate branch of the law known as Equity. The injunction was potentially the most important of these, although it did not come into its own in labour cases until the twentieth century. In the nineteenth, equitable remedies played virtually no role in labour law. Before the creation of the Court of Chancery in 1837, they were unobtainable in Upper Canada. Thereafter, only a few existed (at first excluding injunctions), and even then only in Chancery, until a series of legislative reforms later in the century expanded their availability.[8]

In short, the jurisdiction of superior courts with respect to labour was, although not negligible, nevertheless confined to very particular issues. The central obligations of employment tended to be matters of magistrates' law. This was nicely indicated by McLean, J.'s concurring opinion in *Mitchell* v. *Defries*, where, in an action for assault and battery, Queen's Bench had to decide the scope of the employer's right to punish his servant physically. McLean, J. based his reasons on Burn's *Justice*, a British manual designed to instruct non-lawyer magistrates.[9]

Who then were these magistrates, and how did they exercise their authority? The justices of the peace (the magistrates most relevant in the early period and, throughout the century, in rural areas) were, in aspiration, members of a distinguished and propertied local elite, clothed with authority to keep the peace by a commission issued by the Governor under the Great Seal.[10] They exercised their judicial functions singly, in pairs, or in larger numbers, depending on the nature of the claim before them.

First, magistrates were assumed to possess, by statute, summary jurisdiction to try a number of minor criminal matters, such as assault, and specific disputes related to employment, all without a jury. They exercised this authority singly or in pairs, depending on the terms of the statute conferring jurisdiction. Stated this way, however, it sounds more straightforward than it was, especially during the first half of the century. English statutes were not assembled in the ordered and rationalized manner familiar today. The magistrates' jurisdiction was founded upon a large number of often ancient and overlapping texts. To determine the scope of their jurisdiction would have been no mean feat, even if the magistrates had had the will and capacity to research the materials. Furthermore, many of these laws had long ago lapsed into desuetude,[11] and in any case there was real doubt whether many of them were applicable to the colonies. The magistrates' manuals gave the justices some direction, but even these relied on statutes that had fallen into disuse in England, were declared inapplicable to the colonies, or had, in material respects, been repealed. Moreover, it is clear that magistrates could not possibly have applied some provisions reported as law in the manuals. It seems very likely, then, that magistrates construed their summary jurisdiction in a much more approximate way, using the manuals as an indication of what they could do, but in the end relying on their general sense that small crimes and master-servant relations fell within their purview.[12]

Magistrates' proceedings could be summary indeed. Full descriptions are rare, but their expeditious character is suggested by the events of 1 and 2 May 1843, reported in the pleadings in *Shea* v. *Choat*.[13] An apprentice named Shea was accused of having helped one of the firm's debtors to flee the province and of leaving work without excuse. On 1 May his master laid the complaint before magistrate Asa A. Burnham, a warrant was issued, and the master gave the warrant to a constable. The constable arrested Shea the next day and brought him before the magistrate, who immediately tried and convicted Shea and committed him to jail for one month. Shea served his sentence; this case was an action for false imprisonment initiated after his release.

The more exalted criminal jurisdiction of magistrates, relevant for more serious crimes occurring in the employment context such as theft or conspiracy, was exercised in Quarter Sessions. At first this jurisdiction extended in principle to all felonies and misdemeanours, but in practice Sessions did not try capital felonies, leaving them to the assizes, although magistrates would conduct preliminary hearings.[14] Unlike the magistrates' summary jurisdiction, Sessions was a court of record. It was held four times a year (twice a year after 1868). Initially a grand jury, consisting of at least twelve local landowners, was assembled. The chairman of Sessions would address this jury, often discussing matters of general public interest in the locality. Then the jury would retire to consider indictments. When the grand jury found or presented an indictment, the case would go to trial before the magistrates, with a petit jury determining questions of fact in each case.

During the early part of the century, the courts of Sessions were composed of at least two magistrates sitting together. From 1841 on they were chaired by District Court judges, who as part of the same reform were now required to be lawyers. After that reform, at least one judge would therefore be legally trained. The role of lay magistrates in Sessions gradually diminished, and from 1873 County Court judges were allowed to hold Sessions without an assistant or magistrate sitting with them. The convictions of Sessions were not subject to appeal until the 1850s. Thus, for much of the first half of the century, many serious criminal offences were determined in courts staffed entirely by lay magistrates.

The magistrates, then, exercised a substantial criminal jurisdiction either summarily or in Sessions. Moreover, their jurisdiction to decide what we would now consider civil disputes arising out of employment, such as disobedience, the non-payment of wages, or Shea's improvised absence, could be dealt with by the summary procedures described above if a master-servant relationship existed (a qualification which was itself, in the early part of the period, far from clear, as we will see). But even when there was no such relationship, a civil claim might still come before magistrates (or judges of similar status), exercising civil jurisdiction in the nineteenth-century equivalent of today's small claims courts.

The first of these were the Courts of Requests, established under legislation passed in 1792.[15] These courts were created by the magistrates in Sessions and initially consisted of two or more magistrates sitting together. But given the shortage of magistrates it was difficult to keep up with the demand, and in 1833 the courts were reformed so that they could be staffed by two or more 'commissioners,' not necessarily magistrates, appointed by the Lieutenant-Governor. In 1841 these courts were abolished and replaced by Division Courts, presided over by a District Court judge or a legally trained deputy.

These courts had jurisdiction over small civil claims. In 1833, for example, the Courts of Requests could rule on claims of up to £10. In all these courts procedure was informal. Juries were not used in the Courts of Requests, and were available in the Division Courts only for sums greater than £2 10s. (and then only on demand). Until 1880 there was no appeal.

Slightly larger claims (in 1845 up to £25 in debt, £50 if liquidated) could be brought before the District Courts, most of which were renamed 'County Courts' in 1849. In the early part of the century these were usually staffed by laymen, but from 1841 on, judges were legally trained. Proceedings were more formal than in the Courts of Requests or Division Courts. They used written pleadings based on the English forms of action and, until the 1860s, juries. Wylie suggests that in the first years of the century this greater formality, together with the fact that District Courts sat less frequently and in less convenient locations, meant that the Courts of Requests were often preferred. The District Courts were intermediate between the lower and the superior courts, and after 1845 District Court judgments could be appealed to the superior courts.

These, then, were the institutions most relevant to nineteenth-century labour law. The most important for our purposes were those staffed by lay magistrates. Given their lack of legal training, how did they decide their cases?

In many ways, the magistrates inhabited a different legal universe from that of superior court judges. They often did not have the assistance of lawyers, nor did they work with the raw material of legal analysis: cases, English statutes, and treatises. Instead they relied on their own good sense (or lack of it), on the Upper Canadian statutes, and on the magistrates' manuals – digests of the law most relevant to their tasks.[16] In addition, proceedings before the magistrates did not follow the forms of action that dominated proceedings in the superior courts. Their hearings were informal and the pleadings oral, and could involve the magistrate encouraging the parties to settle.[17] Even after a conviction, he could discharge the accused if that person made good the damage.[18] In practice, proceedings before the magistrates could be used to secure compensation unavailable in a criminal prosecution at the assizes or impossible at common law. Magistrates could, for example, force recalcitrant employees back to work, even though specific performance of the employment contract was unobtainable before the superior courts.[19]

But it is misleading to focus exclusively on the judicial role of the magistrates, for they were much more than judges. During the first half of the century, they were the principal officers responsible for policing in the province. They appointed the constables at the April Quarter Sessions and could swear in special constables when needed. If the constables alone were unable to control disorder, the magistrates could summon the militia. In each case they had the ultimate oversight of the forces of civil order. They also had authority to suppress riots, compel the giving of securities for the peace, and arrest wrongdoers. In some ways, then, their summary jurisdiction was merely one part of a larger responsibility for maintaining order.[20]

During much of the first half of the century magistrates were also, in Sessions, the principal body of local government. They raised and spent taxes, were responsible for poor relief, jail administration, road maintenance, pound regulation, tavern licences, certificates for clergymen for the solemnization of marriage, and the nomination of parish and town officers where there was no town meeting.[21] In the early period they were responsible for regulating markets, including setting the price of bread.[22] Frequently, magistrates in Sessions sought the advice of grand juries on these matters; the juries responded through the same form used for presenting indictments.[23]

In short, especially during the first half of the century, magistrates were not simply judges of inferior courts charged with reading and applying the law – a task which they were in any case poorly trained to do. As the supposed leaders of their communities their role was conceived more broadly, as pillars of local government, maintaining justice, ensuring the peace, and protecting property. Their judicial functions were wrapped up with the more general conception that social order and good government were best secured by entrusting them to men of character and property.

That, at least, was the ideal. Throughout the period observers expressed serious misgivings about the quality of colonial magistrates. In the earliest days, or in sparsely settled districts, the criticism often fixed on the lack of suitable candidates. In 1803, for example, Lord Selkirk noted when travelling through Upper Canada:

The chief difficulty in the interior government of the Country, appears to arise from the want of fit persons to act as Magistrates & Justices of Peace: the great deficiency of education is such that many men of good character & sense cannot be appointed, not being able to sign their name: – the whole Country too having been settled by men of the lowest order with scarcely any men of the rank of gentlemen, they are accustomed to look on each other so much as equals, that the common run cannot feel a proper degree of respect for Magistrates who when they leave the chair are entirely on their own level.[24]

Others fastened on such obvious misconduct as drunkenness on duty.[25] From 1841 on, magistrates were required to file periodic returns, in part because of suspicions that some were pocketing fines.[26] Many complaints concerned partiality or arbitrary behaviour. The appearance of bias was especially likely given the small size of the local elites. It was virtually inevitable that magistrates would rule on matters affecting their friends. Occasionally they even acted in matters in which they themselves had an interest.[27] And quite apart from these more direct forms of partiality, the simple fact that they were men of standing in the community – often merchants, almost always employers – meant that they had a natural inclination to value discipline and obedience, especially in employment relations.

Finally, many criticisms fastened on the sheer inability of amateur magistrates to control disorder and to govern a rapidly changing, mobile, urbanizing, yet still geographically dispersed society. Ultimately, these criticisms led to a gradual erosion of the magistrates' role. In the 1830s and 1840s, a number of cities were incorporated and the powers of local government transferred from the magistrates to a common council or board of police. This was more than an administrative change. The very basis of local authority began to shift from a recognition of worth bestowed from above to a potentially more responsive, more democratic foundation, although one in which property holders retained the predominant say, given the existence of property qualifications for electors and candidates. Although many of the forms of the magistrates' authority remained – indeed, the mayors and aldermen were often clothed with the authority of magistrates – the shift allowed municipal officers to play a role in labour disputes that would have been impossible for the earlier magistrates, one simultaneously more political and more conciliatory.

The place of magistrates in the administration of justice was also transformed. Police forces were created on a professional basis, with ordinary magistrates increasingly confined to their judicial functions. Those functions were themselves undergoing significant change. Beginning in the 1840s, reforms to the District, Division, and Session Courts shifted control into the hands of legally trained judges. In the cities, 'Police Magistrates' were appointed beginning about 1849. These tended to be professional appointments in the sense that the duties of a police magistrate demanded a considerable commitment of energy and ability. They were not necessarily lawyers, however, and they frequently retained the broad conception of their role typical of the rural magistrates.[28] Sitting alone, they could try all offences over which one or more magistrates had jurisdiction, as well as infringements of municipal by-laws. In the same 1849 reform, provision was made for the establishment of Recorders' Courts in cities. These had the same jurisdiction as the Sessions Courts and were presided over by a lawyer. Thus the inferior courts came to be streamlined and consolidated, with lawyers assuming a larger role.

Finally, another kind of officer emerged at the end of the century: full-time or part-time members of the public service, charged with administering specialized regimes relating to, for example, factory conditions or the mediation of labour disputes. They were not lawyers; they were frequently drawn from organized labour and, for balance, employers. The appointments were an outlet for patronage, used to cement the government's relations with its supporters. This meant that the officers' effectiveness varied considerably. It also meant that they had a greater understanding of and often more sympathy for labour than had magistrates.[29] Given the imprecise definition of government service before the creation of a highly rationalized bureaucracy, an able officer also had considerable scope for improvisation and might well serve more functions than those for which he had been appointed.

THE EVOLUTION OF NINETEENTH-CENTURY
ONTARIO LABOUR LAW

Thus far we have focused on institutions of public order. This emphasis, however, tends to obscure the extent to which the law was an expression of social life rather than the product of conscious state policy. It neglects the important social and economic forces driving the evolution of the law.

The most obvious way in which the law adapted to society was through legislative act – although sometimes legislation represented a strongly conditioned response, prompted by domestic circumstances but borrowing its form from English precedents. Adaptation also occurred through the actions of those administering the law. Magistrates and courts were concerned with the fit between law and social fact, sometimes expressly adapting what had come before, always considering how previously enunciated principles should touch ground in the cases before them.[30]

Perhaps the greatest cause of adaptation, however, was the actions of those who had no formal part in the administration of the law, namely, the parties to the employment and near-employment relationships. They influenced law in at least two ways. First, their decisions had an important impact on the content of their legally enforceable relations – the length of contract, method of payment, and even, to an extent, the degree of control exercised by one party over the other. The parties' decisions were not unconstrained, but the constraints varied over time, especially with varying economic conditions. As a result, the characteristic patterns of work relations also changed. Second, the changes in these patterns were often responsible, in turn, for further adjustment in the content of the law. Law almost always exists in an uneasy relationship with the phenomena it regulates. On the one hand, it controls the parties, ensuring that they meet certain imposed standards. On the other, it derives its standards from principles that seem, at least to the judges or lawmakers, to be implicit in the relationship itself – either that, or demanded by a larger social principle.

We will see many of these adaptations throughout this chapter. In the century as a whole, however, there seem to have been four distinguishable periods.

First, there was a brief period of transition before or during the very first years of settlement (in the southern part of the province, from the late eighteenth century into the very first years of the nineteenth). During this time there were few economic opportunities for independent workers (of non-aboriginal origin) in the territory – or at least, there was considerable uncertainty about what those opportunities might be. At the same time, there was very little labour, with the necessary skills, for employers to use. This made for a substantial degree of mutual dependence between workers and employers. In that context, there was an incentive for both to enter into contracts of at least a year in duration, so that each could count on the commitment of the other. These contracts were often concluded outside the territory (in Montreal, Quebec City, or even an immigrant's home country), or in the few centres of European settlement in what became Upper Canada. Along with these moderately long-term contracts were other forms of labour which originated outside the territory but never truly took root in the colony. These included slavery and very long multi-year labour contracts.

The second period began as non-aboriginal agricultural settlement took hold and lasted roughly until the closing of the agricultural frontier in the 1840s. This period was marked by substantial geographic and occupational mobility, as new arrivals worked for others full- or part-time while they amassed capital to buy land or established themselves on their own land. There were often very severe shortages of labour, making for high wages and considerable opportunity for changing jobs. At the same time, many established farmers were cash-poor, so that it was difficult for them to enter into long-term commitments. Thus, much rural work was done by the job or the day, although some workers were hired by the month or year. There was a high degree of labour mobility, and the discipline of those servants who were hired by the month or year was notoriously bad. Frequently the administrative structure of the law was weak, with a single magistrate having responsibility for a large area, relying on part-time constables. During this period, then, many employers and workers had little recourse to law, but relied instead on various methods of self-protection – payment by the job, relatively short employment contracts, the ability to leave and find other work, even physical intimidation. At the same time, there was very substantial immigration during the period, sometimes by paupers without the necessary skills even for farm work. They often ended up in unskilled construction gangs on public works and railways. These sometimes desperate navvies provoked the greatest official anxiety, especially when waves of immigration coincided with periods of economic slowdown and unemployment.

The third period in Ontario labour law, a period lasting until the 1870s, was initiated by the closing of the land frontier. The lack of good land drove up the prices of farms, restricting the movement from labour to land at least within Ontario. The labour supply was now more consonant with demand; workers no longer had the same occupational and social mobility. A more stable class of workers emerged. Moreover, reform of the courts and police made those institutions more efficient, especially in the cities, and they began to play a greater role in employment. The law began to grapple with the problems presented by the new, mass-employment, integrated forms of production of the railways and factories, including the increased prominence of strikes. During this period, the courts drew chiefly upon the instruments of legal control used to repress labour strife in early nineteenth-century England: master and servant and criminal law.

Finally, during the 1870s, this pattern of regulation began to give way to a new, less repressive approach, one marking a fourth stage in the evolution of nineteenth-century employment law. In 1872 trade unions were given a measure of legal recognition, and in 1877 the most draconian provisions of the master and servant legislation were repealed (although collective bargaining still occurred, if at all, because unions had the power to compel it, not because of legal sanction; in Ontario, it was well into the twentieth century before the state intervened to structure negotiations and enforce collective agreements). The province adopted new regimes to deal with child labour, factory conditions, and industrial accidents. Public officials took a more active part in the mediation of industrial disputes. This signalled the beginning of a more subtle approach to labour regulation, one entrusted to elected officials and members of the administrative branch of the state. It supplemented, but did not entirely displace, the use of the police and criminal law to suppress disorder.

The organization of the rest of this chapter is a compromise between chronology and attention to specific legal forms. We will nevertheless see, through those forms, how the broad trends identified here shaped the development of labour law in nineteenth-century Ontario.

Transitional Regimes in a New Territory

In the first years of the colony, there were two common types of work relations that very soon disappeared: slavery and long-term employment contracts.

Both black and Indian slavery existed in the territory at the founding of Upper Canada. Slavery had been practised under the French regime and continued after the Conquest. Many Loyalists had brought slaves with them when they fled the United States. Although some Upper Canadian settlers toyed with the idea of using slavery to overcome the chronic shortage of labour, slaves appear to have been used primarily for domestic labour, not farm work. In any case, by the time Upper Canada was founded, the tide was running against slavery in the jurisdictions to which Upper Canada had closest ties. The English courts had affirmed that slavery was unknown in that country (though this did not extend to the colonies). Of the northern United States, Vermont, Pennsylvania, Massachusetts, Connecticut, Rhode Island and New Hampshire had already passed laws to prohibit slavery or phase it out. New York was soon to do the same.[31]

Very shortly after Upper Canada was created, it acted to abolish slavery, although gradually, without directly attacking existing property rights. In 1793 it adopted a statute providing that any slave brought into the colony would be free. Slaves already in the colony, however, were not emancipated. They remained slaves unless freed by their masters, although their children would be free at the age of twenty-five and their grandchildren at birth. This ensured that slavery would never become a major or continuing source of labour for the colony. But slavery did persist for a time; Riddell notes an advertisement for the sale of a slave in 1806 and a prosecution for the theft of a slave in 1811. Over the years there were some manumissions, usually by will. The last slaves were probably freed by the imperial act of 1833.[32]

Abolition was primarily the achievement of the colony's Lieutenant Governor, John Graves Simcoe, who apparently shared with many of his contemporaries a moral abhorrence of slavery and a belief in the economic superiority of free labour. Those beliefs were not universal, however: in 1798 a bill to reinstate slavery passed the Upper Canadian lower house, although the Legislative Council refused to proceed with it. Legislation for abolition could not be secured in Lower Canada or the maritime colonies because of popular sentiment; there, abolition occurred by judicial action. Of course, racial prejudice survived slavery, in Upper Canada as elsewhere.[33]

Also at the beginning of Upper Canada's history (or in areas far from settlement), employment contracts were often much longer than in later years. One sees, for example, the odd yearly hiring of a carpenter – a term extremely rare once settlement got under way.[34] Clerks posted to remote stores might be hired for three years. In the fur trade, three- or five-year terms were common for all classes of servant around the turn of the century, although North West Company canoemen working from Montreal might be paid by the trip; the Hudson's Bay Company required two years' notice to end a contract. Clearly, there was reason for both parties to accept long terms when the labour was to be performed in remote country, cut off from other sources of employment or supplies of labour. In the Hudson's Bay Company these contracts were combined with a distinctly paternalistic structure of authority. In the North West Company, the framework was less rigid but nevertheless involved strong elements of dependence and obligation.[35] As we will see, however, these regimes were not typical of employment relations in the first half of the century. With important exceptions, paternalistic employment relations disappeared with the full onset of settlement.

One form of labour that had virtually no place in the colony was long-term adult indentured labour, although there were indentured apprentices. The statute of 1793 abolishing slavery prohibited employment contracts of more than nine years.[36]

The Structure of Employment in Nineteenth-Century Ontario

A solid understanding of labour and the law in nineteenth-century Ontario begins with the parties' agreements – the manner, in other words, in which employers and workers structured their relations. These contracts formed the raw material to which statutes and judicial decisions applied, and although their structure and content were influenced by that body of law, they were by no means dictated by it.

These contractual forms were surprisingly diverse, especially in the early part of the century. Although there were common patterns, especially within occupational groups, there was a great deal of variation. Upper Canadian practice also differed significantly from that in England. Extrapolations from English experience, or from legislation derived from English models, are frequently misleading.

This section describes the variety of relationships under which work was done in nineteenth-century Ontario. Since most contracts of employment, with the notable exceptions of apprenticeship and lumber workers' agreements, were oral, the nature of the contract usually has to be deduced from collateral information suggesting the terms of hiring. In this section I will focus especially on the duration of hiring, because this was the principal factor that determined job security, the ability to leave employment, the payment of wages, and obligations of care and support in times of sickness. Indeed, the duration of hiring was largely responsible for fixing the extent of dependence and security inherent in the employment relationship. It was an artificial concept, best understood as the law's presumption of the degree of commitment between the parties: the period during which the employer had agreed to hire, the employee to serve. It bore no necessary relationship to the actual time served (a servant might work on monthly contracts for one employer continuously during her entire working life) and the contracts were often subject to special notice requirements before they could be terminated. Nevertheless, the various lengths of hiring were the principal means by which employment contracts were categorized.

In this discussion I will often take the period used to calculate wages as the best indicator of the duration of hiring for the simple reason that, in the absence of evidence to the contrary, that is generally what magistrates and courts did. It should be remembered, however, that the parties could agree to a duration differing from that used to calculate wages, and both these periods could be very different from the period over which wages were actually paid. A good example is found in Radforth's chapter in this volume: lumber workers' pay was calculated by the month, they agreed to work for a season, and at least part of their pay was withheld until the end of their employment.

FARM LABOUR

The legal forms were especially diverse in the case of farm labour. Much of the work done on Upper Canadian farms fell outside the scope of employment law altogether. Given the prevalence of small holdings, a very large proportion was done by family members. The work was unpaid. Unless the parties expressly agreed otherwise, the magistrates and courts presumed that wives, sons, and daughters contributed their labour out of a sense of family obligation, without intending to enter into contractual relations. This could be especially hard on women and girls, who usually had no property rights in the farm. Widows did receive some protection under the law of dower, but a woman who kept house for her father, brother, or uncle might well be left with nothing if her relative died without making provision for her: she would have no right to the property and no claim to wages.[37]

Another common form of labour, especially during the early years of settlement, was the work bee. In new settlements casual labourers were scarce and expensive, and farmers were poor. When there was a task requiring an intense, short-term application of labour, neighbours would often pool their efforts, congregating on a farm to raise the walls of a house or barn, gather together logs for burning, husk corn, or even, on occasion, bring in the harvest. The host would provide food and strong drink and would contribute his own or his servant's labour at the next bee. Bees were sometimes rowdy and dangerous, not least because of the amount of whisky that was drunk, and they became less common as a settlement became consolidated. Nevertheless, during the first years they were an important form of cooperative labour that fell outside master-servant relations.[38]

A third way of securing agricultural labour, usually also outside the scope of employment law, was sharecropping. Under this arrangement, one person would work another's land, receiving in return a share of the crop. This permitted the owner to have the land cultivated even if he could not work it himself; his tenant, on the other hand, obtained the use of land without needing capital to buy his own farm. Sharecropping could take any one of three legal forms: it could be a lease, under which the tenant took possession of the farm, paying a rent expressed as a per-centage of the crop; it could be a partnership between the owner and the tenant, under which each contributed to a common enterprise, sharing profit and loss; or it could be a contract of service, with the farmer work-ing the farm as the owner's employee and receiving a portion of the crop as wages. The form mattered. If the farmer was a tenant, he would be the owner of the entire crop, could defend his possession of that crop even against the landowner, and could dispose of it as he saw fit as long as the rent was paid when due. If, however, he was an employee, he was sub-ject to much closer supervision and the crops belonged to the landowner. A tenant on shares therefore possessed considerably more independence than an employee sharecropper. In fact, in the southern United States, one of the crucial elements in the post-Civil War subordination of freed-men was a series of court decisions, beginning in 1872, that reinterpreted sharecropping as a contract of employment rather than lease. In Upper Canada the courts generally treated sharecropping as a lease unless the farmer had clearly been hired as an employee. Sharecropping was rea-sonably common but was considered a recipe for trouble, there being frequent disagreements over the division of the crop.[39]

When one thinks of farm workers, however, one tends to think prima-rily of paid farmhands who worked under the close direction of the owner of the farm. Even here there was considerable variation in con-tractual form in Upper Canada. In England much of the paid agricultural labour force was employed on yearly or even longer contracts; indeed, there was a presumption of yearly hirings in husbandry.[40] This was not the only form of farm labour. Thompson identified at least four catego-ries of master-servant relationship in nineteenth-century English agricul-ture: (1) servants on yearly or quarterly contracts who would receive board and lodging in the employer's household; (2) 'A regular labour-force ... more or less fully employed the year round,' but whose members would live independently; (3) labourers paid by the day or by the piece; and (4) 'More or less skilled specialists, who might contract for the job.'[41] The core of the labour force was, however, generally made up of employees working by the year.

In Canada, the situation was quite different, especially once settlement was well under way. There are occasional examples of workers employed on contracts with durations longer than one year, but apart from the special case of apprenticeships (which I discuss separately below), those contracts were invariably concluded in the old country.[42] Even then, it seems likely that in practice Upper Canadian employers would not have been able to insist on the terms of such an agreement, although the contract was binding in law. The law's grip on employment was often tenuous, especially in the first half of the century, as we will see. Specifically with respect to the bringing of servants from England, Susanna Moodie noted: 'They no sooner set foot upon the Canadian shores than they become possessed with this ultra-republican spirit ... if you refuse to listen to their dishonest and extravagant claims, they tell you that "they are free; that no contract signed in the old country is binding in 'Meriky;' that you may look out for another person to fill their place as soon as you like; and that you may get the money expended in their passage and outfit in the best manner you can."'[43]

Yearly contracts were not as rare as multi-year contracts, but they were far from the norm.[44] Most regular farmhands were employed on monthly hirings, even when they were retained for the entire year.[45] Indeed, there are references to regular employees' being paid one monthly wage rate through the growing season and then a renegotiated, lower rate over the winter, if they were kept on at all.[46]

This tendency towards shorter contracts, evident from the earliest years of the century, may seem surprising. One might have expected that there would have been greater use of yearly hirings, because employers would want to assure themselves of a continuous labour force at a time when good servants were hard to find, and workers would want guaranteed work, room, and board over the long Canadian winter. A number of factors, however, militated against long contracts. First, a great many employers would have found it difficult to commit themselves to offering a full year's work. Even those who arrived in Canada with a modest capital usually used it to buy land and buildings and were then very short of cash. Early settlers often recounted having to scrounge money to pay servants or to let servants go because they could not afford to keep them.[47] This, combined with the fact that the work was seasonal in any case, effectively counter-balanced the potential gain from having a stable workforce. Nor did employees, at least those whom farmers would have wanted to hire for a year, crave the stability of yearly contracts. Throughout much of the first half of the century there was a severe shortage of skilled farm workers. Work was plentiful, wages were high, and the employees were consequently much less dependent on any one employer. They were often only in the full-time labour force for a couple of years while they saved enough to buy their own farm or supported families already on the land until their farms came into production.[48] Neither party, then, wished to make the extended commitment inherent in a yearly contract. Employees might be kept throughout the year, but the contracts were generally by the month, tacitly renewed.

Some jobs were also done by the day, a farmer hiring neighbours or recent immigrants to do a specific task. Day labour was especially important during the harvest, when the work was much heavier than normal. During the harvest every farmer was in the same position at the same time, and harvest labour therefore commanded a premium wage. In his advice to prospective immigrants in the 1850s, William Hutton noted that this gave crops like hay, peas, and oats an advantage, because cutting could be delayed until the peak demand for labour had passed.[49]

Finally, some farm work was contracted out to an individual or team of workers, at an agreed price for the job. This was the most common arrangement for clearing land and was occasionally used for ploughing and harvesting. Rates would be calculated according to the number of acres and the difficulty.

Thus, over the course of the year a farm family might employ a number of workers under a variety of conditions. They might pay one man a yearly wage or, more likely, would pay him a monthly wage but count on keeping him for the full year. Another man might be employed for the spring, summer, and fall on a monthly hiring, although his employment might be extended through the winter at a reduced wage.[50] If there were no daughters old enough, a girl would often be hired to help with cooking and cleaning, and tending the chickens, dairy, and kitchen garden. She might be hired by the month, although girls and boys were sometimes hired on long-term apprenticeships. When the demand for labour was high, especially during the harvest, labourers would be hired by the day (if they could be found). The clearing of land or the building of a house would usually be contracted out to a gang of workers for an agreed price. If a barn had to be raised, the family might organize a bee, summoning their neighbours to share the work in return for food, drink, and the expectation that the family would return the favour. Farm labour was organized, in other words, through a highly diverse set of contractual and non-contractual arrangements.

DOMESTIC SERVICE

In Upper Canada, domestic service was treated in much the same way as monthly farm labour. This differed from the English practice. There, domestics – employees living *intra moenia*, within the employer's household – were usually treated as a separate category. Since the law was loath to challenge the master's authority over his home, 'menial' servants were excluded from the English wage-regulation statutes. Most important, the employment of domestics could be terminated by either party upon a month's notice or by the employer upon payment of a month's wages, even if the hiring was by the year.[51]

This rule was repeated in Upper Canadian legal handbooks[52] and would have been applied in the case of yearly contracts. In practice, however, the distinction was of little relevance to the colony. The prevalence of monthly contracts meant that most employees were subject to the same notice. The social basis of the distinction was also much less clear during the first decades of the century. In England there were large numbers of domestics employed in cities, towns, and great houses, doing work quite separate from the primary productive activities of a farm or business. But in the predominantly rural conditions of early Upper Canada, female servants usually performed the same tasks as farm women, doing the cooking and housework but also running the dairy, tending the vegetable garden, and helping generally around the farm. In such circumstances, there was virtually no distinction between a domestic and an outside sphere. Moreover, in country areas, most regular servants lived *intra moenia*. There was little cause, then, to distinguish domestics from others.

ARTISANAL AND INDUSTRIAL LABOUR

In recent years much of the work on labour in nineteenth-century Ontario has concentrated on skilled artisans, such as printers and shoemakers. Many of those studies have assumed that the trades possessed (or would have possessed, were it not for the erosion of workers' control of their craft) a classical artisanal structure: boys would be initiated into the trade through long apprenticeships and would then serve as journeymen under a master's supervision, before becoming masters themselves. That structure did form an important part of the background against which Canadian practice took shape: apprenticeships were used to train young workers, though they were shorter and often more informal than in England; some skilled workers who immigrated to Canada had undergone English apprenticeships; English legal forms were used in Upper Canada; English law was cited in Upper Canadian courts and legal manuals; and colonial workers, especially trade unionists, called upon the traditional structure in their attempt to establish control of their crafts. As a description of the organization of skilled labour in Upper Canada, however, the model is misleading. Although some colonial trades followed it quite closely, most diverged to varying degrees. Certainly the structure lacked the legal support it enjoyed in England.

In England the crucial element differentiating workers in the traditional crafts from others had been the requirement of apprenticeship. According to the Statute of Artificers (enacted in 1562, apprenticeship provisions repealed in 1814; often referred to as the Statute of Elizabeth), workers were forbidden to practise trades then performed in England and Wales (including carpentry, masonry, shoemaking, and tailoring) without having served a seven-year apprenticeship.[53] This set journeymen sharply apart from other workers, giving them a privileged position in the labour market not only because of their skill but also because of the substantial barrier that apprenticeship posed to new entrants. It constituted the foundation for the higher social status of journeymen and their greater pay relative to other workers. In fact, in early nineteenth-century English law, the requirement of apprenticeship was the only factor differentiating skilled from unskilled workers. Otherwise, a journeymen was 'a servant by the day.'[54]

In Upper Canada a number of factors undermined the institution of apprenticeship and blurred the status of the traditional trades. Even in England the requirement of apprenticeship was largely an urban phenomenon. There was no need for apprenticeship if one traded in a country village. Especially in rural areas, skills were often passed down from father to son, and English courts gradually came to accept these casual, non-indentured forms as valid.[55] For its part, Upper Canada was overwhelmingly rural, and in many areas Upper Canadians followed the English country practice. A great deal of skilled work, especially in such trades as carpentry or masonry, was done as a sideline by persons who owned farms. We also know from Lower Canada that skills such as iron moulding or leather work were passed down through families; this must have occurred in the upper province as well.[56] All this would have fallen outside the normal scope of apprenticeship regulation. Referring to the 1880s, Kealey has written of the disdain of Toronto printers for their non-union (and occasionally strike-breaking) small-town counterparts, whom they termed 'country mice.' One suspects that both the disdain and the lack of unionization were part of a single phenomenon typical of nineteenth-century Ontario: less formality in the learning of a trade outside the cities, a less clearly defined craft identity.[57]

Moreover, there was very great doubt throughout the first half of the century whether English apprenticeship law, especially the required seven-year term, applied to the colony in the first place. Skilled labour was in such short supply that the pressures against restrictions would have been overwhelming. As early as 1822, Robert Gourlay remarked that the Statute of Elizabeth 'is not considered to be applicable to this province.' He went on to note that 'a barrister of great respectability' disagreed with his conclusion, but not with the fact that the law was routinely ignored in practice.[58] Indeed, it is evident from surviving indentures that the great majority of apprenticeships were for less than seven years. And, as we will see below, apprenticeships were often used for purposes quite removed from training in a skill.

As a result, there was much less standardization in the use of apprenticeships and, until 1851, none enforced by law. In the latter part of the century many employers dispensed with indentures altogether in situations where they had previously been common, taking unbound 'apprentices' in order to avoid the commitments of a proper apprenticeship.[59] Some of the skilled trades tried to police their qualifications. Nevertheless, the weakness of legal regulation tended to make the distinction between the traditional skilled trades and other occupations much less rigid; differences in status tended to depend on the possession of a scarce and respected skill – whether or not it had been, in England, a skill that required an apprenticeship – and on the actual degree of independence exercised by the worker in the performance of his or her work, rather than on an external, legal requirement.[60]

There was considerable similarity in the forms of hiring used for skilled and unskilled non-agricultural workers. Skilled labour was often hired by the day. The wages of such workers as carpenters, masons, cabinet-makers, dressmakers, milliners, blacksmiths, wheelwrights, and machinists were generally quoted as daily. For carpenters and masons this is true from the very beginning of the century (there is less information on other trades).[61] But daily labour was not the only form of skilled work. There are also frequent references, dating from the early years of the century until at least the 1850s, to the employment of carpenters, masons, and other tradespeople by the month.[62] Weekly hirings existed in some trades (for example, printing) but seem to have been less common.[63]

Skilled workers might also be paid by the product. This could range from what we now think of as piece-work to payment of a lump sum for an entire job, such as building a house. In today's law, these are treated as quite separate, the former constituting a contract of employment, the latter a relationship of independent contractor to client (outside the domain of employment law). As we will see below, the distinction was by no means clear in nineteenth-century Ontario, especially early in the century, and it is best to see these as a range of means by which payment for certain types of skilled work was gauged to product. Shoemakers and tailors were generally paid by the piece.[64] So, in the latter part of the century, were iron moulders in Toronto's foundries, and the puddlers, heaters, and rollers in Hamilton's Great Western Rolling Mills.[65] Bricklayers, coopers, plasterers, sawyers, printers, and railway engineers and firemen were paid either by their time or the task.[66] Carpenters and other construction trades, especially working on their own account in the country, would often contract by the job. Therefore, when one combines the prevalence of piece-work with the existence of weekly or monthly hirings, many 'journeymen' were in fact hired other than by the day.

Outside of the traditional skilled trades, workers generally seem to have been paid by the month, the week, or, most commonly, by the day, with some instances of piece-work. Lumber workers, both in the shanties and in rafting, were generally paid by the month, although hired for a season.[67] Most non-agricultural unskilled labour, and indeed casual labour generally, was paid by the day. This was the case, for example, with labourers engaged in the construction of canals or railways.[68] Semi-skilled or skilled workers in industries without an artisanal tradition, such as sawmills, railways, salt manufactories, and powder companies, were also usually paid by the day, although in later years piece-work became increasingly common.[69] In his contribution to this volume, Craven describes the shift from daily to hourly pay in the Great Western Railway shops in 1872, as part of the nine-hour movement. At about the same time, some Toronto trades such as carpenters and steam-fitters converted to hourly wages. We need more complete information before we know whether this was part of a larger trend towards shorter hirings, although it is clear that daily wages remained common in industrial employment well into the twentieth century.[70]

WHITE-COLLAR EMPLOYMENT

Most manual employees, then, were paid by the month, by the day, or by the piece; few were paid by the year. The duration of hirings could depart from the period used to calculate pay, but the available evidence suggests that yearly hirings were indeed uncommon. There was, however, one class of employee that was often hired on yearly contracts:

white-collar and managerial employees. Employees such as clerks, teachers, and station and harbour masters were generally paid by the year, or hired on contracts that were expressed as yearly but with wages paid more frequently (often quarterly).[71] Once again, yearly wages were indicative of a yearly hiring, although the presumption could be rebutted.

APPRENTICESHIP[72]

There was an additional, very distinctive form of contract common in Upper Canada, one which has appeared obliquely in the discussion above: apprenticeship. Although often assumed simply to be one element in the training of skilled craftsworkers, apprenticeships were much more general in their application and more complex in function. In nineteenth-century Ontario, they were used in virtually all occupational categories: farming, housework, commerce, pharmacy, law, and medicine, as well as such traditional crafts as milling, carpentry, and printing. The best way to understand apprenticeships is to realize that, in addition to the economic benefit to the employer, they could serve two quite distinct purposes. They could be used to teach a child a skill; they could also be used to provide for the care and rearing of children, at a time when there was little public aid to destitute families and when settlers might well lack adequate networks of family support. Apprenticeships placed the master *in loco parentis*, obliging him to provide food and clothing and to care for the apprentice when sick, and giving him power to correct the apprentice as he could his own child. This meant that apprenticeships could serve as a form of foster care. The two purposes were often blended. Indeed, the best form of foster care was one which prepared the child to make his or her way in the world. They were blended, however, in different proportions, and this could take apprenticeship well beyond the place generally attributed to it in artisanal employment.

The use of apprenticeship as a form of foster care is apparent in the circumstances in which children were bound out. Elliott has described the use of apprenticeship as an inheritance strategy: a family with insufficient land to divide between the children would bind one or more to a trade. Parents often turned to apprenticeship when they were unable to provide for the children. Indentures were executed by widows or administrators of an estate for children as young as five years old.[73] In 1799 the Upper Canadian legislature authorized town wardens to bind out orphaned and abandoned children until the age of majority, and this power was exercised frequently.[74] Non-governmental guardians also apprenticed out their charges.[75]

The occupations to which children were apprenticed also revealed various combinations of the dual purposes of apprenticeship. Some children were bound, or bound themselves, to the traditional skilled crafts, and clearly there the acquisition of a skill was paramount. Others, however, were bound to occupations falling outside the artisanal framework. Apprenticeships were often used for farming.[76] In a sample form for the binding out of a girl, first published in 1865 but patterned on an actual indenture, executed by a widow, the apprentice was to be instructed 'in sewing, knitting, and housewifery, the management of the dairy, and all matters connected with the calling of a farmer.' In another, from 1900, the work was simply described as 'household duties.'[77] Others imposed no obligation to train at all.[78] The prevalence of by-employment in nineteenth-century Ontario can be seen in one indenture from 1852, in which a boy was to be instructed 'in the art trade or calling of a miller and farmer.'[79] In all these examples the substance of the master's obligation was to prepare the child for adult life in much the same way that the master would prepare his own children.

Apprenticeships were created by legal documents termed indentures, which were signed by the employer, the parent or guardian (or sometimes the apprentice, either alone or with a parent), and (if required) by two magistrates. The indentures followed the same general wording, although they became less elaborate as the century wore on.[80] Sample forms were often included in published manuals for magistrates or ordinary citizens.[81] A great many indentures were handwritten, although printed forms were also available.

The indentures bound the apprentice to a series of obligations towards his or her master, almost always including 'his secrets keep' and 'his lawful commands every where and at all times readily obey.'[82] The paternalistic character of the relationship was emphasized by terms forbidding the apprentice from contracting matrimony, from absenting himself without leave, and, in the early part of the century, from indulging such moral failings as playing cards, gambling, frequenting taverns, and committing fornication. In England the parents might, to secure the apprenticeship, pay a premium to the master, but this seems to have been very rare in Upper Canada. The only examples I have seen are from the highly skilled occupations of printing and surgery.[83] One indenture from 1865, again in a skilled craft, provided a penalty of $400, payable by the apprentice or his stepfather, if the terms of the engagement were not kept.[84]

In return, the master would normally promise to instruct the apprentice in his trade. Some indentures early in the century also required schooling for the child (four months in one indenture, six in another, twelve months in two others, all referring to the total schooling to be given during the entire course of a multi-year apprenticeship).[85] Room and board would be provided; clothing, washing, and medical care might be specifically mentioned. The indenture might provide for wages, although these were not universal. If wages were paid, they were usually by the year, increasing as time went on. Thus in 1865 one 'carriage and waggon wood worker' was to be paid $30 for the first year, $35 for the second, $40 for the third, and $45 for the fourth year of a four-year apprenticeship.[86] Occasionally the wages were payable to the apprentice's father. Indentures frequently provided for a payment, often in kind, to the apprentice at the end of the engagement, especially if there had been no wages during the term. A seven-year-old girl, apprenticed to a merchant in 1825, was to receive at the end 'two suits of Clothes and a Milch Cow, and Bed;' a boy apprenticed to a carpenter in 1817 was to get 'a decent Suit of Clothing and a Sett of Bench Tools.'[87]

The duration of apprenticeships varied, but was frequently less than the seven years required under the English Statute of Elizabeth. In fact, the only indentures I have seen with terms seven years or longer were for apprenticeships in which the predominant motive was to care for a child. For the learning of a craft, six-year and four-year terms were common; examples of the former occur in printing, cabinet-making, and carpentry, of the latter in blacksmithing, woodworking, carpentry, iron moulding, surgery, and pharmacy, although I have also seen three-year apprenticeships in printing, tinsmithing, and pharmacy.[88] By law, apprenticeships were to last only as long as the apprentice remained a minor, and frequently the indentures' termination date did coincide with the reaching of majority (twenty-one for boys, eighteen for girls). I have, however, seen two indentures that extended beyond the age of majority.[89]

Finally, two features of apprenticeship emphasize its connection to the enterprise of the master, reminding us that although the personal relation of master to apprentice might be important for the latter's care and training, apprenticeship was founded, above all, on an economic relation. First, the indentures did not require that the master personally instruct the apprentice; the master promised to instruct 'or cause to be instructed.' This meant that an apprentice might be bound to the *owner* of a business, to be trained by whatever skilled workers were around. Second, the apprentice could be transferred to another master without the apprentice's consent, as long as the new master carried on the same kind of business. The transfer could occur by act of the master, or by operation of law if the master died during the term of the agreement.[90] This gave some assurance to the person binding out the apprentice that the latter would be looked after, even if the original master was unable to continue, but it also diminished the personal character of the relationship.

Apprenticeships were the longest employment contracts common in nineteenth-century Ontario. They permitted the master to gain the labour of a child or youth for an extended period, while at the same time enabling the apprentice's family (or the town wardens) to provide for the apprentice, often with training in a skill. Apprenticeships were therefore a way of providing practical education and surrogate care for children at a time when there were few state resources to care for the needy. Within the scope of this essay, apprenticeship is important not only because apprentices were a significant source of labour in their own right, but also because apprenticeship held important consequences for skilled workers. Not only did many of them learn their trade through apprenticeships, but also, at a time when changing technology and work practices threatened the traditional crafts, apprentices were a potential source of competition within the shop – a body of partly skilled workers, legally and often personally dependent on the employer, who could encroach on tasks normally performed by skilled labour and maintain production in case of strikes.

The Law and the Individual Employment Relationship

These, then, were the contractual structures through which labour was organized. But how did the law grip those structures? How were they enforced? What kinds of obligations did the law read into them? It seems very likely that for much of the period, especially for the first half of the century, there was little direct enforcement of employment contracts. Instead, the parties relied on their own devices, on means of self-protection and self-help, to order their affairs. The coercive power of the state was used only sporadically to police employers' and employees' conduct.

There were a number of reasons for this. First, in areas of recent settlement, magistrates were thin on the ground. In 1827, for example, there was only one magistrate in Bytown, the unruly centre of the Ottawa River lumber trade. This magistrate would have been responsible for policing as well as judging, and in policing he would have depended on the assistance of part-time constables. In such circumstances, the forces of law and order were often distant, weak, and easily intimidated. In a plaintive letter to the Lieutenant-Governor's aide-de-camp, Bytown's lone magistrate complained that he had been wounded by a riotous mob and added (with some drama), 'No Constable dare approach them, it would, I am persuaded, be instant death.' In 1835 the Bytown magistrates again complained that they could not punish disorderly lumber-workers because if one was arrested, 'all his fraternity will make common cause to aid in his Rescue, setting all law in defiance.' Similar pleas were made in the 1840s. The inadequacy of magistrates' policing was a major reason for the reform of local government during the 1830s and 1840s.[91]

More important than the scarcity of magistrates and their liability to intimidation, however, was their limited geographic reach. The magistracy was an institution of emphatically local justice. Magistrates were propertied citizens of a community, farmers, millers, or merchants, who performed their public duties on the side. For much of the century they had no professional police force to execute their orders or seize wrongdoers; they depended on local constables and the complainants themselves to bring wrongdoers to justice. In country areas, communications were poor, and there was no central agency for pursuing footloose employees. If an accused chose to leave the district, there was little a magistrate could do to find the culprit or bring him to justice. And in the tight labour market often prevailing in early nineteenth-century Ontario, workers – especially single men – were highly mobile. Even without the threat of pursuit, individuals would often move to a distant town or district.

Moreover, especially during the first half of the century, there was little to be gained from proceeding against an employee or, for that matter, an employer. As we will see, absconding workers were liable to imprisonment. This could be used to induce an employee to go back to work, but to what end? A single worker intent on leaving would simply go farther the next time, and in any case the relatively short duration of most employment contracts usually meant that the employee would soon be free of his or her obligations. A prosecution might deter other employees from similar action, but a small employer would seldom find that sufficient to justify his trouble. If, as was often the case in rural areas, the worker was the son or daughter of a neighbour and thus could be found easily, going to court would carry the additional cost of antagonizing neighbours whose co-operation might be needed in the future. On the employees' side as well, the courts would have had little attraction. Employers, especially employers behind in their wages, were often in tenuous financial condition. Farmers were frequently cash-poor, and in the early part of the century might well lack solid titles to their farms. An employee would have to weigh carefully whether the recourse was worth the cost.

For all of these reasons, one suspects that most parties simply looked out for themselves. In fact, the short duration of contracts reflected this. Employers limited their commitments to what they hoped they could fulfil; workers could give notice and leave if they saw better opportunities

elsewhere. There were sometimes more elaborate means of self-protection. From the employer's side, Radforth notes that at least a portion of
lumberworkers' pay was withheld to induce them to remain in the woods
throughout the season. In the 1880s, the Massey Agricultural Implements Company withheld five or ten days' pay and the Cornwall cotton
mills two weeks' pay for the same purpose. Arrears in other occupations,
such as farming and carpentry, may have served a similar function.[92] In
large enterprises, company housing could be used to encourage compliance, since employees who struck or quit would be evicted.[93] Employers
shared information about employees, giving or demanding references
and sometimes maintaining blacklists, although the use of such measures
was limited (especially early in the century) by the scarcity and mobility
of labour.[94] Nineteenth-century contracts also sometimes specified alternative forms of dispute resolution; one sees very occasional arbitration
clauses in labour contracts.[95]

But even to focus on contractual terms is misleading, especially for
employees in the early part of the century. It is likely that their principal
recourse was simply to leave, without notice and with little risk of being
pursued. The accounts of settlers abound with servants' leaving on very
short notice. One gets the impression that, especially in country areas,
many employment relations ran on the basis of live and let live, employers hiring help when it could be found and they could afford it, employees working when they could be absent from their own farms but leaving
on a moment's notice when they were needed at home.

Of course, given the weakness of civil authority in rural areas, there
was also a tougher option if an employer failed, in the worker's eyes, to
live and let live. Farmers were particularly vulnerable to intimidation.
The discussion of arson in Keele's *Provincial Justice* used the example
of a labourer who burned down a yeoman's barn. The charge to the
grand jury at the 1847 Gore assizes cited employment disputes as one
reason for the prevalence of arson.[96] A number of commentators have
noted the persistence in the New World of violent methods of disputing
inherited from the Old, especially among the Irish, methods that often
joined economic and sectarian aims. In Upper Canada, landlord-tenant
disputes and conflict over employment on the canals were coloured by
that history, and one suspects that other employment relations may have
been as well.[97] The possibility of violence constituted a powerful
inducement for farmers to deal with employees in a manner the latter
would tolerate, and may be one reason why farmers often paid workers
for all the time they had worked, even when the circumstances (dismissal for misconduct, or quitting without notice) may have absolved
them from the legal obligation to pay.

The law of master and servant therefore had little practical force in the early part of the century. The following discussion should be read in that light. From mid-century on, however, direct legal regulation of the master-servant relationship and the actions of labour organizations became more significant, as we will see below.

Master and servant law in early nineteenth-century Ontario is an elusive phenomenon. Its content is highly uncertain if one uses the traditional sources of lawyers' reasoning, and those sources are, in any case, an inadequate guide to what happened on the ground. A full understanding would demand careful reconstruction of what individual magistrates did from day to day. Even then, the practice probably varied between magistrates. We do know enough, however, to describe the framework within which magistrates exercised their duties and to suggest some general conclusions about the nature of master and servant law before mid-century.[98]

In England in 1800, the law of master and servant was based on a multitude of overlapping, often archaic, and far from rationally ordered statutes stretching back to the Statute of Labourers of 1351. Many of these provisions had been forgotten, had fallen into desuetude, or had become encrusted with interpretations and practices that departed substantially from the original texts. Master and servant formed, in other words, a body of law that still traced its origins to the statutes but had largely assumed a life of its own, developed through magistrates' practice and shaped by the sporadic intervention of superior courts.[99] The Upper Canadian experience sprang from this tradition, although Canadian conditions forced adjustments to the English law. These adjustments, while easily accomplished in magistrates' practice, were much more difficult to rationalize in the lawyerly discourse of the superior courts. This disjuncture cast doubt upon the introduction of English law into Upper Canada and ultimately contributed to the adoption, in 1847 and 1851, of Upper Canadian master and servant and apprenticeship acts.

The problem emerged as follows. By the beginning of the nineteenth century, the law of master and servant, although based on statute, had become part of the fabric of English law. The labour statutes had been the principal source of English labour regulation for four centuries, throughout the long transition from medieval work relations to those of the emerging industrial era. They had been integral to the structuring of modern work relations in England. They formed the underpinning for the administrative apparatus of English employment law, especially the jurisdiction of magistrates. It was unthinkable, then, that they would not apply to a colony that had, in the first act of its legislature, adopted English law as the rule of decision in 'all matters of controversy relative to property and civil rights' and whose territory had been subject to English criminal law since before the colony's separate existence.[100] Indeed, a number of superior-court decisions during the first decades of the century show plainly that the Upper Canadian courts assumed that English master and servant law was in force.[101]

At the same time, the English statutes contained some provisions that could not be applied in the Canadian context. The most important of these was the requirement in the Statute of Elizabeth that certain trades-people serve a seven-year apprenticeship. As we have seen, this rule was routinely ignored in practice, but how could the courts justify rejecting it without undermining the rest of English labour law? Colonial courts did claim considerable discretion in the reception of England's judge-made law, adopting it only to the extent compatible with colonial conditions. They also asserted a more limited discretion with respect to English statutes, holding that some were so tied to conditions in the old country that they were inapplicable to the colonies. This approach worked best, however, with entire statutes. It was much more difficult to argue that only a part of a statute had been received, especially when the act in question formed part of a single, interconnected regime.[102] The Canadian courts were therefore caught in a dilemma: the apprenticeship requirement made no sense in Upper Canada, yet other provisions of the Statute of Elizabeth were fundamental to English master and servant law. And if the Statute of Elizabeth was confined to England, wouldn't the same be true of all the English labour statutes?

Initially, the superior courts ignored the issue. This was easily done since master and servant cases were decided by magistrates. It was rare that superior courts addressed labour matters, and even when they did, the roots of the law were buried under such a long history of magistrates' practice that it was rarely necessary to reason back to the statutes.[103] When, later in the century, the superior courts were forced to decide whether English labour law applied in Canada, their decisions were tentative and often ambiguous, generally confined to the case before them. In 1831 a majority of the Court of King's Bench suggested that the apprenticeship provisions of the Statute of Elizabeth 'were never part of the law of this province,' but it declined to rest its decision on that basis. In any case, W.C. Keele, commenting on the case in the 1843 edition of his much-used magistrates' manual, suggested that even if the statute's civil provisions were inapplicable, its criminal penalties might still be in force. In 1841 Queen's Bench again ruled that the statute did not apply to the province, although this decision seems to have been ignored. Finally, in *Shea* v. *Choat* (1846), the court ruled the statute inapplicable, this time for good. In its reasons, the court specifically rejected the suggestion that the Statute of Elizabeth could be received in part and excluded in part, but it still left open whether a related act, dating from 1747, had been received into Upper Canada.[104] These hesitations were due to the court's reluctance to strike down the entire law of master and servant, combined with its inability, given the established principles of statutory reception, to justify the selective enforcement of the sections of a single statute. It therefore fudged the issue, enabling the magistrates to continue judging master and servant cases while ignoring the most troublesome provisions.

Indeed, the intricacies of statutory reception meant little to magistrates. For these lay judges, law was what they read in their manuals, and as far as these were concerned, the English authorities were in force. Before 1835, the manual of choice was Burn's *Justice*,[105] itself a British work. After that date, Upper Canadian manuals were available, but they too relied heavily on English authorities. In the most popular of these, Keele's *Provincial Justice* (first published in 1835 but updated in four further editions, the last in 1864), the English law on apprenticeship was reproduced, with only one brief comment in a footnote, right up to the adoption of the Upper Canadian statute of 1851, even after the Court of Queen's Bench had doubted its application.[106] In fact, in *Shea* v. *Choat*, Robert Baldwin used this fact to argue that the English statutes should be applied to Upper Canada. 'The magistrates in almost every part of the province,' he submitted, 'have been in the habit of considering these statutes in force, and have acted upon them in many instances, without their authority being called in question; and they have been treated as in force by Mr. Keele, in his Provincial Justice, a work which is in the hands of every magistrate in the country, and by which the magistrates are generally guided in their proceedings.'[107] He lost his argument. In the wake of the decision the colony adopted its own act, but by then half a century had elapsed, during which magistrates had relied, through their manuals, on the English statutes.

The manuals were fundamental to magistrates' practice; one should not, however, assume too readily that magistrates applied what they read. The manuals contained some material that was patently obsolete. Keele, for example, included provisions drawn from a sixteenth-century statute on conspiracies in every edition from the first to the fifth, complete with the pillory as punishment, even though the pillory had been abolished in Upper Canada.[108] It is, moreover, inconceivable that magistrates would have enforced the seven-year apprenticeship when virtually no one in Upper Canada served such a time. Because of the dearth of records and because of the isolation of many magistrates, it is impossible to know precisely what they did in practice, but it seems clear that they were not overly concerned with the learning of the law. Magistrates saw their role as maintaining order and dispensing justice, within the framework of the law to be sure, but a framework that allowed, in their opinion, ample room for their sense of what should be done.[109] Before mid-century, that framework was largely defined by the English authorities, adapted ad hoc to Canadian conditions.

In 1847 and 1851 the uncertainty over the application of English law was resolved by the legislature's adoption of its own master and servant and apprenticeship acts. The preamble to the 1847 act declared that 'no Statute is in force to regulate the duties between Masters and Servants or Labourers' in Upper Canada. The preamble to the 1851 act observed (somewhat oddly, given *Shea*) that there was no statute 'to provide for binding Apprentices for a less term than seven years' and stated that the purpose of the act was to make shorter apprenticeships 'legal, and the law relating to Apprentices more clearly defined.'[110] For all practical purposes, these acts replaced the previous English statutes, although many principles developed under the old law remained valid. Keele's later editions no longer contained the detail of the English statutes, but instead summarized the new acts, as did other manuals.[111] The new statutes greatly simplified the law, laying aside the seven-year apprenticeship rule and other provisions that had lapsed into disuse, and clarifying the magistrates' authority.

THE CONTENT OF MASTER AND SERVANT LAW

What, then, were the rules governing master and servant? Employment was shaped by a number of regimes, structured around specific recourses. This section concentrates on what was called 'the law of master and servant': the law enforced by magistrates and ultimately derived from master and servant legislation, including the regulation of apprenticeship. It will attempt to reconstruct the broad lines of this law during the first half of the century and under the 1847 and 1851 acts. In addition, it discusses parts of the criminal law that were important in shaping employment relations. Furthermore, it should be remembered that some claims, especially for unpaid wages, could be heard by civil tribunals, especially the Courts of Requests and Division Courts.[112]

In Upper Canadian practice, the most important provisions of master and servant law were those empowering magistrates to punish workers for absence or disobedience, or to order employers to pay unpaid wages.

The recourses under these provisions differed dramatically. Servants could be imprisoned; masters were subject only to civil remedies. This inequality was bitterly attacked by workers and labour reformers. The supporters of the regime defended it on the grounds that masters had property to answer for their obligations, whereas servants had only their liberty. Indeed, the availability of criminal penalties, combined with summary enforcement, accounted for the regime's utility for employers: if they could find their employee, they could impose a quick and severe sanction.[113]

To whom did the regime apply? The answer is by no means simple, for it was only during this time that the distinction between an employee and an independent contractor began to emerge. The English statutes specified long lists of occupations to which they applied, lists repeated in Keele's summaries. For example, the 1747 act governed servants in husbandry, 'Artificers, Handicraftsmen, Miners, Colliers, Keelmen, Pitmen, Glassmen, Potters and other Labourers employed for any certain time, or in any other manner.'[114] This would have covered virtually all manual workers except domestics, who were excluded in deference to the master's authority over his household.[115] The 1847 Upper Canada act got rid of this verbiage by applying simply to 'Servants or Labourers,' although, given the restrictive way in which these terms were now commonly used, this raised a question about whether the act applied to skilled workers (an amendment in 1855 made clear that it did).[116] The 1847 act included domestic servants. Indeed, there is some evidence that it was adopted partly because domestics were considered undisciplined.[117]

Within these occupations, who was a servant? Did the regime apply to everyone who worked as a carpenter, even, for example, if they were paid by the job? Today's labour law applies only to employees, not to independent contractors, a distinction based on the independence of the worker in the performance of the work. In essence, someone who contracts to obey the commands of another person is generally an employee; one who contracts to do a specific job, paid by the job, is an independent contractor. Other indications of independence are the worker's hiring of his or her own employees, or ownership of the means of production.

This distinction was not clearly established in the early years of the century. In *Lowther* v. *Earl of Radnor*, an English case from 1806, a well-digger who was paid by the job and who hired his own labourer was held to fall within the 1747 act.[118] By 1829 some English authorities had begun to distinguish between a servant and someone 'contracting to do specific work,' or to consider that an exclusive engagement with a single employer was crucial to service.[119] Exclusiveness was also important in an 1856 case in which a tailor, paid by the job and having the ability to refuse work, was held to be a servant.[120] The law in Upper Canada was similarly in transition. In 1827 the Court of King's Bench held, without elaboration, that a man hired to work with his oxen for one month was not 'such a labourer as is contemplated by the statutes.'[121] In *Shea*, on the other hand, the Court of Queen's Bench cited *Lowther* as good law (although it hinted that that case might have been too broad in its interpretation). In the 1850s, magistrates apparently applied the act to workers who would not now be considered employees, such as owner-operators of threshing machines and railway contractors.[122] But by 1860 a distinction between contracts of service and contracts by the job seems to have emerged. Dempsey's manual of that year recommended that magistrates not entertain demands for wages 'where the arrangement ... is by the job or contract or savours of such, as for instance, cutting wood by the cord, splitting rails at so much per 100, working threshing machines, painting, &c., by the job, instead of at so much per day.' As late as 1864, however, the York and Peel Sessions was deciding that the act could not be used to recover amounts due to the owner-operator of a threshing machine.[123]

What should we make of all this? Napier has suggested that until the early nineteenth century, English law was concerned with the nature of work rather than contractual form.[124] The English statutes certainly focused on specific occupations. Perhaps one sees, in the halting evolution, a transition from a diffuse sense of social subordination as the basis for master and servant law to the idea that subordination was inherent in a specific contractual form, one in which a person subjected himself to the commands of another. Subordination was gradually redefined, in other words, so that it no longer attached simply to the task performed, but became something that, in theory, one accepted voluntarily. This evolution would have formed part of the larger movement to recast social relations in terms of contracts.[125]

The transition occurred at the level of justification, although it was related in complex ways to the situation on the ground. In Upper Canada, during the first half of the century, contractual theories must have had considerable resonance. Much of the waged labour was performed part-time by farmers or those who reasonably expected to become farmers. The social distance was therefore less, and more transitory, than in England. Moreover, the transactional nature of employment was reinforced by the prevalence of daily and monthly rather than yearly hirings. But if the parties were on a level of greater equality, why was master and servant legislation thought necessary? Why not depend on civil remedies? The Upper Canadian legislation responded, above all, to a specific problem: the desire for effective means of preventing employees, hired for a period of time, from leaving before the end of their contracts. This seems, for example, to have been the chief concern in the lumber industry, the industry uppermost in legislators' minds during the adoption of the 1847 act.[126] Moreover, near equality did not mean absolute equality; property-holders still distrusted those who were not rooted to a particular plot, considering them shiftless and irresponsible. Servants' lack of property was crucial both to the regime's justification and, increasingly, to its scope of application.

There were counter-forces to this evolution. First, the regime provided a quick way of recovering payment for labour and was often used by unpaid workers. This probably accounted for its popularity among those contracting by the job. Moreover, the form of a contract could be affected by things having little to do with the desire for labour discipline. Heron notes the use of subcontracting as a means of lowering wages in industrial employment, although this might have removed the relationship from the master and servant act. Finally, the simple structure of contractual subordination we now associate with large-scale employment – a single employer commanding every employee in the enterprise – was not yet universal. It was reasonably common for skilled workers, for example, even in factories, to hire helpers and provide their own tools, thus blurring the distinction between employees and contractors.[127]

Enforcing the Duration of Employment

The principal aim of master and servant law had been, since its inception, the maintenance of stability in employment. The English acts attempted to do this in a number of ways: by imposing severe constraints on the mobility of workers; by forbidding certain categories of servants from refusing employment; by regulating the length of hiring and the giving of notice; and by punishing workers who left early. Many of these provisions had fallen into disuse long before the founding of Upper Canada.[128] The punishment of workers who left early, however, was very much alive.

The basic rule was that workers who quit their jobs before the end of their contracts or without giving notice were subject to imprisonment. Under the English act of 1747, offenders could be sentenced to one month or, under the 1766 act, from one to three months. Apprentices faced similar penalties.[129] Similarly, under the Upper Canadian master and servant and apprenticeship acts adopted at mid-century, workers could be fined up to five pounds or jailed for up to one month (or three months in the case of an apprentice who refused to make satisfaction to his master).[130] These penalties were imposed. Sentences of a month in prison, or significant fines plus costs, were not uncommon.[131]

These penalties could be used to force the employee back to work. Magistrates would often give employees the choice of returning to their employer or spending time in jail. Even if the employee did choose jail, he would not necessarily be discharged. An employee could not unilaterally terminate his contract; only magistrates could declare the servant's obligations at an end. Upon release from prison, then, he could still be obliged to work for the time remaining. Effectively, then, the master and servant regime permitted employers to obtain specific performance of employment contracts.[132]

Not only could an absconding employee be fined or imprisoned, but he might also forfeit his pay for time he had already worked. Now, there are strong indications that in the early part of the century workers could recover their wages *pro rata*, even if they had not fully performed their contracts.[133] By about mid-century, however, the courts had determined, first in England, then in Canada, that workers who quit early or were fired for misconduct lost their claim to wages.[134] Given the fact that wages were often long in arrears, or that an employee on a yearly contract might only be paid at the end of the year, this could amount to a very substantial penalty.

The employer too was constrained by the term of hiring. He could terminate the relationship at the end of the period of hiring, as long as he gave sufficient notice or payment in lieu of notice. He could fire an employee at any time for misconduct, which the *Canadian Domestic Lawyer* defined as wilful disobedience or habitual neglect of orders, repeated absence, refusal to work or 'submit to the domestic regulations of the house,' or gross moral misconduct. Napier suggests that the English courts upheld dismissals for relatively minor misconduct, and it seems likely that the same was true of Upper Canada.[135] It was more difficult to fire an apprentice. To do that, one had to obtain the consent of the magistrates in Sessions.[136]

The duration of hiring did not, however, mean that the employer had to provide full employment during the period. Although the evidence is fragmentary, it appears that even when hirings were expressed as monthly or weekly, payment was frequently adjusted to the actual time worked, leaving employees without pay for time lost because of sickness or lack of work. The time books of Benjamin Tett's Rideau lumber business (from the 1840s) noted quarter days and half days worked, with no time entered for sick days. An 1872 letter from a surveyor in the Thunder Bay region, commenting on the good wages available for woodsmen employed in mineral exploration and surveying, noted especially that there were no deductions for lost time.[137]

If the employer did breach his obligations, the penalties were by no means as severe as those for employees. The penalty for wrongful dismissal was payment of the wages that would have been paid had the employer fulfilled his obligations: for a yearly contract, payment to the end of the year; for a monthly contract, to the end of the month.[138]

In all these rules, the length of the hiring was crucial. It determined the period of notice required to put an end to the arrangement: three months for yearly contracts, one month for monthly contracts, and one week for weekly contracts.[139] If proper notice was not given, the parties' financial loss was determined largely by the duration of hiring. This meant that master and servant law had a much greater effect on long contracts than on short ones.

In the interest of labour stability, the English statutes had tried to require long terms. The Statute of Elizabeth, for example, established a presumption of yearly hirings, a presumption echoed in some Canadian materials. It was not applied rigorously, however, even in England.[140] By the beginning of the nineteenth century in Upper Canada, the length of hiring was determined either by the parties' express agreement or, failing that, by the period used for the computation of wages, with a maximum term (for oral contracts) of one year. Even then, the courts were willing to depart from the normal criteria. In 1844, Queen's Bench dealt with the claim of a harbour master, paid by the year, who was dismissed one month into his third year. The harbour master assumed, reasonably enough, that he was entitled to wages for the entire year. Robinson, C.J., reluctant to grant such a large award, interpreted the contract as 'for no definite period, at a yearly salary.'[141]

In fact, as we have already seen, there was a general tendency towards shorter hirings in Upper Canada. Wages were usually calculated by the day, week, or month, and although this did not always correspond to the duration of hiring, it was indicative. Because the contracts were shorter, the constraints posed by master and servant legislation were less obtrusive, at least in individual employment relations; we will see their effect on collective relations below. There was one significant exception: apprentices were bound by long-term indentures, which could be brought to an end only in very limited circumstances. Not surprisingly, a large proportion of prosecutions concerned apprentices.[142]

Enforcing Discipline

The law of master and servant – not merely the statutes, but the mass of magistrates' law that had grown up around them – also spoke to employers' disciplinary authority. Employees were expected to obey the lawful commands of their employers. They were also expected to take reasonable care in the master's affairs and to serve the employer's interest and not that of his competitors. These obligations were express in apprentices' indentures, implied in the hirings of servants, and echoed in statutory provisions.[143] If the employee neglected his duties, the employer had a number of recourses, of which some lay within his own power and others within the authority of the courts. We have already seen the strongest recourse available without the intervention of the courts: dismissal. In addition, English law had at one time recognized that a master could beat a servant – 'moderate correction' it was called. By the nineteenth century, however, this was generally denied by the English authorities. The master's right to use force was restricted to apprentices and servants under age, an example of the master's paternal authority over members of the household.[144]

The Upper Canadian authorities leaned in the same direction, though with some ambiguity. It was true that apprentices could be, and were, beaten.[145] Keele suggested in his discussion of assault that a master could also beat a servant, although he did not repeat this in his section on servants, where only dismissal and statutory recourses were mentioned.[146] Similar ambiguity existed in the Queen's Bench decision of *Mitchell* v. *Defries* (1845). There, an adult servant sued his master for assault and battery, alleging that he had been kicked and wounded and his clothes torn. The master claimed that the servant had been lazy and negligent, had 'behaved saucily and contumaciously,' and had been moderately corrected. The majority of the court, in a very brief judgment, declined to say whether a master could beat an adult servant, finding that the assault was in any case beyond moderation. Only McLean, J., citing Blackstone and Burn's *Justice*, held that the servant could not be beaten.[147] We have no way of knowing whether the majority's judgment was simply the easiest way to dispose of a case in the unfamiliar terrain of magistrates' law, or whether it indicated more profound uncertainty. At any rate, instances of masters beating adult servants appear to have been very rare.

Employers could obtain some recourse from magistrates if they wanted to impose discipline short of discharge. The English and Upper Canadian legislation subjected all forms of misconduct, not just absconding, to the same penalties.[148] Thus in theory, an employer could obtain a fine or imprisonment against a servant or apprentice for any misbehaviour. Charges were brought, for example, against a boy for fighting at work and against raftsmen for refusing orders to fetch another batch of lumber.[149] It seems likely, however, that these recourses were of limited use, especially in the first half of the century. The frequent scarcity of labour forced employers to be more tolerant than they would have wished. Masters continually complained of Upper Canadian servants' indiscipline.[150]

For more serious misconduct, employers could also bring the criminal law to bear. The penalties were often more severe for crimes committed by a servant against his master than for those committed in other situations, although the differences were gradually eliminated during the century. It was, for example, a felony to embezzle one's master's goods, although for bankers, merchants, brokers, or attorneys embezzlement was only a misdemeanour. Assault against a master was aggravated assault. Murder was petit treason. As the latter term suggests, one reason for the difference was that when a servant attacked a master, he not only broke the peace but also attacked the subordination inherent in the social order. Blackstone gave another explanation (though one that fails to explain, for example, the different treatment of embezzlement), that the law dealt severely with crimes 'which a man has the most frequent and easy opportunities of committing, and which cannot be so easily guarded against as others.'[151]

Finally, some offences inherited from England had, by their definition, specific relevance for employment. These included breaking machinery, hindering a seaman, or cutting cloth.[152]

Restraining Employers' Misconduct

What recourses were available to employees if they were mistreated by their employer? Undoubtedly the most common recourse was simply to leave, though this amounted to a breach of a servant's obligations. Employees were not entitled to quit, even if mistreated. Their remedy was to complain to a magistrate, who could, if he saw fit, declare them discharged. Given the shortage of magistrates and the isolation of many work sites, this could cause hardship. In his contribution to this volume, Radforth describes the prosecution of twenty-five lumbermen for desertion. After having been given unsound food, they complained and eventually left the shanty. The magistrates convicted them, holding 'that if the Servant did not get proper food, or was otherwise improperly treated by his Master, that his only remedy was to make complaint before a Magistrate, ... that no ill-treatment could justify leaving his master.' Of course, for reasons given above, most deserting employees were never caught; this case was therefore highly exceptional. There was also considerable sympathy for desertion in a situation like this. The Ottawa *Cit-*

izen compared the lumbermen's conviction to slavery. In *Roughing It in the Bush*, Susannah Moodie described the Moodies' hiring of an apprentice who had run away after a beating, suggesting that she thought their actions would attract little social opprobrium even though the law forbade the harbouring of runaway apprentices.[153]

If a servant did decide to pursue legal recourse, a magistrate could grant a discharge.[154] In the case of an apprentice, the magistrate could also (under the 1851 act) fine the master up to five pounds, with prison in default. Presumably the harsher penalty was justified by an apprentice's greater vulnerability.[155] For some actions a master might be sued in the civil courts (as in *Mitchell* v. *Defries* above) or prosecuted under the criminal law. It was assault for a master to correct his apprentice immoderately or 'with an unlawful instrument,' and 'if a master refuses his apprentice necessary food or sustenance, or treats him with such continued harshness and severity as his death is occasioned thereby, the law will imply malice, and the offence will be murder.' Sexual assault on servants or apprentices could give rise to civil actions for seduction or criminal prosecutions for rape. In 1890, Parliament made illicit sexual connection with a female factory, mill, or workshop employee (if under twenty-one and 'of previously chaste character') a criminal offence.[156]

Securing Payment of Wages

The employees' wages were, of course, their reason for working (along with the board included in many relationships). Pay was usually expressly agreed upon, but if not, customary wages would be implied. Wages were often difficult to recover, especially in the early part of the century. During those years there was a shortage of specie in the colony. The owners of marginal farms or financially precarious contractors might delay payment for months or default entirely.[157]

As a result, wages were often paid in kind. This included the routine setting off of debts recorded in store account books; cash-poor farmers paying off their workers in produce or old clothes; paying for land clearing by allowing the clearer to keep the wood or even part of the land; paying for threshing, milling, or weaving by offering a share of the product; or paying workers in chits redeemable only at the employer's store. Store pay could be exploitative. Complaints about it were common in canal construction, prompting the Board of Works to include a clause forbidding it in its contracts. The clause was commonly ignored, however. Although in England the truck acts generally

forbade payment in kind, Ontario adopted no such prohibition, probably because employers' cash poverty made it indispensable in many
circumstances. It is significant that at a union meeting of Cobourg
mechanics and labourers in 1836, a motion to insist on cash rather than
store pay was defeated. Legislation did respond to the prevalence of
non-cash transactions by empowering courts to award an equivalent
money sum.[158] Until 1872 married women faced an added difficulty in
securing their wages: in law, the contract was with their husband and
only he could sue.[159]

If a worker's wages were not paid, he or she (always excepting married women) could claim them before the civil courts, the appropriate
court varying with the amount in issue. One suspects that claims for
small sums would often have come before the Courts of Requests (later
the Division Courts), because these met frequently and did not follow
the highly technical forms of action of the common law. Indeed, after the
definition of service was narrowed about mid-century, anyone excluded
from the definition had to go to the civil courts.

For most employees, however (indeed, early in the century, for many
workers we no longer consider employees), the best recourse lay before
magistrates. Magistrates were generally more available than even the
humblest civil tribunals, and their proceedings were very expeditious.
Like the rest of their labour jurisdiction, their power to award wages was
statutory. It had developed out of the power to fix wages under the
English statutes. It survived long after wage determination had disappeared, and indeed was extended to workers who fell outside the
wage-fixing provisions. When, in Upper Canada, the English statutes
were replaced by the act of 1847, magistrates were again empowered to
award wages up to ten pounds.[160] This recourse was very popular.
Indeed, in the third quarter of the century, claims for wages seem to have
been as frequent as prosecutions of employees for misconduct. The
recourse survived the repeal of the criminal aspects of master and
servant legislation in 1877.[161] It did have its limitations, however:
although a servant could enforce the judgment by distress against a
master's goods, the servant could not have the master imprisoned.

Because of the frequent slide of employers into insolvency – a risk
magnified by the widespread use of subcontracting – workers often
sought statutory preference for wage claims. In the latter half of the
century, this led to mechanics' liens legislation and preferences upon
bankruptcy.[162] There is an intriguing example of the custom of trade
responding to problems arising from subcontracting and cash shortage
in an 1845 Queen's Bench decision. Some workers had taken timber

from the woods under a contract with one operator, who had agreed to deliver the timber to another at the falls on the Petite Nation River. Their wages were to be paid upon delivery at Quebec. When the workers reached the falls, they refused to release the lumber to the second employer until he agreed to take responsibility for the wage bill of the first. The second agreed, and the men and lumber continued to Quebec. On arrival, the second employer denied liability for the debts of the first, resulting in this claim. The defendant's own agent admitted 'that such an arrangement was in accordance with the usual course of the lumber trade, the men always claiming and expecting, under all the circumstances, to be paid their wages out of the proceeds of the lumber when sold at Quebec or Montreal.' The court upheld the claim despite the fact that such liens were not recognized under the common law and the action was of doubtful merit under the law of contract. Clearly the practice was too well established and too useful to decline to enforce it.[163]

Hours of Work and Hours of Leisure

One matter central to today's labour law was subject to very little regulation in nineteenth-century Ontario: hours of work. Employees themselves attempted to govern their hours. Skilled workers often tried to control the pace and scheduling of labour. The fight for a nine-hour day during the 1870s was one of the *causes célèbres* of Canadian trade unionism, uniting workers well beyond their shop or craft.[164] In England the Statute of Elizabeth had specified hours in agriculture (in summer from 5 a.m. to 7 or 8 p.m., with 2½ hours for food and rest; in winter, from dawn to dusk), but there is no indication that these were followed in Ontario.[165] Moreover, hours in Ontario varied considerably between employments. Heron has alluded to the range in manufacturing. Agricultural labourers worked very long days, especially in summer. In the 1840s, canal labourers worked fourteen-hour days, less in winter.[166] I have not found any examples of magistrates ruling on hours, but I suspect that when such issues arose they would have been dealt with under that elastic rubric, 'the custom of the trade,' the magistrates expecting rough conformity to the established practice within the firm or within a particular category of work. That, at any rate, is the basis on which they judged other complaints of unfair treatment.[167]

There was one aspect of work time that was subject to statute, although how rigorously it was enforced, especially in rural settings, remains an open question. Legislation requiring the observance of Sunday was inherited from England and later buttressed by local action.[168]

Employers' Responsibility for Relief from Disease or Accident

I will not deal here with employers' civil responsibility for injury caused by their fault. That complex matter falls outside the scope of this essay and has been addressed elsewhere.[169] I confine my remarks to employers' contractual obligations when an employee was ill or otherwise unable to work. There is very little discussion of employers' legal duties in this area in the available materials. One has to reconstruct them from the sporadic reports of how employees were treated in fact.

Under the Statute of Elizabeth, masters were responsible for providing for servants in illness. The obligation seems, however, to have been one incident of the paternalistic relationship existing in England in agricultural service under yearly contracts. It is doubtful whether the obligation had much currency in Upper Canada, especially given the more transitory nature of agricultural employment and the greater poverty of rural employers.[170] Certainly when labour was done under daily hirings, there was no obligation to pay a sick employee. Employees unable to work were simply sent home.[171] Craven also reports a decision of the Galt magistrates in which an employee on monthly hiring failed to obtain wages for sick days. (But the reasons are ambiguous; the magistrates seem to have based their decision on the employee's failure to appear at work and state the reason for absence.)[172] The best indication of employers' practice, however, is the reliance of employees on voluntary subscriptions to aid fellow workers, even in hirings lasting more than a month. Radforth notes such subscriptions in the lumber industry, Craven on the railways, and Bleasdale on the canals.[173]

In fact, one suspects that employers often did provide some support for ill employees (they certainly contributed, on occasion, to employees' subscriptions), but they did so through a sense of charity rather than obligation. Provision for sick employees was of a piece, then, with the general approach to misfortune in Upper Canada. Above all, individuals and families were expected to provide for themselves and their members. There was some provision for those who were utterly unable to manage, although even here, it was presumed that those who could, should work; thus, children of the destitute were bound out as apprentices. But the relief was generally offered through voluntary means. State assistance was grudging. Individual acts of charity and mutual benefit societies were common.[174]

There was one form of employment in which the assistance of the employer was considered obligatory, however: apprenticeship. Once again, its paternalistic character was reflected in the obligation to provide in sickness and health, and the inability to discharge the apprentice even for incurable illness.[175]

Recourses against Third Parties

Thus far I have discussed recourses directly between master and servant. Often, however, these provided little satisfaction to employers. Even if absconding employees could be located, they rarely had money to pay damages, and even if prosecutions could be used to force them to return, it was extremely difficult to regulate the quality of their effort. But the law also provided a number of recourses against third parties. Sometimes these were based on special agreement, such as those upon a bond guaranteeing the faithfulness of a clerk or those against a parent on his or her covenant in an apprenticeship indenture.[176] These specific actions were of limited scope, but there were others, not dependent on special agreement, potentially obtainable against any future employer of a runaway.

Their origins are hazy, wrapped in the mists of fourteenth-century English law, but, by the nineteenth century, the common law permitted actions against future employers for (1) forcibly taking one's servant, (2) procuring one's employee (in other words, encouraging the employee to desert, without a forcible taking), or (3) retaining a servant that the defendant knew to be a runaway (including failing to surrender an employee after being informed that he or she had deserted). The actions had to be brought before the civil courts. There, the original employer could obtain damages equal to the value of the runaway's services. The action was given a statutory foundation, in the Upper Canadian apprenticeship act of 1851 which entitled a master to obtain the value of an absconding apprentice's labour from those harbouring or employing him.[177]

These actions formed the basis for the advertisements, frequently found in newspapers of the time, informing prospective employers that a servant or apprentice had deserted and warning against hiring or harbouring him. Often the advertiser clearly did not want the runaway back: the employer might offer a reward of a farthing or state plainly that the employee was useless and not worth employing. In other cases (for example, in advertisements in Ottawa Valley newspapers regarding lumber workers), the employer does seem to have wanted the employee to return. I know of one case, from Sandwich (Windsor) in 1806, in which an employer claimed a servant, originally hired on a yearly contract, back from his next employer, a surveyor. According to the surveyor's diary, the original employer had advanced the servant twenty-five pounds on account of his wages and said 'that unless I came responsible for the debt he could not let him go, the said Pascal is therefore discharged.'[178]

There were several reasons for the newspaper advertisements, even if they had little chance of securing the employee's return. First, they acted as a kind of negative reference to the world, informing others that the servant was unreliable. Second, they notified potential masters of the desertion, opening the way for a claim for damages if any of them hired the absconder. Third, impeding a runaway's progress in this small way must have helped satisfy, to some degree, the desire to vindicate one's rights. It might also have had a deterrent effect on other would-be deserters and would have dampened competition among local employers for scarce labour.

THE AUTHORITY OF MAGISTRATES IN MAINTAINING PUBLIC ORDER

This concludes my discussion of the individual employment relationship. There is, however, another aspect of magistrates' authority that deserves mention at this point: their duty to maintain the peace by suppressing riots and disorder. This was used to counter collective action by workers, but it had a broader purpose, serving as a bulwark of public order generally. It is best considered, then, as part of the backdrop against which specific responses to collective action took shape.

As already mentioned, magistrates were not merely judges; they combined a variety of roles, including the direction of police. Until the emergence of more professional police forces, beginning about mid-century, magistrates were responsible for appointing constables and to a large extent supervising them. These officers might be adequate for dealing with individual offenders (though their efficiency was often questioned), but when confronted with mass disorder they were easily overwhelmed. In those situations, magistrates had two additional sets of tools, which they frequently invoked in tandem.

First, they could rely on especially harsh powers to suppress riots. At common law, a riot existed when three or more persons came together, committing acts of violence. It was essential that there be violent acts, 'or at least ... an apparent tendency thereto, which are calculated to strike terror among the people, such as the show of offensive weapons, threatening speeches, or turbulent gestures.' If there was insufficient show of force, those assembled might still be guilty of the lesser offences of rout or unlawful assembly. Under the common law, riots were misdemeanours, punishable by fine or imprisonment. Under the Riot Act of 1714, however, riots by twelve or more were a felony, punishable by death. To trigger the increased penalty, a magistrate or equivalent officer would 'read the riot act' – make a proclamation in the prescribed form. The crowd would then have one hour to disperse. At common law, magistrates had the power to suppress riots and could command all able-bodied men to assist them. Persons acting against a riot could use deadly force. All taking part in the disturbance, even by gestures or wearing badges, were rioters.[179]

Second, magistrates could call in more men to maintain order. Their first option was to swear in special constables. In some labour disputes these were recruited in large numbers.[180] If the specials were insufficient, the magistrates could summon the military. In early years, the troops would be British regulars; later they were Canadian militia. The demand for troops had to be made by a mayor, two magistrates, or certain other officials, and from at least 1855 on the municipality was liable for their cost. The troops' commander often had trouble collecting, however. Not only were town officials stingy, but magistrates sometimes lacked municipal support for their actions. After Confederation, company officials, anxious to secure the intimidating effect of bayonets, sometimes tried to get around reluctant municipal officials by making a direct request to Ottawa, which had jurisdiction over the establishment of the militia. The Dominion authorities routinely refused such requests, insisting that aid to the civil power was a municipal responsibility.[181]

Once called, the troops were in the position of special constables, in theory under the direction of the magistrates. According to army regulations, they should normally have been accompanied by a magistrate. But military discipline remained in effect, and the magistrates' instructions had to be filtered through the unit's commanding officer. Army regulations stated, for example: 'The troops are not, on any account, *to fire* excepting *by word of command* of their officer: and the officer is not to give the word of command *to fire*, unless distinctly required to do so by the Magistrate.' There were nevertheless many instances of the commander's taking effective control by acting in the absence of magistrates or by inducing magistrates to co-operate in his plan of action. Army regulations limited the use of rifle fire, requiring (among other things) a clear warning before the troops opened fire and providing for a graduated increase in the use of force to allow the crowd time to disperse. In fact, troops rarely fired on crowds in Canada, although they did fix bayonets to intimidate rioters.[182]

The militia was summoned in cases of mass disturbance in which the use of regular and special constables was or was expected to be inadequate. For example, troops were deployed in a number of the election and Orange-Catholic riots that raged periodically in Upper and Lower

Canada.[183] They were used along the Ottawa River to control violence by lumberworkers, when drunkenness, grievances against contractors, conflicts between French-Canadian and Irish workers, or the more complex causes underlying the 'Shiners' War' (discussed by Radforth below) led to disorder.[184] In the labour context, however, troops were used most often against canal and railway navvies. Large numbers of would-be workers gathered for the construction of these public or quasi-public works. They were frequently recent Irish immigrants (later Italian) with no capital to buy land and without the skills to obtain jobs as farmhands. There was often not enough work to go around, their contractors frequently delayed or defaulted on wages, and pay reductions or layoffs produced real hardship. Increasingly desperate men would sometimes protest by rioting, taking their case to nearby towns, where they might plunder stores of food. The authorities would respond by reading the Riot Act, increasing the constabulary, stationing troops nearby, and imposing curfews. In 1845 and 1853 the province adopted legislation empowering the Governor in Council to restrict the possession of firearms, establish a force of mounted police, and prohibit the sale of liquor near public works. In 1851 the municipality of Hamilton co-operated with the Great Western Railway to appoint twenty-seven officers to control railway construction labourers.[185]

Information compiled by Pariseau suggests that the military was used about fifty times in nineteenth-century Ontario. Over thirty of these were in the 1840s and 1850s; in later years, the militia's role declined with the creation of more effective police forces. It is difficult to tell how many were instances of labour protest. At mid-century, labour disputes often shaded into other forms of popular disturbance, and Pariseau's detailed work concentrates on later years.[186] Nevertheless, the militia was an important tool in the arsenal of magistrates' responses to mass unrest, although the less extreme remedies of reading the Riot Act or enlisting special constables were more commonly used.

MASTER AND SERVANT LAW AT MID-CENTURY

In the first half of the century individual employment relations had been strongly influenced by the prevalence of small land-holding and the geographical and occupational mobility of the new society. Most farmers were cash-strapped, struggling to get their land into full production, hiring labour when they could, often for limited terms. With few exceptions, lumber and canal contractors, merchants, and master tradesmen had still to acquire large amounts of capital. On the labour side, agricultural workers were aspiring farmers, who possessed their own land or expected to obtain it within a few years. Their presence in the waged labour force was limited – while they accumulated their stake or got their land into production – or sporadic – as they supplemented the income from marginal farms. Domestics often came from similar families and were working for similar reasons, or they were independent immigrants engaged in domestic employment until they too could move on to something else. By-employment was common, so that skilled trades (carpentry, masonry, and milling) were frequently combined with farming. Even work on the canals or in the woods tended to conform to this pattern, serving as a stepping-stone to other kinds of labour (at least so the workers hoped) or supplementing farm income.

The structure of the employment relationship reflected this context. It generally did not involve long-term commitments between the parties. Hirings tended to be short, with no expectation that they would be perpetually renewed. In the great majority, the parties simply exchanged wages and board for work. The hirings looked more like limited, mutually agreeable transactions than encompassing, permanent relationships of dependency. In these circumstances, the old paternalism of some English employment relationships – the paternalism reflected in Blackstone's comment that menial servants were presumed hired by the year 'upon a principle of natural equity, that the servant shall serve, and the master maintain him, throughout all the revolutions of the respective seasons' – seemed, for most employments, obsolete.[187] In practice workers were not presumed to be hired by the year, and the masters' obligations to care for servants were very limited. Families and individuals were expected to be responsible for themselves, doing the work they had agreed to do and in return receiving wages and often room and board, but they otherwise possessed considerable independence. Even that obviously paternalistic relation, apprenticeship, partook of the prevailing ethos: whether children were bound out in order to provide for their welfare or to train them in a skill, the premise was always that they should do what work they could, and ultimately be prepared to make their own way in the world.

Paternalistic employment relations were not, then, as dominant in Upper Canada as some authors have supposed.[188] Paternalism in employment must mean more than merely the acceptance of a social hierarchy or deference to established political authority. These are compatible with paternalistic employment relations, but they may nevertheless exist in circumstances in which employers take no paternal responsibility for their workers – the case of casual labour, as opposed to yearly service, in early nineteenth century English agriculture, for example. Paternalism involves more: the employer's recognition that, as part of the very relation of master and servant, he is responsible for aspects of the employee's life that extend well beyond the performance of work in return for payment (such as caring for employees in time of sickness, or overseeing the moral or intellectual instruction of employees and their families); and, in return, the expectation that the employee owes allegiance to the employer. Paternalism involves, of its nature, commitment in the long term. Some Upper Canadian employment relations were paternalistic in this sense. A few employers struggled, generally in vain, to recreate old-style paternal relations in the new land (the Garden Island enterprises of the Calvin family are the most familiar example). Paternalism was also adopted – 'reinvented' might be the better word – by some employers as a means of retaining scarce tradespeople or creating a compliant labour force.[189] In such circumstances it assumed considerable significance. But we should not take the colourful exception as the norm or lose the clarity of the concept by running it together with all forms of deference, or we will blind ourselves to the specific situations in which it did exist.

During the early period, the role of the law was relatively modest in most work relations. The terms of employment were generally decided by the parties. Both sides relied on self-help and only occasionally resorted to the inferior courts to protect their interests. The law did not treat masters and servants identically – it was primarily concerned with upholding property and doubted the reliability of the propertyless – but it did presume that all parties were self-reliant contractors. There was, however, one crucial situation where this ideal broke down: in the unrest on the canals. There, large numbers of desperately poor workers, unable to provide for themselves or find employment, scarcely fitted the expected pattern of upward mobility. The workers reacted by rebelling en masse. The authorities responded with repression.

The unrest on the canals contributed to the perception, which gathered force about mid-century, that there was a growing class of unpropertied and often impoverished workers who would never find their way onto the land. Others have described the effect of the increasing scarcity of good farmland, combined with continued immigration, on provincial society. Those conditions contributed to a concern for order, for using government to maintain discipline among those who did not possess such a clear stake in society. This in turn helped to generate a whole series of institutional reforms: the creation of elected municipal governments and the expansion of their regulatory role; the founding of professional police forces; the growing displacement of part-time lay magistrates by full-time, legally trained judges; and the enactment of new legislation to govern employment relations.[190]

These developments pointed in two directions. On the one hand, they contributed to more effective, less sporadic regulation of labour discipline. In incorporated towns, full-time police magistrates were appointed to administer justice, so that a single person now saw to the punishment of petty breaches of the peace, including master and servant violations. The existence of professional police, the improvement of communications, and the greater density of settlement made it more difficult for those in conflict with their employers simply to disappear into another township. Municipal authorities tried to bring urban disorder and the unemployed under control by by-laws against such offences as vagrancy and drunkenness. The self-consciously respectable elements of the community began to make a concerted effort to suppress such disturbances as charivaris, Orange-Catholic confrontations, and election violence.[191]

At the same time, the reform of municipal institutions along more democratic lines opened the potential for more conciliatory approaches to labour. This became most apparent in the 1870s, after advances in the political mobilization of workers. It was manifest in the sympathy, albeit qualified, that some mayors and municipal council members showed for labour in a number of late nineteenth-century disputes, and their opposition to the heavy-handed use of the police or militia. Their sympathy towards labour was significant, for mayors and aldermen were also magistrates, who often performed judicial functions and had considerable say over policing, including the summoning of troops. In fact, in the 1870s and 1880s there was often a noticeable difference between the attitudes of appointed officials (for example, police magistrates) and elected officials (mayors and aldermen), the former tending to be much more hostile towards labour.[192] During this period, provincial and federal politicians also came to value the electoral support of labour, a development that eventually led to another series of legislative reforms in the last decades of the century.

The next two sections discuss those reforms, primarily regarding the law's treatment of trade unions. Before addressing collective relations, however, I should first say a word about individual employment law in the factories and on the railways.

As we have seen, the law of master and servant had, in the first half of the century, complemented the transactional nature of employment relations. The emergence of large-scale, integrated forms of production in the second half of the century strained that model. When workers sought employment in those industries, they stepped into highly organized private societies in which labour was controlled and the work process ordered by rules promulgated by the employer without any pretence of negotiation. Rather than engaging in a simple exchange of work for wages, employees seemed to be joining entire institutions which possessed their own complex structures of governance. These structures were enforced primarily by means within the employer's immediate power – by fining employees a portion of their wages or, for more serious offences, by discharging them – without the intervention of magistrates. They were successful because an individual employee wanted the job more than the employer wanted the employee; employees would accept the penalties to retain their jobs. Occasionally, however, these measures came before magistrates as side-issues in claims for wages or defences in prosecutions for leaving work without notice. How did the law treat these new, unilaterally declared forms of regulation? Much research remains to be done, but on the basis of what we do know, we can advance a hypothesis.

The law of master and servant was concerned, above all, with policing the outline of the employee's engagement: the undertaking to serve for a certain time. It paid little heed to what the employee did once he or she was hired or how the work was organized. In practice, that fell to be determined chiefly by the employer, because in any hiring the employee's paramount obligation was to obey. The hiring might impose some vague constraints (stating, for example, the general nature of the job), but in opting to serve, an employee could be assumed to have accepted a number of implicit conditions. Sometimes magistrates used the expression 'the custom of the shop' to capture this phenomenon. The complex rules of industrial employment would almost certainly have fallen within this concept. The law would have ratified their imposition as part of the employer's right to define the tasks of the servant. The law forced the parties to observe their engagements, but did little to alter the effects of the emerging shift in economic power on the terms of those engagements.[193]

In fact, in one context the law moved beyond toleration to give force of law to employers' self-made rules. Special clauses were included in the acts incorporating railways (and later in general railway acts) to grant magistrates jurisdiction over breaches of the railways' internal rules. Under these provisions, employees could be prosecuted to collect fines stipulated by the company's by-laws, or to impose more serious fines or imprison the worker if the fault had endangered persons or property. Workers could be prosecuted for manslaughter if the breach led to death. Craven and Traves suggest that these harsh provisions were designed to enforce discipline in an industry in which personal supervision was often impossible. Workers would be jolted into compliance by the threat of severe retribution. High-profile prosecutions had the added benefit of shifting attention away from the dangers inherent in the fledgling industry, emphasizing instead the vagaries of human nature. Numerous prosecutions did occur, in addition to the docking of wages under the companies' internal systems of fines.[194]

This extension of the law of master and servant to factories and railways showed the tenacity of a model based on individual hirings and individual responsibility and backed by criminal penalties, even in the very different industrial context. This fundamental individualism was also influential in the law's initial encounter with trade unions.

The Law and Trade Unions

From at least the 1830s there had been small, local unions in Upper Canada. Their development had, however, been tentative and episodic, the organizations declining in hard times, expanding in good times, until, by the second half of the century, they began to claim a substantial role in setting the conditions of skilled employment in towns and cities and on the railways. The increasing propensity of skilled workers to seek strength in combination and to strike for their demands posed a significant challenge to Upper Canadian society. On the one hand, the right of workers to come together seemed consistent with eminently liberal principles: the freedom of individuals not to work except on terms acceptable to them and the freedom to associate. But on the other hand, the growth of trade unions seemed to threaten property, both directly through sabotage or riot (here the fear of unions threatened to merge with the fear of popular violence generally, especially during the protests of railway and canal navvies) and in a more amorphous sense, in the risks unions posed to progress and the accumulation of capital. Upper Canada was a society dominated by small property-holders who were devoted to economic expansion, development, and the creation of wealth.[195] Employers were worried about what unions might do to their profits, and these worries fed into a broader anxiety about the effect of unions on economic prosperity. The tensions were reflected in the evolution of the law.

THE INTERSECTION BETWEEN INDIVIDUAL EMPLOYMENT LAW AND TRADE UNIONISM

Many of the recourses we have already seen remained important in the trade union context. Of course, employers and workers still relied on self-help to assert their interests. Workers combined precisely in order to gain more clout over the terms of employment. Masters responded by exploiting the means most immediately at hand: firing union supporters, maintaining blacklists, or, in later years, imposing 'ironclad contracts' (in which an employee would, as a condition of employment, agree not to join a union). The holding back of wages or the provision of company housing were useful in collective disputes, just as they were in cases of individual desertion: striking was, in law, tantamount to quitting; if it occurred without notice, employers could claim that employees had forfeited their wages. They could in any case evict employees from company houses. In fact, as in the individual context, these self-help remedies were undoubtedly more common and perhaps more important than legal recourse.

Prosecutions under the master and servant legislation were used to break strikes. Indeed, in some ways the legislation was more useful here than in disciplining individuals. First, a striking employee could be found much more easily than one intent on leaving for good. Second, some strikes occurred on short notice, in reaction to the firing of a union member, the hiring of a non-member, or the changing of a shop practice. In such circumstances, the effectiveness of a strike might depend on immediate action, making it impossible to allow for notice. When this was the case, the relatively short notice periods of weekly or monthly hirings were of little benefit, especially when, as a Canadian Labor Union delegation complained in 1876, magistrates were willing to impose month-long prison sentences for breach of weekly contracts. Not all strikes were like this, however. There is some evidence that strikers did try to give notice when possible. In 1853, for example, the striking *Globe* printers, in a public defence against allegations by their employer, George Brown, were careful to note that they had given 'the full notice required by the custom of the trade, and worked faithfully as before during the whole interval.'[196]

Third, there were often large numbers of indentured apprentices in the shops. Apprentices were not entitled to quit, even on notice, and masters could prosecute them if they tried.[197] Fourth, master and servant legislation could be used to stiffen the resolve of adult strike-breakers as well. Often, strikers would attempt to persuade strike-breakers, who may not have known of the dispute, to quit work and return home. If they succeeded, the strike-breakers could be prosecuted. In the 1872 Toronto printers' strike, employers signed strike-breakers to one-year contracts, clearly in order to lock them into long-term commitments at a time when weekly hirings were the norm in printing. On occasion, strike-breakers were prosecuted when they subsequently refused to serve.[198] Finally, as we will see, any of these contraventions could furnish an important element in a prosecution for criminal conspiracy, even when the persons prosecuted had not themselves violated the legislation.

In certain kinds of late nineteenth-century strikes it was also common to have recourse to the police and militia (the latter more rarely, given the greater efficiency of the police after the reforms). These disputes generally involved semi-skilled or unskilled workers in such large-employment industries as manufacturing, transportation, or public works. There, the numbers involved and the strikers' frequent use of physical obstruction to stop strike-breakers seemed to pose a direct threat to property. The use of police in such circumstances severely compromised their claim to professional neutrality, however, at least in workers' eyes. Police officers were invariably brought in to defend the employer's property and to protect strike-breakers. They often became closely associated with the effort to maintain production by riding on the employer's street cars or patrolling the employer's plant. Occasionally employers summoned them before any violence occurred, simply because of their intimidating effect and the ideological power of the message that property had to be protected against union violence. When specials were used, they were sometimes recruited and paid by the employer. It was small wonder that policing became the subject of severe criticism by labour reformers.[199]

THE CRIMINALITY OF TRADE UNIONS

The justification for the presence of police was the prospect of criminal conduct during the strike. A range of criminal offences was potentially relevant to labour disputes. Some of these were the ordinary offences proscribing acts of violence or damage to property; later, labour disputes were specifically targeted in various statutes. This law did affect the conduct of strikes. Strikers and their sympathizers were prosecuted for assault, intimidation, and other offences, including riot. Union leaders who believed that their chances of victory could be harmed if the public believed that order was threatened, were careful to portray themselves as law-abiding and peaceable and to distance themselves, at least in public, from acts of violence.[200]

When employers prosecuted, they did not always hope to secure convictions. The prosecutions could serve a purely tactical purpose. In nineteenth-century Ontario private prosecutions were the norm. Under this system, an employer had wide latitude to lay charges. He would then, as prosecutor, control the pace of proceedings. This meant that he could prosecute a strike leader, often on the flimsiest of pretexts, taking the leader away from the strike and casting a pall of illegality over the union's actions. The employer could then use the prosecution as a source of leverage, often without bringing the matter to trial. The literature includes several examples of prosecutions begun and then abandoned.[201]

The invocation of the criminal law therefore played a role in the rough and tumble of strikes. Its significance went well beyond the force of its application, however, for it served as an important focus for public argument over the acceptability of workers' collective action. From the first emergence of trade unions until the legislative reforms of the 1870s, it provided some of the principal terrain on which the legitimacy of unions was debated.

The central question was whether unions, by their very nature, were criminal conspiracies. There was no doubt that the law of conspiracy applied to some conduct by union members. At common law, a conspiracy existed whenever two or more persons combined to achieve an unlawful end or combined to achieve a lawful end by unlawful means. Thus, union members were occasionally indicted for conspiracy when they assaulted or intimidated others. The charge of conspiracy held certain benefits for employers: it gave rise to more severe penalties than assault or intimidation alone; it impugned the conduct of the entire organization, not just the convicted individuals; and it facilitated the prosecution of people who had not taken part directly in the unlawful acts, as long as they belonged to the combination and had consented, even tacitly, to the unlawful acts. The attempt to persuade strike-breakers to leave a struck workplace could, for example, support conspiracy, the strike-breakers' breach of the master and servant law furnishing the unlawful means. The temptation to bring conspiracy actions was especially strong when strikers had given notice before quitting, so that they were not themselves in breach of contract. The disadvantage of conspiracies, from the prosecutor's point of view, was that unlike assault they were tried before the Court of Sessions or, more commonly, the assizes, in each case with jury. A prosecution could easily founder before an unsympathetic jury.[202]

Thus, conspiracy did figure in the law's response to labour disputes. The more doubtful question was whether any combination to raise wages was a criminal conspiracy because its objective – the raising of wages – was in restraint of trade. This, of course, spoke directly to the legitimacy of unions, for it potentially rendered them all criminal, virtually by definition. Twentieth-century Canadian commentators have generally assumed that it did, taking at face value the claim that the 1872 Trade Unions Act liberated unions from that yoke.[203] Many nineteenth-century commentators, including magistrates' manuals, would have agreed with them. A laconic note to the 1809 edition of Blackstone's *Commentaries* is typical: 'Every confederacy to injure individuals, or to do acts which are unlawful, or prejudicial to the community, is a conspiracy. Journeymen who refuse to work, in consequence of a combination, till their wages are raised, may be indicted for a conspiracy.'[204] The trustworthiness of these pronouncements is questionable, however. First, the issue was largely untested in Upper Canada. Conspiracy was predominantly a matter for the superior courts – at the very least the Court of Sessions – and the experience in these tribunals was, as we will see, ambiguous. Second, many of these statements are found in English publications, rely on English statutes, or appear to be copied from standard English works. In this area, English practice was of very questionable authority.

The gist of the second problem was that in England the law of trade unions had been profoundly shaped by statute, first by a series of acts outlawing unions (culminating in the Combination Acts of 1799 and 1800), followed by another series repealing and replacing these measures. These statutes were not in force in Upper Canada. They had, however, dominated English law for so long that it was now difficult to determine what the common law was. As in the law of master and servant, statute and common law had become virtually inseparable in the English discussions.[205] Moreover it was futile to attempt to return to a pristine period before the enactment of the statutes. Common law principles always take shape within a broader discourse of justification, within a general argument about the demands of the social order. Here too, the Upper Canadian discourse had parted company from the English. The early English cases had dealt with a society in which official regulation of prices and markets was common, and any attempt to raise prices therefore suspect.[206] The late eighteenth-century English authorities, including the combination acts, had spoken to a society that was much more industrialized and urbanized than Upper Canada was fifty years later, and in which unions had been seen as a potentially subversive force (especially in the wake of the French Revolution). They therefore expressed an extreme hostility to unions, a hostility that had fallen out of favour by the time Upper Canadians began to address the issues. It would have seemed incongruous to reach back to those authorities, given the very different context. Thus, when the debate over the status of trade unions began in earnest, the Upper Canadians found themselves cut off from English authority, both contemporary and eighteenth-century.

Moreover, the view that unions per se were criminal conspiracies is not supported by the actions of Upper Canadian courts. First, prosecutions were very few, and convictions even fewer, given the number of strikes before 1872. Craven has identified eight labour prosecutions in Toronto, all between 1854 and 1872. Tucker has added two more, in

1837 and 1842, from Kingston. Research for this volume uncovered one more abortive prosecution, in Ottawa in 1864.[207] The results of these cases are inconclusive. Often conspiracy was combined with allegations of unlawful means, making it difficult to sort out the specific treatment of trade unions. Sometimes magistrates did use the broad language found in their manuals. Craven, however, has found two instances in which the accused were acquitted in the absence of unlawful means, suggesting that a combination to raise wages was not sufficient. When convictions did occur, there was always evidence of unlawful means.[208] Clearly, the doctrine that trade unions were all criminal conspiracies was, at the very least, singularly ineffective in punishing workers.

How then should we think about the doctrine, for it did claim a prominent place in legal literature, unions were occasionally damned as conspiracies in newspaper commentaries, and its rejection in the Trade Unions Act has remained one of the enduring landmarks in the history of Canadian labour law? Its significance does not lie in the fact that the doctrine somehow lay in reserve, to be summoned to repress unions when desired, nor did those who invoked the doctrine simply make a mistake about the true state of the law.[209] Each of these suggestions takes too little account of the importance of argument and justification to the evolution of the common law. The debate over criminal conspiracy is best seen as part of a larger, unresolved debate about the legitimacy of workers' collective action. Trade unions were new in Upper Canada. They engaged in activities that many members of respectable society found troubling, not least because of their effects on employers' economic interests. At the same time, the suppression of all workers' organizations would have seemed to many Upper Canadians to be excessive, an illiberal throwback to an age that had largely been repudiated in England. This tension shaped the way the law was interpreted and deployed.

Participation in the debate was by no means evenly distributed. Lawyers, legislators, magistrates, and judges occupied a privileged place, as did landowners and those in business and the other professions. Nor was the debate the only factor determining what people did in strikes. Strikers (and employers) were not beholden to what this dignified forum would accept, although they did care enough to argue the legitimacy of their cause, to portray their actions as peaceable and just, and to lobby for changes to the law. Despite its inequalities and its limited reach, it was a debate in which many members of society, including workers (especially skilled craftsmen), attempted to make their case, and which in turn furnished criteria for evaluating strike conduct.

We begin by reviewing the range of means used by unions to obtain their ends. Conspiracy was almost always joined to other charges in practice, a number of offences being alleged in a single prosecution; it was also inseparable from them in justification.

The basic tool available to unions – and the one central to workers' defence of their organizations – was to refuse in concert to work for less than a certain wage. This was also the most easily justified, since it amounted to the right to set the price at which one would work, combined with the ability to talk about it with one's peers. It was, in other words, little more than an assertion of an employee's freedom of contract. That freedom was generally recognized in Upper Canada and indeed had a solid base in the transactional nature of most master-servant relationships in the colony. William Lyon Mackenzie acknowledged its significance in an 1833 dispute with his printers, when he conceded that the refusal to work for less than a stipulated scale of wages was 'a resolution perfectly correct and reasonable, to be taken in a country where every man has a right to set his own value on his labour' (although he went on to exhort his printers to remember both the golden rule and that 'many of the employed of 1833 will probably be employers in 1844').[210]

But few workers could depend on agreement among themselves alone to secure their demands. Even in printing, masters could find other printers, commonly from country towns, to take the strikers' place. The strikers' next step in pursuing their demands was to speak to the strikebreakers to see if the latter could be dissuaded from working. This was a little more difficult to justify, even if there was no hint of coercion. At the very least the striker was sticking his nose into a transaction between two other parties; he could no longer argue that he was simply setting the price for his own labour. When Mackenzie conceded the legitimacy of his printers' organization, for example, he did so only because its members sought to determine their own wages, not those of all journeymen. The suspicion shown towards meddling in another person's employment was evident in some areas of labour law: master and servant legislation forbade 'any tavern keeper, boarding-house keeper or other person' from inducing servants to confederate to demand high wages; and numerous measures, some adopted by the Parliament of the United Canadas, sought to suppress the activities of crimps (brokers of sailors' labour) in the seaports of Quebec and eastern Canada.[211] Of course, the meddling was considered all the more serious if a contract had already been concluded between the strike-breaker and the employer.

The burden of justification was still greater if the strikers resorted to intimidation or threats. Coercion by strikers almost always met with disapproval, at least in respectable society. Undoubtedly, strikers did rely on intimidation to defend their jobs, especially in occupations where little skill was needed and strike-breakers were plentiful in consequence. Indeed, it was easy for some magistrates concerned with labour discipline to convince themselves that strikers always used intimidation. At any rate, one of the main grounds on which strike conduct had to be justified concerned the peacefulness of the persuasion. Coercion was an elastic concept, and many elements of union action could appear coercive. One of the most common was the insistence by union members that a non-member be fired. At a time when a union's influence was utterly dependent on its ability to mount effective strikes, solidarity within the shop was crucial. Still, for those oblivious to the nature of the struggle, to insist that a specific person lose his job could be seen as a tyrannical imposition. Finally, there were the most spectacular examples of violence in the conduct of strikes: assaults, riot, murder, incendiarism. The last two were extremely rare in labour disputes in Ontario. Nevertheless, their existence in other countries occasionally surfaced in provincial debates.

The application of the concepts of the criminal law – the attempt to decide how the criminal law should be applied to workers' collective action – was conditioned by these various forms of union action. The bald argument that unions were, by definition, criminal conspiracies specifically excluded the need to find pressure or intimidation. This meant that it ran headlong into the liberal premises of freedom of contract. This was patent when the argument was stated frankly (as it rarely was: often authors simply referred to 'conspiracies to raise wages'): '[E]ach [journeyman] may insist upon raising his wages if he can; but if several meet for the same purpose, it is illegal, and the parties may be indicted for a conspiracy.' Many balked at such an oppressive principle. In an 1837 prosecution in Kingston the jury refused to convict on that basis, and there are comments from the Liberal *Globe* and the Conservative *Mail*, even from the Toronto police magistrate who figured prominently in the prosecution that led to the Trade Unions Act, affirming that more was required.[212]

Some arguments could be marshalled in reply. One was that trade combinations inevitably led to disorder, no matter how peaceful they appeared to be. There are hints of this argument both in occasional references to labour outrages abroad and in the loose language often used to refer to the criminality of unions – but aspersions and loose language were shaky foundations for such a specific legal principle.[213] Some headway might have been made by referring to the injury caused by higher prices, but this was unlikely to justify such a draconian measure except to those clinging (in the early part of the century) to the vestiges of price regulation, or the most adamant of Manchester liberals.[214] Moreover, as Tucker has suggested, in the latter part of the century such an approach would have been seen as patently unfair, given Canadian law's tolerant treatment of combinations of capital. In fact, by the time anti-monopoly legislation came to be adopted in Canada, it was largely conceded that rather than exercising monopoly power, unions were a necessary protection for workers against it.[215]

The argument that unions per se were conspiracies was therefore very weak, not so much because it was without foundation in the old authorities, but because it diverged so widely from the normative debate of the time. This drove the discussion of the criminality of unions to focus on other acts. This was evident in the laying of prosecutions. No one wanted to rely simply on the claim that unions were conspiracies; all alleged that other crimes had been committed, such as threatening or molestation, or they coloured their allegations of conspiracy with suggestions of violence or intimidation. This, however, merely opened up a larger set of issues. Everyone agreed that violence or threats of violence were prohibited, but what else crossed the line? There were, for example, perpetual disagreements over what amounted to intimidation or molestation. Did it include virtually any interference with strike-breakers, as some magistrates seemed to believe? Did it involve calling someone a 'scab'? What about insisting that a person be fired and threatening to strike if he was not?[216]

This, then, was the shape of legal argument concerning the criminal law as it applied to unions up until the Toronto printers' strike of 1872, when conspiracy was finally put to the test. That strike is the most discussed event in nineteenth-century Canadian labour history.[217] The proprietor of the *Globe*, the prominent Liberal, George Brown, took his printers to court. The original information alleged a number of offences in addition to conspiracy, but these were dropped by the police magistrate, probably (Craven suggests) because there was not enough evidence. Only conspiracy to raise wages was submitted for trial. Perhaps it was just this – the assertion of the conspiracy claim stripped of any colouration of unlawful means – that exposed, once and for all, its weakness. The case did not come to trial. The Conservative government of John A. Macdonald, relishing the opportunity to embarrass the Liberals in the contest for workers' votes, steered the Trade Unions Act (TUA) through the Dominion Parliament. That act proclaimed that trade unions were not conspiracies by reason merely of being in restraint of trade.[218]

The TUA transformed the debate, although not in the way often assumed. The argument that unions per se were conspiracies was gone, but the disagreements over what constituted tolerable strike conduct remained. Indeed, at the same time as it adopted the TUA, Parliament passed another statute, the Criminal Law Amendment Act (CLAA), which gave statutory form to a series of offences in labour disputes, including threatening, intimidation, and molestation, the latter comprising persistent following, hiding tools, and watching and besetting. Even before its passage, the CLAA attracted complaints from the labour press. During the next three years, these were reinforced by prosecutions of striking shoemakers for conspiracy and threats, and of stonecutters for inducing their employer to fire a man who had accepted work at less than union rates. Although both these prosecutions failed, the Liberals, who were now in power in Ottawa, passed amendments in 1875 and 1876 that tightened the definition of intimidation to require threats of violence, excluded peaceful picketing from the reach of watching and besetting, and made it clear that those involved in disputes could only be convicted of conspiracy when they had used means prohibited by the CLAA. The TUA had not, then, eliminated the issues that had been most important in prosecutions before 1872; arguments over the scope of intimidation and molestation resurfaced. Now, however, the statutory realm had largely displaced the courts: the CLAA furnished the principal terms of debate, and labour used its new-found political muscle to secure change through legislation.[219]

The Regulatory Turn in Ontario's Labour Law

The last three decades of the century were indeed critical years for labour law. Organized more effectively than ever before and able to rely on recent English precedents, unions secured a number of reforms both from Parliament and from the Ontario legislature. These reforms seldom went as far as the trade unionists wanted. Workers' votes might be courted, politicians might be responsive, but unions could not dictate government policy. Nevertheless, the reforms were significant. Furthermore, the nature of the law was changing. New actors – administrative agencies, elected office-holders – played an increasingly prominent role. Their functions involved persuasion and conciliation rather than the adjudication of rights. The common law became proportionately less important; where it remained, it was often hedged about by statute.

One of the most important reforms was the repeal of the master and servant provisions that imposed criminal penalties for breach of contract by a worker. In the mid-1870s, as the controversy over conspiracy, intimidation, and other crimes was dying down, organized labour turned its attention to the long-standing grievance with the master and servant legislation. Workers had long objected to the inequality of the act, which subjected them to imprisonment but their employers only to civil damages. Now the ideological climate was receptive to their cause. There had been a time when the individualism of the law had been tempered by an explicit recognition of the reality of class: the master and servant penalties reflected this, as had, arguably, the 'fellow servant' rule in employers' liability. But the importance of class was now on the wane, and the new orthodoxy tended to aim for (on the face of the law) identical treatment for all. Macdonald had justified the TUA on the grounds that workers' combinations should be treated no differently from those of capital – although this argument was somewhat disingenuous, for the simultaneously enacted CLAA did single out labour disputes. The CLAA was in turn rendered class-neutral by the Liberal government of Alexander Mackenzie in 1876 (although the purported neutrality was specious: no one doubted that controlling unions was still the principal object). Opposition to 'class legislation' had become a powerful rallying cry.[220]

The cry was especially telling when workers were sent to jail for ordinary breaches of contract. In 1877 Parliament passed the Breaches of Contract Act, which repealed the offending aspects of master and servant legislation, as well as the prohibition on incitement to combination by tavern and boarding-house keepers. Like many reforms of the period, it closely followed an English precedent, making labour's case all the stronger; but also like many reforms, it was a genuine response to local pressure. It did not completely eliminate criminal penalties. It had been enacted following a bitter strike on the Grand Trunk Railway. It consequently created a new set of crimes to punish breaches of contract that endangered life, person, or property, threatened the provision of gas and water, or, above all, interfered with the running of railways. It therefore followed in the same line as the special offences applicable to railway employees, and anticipated the concern of later labour legislation with strikes in the developmental or urban infrastructure (on railways, in mines, on street railways, and in the supply of gas and electricity). It was criticized, with some justice, for being class legislation, although in theory it applied to both employers and employees. Its penalties appear never to have been used.[221]

In the 1872 and 1877 reforms, the Macdonald and Mackenzie governments tried to project an appearance of benevolent neutrality, favouring neither workers nor employers, respecting the individual, and allowing employees to pursue their interests in association as long as they had due regard for public order. Indeed, during this period, governments at all levels tried to carve out a role as neutral defenders of the public interest, even-handed in their treatment of employees and employers. This was especially evident in their growing support for, and practice of, 'arbitration' in labour disputes.

'Arbitration' was frequently used to refer to any method for the consensual resolution of labour disputes, ranging from direct discussions to various forms of third-party intervention, including mediation and adjudication. Formal declarations are generally vague about the meaning, often because the speaker's intention was vague: a commitment to arbitration often meant little more than a desire for settlement through discussion, without a strike. In England a wide variety of structures had evolved in different industries over the course of the century, virtually all established by agreement between employers and unions. The British Parliament adopted a series of statutes to promote conciliation, but these were seldom, if ever, used. They invariably required the parties' consent before anything could be done. But when there was sufficient consensus to establish a board, the parties simply created their own, avoiding the cumbersome statutory machinery.[222]

There were few voluntary boards of conciliation or arbitration in Canada. By and large, unions were too weak to compel their employers to create institutionalized forms of accommodation. Employers generally insisted on dealing with their workers as individuals, the most adamant trying to root unions out of their plants by firing union members, maintaining blacklists, or imposing ironclad agreements. Unions had to fight for greater recognition from their employers, and they combined that fight with demands for legislation that would compel 'arbitration.'[223]

Oliver Mowat's provincial government did adopt legislation. In 1873, it passed the Trades Arbitration Act, modelled on an English statute of 1867. Like its model, it was a dead letter. The Mowat government adopted another statute in 1894, this time based on a New South Wales precedent. It too was virtually inoperative. In each case, the problem was the need for the parties' consent before boards could be established or disputes referred. Reluctant employers simply ignored the law. The government would express its faith in conciliatory labour relations, it would give gentle encouragement to boards of arbitration, but it would not force employers to deal with their employees collectively. Even its moral support for arbitration was hesitant. The 1873 act did not apply to future wages (though this was changed in 1890), and farmworkers and domestic servants were excluded.[224]

A more effective form of conciliation, however, began to emerge in the last three decades of the century. Prominent individuals, concerned with the cost of a strike to a community, would try to effect a settlement. Frequently, these volunteers were local aldermen, responding to the concerns of their constituents. They did not have to wait for the parties to agree to an elaborate structure of boards. They simply took it upon themselves to interview each party and explore the potential for compromise.

On occasion they were successful.[225] In the last years of the century, officials or legislators in the federal and provincial governments, perhaps even those appointed under the 1894 Ontario legislation, began to adopt the same approach. The federal government was hesitant at first, wondering out loud whether it had any business intruding into employers' contractual disputes; once again the way was eased by an English precedent, combined with severe strikes in resource and infrastructure industries. Indeed, in 1899 the Prime Minister himself intervened in a strike on the Grand Trunk Railway. The ad hoc conciliation of these years was the progenitor of the regime that came to dominate Canadian labour law in the first half of the twentieth century.[226]

During the 1870s and 1880s, Ontario also adopted legislation to protect workers' safety. These developments have been amply described elsewhere. They prohibited the employment of boys under twelve and girls under fourteen, limited the working hours of women and children, and required such things as lunch breaks for women and children and separate toilets for women; established general norms for safety measures such as protective barriers, proper ventilation, and fire protection; and amended the common law to make it easier for injured workers to sue their employers for damages. One of the principal statutes, the Ontario Factories Act, created an inspectorate to investigate conditions and secure compliance with the act. But the inspectors were few compared to the numbers of factories, and they tended to emphasize education and encouragement rather than prosecution. Thus their effectiveness was limited.[227]

The factory inspectors represented a growing trend towards the use of public servants in the administration of labour law. These officers increasingly intervened in matters touching the substance of the working environment or employment relationship. They did so tentatively, usually relying on mediation and exhortation. In 1897, for example, in retaliation for an American act, Ottawa adopted the Alien Labour Act, which restricted the importation of foreign workers. A number of officers were appointed to enforce the act; like Ontario's factory inspectors, they too emphasized conciliation, in some cases turning their attention to the settlement of strikes.[228] Also in 1897, Ottawa began inserting a clause in post office procurement contracts requiring that wages paid under the contracts be equivalent to those paid competent workers in the locality. This 'fair wages' policy, designed to prevent sweated labour, was later extended to other government contracts. Officers were appointed to determine the appropriate wage and frequently based that determination on the union rate. They also performed other functions, including, on occasion, the mediation of disputes.[229]

All of these measures projected the image of a concerned government, protecting the vulnerable from abuse and striving for reconciliation between masters and men. The same message was delivered by a series of official inquiries on labour matters.

In the 1870s, then, the initiative had shifted from the courts to the legislature. The courts nevertheless maintained a powerful presence. Master and servant law remained in force, although the elimination of the criminal penalties made it, in practice, much less significant. More important, the administration of many reforms – the criminal amendments, mechanics' liens legislation, and changes to employers' liability – was entrusted to the courts. Occasionally judges fought rearguard actions against what they took to be legislative excesses, subjecting mechanics' liens to a restrictive interpretation and discovering ingenious ways to get around the criminal amendments. In one example of the latter, three union members were convicted of conspiracy for calling for a boycott of a particular job unless a man who had served as a strike-breaker was dismissed. Both the trial judge and a unanimous court of appeal held that this resolution was for the purposes of harming an individual, not 'for the purposes of a trade combination,' and that it therefore fell outside the protection of the 1876 statute. This decision led to yet another amendment, in 1890, making clear that the protections did govern workers' refusal to work with other employees. Finally, the courts toyed with the idea of using civil wrongs, backed by injunctions, to forbid conduct that before the amendments had been punished under the criminal law. But the full development of the Canadian labour injunction had to await the next century.[230]

Conclusion

I began this essay by suggesting that the evolution of labour law in nineteenth-century Ontario can be divided into four periods. We can now summarize the nature of that development.

There was, first, a brief transition period, during which labour was frequently performed under legal forms involving a high degree of (sometimes forced) dependency: long-term employment contracts and slavery. With increasing settlement, however, those structures quickly gave way to shorter hirings and much more transactional forms of employment. There were exceptions, but by and large, hirings presumed a high degree of self-reliance and independence. This shaped the labour law of the second period, which covered roughly the first fifty years of the century. During this time, the role of the law was restricted and uneven, owing to the high occupational and geographical mobility of labour, poor communications, and the weakness of the administrative structure of labour law.

The state did have a significant influence on the shape of employment relations, but indirectly, through immigration and land policy.

Then, about mid-century, the pattern began to shift. The emergence of a more stable labouring class challenged the previous order; the assumption that waged labour was merely a waystation along the road to full-time farming seemed less sure. At the same time, the greater density of settlement permitted improved communications and more effective administration of labour law. The province adopted its own master and servant and apprenticeship acts, municipal government was consolidated, full-time police forces were established, and the courts were reformed. The world of the nineteenth-century labourer was closing in. These changes inaugurated the third period, which lasted from mid-century until the 1870s. It was during this time that the courts began to grapple seriously with the challenge of trade unions (though some consideration had been given to them as early as the late 1830s). The challenge was significant. On the one hand, the essence of trade unionism seemed to be founded on the generally accepted individual freedoms of contract and association. But on the other, the logic of the struggle drove workers to try to collectivize the fight, moving beyond the premises of voluntary association. Workers sought to achieve complete solidarity, at least within a trade, by persuasion if possible and, if not, by moral or physical pressure. These tensions played themselves out in the criminal law of the third period.

In the 1870s, organized labour did achieve a significant measure of solidarity, which translated into growing political influence. Politicians sought to establish themselves as brokers between workers and employers. They acknowledged the legitimacy of trade unions, and fashioned responses that began, tentatively, to depart from policing individual transactions and enforcing public order to propose the elimination of 'abuses' in the factory system, or the use of government officers as mediators in labour disputes. During this fourth period, which lasted from the 1870s until the turn of the century, elected officials at all levels seized the initiative, the criminal provisions of master and servant law were repealed, and new forms of intervention, often entrusted to administrative officers and premised on accommodation, were developed.

One can thus discern through the century four successive stages. At the same time there were themes that cut across these periods. One was the application of master and servant law. That law shaped the core of the individual employment relationship throughout the century. English settlers had arrived with conceptions of master and servant relations shaped by that law. The old English statutes or, more accurately, the accumulated custom of magistrates, were applied (sporadically) to employment relations in Upper Canada in the first half of the century. The essential features of that law were retained in the Upper Canadian acts of 1847 and 1851. Under these acts they were applied more consistently and were also used in contexts that were new to Upper Canada: the large-scale industrial organizations of factories and railways and the control of strikes. The abolition of the criminal sanctions in 1877 diminished the role of master and servant law dramatically, but much of its content survived as the foundation of the private law of employment.

Another important theme was the continuity in the criminal law debate over the legitimacy of collective action from the late 1830s till the end of the century (and beyond). The tensions in that law remained remarkably constant, first determining the debate over the crimes of conspiracy, intimidation, threatening, and molestation, then shaping the interpretation (and indeed the amendment) of the statutory reforms of the 1870s, and finally finding an outlet in the law of injunctions.

A third theme is the importance of institutional pluralism in nineteenth-century labour law. The message of this essay has not been one of a unified legal system that responded systematically to labour unrest. It has been much more complex, more diverse, richer in form and possibility. Even the use of 'state' in the singular is profoundly misleading, for it implies a unity of purpose and co-ordination of means that were often manifestly absent. The law of the part-time, non-lawyer magistrate of the first part of the century was often quite different from that of the police magistrate of the second half, and different again from the exercise of magisterial duties by mayors or aldermen – to say nothing of the contrast between all of these and the more elaborate learning of superior-court judges or, towards the end of the century, the conciliatory interventions of government officials. Sometimes these public officers worked in isolation from one another. At other times several might address aspects of the same events: strikers, or repentant strike-breakers, might be prosecuted before a police magistrate for breach of the master and servant legislation; that same magistrate might try allegations of minor criminal offences, referring the more important ones to the assizes; the regular police, supplemented by specials recruited by the owner of a struck enterprise, might patrol the employer's property; the appointed police magistrate and the elected mayor might quarrel over the use of force; a group of aldermen might seek to mediate the dispute.

The result was not a formless cacophony. The arguments did have shape and direction and some degree of commonality, although that shape was often diffuse, open to change and adjustment, and characterized by tensions and disagreements.

One important influence on that shape was what was happening on the ground. The law did not simply remake life in its image, but to some degree sought to fashion stability and order out of the material it found. This was true, for example, of its treatment of apprenticeship, which ignored the requirement of a seven-year term. It was true of the Upper Canadian approach to the employer's responsibility for a sick employee, which was premised on an assumption of individual self-reliance, supplemented by Christian charity. Indeed, the law's general treatment of employment as transactional and not part of a long-term relationship of dependency was conditioned by the way in which masters and servants conducted themselves. No doubt the tribunals found it easy to move in such a direction when similar developments were occurring in England, but one would not want to underestimate the influence of domestic conditions. In the first part of the century, magistrates were, after all, full participants in the economic life of their communities (as were superior court judges). And even later, when legislatures adopted a series of labour statutes based on English originals, the primary impetus was domestic.

This responsiveness to the community does not mean that the law's action was neutral or egalitarian, embodying a consensus unaffected by considerations of power. Magistrates or judges had their own scale of values, influenced by their social position and legal training, that exalted rights of property and defined public order as requiring labour discipline. This conditioned all their decisions, decisions that could (within limits) be enforced. Other persons – labour leaders and politicians responsive to the labour vote – might disagree. They too had means for getting their voices heard, not least through the legislative process or various means of self-help. By far the least influential were women workers, who had no direct access to the legislative process, no representatives on the bench or bar, and indeed greatly inferior rights under the private law for much of the century. The adjustment of the law was therefore a matter of argument – of claim and counter-claim – in which social position, gender, and institutional structure allowed some voices to count more than others.

This struggle occurred not only – indeed not primarily – through mechanisms of coercion, but through arguments of justification. If law were simply about imposition, reasons and rights would be superfluous. It is also about persuasion, about claiming that the norm enforced is a social norm, one which all should obey because it is essential to the social order. The law's reasons matter, and indeed most workers acted as though they mattered, frequently taking the time to justify their own conduct or impugn that of others. In this process, there was always a tendency to try to work if possible with the existing terms of the debate, for two reasons. First, to win the argument it was not enough to have impeccable logic or reasons satisfying to oneself; the reasons also had to be presented as compelling for members of society at large, for that was the only basis on which one could expect others to acknowledge their validity. Second, much less consciously, the parties themselves had been shaped by that debate and had absorbed its language as their own. We saw this, for example, in the argument over the effect of the criminal law on trade unions, in which trade unionists based their appeal on freedom of contract and freedom of association. This, then, is another element that gave shape and direction to the diffuse set of arguments over justice: the need to make the case for a social standard of justice, obligatory for all, and the consequently centripetal tension in all legal claims, even those seeking reform. It is also the reason why the law works by continual adjustment and transmutation, rather than by clean breaks.

We have seen many such mutations in this essay. Indeed, although some aspects of nineteenth-century labour law now seem distant and archaic, we can see the beginnings of others that, by the same process of adjustment, eventually brought us to where we are today.

NOTES

I am indebted to Kurt Johnson, Stephen Lloyd, Joseph Varga, and Carolyn Webber for their able research assistance, and to Blaine Baker, Eric Tucker, the readers for the Ontario Historical Studies Series, and the other contributors to this volume for their trenchant comments on previous drafts. Many others (some of whom I have tried to thank in the notes to this text) helped guide me to additional sources of material. This chapter has benefited from funds from the OHSS, the Social Sciences and Humanities Research Council of Canada, and the Faculty of Law, McGill University.

1 For Britain, see R.Y. Hedges and Allan Winterbottom, *The Legal History of Trade Unionism* (London: Longmans, Green and Co. 1930); Brian William Napier, 'The Contract of Service: The Concept and Its Application' (PhD thesis, Cambridge University 1975); John V. Orth, *Combination and Conspiracy: A Legal History of Trade Unionism, 1721–1906* (Oxford: Clarendon Press 1991). For the United States, Christopher L. Tomlins, *The State and the Unions: Labor Relations, Law, and the Organized Labor Movement in America, 1880–1960* (Cambridge: Cambridge University Press 1985), and *Law, Labor, and Ideology in the Early American Republic* (Cambridge: Cambridge University Press 1993); William E. Forbath, *Law and the Shaping of the American Labor Movement* (Cambridge, Mass.: Harvard University Press 1991).

2 For works on Upper Canada/Ontario, see Paul Craven, 'The Law of Master and Ser-

vant in Mid-Nineteenth-Century Ontario,' in D.H. Flaherty, ed., *Essays in the History of Canadian Law*, vol. 1 (Toronto: Osgoode Society 1981), 175–211; R.C.B. Risk, '"This Nuisance of Litigation": The Origins of Workers' Compensation in Ontario,' in D.H. Flaherty, ed., *Essays in the History of Canadian Law*, vol. 2 (Toronto: Osgoode Society 1983), 418–91; Mark Chartrand, 'The First Canadian Trade Union Legislation: An Historical Perspective,' *Ottawa Law Review* 16 (1984), 267–96; Paul Craven, 'Workers' Conspiracies in Toronto, 1854–72,' *Labour/Le Travail* 14 (1984), 49–70; Eric Tucker, 'The Law of Employer's Liability in Ontario 1861–1900: The Search for a Theory,' *Osgoode Hall Law Journal* 22 (1984), 213–80; Margaret E. McCallum, 'Mechanics' Liens in the Mowat Era,' *Histoire sociale/Social History* 19 (1986), 387–406; Paul Craven, 'The Meaning of Misadventure: The Baptiste Creek Railway Disaster of 1854 and Its Aftermath,' in R. Hall, W. Westfall, L. Sefton MacDowell, eds, *Patterns of the Past: Interpreting Ontario's History* (Toronto: Dundurn 1988), 108–29; R.W. Kostal, 'Legal Justice, Social Justice: An Incursion into the Social History of Work-Related Accident Law in Ontario, 1860–86,' *Law and History Review* 6 (1988), 1–24; Eric Tucker, 'Making the Workplace 'Safe' in Capitalism: The Enforcement of Factory Legislation in Nineteenth-Century Ontario,' *Labour/Le Travail* 21 (1988), 45–85; Lorna F. Hurl, 'Restricting Child Factory Labour in Late Nineteenth Century Ontario,' *Labour/Le Travail* 21 (1988), 87–121; Eric Tucker, *Administering Danger in the Workplace: The Law and Politics of Occupational Health and Safety Regulation in Ontario, 1850–1914* (Toronto: University of Toronto Press 1990); Margaret E. McCallum, 'Labour and Arbitration in the Mowat Era,' *Canadian Journal of Law and Society* 6 (1991), 65–90; Eric Tucker, '"That Indefinite Area of Toleration": Criminal Conspiracy and Trade Unions in Ontario, 1837–77,' *Labour/Le Travail* 27 (1991), 15–54.

3 For family labour, see Marjorie Griffin Cohen, *Women's Work, Markets, and Economic Development in Nineteenth-Century Ontario* (Toronto: University of Toronto Press 1988).

4 For the jurisdiction and evolution of these courts, see William N.T. Wylie, 'Instruments of Commerce and Authority: The Civil Courts in Upper Canada 1789–1812,' in Flaherty, ed., *Essays in the History of Canadian Law*, vol. 2, 3–48; Margaret A. Banks, 'The Evolution of the Ontario Courts 1788–1981,' in Flaherty, vol. 2, 492–572; John C. Blackwell, 'William Hume Blake and the Judicature Acts of 1849: The Process of Legal Reform at Mid-Century in Upper Canada,' in Flaherty, ed., *Essays in the History of Canadian Law*, vol. 1, 132–74. My discussion draws heavily on these accounts. For the inferior tribunals, the best sources are the magistrates' manuals: W.C. Keele, *The Provincial Justice* (Toronto: U.C. Gazette Office or H. Rowsell, in five editions beginning 1835); R. Dempsey, *Magistrate's Handbook* (Toronto: Rowsell and Ellis 1860); R.E. Kingsford, *Commentaries on the Law of Ontario*, vol. 1 (Toronto: Carswell 1896).

5 Keele, *Provincial Justice*, 1st ed. (1835), 408–9; 3d ed. (1851), 27–8 and 469–70.

Craven gives examples of judgments overturned at Sessions: 'Master and Servant,' 198ff.

6 Napier, 'Contract of Service,' 105–6 mentions the use of these in England. *Whelan* v. *Stevens* (1825), Taylor 245 and (1827), Taylor 439, *Briggs* v. *Spilsbury* (1827), Taylor 440, and *Shea* v. *Choat* (1846), 2 U.C.Q.B. 211, were all prosecutions for false imprisonment. Bleasdale mentions another, but it is unclear from her reference whether the defendant was a magistrate or a constable, and whether the action came as a result of a conviction: Ruth Bleasdale, 'Class Conflict on the Canals of Upper Canada in the 1840s,' *Labour/Le Travailleur* 7 (1981), 35. I have come across only two examples of *habeas corpus*, both in a near-employment context concerning slaves in Lower Canada in 1798 (both were decided under the Statute of Elizabeth, although in one the judge declared that slavery did not exist in the province): Robin W. Winks, *The Blacks in Canada: A History* (Montreal: McGill-Queen's University Press 1971), 100.

7 For the rarity of appeals from the District Courts, at least for the period before 1812, see Wylie, 'Instruments of Commerce and Authority,' 18–19.

8 For a discussion of the piecemeal introduction of equity into Upper Canada, see Blackwell, 'William Hume Blake.'

9 (1845), 2 U.C.Q.B. 430 at 431; Richard Burn, *The Justice of the Peace, and Parish Officer*, in multiple editions beginning 1754.

10 For the importance of magisterial appointment to the creation of a local elite, see Colin Read, 'The London District Oligarchy in the Rebellion Era,' *Ontario History* 72 (1980), 195–209; J.K. Johnson, *Becoming Prominent: Regional Leadership in Upper Canada, 1791–1841* (Kingston and Montreal: McGill-Queen's University Press 1989), 61–8. (Note, however, that Johnson's description of magistrates' judicial duties is not wholly accurate. See instead the discussion that follows.)

11 See the fine discussion in Napier, 'Contract of Service,' especially 59ff.

12 This not terribly precise approach to jurisdiction would have been particularly pronounced in the distinction between those things a justice could do alone and those for which two were necessary. Napier, 'Contract of Service,' at 78–84, notes that the English superior courts themselves were less than rigorous in their interpretation of justices' powers, contracting some and expanding others, and especially that they upheld decisions made by a single justice when two were required. For confusion on this point in Upper Canada, see *Shea* v. *Choat* (1846), 2 U.C.Q.B. 211 at 221, where the Queen's Bench ruled that a conviction had been made without jurisdiction in part because one justice had acted where two were necessary. About mid-century, it became common for two or more magistrates to sit together, even when this was not required. According to Dempsey, this court of 'petty sessions' had two advantages: (1) it allowed magistrates to consult on the cases; and (2) it helped remove suspicion of bias. See Dempsey, *Magistrate's Handbook*, at 36–7.

13 (1846), 2 U.C.Q.B. 211 at 211–15.

14 William Blackstone, *Commentaries on the Laws of England*, 15th ed. by E. Chris-

tian (London: A. Strahan 1809), Book the Fourth, 271–2; Keele, *Provincial Justice*, 1st ed., 412; Dempsey, *Magistrate's Handbook*, 43–4.

15 This paragraph and those that follow draw heavily on Wylie, 'Instruments of Commerce and Authority,' 17–18, for the first years of the century, and on Banks, 'Evolution,' for the latter.

16 For a list of common magistrates' manuals, see note 4 above. Apparently, magistrates tended to use Burn's *Justice* until Keele's first edition in 1835. For indications of the extent to which justices relied on these manuals, see (with respect to the 1760s and 1770s) Hilda Neatby, *Quebec: The Revolutionary Age, 1760–1791* (Toronto: McClelland & Stewart 1966), 50–1, or the arguments of Robert Baldwin as counsel in *Shea* v. *Choat* (1846), 2 U.C.Q.B. 211 at 220, where he says that Keele's manual is 'a work which is in the hands of every magistrate in the country, and by which the magistrates are generally guided in their proceedings.' Compare John A. Conley, 'Doing It by the Book: Justice of the Peace Manuals and English Law in Eighteenth Century America,' *Journal of Legal History* 6 (1985), 257–98.

17 See Dempsey, *Magistrate's Handbook*, 45; Craven, 'Master and Servant,' 183 and 201.

18 Keele, *Provincial Justice*, 1st ed., 434–5; 2d ed. (1843), 56.

19 See below and Craven, 'Master and Servant,' 203. It is one of the great assumptions of today's labour law that the common law contract of employment is not subject to specific performance. A court will not, in other words, order an employee to perform the work he or she agreed to do, but will confine the employer's recourse to monetary damages. The operation of master and servant legislation suggests that this premise needs substantial qualification, at least as a description of nineteenth-century law. Although the equitable remedy termed 'specific performance' might not have been available, an employer could achieve the same result through master and servant prosecutions. In effect, contracts of employment were specifically enforceable, but before magistrates rather than Courts of Equity. See M.R. Freedland, *The Contract of Employment* (Oxford: Clarendon Press 1976), 272–4.

20 Blackstone, *Commentaries*, Book the First, 355–6; Keele, *Provincial Justice*, 1st ed., 125–6, 185–7; Dempsey, *Magistrate's Handbook*, 41; W.T. Matthews, 'By and for the Large Propertied Interests: The Dynamics of Local Government in Six Upper Canadian Towns during the Era of Commercial Capitalism, 1832-1860' (PhD thesis, McMaster University 1985), 196–201.

21 D.R. Murray, 'The Cold Hand of Charity: The Court of Quarter Sessions and Poor Relief in the Niagara District, 1828–1841,' in W.W. Pue and B. Wright, eds, *Canadian Perspectives on Law and Society: Issues in Legal History* (Ottawa: Carleton University Press 1988), 179–206; Keele, *Provincial Justice*, 1st ed., 413–14; and see especially Matthews' study of the administrative and policing roles of magistrates: Matthews, 'Large Propertied Interests.'

22 Keele, *Provincial Justice*, 1st ed., 80–1; Matthews, 'Large Propertied Interests,' 132–76; W.T. Matthews, 'Local Government and the Regulation of the Public Mar-

ket in Upper Canada, 1800–1860: The Moral Economy of the Poor?' *Ontario History* 79 (1987), 297–326.

23 Murray, 'Cold Hand of Charity.'

24 Patrick C.T. White, ed., *Lord Selkirk's Diary, 1803–1804: A Journal of His Travels in British North America and the Northeastern United States* (Toronto: Champlain Society 1958), 156. See also Neatby, *Quebec*, 50–1. Note that similar concerns were expressed about non-gentlemen justices in England: Blackstone, *Commentaries*, Book the Fourth, 282.

25 Bleasdale, 'Class Conflict on the Canals,' 35. With respect to the period before 1812, Wylie notes the frequency of complaints but suggests that cases of actual misconduct were few: 'Instruments of Commerce and Authority,' 17–18.

26 Dempsey, *Magistrate's Handbook*, 28–9.

27 Wylie, 'Instruments of Commerce and Authority,' 17; Jean Pariseau, 'Forces armées et maintien de l'ordre au Canada, 1867–1967: Un siècle d'aide au pouvoir civil' (thèse de doctorat, Université Paul Valéry III, Montpellier 1981), 119, and APC 62; Johnson, *Becoming Prominent*, 81. Gregory S. Kealey, *Toronto Workers Respond to Industrial Capitalism 1867–1892* (Toronto: University of Toronto Press 1980), 144, reports the comments of Thomas Moss, future Chief Justice of Ontario, in the House of Commons in 1875, criticizing the 'intimate relations' sometimes existing between magistrates and employers. The nature of these relations is suggested by the background of Angus Bethune, a police magistrate who figured prominently in the law's treatment of cotton-mill disputes in Cornwall during the 1880s. He was a former manager of a flour mill and former mayor, who in the latter post had worked hard to attract cotton mills to the town: Elinor Kyte Senior, *From Royal Township to Industrial City: Cornwall 1784–1984* (Belleville: Mika Publishing 1983), 228–9, 255; Gordon Levine, 'Conflict and Consensus: Labour and the Law in Cornwall's Cotton Mills during the 'Great Upheaval,' 1880–1890,' research paper, 1989, 52n40.

28 For a striking example of this broad conception of their role, see the memoirs of Toronto's long-serving police magistrate, Col. George T. Denison, *Recollections of a Police Magistrate* (Toronto: Musson 1920). See also Gene Howard Homel, 'Denison's Law: Criminal Justice and the Police Court in Toronto, 1877–1921,' *Ontario History* 73 (1981), 171–86; Paul Craven, 'Law and Ideology: The Toronto Police Court 1850–80,' in Flaherty, ed., *Essays in the History of Canadian Law*, vol. 2, 248–307.

29 See the description of the first factory inspectors in Tucker, 'Making the Workplace "Safe,"' 52–6, or Tucker, *Administering Danger*, 138ff.

30 See, for example, Bernard J. Hibbitts, 'Progress and Principle: The Legal Thought of Sir John Beverley Robinson,' *McGill Law Journal* 34 (1989), 460–73.

31 William Renwick Riddell, 'The Slave in Upper Canada,' *Journal of the American Institute of Criminal Law and Criminology* 14 (1923–4), 249–67; Winks, *Blacks in Canada*, 1–113.

32 An Act to prevent the further introduction of Slaves, and to limit the Term of Contracts for Servitude within this Province, S.U.C. 1793, c. 7; An Act for the Abolition of Slavery throughout the British Colonies, 3&4 Will. 4 (1833) c. 73 (UK); Riddell, 'Slave in Upper Canada'; Winks, *Blacks in Canada*, 96–9, 110–13.

33 Riddell, 'Slave in Upper Canada'; Winks, *Blacks in Canada*, 96–113.

34 Agreement between Alexander McDonell and Pierre Ochu, Quebec, 1 May 1793 (my thanks to Joy Ormsby for this reference); H. Clare Pentland, *Labour and Capital in Canada, 1650–1860* (Toronto: Lorimer 1981), 55.

35 For the Hudson's Bay Company, E.E. Rich, *Hudson's Bay Company 1670–1870*, vol. 2: *1763–1820* (Toronto: McClelland & Stewart 1960), 268–9; Jennifer S.H. Brown, *Strangers in Blood: Fur Trade Company Families in Indian Country* (Vancouver: University of British Columbia Press 1980), 23–35. For the North West Company, W.S. Wallace, ed., *Documents Relating to the North West Company* (Toronto: Champlain Society 1934), 91; Robert Rumilly, *La Compagnie du nord-ouest: Une épopée montréalaise*, vol. 1 (Montreal: Fides 1980), 115; Harry W. Duckworth, ed., *The English River Book: A North West Company Journal and Account Book of 1786* (Montreal: McGill-Queen's University Press 1990), xxviii–xxix and 139; Agreement between William M'Gillivray et al. and Noel Lacourse, Montreal, 13 October 1811 (my thanks to Ian Bowering for this reference). Aboriginal labour was employed in the trade on a more casual basis. See, for example, Brown, *Strangers in Blood*, 64–6.

36 S.U.C. 1793, c. 7, s. 1.

37 Craven, 'Master and Servant,' 177–8; J. Whitley, *Canadian Domestic Lawyer, with Plain and Simple Instructions for the Merchant, Farmer, & Mechanic, to Enable Them to Transact their Business According to Law*, 5th ed. (Stratford, Ont.: Thomas Maddocks 1865), 301; Cohen, *Women's Work*, 42–58; Constance B. Backhouse, 'Married Women's Property Law in Nineteenth-Century Canada,' *Law and History Review* 6 (1988), 211–57.

38 See, for example, Catherine Parr Traill, *The Backwoods of Canada* (Toronto: McClelland & Stewart 1966 [1836]), 53 and 58; Susanna Moodie, *Roughing It in the Bush; or, Life in Canada* (London: Richard Bentley 1857), 160–6; William Hutton, *Canada: Its Present Condition, Prospects, and Resources, Fully Described for the Information of Intending Emigrants* (London: Edward Stanford 1854?), 37–8; Catharine Parr Traill, *The Canadian Settler's Guide* (Toronto: McClelland & Stewart 1969 [1855]), 40, 182, 187.

39 Eric Foner, *Reconstruction: America's Unfinished Revolution 1863–1877* (New York: Harper and Row 1988), 594. For examples of both tenancy and employment on shares in Upper Canada, see *Haydon* v. *Crawford* (1834), 3 U.C.Q.B. (O.S.) 583; *Duffill* v. *Erwin* (1859), 18 U.C.Q.B. 431; and *Nowery* v. *Connolly* (1869), 29 U.C.Q.B. 39. In Thomas Radcliff, ed., *Authentic Letters from Upper Canada* (Toronto: Macmillan 1953), 64, a letter from 1832 uses the language of service, although it is not clear whether a court would make the same interpretation: 'Land is

often managed on shares here, from want of money to pay for labour. The man who has land and seed, leaves the management of them to the labourer, who takes half the produce, and draws the rest into the barn of the proprietor.' *Wemp v. Mormon* (1845), 2 U.C.Q.B. 146 is probably an example of an agricultural partnership. For sharecropping as productive of disputes, see Moodie, *Roughing It*, 85 (although a more successful attempt is mentioned at 202); Traill, *Canadian Settler's Guide*, 6.

40 Blackstone, *Commentaries*, Book the First, 425; Napier, 'Contract of Service,' 56–60.

41 E.P. Thompson, *The Making of the English Working Class* (Harmondsworth: Penguin 1963), 235–6.

42 See, for example, B.S. Elliott, *Irish Migrants in the Canadas: A New Approach* (Montreal: McGill-Queen's University Press 1988), 79; Hutton, *Canada: Its Present Condition*, 41.

43 Moodie, *Roughing It*, 100.

44 For examples, see Radcliff, *Authentic Letters*, 187; Moodie, *Roughing It*, 186; A.S. Miller, ed., *The Journals of Mary O'Brien 1828–1838* (Toronto: Macmillan 1968), 125.

45 This is suggested by the fact that farmhands' wage rates were almost always quoted by the month in diaries, books of advice to settlers, etc., throughout the period. This fact alone is indicative but not conclusive; O'Leary, for example, notes the existence of different *monthly* wage rates depending on whether the servant was employed 'for the season of about seven months' or 'for the year round,' making clear that employees paid monthly might still be hired by the year: Peter O'Leary, *Travels and Experiences in Canada, The Red River Territory, and The United States* (London: John B. Day 1877), 104. See also Peter A. Russell, 'Wage Labour Rates in Upper Canada, 1818–1840,' *Histoire sociale/Social History* 16 (1983), 64. But the balance of evidence suggests that most hirings were indeed monthly. Traill states, apparently referring to farm workers: 'Servants in Canada are seldom hired excepting by the month. – The female servant by the full calendar month; the men and boys' month is four weeks only': Traill, *Canadian Settler's Guide*, 7. The frequent turnover of Upper Canadian farm employees strongly suggests contracts of a duration less than one year; the rhythm is incompatible with yearly contracts, at least if they were strictly enforced. Finally, even if one applies the presumptions of early nineteenth-century English law, most Upper Canadian farmhands would be in a position tantamount to that of monthly hires. According to that body of law, servants housed *intra moenia* ('within the walls' – living, in other words, in the employer's household) could be dismissed or could resign on one month's notice, even if hired by the year; most regular farmhands did receive room and board within the household.

46 Hutton, *Canada: Its Present Condition*, 31; Traill, *Canadian Settler's Guide*, 182, 187. The latter is the probable source for Schröder's sample farm diary published in Norwegian: Orm Overland, ed. and trans., *Johan Schröder's Travels in Canada*

1863 (Montreal and Kingston: McGill-Queen's University Press 1989), 128–32. The Tett papers indicate that during the 1870s some men worked for board alone during the winter: Queen's University Archives (hereafter 'QUA'), Tett Papers, Series A, Time Books, vol. 51. See also Judith Fingard, 'The Winter's Tale: The Seasonal Contours of Pre-industrial Poverty in British North America, 1815–1860,' *Canadian Historical Association Historical Papers* (1974), 65–94.

47 See, for example, Miller, *Mary O'Brien*, 217; Moodie, *Roughing It*, 181, 185–6, 211.

48 See, for example, Russell, 'Wage Labour Rates,' 67–8.

49 Miller, *Mary O'Brien*, 36; Hutton, *Canada: Its Present Condition*, 10.

50 This kind of arrangement – one servant kept on at the same wage for the year, another for a reduced wage – is drawn from the sample diary in Traill, *Canadian Settler's Guide*, 182, 187.

51 Napier, 'Contract of Service,' 83, 100–1; Blackstone, *Commentaries*, Book the First, 428.

52 C. Browne and E.M. Chadwick, *Osgoode Hall Examination Questions* (Toronto: Rollo and Adam 1862), 61; Whitley, *Canadian Domestic Lawyer*, 302; Kingsford, *Commentaries*, 338.

53 An Act touching divers Orders for Artificers, Labourers, Servants of Husbandry and Apprentices, 5 Eliz. (1562) c. 4, s. 31.

54 *Hart* v. *Alridge* (1774) 1 Cowp. 54; Napier, 'Contract of Service,' 108–9.

55 Blackstone, *Commentaries*, Book the First, 428; Napier, 'Contract of Service,' 78–80.

56 Peter Bischoff, 'Des Forges du Saint-Maurice aux fonderies de Montréal: mobilité géographique, solidarité communautaire et action syndicale des mouleurs, 1829–1881,' *Revue d'histoire de l'Amérique française* 43 (1989), 9–13. For a similar phenomenon in Upper Canada, see Elliott, *Irish Migrants*, 228–9.

57 Kealey, *Toronto Workers*, 92–3. For the informality of rural training in printing, blacksmithing, and iron moulding, see *Report of the Royal Commission on the Relations of Labour and Capital in Canada: Evidence – Ontario* (Ottawa: Queen's Printer 1889) [hereafter '*Royal Commission – Evidence*'], 37, 107, 146.

58 Robert Gourlay, *Statistical Account of Upper Canada*, vol. 1 (London: Simpkin and Marshall 1822), 236–7. See also my discussion of the reception of the English labour statutes below.

59 See, for example, *Royal Commission – Evidence*, 5, 12, 29–30, 33–4, 41–2, 61–2, 108; the complaint of George Brown's employees in *Mackenzie's Weekly Message*, 30 June 1853, 3. (I am indebted to Chris Raible for this last reference and others dealing with Mackenzie's printers.)

60 Indeed, the limited role of apprenticeship is seen in the lax membership rules for unions. The London Lodge of the Knights of Saint Crispin (shoemakers) required merely that a prospective member should have worked 'an aggregate of 2 years at boot or shoe making ... , and shall at the time be engaged at his trade': Kealey, *Toronto Workers*, 43.

61 White, *Lord Selkirk's Diary*, 138; Survey of Colchester and Gosfield Townships, Journal of Thomas Smith, 28 April 1806, in OA, Lands and Forests Survey Records, Book of Suveyors' Diaries, 1794–1810 (my thanks to Edith Woodbridge for bringing this exceedingly useful source to my attention); Edith Firth, *The Town of York, 1793–1815* (Toronto: Champlain Society 1962), 237; Radcliff, *Authentic Letters*, 206–7; Hutton, *Canada: Its Present Condition*, 30–1; Traill, *Canadian Settler's Guide*, 104–5; Florence B. Murray, ed., *Muskoka and Haliburton 1615–1875: A Collection of Documents* (Toronto: Champlain Society 1963), 294; Charles Marshall, *The Canadian Dominion* (London: Longmans, Green and Co. 1871), 225; QUA, Tett Papers, Series A, Time Books, vol. 51 (boat, barge, and grist mill repairs); Kealey, *Toronto Workers*, 197; Paul Craven and Tom Traves, 'Dimensions of Paternalism: Discipline and Culture in Canadian Railway Operations in the 1850s,' in Craig Heron and Robert Storey, eds, *On the Job: Confronting the Labour Process in Canada* (Montreal: McGill-Queen's University Press 1986), 53–6.

62 Edith Firth, ed., *The Town of York, 1815–1834: A Further Collection of Documents of Early Toronto* (Toronto: Champlain Society 1966), 39; Hutton, *Canada: Its Present Condition*, 30–1, 96. See also, regarding carpenters, Firth, *York, 1815–1834*, 77–9, which suggests that in 1833 carpenters' pay in York was calculated by the day, instalments in varying amounts were paid weekly, and a settlement was made 'when the employer gets in his money.' The carpenters' new union demanded fixed weekly instalments, with the balance paid at the end of each month.

63 Firth, *York, 1815–1834*, xxxiii, 85–6; P.L. Fleming, 'William Lyon Mackenzie as Printer, 1824–1837: Part Two,' *The Devil's Artisan* 6 (1981), 11. Printers could be paid either on piece-work, at so much per 1,000 ems, or by the week: Kealey, *Toronto Workers*, 87–9. The existence of weekly wages, together with the fact that demands for changes in working conditions, from either side, were made on a week's notice, suggests that the hiring was considered to be weekly. When in the early 1890s typesetting machines were introduced into Toronto shops, the printers' union fought to convert entirely to weekly wages: Kealey, *Toronto Workers*, 95–6. For other examples of weekly wages, see Agreement of David Hamill and John Campbell, 23 June 1856, John Campbell papers, Regional History Collection, University of Western Ontario (in carriage making, wages expressed weekly although hiring for the year; my thanks to Jeanne Hughes for this reference); Russell, 'Wage Labour Rates,' 77–8 (tailoring).

64 Radcliff, *Authentic Letters*, 206–7; Traill, *Canadian Settler's Guide*, 105. For piece-work in the industrial production of shoes at the end of the century in Quebec, see Jacques Ferland, 'Syndicalisme "parcellaire" et syndicalisme "collectif": Une interprétation socio-technique des conflits ouvriers dans deux industries québécoises (1880–1914),' *Labour/Le Travail* 19 (1987), 49–88.

65 Kealey, *Toronto Workers*, 66–7; Marshall, *Canadian Dominion*, 225. Kealey describes the method by which piece rates were determined in the foundries, a process emphasizing the artificiality of a sharp distinction between employees on

piece-work and independent contractors: when the employer wished to have (for example) a new pattern of stove cast, the union's shop committee would meet with the boss to determine a single price for the stove; the shop committee alone would then decide the division of that price into piece rates for the different components. Of course, even when work was paid by the piece, both employers and workers paid attention to the total earned in a day, and unions tried to prevent speed-ups by enforcing limitations on daily wages: Kealey, *Toronto Workers*, 67.

66 Radcliff, *Authentic Letters*, 206–7; W.E. Brett Code, 'The Salt Men of Goderich in Ontario's Court of Chancery: *Ontario Salt Co.* v. *Merchants Salt Co.* and the Judicial Enforcement of Combinations,' *McGill Law Journal* 38 (1993), 528n35; above, note 63; Craven and Traves, 'Dimensions of Paternalism,' 56. When, in 1872, Ontario coopers' unions agreed on a price list, they established a schedule of piece rates for many tasks, plus a daily rate for work not included on that list: Kealey, *Toronto Workers*, 56.

67 Radforth, this volume. Monthly pay may have been general for work on the rivers or in the woods: Lord Selkirk noted in 1803 that bateaumen on the Niagara were paid by the month (White, *Lord Selkirk's Diary*, 137); Elizabeth Arthur, ed., *Thunder Bay District, 1821–1892: A Collection of Documents* (Toronto: Champlain Society 1973), 162–3, suggests that in the 1870s wages were monthly for woodsmen engaged in mineral exploration and surveying.

68 Bleasdale, 'Class Conflict on the Canals,' 15; Hutton, *Canada: Its Present Condition*, 31, 40; Radcliff, *Authentic Letters*, 96. William N.T. Wylie, 'Poverty, Distress, and Disease: Labour and the Construction of the Rideau Canal, 1826–32,' *Labour/ Le Travailleur* 11 (1983), 14, suggests that workers on the Rideau Canal in the late 1820s were hired by the month but paid by the day. John Galt, *The Canadas, as they at present commend themselves to the enterprize of Emigrants, Colonists and Capitalists* (London: Effingham Wilson 1832), Appendix, xxxix and xl, and Adam Fergusson, *Practical Notes Made During a Tour in Canada ... in MDCCCXXXI*, 2d ed. (London: T. Cadell 1834), 288, cite monthly wages for the construction of public works, including roads and canals. Surveyors' assistants were paid by the day: Survey of Colchester and Gosfield Townships, Journal of Thomas Smith, 1805 and 1806, passim, in OA, Lands and Forests Survey Records, Book of Suveyors' Diaries, 1794–1810; Russell, 'Wage Labour Rates,' 70.

69 Code, 'Salt Men of Goderich,' 528n33 and n34; Kostal, 'Legal Justice, Social Justice,' 8n47; Craven, this volume; Levine, 'Conflict and Consensus,' 9–10 (during the 1880s, Cornwall cotton mill operatives paid by the piece).

70 *Royal Commission – Evidence*, 1, 29. For other examples of hourly wages at the end of the century, see *Royal Commission – Evidence*, 144 (iron moulders, 1887) and the round robin by tunnel labourers of the St Clair Tunnel Co., 8 March 1890, in Dianne Newell and Ralph Greenhill, *Survivals: Aspects of Industrial Archaeology in Ontario* (Toronto: Boston Mills 1989), plate 9–4.

71 See, for clerks, *Blake* v. *Shaw* (1852), 10 U.C.Q.B. 180; the sample contract in J.

Rordans, *The Canadian Conveyancer and Hand-Book of Legal Forms*, 2d ed. (Toronto: W.C. Chewett 1867), 174–5; Craven, this volume. For teachers, see Firth, *York, 1793–1815*, 198–200; A. Lillie, *Canada: Physical, Economic, and Social* (Toronto: Maclear and Co. 1855), 264–5. For harbour and station masters, see Craven and Traves, 'Dimensions of Paternalism,' 56; *Raines v. Credit Harbour Company* (1844), 1 U.C.Q.B. 174. *Hunter v. Foote* (1862), 12 U.C.C.P. 175 involves a newspaper editor hired on a yearly contract.

72 This section draws on a collection of apprenticeship indentures from Upper Canada and Ontario, assembled from different sources. Except for those in published works, I will cite indentures simply by the name of the apprentice, date, and occupation. My thanks to Bonnie Callen, Gillian Conliffe, Reva Dolgoy, Kathleen Grigg, Jean McFall, Brenda Dougall Merriman, Joy Ormsby, Chris Raible, the staff of the Kitchener Public Library, and especially Jeanne Hughes, for their assistance in locating indentures. For apprenticeships in law, see G. Blaine Baker, 'Legal Education in Upper Canada 1785–1889: The Law Society as Educator,' in Flaherty, *Essays in the History of Canadian Law*, vol. 2, 79–86.

73 Elliott, *Irish Migrants*, 203, 213, 228–31; Michael Gray, 19 April 1803 (farmer); Leonard Lewis, 21 March 1807 (farmer); Hugh M'Donell, 9 May 1817 (carpenter); Whitley, *Canadian Domestic Lawyer*, 5th ed., 310–1, repeated in Rordans, *The Canadian Conveyancer*, 2d ed., 64–5. An Act to provide for the Education and Support of Orphan Children, S.U.C. 1799, c. 3, s. 2 permitted women who had been abandoned by their husbands to bind out their children, with the consent of two magistrates.

74 An Act to provide for the Education and Support of Orphan Children, S.U.C. 1799, c. 3; Keele, *Provincial Justice*, 1st ed., 338; Edward Davis, 1 June 1839 (farmer), in *Waterloo Historical Society Annual* (1969), 80–2. The exercise of this authority required the consent of two magistrates, and of the child if he or she was older than fourteen. The wardens' power existed only if the child's 'relations' were unable to assume support. At least in the 1830s, there were printed forms for use by wardens: Sarah MacClaverty, 2 October 1832 (no occupation). The power remained throughout the century, although vested in the mayor, recorder, or police magistrate in towns, and in the chair of Sessions in rural areas; in fact, it was expanded to include children whose parents were in prison or those who were 'dependant upon any public charity for support': An Act to amend the Law relating to Apprentices and Minors, S. Prov. Can. 1851, c. 11, s. 2; Keele, *Provincial Justice*, 5th ed., 610; Kingsford, *Commentaries*, 339. In England, overseers had a similar ability to bind out poor children, with the consent of two magistrates: Richard Burn, *The Justice of the Peace, and Parish Officer*, vol. 1, 23d ed. (London: Strahan 1820), 107–25; Blackstone, *Commentaries*, Book the First, 426. There are no signs in Ontario of abuses such as those that occurred in the southern United States during presidential reconstruction, when the binding of poor black youths to apprenticeship was one of the devices used to continue the subjugation of blacks: Foner, *Reconstruction*, 201.

75 Neatby, *Quebec*, 235 (in 1791, wardens of a Protestant church in Montreal advertise eight-year-old boy to be bound out); Kingsford, *Commentaries*, 339 (Lieutenant Governor in Council can authorize charitable societies to bind out apprentices); Sarah Louise Chilliman, 16 June 1900 (household duties). For the apprenticeship of children by British charitable societies, see Joy Parr, *Labouring Children: British Immigrant Apprentices to Canada, 1869–1924* (London: Croom Helm 1980), 82–96.

76 Michael Gray, 19 April 1803 (farmer); Leonard Lewis, 21 March 1807 (farmer); James Bolton, 19 October 1829 (farmer). The Statute of Elizabeth had expressly authorized apprenticeship in husbandry; the 1851 Upper Canadian act implicitly did the same: 5 Eliz. (1562) c. 4, s. 25; S. Prov. Can. 1851, c. 11, s. 1.

77 Whitley, *Canadian Domestic Lawyer*, 5th ed., 310–1, reprinted in *Canadian Conveyancer*, 2d ed., 64–5, and 3d ed. (1879), 61–2; Sarah Louise Chilliman, 16 June 1900 (household duties).

78 Mary Ann Thompson, 1 January 1825 (no occupation); Sarah MacClaverty, 2 October 1832 (no occupation).

79 Thomas N.P. Wessels, 22 March 1852 (miller and farmer).

80 I have seen, however, one very brief agreement from 1857, perhaps relying on the obligations set out in the 1851 act to make up for its rather terse phrasing: Richard Balman, 19 March 1857 (blacksmith).

81 Keele, *Provincial Justice*, 1st ed., 24–31; Whitley, *Canadian Domestic Lawyer*, 5th ed., 308–11; J. Whitley, *The Ontario Cabinet Lawyer* (Toronto: A. Lovell 1870), 285–8; Rordans, *The Canadian Conveyancer*, 1st ed. (1859), 21–2, 2d ed. (1867), 61–5, 3d ed. (1879), 60–2; W.H. Richmond, *Richmond's Book of Legal Forms and Law Manual*, 2d ed. (Toronto: Wellington H. Richmond 1854), 11.

82 These are taken from Rordans, *Canadian Conveyancer*, 1st ed. (1859), 21–2, although virtually identical wording could be found in any indenture.

83 Keele, *Provincial Justice*, 1st ed. (1835), 25. I have three examples of premiums in Upper Canadian indentures: Benjamin Tett, 1 November 1818 (surgeon and apothecary); Daniel Bancroft, 17 March 1826 (printer); John Stephen Smith, 10 August 1836 (printer). Baker notes the use of premiums in legal apprenticeships: 'Legal Education,' 81.

84 Alexander Craik, 20 October 1865 (carriage and wagon wood worker).

85 Eliezer Lewis, 15 June 1809 (carpenter or joiner); Michael Gray, 19 April 1803 (farmer); Leonard Lewis, 21 March 1807 (farmer); Hugh M'Donell, 9 May 1817 (carpenter).

86 Alexander Craik, 20 October 1865 (carriage and wagon wood worker).

87 Mary Ann Thompson, 1 January 1825 (no occupation); Hugh M'Donell, 9 May 1817 (carpenter).

88 Richmond, *Richmond's Legal Forms*, 2d ed. (1854), 11; John Stephen Smith, 10 August 1836 (printer); *Dillingham* v. *Wilson* (1841), 6 U.C.Q.B. (O.S.) 85; Hugh M'Donell, 9 May 1817 (carpenter); Richard Balman, 19 March 1857 (blacksmith); Alexander Craik, 20 October 1865 (carriage and wagon wood worker); Charles

Francis, 18 March 1869 (wood worker in waggon and carriage building); Thomas Armstrong, 30 August 1845 (carpenter and joiner); *Royal Commission – Evidence,* 146; Benjamin Tett, 1 November 1818 (surgeon and apothecary); a series of 14 indentures in pharmacy from 1887 to 1907 (Lawrence H. Yeomans, master); Daniel Bancroft, 17 March 1826 (printer); John Fessant Eby, 25 January 1852 (printer); *Shea* v. *Choat* (1846), 2 U.C.Q.B. 211. In 1880s' Toronto, five years was apparently standard for the informal apprenticeships in carpentry and steam fitting: *Royal Commission – Evidence,* 33–4, 55.

89 For the limitation of apprenticeships to the apprentice's minority, see Keele, *Provincial Justice,* 1st ed. (1835), 19; S. Prov. Can. 1851, c. 11, s. 1.

90 S. Prov. Can. 1851, c. 11, s. 3.

91 Richard M. Reid, ed., *The Upper Ottawa Valley to 1855* (Ottawa: Champlain Society and Carleton University Press 1990), 40–1, 53–6 (see 61–2 for similar complaints in 1837). For the impetus for reform, see Matthews, 'Large Propertied Interests,' especially 30ff; John Weaver, 'Crime, Public Order, and Repression: The Gore District in Upheaval, 1832–1851,' *Ontario History* 78 (1986), 175–207. Matthews (at 41–4) describes futile attempts by magistrates to control rioting by canal labourers in St Catharines during the 1840s and gives (at 45) an example from 1846 of a Bytown magistrate being roughly handled. Weaver (at 186) describes a similar event at Brantford in 1843. Miller, *Mary O'Brien,* 216, suggests the difficulty magistrates had asserting their authority in the Lake Simcoe area in 1833 (though without noting the nature of the dispute): 'Poor Edward's magisterial troubles are not over yet. The people have now been abusing the constable. I fear it will take some time to teach them that the arm of the law has reached thus far into the woods.'

92 Radforth, this volume; Heron, this volume; Firth, *York, 1815–1834,* 77–9; Levine, 'Conflict and Consensus,' 10. The fact that following an 1886 strike, the Massey company both reduced the pay period (to every two weeks) and reduced the number of days' wages withheld (from 10 to 5) reveals two forms of arrears: (1) wages accumulated but not yet paid because one had not yet reached pay-day; and (2) wages withheld even on pay-day: Kealey, *Toronto Workers,* 199. See also Craven, 'Master and Servant,' 202, where a magistrate during the 1870s upheld a Galt textile worker's forfeiture of wages held back, when the worker quit before the end of the notice period. See also the holdback in the draft subcontract to a carpenter in Rordans, *The Canadian Conveyancer,* 1st ed. (1859), 104, repeated in the 2d ed. (1867), 168–70, Whitley, *Canadian Domestic Lawyer,* 5th ed. (1865), 45–7, and Whitley, *Ontario Cabinet Lawyer,* 39–41.

93 Craven and Traves, 'Dimensions of Paternalism,' 52–3; Levine, 'Conflict and Consensus,' 10.

94 Radforth, this volume; Kealey, *Toronto Workers,* 66.

95 Construction contracts might, for example, provide for independent assessment of the work before payment: Whitley, *Ontario Cabinet Lawyer,* 23–9; Rordans, *Canadian Conveyancer,* 1st ed. (1859), 99–103; 3d ed. (1879), 170–2. There is an exam-

ple of a similar arrangement for land clearing: Radcliff, *Authentic Letters*, 92. The employment contract of a schoolteacher at York in 1805 provided for arbitration in case of disagreement: Firth, *York, 1793–1815*, 198–200. Actions started before the courts might also be referred to arbitrators for settlement; see, for example, *Briggs v. Spilsbury* (1827), Taylor 440.

96 Keele, *Provincial Justice*, 1st ed. (1835), 40; Craven, 'Master and Servant,' 195. For vulnerability of farmers to local terror, see the comments of Lewis Thomas Drummond regarding railway navvies, quoted in Matthews, 'Large Propertied Interests,' 201–2; and Moodie, *Roughing It*, 183, in which a dispute with a neighbour over the theft of a bull resulted in the neighbour's covertly driving six of the Moodies' hogs into the lake, leaving the family short of meat for the winter.

97 Wylie, 'Poverty, Distress, and Disease,' 25–8; Bleasdale, 'Class Conflict on the Canals,' 19ff.; Elliott, *Irish Migrants*, 146, 188, 252–3; Kealey, *Toronto Workers*, 115ff.

98 The Upper Canadian law of master and servant deserves more complete reconstruction than is possible here. The task is rendered difficult by the lack of detailed magistrates' records and the variation presumably existing in magistrates' practice. An ideal source would be diaries recording the exercise of magisterial functions; one hopes that such documents will eventually come to light.

The Upper Canadian law was, as we will see, ultimately founded on English models. These inspired legislation throughout Britain and its colonies, legislation that often displayed fascinating variations in objective, form, and application. Doug Hay, Paul Craven, and a set of collaborators in other countries are currently engaged in an ambitious study of this legislation, combining detailed local studies (including studies of Canadian jurisdictions) with an overview of the process of statutory diffusion. For an introduction, see Douglas Hay and Paul Craven, 'Master and Servant in England and the Empire: A Comparative Study,' *Labour/Le Travail* 31 (1993), 175–84.

Upper Canadian master and servant law differed considerably from that of the United States. According to Tomlins, the thirteen colonies generally did not embrace the English labour statutes so influential in Upper Canada and tended to reject the use of criminal sanctions to punish absconding workers, except those labouring under indenture or in slavery. The U.S. law's early development was therefore dominated by a stark distinction between bound and free labour, the individual relations of the latter being subject to civil but not criminal penalties. See Tomlins, *Law, Labor, and Ideology*, 239–58.

99 Napier, 'Contract of Service,' 45–101.

100 An Act ... to introduce the English Law, as the Rule of Decision in all matters of Controversy, relative to Property and Civil Rights, S.U.C. 1792, c. 1, s. 3. The English criminal law had been in force in the old province of Quebec before that province was divided into Upper and Lower Canada, although An Act for the fur-

ther introduction of the Criminal Law of England ... , S.U.C. 1800, c. 1, s. 1, altered the criminal law reception date to 17 September 1792.

101 Craven, 'Master and Servant,' 182–5; *Whelan* v. *Stevens* (1827), Taylor 439. See also the Lower Canadian decisions cited by Winks, *Blacks in Canada*, 100. Contrast the situation in the United States: Tomlins, *Law, Labor, and Ideology*, 240, 248–51, 254–8.

102 For the principles and practice of reception, see Elizabeth Gaspar Brown, 'British Statutes in the Emergent Nations of North America: 1606–1949,' *American Journal of Legal History* 7 (1963), 95–136; J.E. Cote, 'The Reception of English Law,' *Alberta Law Review* 15 (1977), 29–92; Hibbitts, 'Progress and Principle,' 465–73. Upper Canadian courts repeatedly rejected arguments that the legislation that had introduced English law into the colony (apparently in general terms) had introduced all English statutes, concluding instead, 'The intention and meaning of the legislature undoubtedly was that resort should be had to such of the laws of England as are applicable to the state of society in a British colony, which is very different in many respects from the state of society in England': *Dillingham* v. *Wilson* (1841), 6 U.C.Q.B. (O.S.) 85 at 86; 'Law Reform,' *Upper Canada Jurist* 1 (1844), 18–24.

103 For examples, see above, note 101.

104 *Fish* v. *Doyle* (1831), Draper 328; Keele, *Provincial Justice*, 2d ed. (1843), 24n; *Dillingham* v. *Wilson* (1841), 6 U.C.Q.B. (O.S.) 85; *Shea* v. *Choat* (1846), 2 U.C.Q.B. 211. See also Craven, 'Master and Servant,' 185–7. Tucker suggests that in *Shea*, Robinson C.J. left open the possibility of the piecemeal reception of the Statute of Elizabeth (Tucker, 'Indefinite Area of Toleration,' 23), but a careful reading of Robinson's reasons, in the light of the argument of counsel, makes clear that he rejected it.

105 Burn, *Justice of the Peace*. For its use before the publication of Keele's first edition, see Neatby, *Quebec*, 50–1; Keele's preface to his 1843 edition, quoted in Craven, 'Master and Servant,' 184. See also McLean, J.'s use of it in *Mitchell* v. *Defries* (1845), 2 U.C.Q.B. 430 at 431.

106 Keele, *Provincial Justice*, 2d ed. (1843), 24 n.

107 (1846), 2 U.C.Q.B. 211 at 220. Craven, 'Master and Servant,' 183, reports an 1839 case in which a magistrate convicted on the basis of an English labour statute.

108 Keele, *Provincial Justice*, 1st ed. (1835), 124; 5th ed. (1864), 835–6. The reliance on provisions known to be obsolete was also typical of English manuals: Napier, 'Contract of Service,' 72.

109 See, for example, Craven, 'Master and Servant,' 200–4; Keele's description of the tasks of the magistrate when deciding apprentice-master cases, *Provincial Justice*, 1st ed. (1835), 20–1. Blackstone suggested that the English courts exercised considerable tolerance for magistrates' errors, but not of 'any malicious or tyrannical abuse of their office': *Commentaries*, Book the First, 354.

110 An Act to regulate the duties between Master and Servant, and for other purposes therein mentioned, S. Prov. Can. 1847, c. 23; S. Prov. Can. 1851, c. 11.

111 Keele, *Provincial Justice*, 3d ed. (1851), 469–70; Richmond, *Richmond's Legal Forms*, 2d ed. (1854), 488–95.

112 When dealing with the master and servant law before 1847, I will ignore the distinction between matters over which a single magistrate had jurisdiction, and those for which two were necessary. In theory, the distinction turned on the specific statute under which the magistrate was acting. For reasons given above (note 12), I doubt that the distinction was rigorously followed in practice. In any case, S. Prov. Can. 1847, c. 23 eliminated the problem, conferring powers on a single magistrate.

113 Napier, 'Contract of Service,' 121–2; Craven, 'Master and Servant,' 176, 188.

114 An Act for the better adjusting and more easy Recovery of the Wages of certain Servants, 20 Geo. 2 (1747) c. 19, s. 1; Keele, *Provincial Justice*, 1st ed. (1835), 408–9. See also the complex terms of the Statute of Elizabeth, 5 Eliz. (1562) c. 4, and An Act for the better regulating Apprentices, and Persons working under Contract, 6 Geo. 3 (1766) c. 25.

115 Napier, 'Contract of Service,' 100–1. In England, there was some variation in coverage because of the terms of different statutes. This probably had little effect in Canada, given the magistrates' complete reliance on manuals that summarized only the most broadly applicable statutes.

116 S. Prov. Can. 1847, c. 23; An Act to amend the Act to regulate the duties between Master and Servant in Upper Canada, S. Prov. Can. 1855, c. 136.

117 Craven, 'Master and Servant,' 189.

118 (1806), 8 East 113; Napier, 'Contract of Service,' 86–7.

119 Napier, 'Contract of Service,' 111.

120 *Ex parte Gordon* (1856), 34 L.J.M.C. 12; Napier, 'Contract of Service,' 114–15. See also Wightman, J.'s reasons in *In re Bailey* (1854), 3 E&B 607, discussed in Napier at 113–14, in which a collier who was paid by the ton and hired his own helpers was held to fall within the statute.

121 *Whelan* v. *Stevens* (1827), Taylor 439. *Lowther* had been cited in argument.

122 *Shea* v. *Choat* (1846), 2 U.C.Q.B. 211 at 221; Craven, 'Master and Servant,' 196.

123 Craven, 'Master and Servant,' 196; Dempsey, *Magistrate's Handbook*, 19 n.(a). See also Whitley, *Canadian Domestic Lawyer*, 5th ed. (1865), 300–1, which emphasized that to have a contract of service the engagement had to be for a particular length of time.

124 Napier, 'Contract of Service,' 100 and 107–8. He also argues, at 117–21, that the later emphasis on exclusiveness may have been descended from feudal notions of allegiance. This may have been true in England, although even there its late emergence, precisely at the time when master and servant was adjusting to a much more atomistic labour market, suggests a very remote relationship, if any. And of course, in Upper Canada the feudal experience was still more remote.

125 For this evolution in England, see Orth, *Combination and Conspiracy*, especially 108–9, 124; Patrick S. Atiyah, *The Rise and Fall of Freedom of Contract* (Oxford: Oxford University Press 1979).

126 Craven, 'Master and Servant,' 187–9. For the concern about lumberworkers quitting, see Radforth's contribution in this volume.

127 Heron, this volume; Kealey, *Toronto Workers*, 67–8. See also above, note 65. Even the terminology seems confused to modern ears. In *Nichols* v. *King* (1848), 5 U.C.Q.B. 324, a party who had contracted to build a highway was referred to as the 'employer' of another person, who contracted to supply wood for culverts at so much per hundred feet. See also Napier, 'Contract of Service,' 113ff., who discusses the law's application to 'butty colliers' (who were paid by the ton and hired their own helpers).

128 Napier, 'Contract of Service,' 45–101.

129 20 Geo. 2 (1747) c. 19, ss. 2 and 4; 6 Geo. 3 (1766) c. 25, ss. 1 and 4; Napier, 'Contract of Service,' 86; Keele, *Provincial Justice*, 1st ed. (1835), 20–3, 408–11. The magistrates could also discharge the servant or reduce the servant's wages.

130 S. Prov. Can. 1847, c. 23, ss. 2 and 5; S. Prov. Can. 1851, c. 11, s. 7; Keele, *Provincial Justice*, 5th ed. (1864), 39–44. The penalties under the 1847 act only applied if the work had actually been started; they were extended to executory contracts in 1855: S. Prov. Can. 1855, c. 136, s. 2.

131 *Shea* v. *Choat* (1846), 2 U.C.Q.B. 211 at 214; Craven, 'Master and Servant'; Radforth, this volume; Reid, *Upper Ottawa*, 76–7; Crowley, this volume; Kealey, *Toronto Workers*, especially at 149.

132 Craven, 'Master and Servant'; Napier, 'Contract of Service,' 86, 99; S. Prov. Can. 1847, c. 23, s. 8; Keele, *Provincial Justice*, 3d ed. (1851), 469–70; and, regarding apprentices: Blackstone, *Commentaries*, Book the First, 426–8; Keele, *Provincial Justice*, 1st ed. (1835), 20–4; 5th ed. (1864), 39–44; S. Prov. Can. 1851, c. 11, s. 7. I have not been able to determine when it became accepted that an employee could put an end to his own contract, although the requirement that he serve out his time would certainly have been undermined by the short duration of many contracts and by the abolition of criminal penalties in 1877 (given that specific performance of employment contracts was unavailable in the civil courts). The extent to which employers insisted that their employees return to them after being released from jail is also unclear. Craven's report of proceedings in the Galt Police Court, 1866–77, suggests that jail and returning to work were treated as alternatives: Craven, 'Master and Servant,' 203. See also the returns of convictions in *[Barrie] Northern Advance*, 19 December 1861, 3, 6 July 1864, 3, and 21 December 1864, 3. In 1866, however, an Ottawa apprentice clearly was fined *and* ordered to return to work: *Ottawa Citizen*, 21 December 1866, 2.

133 In his first edition, for example, Keele says that an absconding servant 'runs the risk' of losing all his wages, and that one fired for misconduct can only collect wages then due: Keele, *Provincial Justice*, 1st ed. (1835), 408. See also Napier, 'Contract of Service,' 49–51; and W.A. Langton, ed., *Early Days in Upper Canada: Letters of John Langton from the Backwoods of Upper Canada and the Audit Office of the Province of Canada* (Toronto: Macmillan 1926), 82–4, where an employer in

the Peterborough area during the 1830s notes that if he can establish that his servant stole from him, 'I need not pay him his wages beyond today.' The master established the theft, and did pay off the worker when dismissing him. See also the debate over the issue in the Ottawa courts in 1854: *Ottawa Citizen*, 17 June 1854, 2 and 1 July 1854, 2. As late as 1862, one magistrate was uncertain whether an absconding servant could claim his wages: Craven, 'Master and Servant,' 198–9.

134 Napier, 'Contract of Service,' 51–2, 83n151; *Blake* v. *Shaw* (1852), 10 U.C.Q.B. 180 (at the trial the jury had attempted to compromise the claim, awarding part of the sum sued for); *Ottawa Citizen*, 15 November 1861, 2; Browne and Chadwick, *Examination Questions*, 61; Kingsford, *Commentaries*, 341. For a similar evolution in the United States, see Tomlins, *Law, Labor, and Ideology*, 273–8.

135 Whitley, *Canadian Domestic Lawyer*, 5th ed. (1865), 302–3; Keele, *Provincial Justice*, 1st ed. (1835), 408; Kingsford, *Commentaries*, 339; Napier, 'Contract of Service,' 83 n. 151. Napier notes (at 84–5 and 99) that immediately before the period, masters had to go before the magistrates to discharge ordinary servants (at least those on yearly hirings in husbandry) as well as apprentices; see, to this effect, 5 Eliz. (1562) c. 4, s. 5. *Spain* v. *Arnott* (1817), 2 Stark. 256 established the employer's ability to dismiss without the intervention of a magistrate.

136 Blackstone, *Commentaries*, Book the First, 426; Keele, *Provincial Justice*, 1st ed. (1835), 20–4; S. Prov. Can. 1851, c. 11, s. 11. One wonders whether this may have contributed to formal apprenticeships falling out of favour late in the century. Employers may have resisted making such a strong commitment to an apprentice, especially given the latters' propensity to abscond.

137 QUA, Tett Papers, Series A, Time Books, vol. 50; Arthur, *Thunder Bay*, 162–3; 'To Journeymen Printers and the Public Generally,' *Mackenzie's Weekly Message*, 30 June 1853, 3 (printers complaining of George Brown's practice of sending printers off for half or quarter days, at their own loss, when work was insufficient). See also the annotation on the inside cover of a Tett time book from the 1880s (mainly of barge records): 'In marking time enter it as it occurs, no time to be given for lost time, and no exceptions made - ' (QUA, Tett Papers, Series A, Time Books, vol. 52). More work needs to be done to determine in what circumstances, and in what employments, deductions were made.

138 Napier, 'Contract of Service,' 85; Keele, *Provincial Justice*, 1st ed. (1835), 408; Browne and Chadwick, *Examination Questions*, 61.

139 Blackstone, *Commentaries*, Book the First, 425–6; Napier, 'Contract of Service,' 84. Domestic service was the one exception; there, dismissal could occur on one month's notice, even if the hiring was yearly: Napier, 'Contract of Service,' 83; Browne and Chadwick, *Examination Questions*, 61; Whitley, *Canadian Domestic Lawyer*, 5th ed. (1865), 302.

140 5 Eliz. (1562) c. 4, s. 3; Blackstone, *Commentaries*, Book the First, 425–6; Napier, 'Contract of Service,' 56–60, 72.

141 *Raines* v. *The Credit Harbour Company* (1844), 1 U.C.Q.B. 174. See also Craven,

'Master and Servant,' 179–80. For contemporary lists of criteria see Browne and Chadwick, *Examination Questions*, 61; Whitley, *Canadian Domestic Lawyer*, 5th ed. (1865), 302; Kingsford, *Commentaries*, 338. Given the criteria applied, it is highly doubtful that the presumption of yearly hirings had any real effect in Upper Canada. For the one-year maximum for oral contracts, see S. Prov. Can. 1847, c. 23, s. 1; Keele, *Provincial Justice*, 3d ed. (1851), 469.

142 During the nineteenth century there was a marked tendency towards shorter contracts in Britain as well. Napier attributes this preference for 'minute contracts' (usually, he suggests, daily contracts) partially to the desire to avoid the effect of master and servant legislation: Napier, 'Contract of Service,' 124–5.

143 S. Prov. Can. 1847, c. 23, s. 2; S. Prov. Can. 1851, c. 11, s. 5. Whitley, *Canadian Domestic Lawyer*, 5th ed. (1865), 302, noted that the obligation to obey did not include 'unjust and unreasonable commands' nor work 'not fairly coming within the scope of his employment,' although nineteenth-century employees doubtless had as much difficulty insisting that these limitations be observed as employees do today.

144 Napier, 'Contract of Service,' 98–9; Blackstone, *Commentaries*, Book the First, 428; Book the Third, 120; Burn, *Justice*, vol. 5, 121. Note the explicit parallel drawn in Blackstone, *Commentaries*, Book the First, 444: a husband is able to chastise his wife 'in the same moderation that a man is allowed to correct his apprentices or children; for whom the master or parent is also liable in some cases to answer.'

145 Keele, *Provincial Justice*, 1st ed. (1835), 20; Neatby, *Quebec*, 235; Moodie, *Roughing It*, 74.

146 Keele, *Provincial Justice*, 1st ed. (1835), 47, 408–11.

147 *Mitchell v. Defries* (1845), 2 U.C.Q.B. 430.

148 20 Geo. 2 (1747) c. 19, s. 2; 6 Geo. 3 (1766) c. 25, s. 4; Napier, 'Contract of Service,' 86–7; Keele, *Provincial Justice*, 1st ed., 21–4, 408–9; S. Prov. Can. 1847, c. 23, s. 2; S. Prov. Can. 1851, c. 11, s. 6.

149 Craven, 'Master and Servant,' 203–4; Reid, *Upper Ottawa*, 174. See also Radforth, this volume.

150 See, for example, White, *Lord Selkirk's Diary*, 180: 'Amns. [Americans] if found fault with are ready to go off, being scarce & knowing their own importance.' See also Traill, *Canadian Settler's Guide*, 6.

151 Blackstone, *Commentaries*, Book the First, 428; Book the Fourth, 16, 75, 203–4; Keele, *Provincial Justice*, 1st ed. (1835), 20, 47, 297, 300, 459; 2d ed. (1843), 244–5; Dempsey, *Magistrate's Handbook*, 20–3; Napier, 'Contract of Service,' 61.

152 Keele, *Provincial Justice*, 2d ed. (1843), 54–5, 439–40, 444; 3d ed. (1851), 291–2; 5th ed. (1864), 734. For an unsuccessful prosecution for machine breaking, see *Ottawa Citizen*, 22 November 1861, 2. For an instance of machine breaking in 1870s Toronto, see Kealey, *Toronto Workers*, 46–7 (those responsible were never apprehended).

153 Blackstone, *Commentaries*, Book the First, 428, especially note 8; Radforth, this

volume; Reid, *Upper Ottawa*, 76–7; Moodie, *Roughing It*, 73–5. The Moodies knew the master.

154 See, for example, 'Return of Convictions,' *Ottawa Citizen*, 20 May 1854, 3 and 'Schedule of Returns of Convictions,' *[Barrie] Northern Advance*, 28 March 1866, 3.

155 Blackstone, *Commentaries*, Book the First, 428; Napier, 'Contract of Service,' 86; Keele, *Provincial Justice*, 1st ed. (1835), 20–1; S. Prov. Can. 1847, c. 23, s. 8; S. Prov. Can. 1851, c. 11, s. 6.

156 Keele, *Provincial Justice*, 1st ed. (1835), 47; Blackstone, *Commentaries*, Book the Fourth, 182, 197n5; Constance Backhouse, *Petticoats and Prejudice: Women and Law in Nineteenth-Century Canada* (Toronto: Osgoode Society 1991), 40–111, especially 58–69; Constance Backhouse, 'The Tort of Seduction: Fathers and Daughters in Nineteenth-Century Canada,' *Dalhousie Law Journal* 10, no. 1, (1986), 45–80; Martha J. Bailey, 'Servant Girls and Upper Canada's *Seduction Act*: 1837–1946,' in R. Smandych, G. Dodds, and A. Esau, eds, *Dimensions of Childhood: Essays on the History of Children and Youth in Canada* (Winnipeg: Legal Research Institute, University of Manitoba 1991), 159–82; Constance Backhouse, 'Nineteenth-Century Canadian Rape Law 1800–92,' in Flaherty, ed., *Essays in the History of Canadian Law*, vol. 2, 200; An Act further to amend the Criminal Law, S.C. 1890, c. 37, s. 4. In 1790 in Montreal, a runaway apprentice was beaten by the master and other workmen until he lost consciousness. The master was fined 10 livres at Quarter Sessions: Neatby, *Quebec*, 235.

157 On the shortage of specie, see Douglas McCalla, 'Rural Credit and Rural Development in Upper Canada, 1790–1850,' in Hall, Westfall, MacDowell, eds, *Patterns of the Past*, 37–54. For difficulty obtaining wages on the canals, see Wylie, 'Poverty, Distress, and Disease,' 15; Bleasdale, 'Class Conflict on the Canals,' 16.

158 Russell, 'Wage Labour Rates,' 68; McCalla, 'Rural Credit'; Douglas McCalla, *Planting the Province: The Economic History of Upper Canada 1784–1870* (Toronto: Ontario Historical Studies Series 1993), 144–7; Radcliff, *Authentic Letters*, 186–7; *Wallen v. Mapes* (1837), 5 U.C.Q.B. (O.S.) 96; *Burnside v. Wilcox* (1838), 5 U.C.Q.B. (O.S.) 328; *Hamilton v. McDonell* (1840), 5 U.C.Q.B. (O.S.) 720; Simcoe County Pioneer and Historical Society, ed., *Pioneer Papers – 1* (Barrie: Simcoe County Pioneer and Historical Society 1908), 29; Langton, *Early Days in Upper Canada*, 19; Galt, *The Canadas*, Appendix, xlii; White, *Lord Selkirk's Diary*, 195–6; Bleasdale, 'Class Conflict on the Canals,' 16–17; Edwin C. Guillet, ed., *The Valley of the Trent* (Toronto: Champlain Society 1957), 279n2; An Act to amend and consolidate the several Acts now in force, regulating the Practice of Division Courts in Upper Canada ... , S. Prov. Can. 1850, c. 53, s. 23; Keele, *Provincial Justice*, 3d ed. (1851), 255; Whitley, *Canadian Domestic Lawyer*, 5th ed. (1865), 197. Compare, however, the 1833 demand of a union of carpenters and joiners for regular part payments in cash; 'a master builder' responded, 'How is it possible that five dollars per week, can be collected every Saturday night, for 20 or 30 men, when money is scarce? and consequently long credit is expected': Firth, *York, 1815–1834*, 77–9.

For the English truck acts, see George W. Hilton, *The Truck System, including a History of the British Truck Acts, 1465–1960* (Cambridge: W. Heffer 1960); Napier, 'Contract of Service,' 73, 115–17; Orth, *Combination and Conspiracy*, 12ff. Room and board, share cropping and bees can also be seen as forms of payment in kind.

159 *Murphy* v. *Bunt* (1845), 2 U.C.Q.B. 284; Backhouse, 'Married Women's Property Law,' especially 236–8. The rigour of this rule was moderated by (1) allowing the wife in some circumstances to sue in her husband's name; and (2) the fact that it only applied to those legally married at a time when, especially among the lower classes, *de facto* unions were common (*Murphy* fell into this category).

160 Napier, 'Contract of Service,' 81–2, 109–10; Keele, *Provincial Justice*, 1st ed. (1835), 408–9; 3d ed. (1851), 469–70; S. Prov. Can. 1847, c. 23, s. 8.

161 See the table in Kealey, *Toronto Workers*, 149; Craven, 'Master and Servant,' 201; Kingsford, *Commentaries*, 341.

162 Dempsey, *Magistrate's Handbook*, 19n(a); McCallum, 'Mechanics' Liens'; The Insolvent Act of 1864, S. Prov. Can. 1864, c. 17, s. 10; Whitley, *Ontario Cabinet Lawyer*, 233.

163 *McDonell* v. *Cook* (1845), 1 U.C.Q.B. 542. For the difficulty establishing liens in other cases, see *Johnson* v. *Crew* (1837), 5 U.C.Q.B. (O.S.) 200; *Milburn* v. *Milburn* (1847), 4 U.C.Q.B. 179; *Land* v. *Malden* (1848), 5 U.C.Q.B. 309. Compare James Willard Hurst, *Law and Economic Growth: The Legal History of the Lumber Industry in Wisconsin 1836–1915* (Cambridge, Mass.: Belknap 1964), 391–409.

164 Bernard Ostry, 'Conservatives, Liberals, and Labour in the 1870's,' *Canadian Historical Review* 41 (1960), 93–127; John Battye, 'The Nine Hour Pioneers: The Genesis of the Canadian Labour Movement,' *Labour/Le Travailleur* 4 (1979), 25–56; Bryan D. Palmer, *A Culture in Conflict: Skilled Workers and Industrial Capitalism in Hamilton, Ontario, 1860–1914* (Montreal: McGill-Queen's University Press 1979), 131–52; Kealey, *Toronto Workers*, 124–53; Eugene Forsey, *Trade Unions in Canada 1812–1902* (Toronto: University of Toronto Press 1982), 95–102; Craven, this volume.

165 5 Eliz. (1562) c. 4, s. 12; Blackstone, *Commentaries*, Book the First, 426–7; Napier, 'Contract of Service,' 118–19. See the other English acts noted by Orth, *Combination and Conspiracy*, 8, 9, 20. Keele, *Provincial Justice*, does not mention any of these.

166 Heron, this volume; Crowley, this volume; Bleasdale, 'Class Conflict on the Canals,' 15. Wylie, 'Poverty, Distress, and Disease,' 18, notes fourteen- to sixteen-hour days in summer for labourers on the Rideau Canal in the 1820s.

167 See, for examples, Craven, 'Master and Servant,' 202. The decision in *Hall* v. *McQueen* was probably typical. There, an employee on a yearly contract in a carriage factory quit early, claiming 'he did not consider that he had received such instructions as were guaranteed by the contract.' The magistrates accepted the foreman's evidence that the employee 'had been used as well in all respects as other hands hired in the same way' and ordered 'that defendant pay costs and continue his

work as usual': *The Markham Economist*, 25 September 1856 (my thanks to Suzanne Knight for this reference). There are occasional references to usual hours of work in some employments. See, for example, the report of the meeting of the Society for the Relief of Strangers in Distress, 4 April 1820: Firth, *York, 1815–1834*, 225.

168 Blackstone, *Commentaries*, Book the Fourth, 63; Keele, *Provincial Justice*, 1st ed. (1835), 307–10; 3d ed. (1851), 456; An Act to prevent the Profanation of the Lord's Day, commonly called Sunday, in Upper Canada, S. Prov. Can. 1845, c. 45.

169 Kostal, 'Legal Justice, Social Justice'; Risk, 'This Nuisance of Litigation'; Tucker, 'Law of Employers' Liability'; Tucker, *Administering Danger*, 38–75.

170 Whitley, *Canadian Domestic Lawyer*, 5th ed. (1865), 303, is the only Canadian legal manual I have found that clearly states an obligation to provide in sickness, and it is limited to household servants.

171 See, for example, Survey of Colchester and Gosfield Townships, Journal of Thomas Smith, 28 April, 4 May 1805, and 21 April 1806, in OA, Lands and Forests Survey Records, Book of Suveyors' Diaries, 1794–1810. The last entry is the contract used with surveying labourers, and provides for an extra two days' pay and rations for employees discharged 'from sickness or other causes ... to carry them to their House.'

172 Craven, 'Master and Servant,' 202. Sick days were also unpaid in the lumber rafting and other activities conducted by Benjamin Tett in the 1840s, presumably (if it followed the custom of the trade) on hirings of at least a month in duration: QUA, Tett Papers, Series A, Time Books, vol. 50.

173 Radforth, this volume; Craven, this volume; Bleasdale, 'Class Conflict on the Canals,' 21. See also Wylie, 'Poverty, Distress, and Disease,' 23–5; Kostal, 'Legal Justice, Social Justice,' 4 and 9.

174 For public relief, see Stephen A. Speisman, 'Munificent Parsons and Municipal Parsimony: Voluntary *vs* Public Poor Relief in Nineteenth Century Toronto,' *Ontario History* 65 (1973), 33–49; Murray, 'Cold Hand of Charity'; Matthews, 'Large Propertied Interests,' 213–31. For mutual benefit societies, Neatby, *Quebec*, 235; Matthews, 'Large Propertied Interests,' 82–4; Craven, this volume; Kealey, *Toronto Workers*, 104, 112–13; Arthur, *Thunder Bay*, 153–5.

175 Keele, *Provincial Justice*, 1st ed. (1835), 24; Whitley, *Canadian Domestic Lawyer*, 5th ed. (1865), 303. A stipulation to that effect was a common feature of apprenticeship indentures, although two from the same employer in the 1860s appear to limit the employer's responsibility: Alexander Craik, 20 October 1865 (carriage and wagon wood worker); Charles Francis, 18 March 1869 (wood worker in wagon and carriage building).

176 Rordans, *Canadian Conveyancer*, 2d ed. (1867), 137–8; Alexander Craik, 20 October 1865 (carriage and wagon wood worker).

177 Blackstone, *Commentaries*, Book the Third, 142; Keele, *Provincial Justice*, 1st ed. (1835), 20; Kingsford, *Commentaries*, 342; Gareth H. Jones, 'Per Quod Servitium

Amisit,' *Law Quarterly Review* 74 (1958), 39–58 (*Dillingham* v. *Wilson* (1841), 6 U.C.Q.B. (O.S.) 85 was an action of this kind); S. Prov. Can. 1851, c. 11, s. 8.

178 Survey of Colchester and Gosfield Townships, Journal of Thomas Smith, 28 April 1806, in OA, Lands and Forests Survey Records, Book of Suveyors' Diaries, 1794–1810. For examples of advertisements, see Firth, *York, 1793–1815*, 141–2; Fleming, 'William Lyon Mackenzie: Part Two,' 5; Reid, *Upper Ottawa*, 150, 172; Radforth, this volume.

179 An Act for preventing Tumults and riotous Assemblies, 1 Geo. 1, st. 2 (1714) c. 5; Blackstone, *Commentaries*, Book the Fourth, 142–7; Keele, *Provincial Justice*, 1st ed. (1835), 90, 221, 393–5; Browne and Chadwick, *Examination Questions*, 172.

180 An Act to amend the Laws relative to the appointment of Special Constables ... , S. Prov. Can. 1847, c. 12; Keele, *Provincial Justice*, 3d ed. (1851), 185–7; Dempsey, *Magistrate's Handbook*, 41; Matthews, 'Large Propertied Interests,' 196–201. In the 1876–7 Grand Trunk Railway strike, for example, 200 special constables were sworn in at Stratford alone: Desmond Morton, 'Taking on the Grand Trunk: The Locomotive Engineers Strike of 1876–7,' *Labour/Le Travailleur* 2 (1977), 26.

181 Burn, *Justice*, vol. 3, 467; An Act to regulate the Militia of this Province ... , S. Prov. Can. 1855, c. 77, ss. 38–9; An Act respecting the Militia and Defence of the Dominion of Canada, S.C. 1868, c. 40, s. 27; Desmond Morton, 'Aid to the Civil Power: The Canadian Militia in Support of Social Order, 1867–1914,' in Michiel Horn and Ronald Sabourin, eds, *Studies in Canadian Social History* (Toronto: McClelland & Stewart 1974), 417–34; Pariseau, 'Forces armées'; Morton, 'Taking on the Grand Trunk,' 17ff.

182 Keele, *Provincial Justice*, 5th ed. (1864), 725; Pariseau, 'Forces armées,' 33–8. Quotation from regulation on the suppression of riots from *The Queen's Regulations and Orders for the Army, 1857* (London: Eyre and Spottiswoode 1857), s. 9, reproduced in Pariseau, 'Forces armées,' Appendix E-16 (emphasis in the original). For an example of the commander's de facto authority, see Pariseau, 'Forces armées,' APC 36. For a good example of how bayonets were used, see Morton, 'Taking on the Grand Trunk,' 19–26.

183 Morton, 'Aid to the Civil Power'; Pariseau, 'Forces armées,' 17–18; Kealey, *Toronto Workers*, 115ff.

184 Pariseau, 'Forces armées,' APC 30; Radforth, this volume; Reid, *Upper Ottawa*, 53–6, 61–2; Matthews, 'Large Propertied Interests,' 201–2.

185 For discussions of unrest among navvies and the response by the state, see Wylie, 'Poverty, Distress, and Disease,' 25–9 (for the Rideau, as a military project, authorities simply used the troops on site to maintain order); Bleasdale, 'Class Conflict on the Canals'; Matthews, 'Large Propertied Interests,' 41–4, 201–3; Weaver, 'Crime, Public Order, and Repression,' 188. See also Pariseau, 'Forces armées,' APC 52 (laid-off Italian and Irish railway construction workers riot in 1884 near Napanee); APC 54 (in December 1884, Italian immigrant labourers, who had not been paid for two months and were now facing the onset of winter, riot; the matter is resolved in

part when the townspeople collect money to aid the most needy); An Act for ... the prevention of Riots and violent Outrages at and near Public Works while in progress of construction, S. Prov. Can. 1845, c. 6; An Act to prohibit the sale of Intoxicating Liquors on or near the line of Public Works in this Province, S. Prov. Can. 1853, c. 164.

186 Pariseau, 'Forces armées,' especially at 17–18 and 158–60.

187 Blackstone, *Commentaries*, Book the First, 425. Kingsford's discussion of master and servant alongside husband and wife and parent and child (copying Blackstone) was therefore highly anachronistic: Kingsford, *Commentaries*.

188 For exaggeration of the extent of paternalism, see Bryan Palmer, *Working-Class Experience: The Rise and Reconstitution of Canadian Labour, 1800-1980* (Toronto: Butterworths 1983), 12–20. Pentland also stresses the prevalence of paternalistic relations, although he is somewhat more cautious about its existence in Upper Canada. Much of his discussion concerns Lower Canada (where the seigneurial system created a very different context) and the Maritimes (where English settlement dated from an earlier era). His Upper Canadian examples are drawn chiefly from the first years of the century, many falling within the brief transitional period identified at the beginning of this essay. See Pentland, *Labour and Capital*, 24–60; and for a useful corrective, Russell, 'Wage Labour Rates,' 67 and 79. The common assumption that mid-century developments took place against the backdrop, in Upper Canada, of 'paternal' or 'personal' master-servant relations therefore needs to be qualified. See, for example, Tucker, 'Indefinite Area of Toleration,' 30–1 and 37.

189 For employment relations in nineteenth-century English agriculture, see Thompson, *Making*, 235–6. For Calvin, see D.D. Calvin, *A Saga of the St Lawrence: Timber and Shipping through Three Generations* (Toronto: Ryerson 1945); Palmer, *Working Class Experience*, 15–18. For the reinvention of paternalism, see Craven and Traves, 'Dimensions of Paternalism'; Craven, this volume.

190 Matthews, 'Large Propertied Interests'; Weaver, 'Crime, Public Order, and Repression'; H. Boritch, 'Conflict, Compromise and Administrative Convenience: The Police Organization in Nineteenth-Century Toronto,' *Canadian Journal of Law and Society* 3 (1988), 141–74; Craven, 'Law and Ideology.'

191 Nicholas Rogers, 'Serving Toronto the Good: The Development of the City Police Force 1834–84,' in Victor L. Russell, ed., *Forging a Consensus: Historical Essays on Toronto* (Toronto: University of Toronto Press 1984), 116–40; Matthews, 'Large Propertied Interests,' 180–213; Weaver, 'Crime, Public Order, and Repression'; Boritch, 'Conflict, Compromise'; Craven, 'Law and Ideology.'

192 Morton, 'Taking on the Grand Trunk,' passim; Kealey, *Toronto Workers*, 198ff.; Pariseau, 'Forces armées,' APC 68; Homel, 'Denison's Law,' 176.

193 For cases that are suggestive along these lines, see above, note 167. See also Napier, 'Contract of Service,' 66–9, 96–7; Tomlins, *Law, Labor, and Ideology*, 284–90. Fines for defective work had also existed outside of industrial employment. See, for example, Survey of Colchester and Gosfield Townships, Journal of Thomas Smith,

21 April 1806, in OA, Lands and Forests Survey Records, Book of Suveyors' Diaries, 1794–1810.

194 Craven and Traves, 'Dimensions of Paternalism,' 49–52; Craven, 'Meaning of Misadventure.'

195 Michael Bliss, *A Living Profit: Studies in the Social History of Canadian Business, 1883–1911* (Toronto: McClelland & Stewart 1974); Code, 'Salt Men of Goderich.'

196 Kealey, *Toronto Workers*, 149–50; 'To Journeymen Printers and the Public Generally,' *Mackenzie's Weekly Message*, 30 June 1853, 3. In addition to the master and servant legislation, the special provisions applicable to railway employees were invoked during strikes. See Tucker, 'Indefinite Area of Toleration,' 47–8.

197 For the fining of apprentices for desertion in a strike, Kealey, *Toronto Workers*, 70. For the use of apprentices to maintain production, Fleming, 'William Lyon Mackenzie: Part Two,' 5.

198 Kealey, *Toronto Workers*, 70 (discussing an 1867 strike in which moulders were recruited on yearly contracts, without knowing of the strike); Craven, 'Workers' Conspiracies,' 66; Tucker, 'Indefinite Area of Toleration,' 34n71.

199 Bleasdale, 'Class Conflict on the Canals,' 34–5, 44; Kealey, *Toronto Workers*, 198, 202–5; Boritch, 'Conflict, Compromise,' 158–60; Pariseau, 'Forces armées,' APC 68; Matthews, 'Large Propertied Interests,' 201; Weaver, 'Crime, Public Order, and Repression,' 188; Morton, 'Taking on the Grand Trunk,' passim (during the 1876–7 Grand Trunk strike, Stratford's special constables were railway employees). Employers sometimes supported the cost of the militia as well: Morton, 'Aid to the Civil Power,' 419.

200 One early Upper Canadian statutory crime directed specifically at labour disputes was S. Prov. Can. 1841, c. 27, ss. 35–6, probably copied (without much domestic impulsion) from an English model. See Tucker, 'Indefinite Area of Toleration,' 35n73. The use of the criminal law during strikes was only a small part of that law's application. One should guard against interpreting criminal law generally on the basis of its exceptional application to master-servant confrontations. See the important caution in Greg Marquis, 'Doing Justice to "British Justice": Law, Ideology and Canadian Historiography,' in Pue and Wright, *Canadian Perspectives on Law and Society*, 50.

201 Craven, 'Workers' Conspiracies,' 56; Tucker, 'Indefinite Area of Toleration,' 48–9; Morton, 'Taking on the Grand Trunk,' 18–9, 29; Levine, 'Conflict and Consensus,' 22–3.

202 See, for example, Tucker, 'Indefinite Area of Toleration,' 19–20, 36–7. On nineteenth-century juries generally, Paul Romney, 'From Constitutionalism to Legalism: Trial by Jury, Responsible Government, and the Rule of Law in the Canadian Political Culture,' *Law and History Review* 7 (1989), 130–41.

203 See the discussions cited in Craven, 'Workers' Conspiracies,' 49 n. 2. Craven himself argues against this.

204 Blackstone, *Commentaries*, Book the Fourth, 137n4. See also Blackstone, *Com-*

mentaries, Book the Fourth, 159–60n8; Keele, *Provincial Justice*, 2d ed. (1843), 54, 124, 488; 5th ed. (1864), 182; Dempsey, *Magistrate's Handbook*, 22n(c); Browne and Chadwick, *Examination Questions*, 177; and the comments recorded in Tucker, 'Indefinite Area of Toleration,' 30.

205 This is made abundantly clear by Orth's detailed account: *Combination and Conspiracy*, passim. See also Craven, 'Workers' Conspiracies,' 60ff.

206 This was true, for example, of the case on which most later commentators relied: *R.* v. *Journeymen-Taylors of Cambridge* (1721), 8 Mod. 10. See also Orth, *Combination and Conspiracy*, 5–60.

207 Craven, 'Workers' Conspiracies'; Tucker, 'Indefinite Area of Toleration,' 19–20, 26–7. The Ottawa case arose out of a strike by stonecutters working on the new Parliament Buildings. The prosecution based its submissions on the illegality of unions in England before recent legislative reform there (although without addressing the influence of statute on that previous law), and claimed strong provincial government support for the prosecution. The magistrate referred the charges for trial in the Recorders' Court. The matter was apparently settled after the men went back to work (*The [Ottawa] Union*, 19 May 1864, 2). Regarding the incidence of strikes, Palmer has identified just under two hundred strikes in Ontario before 1879: Bryan D. Palmer, 'Labour Protest and Organization in Nineteenth-Century Canada, 1820–1890,' *Labour/Le Travail* 20 (1987), 68 and 71.

208 Craven, 'Workers' Conspiracies'; Tucker, 'Indefinite Area of Toleration,' 20.

209 See Tucker, 'Indefinite Area of Toleration'; Craven, 'Workers' Conspiracies.'

210 *Colonial Advocate* (17 October 1833), quoted in Firth, *York, 1815–1834*, 85–6; Fleming, 'William Lyon Mackenzie: Part Two,' 11. For more on Mackenzie's attitudes to unions, see Frederick H. Armstrong, *A City in the Making: Progress, People and Perils in Victorian Toronto* (Toronto: Dundurn Press 1988), 122–34. Contractualism also furnished the rhetoric that the Toronto Typographical Society marshalled against George Brown's hard line in an 1853 dispute: 'poor men thank God ours is the land of *liberty*, and as freemen, *we*, and not Mr. Brown have the right to set a price upon *our labour*. Mr. Brown has two commodities to dispose of in this market, we have but one – his, *politics* and *papers*; ours, *labour*, he is anxious to dispose of ours for us – we have no desire to engage his services' (*Mackenzie's Weekly Message*, 14 July 1853, 3). Marquis has argued forcefully for a reevaluation of the significance of this discourse: Marquis, 'Doing Justice to "British Justice,"' 43–69. Similar appeals to manly independence and contractualism lay at the core of Canadian labourism: Craig Heron, 'Labourism and the Canadian Working Class,' *Labour/Le Travail* 13 (1984), 45–76; Ian McKay, '"By Wisdom, Wile or War": The Provincial Workmen's Association and the Struggle for Working-Class Independence in Nova Scotia, 1879–97,' *Labour/Le Travail* 18 (1986), 13–62.

211 *Colonial Advocate* (17 October 1833), quoted in Firth, *York, 1815–1834*, 85–6; S. Prov. Can. 1847, c. 23, s. 3; Judith Fingard, *Jack in Port: Sailortowns of Eastern Canada* (Toronto: University of Toronto Press 1982), especially 32ff and 194ff. See

Mackenzie's comments on the point at which union action becomes illegitimate, which deal especially with the enforcement of a union monopoly and the refusal to work with non-members: Armstrong, *City in the Making*, 130–1. English judges drew a similar line at mid-century: Orth, *Combination and Conspiracy*, 94, 98.

212 Browne and Chadwick, *Examination Questions*, 177. See also Blackstone, *Commentaries*, Book the Fourth, 159–60n8; Keele, *Provincial Justice*, 1st ed. (1835), 488; Tucker, 'Indefinite Area of Toleration,' 19–20, 29, 38; Craven, 'Workers' Conspiracies,' 56–7, 64.

213 For references to outrages, Craven, 'Workers' Conspiracies,' 57; Tucker, 'Indefinite Area of Toleration,' 27.

214 For a possible example of the former, see the argument by counsel in the 1842 Kingston prosecution, Tucker, 'Indefinite Area of Toleration,' 27. George Brown may be the best example of the latter: J.M.S. Careless, *Brown of the Globe*, vol. 2: *Statesman of Confederation 1860–1880* (Toronto: Macmillan 1963), 289; Kealey, *Toronto Workers*, 131–3. For the persistence of market regulation in Upper Canada, see Matthews, 'Large Propertied Interests,' 132–76; Matthews, 'Regulation of the Public Market.'

215 Tucker, 'Indefinite Area of Toleration,' 37. For a masterful discussion of the law's response to combinations of capital in the 1870s, see Code, 'Salt Men of Goderich.' In the 1880s, combines legislation exempted unions (although the Senate, in a bit of mischief, at one point deleted the exemption): Kealey, *Toronto Workers*, 267–8.

216 The flavour of these discussions can be captured well from Kealey, *Toronto Workers*, passim (see, for example, 48, where Kealey describes the 1871 conviction of a picket captain for calling a strike-breaker a 'scab,' and 148 where, as late as 1876, John A. Macdonald argued that intimidation could include a threat to injure a man's reputation); Homel, 'Denison's Law,' 176 (convictions for calling another a 'scab'); Craven, 'Workers' Conspiracies'; Tucker, 'Indefinite Area of Toleration'; Eric Tucker, 'Through the Prism of the Law: Labour Conflict in Ontario in the 1880s,' unpublished manuscript, 28 November 1991. See also Bliss, *Living Profit*, 79 (according to business journals, picketing and 'impertinent questions' amount to intimidation).

Similar discussions of unlawful means occurred in England and the United States: Orth, *Combination and Conspiracy*, for example at 98, 130–33, 146–7; Tomlins, *Law, Labor, and Ideology*, for example at 143, 168, and 201–12. Tomlins argues that a republican hostility to the mere existence of self-constituted societies was one of the early bases for the conspiracy doctrine in the United States (see 110, 124–6, 130ff.). Doubtless American lawyers adopted a distinctively republican idiom, but one suspects that the substantive grounds of objection were not all that different from those in Upper Canada. It was not the mere fact of association that offended republican principles, but the attempt to regulate the activities of *all* employees, members and non-members. It was that attempt that seemed to represent an arrogation of governmental authority. Objection to the 'existence' of such societies therefore merged with objections to their 'behavior and goals,' blurring the distinction Tomlins wishes to establish (at 110).

217 Ostry, 'Conservatives, Liberals, and Labour'; Kealey, *Toronto Workers*, 128–34; Sally F. Zerker, *The Rise and Fall of the Toronto Typographical Union 1832–1972: A Case Study of Foreign Domination* (Toronto: University of Toronto Press 1982), 78–88; Craven, 'Workers' Conspiracies,' 59–68; Tucker, 'Indefinite Area of Toleration,' 38–41; Chartrand, 'First Canadian Trade Union Legislation.' The summary that follows draws chiefly on Craven and Tucker.

218 The Trade Unions Act, S.C. 1872, c. 30. The drafting of the act suggested that only unions registered under its provisions would benefit, but this limitation was of no practical significance. Despite the fact that registration was ignored, the conspiracy measures were treated as though they applied to all unions.

219 An Act to amend the Criminal Law relating to Violence, Threats and Molestation, S.C. 1872, c. 31 (commonly called the Criminal Law Amendment Act), amended by S.C. 1875, c. 39 and S.C. 1876, c. 37; Kealey, *Toronto Workers*, 137–48; Tucker, 'Indefinite Area of Toleration,' 41–7. Both The Trade Unions Act and The Criminal Law Amendment Act were based on English precedents: The Trade Union Act, 1871, 34&35 Vict. (1871) c. 31 (UK); An Act to amend the Criminal Law relating to Violence, Threats, and Molestation, 34&35 Vict. (1871) c. 32 (UK).

220 Tucker, 'Indefinite Area of Toleration,' 36, 41, 46. For a summary of the fellow servant rule, see Tucker, 'Law of Employers' Liability,' 218–20. Briefly, the rule states that the employer is not liable for accidents caused to one of his employees by the fault of another employee. Most commentators suggest that the rule is based on a highly individualistic social philosophy. That is true, but the individualism is tempered by a strong suspicion of class solidarity – an empirical assumption that there is a class-based tolerance for misconduct – reflected in the fact that the employer need not prove that the injured employee knew of the other's negligent propensities.

221 The Breaches of Contract Act, S.C. 1877, c. 35. For the circumstances of its adoption, see Morton, 'Taking on the Grand Trunk;' Kealey, *Toronto Workers*, 148–53; Tucker, 'Indefinite Area of Toleration,' 47–51. The English precedent was the Conspiracy, and Protection of Property Act, 1875, 38&39 Vict. (1875) c. 86 (UK). One reason it was not used might have been the short duration of contracts in the organized railway trades; Edward Blake suggested that those contracts were 'minute contracts': Canada, House of Commons, *Debates*, 27 March 1877, 1016. Five convictions occurred in the Ottawa Valley, apparently under the old master and servant provisions regarding absconding, after those provisions had been repealed: *Ottawa Citizen*, 18 December 1878, 2 and 13 January 1879, 3.

For the later legislation, see Jeremy Webber, 'Compelling Compromise: Canada Chooses Conciliation over Arbitration, 1900–1907,' *Labour/Le Travail* 28 (1991), especially 26–9.

222 For the English experience, see Sidney and Beatrice Webb, *Industrial Democracy* (London: Longmans, Green, and Co. 1897), 173–246; Carroll D. Wright, *Industrial*

Conciliation and Arbitration (Boston: Rand, Avery and Co. 1881), 9ff.; W. Steward Martin, 'A Study of Legislation Designed to Foster Industrial Peace in the Common Law Jurisdictions of Canada' (PhD thesis, University of Toronto 1954), 49ff.

223 For labour's support for arbitration, see Forsey, *Trade Unions*, 442–4 (and elsewhere for local unions); Gregory S. Kealey and Bryan D. Palmer, *Dreaming of What Might Be: The Knights of Labor in Ontario, 1880–1900* (Toronto: New Hogtown Press 1982), 330ff; Paul Craven, *'An Impartial Umpire': Industrial Relations and the Canadian State 1900–1911* (Toronto: University of Toronto Press 1980), 142–9; McCallum, 'Labour and Arbitration,' 73ff.

224 The Trades Arbitration Act, S.O. 1873, c. 26, amended by S.O. 1890, c. 40; The Ontario Trade Disputes Conciliation and Arbitration Act, S.O. 1894, c. 42, amended by S.O. 1897, c. 25; Martin, 'Study of Legislation,' 78–91, 149–61; McCallum, 'Labour and Arbitration.' The English and New South Wales models were The Councils of Conciliation Act, 1867, 30&31 Vict. (1867) c. 105 (UK); Trade Disputes Conciliation and Arbitration Act, S.N.S.W. 1891–92, No. 29.

225 For examples, see Martin, 'Study of Legislation,' 88; Kealey, *Toronto Workers*, 203; Levine, 'Conflict and Consensus,' 24–6, 34–5. It was quite common for trade unionists to attempt to mediate disputes involving other unions, or for representatives of labour centrals to offer their services. See Kealey, *Toronto Workers*, 48, 92, 235–6.

226 The speculation regarding intervention under the 1894 act is based on Martin, 'Study of Legislation,' 156, and on Atherton's note that one of the persons chiefly responsible for the federal conciliation policy had been chair of the board under the 1894 act: James J. Atherton, 'The Department of Labour and Industrial Relations, 1900–1911,' MA thesis, Carleton University 1972, 49. Crowley, this volume, notes that officials of the Farm Labour Bureau conciliated disputes. For hesitations and the British precedent, see Canada, House of Commons, *Debates*, 27 May 1899, 3776–9. For Laurier and the relationship to subsequent developments, see Webber, 'Compelling Compromise.'

227 The principal statutes were The Ontario Factories Act, S.O. 1884, c. 39 and The Workmen's Compensation for Injuries Act, S.O. 1886, c. 28. See Risk, 'This Nuisance of Litigation'; Tucker, 'Law of Employers' Liability'; Tucker, 'Making the Workplace "Safe"'; Hurl, 'Restricting Child Factory Labour'; Tucker, *Administering Danger*; Backhouse, *Petticoats and Prejudice*, 260–92.

228 S.C. 1897, c. 11. The story of the act remains largely to be told. For a beginning, see Atherton, 'Department of Labour,' 238–72; Webber, 'Compelling Compromise,' 21–4.

229 For the origins of this policy, see Craven, *Impartial Umpire*, 191–4.

230 For mechanics' liens, see McCallum, 'Mechanics Liens'; Kealey, *Toronto Workers*, 140ff. For conspiracy, see Tucker, 'Through the Prism of the Law'; *R. v. Gibson* (1889), 16 O.R. 704; S.C. 1890, c. 37, s. 19. For injunctions, see Tucker, 'Through the Prism of the Law;' Kealey, *Toronto Workers*, 93.

The threshing machine

Throughout the nineteenth century, much of Ontario's manufactured output came from small establishments like this wagon works and bicycle shop.

The boys in the front row of the Heintzman and Company piano-making workforce were probably apprentices.

The Shantymen

IAN RADFORTH

During the first half of the nineteenth century the forest industry was among the most important sources of waged employment in Ontario, and for countless farm families it was a crucial source of cash income. Even during the second half of the century, the forest industry continued to play an important role as an employer in Ontario's large, rural economy, and the output of the shantymen* provided raw materials for the manufacturing employees in hundreds of sawmills. As the distinctive resource economy of the north began to develop from the 1880s, forest work had a leading part there, too. And in terms of legends and images, the shantymen were no less important. The exploits of that colossal fighter and woodsman of the Ottawa, Joe Muffraw, inspired generations of woodsmen. When the Prince of Wales visited Ottawa in 1860, he rode the timber slide at the Chaudière Falls in the company of raftsmen and was greeted by hundreds of colourfully clad voyageurs and shantymen – the quintessentially Canadian occupational groups of the era.[1]

Given their importance to employment and legend, it is surprising how poorly the shantymen of Ontario have been served by historians. A.R.M. Lower provides only sketchy chapters on workers in the industry; his prime interests lay elsewhere – in the industry's exploitative ethic and the structures of the trade.[2] Several lumbermen – that is, the owners of businesses – have received quite thorough treatment in company histories and in many superb entries in the *Dictionary of Canadian*

---

* A note on teminology: 'Shantyman' in nineteenth-century Ontario referred to any worker engaged in lumbering, although it sometimes referred only to those working in the woods as distinct from river drivers and raftsmen, who worked on the waterways. 'Lumberman' always meant an owner or top manager. 'Lumberer,' 'logger,' and 'woodsman' were used interchangeably with 'shantyman,' but 'woodsman' was much more common. 'Lumberjack,' 'woodsworker,' and 'bushworker' were virtually never heard in the province during the nineteenth century.

Biography.[3] To be sure, workers are discussed with some skill in a few reminiscences, popular histories, and local studies.[4] Few such studies, however, provide context and sustained analysis, or attempt a synthesis. The most useful work on woodsmen is by Douglas McCalla, who has studied their place in the economy of Upper Canada, and by regional historians of the Ottawa Valley – Michael Cross, Chad Gaffield, and Richard Reid.[5] For Ontario we lack the kind of overview given by Graeme Wynn in his *Timber Colony: A Study in the Historical Geography of Early New Brunswick* or by René Hardy and Normand Séguin in *Forêt et société en Mauricie: La formation de la région des Trois-Rivières, 1830–1930.*[6]

Recovering the history of the shantymen means more than simply providing coverage for an important but neglected occupational group in nineteenth-century Ontario. By giving the shantymen their rightful place in the broader history of Ontario labour, we can help to correct the bias in the literature, one that has given disproportionate attention to craftsmen, a comparatively small group compared to the seasonal and day labourers in the forests and on the farms, construction sites, docks, schooners, and steamships. Furthermore, a study of woodsmen brings to light a fascinating way of life – that of men working and living for a whole season in camps away from their families and communities. The shantymen lived and toiled in an all-male environment, where many of the tasks usually done by women were here arranged by the companies and done by other men. The unusual way of life in shanty and rafting operations has long had a romantic appeal celebrated in the songs of the shantymen themselves and in histories, both popular and scholarly. In many respects, it *was* a colourful occupational group whose ways ought not to be forgotten – although there is little danger of that. Yet woods operations also had their businesslike side, and the work routines were exactly that: routines that could grow monotonous. Both aspects of that way of life need to be recalled and reconstructed.

This chapter surveys the history of the shantymen and their work throughout the nineteenth century and in several parts of the province, but most notably in the Ottawa Valley and on the Canadian Shield. It draws selectively, and critically, on the secondary literature, and it presents the results of new research, notably in hitherto little-used archival sources. The records of quite a few lumber companies that operated in nineteenth-century Ontario have been preserved, and some have proved to be quite rich and to provide an unusual vantage point. To be sure, the company sources seldom record directly the voices of the woods worker himself, but they do offer a perspective that is remarkably close to the ground. In some cases, camp foremen and backwoods supervisors reported almost daily on activities in the woods, on the river, or during labour recruitment drives. I have relied heavily on some of the best of these kinds of records.

This research has led me to the conclusion that the work lives of the shantymen in nineteenth-century Ontario were characterized both by variety and movement and by stability. The work itself drew on many kinds of skills and offered the workers great variety – the carefully defined responsibilities of members of felling gangs, the cooperative spirit of the mid-winter sleigh haul, the frantic rush and motion of the spring river drive. Similarly, the shantymen's contact with the world beyond the workplace changed with the season; most spent the winter in remote districts, cut off from families and taverns, whereas in spring and summer the drivers and raftsmen had access to liquor and opportunities for conflict in the towns and villages they passed through as they moved downstream. Those who found jobs in the woods and on the river came from a wide range of backgrounds – French-Canadian, Irish, Scottish, German, Polish, and aboriginal – and they integrated woods work into their lives in a number of ways. Some were specialists who worked year-round in the industry; others came from various walks of life and stayed in the woods for a few weeks or several months. The recruiting of seasonal workers was virtually a continuous activity for employers. Yet stability prevailed as well. Over the course of the century there were few technological or managerial innovations that disrupted the well-understood methods of conducting a logging campaign. Similarly, once a crew was on the job, instances of overt conflict between men and bosses were rare. Furthermore, throughout the entire century, woodsmen were immersed in an intensely masculine world, and their dangerous work and crude living conditions always encouraged them to project an image of rugged masculinity.

COMMERCIAL LUMBERING

The forest has always had a value to the inhabitants of Ontario. It was the habitat for the animals that the aboriginal peoples hunted, and it supplied the building materials for Huron longhouses and the Loyalists' first log homes. We are concerned here, however, with commercial lumbering. Even that supported diverse activities throughout the nineteenth century. In part, logging and sawmilling were done locally to meet the many needs of the farmers and townsfolk who settled the province. From the local sawmiller the comparatively well-off or better-established settlers bought clapboard siding for their frame houses. Local craftsmen turned out countless products for farm, home, and community – from wagon wheels to bedsteads to coffins. Along with grist mills, sawmills were ubiquitous structures in the tiny commercial centres that provided a manufacturing base for nearly every village and town in the pioneer districts. This local wood industry had an essential part in the growth of the internal commercial economy of Old Ontario, a sector that economic historians have shown was crucial to the growth and development of the province as a whole.[7] That said, this chapter will not deal with the lumbering associated with sawmills that served strictly local markets. Those local mills were not supplied by a distinct occupational group of woodsmen. For the farmers (and their sons and hired hands) who did most of the work, harvesting trees on their woodlots or on nearby crown lands was just one of the many tasks of farm life. Thus the history of lumbering for local markets properly belongs to the history of farming and settlement.

But in nineteenth-century Ontario, lumbering was also a staple trade that provided wood products for export. From the beginning of the century there was an external demand for high-grade timber. Industrializing Britain imported huge quantities of wood products for diverse needs: to build railways and ships, houses and shops, to fashion moulds for the rapidly expanding metal industries, and to manufacture barrels then so essential to the transportation of many kinds of goods. Timber from Ontario was included in shipments from Quebec, and it competed in English markets with wood from New Brunswick and other colonies, as well as from foreign sources, mainly the Baltic countries. As early as the 1830s there was also an American demand for Ontario wood. The convenient local forests that had supplied sawmills in parts of the northeastern United States had been depleted, and when settlement began later in the century on the grasslands of the Midwest the American demand for Ontario wood soared. The volume of lumber and sawlogs exported to the United States far outstripped that of square timber shipped to Britain, even in the peak year, 1864.[8]

There was a distinct pattern to the wood exports of nineteenth-century Ontario. The British orders included substantial quantities of oak staves for cooperages and masting timber for the Royal Navy and merchant marine. The strongest demand in England, however, was for red and white pine shipped in the form of square and waney timber or deals. Timber exported in these forms would then be sawn to order in the large mills of England, most of them in the vicinity of the great timber port of Liverpool.[9] The British market was known for its discriminating buyers, and only the clearest Canadian pine found a ready market. By contrast, the American demand was for quantity rather than quality. And American buyers at Oswego, Albany, Buffalo, and Chicago were more interested in standard-dimension contruction lumber already prepared in Ontario sawmills. On the other hand Michigan importers at sawmill centres such as Tawas and Bay City imported sawlogs to supply their own mills.[10] The value of sawn lumber exports to the States overtook the value of square timber bound for Britain in about 1870, and by the 1880s four-fifths of the exports were in the form of sawn lumber.[11] The export of square timber from Canada began to decline significantly in the 1870s and had all but disappeared by the beginning of the twentieth century. The demise of that trade coincided with a peak production of sawn lumber and the rise of a pulp and paper industry in northern Ontario.[12]

The lumber business was carried out by a host of firms of widely varying sizes and organizational structures. In the earliest days of the trade with Britain, timber was but one line of general wholesale merchants at Quebec. Small-scale entrepreneurs would raft some timber down the St Lawrence, hoping to make a sale. When in 1806 Napoleon's blockade of European ports cut off vital supplies of Baltic timber bound for English markets, the large, well-established British importers sought secure sources of supply in the colonies. Several importers set up branch offices at Quebec. All bought rafts of timber on the open market, but some contracted with producers to ensure future supplies, and a few became directly involved in production upstream.[13] Thus, from early in the century lumbering was conducted by concerns that ranged from large, long-established merchant houses, to operators with solid contracts, to the small, independent entrepreneur taking risks on his own account. Though small-scale producers never disappeared from the business, the lion's share of timber came to be made by several larger firms that could better withstand the fluctuations in demand, prices, and other factors. Producers of modest means were more apt by the 1840s to act as jobbers or subcontractors, undertaking lumbering and/or rafting for one of the bigger fish. The owners of the large firms were almost all English-speaking, whereas some of the smaller firms were run by French Canadians.[14]

Similarly, business operations were complex among the sawlog and lumber producers. Some of the larger concerns had their roots in the square-timber trade, the owners having shrewdly diversified.[15] There were also operators who specialized from the start in sawlogs and sawmilling. Many of them had moved up from the States when the forest resource in their home districts ran out.[16] Others were Canadians who had expanded from humble beginnings in local sawmilling, or in rare instances from furniture making. Still others might best be dubbed continentalists because they were just as much at home operating on either side of the border.[17] And here, too, there could be found jobbers and small contractors, many of whom contracted to clean out a patch of bush in a remote corner of a big firm's forest domain. Even keepers of country general stores entered the business, selling timber to buyers who assembled rafts and shipments from a host of local suppliers. Whatever the scale of a firm, it was invariably financed as an individual or family investment or a joint partnership.[18]

There was no guarantee that large firms could handle the erratic conditions of the lumber business, as John Egan, the 'Napoleon of the Ottawa' discovered in the 1850s when his huge timber business came crashing down. Historian A.R.M. Lower likened lumbering to gambling, so high were the risks.[19] Good prices one year encouraged new entrants and expanded lumbering operations the next, with the inevitable result that a glut of timber on the market forced prices down. This problem was recognized very early in the century by George Hamilton, then in the timber business at Quebec. He regularly assessed the situation for his business contacts and made recommendations. In November 1804 he wrote one of them: 'Staves I look upon it will be cheap next year as the Prices this Year will encourage the manufacture of them. For the Contrary Reason I think Oak, Pine, Pine Planks and Boards will be dear, as they have been uncommonly low and of Course will discourage the Cutting.'

Adding to the risks was bad weather, which could, for instance, delay or prevent delivery of rafts at Quebec. 'It is proverbial of lumbermen to have something always to complain of,' wrote William Stewart, a lumber merchant at Bytown, in Febrary 1842. 'They can justly complain this year for want of snow and last year it was too much ... If snow do not come soon a great portion of the timber must remain in the woods.' Too little snow made it too difficult to haul the wood on land and reduced the spring run-off for river operations, which could result in wood being 'hung up' in the back country. Such was the case in the spring of 1868. The *Bytown Gazette* reported that so much wood had failed to reach Ottawa that the sawmills could not operate their night gangs, thus 'depriv[ing] many families in this locality of the means of subsistence on which they have heretofore relied.'[20]

Commercial lumbering took place almost wholly in what were originally called the 'wild lands of the crown.' At the beginning of the nineteenth century, most of the cutting was done without legal sanction. Pine and oak timber were theoretically reserved for the crown, but the provincial executive, acting in the name of the crown, granted few cutting licences. In the mid-1820s the Upper Canadian executive came to realize the revenue potential of the forest, and beginning in 1826 the government charged dues on the volume of timber actually cut each season. Although there were ways to cheat, most firms paid some dues when their rafts passed the gaze of the timber officials at Bytown and other rafting centres such as Belleville near the mouth of the Trent River. By mid-century operators had to acquire from the Department of Crown Lands in the United Canadas a licence to cut timber on a specified area, for which the government charged a ground rent in addition to dues on timber cut. Later still, the Ontario Department of Crown Lands auctioned timber berths to the bidder willing to pay the highest 'bonus.' (The other charges remained in place, too.) In Upper Canada, the timber revenues were important in so far as they gave the executive branch of government independence from the elected Assembly. During the two decades after Confederation, the various charges on lumbering were the largest single source of provincial revenue apart from the Dominion subsidies. For their part, the companies gained relatively inexpensive access to abundant supplies of timber without having to purchase the lands or assume any permanent commitment to their care. The lumber companies also benefited from provincial expenditures on transportation – booms and slides on waterways, colonization roads that enabled the lumberers to carry supplies into their backwoods camps, and subsidized railways that transported timber and sawn lumber. In fact, the lumbermen's advantages were criticized by many settlers and mining interests that were competitors for the use of the lands. In the latter years of the century a conservation movement began to raise questions about the damage to the environment caused by lumbering. Yet, with their considerable economic and political influence, the lumbermen prevailed.[21]

At one time or another during the nineteenth century, lumbering took place in nearly every corner of southern Ontario and throughout the more accessible parts of the North as well. The main artery of the trade in the first half of the century was the Ottawa River, which gave access to a vast lumbering region on both sides of the provincial boundary. Massachusetts-born Philemon Wright is given credit for bringing down to Quebec in 1806 the first Ottawa raft. It was made up of timber from around his settlement at Hull. Raft traffic on the Ottawa increased greatly during the following few decades, as lumbermen reached farther up the river and back into the woods, following the many tributaries. The early campaigns were mainly high-grading operations, which took only the choicest timber along the water's edge. Stream improvements, often the joint projects of several lumber companies, smoothed the passage of rafts and gave access to additional districts. Well before mid-century, lumbering was also taking place along the shores of the lower Great Lakes and the rivers draining into them. Logging activities could be found from the Rideau Lakes district in the east to Essex and Kent counties in the far southwest of the colony. Waters draining into southern Georgian Bay began to be used by lumbermen in the export trade as early as the 1850s.[22]

During the 1850s, railways were opening new districts, as lines shot northward from the front along Lake Ontario. In the latter quarter of the century the trade shifted increasingly to the north and west. Operations in northern Georgian Bay and along the north shore of Lake Huron began in earnest in the 1880s, once the more convenient sources of supply in Michigan and other lake states had been depleted. The building of the Canadian Pacific Railway through northern Ontario during the 1880s created its own demand for construction timber and provided access to fine pine forests to the west of the Lakehead. During the 1890s Michigan lumbermen boomed vast quantities of northern Ontario sawlogs to their mills south of the border. Also during the 1890s, the last of the first-class virgin pine timber in southern Ontario was opened to exploitation when the Ottawa lumber baron J.R. Booth built a railway through the Madawaska Valley and Algonquin Park, and on to Parry Sound. Altogether it was a geographically extensive business, always on the move, as the forests were depleted. Once the demand warranted the expense of operating in a new district, the trade moved on without a backward glance.[23]

SOURCES OF LABOUR

Thousands of men were attracted to lumbering and rafting jobs each season. The precise numbers will never be known. Douglas McCalla has shown that contemporary statements about the size of the labour force were apt to be much exaggerated by lumbermen who had an interest in inflating the industry's importance. Thus, rather than the 8,000 men said to work in the timber trade of Upper Canada in 1836, 3,500 appears to be a more accurate calculation.[24] Towards the end of the century, 25,000 was a frequently cited figure for the number of woodsmen working in Ontario, but that figure is quite likely too large as well. Still, the industry did create significant numbers of jobs in rural areas where other kinds of work were generally lacking and at a time of year – winter – when work on the docks, construction sites, and farms was much reduced.

The labour force may be divided into two groups: specialists and occupational pluralists. Rafting was done almost entirely by specialists who worked exclusively in the timber trade. Raftsmen worked in spring and summer on the river, and then took jobs as woodcutters in wintertime. They worked virtually year round. Some signed contracts in September that specified a term of employment lasting through the following summer. Others had at least two contracts, one for the fall and winter in the woods, and another (possibly with a different firm) covering late spring and summer on the river. Other specialists worked in the sawlog camps in winter, and then in spring and summer found jobs either on the river drive and related activities or in a sawmill.

The demand for labour in the woods was always far greater in fall and winter, and so the specialists were joined by about an equal number of men who were employed by the season. Some of them came from canal and road construction projects, or from labouring jobs in the ports of Ontario and Quebec. The largest group, however, came from farms.

Farmers were especially likely to hire as teamsters for the midwinter sleigh haul of timber. It was then that they had the least to do on their farms and, where possible, they might take a team with them to the bush and earn income in addition to their wage. Yet many farmers and especially their sons hired on as early as September, so eager were they to earn wages. This practice, which lasted throughout the century, was described in 1835 by lumberman John Neilson of Quebec: '[Shantymen] are mostly young men who have been working for their parents or in the towns; those that are married have left their wives and their younger children upon their farms that have been doing little things during their absence. The moment they return they set to work.'

As Marjorie Cohen has pointed out, the non-waged winter work of women and children on the farm freed the men to seek wage labour in the forests. Women's indirect contribution to commercial lumbering and the growth of a wage labour market was thus considerable, however dismissive a man like Neilson may have been of the 'little things' they did on the farm. The feelings of individual women about a winter alone undoubtedly varied. Life could be dull and survival a struggle for women isolated with their children on farms, as a pioneer woman in Muskoka explained in 1878: 'On the first approach of cold weather he starts for the lumber-shanties, and engages himself to work there ... It is certainly a very hard and anxious life for the wife and children, left to shift for themselves throughout the long dreary winter, too often on a very slender provision of flour and potatoes and little else.'[25]

Most of the earliest woods employees in the Ottawa Valley were Americans brought in because of their skill and experience in lumbering. Soon, however, local men picked up the techniques. John Neilson maintained that the 'United States people introduced their fashions,' but since 'the people of the country could be employed at a lower rate,' they were almost immediately given preference so that they soon came to 'carry it on almost exclusively.' Neilson described the 'wood-cutters and the raftsmen' as 'a mixture of native French Canadians and the new comers [i.e.], settlers from the old country.'[26] Throughout the rest of the century French Canadians from both sides of the Ottawa River continued to provide a large part of the woods labour force everywhere in Ontario, including in the remote northwestern part of the province, where few French Canadians actually settled. Even in Michigan, the square timber business is said to have had 'a distinctly French-Canadian flavour,' thanks to the annual influx of what was known locally as 'the red-sash brigade.' By mid-century, many rural Quebec men had excellent skills that they passed on routinely to the youths. Logging jobs in the upper province proved attractive to many in rural Quebec because there were nearly always more shantymen than jobs there. Especially when distant Ontario operators paid men their transportation costs and offered higher wages than local Quebec firms, the Ontario operators were assured of applicants from the lower province.[27]

Naturally, people of British background, who made up the great majority of the province's population in the nineteenth century, also could be found in large numbers in the shanties. Glengarry Scots and Ottawa Valley Irish long maintained a reputation for their abilities in lumbering. Few immigrants from the British Isles arrived in Canada with woods skills, but many acquired them as pioneers or on farm woodlots. Immigrants direct from the boat had to serve a kind of apprenticeship in commercial lumbering before they had enough experience to work on, for instance, felling gangs. George Hamilton explained in 1835 that recent immigrants were 'brought to the use of the axe by road making, or cutting down the small trees and underbrush, when the hauling is done with oxen.' Another lumberman, William Patton, told the same inquiry: 'During the first winter [immigrants] obtain employment either among the Farmers as substitutes for such of their men (who from being more acquainted with the ways of the country) go to the Shanties, or are employed in transporting Provisions for Shanties and looking after the cattle [i.e. oxen], the second and third winter as Teamsters, after which they become useful, and are employed as Axemen.'[28]

Ethnic diversity in the woods was increased by the presence of considerable numbers of Poles and Germans who began to settle in Renfrew County about the middle of the nineteenth century. Once again, the immigrants lacked logging experience when they arrived, but as frontier settlers in heavily wooded parts of the Ottawa Valley, they soon acquired it. Because of the poverty of these immigrants, especially the Poles, who came to Renfrew without cash and settled on marginal farm lands, for several generations there were wage-seeking descendants in the timber camps.[29]

Native men from various bands throughout the north found jobs in the woods of their own districts, especially where logging took place on reserve lands and where there were no clashes over land rights. Some native men had a reputation for being expert guides in the woods, and they played a crucial role in timber cruising, that is, guiding whites while they assessed the timber resources of an area. The Mohawk were much sought after as expert pilots for the timber rafts when they had to descend treacherous parts of the St Lawrence.[30]

The neat dovetailing of woods work and farming was played up by defenders of the timber trade in reply to critics who bemoaned the demoralizing effects of lumbering and the ways in which it distracted men from their responsibilities on family farms. Lumbering facilitated settlement on the land, explained George Hamilton in 1835: 'Emigration to the Colonies in North America is promoted by the Timber Trade; in the first place it affords the Emigrant a cheap conveyance in the Ships coming out in ballast, and at the end of his voyage it affords him wholesome work at good wages, the work at which he is employed fits him to clear land for himself, and the wage that he receives, enables him to purchase the land.'[31] There was some truth in this assessment. Before the 1860s, countless emigrants did find cheap passage in the timber or 'coffin' ships. Upon arrival the men took woods jobs that helped them realize their goal of becoming independent on the land. Woods work was but a stepping-stone, though their sons might take it up too to help them establish their own farms. In this way, then, the connection between lumbering and farming continued to be close long after the pioneer stage had passed. The tie was even tighter in certain districts. In fertile agricultural pockets within the Ottawa Valley, for instance, farmers prospered by supplying 'the shanty market,' that is, selling hay, oats, pork, potatoes, peas, and beans to the lumber camps for consumption by men and beasts.[32]

In parts of Ontario and Quebec where the land could support only struggling, marginal farms, there was a continuing connection between seasonal waged work in the woods and family farming. Historians refer to local economies of this sort as part of the agro-forest system. Sometimes wage employment in the forest is presented in a favourable light, for having provided a helpful supplement to farm incomes, one that ensured the very survival of such communities. More persuasive, though, is the view that the forest employers, rather than the farmer–woods workers, benefited most from the system. The lumber firms could recruit men from marginal farm districts and pay them a low, seasonal wage. Their farms would help the men and their families survive during the off-season in the woods, when the lumber firms did not need much labour. And each fall and winter, the companies would be assured of having an adequate labour pool because the marginal farms did not produce enough to permit even a basic level of comfort. It was a treadmill for reproducing rural poverty generation after generation, even as it kept the timber camps well manned.[33]

THE SEASONAL ROUND OF WORK

All commercial woods work was based on the labour of gangs of men working from shanties, that is, camps in the woods, located within walking distance of the timber. A gang usually had five men, and a shanty was made up of two to ten gangs, the number depending on such factors as company resources, local traditions, and, especially, the amount of accessible timber of the species, quality, and size desired. Lumbering methods became well established early in the century. They were second nature to the experienced man, and he taught the ropes to greenhorns. That well-understood way to proceed changed remarkably little over the course of the century. In the woods end of the business at least, this was a thoroughly conservative industry.

During the nineteenth century, employers made no formal attempts to innovate, either as individual firms or in co-operation with one another, as their successors did in the next century.[34] To be sure, dramatic innovations in related forest industries such as sawmilling and pulp and paper affected logging, mainly by increasing the demand for timber and making it profitable to enter remote or hard-to-reach forests that had hitherto been too expensive to exploit. Such developments had little direct effect on lumbering methods, however. Small improvements in basic logging methods were sometimes made, including the odd advance introduced from the outside. Boat builders, for instance, tried to develop a market among firms operating on the river.[35] Men and firms that had logged in the even bigger timber of Michigan brought modest innovations with them. Generally, however, I want to stress that once the methods were established, lumbering firms preferred to stick to the methods that worked for them.[36] What worked was a system that relied heavily on nature to facilitate each step in the lumbering process. The activities had a distinctly seasonal rhythm.[37]

Crews for the annual lumbering campaign began to assemble about the beginning of September. At that time of year, there were men available (rafting having been completed shortly before), the worst of the heat and fly season was over, and there still remained enough time to fell and prepare plenty of timber before the snow became too deep. Once a shanty had been built – and that didn't take long because they were crude temporary structures – then the felling gangs, usually of five men each, would set out every day to cut timber.

The cutting gangs came under the authority of the shanty boss, sometimes called the camp foreman. A good boss was an experienced shantyman whom the owners had singled out for his skill at handling logs and men. Before cutting began, he helped cruise the timber limit, assessing the quality and location of the timber, and he chose the site for the shanty and planned a network of roads and trails for bringing in supplies and transporting timber out. During the cutting season he assigned the gangs to specific sites and rotated them to new ones once the timber had been felled. In the woods the shanty boss was in charge. To be sure, he corresponded with headquarters regularly, perhaps daily where and when access was good, and was visited from time to time by an owner or by a woods superintendent, or 'walking boss,' who moved among the company's camps. Nevertheless, the foreman was *the* day-to-day authority at the shanty. He had the power to hire and fire, and he did much to set the tone for relations among the men and the spirit of the shanty.

During the felling season, the head of the gang, or 'head chopper,' was responsible for selecting the best trees for the purpose – generally, tall, straight ones that appeared to have little or no rot. He made the undercut, which largely determined where the giant would fall. Since placing the tree in the right spot facilitated the subsequent steps and helped ensure safety on the job, this was an important task requiring experience and sound judgment. A pair of choppers usually worked together making the deep cut that would bring the tree down. Until the 1870s they did so using single-bit or double-bit axes, taking pride in the accuracy of their blows and learning to trust a partner not to break the rhythm and cause an accident. During the 1870s the two-man cross-cut saw was introduced to Ontario woods operations for the purpose of felling. When the saw was properly filed and set with raker teeth that removed sawdust, a pair of skilled sawyers, one hauling on either end of the saw, could fell a tree more quickly and with less energy than two axemen. It is worth noting that this innovation, perhaps the most significant in woods work during the century, involved a new use for a fairly simple hand tool that had been in the tool kit of workers in wood since biblical times.[38]

Once the tree had been laid low, then the choppers (always using axes) would 'top' the tree, removing the crown, and hack off every branch of the trunk. For crews in sawlog operations, the next steps were straightforward. The trunk was made, or 'bucked,' into log lengths, usually of sixteen feet with an extra half foot in case the ends were damaged in transport. Here, too, the two-man cross-cut saw replaced the axe during the 1870s. The bucking crew of two men completed the five-man felling gang. Output was about sixty logs a day for one gang.[39] The work demanded strength and stamina, as well as some experience with axe and saw.

For gangs making square timber, the work at this stage was more complicated because it was at the stump that the wood was put in its final form for export. To convert a rough log into a smooth stick of square or waney timber, the crew worked together, each member doing a specific job. The 'rosser,' using a rossing iron that resembled a short hoe, scraped a two-inch-wide strip of bark off the tree, from one end to the other– some thirty to sixty feet. The liner then used a chalk line to draw a straight line the length of the cleaned strip. The scorer swung his axe, making notches that would guide the work of the highly skilled 'hewer.' Using his broad axe, a special tool with a twelve-inch blade, the hewer gave the side of the log a flat surface. This was the most skilled task of all, for he had to hew the surface perfectly smooth. Once one side had been made flat, the crew rolled the log, repeating the process on all four sides until the stick was square. A talented hewer could strike his blows so accurately that the stick ended up as smooth as a table top, looking as though it had been planed. The final result was a stick or 'balk' of square timber that was at least twelve inches square (and sometimes much more) and thirty to sixty feet long.

Some indication of the way in which the skill required for the positions in a square timber gang was valued is given by the pay assigned the various positions. In October 1870, Mossom Boyd and Company, a long-established and large firm operating in the Kawarthas and Haliburton, paid hewers $30 per month, liners $20, and scorers $15–$18. In the fall of 1877, Gillies Brothers, a major operator in the Ottawa Valley, paid its hewers $38 per month, liners $22, scorers $17.50–$19, and teamsters and general hands $14–$16.[40]

Observers frequently criticized the waste involved in square timber operations.[41] Many felled trees were discarded at the stump because rot or imperfections of colour showed up once the work was underway. About one-third of the log was hewn away and left as so-called waste, or 'slash.' When dry, such material helped fuel forest fires. Commentators urged that the technique be abandoned but the actual decline of the square timber trade had more to do with falling demand, shrinking supplies of prime timber, the high labour costs of such labour-intensive, skilled work, and the persistently rising demand for sawlogs and lumber in American markets.[42]

Once the sawlogs and timber had been made, the next step in the seasonal round of activities was to move the wood from the stump to a dump site, or point from which long-distance transportation would start. On nearly all square timber operations, the sticks were 'skidded,' or pulled by a chain, one at a time along trails to the dump – either the surface of a frozen lake or the edge of a river. At least until mid-century, oxen were the most common beasts of burden, a pair being used to pull each stick, one end raised behind the beasts, the other dragging along the ground. The ox's strength was an obvious advantage, and when the work was done oxen could be slaughtered and salted to feed future shanty crews. A drawback was that the teamsters who drove them found them hard to handle and much preferred heavy work horses, such as Percherons and Clydesdales. In many operations the teamsters brought their own horses with them from their farms, thus reducing the number of horses the companies had to supply. Moreover, teamsters that knew their horses well got the most from the animals. A simple, spoken command from the teamster would set the horse to the task at hand. Horse handling was a skill much needed in the shanties, and one that countless men from farms could readily supply.

In sawlog operations, backwoods transportation was more elaborate, and it grew somewhat more so towards the end of the century. The work was divided into two distinct phases. From late October through December, teamsters would arrive to skid the logs along trails cut from the stump to 'skidways,' that is, a type of 'landing' or place where wood was piled temporarily. In sawlog skidding, a horse pulled one or two logs, depending on their size, by means of a skidding chain that ran around one end of the logs, lifting them above the ground. The other end of the chain was hooked onto a crossbar, or 'whippletree,' which was attached to the horse by chains and leather straps. The teamsters followed skidding trails cleared early in the autumn either by themselves or by comparatively inexperienced (and lower-paid) men and boys hired specifically for the task. As the snow fell on the ground it helped to reduce friction and to speed operations, and it buried stumps and other obstructions on which logs might snag. Once the teamster reached the skidway with his load, he stopped to pile it, sliding the logs up poles leaning on an angle from the ground to the top of the skidway. Again, in some of the larger operations, especially later in the century, inexperienced men were hired as 'general hands' to perform the back-breaking grunt work of piling.

On sawlog operations the second phase of backwoods log transportation was known as the sleigh haul. It began shortly after New Year's, once freezing weather had set in and the snow conditions were optimal. Sawmill employees who generally had been laid off in December were available to supplement the shanty crews. From the skidways, crews loaded a dozen or more logs onto wooden, horse-drawn sleighs with iron (later steel) runners. The loading equipment was simple. A 'decking line,' or rope, was looped around the log, and a horse pulled on it, raising the log above the ground to the sleighs, while men steadied it as it moved. A canthook was often used for the purpose – a simple wooden pole, three inches in diameter and four feet long with an iron hook on the end. Once the sleigh was loaded, a teamster standing on top of the load, drove a team of powerful horses that pulled the sleigh along the haulways or roads.

The main hauling roads were carefully prepared at the beginning of the season, and maintained each night, by a crew that made sure the ruts carved out for the sleigh runners had a rock-hard, glare-ice surface. Once again, on larger operations later in the century, greater care was taken to maintain the roads and ensure the rapid and safe movement of the sleighs. Young lads known as 'chickadees,' cleared the roads of manure throughout the day. 'Sandpipers' poured hot sand on downhill slopes to slow down the sleighs and prevent their toppling over. Towards the end of the century, most shanties had a blacksmith to maintain the chains, whippletrees, and other paraphernalia in top working order. Just before New Year's he toiled long hours re-shodding the horses in clogs designed to grip the ice of the haul roads.

Once the teamster and sleigh reached the dump site, the logs were unloaded by crews using a decking line and canthooks. Yet again the logs were piled, this time in 'rollways' on the banks of streams or on the flat, frozen surface of a lake. Hauling ended about mid-March, once the warmer weather had made sleighing less efficient or all the logs had been moved.

At the end of the hauling season the crews usually enjoyed a hard-earned rest or broke up. The next step in the seasonal round required the high water of springtime, and that usually meant waiting until mid-April. Many men returned home, while others sought pleasure in lumbermen's hotels until their work resumed.

During the river drive, newly organized crews marshalled the power of the spring run-off to flush the timber down creeks and streams in the backwoods. Dams built earlier, perhaps during the previous summer, would be used to hold back the freshets, and then, just as the river drivers broke apart the rollways, the water would be released, sending the timber crashing into the white water below. River drivers lined the banks of the creek and with their pike poles, wooden poles about ten feet and more in length with an iron spike on the end, they would push towards mid-stream any log that threatened to catch on the bank and create a logjam. The men camped in tents alongside the creek, moving downstream each day with the logs. During the drive, men and provisions were carried downstream in pointer boats, long narrow vessels with pointed ends that could be steered with one oar. The drive lasted at most a few weeks, depending on local geography and weather. Once the logs reached a major waterway, they were floated downstream at a more leisurely pace. In order to cross lakes en route, the logs were sometimes corralled into booms which were towed by a steam vessel, or they were drawn by barges or 'alligator boats' using a steam- or horse-powered winch or capstan. In the biggest booming operations, which were on Lake Huron during the 1890s, gigantic loads were towed across the lake to sawmills in Michigan.

There is a sense of romantic adventure often associated with the river drive. To be sure, the work was inherently more exciting than that of the shanties – because of the white water, the danger, and the short duration of the drives, which allowed no chance for monotonous routine. As they moved downstream, there was liquor to be had in the taverns of the towns, and drinking frequently led to brawls that gained the river drivers a bad reputation. Once established, it was a rough, manly image the river drivers liked to cultivate in their songs and their behaviour. One such song, entitled Conroy's Camp, begins:

> We left the camp at half-past eight.
> When we got to Waltham it was late,
> And Fleury said, 'Come on in, boys,
> We'll drink some beer and make some noise.'[43]

The song then proceeds, verse by verse, to describe and poke fun at the antics of Conroy's crew, up the Ottawa.

In the square timber sector, there was less river driving because the giant sticks could not be as easily moved and damage to them would not be tolerated by the buyers. Square timber tended to be floated down wider streams to a main river, most notably the Ottawa or the Trent. From Belleville, the timber was taken by schooner to Garden Island at the east end of Lake Ontario, where the Calvin Company specialized in constructing and manning the timber rafts that descended the St Lawrence to Quebec. In the 1850s and 1860s that firm annually hired a summer seasonal work force of some three hundred Irish, French-Canadian, and native workers. These men, and their counterparts on the Ottawa, built rafts by chaining together about twenty sticks of square timber to form a 'crib.' The cribs would then be assembled into rafts that could be floated long distances – from Kingston or well above Bytown to Quebec. When rapids were encountered en route, the rafts had to be broken down into cribs and then reassembled below. Square timber rafts sometimes had as many as five thousand sticks in a frame 150 by 1,500 feet. The raftsmen lived aboard as they travelled downstream, making perhaps two or three trips between May and late August. Sometimes they had to row furiously and steer with precision to keep the raft in the centre of a strong current and thus bring it safely down a set of rapids. Both on the Ottawa and the St Lawrence, the Iroquois and especially the Kahnawake were highly regarded for their courage and their white-water skill. On smoother stretches of the great rivers, the pace changed entirely, and for the men there was little to do but soak up the summer sun.[44]

Like the river drivers, many raftsmen came into contact with the general population living in the settlements along the rivers and gained a reputation for causing disturbances. The *Bytown Gazette* enjoyed reporting on many such activities. Thus, for example there was a report of a raftsman in 1866 who was injured by a fall from a moving coach, the accident, according to the paper, having been caused by an overindulgence in 'Lower Town Tangle Leg.' On another occasion a gang of raftsmen were chased by the police after being caught in the company of four 'unruly women' on the Richmond Road, the centre of prostitution in Ottawa. The gang, however, was said to have 'escaped the honor of figuring before the police magistrate, by the superior skill they displayed in skedaddling through the bush ... to their encampments on the river.' At Pembroke it was once reported that a party of raftsmen from the Upper Ottawa had become abusive after they had 'imbibed too much forty rod.' After the magistrate had intervened and imposed a fine, 'the ringleader' loaded a musket and roamed about 'to the terror of some of the residents.' Finally, 'he went in a spirit of bravado to fire off the piece, when the barrel burst, and tore out the whole front of his stomach.' Showing his class sympathies, the journalist concluded that this explosion had put 'an end to his ruffianly conduct and miserable existence.' By contrast, the Calvin Company records make it clear that its crews regularly travelled downstream by raft and upstream by steamer with seldom a mishap or diversion.[45]

The seasonal round of activities ended when the last rafts reached the timber coves at Quebec City. At that point, specialized workers who lived at Quebec broke up the rafts and cribs and loaded them through the bows of the timber ships. The raftsmen had at least a couple of weeks before they returned to the shanties to begin felling once again.

DANGERS ON THE JOB

Lumbering has always had a reputation for being a dangerous occupation. In twentieth-century Ontario, when statistics for fatalities from workplace accidents are available, logging has long rivalled mining as the province's most dangerous industry.[46] No such statistics are available for the nineteenth century, but other kinds of evidence suggest that, especially in river operations, the annual toll must have been atrocious. Certainly nearly every step of the seasonal round of lumbering activities provided all too many opportunities for mishaps and disasters.

Autumn road-clearing gangs and felling crews faced two main hazards: their tools and the trees. They worked with sharp, heavy tools that could cause serious wounds or blows. Such was the case of a shantyman working in the Ottawa district in 1876 who was reported to have hit himself in the arm with his axe. He bled to death. Another shantyman, an experienced and respected hewer by the name of John Sinclair, tripped while returning to the shanty one evening in November 1876. He was carrying his broadaxe at the time, and it cut him so severely in the arm that he too bled to death within a few hours. 'It is a sorrowful afair,' wrote the woods superintendent to Gillies Brothers. 'To us the shock is great – but will be felt more so by his poor widow and family.'[47]

In addition, the crews always had to be alert to the dangers of falling branches and trees. An inquest held at Calumet Island in 1863 found that a fatal accident had occurred when a young man of 'French Canadian and Indian descent' had been clearing logging roads for an ox team that was hauling timber. Though no one had witnessed the accident, it appeared that a heavy branch had fallen on the man, fracturing his skull. He was taken to the shanty, but he had died by the time a doctor examined him. The lad had no known relatives in that part of the country, and he was known only as Vincent. On another occasion the *Bytown Gazette* published an epitaph to Robert Wilass, an old raftsman, killed in the woods by the fall of a tree:

> By cutting down pine he made his money and mirth;
> Pine down cut him off this earth;
> By pine he lived – by pine lost his breath;
> Pine made him bed – Pine enclosed him in death.[48]

The jobs of other workers in the woods were not quite as dangerous, but still there were hazards. The lifting and rolling of sticks of timber and logs could result in hernias and back injuries. When skidding, shantymen had to be ready to jump clear if the logs were stopped abruptly by stumps or other obstructions. On the sleigh haul, loads could get out of control when they rushed downhill faster than the horses. The only hope for the teamster, perched high on the load, was to get clear of the toppling sleigh by jumping far to the side and into whatever lay in the bush at the side of the road. Even more risky for teamsters was crossing frozen lakes and rivers with loaded sleighs. Early – too early – in the winter season of 1875–6, one of the Gillies' foremen reported that a teamster had drowned while crossing the ice. 'Sir,' he wrote, 'it is my Panefull Duty to acauant You of the Death of Andy Gurrey, who was drown this day at the Foot of the Island Rapid whilst crossing a Span of horses.'[49]

Sometimes unusual accidents happened in the woods. In 1870 Duncan

McNab was killed in Barnett and McKay's shanty when he went to feed his horses in the morning. While he was getting hay from the loft of a shed – no doubt built hastily and rudely like most camp structures – the roof collapsed, crushing him beneath it. Shantymen were also known to have hunting accidents with shotguns and to get frostbite while working or walking out of camp or while lost in the woods. Perhaps the most extraordinary death reported by the *Bytown Gazette* involved a shanty cook who had been lost in the woods for some days and nearly starved to death. It was said that upon his return to camp he had died from 'excessive eating.'[50]

Notwithstanding the many dangers of shanty work, the evidence suggests that woods operations were in fact seldom disrupted by accidents. The thousands of daily reports from shanty bosses and woods superintendents reporting on day-to-day operations in camps almost never mention an accident. Now, it is possible that accidents were treated rather cavalierly by bosses and men alike because the dangers of woods work were taken for granted and manly self-images interfered with frank reporting. On the other hand, there may have been lower rates of accidents in the woods than in a later period – say, the first half of the twentieth century. The proportion of inexperienced immigrants working in the woods grew after 1900, and, moreover, the pace of woods work increased as managers introduced piece-work and other methods of driving the men.[51] By contrast, in the timber and sawlog camps of the nineteenth century, the crews were largely made up of men who were handy with an axe after many seasons of work on farm woodlots or in lumbering. They were under less pressure to work fast because production quality was more important than it was later in pulpwood camps, and, accordingly, the men were paid for their time rather than their output. Furthermore, the use of five-man gangs for felling gave the workers a chance to rest and to watch for hazards developing overhead while the other gang members completed their tasks. The working conditions in the woods, then, were quite possibly safer before the coming of the efficiency measures associated with early twentieth-century corporate capitalism.

Operations on the river, however, are another matter. There can be no doubt that rafting and river driving were highly dangerous. Reports frequently reached the wider public of drownings. Until late in the century, when more stable craft became common, canoes often capsized in white water. 'We deeply regret to have to announce,' said the *Bytown Gazette* on 22 May 1852, 'that on Saturday last four men in the employment of Daniel McLachlin, Esq., M.P.P., were drowned at the Mountain Chute on the Madawaska River, in attempting to run a chute in a canoe.' The sudden arrival of high water caused by spring floods and broken dams could also catch rivermen by surprise. In May 1857 it was reported that a dam at Crotch Lake, a feeder lake for the upper Mississippi River in eastern Ontario, had given way after a few days of heavy rain. Twelve men engaged in stretching a boom below the dam were engulfed by a wall of water and floating timber. Ten of them drowned.[52] The breaking of log jams was notoriously dangerous because once the kingpin was pried loose, the entire pile was apt to break apart at once. The *Canada Lumberman* reported such occurrences, as on 15 July 1885, when seven men were said to have 'drowned while endeavouring to remove a key log in a log jam on the Mattawa River.'

The *Bytown Gazette* occasionally commented on the high accident rates on the river (a point not made about the woods). In an 1853 report on the drowning of a foreman by the name of Jeffries, who had been working for Wadwarth at Landon Chute, the newspaper added: 'This accident makes either the 9th or 10th life loss on the Madawaska this season.' On a few occasions safety conditions at the Chaudière slides also drew comment. For instance, improvements constructed in 1855 were said to secure 'the safety of the poor raftsmen.' Yet the death of a raftsman there nine years later brought a demand for changes: 'Experienced raftsmen say that had an "apron" been attached to the drop where the accident took place, it would not have resulted.' A few days later such an apron was built at the foot of the slide, and the *Gazette* reported, perhaps too optimistically, that 'cribs pass over now in safety.'[53]

Sometimes the river drivers' own carelessness was cited as the cause of the frequent accidents on the drive. Reporting on three drownings on the Madawaska in spring 1852, the *Gazette* commented: 'It is really lamentable to observe the consequence of the reckless daring and wanton disregard of life which is so often exhibited by those employed driving lumber. If unnecessary risk and exposure to danger were avoided, fewer accidents would be heard amongst raftsmen.'[54]

There may have been some truth in the *Gazette*'s charges of recklessness. Unfortunately, company records shed little light on this matter. The correspondents rarely mention the habits of the river men; clues are at best oblique. In 1861, high water during the river drive on the Upper Ottawa prompted McIntyre, an official with H. Bronson and Company, to instruct the supervisory staff to take special precautions. In one letter, the official noted that five men had drowned the previous week, and he urged a foreman: 'Play safely, Boyd, rather than fast ... Save your men and save your logs.' In a letter to another foreman, McIntyre wrote: 'Be careful Mc about your men. Save them first. Save your logs next and then get along as fast as possible.'[55] Evidently the official felt the men on the spot were likely to put speed before safety. Why they might be tempted to do so is not explained. Was it because of the men's competitiveness, the foremen's goading, or a pervasive bravado and recklessness associated with their sense of manliness?

The views of the river drivers and raftsmen themselves are preserved mainly in their many songs about accidents on the river.[56] Ballads about men crushed while breaking log jams or about drownings on the river were among the shantymen's most popular songs and far outnumbered those concerning accidents in the woods. These vibrant, sometimes haunting songs were an important way in which the woodsmen dealt with the extraordinary dangers of the work. In some songs the men exurberantly boast of their courage (perhaps as a way to screw up their courage!), and in others they lament the dangers, recklessness, and loss of life.

Certain themes recur. The men are portrayed as brave and as skilled at their jobs. Monroe, the tragic victim of the famous ballad 'The Jam on Gerry's Rocks,' was 'a young riverman so manly, true, and brave.' The hero and victim of another ballad was Charlie Williams, who 'held a peavey with the driver's hand and skill.'[57] Victims have no warning before either they are lost in a flash when the jam breaks or they plunge into the watery depths and struggle helplessly for shore. Their fellow workers do all they can to recover the bodies of the drowned so as to give them a proper burial, and along with the loved ones of the deceased, they mourn and feel a sense of loss.

As for the cause of the accidents, usually in the songs it is admitted that the work is dangerous. In the ballad about Jimmy Whelan's demise (possibly in 1878 on the Mississippi in eastern Ontario), the foreman selects Jimmy to break a jam because he had 'always been an active youth / While danger's lurking near.'[58] Nevertheless, in most of the ballads the rivermen are not at fault; the accident is caused by fate or the hand of God. The ballad about the 1894 drowning near Kinmount of Bill Dunbar ("a powerful able man") and his companion makes the point that the ice ought not to have broken through when his sleigh crossed the lake, 'it being the depths of winter.'[59] In 'The Jam on Gerry's Rocks' the crews are wary about breaking a jam on the sabbath: 'For to break a jam on Sunday they did not think it right.'[60] By contrast, another popular ballad stresses the experience and skill of young Johnny Stiles, but points as well to his recklessness:

> On the river there never was better,
> As I said, my young friend, Johnny Stiles.
> He had drove her far oftener than any,
> But he always seemed careless and wild.

Young Johnny paid dearly for his carelessness. Like several of the ballads, this one ends on a gruesome note, possibly meant as a warning to others. When the crew pulls Johnny's body from the river, 'it looked like poor Johnny no more':

> For his flesh it hung down in large ringlets,
> In pieces the size of your hand.
> On earth we found rest for his body,
> May the Lord keep his soul in command.[61]

At least according to the ballads of the shantymen, then, accidents were more often attributed to chance, but carelessness could also play a role. Bravery is celebrated, recklessness is not. After all, each man's safety depended on the caution and skill of his fellow crew members.

Few safety precautions were taken by the men themselves. Agility was what counted most. It enabled river drivers to ride a log or dance across a boom of floating timber and jam-breakers to leap clear just in the nick of time. To enhance their agility, river drivers were said to take care with their footwear. They paid high prices for a good pair of calked boots with sharp studs, thick soles, and well-fitted uppers that supported the ankles.[62] A fellow's safety and, perhaps more important still, his reputation as a skilled river driver rested to a large extent on his quickness and sureness of foot. The ability to swim or a flotation vest might have saved many lives on the river, but neither was much prized by the men. Accounts in the press sometimes noted that a drowning man could not swim, as in a report concerning two men lumbering on the Madawaska in May 1866.[63] A drowning man 'who was unable to swim' had cried out to a friend by the name of Howard, who jumped to the rescue. 'The drowning man immediately seized Howard,' explained the writer, 'and they sank together.' In a ballad about a young man from Peterborough who lost his life on the Black River, a line is repeated: 'As he could not swim, to the bottom sank on the cold Black River stream.'[64] The impression is given that swimming was not something one learned; rather, it was a talent that God had granted only to a few. Certainly it was not a requirement of the job.

During the nineteenth century woods workers had no feeling that they might be entitled to a safe workplace or to financial compensation for injuries. In Ontario, the foundations of the modern, state-sponsored system of workers' compensation were not laid until the second decade of the twentieth century. During the earlier century, shantymen passed the hat to collect for injured workmates or their widows. Bravado and ballads provided psychic compensation where agility, skill, and luck gave out. Fortunately for the employers, the shantymen's daring and their lack of any sense of their rights relieved the companies of the obligation to pay for safer methods and equipment and to provide just compensation for injuries incurred on the job.

IN THE SHANTIES

An integral part of the work of the men in the woods was shanty or camp life. Unlike workers in many other occupations, who left their work-mates at the end of the day, woodsmen stayed together, sharing accommodations, food, and free-time amusements. The essential features of shanty life – the close, all-male community, the considerable isolation, the traditional routine – changed remarkably little during the course of the nineteenth century.

Accommodations in the woods were invariably primitive. From the earliest shanties to the more elaborate camps of big operators during the last decade of the century, the buildings were crudely and inexpensively constructed by the shantymen themselves. The companies' aim was to keep costs to a minimum. The essentials were supplied by the materials that came immediately to hand in the backwoods from logs for walls to fir boughs for mattresses, thus the expense of transporting large quantities of goods into remote locations was eliminated. A minimum amount of care was taken with construction because the camps were used only for a season or two until the timber within walking distance had been depleted. The shantymen expected primitive conditions when they set off for the bush each fall. In the nineteenth century, as opposed to the twentieth, it appears Ontario woodsmen put little or no pressure on their employers to improve the basic accommodations.

In all small operations and even most large ones, at least until the last decade of the century camboose shanties were the norm. Charles Macnamara, a head office employee of McLachlin Brothers of Arnprior, made a point of documenting camboose shanties in words and photographs. The typical shanty housing fifty to sixty men, he wrote, 'was a low log building about 35 feet by 40 feet, with side walls six feet high and gables about 10 feet at the peak.' The walls were built of logs notched so as to interlock at the ends. Gaps between the logs were chinked with moss. The shanty was roofed 'with "scoops" that is, logs hollowed out like troughs ... The joints between them were covered with other scoops turned hollow side down, and the ridge of the roof, where the scoops butted together, was also covered with inverted scoops.' There was a single door. In rare instances, there were windows, but usually it was thought that enough light (and more than enough ventilation!)

came from the large (twelve-foot by twelve-foot) opening in the roof. It also allowed smoke to escape from the central fire pit, or 'camboose.'[65]

The heart of the shanty was the camboose, a twelve-foot by twelve-foot area that was built up a foot or two from the ground with logs and filled with sand. There a large fire burned day and night to heat the shanty and allow for cooking. Bread was baked, salt pork boiled, and pea soup simmered in large iron kettles and pots suspended over the open fire or set in the hot sand. Around the edge of the camboose stood simple benches, where the men could sit to eat, warm themselves, or mend their clothing and sharpen their axes by the light of the fire. Along three walls of the shanty were bunks roughly constructed of saplings. They ran two tiers high and were built as muzzle-loaders; that is, the men shoved themselves into the bunks so their heads were against the wall and their feet to the fire. The men slept two to a bunk, sharing a double grey woollen blanket. Along the wall with the door stood the woodpile, wash basins and water barrel, the cook's work table, stores and utensils, and a rough desk for the clerk with handy shelves to hold 'van' supplies – mittens, tobacco, moccasins, longjohns, red flannel sashes, and so on, that would be sold to the men.

In the case of camboose shanties, the only other building in the camp was a log barn for the oxen or horses and their fodder. During the 1890s, big operators, perhaps borrowing from Michigan, tended to opt for a new kind of camp composed of a cluster of buildings, each with a special purpose. Thus, in addition to the barn, there was usually a blacksmith's shack; a cabin where the clerk kept accounts, sold van goods, and slept along with the foreman; a separate cookery where the cook worked and slept along with his assistants, and where they served meals to the men; a cellar for storing root vegetables and salt pork; and perhaps two or three sleep camps or bunkhouses. These bunkhouses were as crude as the camboose shanties and similarly built of logs, but they were heated by a wood stove, usually a tin barrel turned on its side. A tin chimney replaced the large opening in the roof. In the cookery stood a big, wood-burning cookstove and many long tables with benches where the men ate sit-down meals.

These new arrangements represented a modest step towards a further division of labour, most notably the addition of cookees who assisted the cook by peeling potatoes and the like, serving meals, and washing up. The changes also increased the social space between some members of the camp. At night the foreman and clerk, and the cooking staff retired to their respective quarters outside the main sleep camps. Nevertheless, what should be stressed is the close quarters and shared experience of the shantymen. However firm the hierarchy on the job, it was partly offset by the propinquity and fraternity of the shanty. From chore boy to shanty boss, all ate from the same pot and drank from the same dipper.

The shanty diet was determined by both tradition and remoteness. Though the food was not always appetizing or of good quality, it was usually plentiful. It was also rich, as was believed to be suitable for men doing heavy labour. The basis of the diet was salt pork, which was easier to store than beef and usually cheaper. During the second half of the century most of it was imported from Chicago, although local sources were not unimportant. It was fried in strips or, more commonly, simmered as part of a stew, pork and beans, or pea soup. Bread was also a staple. Macnamara remembered the bread baked in sand as being 'particularly fine,' and having 'a delectable nutty flavour.' Dried foods – peas, beans, apples, currants, and biscuit or hard tack – were light to transport and kept well, and so they provided the other basic ingredients. Sometimes there was also pickled herring or dried cod. Molasses, sugar, and tea were considered luxuries even at mid-century, but later they became commonplace, as did mustard, cloves, and cinnamon for flavouring. Scurvy, or 'blackleg,' was known in some camps; it was caused by the lack of vitamin C in the diet.[66]

With the exception of fish and game given to the cook by the shantymen themselves, all food had to be brought in from the outside. In the fall of the year, and again in mid-winter when the ice conditions were good, the tote roads into the camps were often busy with local farmers and teamsters hauling in supplies and, incidentally, carrying correspondence and keeping the shanties in touch with the outside. The big firms ran their own farms in conjunction with the shanties, largely to pasture the horses during the off-season and to grow hay and oats for the horses and oxen, and sometimes root vegetables for the shantymen. In areas of intensive lumbering in the lower Ottawa Valley, independent farmers provided food and forage for the shanty market. By the end of the century, railway construction and advances in bulk food processing and packaging enabled some operators to provide even greater variety in camp diets. Yet in most camps the traditional foods were all that the men expected, even at the end of the century. It was not until the acute labour shortages of the First World War that the logging operators methodically set out to make the diets less monotonous as part of an attempt to attract workers and keep them.[67]

Every shanty worthy of the name had a cook. Only small shacker operations – that is, those conducted on a more or less ad hoc basis by fewer than a dozen men – tried to get along without one. Naturally, it took the time of at least one person to cook meals for a standard shanty of fifty men. Moreover, cooking was acknowledged to be a skilled occupation and was paid accordingly. Cooks were virtually always male, not because of the job itself, which, after all, closely resembled tasks designated as 'women's work' in the home, but because the rest of the crew was male and the camp was far removed from what were considered to be the necessary moral restraints of family and church. Moreover, male cooks guarded their well-paid jobs from women competitors. Female cooks or cookees were sometimes found at the depot camp (the base camp) if there were farms and hence farm families nearby. Even early in the century, it was recognized that company farms were best run by families and that the women might play a role in feeding shantymen at the depot camp. When John Donnally took over responsibility for Hamilton and Low's Rouge River operations in 1835, he was told to consider having a family at the depot because the firm was 'convinced in cooking affairs & Cows that a woman is of service and profit.'[68]

Each fall, camp life soon settled into a routine. During the autumn felling season, the work day lasted until dusk, and in mid-winter, when the rush was on to haul the timber before the thaw, hauling crews worked by torchlight until the mid-evening. Most evenings, the men were so exhausted that once they had eaten they tumbled into their bunks. Sunday provided a day off – at least when the urgency of completing the sleigh haul wasn't stronger than the sabbatarian inclinations of the owners. It was a time to restore energies by taking it easy or by going hunting or fishing. Clothes were repaired, axes and saws sharpened.

Was sex a part of the nightly shanty routine? Probably not for the vast majority, but this question is difficult to answer. Sexual relations and practices in the lumber camps are hard to document and assess. Given the scarcity of evidence so far come to light, it seems likely that among campmates there was no openly acknowledged sub-culture of sexual intimacy in the all-male shanties. Nevertheless, furtive same-sex liaisons did occur; we have evidence of at least one charge of buggery involving two Ontario shantymen. Without further evidence, it is open to speculation whether this kind of incident hints at widespread but well-hidden practices, or whether it was an example of rooting out unusual behaviour. The only sexual relations among the shantymen that were discussed openly were with female prostitutes. In the press of the day, such activity was regarded as a safety valve that released tensions pent up during long periods of celibacy in the shanties.[69]

The routine of shanty life was sometimes interrupted by a visitor. In some camps a priest made a brief appearance to hear confessions and say mass or a preacher would turn up to deliver a sermon and lead a hymn sing. Priests and preachers alike asked the men to subscribe to missionary and hospital work, and the clerks would deduct the designated amount from the season-end pay. In the surviving company records such subscriptions are not noted with much frequency. In all likelihood, clerical visits were rare in many camps and unknown in others. During the late 1870s and 1880s a few reports in the *Canada Presbyterian* indicate some commitment to the shantymen's mission, an endeavour given support by Presbyterian congregations at Ottawa. But such outreach must have been limited. One missionary based at Mattawa emphasized the difficulties in reaching a large population scattered among remote shanties, and he admitted that even where contacts were made, the results varied: 'Frequently the Word is listened to earnestly and a deep impression is made,' but other times 'through prejudice or ignorance little good will be accomplished.' Fundamentalist and moral reform organizations that specifically targeted bushworkers were not formed until shortly after 1900.[70]

Physicians' visits, too, were virtually unknown in camps until the new century. When a man became seriously ill, his camp mates were apt to take up a subscription (docked from their final pay) in order to send him home. Thus, when Christof Bernier fell ill in November 1869 in Britten's shanty, the superintendent informed Mossom Boyd that the men had 'together subscribed $14 to defray his expenses back to Quebec.' But doctors might make a special trip to a camp where typhoid or smallpox had broken out in order to deal with the sick and attempt to arrest the disease before it spread beyond the camp. At the time of the smallpox epidemic of 1885, all men living in lumber camps in Ontario were required to be vaccinated – a rare instance of state intervention in the lives of the shantymen.[71] The idea that doctors might make regular check-ups of the men in the camps was broached during the nineteenth century. Dr C.A. Duke wrote Gillies Brothers from Baie de Pères in July 1889 suggesting that all the men in his district subscribe twenty-five cents a month each, and that in return for that payment, the doctor would visit all shanties once a month and tend to any emergencies. As a precedent he cited a system adopted by the Canadian Pacific Railway. Gillies did not accept the suggestion at that time. However, after smallpox spread widely from the lumber camps in 1900, the province required that a similar system be imposed throughout the logging districts.[72]

Rather than being broken by outsiders, the camp routine, was more apt to be broken by the men themselves. Saturday night was the time for lively diversions. Nearly every camp had a fiddler, and singing and buck dances were popular pastimes. James Hillis, who in 1883 at the age of sixteen got his first woods job with Boyd Caldwell and Company, recorded his experiences in later life.[73] He notes 'how proficient some of those log-rollers were with the violin when they couldn't read a note of music,' and he recalls that 'community dances provided a background for their agility at square dancing as well as clog.' Singing was the specialty of men who had a voice and a knack for remembering long ballads and adapting them to their crew's experiences. Sing-alongs could be times for exuberance, and the lively tunes of many a shanty song, melodies drawn from Irish, French-Canadian, and American folk songs, as well as those of sailors around the globe, express a great zest for life.

In his recollections, Hillis vividly recalls some of the Saturday-night tricks played on him that first season as part of his initiation into shanty life. When he played one of the popular test-of-strength games, it was rigged so that he fell backwards into a tub of icy water. 'This trick raised my Irish blood,' he says, and he was about to raise a ruckus until he was assured that every newcomer had the same trick played on him. On another occasion, when playing hit-ass, a popular game where a blindfolded man had to guess who had walloped him on the rear, unbeknownst to Hillis, his face had been blackened with soot, much to the amusement of his senior camp-mates. Hillis also describes the elaborate preparations made in order to terrify young greenhorns. For several evenings running, men would return to the shanty from the dark woods saying they had glimpsed a bizarre animal. Then, on Saturday night, after various horror stories had been told around the camboose fire, the cook would say, '"Listen!" Sure enough, there would be a queer noise on the roof near the smokestack. Everyone in the group would become excited and jump to his feet as the racket above grew worse. Then, in an instant, they would all behold a large, dark furry animal with huge eyes tumble from the chimney to fall with a thump at their feet.' The terrified lads had been tricked by a man dressed in a bull hide.

These kinds of initiation rites denote a strong sense of group identity among the shantymen. When a young lad signed onto a crew, he was doing more than merely taking a job; he was joining a fraternity that had its own rules and ways of doing things and a sense of boundaries between itself and others. Internal discipline prevailed, as did outward conformity. Charles Macnamara put it this way: 'There was a code of conduct and even rules of etiquette to which the newcomer had to conform or he was soon "given his time" and sent down. The men who did not fit in were eliminated, and the gang settled down for the winter as a more or less harmonious community.'[74] At the camp level, the process of winning conformity was probably straightforward, as Macnamara indicates. But for some individuals it must surely have been painful. Precisely how a man was made to conform is a matter that has not been much explored by historians, and the sources are extremely scanty. It is reasonable to assume, however, that ethnic differences must have made for difficulties. Poles from Renfrew County and many a lone French Canadian must have had trouble being one of the boys. Where men from such minorities were numerous enough, it was common practice to make up a Polish shanty or a French *chantier*, and in this way the problems of fitting in were circumvented. The Polish and French camps then set their own standards for conformity (although in many respects the patterns of camp life varied little from those in the camps of the English-speakers).

When the shanty crew broke up in spring, the men dispersed. Many returned to their homes, of course, but for others camp life of a different sort began. River drivers, their clothes soaked day and night, shivered in tents pitched on the bank of the stream and near their work. Conditions here were even more primitive, but at least the season was short. For raftsmen on the Ottawa, makeshift quarters were rigged upon the rafts themselves, the men living aboard for the few weeks it took to ride down to Quebec.

In comparison with shantying, river driving and rafting brought many more chances of contact with the wider world – the local communities they encountered as they moved downstream. In Upper Canada, John Langton described the river drivers as follows: 'They are a light-hearted set of dare devils and the greatest rascals and thieves that ever a peaceable country was tormented with ... Hen roosts have quite disappeared from the riverside, and lambs and little pigs have to be kept under lock and key.'[75]

Other observers have recalled the annual visit of the river drivers with unalloyed delight. Jim MacDonald remembered how, as a boy living near the Little Thessalon River on the north shore of Lake Huron, 'It was an event to remember when that first log reached the pond each spring.' He and his pals liked to watch the men at work, and they 'looked forward to the evenings when sluicing might be finished early and the drivers assembled in the street to play a rousing game of "duck-on-the-rock" with them.'[76] Among the women in the villages along the river drivers' route, some looked forward to their arrival, while others felt threatened by the groups of carousing men. In contrast to shantymen in the backwoods, the river drivers' and raftsmen's contact with communities meant that they were much more likely to drink alcohol and become embroiled in fights. Local newspapers appear to have followed the movements of the river men closely, and a study of the local press would help clarify both the image and reality of the river driver's life.

The raftsmen especially gained a reputation for rowdiness. Several witnesses before the Committee on Trade that investigated the timber trade of the Canadas in 1836 stressed the contrast between the habits of men when they worked in the shanties and when they were rafting. No group were 'so hard wrought or allowed so little relaxation or indulgence as the actual *chantier* men,' stated one observer. By contrast, 'during the rafting season some dissipation may occur; ardent spirits are freely used, in consequence of the constant exposure to wet, and an erroneous impression that they afford the best counteraction to it.' The deal manufacturer of Hawkesbury, George Hamilton, insisted: 'There is no dissipation or idleness in the woods; hard work and plenty to eat is the order of the day.' Raftsmen, once paid off at Quebec, boarded steamboats to return home after many months away. 'Very frequently at the Bars of those Boats [they] procure the means of intoxication, [and] ... broils and riots proceed.' Hamilton thought that this unfortunately created the wrong impression among observers, who erroneously assumed that 'all rafts men are at all times and seasons, and in all situations, a set of demoralized ragamuffins.'[77]

As Hamilton suggests, it was easy for social commentators in the nineteenth century to exaggerate the depravity of the woodsmen. An important Victorian source of information and comment on the shantymen was the Protestant missionary in the field. Of course, missionaries were especially apt to dwell on questions of morality. D.L. Mackechnie, a Presbyterian proselytizer in the upper Ottawa region during the 1880s, told the readers of the *Canada Presbyterian* about the 'ungodliness among the lumbering class.' He condemned their 'most obvious sin,' profanity: 'The man who does not swear is an exception to the general rule. Sometimes men vie with each other in using the most awful oaths.' Mackechnie attributed their bad habits to the 'strange and undesirable life ... The men are away the greater part of their time from society, from religious privileges and from their homes and families. There is a tendency to roughness in appearance and manners. The absence of the refining and softening influence of woman is greatly felt. The sight of a woman in some of the shanties furthest off would be as strange a spectacle as the appearance of a white man in some village of Central Africa.' Given the late Victorians' view of the sexes as sharply distinct and mutually complementary, such a commentary on the all-male shanty was likely to find a resonance among the middle class.[78] Interestingly enough, the songs of the shantymen themselves neither lament the absence of women nor condemn immorality. Instead, they show a robust enthusiasm for the ways of the all-male camps.

Earlier scholars noted the predilection of nineteenth-century outside observers to focus on the bad morals of the shantymen and raftsmen. A.R.M. Lower was correct in pointing to a class dimension to many of the criticisms of forest workers, whom he describes as 'men impatient of control, fond of their liberty and equipped with all the improvidences that are the despair of an orderly, thrifty, money-getting and commendable society, in short to that respectable bourgeois society to which all the critics of the shantymen belonged.' In connection with the woodsmen, mainly of New Brunswick during the first half of the nineteenth century, Graeme Wynn has explored the intellectual traditions that led to the generally inapt depiction of lumberers as 'deplorably dark and demoralized.'[79]

Nevertheless, there is evidence to suggest that many (though not all) shantymen did on occasion drink heavily, carouse, and fight. When cutting loose in town, they thrived on defying Victorian conventions. In the tradition of the frontier thesis, Lower puts this down to 'the woods [which] gave rise to their own manner of life and their own manner of men,' and he holds that frontier conditions inevitably produced a *'joie de vivre'* which manifested itself in 'wine, women, song, and fisticuffs ... In this respect, the shantyman was no different from the sailor or the soldier, or from his counterparts, the prospector, the miner, the cowboy and other such frontiersmen.'[80] Michael Cross considers the violence of Ottawa lumberers to be partly ethnic in origin – the Irish 'were prone to violence, the violence of the drunken, of the desperate, of the insecure,' and on the river they clashed with their rivals, the French-Canadian raftsmen. To this he adds an argument about the lack of social restraints on the frontier.[81] More satisfactory is Richard Reid's argument linking fighting among Ottawa lumberers to their 'all-male society which accorded greatest status to strength, stamina, courage, cunning, and ferocity.' In this vein, he argues, 'Fighting demonstrated an individual's standing in his male environment, and by extension, the status of the group which he represented.' Reid points to the most famous Ottawa Valley fighter, Joseph Muffraw, who made his mark in the 1820s and was thereafter a hero and a legend, especially among French Canadians. 'The hero worship accorded him by many fellow French Canadians,' says Reid, 'reflected the status which an individual could obtain by feats of strength, courage, and endurance.'[82] A rugged masculinity was essential to the image the river men liked to project.

FINDING WORK

Historians know very little about how labour markets operated in nineteenth-century Ontario. Apart from some broad strokes made by Clare Pentland, the picture for particular occupational groups is virtually blank, the one exception being the case of domestic servants.[83] We are fortunate, however, that some unusually rich sources are available for the shantymen – the records of firms that devoted considerable resources to assembling seasonal crews.

Direct evidence from the woodsmen about how they found jobs is scarce, but we do have some letters by men applying for work in the forest industry. These are the nearest we can get to the voices of the men themselves. Several collections of lumber company records contain at least a few such letters, most of them scrawled in an awkward hand with a blunt pencil on cheap paper. In 1870 Robert Hay of Jacques and Hay, the furniture makers, received an application from a C.H. Hays of Vesto, Simcoe County, who was seeking work in the firm's nearby logging operations: 'i was hauling All last winter fore Mr. Warner [of] brentwood and i would like to git a job this winter to. i was goying to Warner a gain this winter but i heard that he has left. And i wood like to Know If there will be any chance fore teams, please wright.'

Thomas Hall of Smith's Falls wrote to Gillies Brothers on 7 November 1872: 'i rite this few Lines to Sea if thair Will be any Chanch to take a team up to the Bush this Winter. i have a splend team that is bought this fall for thrashing, and I will be done thrashing in a bout three weeks and if yous have not hired all your Lads i Wood Like to Get a Sha to Go up and try my hand. Pleas drop me a few Lins and if not Required i Shall Look elsewhere. no mar at Present. But i remain Yours truly ...' Notwithstanding all the irregularities of spelling, Hall has no problem making his meaning clear. It is interesting to see that he does not hesitate to sell himself – or, more precisely, his 'splend team.' Moreover, even as he asks for work his pride is maintained; he makes it known that he can look elsewhere. He's interested in a job, but not begging for one.[84]

Other writers wanted to know the wages and other terms of employment before committing themselves. Edward Gorman, writing to Gillies Brothers on 27 October 1879 from Onslow, a farm community in Renfrew County, proposed terms he would find advantageous: 'I write you these few lines to engage work for the winter & if it would suit you I would take a load of my own oats up. You can let me know what time I could go. I would like to go earlier than I did last year. I am Sir your obedient Servant ...' Gorman is inclined to bargain and confident that he will be wanted.[85]

Only applicants for especially skilled positions – most notably in the sawmill – were likely to specify their experience or provide references. In April 1879 Gillies Brothers needed a steam engineer for their Braeside mill. Writing from Carp, George W. Green stated he had 'good references' and was 'strictly Temperate.' Nevertheless, he lost the job to Nelson Martin of Hull, who said that the previous summer he had served as engineer on the steamer *T.B. Maxwell* at Toronto. Copies of outgoing correspondence of forest industry firms sometimes contain lettters of reference for former employees. The Calvin Company wrote in May 1848, 'Mr Charles Newson has passed this winter as Cook in our shanty and has given satisfaction and as far as we know has acted with Honesty and propriety.'[86]

A few telegrams from woods workers to employers also survive. Not surprisingly, they are very much to the point. In October 1883, Mossom Boyd and Company received one from a Mathieu Bonenfant who was then at Trenton: 'Have you work for me and friend, both worked for Johnson last winter.' The firm replied, offering jobs to as many as eight men, sight unseen.[87]

In general, the small number of surviving letters of application suggests that only a fraction of woodsworkers found jobs by writing to lumber companies. Many who sought woods jobs were illiterate or at least uncomfortable writing letters. The large numbers of French Canadians coming to woods jobs from Quebec were especially unlikely to write to anglophone employers. Why it was that some workers did make written application is not usually evident, but one such applicant, T. Lachaud who described himself as 'a first class Cook for Shure,' explained to Mossom Boyd and Company in August 1888 that he did 'not use to hire at any hotel so you will not find strange about me writing to you for a job.'[88] Indeed, it was customary for job seekers either to rely on local networks of neighbours and kin or to frequent certain hotels and boarding houses well known as hiring halls for the woods. In either case, the ability to write was not required. These methods of matching applicants to positions are best examined from the employers' perspective because it was they who left a paper trail which we can follow.

FINDING MEN

When employers needed men for their woods operations they relied on a number of recruitment methods, some of them requiring more initiative and effort than others. Though woods work had a strong appeal for rural men, in some years other opportunities drew the men away, making recruitment a harder chore for employers. Moreover, the seasonality of lumbering meant that assembling a workforce was in many instances virtually a constant activity.

One of the employers' easiest means of recruiting labour was to sit back and let applicants appear at the office. And in fact local lads and men tramping in search of work frequently did appear on the doorstep at headquarters. These offices were located either in a large town or city, such as Ottawa or Toronto, or on the site of the company's sawmill. The headquarters staff regularly sent men to the backwoods with notes of introduction, stating wage rates and either recommending that the bush superintendent or foreman hire the man or saying that he had already been hired. In November 1871 a clerk in the Mossom Boyd office at Bobcaygeon wrote such a note to the firm's bush superintendent, Norman Barnhart:

Angus McElnernry – hired by *me* for you @ $22 per month. This man appears somewhat superior, and can act as either Cook or Clerk, or both, and represents himself as competent to fill the place of A 1 Cook, having had four years experience.

If he is up to the mark, I hope you will keep him on.

In this instance we learn something about the chain of authority; the applicant was hired at the office, but the bush boss had final say. In the case of the Jacques and Hay Company at Toronto, senior partner Robert Hay was in constant touch with job seekers in the city and would inform the manager of woods operations at New Lowell, in Simcoe County, about the condition of the urban labour market. Thus, in December 1863 he wrote: 'We have had Calls from one or two parties who own teams wishing to get employment at Logging. Do you want any help of this kind? Or can you procure as much as you want in your neighbourhood?' The decision to hire was left to the man on the spot.[89]

The letters of introduction from headquarters sometimes contained advice regarding new hands. Robert Hay couldn't resist including his own assessment of the qualities of the men he sent north. One might be described as 'a very likely looking man' and another ('Scotch Billy,' the chopper) as 'a Hard case.' Similarly, Mossom Boyd would occasionally add his opinion, as in an 1870 letter introducing 'one of the best liners that can be had ... He understands making Timber as he lined several years for me before. Let him make Timber his own way – especially board Timber.'

In the case of Gillies Brothers, letters of introduction sometimes included brotherly advice. James Gillies wrote in January 1871 from his office at headquarters in Carleton Place to his younger brother, John, who was supervising operations up country: 'I have sent up Robert McCallum to cook all through. His pay is to be $18 per month. He is very short in the grain and passionate. You will have to be cautious how you talk to him. At least until you get used to him.'[90]

The stream of applicants at headquarters was not always steady. In the mid-1860s at Toronto, for example, the labour market was tight. In the fall of 1865, Robert Hay informed his manager up-country: 'I have been speaking to a number of people about a Blacksmith. I think a good one will be difficult to get hold of at this particular time.' By the same token, job seekers might give up on applying for work when word got around that a firm was not hiring. In January 1877 James Gillies wrote from Carleton Place to Braeside, informing the office there that it might take a while to hire a man with a superior team because he (Gillies) had 'refused all applicants all fall and lately there are none calling.'[91]

Another common recruiting method that required little effort on the employer's part was to have shanty foremen bring their own men. Shanty bosses often hired men near their home bases. Loyal crews made up in this way were known as the foreman's 'following.' Greenhorns might also be recruited from informal networks in the boss's neighbourhood, and in this way the crew of a single camp might all be Glengarry Scots or Richelieu Valley *Canadiens*. In August 1898 the Collins Inlet Lumber Company conveniently recruited men for operations on the north shore of Lake Huron by writing to Thomas Kirby, a foreman living in the off-season at Parry Sound: 'I would like to have you here with your men not later than next Thursday the 25th or earlier if possible. Get about forty men now, & we will enlarge to fifty men a little later or when you get going good.'

In other instances, companies would contact long-standing employees at their off-season homes and ask them to bring a gang. Farmers with their own teams were especially likely to be recruited in this way. In November 1834 William Stewart asked one such employee, Alex Corbet of Lancaster Township in Glengarry County, to go up the Ottawa Valley to 'team,' along with his neighbours, Allan Roy McDonell and Finley McDonell. 'You will take up three other spans,' Stewart wrote. 'Good smart fellows that know how to team and who have good horses.' Why Stewart recruited in that particular township is indicated in the request that concludes the letter: 'I wish you to speak to M. McLeod, 9th Concession, my brother in law. He may likely come up for one.' When recruiting raftsmen in 1861, the Calvin Company relied on a former foreman, Francis Ladrigg, to send workers from Coteau Landing in Canada East. The firm assured Ladrigg 'We will of course remunerate you for your trouble in getting them for us whenever we telegraph you.'[92]

Not only was this an easy way to recruit men, but the hope was that neighbours, friends, and relatives would cooperate well on the job, and that a foreman's following would remain loyal and stay the run. The strategy could backfire, however. When a foreman had to leave camp, there was the risk that all the men would follow. In April 1871 Mossom Boyd was informed that Dan MacIntosh, a shanty boss in the vicinity of Haliburton, had been taken ill, had gone home, and would not return.

'His men are all at the Shanty,' the report continued, 'and probably there may be some little difficulty to keep them in consequence of his not coming.'[93]

From reading the correspondence about hiring matters, one gets a sense of the informal networks in which employers and employees participated in an effort to place individual men 'Thomas Shillington called here today at noon and wanted to know if you could give him a job,' wrote James Gillies at Carleton Place to his brother John at Braeside in March 1875. 'He said that he would drive as a common hand or do anything you might want him for and also that he had a team that he could send up any day if you need any. Please write him to Lanark and give him an answer at once.' It is interesting to see the Gillies taking the trouble about such a matter, but they evidently knew Shillington, and James thought John might need his services. From the other side of the employment relationship, there could be similarly helpfulness and consideration. John Gillies received a letter in March 1880 from W.P. Roche, a former sawmill employee from Waltham who expressed concern for the Gillies' in their attempts to fill his place: 'I am sorey I cant go back this summer to file for yous but I think if you can get McPherson to take my place he would get along all right. Last fall he could File as well as I could. All he has to do is to be a little careful in the start and get every thing right.' Company loyalty and craft pride are equally present here. As a postscript, Roche added, 'If yous think of hireing an old filer I would advise yous to write J. Cheney, Purley & Pattee forman and if he recommend a man to you he will be a good one.' These information networks, then, could bridge both the division between master and men and rivalries among companies.[94]

It is difficult to gain any definite picture of how large a proportion of the logging crews was made up of men who developed a sense of attachment to a firm or foreman. The surviving employment records are too fragmentary to establish province-wide patterns. But one unusually complete set of woods employment records for the Mossom Boyd Company's Burnt River operations in the 1890s provides one piece of the puzzle.[95] When the crew list of 82 names for the 1890–1 winter season is compared with the comparable list of 53 names for the 1895–6 season, 15 names are found to be repeated. In the course of a half dozen years, then, about 15 men, or 18.5 per cent, of the crew appear to be still returning to work with the same firm in the same operation. The remainder of the crew had had to be recruited in the interim. Of course we cannot know whether this proportion of returnees was typical, although a general reading of qualitative evidence suggests that it might be. One shortcoming of the sources is that most of the surviving records deal with

recruitment problems or active efforts. The regular employees who did
not create recruitment difficulties left little trace in the records. Unfortunately for the historian, the experienced and loyal core of the crews is the
most elusive group.

AGGRESSIVE RECRUITING

Employers routinely had to go beyond informal job placement networks
and undertake aggressive recruiting campaigns. Only in exceptional circumstances though, did companies resort to paying for advertising space
in newspapers. In 1882–3 William Carpenter began setting up new lumbering operations at the Lakehead, in large part to supply construction
contractors on the Canadian Pacific Railway. In addition to his recruiting
efforts in Simcoe and Bruce Counties, he advertised in the Toronto
Globe for an essential employee:

Wanted

A first class Circular Sawyer who must be a good filer, active, and *strictly temperate* to go to Fort William, Lake Superior, on first Boat after opening of navigation. Apply stating wages and references.

A close reading of the *Bytown Gazette* for a twenty-year period (1853–
73) turned up only two want ads for shantymen, and both were for foremen – once again, essential employees. The assumption of employers
appears to have been that even for highly skilled woodsmen – hewers
and the like – there was little point to spending money on newspaper
advertisements, perhaps because so many of such men did not (or could
not) read them. And thus, other recruiting techniques were used.[96]
Recruitment drives were made annually by company personnel, usually by the bush superintendent. They would first tour the towns in the
general vicinity of their mills or timber limits of long standing. Here
men would know to congregate at the times, such as October, December, or April, when the companies were most likely to be hiring. Thus,
for example, Norman Barnhart, superintendent for Mossom Boyd,
would make tours of towns in the Kawarthas, like Peterborough and
Lindsay, which were not far from the base at Bobcaygeon, or villages
farther north near active lumbering operations, such as Haliburton, Kinmount, and Gooderham. In April 1887 Barnhart reported from Peterborough that there was 'a lot of hiring going on here,' and he referred to
other recruiters who were sending men to the French River, far to the
north. In the fall of the same year, he referred to stiff competition at
Peterborough and Lindsay from recruiters who were sending men to

Parry Harbour and other places in the Georgian Bay area. Local newspapers occasionally reported on the presence of recruiters. In November 1894 the *Orillia Times* informed its readers, 'Great numbers of men have gone to the shanties this fall,' and noted, 'Mr. Samuel Symington is hiring men for camps at Moon River and Wahnapitai, Mr. Doolittle for Ahmic Harbor and Whitestone.' The item was picked up by the *Forester*, the local paper at Huntsville, for the benefit of woodsmen and employers there.[97]

Once the labour supply in local towns had been exhausted, company recruiters would scour the farm communities of their districts. After Barnhart's disappointments in Peterborough and Lindsay in 1887, he wrote saying that he didn't 'see anything else to be done only to try around the Back country.' He personally travelled the concessions and reported from Gelert that he had promises from a few men. In 1880, when too few men turned up at Carleton Place to team for Gillies Brothers, James Gillies sent an employee, John Dougherty, to recruit on the back roads of Renfrew County. Gillies reported that Dougherty had had some success, but added that that year men seemed to prefer to go to Booth's or 'somewhere else.' Off-season farmers and their sons who brought teams with them could not travel far and were thus confined to a limited number of employment options. But men selling just their labour power were, of course, more mobile. They could sign up with operators from farther west whose supply of local labour was strictly limited and who were thus willing to pay higher wages.[98]

When local supplies of labour proved inadequate, firms had to recruit from farther afield. In the central part of the province, Toronto was a recruitment centre where woodsmen congregated and employers sought placements. In mid-century, the woods labour market of the city was not highly organized. Thus, when Jacques and Hay needed men for the firm's Simcoe County shanties, Robert Hay himself had to scour the haunts of job-seeking woodsmen. At one point he reported to his woods manager that he had been unable to find choppers, but promised to 'call at the Houses they put up at every day, and see if I can engage them for you.' Another time he reported having 'called several times at the Taverns where choppers put up.' It is difficult to imagine this leading manufacturer and member of the local establishment visiting such taverns, but evidently he thought it the best way to proceed.[99]

Usually, though, when the larger Ontario woods employers found the local supplies of shantymen depleted, they turned to the woodsmen of Quebec, either undertaking a recruitment drive in the lower province or making arrangements with hiring agents at Ottawa, where an employment system developed early. A series of telegrams that Barnhart sent to the Mossom Boyd office at Bobcaygeon in 1882 illustrates just how active and mobile the bush superintendents had to be when assembling crews. On 14 October Barhart wired from Chicoutimi that he had hired thirty men at Murray Bay, though men were scarce and wages high. A few days later he arrived in Lindsay with a crew of sixty men. On 26 October he wired from Quebec that some thirty more men had been hired and more could be had. Four days later he was at Peterborough complaining that he could not get teams except at exorbitant wages. The following day he sent the last of his October wires, stating that he was leaving from Haliburton with twenty-two men. This kind of aggressive, far-reaching recruiting was greatly facilitated by railways and the telegraph during the second half of the nineteenth century.[100]

Recruiters often relied on priests to find them men. In the all-Catholic communities of rural Quebec, the *curé* was the centre of an information network that reached out to every family in the parish.[101] A half century later, recruiters from Ontario lumber firms were still relying on priests to find workers.[102] After Sunday mass, the priest would speak to men he judged to be in need of work and able to leave their families. His knowledge of family situations and his regular contact with his parishioners gave him a strategic position in the local labour market, a position upon which recruiters depended.

THE OTTAWA EMPLOYMENT AGENTS

Even more common than these extensive recruitment drives were attempts by Ontario employers to hire Quebec and other woodsmen at Ottawa, which by the 1870s had become known as 'the great employment bureau of Ontario and Quebec.' The trade was served by numerous lumbermen's employment agencies, some of them handling thousands of men annually from substantial and permanent establishments. Among the best known were A. Chevrier, E.E. Lauzon, George Martel, and W.O. McKay, all of Lower Town.[103]

Early in the century, Ottawa – or rather Bytown – had established itself as an important meeting place for men seeking woods and rafting jobs and for employers and their agents. Woods agents could service both the large timber firms, which were then based at Quebec, the export point, and timber operators far up the Ottawa River. Among other tasks, such as provisioning the shanties and overseeing rafting operations, the agents matched job seekers with jobs. The best-documented example of this kind of agent is William Stewart. Born in Scotland and raised in Glengarry, Stewart arrived in Bytown in 1827, when it was still a construction camp, to open a store that sold dry goods and shanty supplies and offered a taproom. Before long he was operating his own timbering and rafting concern, selling rafts at Quebec, and playing an active part in local and provincial politics and social affairs.[104] Stewart recruited men for operators up country. Thus, in November 1834 he wrote to prospective teamsters in Glengarry saying that he was doing so at the request of Mr William Kelly. A few years later he had to inform another operator, John Ker, that raftsmen were scarce and wages high: 'As to men there is not any to be had here ... I hired one today @ $16 [per month] & a Bonus. I'm waiting the arrival of Boats from below and will try. But you better try in your vicinity and don't discharge those you have.' A year later, when he was supplying another rafting concern, he reported even more vexing labour market conditions: 'I am now ... in the way of sending one Robert Thomson as Pilot and McIntyre and 4 or 5 men to you. They are old Countrymen @ $18 per month & as savey as the devil. You must keep them up to their work. I charged their minds that they must do it & no mistake. You never saw such work in getting men. Some of Egan's foremen paid yesterday $22 indiscriminately.'

Stewart would also make reports to Quebec timber merchants, informing them of the availability, price, and quality of men. He provided such information along with other details of day-to-day activities up the Ottawa. Apparently the merchants at Quebec liked to keep abreast of matters upstream that might affect costs, and in this, Stewart could be useful. Thus, in April 1840 Stewart reported to Wood and Gray, a Quebec firm with which he had extensive dealings: 'Generally Lumbermen are badly off for men. The demand is so great that any boats that can be picked up get any wages they choose to ask. When the Navigation opens I hope there will be a supply from below.'[105]

By the 1850s it had become common practice for employers at Bytown to hire men at the many Lower Town boarding houses and hotels that catered to the trade. Year-round woodsmen and raftsmen made such establishments their homes between jobs; seasonal workers in the trade put up there upon arriving in Ottawa from their homes in Quebec and eastern Ontario. Their stays might become extended because of the enterprising landlords who offered their boarders plenty of grog and the opportunity to play games of chance, thus inducing them to stay on and run up larger bills. Because the men themselves had no money to pay their bills, their employers either had to pay them when they had no other way of filling their crews or offer higher than the going wages.

Naturally, employers objected to what one of them called 'an organized system of imposition.' In an 1853 letter to the *Bytown Gazette,* 'Lumberer' described the system and its defects from the perspective of the employer:

The Canadian Raftsmen come up to Bytown, generally, in gangs of a dozen, or two dozen, and 'put up' or stop at these Boarding Houses, where every inducement in the shape of Grog, Bagatelle Tables, and so forth is kept, to run up a 'score,' – so that when I or any other unsophisticated Lumberman goes to hire them in the spring or the fall, we have to literally buy them out, and pay down large sums before they stir. In the meantime, while even on the way up [to the job site], it is quite easy for them to clear out, and leave, which they often do. Those who do not drink or play at Pigeon-hole are induced to stop, by the hope of higher wages, which the cunning Landlord holds out.[106]

The 'unsophisticated' employer was thus faced with the increased cost of paying hotel bills or with delays in hiring and getting operations underway.

From the men's point of view, one can understand the appeal of these drinking and gambling establishments, especially when groups of young men hailing from the same district came together, as was apparently the practice. Moreover, for the men there was the distinct possibility of taking pleasure at no financial cost. Such was the case in April 1850. According to the *Bytown Gazette*, a few raftsmen waiting briefly at Stewart's Tavern had gone on a drinking 'spree' and run up a substantial bill of twenty dollars. They were fortunate to have an employer or agent by the name of Conroy pay their bill. Alternatively, shantymen had a good chance of escaping into the backwoods or down the Ottawa, thus leaving the hotel keeper in the lurch with the unpaid bill or the employer who had agreed to pay it. Then again, it was possible that employers eager to pry workers loose from their comforts might raise their wage rates, just as landlords suggested. Of course, an unwitting boarder might find either that most of his wages went to paying the hotel bill or that he faced a jail term for failing to pay a bill. Even then, a resourceful shantyman might persuade a police court magistrate that his departure had been unavoidable. When Oliver Jeauvé was arraigned in the Ottawa police court in February 1862, he insisted that when he had got within five miles of the shanty (with some cash advanced by his employer, Alex McDonald of Sand Point) he had reversed his course and returned to the city because he did not feel well. Unfortunately for Jeauvé, the magistrate did not believe the story and sent him to jail for one month.[107]

But even from the perspective of the boarding-house and hotel keepers there were some disadvantages to an arrangement that generally proved lucrative. In 1859 sixteen landlords decided to form an association aimed at eliminating certain abuses. It was reported that they had discovered that the men who skipped out on hotel bills were the same ones who made a habit of quitting their jobs. The plan was to pool information and maintain a black-list for the benefit of cooperating employers and landlords. The hotel keepers pledged to refuse accommodations to anyone on the list. Moreover, implicitly admitting to past abuses themselves, the sixteen landlords agreed that they would refrain from encouraging the men to 'run large bills and thus impel them to demand more wages than the regular rate.'[108] Having made these promises, the landlords asked the employers to patronize their establishments when seeking men. In this way these landlords would get the business of the more reliable men and be able to increase their incomes by charging the employers for services rendered as employment agents.

Whether or not the strategy of the agents met with any success is not evident. What is clear is that by the 1870s a few landlords had emerged as the leading employment agents at Bytown, handling the bulk of the business and treating other boarding-house and hotel keepers more or less as subagents. Thus, large employers would do their business mostly with one agent, who in turn might recruit from a roster of landlords in Lower Town. Several of the leading employment agents were bilingual French Canadians who could talk both to the English-speaking lumber operators and the French-speaking applicants.

The agents provided diverse services to both employers and men. For the employers, the agents found men, sometimes by drawing on the stream that flowed through their offices, and sometimes by searching farther afield. Adrien Chevrier wrote to Gillies Brothers in December 1879 saying that he had 'written to three places to have some teams,' and a few weeks later he said he had been 'obliged to go in country to hire them, but it was very hard to hire them.' On occasion an agent would be pleased to report his success, as when Léandre Chevrier wrote Gillies Brothers to say that the two hewers he had found 'are very good ones. There is one left handed and the other right handed' – an ideal combination. The agents processed each man, filling in standard printed contracts that stated the wages and bound the men to stay a specific length of time. The agents also saw to the employee's transportation to camp and his accommodations en route. Chevrier informed Gillies Brothers that the hewers he had found would be put on the 4:50 train going north and that they would 'stop overnight at Young's Hotel in Sand Points.' Chevrier or an assistant probably purchased the train tickets, accompanied the hewers to the station, and provided a letter of introduction to the hotel keeper so he would know Gillies Brothers would pay the bill. Such close supervision was usually maintained because of the risk that the men might be tempted away by some other job offer or by a last-chance visit to a barroom. For all this service, the agent would extract from the employer a fee – perhaps two dollars a hiring.[109]

The fee could be well worth paying, as was evident in the extraordinary case of lumberman James Leamy, a leading citizen of Ottawa in the early 1860s. Early one morning in November 1862 Leamy had been doing a job usually performed by an agent – collecting his newly hired men at a Lower Town hotel, Longway's, on St Patrick St. One of his men, a hewer by the name of Crickway, was, in the words of the *Bytown Gazette* 'somewhat intoxicated.' As he was attempting to climb aboard the stage coach, Leamy 'seeing Crickway's helpless condition went to assist him to mount.' Now, unfortunately for Leamy, the hewer was carrying a shotgun, a hunting weapon he was taking to the bush. 'Crickway slipped or staggered,' reported the *Gazette*, and, 'sad to relate, the gun which he held in his hand went off, discharging its contents (duckshot) into Mr. Leamy's head, scattering the unfortunate man's brains about the sidewalk and over the front wall and windows of the hotel.'[110]

Eventually the leading employment agents and the employers found ways around what they had earlier seen as abuses. Through their connections with employers in the lumber business, the employment agents could exercise some control over the accounts of boarders. Written into employment contracts of the 1870s and later were provisions intended to ensure the payment of hotel bills. On the standard, printed engagement forms that lumbermen's agents completed, there was a column headed 'Board Bill' and another 'Where Owing.' Thus, for example, on a form completed on 19 June 1890 by Ad. Chevrier, Lumberman's Agent, it was noted that William McDonald, hired as a 'General Hand' on a raft leaving Long Sault for Quebec, owed $50 to A. Chevrier; Joseph Bourque, hired in the same capacity, owed $23.75 to George Martel, a boarding-house keeper with whom Chevrier dealt.[111] Such bills were a first charge against wages earned, and an employer was expected to deduct the amounts owing from the employee's pay and remit the funds to the hotel keeper. Such a system made it possible, then, for hotel keepers to offer services to workers knowing there was a good chance that their bills would eventually be paid.

Under the new arrangements, it was the woods and raftsmen themselves who paid for the agents' and employers' reduced risks. If a man staying at a Lower Town hotel after 1870 ran up a bar bill and gambling debts, he usually had to pay them off. No doubt some men, having enjoyed several drinks, lost control over their finances and ended up working for many weeks simply to pay off their hotel debts. Certainly the surviving employment records show that a small proportion of the crews had to pay substantial debts each season. Of course there is the strong possibility that many of these men were not the unwitting victims of exploitative hotel keepers, but single men who chose a life of seasonal bouts of hotel living and hard drinking alternating with periods of hard work.

A few of the men who ran up high debts tried to escape from paying them, and hotel keepers and lumbermen's agents did on occasion chase after payments for board owing. It was not uncommon for men to switch employers early in a contract without carrying their unpaid board bills forward. Thus, for example, W.O. MacKay, a lumberman's agent at Ottawa, on 23 January 1880, wrote to Gillies Brothers as follows: 'Will you be so kind as to charge Patrick Millway with $43.25 amount of order given to me, upon going for Messrs Perley & Pattee [another lumber firm] on the 18th Sept. last from which he has deserted and hired to your agent on the Coulonge.'[112]

In addition to furthering the firm's interests, the tracking down of a deserting employee might entail an element of paternalism. The Calvin Company at Garden Island wrote to Cook and Company in 1849, to say that a Mr Mooney had gone up to work for Cook, leaving a debt to the firm and 'his family here for us to support.' The plan was to have Cook and Company deduct ten or twelve dollars a month from Mooney's wages and remit them to Garden Island.[113]

On occasion employers threatened or took legal action against deserting shantymen or rival employers who hired runaways. Firms placed notices in newspapers such as the *Bathurst Packet* and the *Bytown Gazette* declaring that certain men had deserted with bills owing and threatening legal action if other firms hired them.[114] The police at Ottawa helped apprehend deserters who had returned to the city. Only in rare instances when bills were extremely large did hotel keepers resort to the courts for an order to garnishee wages; their own arrangements with employers were less costly and troublesome.[115] By the same token, only a few men made a game of avoiding payment of bills. Joseph Vinanca and Charles Lamoth, alias Degré, were said to 'have been running away from their employers all spring in order to try and get out of paying their Board Bill.' Usually however, the system worked well from the point of view of the agents and employers.[116]

ESTABLISHING THE TERMS OF EMPLOYMENT

An important part of the hiring process was establishing the terms of employment, particularly wages. There is a small amount of evidence of outright wage bargaining between employers or their agents and the men. One example comes from the correspondence between W.H. Carpenter, a Kincardine merchant who began recruiting for his new operations at the Lakehead in 1882, and Colin Beaton of Angus who recruited in Simcoe County for Carpenter. In response to Beaton's insistence that a cook would have to be paid substantially more than the two dollars per day offered, Carpenter replied, 'I think wages must be very much *higher* in your part of the country.' He had calculated 'to pay all we can afford and make money ourselves, but we do not think it necessary to raise wages over what men can gain for us.' He concluded by saying that if the cook Beaton had in mind could get five dollars per day, 'He would be foolish not to take it.' Daniel Phealen, a teamster living in Lanark Village, rejected outright the wages offered by Gillies Brothers in December 1879, and he proposed a higher rate. Two years later William Gillies complained that teamsters at Ottawa were refusing $1.25 per day and 'holding stiff for $1.50,' a price he had become resigned to paying.[117]

On occasion, prospective employees could bargain for other terms as well. Robert Hay reported in November 1863 that he had found an ox teamster, which is what his woods manager wanted, but the man said he would rather chop for $16 per month or drive horses for $15 than drive oxen for $18. In December 1873, James Gillies reported that several teams from the neighbourhood of Perth had visited Carleton Place and reluctantly agreed to the wage offered – $1.10 per day – 'providing that they get a winter's job.' A measure of security and a chance to save some money made the job more attractive.[118]

In the mid-nineteenth century, offers were occasionally sweetened, sometimes quite literally. Luxuries then not part of regular shanty fare such as tea or sugar might be included in contract terms as a supplement to wages. Even in later decades a pound of chewing tobacco might be mentioned in contracts as part of 'wages.'[119]

Generally speaking, however, lumbermen and their agents sought to avoid bargaining with woodsmen over wages. A firm would establish a wage rate based on previous experience and taking into account what the firm could afford and the market would bear. Once a rate had been established, it was only with great reluctance that changes would be made. Recruiters might complain continually about competitors – especially ones from farther west or from the United States – who were offering more and taking the best men. Nevertheless, the solution was to recruit farther afield or to wait until the labour supply had been infused with new entrants. Thus, for example, in the exceptionally tight market during the fall of 1887, when Mossom Boyd was greatly expanding its woods operations, Norman Barnhart had repeatedly tapped the market in the Kawarthas and Haliburton and had reached out to Quebec and even New Brunswick. Yet Mossom Boyd continued throughout to offer a basic wage of sixteen dollars per month, even though its competitors were offering much more. Similarly, when Robert Hay met with wage resistance when attempting to recruit shantymen at Toronto he advised his woods manager to look elsewhere: 'I have ... spoken to several [choppers], but they smile at the wages offered. I do not think you need expect any at $16 per month from this quarter. Perhaps Barrie would be a better place to look after cheap labour.' It must have been with some considerable pleasure that ordinary woodsmen turned down the appeal of one of Toronto's leading citizens![120]

Lumber firms were especially anxious to avoid offering a better rate to men hired late in a season, for fear those hired earlier would complain and insist on increases. John Gillies once reported to his brother that he had failed to hire the man he had wanted because that teamster insisted on getting at least one dollar a day when earlier recruits had been promised only eighty-five cents. 'I did not want to send up a team at them wages now,' commented Gillies, 'as it would play puck with the others.' Another time, when the Gillies were not so careful, they got blasts from two teamsters who discovered they were getting less than the others. 'When I hired with you last fall youse promised me as high wages as was going,' wrote James Doyle. 'I went and worked 58 days and was paid 85 cts per day. You have paid $1 per day to McGarry and McAffery. I write youse now for 15 cents per day for 58 day – $8.70.' The other teamster, Nathaniel Olmsted, was similarly insistent, and his pride was obviously injured because he added that he and his team had 'always been doing their best to Satisfy you in every way.' Examples of individuals standing up for their rights in this way are few, however. At least in the second half of the century written contracts made clear what the rates were to be, and the companies rarely adjusted them in mid-season.[121]

The details in written contracts varied from employee to employee. One matter that was always specified was length of stay. Some men would sign on until spring, 'clear in spring' being the common phrase to denote that the firm would settle up with the man about mid-March, once spring came and no more wood could be hauled to the dump sites. Others might sign on in the fall and be committed until the timber had been driven to the creek mouth or some other local point in readiness for rafting or other long-distance travel. Thus, a contract might read, 'Through to Big Chute,' and would involve staying until about mid-May. Many woodsmen had farms to attend to in spring and summer, and so they could not consider a long run. It appears that a shantyman stated his preference for length of run and, depending on the needs of the firm, the employer either agreed or hired someone else.

Sometimes, especially from mid-century, contracts included several provisions that firmly established the superior powers of the employer. One from 1850–1 set out the wages for each crew of shantymen and raftsmen and stated five 'rules and regulations,' including that the men were to receive no wages until their raft reached Quebec, even if they were discharged months before for any reason Mr Boyd might 'think proper.' Fines were also specified: '2 Shillings and sixpence for every day not working whilst in the shanty unless stopt by inclemency of weather.' Thus, twelve days missed for any reason, including illness, amounted to the loss of an entire month's pay. Even late in the century, workers who were ill had their pay docked and were charged board, usually at one dollar a day, for days not worked. Some employers succeeded in paying men in scrip or due bills redeemable at the company store in a sawmill centre where prices were apt to be inflated. Regular merchants accepted such funds only after discounting them by 15 to 50 per cent.[122]

During the last quarter of the nineteenth century, contracts throughout most of the industry became standardized and simplified. Hiring agents used commercially printed contract blanks that dealt mainly with wages and payments. These forms had columns headed 'Wages,' 'Advances,' and 'Monthly Payment.' The monthly wage rate was entered in the first column. Under 'Advances' the employer would note how much cash the employer or agent had advanced to an employee at the time the contract was signed. The amounts of advances varied considerably, with some employees taking nothing and others as much as a month's wages. Individual circumstances, of course, varied. Some men wanted cash to pay off a debt, send home to their family, or pay for a spree, while others had no pressing need for funds. And so a high advance does not necessarily denote an employee with bargaining clout. Under 'Monthly Payment' would be entered either an amount paid in cash every month to the worker, or an amount to be sent to someone else, almost always a wife, mother, or father. Here, too, individual circumstances varied and bargaining was not necessarily part of the transaction.

Naturally, it was to the advantage of the firm to minimize monthly payments because companies were frequently short of cash themselves and, moreover, they could always put unpaid wages to use. 'Of late Mr. Boyd has been finding fault with me for permitting such free advances to men,' explained a beleaguered accountant in March 1872. 'Had I carried out his wishes the men would have had no money paid them while in the woods.'[123]

From the employer's perspective, cash payments to raftsmen were especially troublesome because raftsmen had comparatively easy access to taverns en route and their drinking could delay operations. When a clerk at Harris, Bronson and Company informed a rafting supervisor on the Ottawa that he had hired several Irish raftsmen ('rugged looking fellows'), he begged the man on the spot to be sure to 'let no money out to them. It is a curse rather than a benefit.' On another occasion, in 1863 a Quebec agent for the Calvin Company wrote to the Garden Island office: 'On paying the Raftsmen the other day, I gave Bapt. Nobert $4 to take him back to the Island. He got drunk immediately and returned to the office next morning minus all his money and plus a broken nose. I repeatedly refused to give him any more money, but as there is no other prospect of his getting out of Quebec, I am going to pay his passage.' For employers, raftsmen in town with cash in their hands were thought to be a recipe for trouble.[124]

SHANTYMEN'S REMITTANCES

It was a routine matter for companies to send money to families of employees at the employee's request. Usually the amount was simply written on the engagement form and either the office at headquarters or the shanty clerk sent money orders according to schedule. When Mossom Boyd hired one F. Filworth in October 1871, the office informed the woods superintendent: 'His wife is to have half his wages monthly – which note and send order when due.' In November 1891 Thomas Lunan, bush superintendent for Gillies Brothers, had letters from an Alphonse Deschênes acknowledging receipt of eighteen dollars on his son's account, and from the mother of Henry Leitch acknowledging six dollars received.[125] On occasion, problems arose with the remittances. Emelia Lefèvre of Montreal, for one, complained in 1877 that she had been waiting for money on her husband's account 'for a great many things since many days.' She explained that she had 'no work' and 'a real want of money.'[126]

It is not easy to measure the significance of remittances. For one thing, the extent of the practice is difficult to assess. Records from Mossom Boyd's Burnt River operations during the 1880s give an indication of what may have been a pattern.[127] In 1883–4 the camps had 101 employees, 46 of whom sent home orders totalling $2,256, or nearly half the total pay of the crews. A year later in a crew of 64 there were 13 orders totalling $206, when total pay was $2,060. In 1886–7, 70 men out of a total group of 190 sent orders home. The orders represented $2,865 out of total pay of $7,832. In each of these instances, then, a substantial minority of the men sent home amounts equivalent to at least 10 per cent of the total payroll. These remittances must have made a difference to the lives of those back home, as is indicated by the complaints of relatives who hadn't received the expected sums.

These remittances are significant, too, in so far as they shed light on the sense of responsibility that many shantymen felt for their families.

Although the men were isolated from their wives, children, and parents for considerable periods of time, they continued to provide support for them. Married men must have derived some satisfaction from knowing that they were continuing to fulfil their masculine, breadwinner responsibilities, even when they were absent. Moreover, their active if distant contributions must have helped ease their return to a place of authority within their families at the end of a season of woods work. It is important to note as well that even some single men in the shanties, men so often mythologized as footloose and irresponsible, sent money home regularly. Here was an expression of masculine identity quite distinct from the forms of manliness associated with ruggedness, dangerous work, or the fellow feeling of the work crew and shanty. By the same token, there must have been many men who felt no obligation to send home remittances and more than a few who saw their earnings as strictly their own to enjoy.

THE TRIP TO CAMP

Once an agreement had been struck, and plans made regarding remittances, then it was off to the shanties and rafting grounds far upstream. The comings and goings of the lumbering crews were much commented on in the press because movements of such large numbers of men altered the pace and tenor of community life. In December 1882 the arrival in Midland of '120 good, able-bodied men for the bush' was noted with pride: 'These men have come all the way from the Gaspe, induced by the high wages paid in this lumbering district.' A few months later the Belleville *Intelligencer* reported that a large number of shantymen had returned from the woods with news of their accomplishments and prospects for the trade. 'They assert that the cut is very large and that the drive will be an early one.' In mid-March 1866 the *Bytown Gazette* reported the appearance of teams and shantymen returning from the 'winter's campaign.' The paper commented, 'The sight of the city evidently warmed up their hearts, for they cheered lustily as they proceeded.' In early September the same paper noted that the back streets of the Lower Town were being depopulated by the movement of shantymen back to the woods. One time the paper described the departure of a group of fifty shantymen: 'Before leaving they improvised a pike pole dance, near the old By-Ward market building, which attracted a large crowd, who seemed highly amused.'[128]

The men themselves appear to have counted their annual contract signing and trips to camp worth recording and even celebrating in song. The negotiations of canny shantymen recruited at Toronto and their movement to the camps of Michigan in 1892 are decribed in one such song, 'Michigan–I–O':

'Twas in the city of Toronto in eighteen ninety-two
I met with Isaac Colbourne, a lumberman you know.
He said, 'My hearty good fellows, how would you like to go
And spend a winter lumbering in Michigan–I–O?'

To him I quickly made reply and unto him did say:
'Me going out to Michigan depends on what you pay.
Oh, if you'll pay good wages and pay our passage to and fro,
Perhaps I'll go along with you to Michigan–I–O.'

'Twas on those conditions he 'listed quite a train,
Full thirty-five or forty, all able-bodied men.
Our passage being pleasant on the way we had to go
Till we arrived in Saginaw in Michigan–I–O.

A similar tale is told of a group signing on at Bobcaygeon for Allan Gilmour and Company, which had purchased a new limit in Muskoka shortly after Confederation:

Now we left our own homes, for the woods we were bent –
The first night in Bobcaygeon with pleasure we spent.
We put up at Harve Thompson's that night for a time
Who was hiring teams for the New Limit Line.

Now the name of those fellows in 'Caygeon that night
Was O'Neil, Georgie Ell, Pat Breck, and Jim White.
Harve gave each a fiver and with them did sign
For to pay our way through to the New Limit Line.

So we left there next morning precisely at eight
So as to reach Minden before it got late.
Oh, we landed in Minden that night just at nine
With our hearts full of joy for the New Limit Line.

The song follows their movements through Dorset and into Muskoka and then describes events that occurred at camp. Although the details refer to particular crews and times, the lyrics were frequently changed by the singers to suit first-hand experiences that in a general way were widely shared. Noting some of the terms of their deal with their employers was important to the shantymen, just as describing their long journey into remote areas was an essential part of their experience, their odyssey.[129]

SHANTYMEN, RAFTSMEN, AND CONFLICT

As we have seen, once the men were on the job, lumbering entailed a set of routines that were familiar to shantymen, season after season. The routine was seldom broken by conflicts. In their accounts of day-to-day activities in the shanties, bosses rarely noted a disruption caused by disputes with or among their men. They did report on other kinds of disruptions. Daily they worried about the weather – would the cold hold long enough, the storms soon depart? Equipment breakdowns and shortages of hay and oats created frequent snags that threatened to set their plans askew. There is no reason to suppose that shanty bosses suppressed news of trouble with the men, given that they reported other difficulties, even ones resulting from their own mistakes. Certainly employers of shantymen and raftsmen in nineteenth-century Ontario never had to deal with the labour-management conflict that developed when collective bargaining broke down, since there was no collective bargaining. In fact, unions were unknown in the bush and on the river, although some people must have encountered the Knights of Labor when sawmill workers in Muskoka and at Ottawa organized and struck in the late 1880s and early 1890s.

To be sure, there were instances of conflict, and it is worth scrutinizing a few of them, bearing in mind that they were exceptions. Woodsmen and raftsmen did not always get along among themselves, and inevitably there were clashes between individuals. Particularly during rafting, when men could get liquor more easily, fights sometimes broke out. One such incident was reported in the *Bytown Gazette*, probably because it involved a local clerk who bested his raftsman assailant in court. The accused was convicted and fined ten dollars. Another dispute entered into the public consciousness because the assailant died. In early September 1847 the *Bathurst Courier* reported that Hyacinthe Blachette had stabbed Pierre Aubichon in a fight at William Morris's camp on the Petawawa. The men had arrived in the camp two days before, bringing alcohol with them. Drinking had led to fighting and eventually to the murder of Aubichon.[130]

Some of the disputes among workers involved larger numbers of men. The *Canada Lumberman* reported in February 1882 that two rival camps at Hubbard Lake claimed the same landing, that is, the same dump site for their logs. Group pride and a competitive spirit evidently played their parts: 'The result was a kind of guerrilla warfare, until the men at one of the camps cleaned out the other – the foreman of the vanquished camp taking to town in his shirtsleeves.' In some of the clashes there was an element of ethnic differences. In the summer of 1876 it was reported that a fight had broken out between rival gangs of raftsmen when a crew of French Canadians discovered that a raft run by Indians had arrived at Ottawa a day sooner than theirs. Such ethnic clashes entered into the folk tradition of the woodsmen. The ninth verse of the song 'The New Limit Line' depicts an incident on the Gilmour limits in Muskoka. The crew of local boys hauling timber behind their lead teamster were confronted by a defiant outsider, a French Canadian who challenged the pecking order:

> Our lead was St. Thomas, from Nogies Creek mouth,
> But a Frenchman called Sweenor he tried to run him out,
> But our Bobcaygeon boys they all got combined –
> They ran Sweenor to hell from the New Limit Line.[131]

The most notorious clash involving ethnic groups was the Shiners' War among Ottawa raftsmen, which reached a climax during the period 1835–7. Observers at the time contended that it was in large part an attempt by organized Irish raftsmen to raise their wages by driving French Canadians from the river. Curiously enough, those same observers pointed out that certain employers were inciting the Irish, who were said to act as the employers' troops in battles that had their origins in clashes over timber limits.[132] Historian Michael Cross accepts both arguments, but he believes that in the frontier situation where there were virtually no forces of social control, one employer in particular, Peter Aylen, cynically manipulated the Irish raftsmen as part of his bid for social prestige.[133] A more compelling explanation for the violence has recently been advanced by Richard Reid.[134] He casts serious doubt on the claim that this was a fight over jobs, by noting that at the peak of the violence local employment opportunities were expanding. He also points out that the Irish cannot have been victorious, as is usually said, for both Irish and French Canadians continued to work in large numbers on the river, and their relations were generally harmonious. Reid suggests that the Shiners' War makes sense only when partisan political rivalries are taken into account. Peter Aylen was a Reformer who rallied Irish Catholic raftsmen as part of his political campaign to win power and defeat the Conservatives, who relied on Orange and French-Canadian bullies. It is at least clear that this exceptional moment of widespread violence among lumberers was no straightforward instance of class conflict. The alliances were cross-class, and the divisions were essentially ethnic and, quite possibly, partisan.

These were conflicts among workers, but sometimes, of course, a boss clashed with an employee or two. In 1881 a woods superintendent for Gillies Brothers reported that one of his foremen was so fed up with the incompetence of greenhorn teamsters that he had discharged them, because he could not 'get them to do fair work.' A woods boss wrote from Glanmorgan in 1898 to Mossom Boyd expressing his impatience with a clerk with whom he found 'it very difficult to get along.' What's more, the clerk was 'continualy making mestakes, and ha[d] no memory.' One employer, a Mr Findlay, succeeded in having charges laid against Baptiste Laframboise, an allegedly insubordinate raftsman who had been hired to run the Chatts Rapids. The story according to a police court reporter was as follows: 'When in the midst of a number of islands, where if every man does not do his duty, the chances are that the raft will be knocked to pieces, Laframboise refused to row. He also made an attempt to assault the foreman.' Fortunately for the raftsman, the magistrate held that as the offence had not been committed within the City of Ottawa, he had no power to act.[135]

The records of lumber companies reveal several cases where men were disciplined for being drunk on duty. A walking boss for Wright docked one such man a half day's pay. When drunks caused fights they were more likely to be fired. Writing from Usborne Depot in 1873, James McEvoy reported that he 'was obliged to discharge James Smith for getting drunk and raising disturbance.' Moreover, on the Monday morning he was still so drunk 'he could Scersly waulk.' Charles R. Stewart, bush superintendent with Mossom Boyd, wrote from Haliburton in 1869 complaining about a shanty cook by the name of Ingram who had gone on 'a two days drunk.' Stewart believed he 'should have discharged him,' but there was no one to take his place (and a cook was essential). Furthermore, Stewart considered Ingram 'a good cook.' And so Stewart had scolded him, saying that 'if he was not sober in the morning [he] would kick him out of the township, and forbid the tavern keeper to give him more drink.' On the morrow, the cook was reported 'penitent' and he 'solemnly promise[d] he w[ould] not take whiskey until next spring.'[136]

One instance of a conflict between employers and a raftsman is told so vividly by Ruggles Wright in his diary entries of August 1833 that it bears repeating here. While the Ottawa raftsmen were awaiting their pay at Quebec, they had 'got to quareling in consequence of some being drunk.' One of them by the name of 'Etien Lafleur got behind W. Wright [Ruggles' brother William] and Struck him with an ax in the head.'

Lafleur appeared to clear out, leaving his victim – his employer – for dead. The next day's diary entry records, however, that early in the morning Lafleur was discovered still aboard the raft, crying. According to Ruggles, Lafleur had been 'desperately wounded in the Grine with a picket when running across the raft to escape the night before.' Ruggles and a brother thought the fellow 'to miserable an object to take before the police,' and so they gave him a reprimand and pardoned him. Lafleur 'swore by all that was good that he recollects nothing, that he never would drink any more, [and] beged on us to assist or he must die.'[137]

When groups of workers took action against their bosses, they usually appear to have been objecting to the quality of shanty fare. In November 1883 W. Ritchie, camp foreman for Mossom Boyd, wrote from South River reporting on 'a break up in the gang of men – concerning the Board.' The men had 'refused for to work without having Beef.' Five log makers had left as a result, and 'the Balance of the gang remain at their work on conditions that I will get Beef for a chainge when I can.' Ritchie thought the company should approve his purchase of beef, even at high prices, because replacements for the men would have had to be paid higher wages. Since there is no follow-up correspondence, it appears likely that the foreman was given permission to buy the beef and the remaining men were satisfied.[138]

Another dispute over camp fare was not resolved as easily. In 1854 John Egan and Company had twenty-five shantymen arrested and charged for quitting work and thus breaking their contracts. In the Ottawa police court the defendants explained that 'the pork with which they were supplied in the shanty was unsound, and unfit for use; so much so, that they could not eat it, and had lived for several days on nothing but bread and tea.' Although the men complained several times, the foreman did not get better pork, and so they refused to work. According to the men's testimony the foreman then told them 'that if they could not work on such victuals they might leave.' The magistrates decided that according to the Master and Servant Law they had no power to inquire into the reason for the employees' departure. By leaving before the end of their contracts, the men had broken them. Each of the workers was fined one shilling or sentenced to a week in jail.[139]

Another cause for the occasional labour-management conflict involving whole crews was an employer's attempt to alter the terms of an existing contract. It was well understood that trouble was likely to result from such attempts. In December 1847 Thomas Graham, a Quebec timber dealer, wrote Douglas Cameron, a small lumberman operating out of Glengarry County, regarding the need to reduce shantymen's wages in mid-season. Graham complained that business was slack, he was losing money, and unemployment was so bad at Quebec there were 'Plenty of men here just now would be glad to work for their board.' He instructed Cameron as follows: 'You must make a Second arrangement with your men. They may think it hard but it is worse on me to be paying money for nothing. So you had better mind what you are about.' Unfortunately, we do not know how Cameron fared.[140]

In another instance early in the century, Ruggles Wright was reluctant to break his contract with his many raftsmen by failing to pay them as soon as the rafts reached Quebec. In June 1833 some of his rafts and men had arrived at Quebec, but the bank would not, or could not, provide Wright with the necessary cash – totalling over £1,287 – to pay them off. He reported, 'The hands were dissatisfied, thought it was my doing, in keeping them out of their money.' After a few days Wright managed to get hold of some funds and began paying them part of their earnings, except for those who would not be put off, 'consider[ing] it an unpardonable Sin.' It was a few weeks before he finally settled with the last of them, whom he shrewdly treated 'to rum and gin.'[141]

In his book *Up to Date; or, the Life of a Lumberman*, George Thompson includes a chapter entitled 'Trouble with the Men,' where he describes 'the first and only big strike that ever occurred in the bush.'[142] The dispute happened one October (probably in 1873) among the men Thompson was superintending for a large concern operating on a tributary of the Trent River. Towards the end of the month, the manager or head of the firm wrote to instruct Thompson to cut the shantymen's wages by 20 per cent, because of the falling price of labour that autumn. 'Now such a thing as a cut in the men's wages had never before been heard of in the bush,' writes Thompson, and he continues:

The view the men took of it was that they were being imposed upon, for they knew that they could have obtained the same rate of wages from other firms when they engaged with men, and being away back in the bush they knew nothing of the drop that had not only occurred in wages, but in timber and lumber; neither did they care. They claimed a bargain was a bargain; they had signed papers for the run or until the shanties closed in the spring, and they were prepared to carry out their part of the contract.

As Thompson tells the story, he knew there would be trouble, and so he insisted that the head of the firm himself come to the headquarters camp to announce the wage cut. On 1 November, the manager did appear with 'a big force of men' who had agreed to take the lower wage and the jobs of the workers. Work stopped for several days as the strikers came to realize the cut would go through; then they insisted they be paid their back wages. Altogether about two-thirds of the work force were paid off, and then the climax came.

Thompson, the manager, and the camp clerk were sitting in the office at headquarters camp when a group of the men who had just been paid off came in, asking how they were supposed to transport their trunks ten miles down the lake. The author continues: 'His nibs replied that he did not care a ——— how they got them down. Quick as a flash his nibs got a blow on the neck from one of the men, and then I knew we were in for it.' The manager was incapacitated with terror, and in an unmanly way 'did not speak or attempt to get up from his seat or in any way try even to defend himself.' Not surprisingly, given whose account this is, it was Thompson himself who sprang to the rescue and saved the day:

I instantly drew my revolver and fired in among the men, being careful not to hurt any one. This had the desired effect; the men tumbled out of the office in short order, and immediately got their trunks, emptied their clothes out and made a bon fire of the trunks right in front of the office, and with curses and yells took their departure.

To complete the story, Thompson reports that the firm lost a fortune on its timber that season because the replacement workers were incompetent and the original men that remained on the job put rotten timber into the raft so that it could not be sold. 'It was a lesson to his nibs,' concludes Thompson, 'for never after did he mention anything about reducing the men's wages. The timber that season was the last our firm ever put on the Quebec market.'

Now, this is a well-told story, but one wouldn't want to give too much credence to certain details concerning the heroism of the author himself. Nevertheless, the essentials of the account have a ring of authenticity. Here were men determined to resist a wage cut and to see their contracts fulfilled. When that proved impossible, two-thirds of them insisted on their wages, got what was owing, and expressed their anger. The other third swallowed the wage cut but used their control over production and quality to sabotage the operation. For the firm, the grim results of an ill-chosen policy were only too evident. It is quite possibly for this reason that firms almost never tried to reduce wages in mid-term.

What of the men themselves? Did they tend to live up to the terms of their contracts? Indications are that shantymen and raftsmen did so, although admittedly the evidence is fragmentary and difficult to interpret. An important source for shedding light on the issue of desertion is the *Bytown Gazette*, which published the paid notices of woods employers regarding runaway employees, as well as police court reports of breaches of the Master and Servant Act. The employers' notices were intended to prevent the runaway from securing a job from another employer in the trade and perhaps to recoup expenses incurred by the employer in hiring him. Some announcements also included a warning to any employer who was found to be harbouring the man in question. A typical notice reads:

Lumberers on the Ottawa and elsewhere are hereby cautioned from taking into their employment Louis Charout and Theofile LeClair, my hired men, they having left my shanty without my knowledge or consent, and are considerably indebted to me. Any person found employing them or continuing them in their service after the date of this notice will be prosecuted. John Thompson. Nepean, 26th September, 1846[143]

During the twenty-six-year period from 1846 to 1872, the *Bytown Gazette* published sixteen notices concerning a total of 78 men who had broken their contracts by quitting their jobs in mid-term. Three of the announcements concerned large groups (18–20 men), possibly whole crews that had deserted; the remainder announced alleged desertions of from one to five employees. The incidents were spread more or less evenly throughout the period. To be sure, the notices indicate that some men did leave their jobs against their employers' wishes and probably in violation of their contracts. Yet sixteen alleged incidents involving just 78 men over twenty-six years is not many, given that during the same period tens of thousands of contracts must have been made in the trade.

The police court reports in the *Gazette,* which provide further evidence, tend to confirm the low incidence of desertions. The period covered is a different one: the fourteen years from 1864 to 1878. My research located twenty-one reported cases involving lumbermen and their employees; all but six of the cases concerned only one alleged deserter. The resolution of each case is not always apparent, but in at least four instances the case against the employee was dismissed. Here, too, then the figures are hardly impressive when compared to the tens of thousands of contracts.

It is possible, of course, that these reported incidents are only the tip of the iceberg, that for one reason or another few of the many desertions resulted in employers' making public notices or taking men to court. Employers may sometimes have felt that it was futile to make a public announcement. If the alleged deserters could not be caught, then they could not be taken to police court. Lumbermen sometimes went to extremes, however, to apprehend a runaway. Take the case of Olivière Jeandreau, hired for the 1866–7 season by one John Sullivan. According to Jeandreau's testimony in police court, when he had quit the shanty after being 'badly used' he had been 'followed by a man and two dogs and was captured.' Back at the shanty he was beaten, and in the court-room he 'exhibited a mark on his head, not yet well, that he received on the occasion.' Jeandreau also declared under oath that Sullivan 'had his rifle loaded and said if he attempted to go away again he would kill him.' Jeandreau was discharged.[144]

Notwithstanding the evidence regarding these few dozen runaways, it appears likely that desertions were in fact rare. Certainly in the surviving records of lumber companies, where there are countless detailed reports of day-to-day mishaps and difficulties, there are almost no reports of employees' quitting their jobs and breaking their contracts. For woods-men, there were strong disincentives to quitting in mid-stream. They might lose their back wages, and because so many of the shantymen were paid only at the end of their contracts, the amounts owing would have been too large to forgo.

The runaways that employers pursued were mainly those who quit early in the game, before they had worked off the cash advances or the expenses their employers had incurred for hotel bills or transportation. Employers had another advantage in that because hiring was concentrated at Ottawa they had a fair chance of finding runaways when they came to town in search of work. So it was with two woodsmen hired by J.R. Booth who were said to have broken their contracts in November 1869. It was reported that Police Sgt Davis had succeeded in apprehending them at Ottawa, where they awaited trial. Once caught, the alleged deserters could then be brought to court and their employers could have the satisfaction of seeing the men fined or jailed. Many convicted run-aways were fined twenty dollars – more than a month's wages for many of them – or sentenced to twenty-one or thirty days in jail. A typical report from the police court concerned 'a little shanty cook of the name of Bouchette, about three feet in his boots.' Convicted of breaking a con-tract with lumberman Peter McLauren, he was given a fine of twenty dollars or twenty-one days in jail. 'Minus the needful,' the reporter com-mented wryly, 'he was sent to limbo.'[145] In this way, then, the state helped employers to discipline even that small minority of woods work-ers who believed they had something to gain by quitting a contract. The substantial fines and jail sentences must have deterred others from light-ing out from their camps.

LOOKING BACK, LOOKING FORWARD

This chapter began by arguing that the world of Ontario's shantymen in the nineteenth century was one of variety and movement, as well as remarkable stability. Many of the fundamental patterns of woods work endured well into the next century, although eventually – mainly after the Second World War – there were to be sweeping changes.[146] Throughout the nineteenth century, the workforce came from diverse sources. For many young men and immigrants, working in the woods was a way of earning cash so that they could settle on the land. For farmers on marginal lands, woods wages meant the difference between permanency and migration, making a go of a farm or having to move elsewhere. For some fellows – mainly single labourers – the timber camps provided jobs in winter, a time of year when there was little other work. And for still others, woods work, river driving, and rafting made up a year-round job and defined who they were. It was not until the second half of the twentieth century that the logging labour force came to consist mainly of a stable population of men who lived permanently in the logging districts and who thought of lumbering as a career.

The recruiting of workers amounted to an enormous and virtually continuous task for employers in the highly seasonal operations characteristic of nineteenth-century Ontario lumbering. Earlier than most other industries, lumbering developed an organized way of handling the supply and recruitment of labour. Before mid-century the merchants who bought and sold timber sometimes acted as employment agents: in the 1850s and 1860s certain hotel keepers, notably at Ottawa, came to specialize in hiring men, and their establishments became well-known hiring halls. As far as we know, only the main Atlantic ports then had structures as specialized and elaborate to deal with the highly fluid labour force of sailors. Possibly, given the importance of the port of Quebec to the timber trade, lumbering borrowed directly from the examples provided in shipping.[147]

The work of the shantymen involved a variety of tasks and distinct seasonal rhythms. In terms of skill the men ranged from the masterful hewer, well paid for his expert handling of a broad axe, to the men who did the grunt work of piling logs. During the mid-winter sleigh haul, the pace could be furious and the hours long, because the ideal cold weather lasted for only a short season. When the timber rafts were passing down smooth stretches of river, life seemed easy; at rapids, there was hope of survival only with strenuous effort. A heavy dependence on natural conditions and seasonal changes has remained characteristic of the industry to this day, although mechanization during the third quarter of the twentieth century reduced the extent of the dependence.

An outstanding example of stability in the nineteenth-century industry was the techniques of the shantymen. Although the industrial revolution swept through many industries, including even the sawmilling and pulp and paper branches of the forest industry, logging remained heavily dependent on simple tools and the muscles of men and beasts. The essential tools of the trade were still the axe, hand saw, cant hook, pike pole, and oar. To be sure, there were some innovations, such as the use of the two-man cross cut saw for felling and the switch from canoes to pointer boats, but the basics remained little changed. The most significant development in technique was not an innovation at all: it was the decline of square timbering. That reduced the demand for hewers, and hence the recognition (through high wages and status) traditionally granted the expert axeman. The fundamental methods of the trade in Ontario, however, were largely unchanged throughout the nineteenth century.

Labour relations, too, held their basic shape throughout the century. Unions were unknown in the woods and on the river. They did not come to the industry until the next century, when there developed acute labour shortages, a core of radical activists, and state policies that helped to promote collective bargaining. Even spontaneous group protests or strikes – aimed at bad food or wage cuts – were exceptional events. Individual protest, however, was never absent from logging. But throughout the nineteenth century a man wanting to challenge a boss or quit his job had to weigh the advantages against the fact that by doing so he would lose back pay and might be charged and convicted for having broken his contract.

Through the years the shantymen have retained a reputation for toughness, bravado, and, when in town, carousing. Hard work in remote places, very dangerous jobs, and the all-male life of the camps contributed to the shantymen's image and culture. And yet for many men, lumbering was simply a job at a time of year when jobs were scarce. The work was demanding but familiar, even monotonous. A sojourn away from home was less a means of escape from family life than a chance to advance the well-being of the family. Today, logging continues to provide men with a range of experiences and opportunities, even as rugged masculinity remains the hallmark of the woodsman.

NOTES

For helpful advice, I thank Paul Craven and the other authors of this volume, the Toronto Labour Studies Research Group, and the Early Canadian History Group.

1 The economic importance of the forest industry is evaluated in Douglas McCalla, 'Forest Products and Upper Canadian Development, 1814–42,' *Canadian Histori-*

cal Review 68 (1987), 159–98; and Peter W. Sinclair, 'The North and the North-
West: Forestry and Agriculture,' in Ian Drummond, *Progress without Planning:
The Economic History of Ontario from Confederation to the Second World War*
(Toronto: Ontario Historical Studies Series and the University of Toronto Press
1987), 77–8. On Muffraw (also Montferrand), see Gérard Goyer and Jean Hamelin,
'Joseph Montferrand,' *Dictionary of Canadian Biography* [*DCB*], vol. 9, 562–3. On
the Prince of Wales, see *Bytown Gazette*, 15 Aug. 1860.

2 A.R.M. Lower, *Great Britain's Woodyard: British America and the Timber Trade,
1763–1867* (Montreal and Kingston: McGill- Queen's University Press 1973);
idem, *The North American Assault on the Canadian Forest* (Toronto: Ryerson Press
1938); idem, 'The Trade in Square Timber,' University of Toronto Studies, History
and Economics, *Contributions to Canadian Economics* vol. 5, (1933), 40–61, repr.
in W.T. Easterbrook and M.H. Watkins, eds., *Approaches to Economic History*
(Toronto: McClelland & Stewart, Carleton Library 1967).

3 For company histories, see John H. Hughson and Courtney C. Bond, *Hurling Down
the Pine* (Old Chelsea, Quebec 1964); Charlotte Whitton, *A Hundred Years A-
Fellin' : The Story of the Gillies on the Ottawa* (Ottawa: Runge 1943); James T.
Angus, *A Deo Victoria: the Story of the Georgian Bay Lumber Co., 1871–1942*
(Thunder Bay: Severn Publications 1990); Louise Dechêne, 'Les entreprises de
William Price, 1810–1850,' *Histoire sociale/Social History* 1 (1968). From the
DCB see Richard Reid, 'John Egan,' *DCB*, vol. 8, 268; Henri Pilon, 'Joseph Aug-
mon,' *DCB*, vol. 10, 23; Michael S. Cross, 'Daniel McLachlin,' *DCB*, vol. 10, 480–
1; David S. Macmillan, 'Allan Gilmour,' *DCB*, vol. 11, 348–50; Robert Peter Gillis,
'Henry Franklin Bronson,' *DCB*, vol. 11, pp 112–13; idem, 'John Hamilton, *DCB*,
vol. 11, 379; idem, 'William Goodhue Perley,' *DCB*, vol. 11, 681–3. In a category
by itself is the fine study by Gwenda Hallsworth, '"A good paying business": Lumbering on the North Shore of Lake Huron, 1850–1910 with Particular Reference to
the Sudbury District' (MA thesis, Laurentian University 1983).

4 Among the best are Carl Kauffmann, *Logging Days in Blind River* (private 1970);
J.E. MacDonald, *Shantymen and Sodbusters: An Account of Logging and Settlement in Kirkwood Township, 1869–1928* (private 1966); John Macfie, *Parry Sound:
Logging Days* (Erin: Boston Mills Press 1992); Donald MacKay, *The Lumberjacks*
(Toronto: McGraw-Hill Ryerson 1978); Chris Curtis, 'Shanty Life in the Kawarthas, Ontario, 1850–1855,' *Material History Bulletin* 13 (1981), 39–50; Christian
Norman, 'A Company Community: Garden Island, Upper Canada at Mid-Century,'
in Donald H. Akenson, ed., *Canadian Papers in Rural History*, vol. 2 (1980),
113–34.

5 McCalla, 'Forest Products'; Michael S. Cross, 'The Shiners' War: Social Violence
in the Ottawa Valley in the 1830's,' *Canadian Historical Review* 54 (1973), 1–26;
idem, 'The Lumber Community of Upper Canada, 1815–1867,' *Ontario History* 52
(1960); idem, 'The Dark Druidical Groves: The Lumber Community and the Commercial Frontier in British North America to 1854' (PhD thesis, University of Tor-

onto 1968); Chad Gaffield, 'Boom and Bust: The Demography and Economy of the Lower Ottawa Valley in the Nineteenth Century,' *Canadian Historical Association, Historical Papers* (1982), 172–54; Richard Reid, ed., *The Upper Ottawa Valley to 1855: A Collection of Documents* (Toronto: The Champlain Society 1990); Sandra J. Gillis, 'The Timber Trade and the Ottawa Valley, 1806–1851,' (Ottawa: Parks Canada Manuscript no. 153, 1975).

6   Graeme Wynn, *Timber Colony: A Study in the Historical Geography of Early New Brunswick* (Toronto: University of Toronto Press 1981); René Hardy and Normand Séguin, *Forêt et société en Mauricie: La formation de la région des Trois-Rivières, 1830–1930* (Montreal: Boréal 1983).

7   McCalla, 'Forest Products'; idem, 'Rural Credit and Rural Development in Upper Canada, 1790–1850,' in Roger Hall, William Westfall, and Laurel Sefton MacDowell, eds, *Patterns of the Past: Interpreting Ontario's History* (Toronto and Oxford: Dundurn 1988); idem, 'The Internal Economy of Upper Canada: New Evidence on Agricultural Marketing before 1850,' *Agricultural History* 59 (1985).

8   Lower, *Great Britain's Woodyard*; idem, *North American Assault*, 89–12; Wynn, *Timber Colony*, chap. 2; R.G. Albion, *Forests and Sea Power: The Timber Problem of the Royal Navy, 1652–1862* (Cambridge, MA.: Harvard Economic Studies, no. 29, 1926); J. Potter, 'The British Timber Duties, 1815–60,' *Economica* 22 (1955), 122–36; R. Marvin McInnis, 'Canada in the World Market for Forest Products, 1850–1895,' paper prepared for the Second Canadian Business History Conference, Victoria, 1988; W.E. Greening, 'The Lumber Industry in the Ottawa Valley and the American Market in the Nineteenth Century,' *Ontario History* 72 (1970), 134–6; R.F. Palmer, 'Oswego: Lumber Trade Capital of the U.S.,' *Inland Seas* 40 (1984), 30–39; Paul L. Aird, *In Praise of Pine: the Eastern White Pine and Red Pine Timber Harvest from Ontario's Crown Forest* (Chalk River, Ont.: Canadian Forestry Service, Petawawa National Forestry Institute, Report PI–X–52, 1985).

9   D.M. Williams, 'Merchanting in the First Half of the Nineteenth Century: the Liverpool Timber Trade,' *Business History* 8 (1966), 103–21; Braithwaite Poole, *The Commerce of Liverpool* (London: Longmans 1854).

10   Theodore J. Karamanski, *Deep Woods Frontier: A History of Logging in Northern Michigan* (Detroit: Wayne State University Press 1989); Jeremy W. Kilar, *Michigan's Lumber Towns: Lumbermen and Laborers in Saginaw, Bay City, and Muskegon, 1870–1905* (Detroit: Wayne State University Press 1990); W.R. Williams, 'Big Tugs and Big Rafts: A Story of Georgian Bay Lumbering,' *Inland Seas* 3 (1947), 11–16; Robert C. Johnson, 'Logs for Saginaw: The Development of Raft-Towing on Lake Huron,' *Inland Seas* 5 (1949), 37–44; idem, 'Logs for Saginaw: An Episode in Canadian-American Relations,' *Michigan History* 34 (1950), 213–33.

11   McInnis, 'Canada in the World Market,' 9–20.

12   John A. Guthrie, *The Newsprint Paper Industry: An Economic Analysis* (Cambridge, Mass.: Harvard University Press 1941); Robert E. Ankli, 'The Canadian

Newsprint Industry, 1900–1940,' in Bruce R. Dalgaard and Richard K. Vedder, eds, *Variations in Business and Economic History: Essays in Honour of Donald L. Kremmer* (Greenwich, Conn.: Aijai Press 1982).

13 Lower, *Great Britain's Woodyard*; John Keyes, 'The Dunn Family: Two Generations of Timber Merchants at Quebec, 1850–1914,' paper presented to the First Canadian Business History Conference, Peterborough, 1984.

14 Reid, *Upper Ottawa Valley*, liv–lv.

15 Examples include the Hamiltons of Hawkesbury (see Gillis, 'John Hamilton,' 379) and the Gillies (see Whitton, *Hundred Years A-Fellin'*, 59–60).

16 Reid, *Upper Ottawa Valley*, lxxii; Angus, *A deo victoria*, 17–46.

17 John Gillies (1811–88) began as a backwoods farmer in Lanark County (see Whitton, *Hundred Years A-Fellin'*, 36–8). I discuss a furniture firm that diversified into logging in 'Confronting Distance: Managing Jacques and Hay's New Lowell Operations, 1853–74,' in Peter Baskerville, ed., *Canadian Papers in Business History* I (Victoria: Public History Group 1989), 75–100. Continentalists are described in Hallsworth, '"Good Paying Business,"' 52–4; an example is McArthur Brothers, who had operations near Sudbury and Saginaw, Michigan, and branches in Montreal, Detroit, and London, England.

18 Small operators are discussed by McCalla in 'Rural Credit'; on financial arrangements, see Hallsworth, '"Good Paying Business,"' 60–65.

19 Reid, 'John Egan,' 268–9; Lower, *North American Assault*, 138.

20 Archives of Ontario [AO], Hamilton Brothers Records, George Hamilton Letterbooks, mfm, G. Hamilton to Dennis Caulfield of Newry, 28 Nov. 1804; AO, William Stewart Papers [Stewart Papers], William Stewart to Wood & Gray of Quebec, 8 Feb. 1842; *Bytown Gazette*, 8 May 1868.

21 Regulation of the timber industry is discussed in Thomas Southworth and Aubrey White, 'A History of Crown Timber Regulations from the Date of the French Occupation to the Year 1899,' in Ontario, Department of Lands, Forests, and Mines, *Annual Report* 1907; Richard S. Lambert with Paul Pross, *Renewing Nature's Wealth: A Centennial History of Lands, Forests and Wildlife Administration in Ontario, 1763–1967* (Toronto: Department of Lands and Forests 1967); H.V. Nelles, *The Politics of Development: Forests, Mines, and Hydro-Electric Power in Ontario, 1849–1941* (Toronto: Macmillan 1974), 1–19. On colonization roads, see George W. Spragge, 'Colonization Roads in Canada West, 1850–1867,' *Ontario History* 44 (1957), 1–17. On the conservation movement, see R. Peter Gillis and Thomas R. Roach, *Lost Initiatives: Canada's Forest Products, Forest Policy and Forest Conservation* (Westport, Conn.: Greenwood 1984); Bruce Hodgins and Jamie Benedickson, *The Temagami Experience* (Toronto: University of Toronto Press 1988).

22 Reid, *Upper Ottawa Valley*, xviii–xix, xlvi–xlix; Bruce Elliott, '"The Famous Township of Hull": Image and Aspirations of a Pioneer Quebec Community,' *Histoire sociale/Social History* 12 (1979), 339–54; Edwin C. Guillet, ed., *The Valley of*

the Trent (Toronto: Champlain Society 1957); Hallsworth, '"A Good Paying Business,"' chap. 1

23 Hallsworth, '"A Good Paying Business,"' 127–9; C. Grant Head, 'An Introduction to Forest Exploitation in Nineteenth Century Ontario,' in J. David Wood, ed., *Perspectives on Landscape and Settlement in Nineteenth Century Ontario* (Toronto: McClelland & Stewart 1975).

24 McCalla, 'Forest Economy,' 182.

25 Testimony of John Neilson, 'Select Report on Timber Duties,' 1835, *British Parliamentary Papers* 19, 138; Marjorie Griffin Cohen, *Women's Work, Markets, and Economic Development in Nineteenth-Century Ontario* (Toronto: University of Toronto Press 1988), chaps. 3 and 4; Harriet B. King, *Letters from Muskoka, by An Emigrant Lady* (London: Richard Bentley and Son 1878), 137.

26 Neilson testimony, 139.

27 Karamanski, *Deep Woods Frontier*, 46–8. On rural conditions in Quebec and recruitment of seasonal labour, see Allan Greer, 'Fur-Trade Labour and Lower Canadian Agrarian Structures,' Canadian Historical Association *Historical Papers*, 1981, 197–214; Hardy and Séguin, *Forêt et société*, chap. 3.

28 Testimony of George Hamilton and William Patton, *Journals of the Legislative Council of Lower Canada*, 1836, App. C., 'Second Report of the Special Committee on the Trade of the Province' [Committee on Trade], n.p.

29 Henry Radecki with Benedykt Heydenkorn, *A Member of a Distinguished Family: The Polish Group in Canada* (Toronto and Ottawa: McClelland & Stewart and Dept. of the Secretary of State of Canada 1976), 21–2; Brenda Lee-Whiting, *A Harvest of Stones: The Germans of Renfrew County* (Toronto: University of Toronto Press 1985).

30 This topic needs further study, but see Royce Richardson, ed., *Drum Beat: Anger and Renewal in Indian Country* (Toronto: Assembly of First Nations 1989); Hodgins and Benedickson, *Temagami Experience*; W.R. Wightman, *Forever on the Fringe: Six Studies in the Development of Manitoulin Island* (Toronto: University of Toronto Press 1982).

31 Testimony of George Hamilton, Committee on Trade, n.p.

32 Robert Leslie Jones, *History of Agriculture in Ontario, 1613–1880* (Toronto: University of Toronto Press 1946), chap. 7; McCalla, 'Forest Economy'; John Buchanan, Chief Agent of the Emigration Department at Quebec, 'Bytown and Ottawa River Settlements,' in *Bytown Gazette*, 6 Sept. 1851; Bruce Elliott, *Irish Migrants in the Canadas: A New Approach* (Kingston and Montreal: McGill-Queen's University Press 1988).

33 Gaffield, 'Boom and Bust'; Graeme Wynn, '"Deplorably Dark and Demoralized" Lumberers? Rhetoric and Reality in Early Nineteenth Century New Brunswick,' *Journal of Forest History* 24 (1982), 192–5.

34 Ian Radforth, *Bushworkers and Bosses: Logging in Northern Ontario* (Toronto: University of Toronto Press 1987), chaps. 4 and 9.

35 Ontario Ministry of Natural Resources Library, 'The Pointer Boat,' typescript prepared by the Operations Branch, Department of Lands and Forests, 1963; R. John Corby, 'The Alligator or Steam Warping Tug: A Canadian Contribution to the Development of Technology in the Forest Industry,' *Industrial Archaeology* 3 (1977), 15–33.

36 See Wynn, *Timber Colony*, 54; Lower, *North American Assault*, 27.

37 The description of lumbering techniques is based on Wynn, *Timber Colony*, and Lower, *North American Assault*; MacKay, *The Lumberjacks*, passim; and Angus, *A deo victoria*, chap. 7.

38 Lower, *North American Assault*, 33.

39 Ibid.

40 National Archives of Canada [NAC], MG 28 III 1, Mossom Boyd and Company Records [Mossom Boyd Records], A1(b) Shanty Operations, 1. Letters from foremen, 1869–1912, vol. 99, Charles Thomson to A. Elliot, 20 Oct. 1870; AO, Gillies Bros. Lumber Company Records, D-10, Misc., 1875–1924, MU 3270, Engagements, 1877.

41 Ontario, Department of Crown Lands, *Annual Report* 1879, x–xii; Lambert, *Renewing Nature's Wealth*, 160.

42 McInnis, 'Canada in the World Market,' 15–20.

43 Edith Fowke, *Lumbering Songs from the Northern Woods* (repr. Toronto: NC Press 1985) 166.

44 On the rafting workforce and the Calvin Co., see Queen's University Archives (QUA), Calvin Company Papers, vol. 81, 'Records for Blacksmith Shop, Shipyard and Raftsmen'; D.D. Calvin, *A Saga of the St. Lawrence: Timber and Shipping through Three Generations* (Toronto: Ryerson Press 1945), chap. 3. More general studies of the Calvin Co. include Norman, 'A Company Community'; Donald Swainson, *Garden Island: A Shipping Empire* (Kingston, Ont.: Marine Museum of the Great Lakes at Kingston 1984); Donald Swainson, 'Dileno Dexter Calvin,' *DCB*, vol. 11, 139–41. The reputation of the Caughnawaga is discussed in Queen's University Archives; A.R.M. Lower Papers, box 62, File F77, notes on interview with Hon. Geo. Bryson, Ottawa, summer 1927; Adam Shortt, 'Rafting on the St. Lawrence,' *Queen's Quarterly* (Jan. 1902); E.J. Devine, *Historic Caughnawaga* (Montreal: Messenger 1922); Tony Hall, 'Native Limited Identities and Newcomer Metropolitanism in Upper Canada, 1814–1867,' in David Keane and Colin Read, eds, *Old Ontario: Essays in Honour of J.M.S. Careless* (Toronto: Dundurn 1990); Louis Jackson, *Our Caughnawagas in Egypt* (Montreal: Drysdale 1985).

45 *Bytown Gazette*, 29 Sept. 1866, 30 June 1864, 16 June 1866.

46 Radforth, *Bushworkers and Bosses*, 66–67, 204–6.

47 *Bytown Gazette*, 15 Nov. 1876, 21 Oct. 1874; Gillies Bros Records, MU 3247, McEvoy to Gillies Bros, 3 Nov. 1876.

48 *Bytown Gazette*, 17 Nov. 1863, 21 Nov. 1866, 29 Sept. 1849.

49 AO, Gillies Bros Records, MU 3246, C.J. Grierson to Gillies Bros, 1 Nov. 1875.
50 *Bytown Gazette*, 6 Apr. 1870, 8 Mar, 1878.
51 Radforth, *Bushworkers and Bosses*, chs. 2 and 4.
52 *Bytown Gazette*, 15 May 1857.
53 Ibid., 18 May 1853; 20 and 25 May 1855.
54 Ibid., 22 May 1852.
55 NAC, Bronson Co. Records, MG 28 III 26, Business Correspondence, 1857–1900, vol. 91: McIntyre to H.P. Boyd, 15 May 1861, and McIntyre to N.L. McCaushin, 30 May 1861.
56 All songs referred to in this chapter are taken from the folklorist Edith Fowke's *Lumbering Songs*. Between 1957 and the late 1960s Fowke recorded the songs of old-timers from the lumber camps in Ontario or just north of the Ottawa River in Quebec. Passed from one generation to the next, these songs are as close as we are likely to get to the voice of the nineteenth-century shantymen. It is worth adding that they were traditionally sung in the shanties during periods of relaxation. They are thus songs of an occupational group but not, strictly speaking, work songs sung while actually performing tasks.
57 Ibid., 'The River through the Pine,' 131.
58 Ibid., 'Jimmy Whelan,' 111.
59 Ibid., 'Bill Dunbar,' 144.
60 Ibid., 'The Jam on Gerry's Rocks,' 96.
61 Ibid., 'Johnny Stiles,' 108.
62 MacDonald, *Shantymen and Sodbusters*, 82–4.
63 *Bytown Gazette*, 29 May 1866.
64 Fowke, *Lumbering Songs*, 'The Cold Black River Stream,' 146.
65 Charles Macnamara, 'The Camboose Shanty,' *Ontario History* 51 (1959), 74. See also Bernie Bedore, *The Shanty* (Arnprior, private 1975). For a wider view, see Randall E. Rohe, 'The Evolution of the Great Lakes Logging Camp, 1830–1930,' *Journal of Forest History* 30 (1986), 17–28.
66 Macnamara, 76; Canada, Royal Commission on the Relations of Labour and Capital, *Report – Evidence, Ontario* (hereafter RCRLC), vol. 5, 1189.
67 Radforth, *Bushworkers and Bosses*, 98–9.
68 AO, Hamilton Brothers Records, Outgoing Correspondence, 1835–40, 'Instructions from Messrs. Hamilton & Low to Mr. John Donnally for Management of Rouge business,' Oct. 1835, cited in Reid, *Upper Ottawa*, 123.
69 The case of buggery is noted by Steven Maynard, who suggests that court records may prove revealing about sexuality in the logging camps; see his 'Rough Work and Rugged Men: The Social Construction of Masculinity in Working-Class History,' *Labour/Le Travail* 23 (1989), 159–69.
70 *Canada Presbyterian*, 3 June 1885. (My thanks to Christine Burr for this and subsequent references to this journal.) Radforth, *Bushworkers and Bosses*, 95–6, 102–3.
71 NAC, Mossom Boyd Records, vol. 102, Charles Stewart to Mossom Boyd, 26 Nov.

1869. Physicians' reports include: vol. 99, Dr Macdonald to A. Elliot, 30 Aug.
1870; vol. 105, Dr D. Williams to Mossom Boyd, 7 Dec. 1900. A copy of the government order may be found in AO, RG 10, Department of Health Records, 1B4, vol. 464, Scrapbook #1, item #50. The wider context is given in Barbara Lazenby Craig, 'State Medicine in Transition: Battling Smallpox in Ontario, 1882–1885,' *Ontario History* 75 (1983), 319–47.

72 AO, Gillies Bros Records, MU 3258, 15 July 1889. For context, see Radforth, *Bushworkers and Bosses*, 104–5; and Paul Bator, 'The Health Reformer versus the Common Canadian: The Controversy over Compulsory Vaccination against Smallpox in Toronto and Ontario, 1900–1920,' *Ontario History* 75 (1983), 348–73.

73 James M. Hillis, 'Life in the Lumber Camp: 1883,' *Ontario History* 59 (1967), 157–62.

74 Macnamara, 'Camboose Shanty,' 78.

75 John Langton, *Early Days in Upper Canada*, ed. by W.A. Langton (Toronto: Macmillan 1926), 205.

76 MacDonald, *Shantymen and Sodbusters*, 95.

77 Testimony of G. Brown, question #2, and Testimony of George Hamilton, Committee on Trade, n.p.

78 *Canada Presbyterian*, 3 June 1885.

79 Lower, *Great Britain's Woodyard*, 194; Wynn, ' "Deplorably Dark and Demoralized," ' passim.

80 Lower, *Great Britain's Woodyard*, 194.

81 Cross, 'Shiners' War,' 5.

82 Reid, *Upper Ottawa Valley*, xxxiii–xxxiv.

83 H. Clare Pentland, 'The Development of a Capitalistic Labour Market in Canada,' *Canadian Journal of Economics and Political Science* 25 (1959), 450–61.

84 Simcoe County Archives [SCA], Jacques and Hay Collection, C.H. Hays to Robert Paton, 24 Nov. 1870; AO, Gillies Bros Records, MU 3248, Thomas Hall to Gillies Bros, 7 Nov. 1872.

85 AO, Gillies Bros Records, MU 3249, Edward Gorman to Gillies Bros, 27 Dec. 1879.

86 AO, Gillies Bros Records, MU 3249, File: April 1879; QUA, Calvin Co. Papers, Series A, vol. I, p. 51, Calvin, Cook & Co. to Mssrs Smith and Goodward, 11 May 1848.

87 NAC, Mossom Boyd Records, vol. 93.

88 Ibid., vol. 104, T. Lachaud to Mossom Boyd, 7 Aug. 1888.

89 NAC, Mossom Boyd Records, vol. 94, Connell to Mossom Boyd, 7 Nov. 1871; SCA, Jacques and Hay Records, Robert Hay to Paton, 29 Dec. 1863.

90 SCA, Jacques and Hay Records, Robert Hay to Paton, 7 Nov. 1863, 25 [Nov.] 1873; NAC, Mossom Boyd Records, vol. 94, Mossom Boyd to Norman Barnhart, 29 Nov. 1870; AO, Gillies Bros Records, MU 3241, James Gillies to Gillies Bros, 3 Jan. 1871.

91 SCA, Jacques and Hay Records, Robert Hay to Paton, Oct. 1865 and Sept. 1866; AO, Gillies Bros Records, MU 3248, James Gillies to Gillies Bros, 6 Jan. 1877.

92 AO, Collins Inlet Lumber Co. Records, MU 7252, C.W. Pitt to Thomas Kirby, 19 Aug. 1898; AO, William Stewart Letter Books, MU 1729, William Stewart to Alex Corbet, 17 Nov. 1834; QUA, Calvin Co. Papers, Series A, vol. I, Calvin & Beck to Francis Ladrigg, 29 April 1861.

93 NAC, Mossom Boyd Records, vol. 99, M.A. Elliot to Mossom Boyd, 16 Apr. 1871.

94 AO, Gillies Bros Records, MU 3241, James Gillies to John Gillies, 6 Mar. 1875; MU 3250, W.P. Roche to John Gillies, 21 Mar. 1880.

95 NAC, Mossom Boyd Records, vol. 112, 'Balance Sheets,' Burnt River Operations, Winter 1890–1 and 1895–6.

96 AO, Carpenter Letterbooks, Feb. and Mar. 1883; *Bytown Gazette*, 23 Oct. 1852 and 28 Aug. 1868.

97 NAC, Mossom Boyd Records, vol. 95, Norman Barnhart to Mossom Boyd, 14 Apr. 1887, 2 Sept. 1887; *The Forester*, 30 Nov. 1894.

98 NAC, Mossom Boyd Records, vol. 95, Norman Barnhart to Mossom Boyd, 5 Sept. 1887; AO, MU 3241, Gillies Bros Records, James Gillies to Gillies Bros, 24, 30, and 31 Dec. 1880.

99 SCA, Jacques and Hay Collection, Robert Hay to Paton, 3 Nov. 1869 and 8 Nov. 1873.

100 AC, Mossom Boyd Records, vol. 93, 'Telegrams, 1882.'

101 Ibid., vol. 95, Norman Barnhart to Mossom Boyd & Co., 24 Oct. 1887.

102 Radforth, *Bushworkers and Bosses*, 36.

103 *Canada Lumberman*, 1 May 1903. On Lower Town in Ottawa, see John H. Taylor, *Ottawa: An Illustrated History* (Toronto: National Museum of Canada and James Lorimer & Co. 1986), 27.

104 R. Forbes Hirsch, 'William Stewart,' *DCB*, vol. 8, 840–1.

105 AO, William Stewart Letter Books, William Stewart to Alex Corbet, 17 Nov. 1834; Stewart to John Ker, 29 Apr. 1841; Stewart to Gerard I. Nagle, 5 Apr. 1842; Stewart to Wood and Gray, 11 Apr. 1840.

106 *Bytown Gazette*, 9 Apr. 1853.

107 Ibid., 27 Apr. 1850, 27 Feb. 1862.

108 Ibid., 7 Sept. 1859.

109 AO, Gillies Bros Records, MU 3249, Ad. Chevrier to Gillies Bros, 17 Dec. 1879, 9 Jan. 1880; MU 3247, Léandre Chevrier to Gillies Bros, 11 Nov. 1876.

110 *Bytown Gazette*, 8 Nov. 1862.

111 AO, Gillies Bros Records, MU 3266, 'Engagements, '19 June 1890.

112 Ibid., MU 3249, W.O. MacKay to Gillies Bros, 23 Jan. 1880.

113 QUA, Calvin Co. Papers, Series A, vol. 2, I.S. Beck to Messrs H. Cook & Co., 14 Dec 1849.

114 An example from the *Bytown Packet*, 10 Oct. 1846, is reprinted in Reid, *Upper Ottawa Valley*, 150.

115 A rare example of an order to garnishee is in AO, Gillies Bros Records, MU 3249, Court Order re: Euclide Bourgeois of Hull, 24 June 1890.

116 AO, Gillies Bros Records, MU 3258, C. Lamache to Gillies Bros, 14 July 1890.

117 AO, Carpenter Letterbooks, W.H. Carpenter to Colin Beaton, 23 Mar. 1882; AO, Gillies Bros Records, MU 3249, Daniel Phealen to Gillies Bros, 9 Dec. 1879; MU 3250, William Gillies to Gillies Bros, 21 Dec. 1881.

118 SCA, Jacques and Hay Collection, Robert Hay to Paton, 7 Nov. 1863; AO, Gillies Bros Records, MU 3244, James Gillies to Gillies Bros, 19 Dec. 1873.

119 See, for example, AO, Gillies Bros Records, MU 3238, John Gillies Shanty Book, 1856; MU 3266, 'Engagements,' 1880–81.

120 NAC, Mossom Boyd Records, vol. 95, '1887'; SCA, Jacques and Hay Collection, Robert Hay to Paton, 8 Nov. 1873.

121 AO, Gillies Bros Records, MU 3249, John Gillies to Gillies Bros, n.d.; MU 3249, James Doyle to Gillies Bros, 19 Apr. 1879, Nathaniel Olmsted to Gillies Bros, 8 Mar. 1879.

122 NAC, Mossom Boyd Records, vol. 875, Notebook 1850–1, as cited in Curtis, 'Shanty Life,' 43; RCRLC vol. 5, 1188–9.

123 NAC, Mossom Boyd Records, vol. 94, Connell to Norman Barnhart, 18 Mar. 1872.

124 NAC, Bronson Co. Records, vol. 91, McIntyre to H.P. Boyd, 27 Apr. 1890; QUA, Calvin Co. Papers, Series A, vol. 7, John Storey to Calvin & Beck, 31 Oct. 1863.

125 NAC, Mossom Boyd Records, Robert McConnell to Norman Barnhart, 14 Oct. 1871; Gillies Bros. Records, MU 3256, Alphonse Deschênes to Thomas Lunan, 9 Nov. 1891. See also OA, Madawaska Improvement Company Records, MU 1996, Operating Records – Cash Book, 1890.

126 AO, Gillies Bros Records, MU 3248, Emilia Lefèvre to Gillies Bros, 12 May 1877; see also MU 3249, Eustache Charbonneau to Gillies Bros, 15 Dec. 1879, MU 32532, Mrs. Robert McCane to Gillies Bros, 17 Dec. 1884; RCRLC vol. 5, 1137; AO, Hawkesbury Lumber Company Records, MU 1282, Employment Contracts, Eli Menard to Hamilton Bros, 17 Nov. 1887.

127 NAC, Mossom Boyd Records, vol. 112, 'Balance Sheets,' Burnt River Operations, 1883–4; 1884–5; 1886–7.

128 Canada Lumberman, 1 Dec. 1882; Intelligencer cited in Canada Lumberman, 15 Mar. 1883; Bytown Gazette, 16 Mar. 1866, 9 Sept. 1870, 26 Nov. 1878.

129 Fowke, Lumbering Songs, 'Michigan–I–O,' 28; 'The New Limit Line, '54–5.

130 Bytown Gazette, 9 Aug. 1870, 28 Aug. 1847. See also Bathurst Courier, 7 Sept. 1847, reprinted in Reid, Upper Ottawa Valley, 70–1.

131 Canada Lumberman, 1 Feb. 1882; Bytown Gazette, 3 Aug. 1876; Fowke, Lumbering Songs, 'The New Limit Line,' 55.

132 NAC, Upper Canada Sundries, vol. 152, George Hamilton to Lt.-Col. Rowan, 1 June 1835, G.W. Baker to Rowan, 15 June 1835.

133 Cross, 'Shiners' War,' passim.

134 Reid, *Upper Ottawa Valley*, xxxvi–xl.

135 AO, Gillies Bros Records, MU 3250, George Gordon to William Gillies, 13 Nov. 1881; NAC, Mossom Boyd Records, vol. 96, William Creswell to Mossom Boyd & Co., 8 Feb. 1898; *Bytown Gazette*, 13 June 1865.

136 NAC, MG 24 D 8, Philemon Wright and Family Papers (Mfm. M–234), unsigned diary, 18 Mar. 1859; AO, Gillies Bros Records, MU 3246, James McEvoy to Gillies Bros, 5 Jan. 1873; NAC, Mossom Boyd Records, vol. 102, Charles R. Stewart to Mossom Boyd, 26 Oct. 1869.

137 NAC, Wright Papers, Ruggles Wright Diary, 23 and 24 Aug. 1833.

138 NAC, Mossom Boyd Records, vol. 105, W. Ritchie to Mossom Boyd, 7 Nov. 1883.

139 *Bytown Gazette*, 17 June 1854.

140 OA, Douglas Cameron Papers, MU 466, Thomas Graham to D. Cameron, 20 Dec. 1847.

141 NAC, Wright Papers, Ruggles Wright Diary, 22 June 1833 – 17 Aug. 1833.

142 George Thompson, *Up to Date: Or the Life of a Lumberman* (Peterborough, private, c. 1895) chap. 6.

143 *Bytown Gazette*, 10 Oct. 1846.

144 Ibid., 31 May 1867.

145 Ibid., 6 Nov. 1869, 28 July 1864.

146 Twentieth-century developments are discussed in Radforth, *Bushworkers and Bosses*.

147 Judith Fingard, *Jack in Port: Sailortowns in Eastern Canada* (Toronto: University of Toronto Press 1979). In contrast to shipping, the state was not involved directly in Ontario lumbering labour markets of the nineteenth century.

Axemen notching pine at the McLachlan Brothers Lumber Company camp on the
Black River, 1900

Squaring timber with broad axes, 1890

River drivers at Muskoka timber slide, 1895

Camboose shanty

An evening's entertainment at a camp near Rainy Lake, west of Fort Frances, 1899

Religion, Leisure,
and Working-Class Identity

LYNNE MARKS

In the 1880s small towns and large cities across Ontario were invaded by the Salvation Army, which heralded its message of salvation with brass bands and rowdy parades that attracted crowds of working-class Ontarians. While its religious message was a familiar one in Protestant Ontario, the Salvation Army shocked many sedate middle-class churchgoers, who associated Christianity with dignified services in Gothic churches, not wild emotional exhortations in streets and rough 'barracks.' Working-class Ontarians, however, felt increasingly uncomfortable in the elaborate churches, dominated by the middle classes, that had come to define late nineteenth-century Ontario Protestantism. Many flocked to the Salvation Army, which provided them with religious solace in their own cultural idiom and also served as a vehicle for an emerging working-class sense of pride and identity.

While many middle-class observers attacked the Salvation Army as vulgar and disorderly, others, particularly middle-class Methodists, defended the Army as a return to an older, truer version of evangelical Christianity, which the Methodists had abandoned. During the early nineteenth-century 'golden age' conjured up by these commentators, Methodism too had been attacked as vulgar, overly emotional, and disorderly. Like the Salvation Army of the 1880s, it had provided a place for the dispossessed and a vehicle for their repressed aspirations.

Of course, Christianity has not just provided a space for the downtrodden. It has also, and in fact more commonly, instilled in its adherents a respect for, and indeed a belief in, the social and economic ideals of the systems which oppress them. When labour historians have studied religion at all, they have emphasized its repressive elements.[1] However, like the various leisure activities and associations which have been of more interest to labour historians, religion could either reinforce dominant values and structures or strengthen and channel social opposition among oppressed groups.[2]

In this chapter I will explore the ways in which a person's religious and leisure activities could reflect both opposition and accommodation to the dominant culture of nineteenth-century Ontario.[3] Religion and leisure are the spheres in which nineteenth-century Ontarians possessed the most choice about their lives. A person could, for example, more readily choose whether to go to a bar or a church on Sunday than whether to stay away from work on Monday. It is true that choices regarding religion and leisure were not completely freely made. Some options were simply not available to those working twelve-hour days, or to those of a particular gender or race. None the less, the religious and leisure activities of various social groups did reveal active choices, not only about beliefs and tastes but also about whom one felt most comfortable spending one's non-work hours with. The choices that were made can tell us a great deal about group identity.

In the nineteenth century, particularly in the latter years of the century, Ontarians could choose from an ever larger range of religious and leisure options. In the early part of the century, entertainment was usually organized locally, and the choices were limited. Local logging or house-raising bees provided opportunities for drinking, dancing, and socializing among otherwise isolated settlers; sports matches were organized in various communities; and Methodist camp meetings let Upper Canadians get together for sociability as well as worship. Entertainment also entered Ontario from more 'developed' regions. From early in the century small travelling theatre companies performed in local hotels; by mid-century larger towns were building theatres to accommodate both local amateur performances and the increasing numbers of theatre companies – of varying quality – that toured the province.[4] Audiences flocked to see Shakespearian plays, the ever popular melodramas and minstrel shows, and travelling circuses.[5] In most towns and cities, mechanics' institutes provided opportunities for more serious self-improvement, and in the last decades of the century there was a proliferation of commercial entertainment. Urban entrepreneurs built dance halls and amusement parks, and from the 1880s on even small communities boasted the popular 'roller rinks.' Nevertheless, the activities of voluntary associations remained central throughout the century. The meetings, socials, concerts, dances, and other events organized by local literary societies, sports clubs, fraternal orders, temperance societies, bands, fire companies, and a range of church-based women's, young people's, and other associations competed for the limited spare time of Ontarians in small towns and large cities alike. On public holidays such as Victoria Day, local voluntary efforts provided a range of entertainments of which trade processions, band music, torchlit parades, serious dramas, lacrosse and baseball games, three-legged races, and the chasing of greased pigs were only a few.

Since any attempt to discuss all the religious and leisure options in nineteenth-century Ontario would risk becoming nothing more than an ever growing list of possibilities, I will concentrate instead on the elements of religious and leisure life that clearly reveal the complexities of class, gender, and alternative-group identities. In examining leisure activities, I emphasize the two apparent extremes of nineteenth-century culture – the rough and the respectable. The clearest symbol of the distinction between these two extremes was the use of – or abstinence from – alcohol. But class was only one of several possible dividing lines between rough and respectable. An examination of the popular fraternal orders reveals that, at least among men, the distinction between these supposed extremes was murkier than previously believed.

The dominant faith of nineteenth-century Ontario was Protestantism, though in some townships and villages Catholics did make up the majority. In my discussion of religious life I will concentrate on the Protestant majority. This Protestant focus in part is due to the gaps in the literature. In Ontario, where the majority of Catholics were of Irish origin, historians have studied the close links between Catholicism and Irish identity. The most impressive example of such work is Brian Clarke's recent study of popular Irish Catholicism in Toronto. However, more research needs to be done into the social implications of Catholicism in nineteenth-century Ontario.[6] In exploring religious issues then, this chapter does not claim to examine the experience of the entire working class. Instead, it will concentrate on the ways in which various forms of Ontario Protestantism – ranging from Anglicanism to the Salvation Army – either reinforced or undermined a range of group identities among Protestant workers.

Although class will be a central form of group identity to be examined here, when discussing the early decades of the nineteenth century it is more accurate to speak of largely rural 'popular classes,' than of a working class, which did not emerge until Ontario's industrial revolution in the second half of the century. Moreover, throughout the nineteenth century (as today) Ontarians defined themselves not simply by class, but also by various other identities, which included ethnic origin, religious denomination, gender, age, and marital status. Since religious and leisure activities usually reinforced more than one form of group identity among the participants, the social legacy of such activities is complex and often contradictory.

The complexity of this legacy did not decline with the emergence of a distinct working class. The story to be told here is not a linear one – religious and leisure activities did not gradually divide out along class lines, providing increasingly important vehicles for class consciousness. Both early and late in the century, some religious and leisure activities expressed and nurtured some form of oppositional consciousness, sometimes by class and sometimes by gender. Even at such times, however, participation in these activities also demonstrated the existence of alternative loyalties and identities which could cut across and even negate any possibilities of radicalism. As we will see, the Knights of Labor of the 1880s showed most clearly how religious beliefs and associational practices could reinforce a distinct class politics. However, in the decades immediately before and after the 1880s, religious and leisure activities seem to have been influenced less by class identity than by other forms of identity based on age, sex, and ethnicity.

BELIEF AND UNBELIEF, ORDER AND DISORDER IN UPPER CANADA

In the early decades of the nineteenth century, both religion and the absence of religion could be viewed as subversive of the established order. As John Webster Grant has noted, many colonists in early Upper Canada professed no religion at all. In the first decades of the nineteenth century, ministers bemoaned the religious indifference of many Upper Canadian settlers. Many echoed the Rev. William Proudfoot, a Presbyterian minister who settled in the London area in 1833 and noted with surprise 'the number of persons who do not even make a profession of religion.'[7] As late as the first census of 1842, almost 17 per cent of the population claimed to have no religious preference or creed, a proportion that had declined to less than 2 per cent by 1861.[8] No doubt some of those claiming to have no religious adherence had not had any religious connection in either England or the United States before emigrating to Upper Canada. In other cases, however, emigrants who settled in the Upper Canadian backwoods, where ministers were few and far between, simply shrugged off the restraints of religious practice, either intentionally or unintentionally. But Christian customs were not entirely ignored, even by the irreligious. Most do not appear to have worked on the Sabbath, perhaps, as the Rev. Mr. Proudfoot suggests, because they 'dare not outrage public feeling,' or perhaps simply because a day of leisure was welcomed in the hard-working lives of the early settlers.[9] Visiting ministers and missionaries were shocked at the kinds of entertainment many indulged in on Sundays. In 1810 William Case, a Methodist minister, complained that in western Upper Canada the Sabbath was chosen as 'a day of wicked amusements,' when people spent their time at parties, and in dancing, hunting, and fishing.[10] Similarly John Howison noted in 1821 that in places without religious services Sundays were spent 'in idleness and amusement.'[11] Such views were expressed by visiting ministers from a variety of denominations well into the 1840s.[12]

While such activities can be viewed as simply a passive neglect of religious practices resulting from the shortage of clergy, in some cases this behaviour may also have expressed an active rejection of religious authority, as part of a desire for greater social freedom and equality, sought by some in the backwoods of Canada.[13] Certainly not all settlers welcomed efforts to reimpose the moral restraints and clerical direction of Christianity. Samuel Stearns Day, a Baptist theological student, noted that in the early 1830s, when he tried to start a Sunday school in what he described as 'a very degraded neighbourhood' south of Hamilton, he found that 'very many manifested either an entire indifference concerning Sabbath School, or an opposition to it. They are *bitter* against *tracts.*'[14] Many early Methodist preachers who travelled through the backwoods spreading the gospel also noted that some settlers received their message with hostility. Sometimes there were even threats of violence.[15]

The accounts by early Methodist ministers of such persecutions usually ended most appropriately, with hecklers being swept up in the revival led by the visiting preacher.[16] While such happy endings may be seen as victories for Christian morality, they were not necessarily considered as such by the Upper Canadian elite. As William Westfall has shown, this predominantly Anglican elite was extremely hostile to 'experiential' religious denominations like Methodism. For the central tenet of Methodism was the need for conversion, an intense, emotional experience in which individuals recognized the depth of their own sinfulness and felt themselves saved by God's grace. The personal nature of such an experience was in itself antithetical to the Anglican world view, in which the church existed not so much to encourage individual conversion, as to reinforce an ordered, hierarchical society.[17] The Anglican elite often viewed the emotionalism of Methodism and other revivalist denominations as a threat to the social order.[18]

Nathan O. Hatch has noted that in the United States during the Second Great Awakening of the early nineteenth century, Protestant religious groups that preached an implicitly and sometimes explicitly democratic and egalitarian message encountered considerable hostility from the established denominations.[19] Nancy Christie has argued that in Upper Canada in the same period, Methodist and Baptist evangelicals challenged the hierarchical Tory Anglican social order which men like

John Strachan were attempting to impose on the new colony. Evangelical preachers certainly hoped to bring the godless backwoods settlers to adopt a more moral, ordered, Christian life. Nonetheless, the young uneducated Methodist preachers, generally of humble background, who travelled from place to place, preaching in barns, private homes, and fields could not help but undermine the social order preached by and implicit in the very presence of an educated Anglican cleric before a congregation made up of the rich in their private pews, and the poor in the galleries.[20] John Strachan thundered against the 'uneducated itinerant preachers, who leaving their steady employment, betake themselves to preaching the Gospel from idleness, or a zeal without knowledge.'[21] Strachan was aware that the itinerants who preached because they felt called by God to do so – regardless of education or family background – not only challenged the prestige and authority of an educated clergy, but also undermined the very concept of an ordered and hierarchical society.

Some Methodist sects did not just challenge the Anglican belief in an educated upper-class clergy – they also denied that only men could preach the Gospel. Women preachers had been accepted in eighteenth-century British Wesleyan Methodism. However, the growing respectability of this denomination by the end of the century led to the suppression of female preaching. In early nineteenth-century England, only the Bible Christians and the Primitive Methodists – two Methodist sects with primarily working-class members – still believed that women too could receive God's call to preach. As Elizabeth Muir has shown, some of these women journeyed from England to preach in the backwoods of Upper Canada. Like male itinerants they travelled from place to place preaching God's word, sometimes in the company of preacher husbands, and sometimes on their own.[22]

The Anglican elite's hostility to the Methodist itinerants was based not only on their overturning of hierarchies of class, education, and occasionally gender, but also on their influence in the colony. Members of all denominations thronged to hear these ministers. Christie argues that part of their appeal was that they preached in familiar places where their hearers felt at ease and on an equal footing with the other worshippers. She also notes that Methodist preachers used common, simple language in their sermons and set their hymns to the tunes of popular songs, making their services far more appealing to the popular classes than the learned rational discourses of Anglican divines.[23] Methodist appropriation of some of the trappings of popular culture does help to explain its popularity among Upper Canadian settlers. But it must also be recalled that the Methodists were often the only ministers who would venture into many isolated parts of the colony. Though some settlers were Christians who welcomed the rare visit of a man (or woman) of God, for others the services no doubt were welcome social occasions, and ones that strengthened the local sense of community.[24] Anna Jameson noted how after a church service in Woodstock in the 1830s the congregation, most of them settlers who had come from many miles around, 'remained some time assembled before the church-door ... many were the greetings and inquiries; the news and gossip of all the neighbourhood had to be exchanged.'[25]

Methodist camp meetings, in which services, often of several days' duration, were held in a field or woods, also attracted people from miles around and provided an opportunity for meeting neighbours, forming new friendships, and generally socializing. This may have been particularly important for isolated young people. One observer noted at the end of a camp meeting she had attended that 'the young lads were sparking the girls, and the girls laughing and flirting with them.'[26]

While the social aspects of Methodist and other evangelical services no doubt helped to draw an audience, the religious message was also crucial. This message was delivered by highly charged emotional methods. At a service in the Niagara District in 1813, for example, an American, Rev. T. Harmon, 'exhorted the people ... His voice ... might have been heard a mile. He uncovered the depravity of the human heart, and thundered the terrors of sin ... There was a shaking among the people.'[27] At meetings led by Harmon and other Methodist itinerants, the listeners often fell to the floor, overcome by emotion.[28] In the highly charged atmosphere created by revivalist preachers, it was not uncommon for people to weep, cry out, jump up and down, roll on the ground, and even foam at the mouth. The emotional pitch often reached its height at camp meetings, where for days at a time the crowds were exhorted about the threat of hellfire and the importance of salvation.

Anglicans decried the emotional excess and potential for disorder of such events. As Westfall has noted, even the Methodists themselves grew increasingly concerned that their own preachers could not always control the emotions generated by revivals. At camp meetings, once emotions reached fever pitch, anything could happen: women could have hysterics, disrupting the proceedings; some participants could feel so moved by the spirit of God as to interrupt the preacher with their own cries and exhortations.[29] George Rawlyk has pointed out that since at revivals all participants could be filled with God's spirit, these events provided an opportunity for those who were usually subordinate to speak out and play a more active role.[30] This could be true of women, young people, and the popular classes. Certainly many camp meetings, like one held near Adolphustown in 1804, saw not only 'parents praying for their children,' but also 'children for their parents'.[31] As Cecilia Morgan has noted, such a reversal of traditional hierarchies was strongly condemned by Anglican observers, who were horrified that 'children are encouraged to judge the belief of their parents, to belie them, and to hold them up to the malicious hatred of the low, the ignorant, the vile, and the most ferociously savage.'[32]

Such observers also feared that converted women would put their religious duties ahead of their family obligations, again undermining the proper order and hierarchy.[33] The importance in Methodism of individual salvation did serve to justify converted women in defying unconverted husbands. Women who refused to obey husbands who opposed their religious activities were praised in the Methodist press, while their husbands' efforts to enforce patriarchal authority were attacked. Nathan Bangs, an early Methodist itinerant, described one such incident in which the husband, 'upon hearing that his wife was in a prayer meeting, rushed violently into the room, seized his wife, and dragged her to the door, when attempting to open it he was himself seized with trembling, his knees failed him, and he fell helpless upon the floor ... He rose not until the Lord released him from his sins and made him a partaker of his pardoning mercy.'[34] As Morgan notes, though the primacy of salvation within Methodism gave women and children some space to question patriarchal authority, this space remained limited. Once a husband was converted, it was assumed that he should return to his rightful place as the head of his household.[35] None the less, Methodism did provide at least some opportunity for women and children to assert themselves as active individuals both in the home and at religious services.

While Anglican observers attacked what they viewed as the Methodist challenge to the proper hierarchy within the family, they were even more concerned with Methodism's 'levelling' tendencies in society as a whole.[36] The willingness of uneducated Methodist ministers to appeal to the 'lowest common denominator' in their services was a concern here, as were fears about over-emotionalism and disorder. The elite also considered the American origins of most early Methodist preachers as a particular threat to the social hierarchy.[37] In fact, though, most evangelical ministers did not preach an overtly republican message and advocated obedience to the temporal authorities. None the less, their spiritual message did stress the importance of salvation for all and thus the equality of all souls, at least in the spiritual realm.[38] Certain scholars have suggested that this may have encouraged the spread of democratic ideas: for example, E.P. Thompson and Bernard Semmel have argued that in Great Britain Methodism's message of spiritual equality did spill over into the secular realm.[39] Westfall, however, suggests that the otherworldly emphasis of Methodism could negate its political influence since many adherents ignored the secular world to concentrate on spiritual matters. For Christie, however, this otherworldly emphasis does not preclude a political influence. She argues that particularly before 1812, Methodism's emphasis on otherworldly concerns led its members to reject the social distinctions of the secular world.[40]

Whether or not secular distinctions were completely abandoned, for Methodists and other evangelicals of the early nineteenth century the most important distinctions do appear to have been religious, not social. The gap between the converted and unconverted loomed large.[41] This distinction was illustrated most clearly at the camp meeting. In the early years of the century, believers sat in a circle around the preachers, while the unconverted stood behind them. In later years, unbelievers and scoffers were often kept away from the saved by high fences erected around the camp meeting grounds.

CHURCH DISCIPLINE

While the distinction between the converted and the unconverted may have led many of the 'saved' to ignore the values and hierarchies of the secular world, salvation did not mean an abandonment of order. The emotionalism of the conversion experience was followed by entry into a community of believers, all of whom were expected to adhere to a strict code of conduct. It was their adherence to the rules of this code that most clearly separated believers from worldly sinners. The evangelical code extended beyond what we today would consider the religious realm to incorporate family life, business, and leisure. Those who transgressed were subject to various sanctions, the ultimate penalty being exclusion from the group.

The most strongly revivalist denominations, the Methodists and the Baptists, both subjected their church members to firm discipline in the first half of the nineteenth century, as did the Presbyterians, who in other respects were more sympathetic to Anglican notions of order than to the Methodist emphasis on the emotional experience of conversion. Each denomination had its own means of enforcing discipline.[42] Among the Methodists, members received mutual support and supervision in small groups, or classes, as they were known. At weekly class meetings, which were overseen by class leaders, the members offered each other criticism and guidance regarding their behaviour and spiritual growth. Among Presbyterians, the behaviour of members was overseen exclusively by the minister and church elders (the Session), who had the power to demand public confession or to excommunicate erring members. Baptist deacons and ministers also had special power to enforce discipline, but Baptist discipline cases were discussed at monthly covenant meetings. Both female and male members appear to have taken an active part in such meetings.[43]

Since no records were kept of Methodist class meetings, our knowledge of early church discipline comes exclusively from the Session minutes of Presbyterian elders, and the church minutes of Baptist congregations.[44] The focus of church discipline was similar in both denominations, but there was one important difference. In Upper Canada the Presbyterians, closely linked to their Scottish or Irish origins, were a far more ethnically homogeneous group than the Baptists.

None the less, the issues dealt with in both denominations were remarkably similar. In both denominations the largest number of discipline cases pertained to non-attendance at church services, particularly communion. Repeated absences led to visits from deacons or elders, and ultimately to exclusion. This policy was enunciated clearly by the Port Burwell Baptist church, which noted in 1846, '[If] any member after being laboured with twice for non-attendance and then miss three months from Covenant meetings in succession they then shall be excluded from the Church unless they have a lawful excuse.'[45]

Church supervision also extended far beyond attendance at services. The business practices of members were carefully monitored. Not surprisingly, stealing was strongly condemned. In some clear-cut cases of wrongdoing, members were excommunicated. Failure to pay debts was also viewed as a serious offence. People who left town without settling their debts, a fairly common practice in the boom-and-bust economy of nineteenth-century Ontario, were routinely excommunicated by Baptist congregations.[46]

The leisure hours of church members were also closely regulated. The activities that were censured reveal as much about the amusements of Upper Canadians as they do about the moral standards of the churches. Drinking was the most common leisure offence to come before the churches. As other scholars have demonstrated, alcohol consumption was extremely high in Upper Canada, and drinking was simply part of everyday life.[47] Even within the churches it was not drinking per se that appears to have been censured, but rather drinking to excess, or to the point of drunkenness. Even the Rev. William Bell, a zealous Presbyterian minister, was a moderate drinker in his early years in Upper Canada.[48] The Presbyterian and Baptist discipline records are full, however, of those who did not use liquor in moderation. This practice was not confined to those on the fringes of the congregation. In several cases the records note sorrowfully that an elder or deacon had been seen drunk.[49] In these and other cases, the member was generally given the opportunity to reform, but repeated offences usually led to excommunication. Though the majority of drinkers who came to the attention of the churches were men, a significant minority were women.[50] In 1847 a Mrs Hillas of the Baptist church in Dundas denied the charge of 'drinking too much spiritous Liquors,' although one member of the congregation claimed to have seen her 'go to a Tavern and call for a glass of Liquor and drink it,' and others claimed to have seen her 'under the influence of too much liquor.'[51] This and other cases of repentant women drinkers are at odds with the later nineteenth-century concept of drinking as a purely male vice. Other charges against women are more in keeping with nineteenth-century concepts of femininity, such as accusations of dancing, which appeared regularly in both Baptist and Presbyterian records.[52] In some cases the churches found it difficult to discourage women from dancing, as was true of Rachel Mackenzie of Wicklow, who, as the Baptist church minutes noted, had 'been previously laboured with for the sin of dancing.'[53]

Another common focus of church discipline was interpersonal relations. Since church members were expected to live together in peace, church leaders often found themselves trying to mediate in quarrels between friends, neighbours, and business associates.[54] The parties who were considered to be at fault were admonished, and if they were found guilty of slander they were faced with more serious censure.

Sexual relationships rivalled drunkenness as a subject of discipline among both the Baptists and the Presbyterians. Both men and women were disciplined or excommunicated for fornication and adultery.[55] Among both Presbyterians and Baptists transgressors could be expected to make public penance. Among the Baptists such cases, like others, were judged by the entire congregation. When 'Sister Nancy Finton charge[d] Sister Matilda Gleason with having carnal connection with Hiram Card in the same bed that she was in and she had told it before the World and it had become public talk ... both women [were] brought before the Church to give their account of the incident. Members were split in their opinions as to who was the guilty party.'[56]

Though such public scrutiny of people's private lives cannot have been particularly welcome, the willingness of both denominations to oversee family life was sometimes useful for oppressed wives or children. Since the churches sought to uphold the ideal of a united peaceable family, when members of a family quarrelled, efforts were made to reconcile them. Families that demonstrated a lack of interest in reconciliation by refusing the church's mediation efforts could be excommunicated.[57] In some cases the threat of excommunication may have discouraged husbands from deserting their families, or encouraged them to return. Brother Swan of Boston, for example, was told by the church that he had to 'make a confession to his wife and the public for his wrong in leaving her and become reconciled with her in order to retain his membership and that he shall have a month to do it in.'[58]

Both the Presbyterians and the Baptists also sometimes censured husbands for beating their wives. In Woodstock the Baptist church stated that 'for the sake of the cause of their own conscience' they would 'withdraw the hand of fellowship' from a member accused of excessive drinking and wife abuse.[59] In other cases churches refused to uphold such accusations. For example, in Vittoria, when a member of the Baptist church, Daniel Bennet, who was accused of 'whipping his wife and abusing his child,' denied that he had hit his wife and claimed that he had 'only chastized his child,' others agreed with him that the child was bad and had only been chastised, not abused. In this case the female church member who brought the charge was the one who was excommunicated.[60] It seems likely that wife-beating cases brought before the all-male Presbyterian sessions would have received even less sympathy than those judged by the mixed-sex Baptist covenant meetings.[61]

None the less, as we have seen, church discipline could sometimes give protection to an abused wife. In this period the churches also tried to provide some material aid for deserted or widowed women who were part of their community of believers. Other church members could also appeal to the churches for material relief, but the bulk of such relief appears to have been provided for 'dependent' women.[62] In Perth, for example, the Presbyterian Free Church helped support several destitute widows with special congregational collections.[63] In some Presbyterian churches women's associations were primarily responsible for raising and distributing poor relief.[64]

Women might thus receive at least some protection from poverty and abuse as dependent family members. To what extent, though, were women considered to be independent actors within the family? In certain cases the husband's position as household head was clearly affirmed. The efforts of St George's Baptist church to mediate between Mary Hammil and Stephen Pembleton came to a halt when Mr Hammil 'objected to his wife saying anything.'[65] Though women were generally expected to obey their husbands, in the spiritual realm they were viewed as independent and responsible beings. In a number of cases it was made clear that the excommunication of a man did not apply to his wife, who remained a member in good standing.[66] Women who left a church to join their husband's denomination were not excused on the grounds of wifely obedience, but were viewed as erring sinners.[67]

The evangelical churches appear to have granted married women some autonomy, at least in the spiritual realm. But these women and their husbands did not live only in the spiritual realm. To what extent did worldly matters impinge on these communities of believers? Among the Baptists, efforts appear to have been made in the early years to remain aloof from politics.[68] For example, it was not until 1849 that the Vittoria Baptist church decided that 'the exercise of political rights possessed by the members of this Church ... will henceforward be no reproach to their Christian standing in the church.'[69] While remaining aloof, the Baptists wished to be seen to be loyal to the government. For example, in the aftermath of the Rebellion of 1837 the Port Burwell church made it clear that members who opposed the government would be excommunicated.[70]

Despite such protestations of loyalty, the evangelical churches were certainly willing to complain when they felt that government regulations impinged on the spiritual needs of their members. The Smiths Falls Presbyterian church had particular difficulties with the Rideau Canal, which the government permitted to operate on Sundays. The Session complained that lockmasters and labourers on the canal, some of whom were members of the church, were forced to work on the sabbath. But the Session's attitude to these workers revealed at best a limited recognition of their financial difficulties. In 1843 canal workers who would not resign their jobs were suspended from the church for breaking the sabbath. But two years later when four canal workers told the Session that they had no choice but to work, since they had no other income, the Session agreed to restore their church privileges.[71]

While the evangelical churches did make some compromises with the forces of the new wage-labour economy, some congregations at least tried to ensure that members who were employers of labour lived up to the same scriptural precepts as those imposed on other members. Before 1850 certain churches censured employers who treated their employees unjustly. Baptist employers who failed to pay the wages they owed could be excommunicated. In St George in 1836 'a meeting [was] convened to consider a charge laid by Bro Crandal against Bro. Jeremiah Wilson for refusing to give him his pay for 30 bushels of wheat as agreed and still persists in the same and therefore the church withdrew the hand of fellowship.'[72] The Dundas church suspended a member who had hired some men from Hamilton to work for him and then refused to pay them.[73] The Beamsville church heard a complaint against Sally Kenada for 'abusing those that took labour with her,' but it is not clear what action was taken against her.[74] These practices seem closely related to more common discipline proceedings, such as the censuring of those who did not pay their debts and who unjustly abused their dependents.[75] None the less, such efforts also suggest a willingness to take on at least some injustices of the emerging wage-labour economy.

It is clear, therefore, that before mid-century both the Presbyterian and Baptist churches intervened in the lives of their members in a range of areas that extended far beyond what we might define as the sacred sphere. Church members were required to live up to Christian teachings not only at church, but also at home, at work, in leisure activities, and in their relations with friends and neighbours. How did people respond to such close supervision? In Upper Canada churchgoing was voluntary, and disgruntled church members were free to leave the church if they were displeased with the way they were treated. Some did refuse to accept the discipline of the churches. Efforts to regulate leisure activities were sometimes challenged. When Mr Gardiner Wait was confronted by members of Wicklow Baptist church for having 'been seen to drink whiskey to a considerable extent,' he told the visitors that 'he would drink as long as he could get it.'[76] Similarly Mr Butler of Vittoria informed the local church that 'it was no persons business about his drinking as long as he paid for it.'[77] It appears to have been fairly common for Baptists to be excommunicated for failing to accept church discipline. While such members could not join a Baptist church in another community, since they required a letter from their original church, many appear to have joined churches of other denominations. This was also an option for Presbyterians. However, since Presbyterian communities were united not just by religious but also by ethnic bonds, the pressure to submit to church discipline appears to have been stronger than in the case of the Baptists. In Crerar's study of Session discipline in the Bathurst District, relatively few church members defied church discipline, except when a particularly arbitrary Session provoked a general revolt within a congregation.[78]

Despite such differences the Baptists, Presbyterians, and Methodists had all shifted away from the supervision of personal behaviour by the 1850s, and 1860s. Among the Methodists, increasing numbers of church members refused to attend class meetings, where their personal behaviour could come under group scrutiny.[79] While Baptist and Presbyterian churches were still censuring an occasional drunkard into the 1890s, and all three denominations continued to drop those who did not attend services from church rolls, the regular recounting of misdeeds fades from congregational records and Session minutes after mid-century. The common abandonment of most church discipline points to the influence of broader social forces. By the 1850s and 1860s many evangelicals, heeding their churches' exhortations about thrift, sobriety, and hard work, had become wealthy. Their success was only part of a gradual transition in this period from an agrarian society to an increasingly stratified urban one. Neil Semple has argued that as the gap between wealthier and poorer members of various Methodist congregations widened, the better-off became more and more reluctant to subject their behaviour to the scrutiny of the less well-off, who may sometimes have been their employees.[80] It would certainly not be surprising if employers, whether Methodist, Baptist, or Presbyterian, were eager to shrug off a religious code that could censure them for mistreating their employees.[81] The weakening of church discipline can also be viewed as part of a larger shift away from community control over private life which was occurring in this period.[82] At the same time, however, as middle-class church-goers were rejecting the right of the churches to control their private behaviour, they were becoming increasingly involved in temperance and Sabbatarian associations which sought to control the behaviour of others. Their primary targets were those within the working class who were considered to be moving away from the churches, and whose behaviour, particularly drinking and sabbath-breaking, did not adhere to the contemporary code of churchgoing respectability.

RESPECTABILITY AND CHURCH BUILDING

The fading of church discipline in the evangelical churches in the latter half of the nineteenth century was accompanied by a toning down of the emotional excesses which had set them apart from the more conservative Anglican tradition. Most Protestants continued to define themselves as evangelical Christians, but the methods used to bring people to a recognition of their own sinfulness and their need to seek salvation through 'the transforming power of faith in Christ' had changed.[83] While the revivalist tradition remained important, particularly among Methodists, too much emotionalism was shunned.[84] The salvation of souls could no longer justify the flouting of social conventions.[85]

As Protestants of all denominations became more integrated into the larger world, church membership came to mean both more – and less – than membership in a distinct community of believers. No doubt religious belief remained central to many, if not most churchgoers, but church attendance was increasingly also viewed as a badge of respectability within the wider community.[86] In the 1882 anniversary sermon in the Canada Methodist church in Ingersoll, the minister complained that many attended church for appearance' sake since 'being a pew holder in the house of God gives a man a distinction both socially and politically,' and a few years later a Stratford man wrote to the local paper, that 'Christianity is not now what it used to be. It is now considered respectable, and even fashionable, to belong to an orthodox church.'[87]

This increasing emphasis on the external meaning of church attendance is seen in a growing preoccupation with financial matters in the churches. After mid-century, Ontario Protestants (and Catholics) were increasingly dissatisfied with the modest structures erected by the early settlers and devoted more of their energy to raising money to build new and more elaborate churches. Though many churches continued to provide at least some poor relief to their members, the budgets for poor relief were minimal compared to the money being spent on church building and improvement. Women's church associations continued to distribute some money to the poor, but once again, their primary activity was fund-raising for church building projects.[88]

Urban congregations erected grand new churches, such as Jarvis Street Baptist Church in Toronto, built in the early 1870s in the popular Gothic style. New churches also sprang up in smaller communities. Congregations which did not build completely new edifices did not stand still. In the early 1880s the Methodist church in the small town of Thorold spent three thousand dollars on 'improvements,' which included handsome new pews, a new pulpit desk, and a number of other changes described in the *Thorold Post*, as follows: 'The walls of the church have been pannelled in oil, while the roof has been papered with paper of beautiful tints ... instead of the old fashioned windows with small panes, there are handsome ones, divided in two ... with a stained border and diamond at top ... The floor is carpeted with a handsome, all wool carpet, while the platform and the altar are covered with tapestry carpet ... The building is lighted by several chandeliers.'[89]

Westfall has argued that in this period the construction of new churches, particularly in the Gothic style, was intended 'to proclaim the reality and power of the sacred as a force in a secular world.'[90] No doubt spiritual motives played a part in the decisions to build new churches. However, such decisions were also coloured by social and economic concerns. The self-interest of wealthy and socially prominent church members was clearly involved in the building of beautiful new churches and the improvement of old ones. After the middle of the nineteenth-century churchgoing among all Ontario denominations increasingly demonstrated not only belief in the sacred but also respectability within the secular world. For the rich and socially prominent, such respectability was reinforced through worship in larger and more elaborate churches.[91]

No doubt many workers, Catholic and Protestant alike, also enjoyed worshipping in the beautiful new churches, which would have been a welcome respite from their cramped and drab home environments.[92] Sunday attendance in impressive Gothic-style churches may have strengthened their faith by associating the sacred with the grandeur and beauty of its surroundings. At the same time, for many poorer workers, any sense of holiness may have been undermined by a disturbing feeling that they had no place in these impressive edifices unless they had contributed financially to the beauty around them.

Church membership has always carried with it financial obligations, obligations which made the poor less able to participate. But at least in the evangelical churches before mid-century, financial matters did not generally overshadow spiritual ones. It is not until the 1840s that there is evidence of anyone being excommunicated from a Baptist congregation for failing to contribute to the church. In 1844 Richard Havens and his wife were excommunicated from the St Catharines church for not 'walking in unison with the church,' which was a fairly common complaint. However, they were also censured for 'refusing to contribute toward the support of our pastor or liquidating a debt necessarily incurred in erecting a suitable place of worship while professing adequate means to so to do.'[93]

By the 1860s the Session minutes of Erskine Church in Ingersoll demonstrate the effect of growing financial pressure on church members. One member, William Bainbridge, stated that he had stopped attending services because he was unable to pay his church dues. The members of the Session who visited him assured him, 'If he could not pay the church door would not be shut against him, members would not frown on him (as he seemed to fear).'[94] Despite such assurances Bainbridge and others like him knew that while the church door might not literally be shut against them, their failure to contribute to the church would make things quite uncomfortable. This may have always been true to some extent, but the church building craze of the latter part of the nineteenth century increased the financial pressure on local congregations. In the minutes of both large and small churches of all denominations, there is constant discussion of the bills for improvements or paying the mortgages on elaborate new churches.[95] Churches published annual reports, which listed the names of contributors and the amounts contributed. Even though non-contributors were usually not listed, in most communities they would certainly not have been unknown.

The constant pressure to contribute to the church could make the poor very uncomfortable, and the need to finance church improvements limited efforts to make the churches more welcoming to those who could not afford to contribute. The extent to which pew rents limited church accessibility, or at best created a two-tier system of church involvement by restricting the poor to the free seats at the back or in the galleries was hotly debated in a number of denominations in this period. Some churches did abolish pew rents, replacing them with the weekly envelope system.[96] But pew rents were not an absolute barrier to church attendance by the working class. Skilled workers and even some semi- and unskilled workers did pay pew rents in various denominations.[97] However, even the payment of pew rents did not guarantee equal treatment since the pews towards the back of the churches and in the galleries cost less than those towards the front. At the Methodist church in Thorold the board of trustees fixed the rent for the first ten pews at nine dollars each a year, the next four at eight dollars, and the next three at six dollars.[98] Church space clearly indicated local hierarchies.

Neil Semple believes that the churches' increasing need for money also influenced the Christian message they delivered. He argues that in the case of the Methodist Church, John Wesley's message concerning the spiritual dangers of wealth was replaced by a willingness to give a religious quality to wealth, at least if some of this wealth was used to support the church. Semple argues that in return for the support of the business elite 'the church bolstered the respectability and virtue of the business ethic and re-emphasized the traditional link between sin and poverty.'[99] Though the relationship may not have been as direct as Semple suggests, it is clear that the building of churches in the late nineteenth century did more than create symbols of the sacred within an increasingly secular world. The new churches were also symbols of the secular ambitions of many of their members. Whereas evangelical churches had earlier seen themselves as shared communities of believers, isolated from the outside world, the cost of building elaborate edifices brought the social and economic distinctions of the secular world more firmly into such communities.

CHURCH MEMBERSHIP

Did the increasing financial power of the wealthy within the churches actually discourage the working class from attending church? It is certainly true that at least on the surface Ontario society was more Christian in the second half of the nineteenth century than it had ever been. Everyone schooled in the province had been exposed to at least some religious teaching, either Catholic or non-denominational Protestant.[100] From the 1861 census on, almost every Ontarian claimed to be an adherent of a Christian denomination. None the less, having some sense of Christian belief and being a church member were two different things. Many Ontarians did not even attend church, let alone become a member in this period. Surveys conducted by the *Globe* in the last decades of the century reveal that in Toronto about 45 per cent of the population had attended church at least once on a given Sunday.[101] Over half therefore had not. Nor did smaller towns appear to have been noticeably more pious.[102]

In the last few decades of the century there was considerable anguished rhetoric from church leaders about the apparent abandonment of the churches by Ontario's growing working class, as well as by young people of all classes. How legitimate were such fears? Who was really attending Ontario's ever larger and more elaborate churches? While there have been no studies of church membership in large cities, some work has been done on church involvement in smaller communities. The following discussion is taken primarily from my study of church participation in two small Ontario towns: Thorold, located on the Welland Canal in the Niagara Peninsula, and Campbellford, located east of Toronto between Peterborough and Belleville. Doris O'Dell's study of church participation in late nineteenth-century Belleville also contains useful information on this topic.

In smaller towns like Thorold, Campbellford, and Belleville, where one might expect class differences to be less stark than in large cities, middle-class townspeople were more likely than their working-class counterparts to be church members. None the less, a significant proportion of working-class townspeople in smaller communities were church members. In late nineteenth-century Thorold and Campbellford, while a higher proportion of middle-class families contained church members than was the case with working-class families, approximately 40 per cent of all working-class Protestant families had at least one church member.[103] Working-class Baptists were the most likely to be church members, but workers made up a signficant proportion of the membership of all Protestant churches. In small towns like Thorold and Campbellford, which had only one church of each denomination, a working-class churchgoer would have to worship in the same church as his or her middle-class neighbours. But as O'Dell has shown, in larger towns like Belleville, workers could and often did worship separately in churches with predominantly working-class memberships.[104]

Whether working-class church members worshipped together with middle-class townspeople, or separately in their own churches, their presence suggests that at least outside the large cities, the fear that the working class was abandoning the churches may have been somewhat exaggerated. Christian belief was clearly important to the many workers who made the commitment of joining a church. Religious faith no doubt provided solace, a sense of meaning and hope for women and men who lived lives of endless toil and economic uncertainty. Like their middle-class counterparts, at least some working-class church members may also have sought the respectability conferred by churchgoing.

Whereas concern about the absence of workers from church congregations may have been somewhat overblown, fears about the loss of young people, or at least of young males, were well founded. American scholars have noted the feminization of church congregations in the nineteenth century and have attributed this phenomenon to the contemporary views of women's nature. Women were assumed to be more moral, more spiritual, and thus more religious than men, and were certainly taught that this was true.[105] The dominant gender ideology may partially explain the predominance of women in late nineteenth-century Ontario church congregations. However, that phenomenon was due as much to the absence of young males from the churches as to any particularly feminine piety.

The records of Thorold and Campbellford churches demonstrate that women predominated within the churches, not because all the men stayed away, but because very few single men of any social class were church members.[106] It is difficult to know, however, whether this was a new phenomenon in the late nineteenth century. Cecilia Morgan has shown that fears about the un-Christian lives of many young men were a common theme in early nineteenth-century periodical literature, suggesting certain commonalities over the course of the century.[107]

If young single men were not church members, why did so many choose to join the churches after they married? Some clues are provided by an examination of contemporary concepts of masculinity. A central masculine ideal was that of family provider, the man who worked hard to support his family. For married men the ideal of being a good provider or breadwinner was an inherent part of respectability. The solid respectability expected of the family provider was strengthened by membership in a church. Before they married, few young men appeared interested in seeking that respectability. Age and marital status were therefore more significant than class in explaining church involvement, or the lack of it, at least among men. None the less, it is also true that members of the working class were less likely than members of the middle class to join Protestant churches.

THE SALVATION ARMY

Did the many workers who were not church members see themselves as Christians, and if so, were there any other outlets for their religious feelings beyond the middle-class churches? One such outlet was provided by the Salvation Army, a working-class religious movement of the 1880s.

The Salvation Army was founded in London, England, in 1878, but it had emerged from an earlier organization known as the Christian Mission, which was founded in 1865 by William Booth, a former Methodist preacher. The dominant principle in Booth's life was said to be the need to convert the poorest groups in society, who were generally untouched by the churches.[108] Although Booth's earliest efforts were based in the traditions of Methodist revivalism, his work soon became distinctive for his willingness to use a variety of unconventional methods to reach the poor. One essential method was the adoption of the organization and trappings of the military. The Army structure was firmly hierarchical, all members being expected to obey the orders of superior officers. Supreme power was vested in Booth, who as General commanded an Army which, by the 1880s, had spread around the world. The Army's military trappings included brass bands and uniforms as well as a distinctive vocabulary in which prayer services were called 'knee drills' and saying 'Amen' was known as 'firing a volley.' Those who joined the Salvation Army were known as soldiers, preachers were called officers, and congregations were corps. A Canadian Salvationist gave a telling reason for this military vocabulary:

It is well known that in many parts of the world – in this country indeed – a strong prejudice exists in the minds of a vast majority of the people against the terms church, cathedral, holy orders, priest, preacher, deacon, elder and such like, and on no account will they have anything to do with them. By calling our body an Army, the places of worship, barracks and the officers, general, major, captain etc., we avoid these prejudices and obtain the attendance of the people.[109]

In its early years in Canada the Salvation Army certainly had considerable success in attracting working-class members. The movement, which entered Ontario in 1882, spread rapidly through the province. By 1884 there were Salvation Army corps in seventy-three Ontario towns, and at the height of its popularity in mid-decade it had enrolled over 25,000 soldiers across the country, most of them in Ontario.[110] The membership figures exclude most of those who thronged to Army meetings in the early years of the movement. For the majority of the unchurched the Salvation Army provided entertainment but did not lead to conversion, while for many others their conversion by the Salvation Army was short-lived or led to a return to their previous denomination.[111]

Despite the short-term nature of many conversions the Army was at first very successful in attracting both working-class women and men to its meetings and in encouraging them to enrol as soldiers. The newspapers reported that the Army could attract the 'lower orders' or the 'unchurched masses.' According to the *Toronto Mail*, Salvation Army soldiers were 'chiefly working people, who give what little leisure they have to helping the cause.'[112] The few surviving converts' rolls also suggest that even in smaller communities those attracted to the Army were almost exclusively working-class.[113] A study of the officers' roll reveals that the majority of officers were also working-class.[114]

The newspaper reports also make it clear that the majority of Salvation Army soldiers were women.[115] A high proportion of female Salvationists were domestic servants, which is particularly striking, given the scarcity of servants on the membership rolls of the mainstream churches.[116] Female servants not only joined the Salvation Army; many also went on to be officers or preachers. Whereas by the 1880s preaching by women had been prohibited even in those few mainstream churches that had previously allowed it, the Salvation Army not only allowed, but encouraged, women to be preachers. As in earlier Methodist groups, any who felt called to preach were expected to answer God's call.[117] Women made up more than half of Salvation Army officers in Ontario. These 'Hallelujah Lasses,' as they were known, often led the Army's assault on new communities, and were clearly a great attraction. The arrival of a new female officer in Kingston led to larger crowds than 'when the Governor General and the Princess were here,' with the hall being 'jammed to the doors.'[118]

Though the novelty of female officers added to the Salvation Army's appeal, the Army also made use of a variety of tactics to attract working-class crowds. Officers were told that meetings must be interesting and lively and were encouraged to use innovative methods. Some of their methods were not very different from those of the early Methodist itinerants; others appropriated newer elements of working-class culture. Salvation Army officers led open-air meetings and parades with colourful banners and the music of tambourines, triangles, and drums; they sang hymns to the tunes of popular songs and organized a variety of events, many of which provided a religious alternative to popular amusements. A Kingston Army service ('superior to any show on earth') was advertised as a counter-attraction to the visiting circus. Other such events included Hallelujah Sprees, Popular Matinees, Hallelujah Pic-nics, Free and Easy Meetings, and Grand Tea Fights.

Another element of the Salvation Army's appeal lay in its clear, class-based critique of the mainstream churches. The very existence of the Salvation Army points to a belief that the churches had failed in their responsibility to minister to all classes. Many Salvationists and their supporters were, however, much more explicit in their opposition to the churches. In the first few years after the Army arrived in Ontario, the newspapers were filled with letters both attacking and defending the Army. The defence of the Army frequently included an attack on the churches as middle-class institutions which concentrated on building elaborate structures while ignoring Christ's true teachings. The letter from 'Spectator' of Belleville is fairly representative:

Of all the denominations whose worship I have attended that which suffers least by comparison with the precepts and example of Christ is the Salvation Army ... As to the empty pews in the churches, they were so before the Army came to this city, and why? Because Sunday after Sunday they serve out the dry bones of sectarianism for the living truths of Christianity ... I see the haughty 'Miss Shoddy' sweep up the aisle and recoil in poorly concealed discomfort lest her costly robes should touch the threadbare garments of some poor sinner who had the temerity to enter therein. I hear the doctrine of Dives preached in the name of Christ ... I see the Almighty blasphemed by the erection in His name of costly edifices, wherein are exclusive and costly people who worship in a costly style, while orphans cry for bread.[119]

'A Salvation Army Soldier' from Woodstock defended the Army, which 'reaches classes of people who have precious souls but whose burden of sin the clergy will not touch with even their little finger!' while attacking the 'pew-renting and so-called respectable congregations of town and country, whose very respectability has crushed many a bruised reed.'[120] James Smith, a London Salvationist, wrote of 'the Salvation Army, who without money and without price are nobly bearing their crosses, fighting the Lord's battles; while the sluggish churches and overpaid ministry thereof have been asleep and drunken in their opulence.'[121]

Some supporters of the Salvation Army made direct comparisons between the Army and the Methodists of days gone by. The willingness of the earlier Methodists to reach out to the unconverted was pointedly compared to the overly respectable contemporary Methodist churches, with their 'purple and fine linen' members who had no interest in converting the poor.[122] The Army's evangelical emphasis on the salvation of souls, with its assumption of spiritual equality certainly echoed that of early Methodists. But by the 1880s Ontario society was far more divided by class than it had been in the early decades of the century. Under those circumstances the Army's emphasis on spiritual equality may have tapped into or strengthened an emerging class consciousness. Like other evangelical movements, the Army explicitly discouraged its followers from taking part in political movements, and urged them instead to concentrate on the state of their own souls and the salvation of others. Nonetheless, the Army's message of spiritual equality may have spilled over into the secular realm, fuelling working-class anger at a society characterized by profound inequities.[123] At the very least this message would have reinforced a sense of self-worth among the Army's working-class adherents, who were increasingly subordinated and devalued within the larger society.

The Army's use of emotionally charged methods of bringing 'the perishing' to salvation mirrored the earlier revivalist movements, with converts jumping up and down, shouting, and going into trances. By the 1880s, however, 'emotionalism' had become anathema even to Ontario Methodists, who had once preached a fire-and-brimstone message across Upper Canada. Most middle-class Protestant Ontarians still saw themselves as evangelical Christians but believed that revivals should remain within the bounds of moderation and respectability. For this reason alone the intensely emotional appeal of Army services was interpreted as a working-class challenge to respectable middle-class churchgoing by middle and working class alike.

Membership in the Army may not have implied among all soldiers an active opposition to the middle-class-dominated churches, but it would certainly have revealed an alienation from middle-class institutions in which workers were both subordinated and marginalized.[124] The Salvation Army gave Ontario workers a religious alternative which spoke to them in terms of their own cultural values, and provided a separate religious space in which they could feel comfortable and in control.[125] The popularity of the Army points to the existence of some form of distinct culture and class identity among Ontario workers, and the Army's activities themselves undoubtedly reinforced that consciousness.

Nevertheless, the Salvation Army's success points not only to working-class consciousness, but also to working-class religious faith. The Army's message may have been delivered in working-class cultural forms, but it remained the message of evangelical Protestantism. This message was clearly a familiar one to those workers who were swept up in the Salvation Army. Some Salvation soldiers had formerly been church members and had either drifted away from the churches or found the Army's 'blood and fire' methods more appealing than sedate church services.[126] Even those who had never even attended Sunday school lived in a society permeated by Christianity, in particular Protestantism. The instant popularity of the Salvation Army certainly suggests that the basic message of evangelical Christianity was a familiar and welcome one to most workers, when presented in a style and language with which they could identify.

The Army's message had a particular appeal to working-class women. The fact that women were over-represented in the Army, just as they were in the mainstream churches, does not appear, however, to have been due to any shared, cross-class feminine religious feelings among 'Hallelujah lasses' and church ladies. For the behaviour required of women in the Salvation Army was quite different from the more passive ladylike piety expected of women in the mainstream churches. However, there were parallels between the opportunities available to women in the Army and in the revivalistic movements of Upper Canada.

Like male soldiers, female soldiers, or 'Hallelujah lasses,' were expected to stand up in crowded halls, give testimony to their faith in Jesus, and describe the misery of their past lives. They also marched through the streets, beating drums or tambourines to attract attention to the cause. The Army also gave many such women the opportunity to defy more concrete gender-based constraints. Many female soldiers challenged both the authority of their husbands and fathers and their relegation to the narrow confines of the domestic sphere.[127] For example, 'Drum-Major Annie' of Petrolia proclaimed the importance of her efforts to save the souls even of unappreciative and undeserving men, defending such efforts as much more important than 'wash[ing] the crude oil out of the shirt of some dirty beast.'[128]

Female soldiers who became officers posed an even greater challenge to dominant feminine roles by usurping the traditional male position of religious leader. Many such officers became captains, and thus took charge of local corps that could include up to several hundred soldiers and adherents. Though they were expected to follow the directives issued by headquarters in Toronto and were subject to transfer at any time, their work nevertheless required considerable initiative and effort. Not only did they preach to crowds every night of the week and three times on Sunday, but they also led parades, visited converts, managed the corps's finances, and planned innovative methods of drawing crowds.

Before becoming officers, the majority of female Salvationists had worked outside the home, labouring for long hours in factories, or as servants or seamstresses.[129] Since the image of the fragile passive Victorian lady in the home may thus have had little relevance to them they may have been more willing than middle-class women would have been to flout the prevailing gender roles. Certainly the participation of women in the Army hints at the existence of a distinct working-class conception of femininity, which more readily acknowledged women's strength, assertiveness, and involvement in the public sphere. At the same time, however, Salvation Army women could claim that their activities were justified by a most appropriately feminine Christian submission to God's will. For many such women feminine self-denial may have provided more of a justification than a motivation for their willingness to play an active public role.

But if some female Salvationists thought their Army activities demonstrated an appropriate feminine piety, many middle-class observers felt otherwise. For critics like the Rev. A. Wilson of Kingston, 'female preaching and fantastic dressing, the outrageous talk and singing of doggerel hymns' combined to render the Army completely unacceptable.[130] The Army's class-based critique of the churches was more than fully reciprocated by ministers and other middle-class observers across Ontario. These men believed that the respectable trappings of the mainstream churches were integral to Christianity. The Army was frequently accused of treating Christianity with vulgarity, levity, and frivolity, and Army activities were disparagingly likened to working-class entertainments.[131] A common, and telling, comparison described the Army as worse than 'a negro minstrel show.'[132] The adoption of the cultural forms of the marginal and the devalued, whether by class or race, placed the Army beyond the pale of true Christianity, which in the dominant discourse of the period was inextricably linked with middle-class culture.

Like John Strachan's critique of the Methodist itinerants of over fifty years before, the hostility to the Army was also fuelled by fears of disorder and loss of middle-class control. Common complaints about the Army included the lack of order at their meetings, and in particular their habit of marching through the streets with drums and tambourines. In Ingersoll a letter to the editor complained of the 'infernal drum beating and parades' that forced 'ladies' off the sidewalk into the gutter, and the *Newmarket Era* attacked the 'abominable nuisance of singing and howling ... after orderly people have retired to rest' and the 'drum and symball (*sic*) playing and singing, on the streets on Sunday.'[133] Middle-class citizens often tried to regain control of public places by petitioning town councils to pass by-laws prohibiting the Army from marching and beating their drums. In some cases Salvationists were arrested for refusing to comply with such laws.[134]

Outraged middle-class churchgoers and town councils were not the only Ontarians to oppose the Salvation Army. In most towns the Army also encountered considerable hostility from the local young men, who appear to have been predominantly working-class. This opposition took a variety of forms – throwing rocks and rotten eggs, putting cayenne pepper on a stove during Army meetings, assaulting officers, and scoffing and heckling during meetings.[135] A public confrontation between the Army and these men took place in Ingersoll in December 1883.[136]

During the parade of the Salvation Army on Monday evening an 'indescribable' meeting took place between this and another body headed by a brass band composed of members of our town band and others. When the Salvationists started from the market square the other body, composed principally of working men to the number of several hundreds, also started from an opposite point, the band playing vigorously ... [when] opposite the Salvationists ... both bodies commenced to play with renewed vigour and to emit the most hideous yells.

Such attacks revealed a hostility towards the Army for its efforts to transform the lives of working-class men.[137] Young men may have been particularly hostile to the Army's claims that through conversion they were able to transform the life of the most hardened drinker to one of piety and sobriety. Opposition to the Army also may have been based in a popular anti-clericalism and perhaps an anti-religious sentiment among certain young men.

SOME ASPECTS OF 'ROUGH' CULTURE

Although the attacks on the Salvation Army were particularly severe, there was a long history of 'rough' challenges to the churches in Ontario. The early Methodist itinerants were accustomed to the jeers of hostile onlookers, and the fences erected at early camp meetings were intended to keep out those who attended merely to ridicule the proceedings and to harass both preachers and believers.[138] Nineteenth-century police court proceedings regularly included reports of young men and boys arrested and fined for disturbing public worship.[139] Those who were charged with such offences were part of a particular subculture. Their disturbing of public worship was symptomatic of their larger rejection of the values and manners of 'respectable' churchgoers, particularly those adhering to the evangelical moral code.

This 'rough' subculture was largely male. Its members appear to have been predominantly young men – often the same men who were absent from church rolls. This culture was to some extent a cross-class male youth culture, especially in small towns.[140] However, it was also associated, especially in larger towns, with particular segments of the working class. At the extreme this rough culture was distinct from the more respectable masculine culture of home and church. Nevertheless there was also considerable overlap between the two cultures, and most married men, both middle- and working-class, were able to incorporate elements of both lifestyles within the bounds of acceptable definitions of masculinity.

At the centre of 'rough' culture were the local taverns. Women may have entered taverns earlier in the nineteenth century, but increasingly after mid-century they were exclusively male spaces.[141] Different taverns did serve different clienteles, some of which were 'rougher' than others, but there were certain similarities among them. Most of them offered lodging for men away from home; they also sought to provide comfortable furnishings and innovative decorations, although few could compete with the menagerie kept at Joe Beef's famous Montreal tavern.[142] None the less, even such decorations as the 'genuine Indian war clubs' displayed at Franklin's hotel bar in Thorold would have appealed to young men of all classes who sought excitement beyond the home circle.[143] For many working-class men, both single and married, whose homes may have offered little in the way of domestic comfort, the tavern provided warmth and entertainment after long hours at work.[144] The taverns clearly also afforded an opportunity for male sociability.[145] Alex Bolton, who later joined the Salvation Army, left us what may be a somewhat jaundiced description of young men's tavern culture in Ingersoll in this period. He was a blacksmith who boarded at a local hotel, the Carroll House, and apparently spent his free time, including Sundays 'in the bar-room drinking, swearing, and telling yarns and sometimes fighting.'[146]

Participants in tavern culture defended their right to drink against the increasingly powerful temperance movement of late nineteenth-century Ontario. Municipal authorities found it impossible to enforce local bans on liquor sales (under the Scott Act), owing to a solidarity within the masculine drinking culture. Witnesses routinely lied, claiming that they had been served nothing but beef tea or 'pop' in hotel bars.[147] Those willing to inform on hotel keepers who sold liquor were threatened with violence and were sometimes attacked. Two Ingersoll men who gave evidence in Scott Act trials had their homes broken into and were beaten up.[148] When several local hotel keepers were to be charged with violating the Scott Act, the Ingersoll town council, expecting a riot in response, swore in six special constables.[149] In Woodstock two men who had testified at Scott Act trials were attacked by a crowd of two hundred 'rowdies' and prevented from leaving town.[150]

The organized power of 'rough culture' was not only mobilized to defend drinking rights; it could also be used to mete out 'rough justice' on a range of issues by such means as charivaris and whitecapping. Rough justice may have been more popular in the earlier decades of the century, but it persisted throughout the century, particularly in smaller communities.[151] As Bryan Palmer has noted, the tradition of the charivari extends back to medieval times. Charivaris were popular attempts to enforce community norms. In nineteenth-century Ontario, they were often concerned with domestic mores. When an older man married a considerably younger woman, or when two older people married, the couple could expect to be serenaded with 'rough music' from kettles, horns, and drums. These serenaders could often be appeased by financial compensation from the newly-weds, as in a case reported by the Aylmer *Times* in the winter of 1869:

The 'ear of night' was shocked by a variety of discordant sound calculated to disturb the nuptial repose of a[n] [older] couple who recently dropped into each other's arms for 'better or worse.' Benedict was profuse in his generosity and promptly contributed to the wants of his thirsty tormentors by inviting the unwelcome musicians to a neighboring hotel, which invitation, we need hardly remark was as promptly complied with, and the band dispersed.[152]

Such events did not always end so cordially. The bridegroom often refused to pay up, sometimes shooting into the crowd, which might retaliate in kind. Not surprisingly, these events could result in fatalities.[153]

In the late nineteenth century a newer form of community control, known as whitecapping, emerged throughout North America. The White Caps went around disguised, often in masks, hoods, and robes, beating and otherwise abusing those known to have offended against the moral standards of the community. A prime target were wife beaters. In Lambton, Ontario, William Lawson, a chronic wife abuser was whitecapped by his neighbours, who held his head under the pump until he was 'half-drowned' and paraded him up and down the streets of the town.[154] Adulterers and child abusers could also be targets of White Caps. These groups were not always consistent in their choice of targets. In Georgetown they harassed the Salvation Army, apparently for its attacks on the 'rough' habits of local men. In other communities White Caps tried to enforce an almost evangelical morality,[155] attacking prostitutes and encouraging drinkers to reform – under threat of violence. In Smiths Falls, in the late 1860s, a group that called itself the 'Thrashers,' and whose behaviour resembled that of White Cap groups, unmercifully whipped known drinkers.[156]

Despite the growing temperance sentiment in Ontario in this period, such methods were not condoned by the respectable community. The Thrashers were strongly condemned by local editors and were fined for their efforts.[157] Many other participants in charivaris and whitecapping also found themselves before magistrates, particularly in the latter half of the century.[158] In the same period that the evangelical churches were exercising less and less control over the private lives of their members, other forms of community control over private life were also becoming less acceptable. While such changes can be attributed to the growing distinction between public and private life, they were also related to a greater reliance on the legal system. Extra-legal means of enforcing community standards were increasingly frowned upon, and people were expected to turn to the police and the courts for redress.[159]

Palmer has argued that in the earlier nineteenth century when charivaris were more socially acceptable, the participants may have included members of the local elites, but that as social tolerance of such activities lessened, the participants were increasingly drawn from the working or popular classes.[160] In the earlier decades of the century women appear to have taken part in charivaris, but such activities were increasingly male in later years. Those charged with participating in charivaris later in the century were mostly young men, or boys. As Palmer notes, whitecapping was an almost exclusively male activity from the beginning.[161] Not only the elite but also the respectable married churchgoing working man may have shunned such activities for their association with a distinct 'rough' culture. The distinction between rough and respectable was not, however, always clear-cut, for respectable working men employed the methods of the charivari in some labour disputes. On occasion women could also take up such methods. For example, as Palmer notes, in the course of a weavers' strike in Hamilton in 1890, the female strikers attempted to intimidate scabs by shouting and blowing horns.[162]

'Rough' culture could thus express a particular form of youthful masculinity or could serve to assert the working-class interests of both women and men. The participants might be trying to enforce Protestant moral codes, or rioting in defence of their right to drink. The contradictions of rough culture and its relationship to more respectable norms can also be seen through an examination of that ubiquitous nineteenth-century organization, the fraternal order.

FRATERNAL ORDERS, TEMPERANCE LODGES, AND ORANGEMEN

Fraternal orders enjoyed a growing popularity in Ontario over the course of the nineteenth century. Like most other voluntary associations, such as fire companies, bands, and sports clubs, most fraternal orders admitted only men.[163] Some associations, like the Sons of England and the Sons of Scotland, welcomed only those with the same ethnic background; others, like the Sons of Temperance and the Royal Templars of

Temperance, admitted only those who adhered to temperance principles. But the majority of lodges were open to all white men, although as a result of the hostility of the Catholic Church to 'secret societies,' most lodge members were Protestant.[164] Many lodges provided a range of financial benefits, including the services of a lodge doctor, and payments in cases of sickness. Increasing numbers also offered life insurance. Others had no organized benefit plans, although they preached the virtue of helping lodge brothers in distress. All lodges were centred on some form of secret ritual, which stressed the virtues of mutual support and assistance and included elaborate initiation rites. Most also contained a series of degrees by which a member could rise in the lodge hierarchy.

There has been considerable debate among historians, both in Canada and the United States, about the class composition of fraternal orders.[165] Bryan Palmer has argued that in Canada the lodges had a primarily working-class membership, and that the mutual support and brotherhood of the lodges expressed working-class culture and fostered working-class bonds.[166] It does appear, however, that most fraternal orders had both working-class and middle-class members. Some orders, such as the Masons, had a more middle-class membership than others, but middle- and working-class men could be found both as members and office-holders in most lodges.[167] As a result, fraternal orders tended to promote a cross-class fraternalism that could inhibit the development of a distinct working-class consciousness. In *Constructing Brotherhood: Class, Gender and Fraternalism*, Mary Ann Clawson has added a gender dimension to this analysis, arguing that because the lodges were exclusively male they gave men a popular alternative to a woman-centred domesticity and encouraged them to define themselves primarily by gender rather than class.[168]

In many ways the fraternal orders were cross-class bastions of masculinity. Most fraternal rituals affirmed explicitly masculine virtues such as courage, brotherhood, and independence.[169] As Darryl Newbury has shown, the fraternal mottoes also reinforced the ideals of manliness. The motto of the Knights of Pythias, 'Be Generous, Brave and True,' and that of the Independent Order of Foresters 'Moral Courage, Physical Fitness and Stability of Character,' expressed the ideals of respectable manhood in nineteenth-century Ontario.[170] As Mark Carnes has argued, for many young American men initiation into a fraternal order was a significant rite of manhood in the nineteenth century. Newbury has shown that the majority of fraternal members joined the orders at relatively young ages, thus heightening the significance of fraternal orders in the passage to manhood.[171]

The fraternalism advocated by these lodges certainly encouraged the development of strong bonds among men. Fraternal culture offered a sociability and camaraderie that enticed many men away from home and family. In the early years of the century, lodge culture was not much different from tavern culture. Most lodge meetings were lubricated with alcohol, and some took place in taverns. Over the course of the century, however, lodges became increasingly interested in respectability, and alcohol was banished from lodge rooms. It was not, however, completely banished from the many all-male social events organized for lodge members. For example, after the election of their officers in December of 1889, the Thorold Oddfellows 'adjourned to the Welland house, where a sumptuous oyster supper had been prepared by host Winslow to which full justice was done. Toast and sentiment, song and story, all united to form an evening's unalloyed pleasure.'[172] Such lodge suppers were often held in hotels. Though some of these events were conducted on strict temperance principles, alcohol continued to play a part in the conviviality of many lodge dinners.[173] Whereas drinking among local 'roughs', both in taverns and on the streets, was generally frowned upon, the drinking among middle- and working-class fraternal brothers at such dinners occasioned little comment.

Women, however, were not completely happy with associations which took their husbands away from the home and gave them an alternative, all-male sphere of sociability.[174] Various jokes and stories in local papers reveal a feminine hostility to men's ability to use the lodge as a means of getting away from home and family. Such stories also express women's displeasure at their husbands' coming home drunk from their lodge evenings.[175] One group of fraternal orders, however, did send the husbands home sober, and they often included wives and daughters in their membership. These were the temperance lodges, such as the Sons of Temperance and the International Order of Good Templars. These associations were not simply instruments of middle-class social control, but could also serve the interests of the working class.

In the 1830s and 1840s, the early years of temperance agitation in Ontario, temperance work was viewed as scarcely respectable. Most of those involved in such work were farmers, workers or artisans, and their leaders were often 'self-made' men from similar backgrounds.[176] During the 1830s advocates of temperance only encouraged people to avoid excessive drinking. By the 1840s, however, agents for the evangelically inspired Montreal Temperance Society were drawing huge crowds of working men and women with their appeal for 'converts' to sign pledges of total abstinence from alcohol. The religious fervour of the campaign, complete with temperance tracts and days of prayer, has led Jan Noel to describe the efforts of the Montreal Society as resembling 'a travelling religious revival with a temperance theme.'[177] Abstinence was described in the temperance literature as a social panacea, and many Ontarians 'signed the pledge' as a route to personal dignity, self-help, and family harmony.[178]

Since social drinking was still accepted among the elite in this period, temperance advocates were dismissed as vulgar fanatics. Teetotalism was considered to have some value among the popular classes, but to be completely unnecessary for gentlemen.[179] Among the 'gentlemen' who opposed temperance agitation were many ministers from a range of denominations. At the same time, however, many Baptists, Methodists, and Free Church Presbyterians were active in the evangelically inspired work of the Montreal Temperance Society.[180]

Even those ministers were less than pleased, however, with the new temperance organizations which emerged in Ontario in the late 1840s and early 1850s. These new temperance lodges had a far more secular approach than the Montreal Society. The Sons of Temperance, which was founded in the United States in 1842 and entered Ontario in 1848, was intended originally as a self-help organization that would keep men away from alcohol by providing an alternative social world with the ranks, ritual, and financial benefits of a fraternal order as well as numerous 'dry' social events. Such events included activities that evangelicals could not accept, such as dances.[181] While members of the Sons, like members of other lodges, were expected to believe in God, the Sons and other temperance lodges eschewed the Christian rhetoric of the Montreal Society, espousing instead what Sharon Cook has termed 'an indeterminate Christianity.'[182]

Although the Sons of Temperance did not admit women until 1866, women could join the sister organization, the Daughters of Temperance. The class background of the early female members is not known, but scholars have shown that in the early years the Sons of Temperance attracted a primarily working-class membership.[183] In the 1850s temperance became more respectable as it came to be associated with the emerging dominant bourgeois ethic of progress, industry, and self-improvement.[184] Although this shift drew some members of the middle class into the temperance lodges, into the 1880s and 1890s working-class men and (by this period) women made up a significant proportion of their membership. While middle-class men also became active in these associations middle-class women appear to have preferred the more evangelical Women's Christian Temperance Union.[185]

Did middle- and working-class men join the temperance lodges for the same reasons? No doubt they had some of the same motivations, but there also appear to have been some class differences. Scholars have argued that most of the working-class members had little interest in the prohibition campaigns waged by the temperance lodges in the second half of the century.[186] Many workers recognized that temperance was of value for themselves and their families and that it upheld a sense of working-class pride and self-respect. But most workers do not appear to have supported prohibition, which was seen as class legislation, an attempt to abolish one of the few leisure activities available to working-class men, without providing an alternative.[187]

While many working-class members of the temperance lodges may have been uninterested in or hostile to prohibition campaigns, they were drawn to other activities offered by the lodges. In particular, both middle- and working-class male members found the lodges useful in their own efforts to remain temperate. In these associations potential drinkers were not only offered a social environment removed from the drinking culture of the hotels, but were supervised carefully to ensure that they did not 'backslide.' A common feature of lodge meetings was the expulsion of members who had violated their pledges by taking a drink. Erring but penitent members were generally readmitted.[188]

Most members of the temperance lodges were Protestant, since Catholics were expected to avoid 'secret societies.' None the less, from at least the 1840s the Catholic hierarchy organized temperance societies both to encourage abstinence among their parishioners and to provide alternative 'dry' amusements to those offered by the temperance lodges.[189] Such societies were very much visible at public events. In Ottawa, St Patrick's Day parades usually included members of the St Patrick's Temperance Society, as well as other local Catholic temperance societies.[190] In small communities priests often took the lead in promoting temperance among their parishioners. In Thorold, for example, Father Sullivan set up a temperance society in the 1870s. Though this society seems to have disappeared by the mid-1880s Father Sullivan continued his efforts to keep his parishioners away from the temptations of local rough leisure. In 1884 he organized the Catholic Mutual Improvement Society among young men, 'point[ing] out the dangers [young men] incurred by having so much idle time on their hands during the winter which could be profitably spent in improving their mental condition.'[191] The year it was organized this society presented 'a grand temperance drama' to an appreciative audience.[192] Sometimes Catholic and Protestant temperance groups came together in support of the cause. At a temperance meeting held in Ottawa in the fall of 1870, a reporter noted that 'Catholics were seen sitting together with Methodists and Unitarians.'[193]

The fact that such unity was noteworthy, however, demonstrates clearly the distance between Catholics and Protestants. Nothing symbolized this distance more strongly than one particularly popular and powerful fraternal order, the Orange Lodge. Although the Orange Lodge originated in Ireland, in Ontario it attracted Protestants of various backgrounds, all of whom were united by their commitment to uphold Protestantism and the British Crown. They were also united by a strong anti-Catholicism. This anti-Catholicism was endemic among nineteenth-century Ontario Protestants, but the Orange Lodge expressed a particularly virulent strain. The hostility was cordially reciprocated by the Catholics, particularly the Irish Catholics who made up the vast majority of Ontario Catholics during the nineteenth century. As scholars have demonstrated, Ontario Catholics and Protestants were able to coexist fairly peacefully from day to day.[194] However, the frequent clashes between the Orange Lodge and its Irish-Catholic equivalent, the St Patrick Society, revealed the underlying tensions. In the larger cities, particularly Toronto, the giant processions held on St Patrick's Day and the Orangemen's celebration of the Battle of the Boyne on 12 July, often served as flashpoints for Orange-Green riots.[195] The fear of such riots could lead the authorities to step in. In 1852 when rumours surfaced in Renfrew that the 12 July celebrations were likely to end in violence, over a hundred soldiers were sent to that small town to keep the peace.[196] While large riots were certainly not everyday affairs, Orange-Green enmity was kept alive in small towns and rural areas as well as in the cities by the burning of Orange Lodges and Catholic churches and by small-scale fights and even murders.[197]

By the 1880s such violence was on the decline.[198] None the less, the Orange Lodge continued to be regarded with suspicion by the authorities. Orange violence was associated not only with religious sectarianism, but also with drunkenness. The leaders of the lodge attempted to reduce the drinking associated with the lodges, but such drinking clearly remained a concern.[199] The annual 12 July Orange procession seldom passed without local editors' commenting on the extent to which Orangemen were (or were not) 'found unruly or under the influence of liquor.'[200]

Drinking among Orangemen was subject to editorial censure not received by the other lodges, which drank more 'respectably' behind closed doors at convivial lodge dinners. The possibility of Orange-Green violence may in part explain such concern, but the fact that Orange Lodges included a far higher proportion of working men than most other fraternal lodges may also explain such suspicion.[201] Scholars like Kealey and Palmer have celebrated the Orange Lodge as a fraternal order which helped lay the basis for a distinct culture among Ontario workers, and clearly the Orange Lodge was further removed from 'respectable' culture than the other fraternal orders. But as Houston and Smyth have noted, the order did have some middle-class members. Though these members would have had to accept a 'rougher' culture than that of most lodges, they would have noted similarities with other lodges. The exclusive masculinity of the Orange Lodge paralleled that of other fraternal orders, and while the religious bigotry of the lodge may have been unusually strong, the ethnic orders such as the St George's Society and the St Andrew's Society also fostered ethnic as well as gender exclusion.

As Newbury has noted, such traditions were not particularly beneficial ones for Ontario's emerging working class. From the Masons to the Orange Lodge, the fraternal orders taught their working-class members the values of fraternity and mutuality, but they also instilled less positive lessons. They taught that brotherhood included only men and that often it did not cross ethnic or religious boundaries.[202] Newbury has argued that Ontario workers took both the positive and negative legacies of the fraternal orders with them when they organized their own unions.[203] It is certainly clear that the gender exclusivity of the fraternal order was also found in the union hall. The masculinity of union culture was reinforced by the use of alcohol, mirroring fraternal patterns. While union leaders opposed the overuse of alcohol, arguing that capitalist hegemony could best be challenged by a sober, disciplined, respectable working class, many union meetings took place in the all-male environment of the tavern. The tavern did provide one of the few meeting places open to working-class men, who could attend union meetings in taverns and retain their sense of respectability, just as both middle- and working-class men could remain respectable while taking part in convivial fraternal lodge events at which alcohol was served.[204] But only men could enter taverns and retain their respectability. The absence of women from most nineteenth-century unions can be traced to a number of causes. None the less, the use of taverns for union meetings could not help but heighten a gender exclusivity already familiar to the many union men who regularly attended fraternal lodge events, an exclusivity which would not have encouraged an openness to women joining either the trade or the union.[205]

THE KNIGHTS OF LABOR

One major labour organization of the 1880s was able to incorporate the more positive legacy of the fraternal orders into an inclusive labour organization which expressed an alternative vision for Ontario workers. This organization, the Knights of Labor, also drew on other elements of nineteenth-century religious and leisure culture shared by middle and working class alike in fashioning what Kealey and Palmer have termed a distinctly working-class 'movement culture.'[206]

The Knights of Labor, which struggled to improve conditions for workers at the local level while offering a broader critique of industrial capitalist society, was founded in 1869 in Philadelphia. Within the Knights, workers were organized into local assemblies, either by trade or in mixed assemblies. The meetings of the local assemblies incorporated rituals similar to those of the fraternal orders, while also providing various educational and social activities for their members. The Knights supplied a trenchant critique of the dominant social and economic system which treated workers as cogs in capitalist industry, allowed them no human dignity or respect, and ground them down into poverty. The Knights saw themselves as struggling towards a more just, egalitarian, and cooperative social system for both male and female workers.

It is not surprising then that, unlike most unions and fraternal orders, the Knights welcomed women into the order, both in women's and in mixed assemblies. The order also welcomed both Catholics and Protestants and was careful to avoid sectarian controversy.[207] The many fraternal brothers who joined the Knights found the familiar fraternal ideals of brotherhood and mutual assistance there, without the exclusionary trappings linked to such values within the lodges. The order also drew on other elements of respectable leisure culture beyond the fraternal orders. Kealey and Palmer have claimed that the culture it appropriated was primarily working class. However, the evidence seems to point more clearly towards Leon Fink's assertion that the Knights drew on the dominant cross-class respectable culture, seeking to affirm working people's place within this culture in the face of a decline in the living standards of the working class and an increase in the pretensions of the middle class.[208] The Knights reshaped the standards of respectable behaviour in class-specific ways. For example, as Fink has argued, the Knights did not view temperance as a way of quelling social disorder: they advocated temperance as a means of strengthening workers' self-respect and making available to them the energy, money, and resources necessary to battle social injustice.[209]

A brief look at the Knights' involvement in leisure and associational life suggests the validity of Fink's assertion. Although Kealey and Palmer believe that the social events organized by the Knights incorporated residual forms of a working-class way of life, in fact such events were part of the leisure activities of all classes.[210] Interestingly enough, a significant difference between Knights of Labor events and other similar activities was that in some ways the Knights were more concerned about respectability than the more mainstream organizations. For example, the

Knights, who venerated family life and sought to attract more women into the Order, did not meet in taverns. By meeting in local halls instead, the Knights not only highlighted their temperance principles but also made their meetings accessible to women. The Knights also do not appear to have organized the all-male oyster suppers popular with fraternal orders and sports clubs. When the Petrolia Assembly organized an oyster supper, it was attended by Knights of both sexes.[211]

Dances, an obvious mixed-sex social event, were popular with the Knights. In Thorold, dances put on by the two male assemblies were followed by one organized by Advance Assembly, the local women's assembly. In due recognition of female modesty, however, the public organizers of the dance were male Knights.[212] Acceptance of the dominant gender ideology was even more evident at a Knights of Labor parade in St Catharines, where 'lady Knights' rode in carriages, while their brothers marched beside them.[213] Female Knights also organized social events like those popular with the predominantly middle-class women's church organizations. For example, Advance Assembly in Thorold organized both a strawberry social and a concert, complete with recitals and musical performances by members.[214]

At first glance, the leisure activities organized by the Knights were strikingly similar to those of respectable mainstream culture, but there were also significant differences. At the St Catharines parade in which the 'lady Knights' rode in carriages, the local assemblies carried banners calling for an eight-hour day; for while many Knights sought the same respectable leisure opportunities as their middle-class counterparts, they had first to struggle for the time and resources to enjoy them.[215]

A closer look at leisure events organized by the Knights suggests other significant differences from the mainstream. Many of the dances organized by local Knights were intended as benefits for injured fellow Knights.[216] The mutuality of such events contrasts sharply with the colder charity dispensed by churches, municipal councils, and middle-class charitable organizations. The strawberry socials and concerts represented an assertion of working-class respectability, as well as a willingness among working-class women to organize for themselves, and in their own interests, events which were normally dominated by the local middle class.[217]

The clearest indication of the Knights' distinct working-class appropriation of dominant values can be seen in their attitude towards Christianity. Although both the early Methodists and the Salvation Army used Christianity to challenge the subordinate position of the popular and working classes and of women, such challenges never explicitly moved beyond the spiritual realm. The Knights, on the other hand, used

Christianity to fuel a clear class-based critique of the dominant social and economic order.[218] A poem in the American Knights of Labor paper the *Journal of United Labor* proclaimed:

> We'll fight in this great holy war till we die
> No longer in silence we'll whimper and sigh
> No longer we'll cringe at the proud tyrant's nod
> But defy him, and fight 'neath the banner of God ...
> King Labor is ruler of earth of God's word.[219]

The editor of the *Palladium of Labor*, a Canadian Knights of Labor paper, also used religious language to attack social injustice. He was particularly fond of arguing that true Christianity was allied with the workers' cause: 'The doctrines of Jesus Christ, the carpenter – who would have been called a tramp and a Communist had he lived in these days – if applied to the present conditions would solve the question satisfactorily.'[220] Christ was also described as 'the greatest social reformer that ever lived. He had nothing but words of bitter scorn and scathing indignation for the idle and luxurious classes who oppressed the poor.'[221]

The Knights also asserted their rights as Christians in a society which increasingly ignored Christian ideals when they conflicted with capitalism. For example, in 1888 the Dominion government permitted the Welland canal to be opened on Sundays for a few hours in the morning and the evening. Mountain Assembly No. 6798 of Thorold unanimously passed a resolution condemning this action, declaring 'that such order will conflict with both the social and religious liberty of many of our members who are the servants of the government and as such will be compelled to perform duties which their consciences cannot approve of.'[222] In Petrolia, in southwestern Ontario, it was apparently common practice for certain companies to operate their oil wells on Sundays. Soon after the Knights of Labor arrived in town, they wrote to all the offending companies requesting that they cease this practice:

The laws of both God and man demand the due observance of the Lord's day, and the moral sentiment of the entire community ... It is believed that it is only necessary to appeal to the respect and reverence which, living as you do in an enlightened and Christian community, you must feel for God's law ... in order to secure your unhesitating consent to this reasonable request of your fellow citizens.[223]

In affirming that everyone had a right to the religious liberty and day of rest ordained 'by God's law,' the Knights were using Christian principles to affirm the dignity and worth of all, within a society characterized by hierarchy and inequality.[224]

While the Knights went far beyond the Army in using Christian values to criticize the social and economic order, their critique of the churches themselves parallels that of the Army. The *Palladium* argued that Ontario's increasing economic prosperity had led to the building of elaborate churches which strengthened the control of the moneyed classes over them: 'Many of our places of worship have become simply Sunday Clubs or opera halls, intended to attract rich congregations, where the poor are neither invited nor welcomed.'[225] One social critic featured in the paper noted, 'If a man hasn't money to pay a high pew rent ... he ain't wanted in the church'; another contributor sketched a picture of the contemporary churches with 'the rich man in the front seat' while at 'the back of the church, or away up in the strangers' gallery [you] will see the blacksmith, the machinist, or the carpenter.'[226] A 'Canadian Girl' pointed to the material basis of church membership among the commercial classes, attacking a dry goods merchant for the low wages he paid his clerks and asserting that for this man and other like him their 'pretensions to Christianity [were] a blasphemy, their attendance at divine service a mockery, their [church] donations, an advertisement, or as they would be pleased to term it "a masterly stroke of business."'[227]

While many Knights never attended the churches satirized by the *Palladium*, because they no longer felt at home there, most appear to have held some basic Christian beliefs.[228] Only by assuming a basis of shared belief could the Knights have used Christianity as they did in challenging both contemporary institutional Christianity and the inequities of the larger social and economic system of which it was a part.

CONCLUSION

The 1880s were the first decade in which members of Ontario's emerging working class clearly identified themselves as a class with distinct values and interests separate from and opposed to those of the capitalist class. This consciousness was seen not only in work-place action, but at Knights of Labor dances and lectures, as well as in the crowds that thronged to Salvation Army parades and services. By the end of the decade this class consciousness had ebbed, the Knights had collapsed, and interest in the Salvation Army had declined.[229]

Neverthless, institutions like the fraternal orders, which appealed primarily to gender and ethnic ties, continued to attract members. The enduring force of religious and ethnic divisions among Ontarians is demonstrated most clearly by the emergence in the early 1890s of the virulently anti-Catholic Protestant Protective Association. The PPA's lectures 'exposing' the evils of convent and confessional drew crowds across the province.[230]

Meanwhile the appeal of the all-male leisure culture of taverns and lodge halls began to show a few cracks as some men were drawn away by the attractions of emerging commercialized leisure alternatives. In the last decades of the century enterprising capitalists began to erect public dance halls and roller skating rinks in cities and towns across Ontario. For those who could afford the price of admission, dance halls and rinks provided young men and women with a place to meet and socialize beyond church and home.[231]

We still know very little about the beginnings of commercialized entertainment in Ontario, and its implications for the emergence of a mixed-gender leisure culture.[232] More generally, much more work remains to be done before we can have a clear understanding of religious and leisure practice in Ontario, particularly in the first half of the nineteenth century. A particularly intriguing issue about which we know very little is the social and cultural implications of the high proportion of non-believers in Upper Canadian society.

In this study we have seen that the social distance between the 'rough' tavern and the respectable lodge dinner was not as far as one might expect. However, we still need to know more about the links between these two apparently distinct cultures. The meaning of nineteenth-century masculinity seems to be a key to understanding this issue, but as yet we know far more about nineteenth-century femininity than masculinity.

The social history of religion is beginning to emerge as a serious subject of study in Ontario. A great deal remains to be done. Protestant church attendance patterns in small towns have received some attention: the urban experience remains largely unknown. The nature and meaning of church involvement among Catholics have also been largely neglected.

A more comprehensive understanding of nineteenth-century religious and leisure practices will be valuable in itself. However, as we have seen, the social and cultural meaning of such practices is of particular significance. We must know who went to church and to lodge meetings, and who did not, in order to understand how Ontarians saw themselves and related to each other. It is important, however, not only to know who was present in these and other settings; we must also know what the participants learned and celebrated there if we wish to understand the complexities of group identity in this period.

Group identity and consciousness were not only created in the workplace. By the second half of the century the class consciousness that developed there during the week could be reinforced by the Sunday hierarchy of rented pews and free seats. Such consciousness could in turn lead workers to the Salvation Army barracks as well as to the Knights of Labor assembly. Religious and leisure practices could diminish as well as intensify class tensions. Earlier in the century participation in a close-knit community of believers encouraged Ontarians to see conversion, not class as a primary basis of social differentiation. The fact that in such communities employers and workers alike could be censured for a range of offences further reinforced a sense of religious cohesion. In other milieus alternative identities came to the fore. In the culture of tavern and lodge, class identity could be undermined or at least defined in exclusively masculine terms.

The identities traced here were certainly not static or one-dimensional. They shifted in response to social and economic change. However, religious and leisure activities did not simply serve as barometers of group values and identities developed elsewhere. The tavern, the church, and other religious and leisure institutions also shaped the shifting and multidimensional nature and meaning of group identity and consciousness in nineteenth-century Ontario.

NOTES

I would like to thank John Blakely, Paul Craven, the other contributors to this book, the series editors and the anonymous reviewers for their helpful comments on various drafts of this chapter; and Chris Dorigo for her skilful research work. Some of the material about the Salvation Army and the Knights of Labor in this chapter first appeared in 'The Knights of Labor and the Salvation Army: Religion and Working-Class Culture in Ontario, 1882–1890,' *Labour/Le Travail* 28 (Fall 1990).

1 Social historians and labour historians have largely ignored the study of religion in Ontario. Recently, however, some scholars have begun to study this topic. See, for example, Doris Mary O'Dell, 'The Class Character of Church Participation in Late Nineteenth-Century Belleville, Ontario' (PhD thesis, History, Queen's University 1990); Mark Rosenfeld, '"She Was a Hard Life": Work, Family, Community, Politics and Ideology in the Railway Ward of a Central Ontario Town, 1900–1960' (PhD thesis, History, York University 1990); and Lynne Marks, 'Ladies, Loafers, Knights and "Lasses": The Social Dimensions of Religion and Leisure in Late Nineteenth Century Small Town Ontario' (PhD thesis, History, York University 1992).

2 For a discussion of working-class leisure and its implications for working-class culture and consciousness see, for example, Bryan Palmer, *A Culture in Conflict* (Montreal: McGill-Queen's University Press 1979), and E.P. Thompson, *The Making of the English Working Class* (New York: Penguin Books 1963).

3 Religion and leisure could of course serve other social functions as well. Most notably, they could help create a sense of community among particular social groups. This social function is discussed by many sociologists of religion, and is studied extensively in S.D. Clark's *Church and Sect in Canada* (Toronto: University of Toronto Press 1948). In fostering a sense of community, religious and leisure forms could of course help to create a community of resistance or, alternatively, integrate what might become an opposition group into the larger community and society.

4 See Mary M. Brown, 'Entertainers of the Road,' in Ann Saddlemyer, ed., *Early Stages: Theatre in Ontario, 1800–1914* (Toronto: University of Toronto Press 1990).

5 See Gerald Lenton-Young, 'Variety Theatre,' in Saddlemyer, ed., *Early Stages*.

6 Brian P. Clarke, *Piety and Nationalism: Lay Voluntary Associations and the Creation of an Irish-Catholic Community in Toronto, 1850–1895* (Montreal and Kingston: McGill-Queen's University Press 1993). See also Murray Nicholson, 'Irish Tridentine Catholicism in Victorian Toronto: Vessel for Ethno-religous Persistence,' Canadian Catholic Historical Association (CCHA) Study Session, *Papers* 50 (1983); Terrence Murphy and Gerald Stortz, eds, *Creed and Culture: The Place of English-Speaking Catholics in Canadian Society, 1750–1930* (Montreal and Kingston: McGill-Queen's University Press 1993); and Mark McGowan and Brian Clarke, eds, *Catholics at the 'Gathering Place': Historical Essays on the Archdiocese of Toronto, 1841–1991* (Toronto: CCHA 1993).

7 'Proudfoot Papers,' *Ontario History* 26 (1930), 551. Also see John Webster Grant, *A Profusion of Spires: Religion in Nineteenth-Century Ontario* (Toronto: University of Toronto Press 1988), 33–4.

8 See Grant, *A Profusion of Spires*, 224.

9 See 'Proudfoot Papers,' *Ontario History* 26 (1930), 522.

10 S.D. Clark, *Church and Sect*, 95.

11 Ibid., 113.

12 Ibid., 113–14.

13 Such desires are discussed by Susanna Moodie in *Roughing It in the Bush* (Toronto: McClelland and Stewart 1989), 197–201.

14 Samuel Stearns Day diaries, 22 April 1832, typescript excerpts in Canadian Baptist Archives, Hamilton (hereafter CBA).

15 See, for example, John Carroll, *Case and His Cotemporaries*, vol. 1 (Toronto 1867), 97, 183.

16 Ibid., 96, 184.

17 See William Westfall, *Two Worlds: The Protestant Culture of Nineteenth-Century Ontario* (Montreal: McGill-Queen's University Press 1989).

18 See, for example, Westfall, *Two Worlds*, and Nancy Christie, '"In These Times of Democratic Rage and Delusion": Popular Religion and the Challenge to the Established Order, 1760–1815,' in George Rawlyk, ed., *The Canadian Protestant Experience, 1760–1990* (Burlington: Welch Publishing Company 1990).

19 See Nathan O. Hatch, *The Democratization of American Christianity* (New Haven and London: Yale University Press 1989).
20 See Christie, '"In These Times,"' 20.
21 Quoted in Westfall, *Two Worlds*, 24.
22 Elizabeth Gillan Muir, *Petticoats in the Pulpit: The Story of Early Nineteenth-Century Methodist Women Preachers in Upper Canada* (Toronto: United Church Publishing House 1991).
23 Christie, '"In These Times,"' 32. In *The Democratization of American Christianity* Hatch notes similar practices among the popular Protestant groups of the Second Great Awakening.
24 See, for example, Carroll, *Case and His Cotemporaries*, 93.
25 Anna Jameson, *Winter Studies and Summer Rambles in Canada* (Toronto: McClelland and Stewart 1923), 137.
26 Susanna Moodie, *Life in the Clearings* (Toronto: Macmillan 1959), 110.
27 Quoted in Clark, *Church and Sect*, 152.
28 Ibid., 152.
29 Westfall, *Two Worlds*, 60–6.
30 George Rawlyk, *Ravished by the Spirit: Religious Revivals, Baptists and Henry Alline* (Kingston and Montreal: McGill-Queen's University Press 1984), 119–32.
31 Quoted in Clark, *Church and Sect*, 154.
32 Quoted in Cecilia Morgan, 'Languages of Gender in Upper Canadian Religion and Politics, 1791–1850' (PhD thesis, History, University of Toronto 1993), 172.
33 Morgan, 'Languages of Gender,' 173–4.
34 John Carroll, *Past and Present; or, A Description of Persons and Events Connected with Canadian Methodism* (Toronto 1860), 21.
35 Ibid., 184–5.
36 See, for example, ibid., 164–5, and Christie, '"In These Times,"' 38.
37 See Clark, *Church and Sect*, and Christie, '"In These Times."'
38 George Rawlyk has suggested that this evangelical message of spiritual equality existed in a more radical form in pre-1812 Upper Canada than in the United States at this time. See G.A. Rawlyk, *The Canada Fire: Radical Evangelicalism in British North America, 1775–1812* (Montreal: McGill-Queen's University Press 1994).
39 Thompson, *The Making of the English Working Class*, 399, and Bernard Semmel, *The Methodist Revolution* (New York: Basic Books 1973), 193. Hatch suggests that this was also true in the United States. See Hatch, *The Democratization of American Christianity*.
40 Westfall, *Two Worlds*, 44–5; Christie, '"In These Times,"' 28. She argues that the Methodists became more conservative after 1815, as British Wesleyans replaced American Methodists, but that older patterns persisted much longer in rural areas.
41 Christie, '"In These Times,"' 38.
42 The Methodists, Presbyterians, and Baptists in this period were in fact each divided into several subdenominations.

43 This may not have been true in all churches, but it was certainly the case in many smaller communities. See Judith Colwell, 'The Role of Women in the Nineteenth Century Church of Ontario' (unpublished paper, 1985, Canadian Baptist Archives, hereafter CBA), 8–9.

44 The following discussion is based primarily on a study of Baptist congregational minutes in the Canadian Baptist Archives, and on Duff Willis Crerar's thesis on Presbyterian Session records, 'Church and Community: The Presbyterian Kirk-Session in the District of Bathurst, Upper Canada' (MA thesis, University of Western Ontario 1979).

  Information on the Baptist records for Vittoria, Boston, and Beamsville is from the notes taken by Murray Meldrum and held by the Canadian Baptist Archives.

45 Port Burwell Baptist church minutes, 13 June 1846, CBA.

46 See, for example, St George Baptist church minutes, February 1845, CBA; St Catharines Baptist church minutes, 13 December 1844, CBA; Vittoria Baptist church minutes, March 1849 (from Murray meldrum notes), CBA.

47 See Janet Noel, 'Dry Millennium: Temperance and a New Social Order in Mid-Nineteenth Century Canada and Red River' (PhD thesis, University of Toronto 1987).

48 See Crerar, 'Church and Community,' 54–5.

49 See, for example, Dundas Baptist church minutes, 5 and 12 December 1847 and 20 May 1849, CBA.

50 See, for example, Crerar, 'Church and Community,' 84; Dundas Baptist church minutes, 30 December 1842, CBA; Beamsville Baptist church minutes, 22 September 1810 (Murray Meldrum notes), CBA; Wicklow Baptist church minutes, October 1819, CBA.

51 Dundas Baptist church minutes, 10 January 1847, CBA.

52 See Crerar, 'Church and Community,' Appendix; Boston Baptist church minutes, 10 December 1843 (Murray Meldrum notes), CBA; Vittoria Baptist church minutes, February 1850 (Murray Meldrum notes), CBA; Wicklow Baptist church minutes, 5 February 1850, CBA.

53 Wicklow Baptist church, July 1823, CBA.

54 See Crerar, 'Church and Community,' appendix; Cramahe Baptist church minutes, 5 July 1818, CBA; Woodstock Baptist church minutes, 8 March 1824, CBA; Beamsville Baptist church minutes, 6 October 1808 (Murray Meldrum notes), CBA.

55 A more quantitative analysis of the church discipline records is required before it can be said whether there were more men or women accused of fornication or adultery.

56 Wicklow Baptist church minutes, 22 and 25 July 1849, CBA.

57 See, for example, Hamilton Baptist church minutes, 28 March 1851, CBA.

58 Boston Baptist church, 18 May 1839 (Murray Meldrum notes), CBA. Also see Colwell, 'The Role of Women,' 4.

59 Woodstock Baptist church minutes, November 1822, CBA; also see Crerar, 'Church and Community,' 70.

60 Vittoria Baptist church minutes, August 1831 (Murray Meldrum notes), CBA.

61 However, Crerar (in 'Church and Community') does not describe enough wife-beating cases for this assertion to be definitely proved. More research is needed on this subject.

62 One interesting exception was the case in St Andrew's Presbyterian church in Perth, where the congregation took up a collection for thirty-seven members who had been ruined by the collapse of a bank. See Crerar, 'Church and Community,' 82.

63 Crerar, 'Church and Community,' 113. For poor relief to widows among Baptists see Colwell, 'The Role of Women,' 4.

64 Crerar, 'Church and Community'.

65 St George Baptist church minutes, 14 July 1825, CBA.

66 See, for example, Hamilton Baptist church minutes, 7 December 1849, and Dundas Baptist church minutes, 8 July 1843, CBA.

67 See, for example, St Catharines Baptist church minutes, October 1837, CBA.

68 See, for example, Dundas Baptist church minutes, 31 December 1837, CBA.

69 Vittoria Baptist church minutes, January 1849 (Murray Meldrum notes), CBA.

70 See Port Burwell Baptist church minutes, 28 April 1838, and 30 January 1839, CBA.

71 Crerar, 'Church and Community,' 76.

72 St George Baptist church minutes, 6 January 1836, CBA.

73 Dundas Baptist church minutes, 9 March 1851, CBA.

74 Beamsville Baptist church minutes, September 1830 (Murray Meldrum notes), CBA.

75 In the pre-industrial period, employees were often perceived as extensions of the family.

76 Wicklow Baptist church minutes, 20 September 1849, CBA.

77 Vittoria Baptist church minutes, August 1850 (Murray Meldrum notes), CBA.

78 See Crerar, 'Church and Community.' This may have been particularly true in smaller more homogeneous communities, although Crerar does not make this distinction.

79 Neil Semple, 'The Impact of Urbanization on the Methodist Church of Canada, 1854–1884,' Papers, Canadian Society of Church History, 1976.

80 Semple, 'The Impact of Urbanization.'

81 Crerar sees the fading of church discipline among Presbyterians as a matter of acculturation, with the new immigrant Free Church retaining discipline longer than the second generation Old Kirk, which largely moved away from church discipline in the 1850s (Crerar, 'Church and Community'). While this explanation may have some legitimacy, it does not explain why one can see a similar pattern among Baptists and Methodists in the 1850s.

82 Such a change reflected the distinction between public and private life that was

becoming increasingly important to the urban middle class in this period. For a dis-
cussion of this shift in the United States see, for example, Mary Ryan, *Cradle of the
Middle Class: The Family in Oneida County, New York, 1790–1865* (Cambridge:
Cambridge University Press 1981).

83 The definition of evangelical is taken from Grant, *A Profusion of Spires*, ix.
84 See Phyllis Airhart, *Serving the Present Age: Revivalism, Progressivism, and the
Methodist Tradition in Canada* (Montreal and Kingston: McGill-Queen's University Press 1992), chap. 1, and Westfall, *Two Worlds*, 67, 193.
85 See, for example, Clark, *Church and Sect*, and Semple, 'The Impact of Urbanization.'
86 See Clark, *Church and Sect*, and Semple, 'The Impact of Urbanization.'
87 *Ingersoll Chronicle*, 2 November 1882; *Stratford Beacon*, 2 April 1886. In *Of
Toronto the Good, A Social Study, The Queen City of Canada as it is* (Montreal
1898), C.S. Clark argues that '[church attendance] carries with it a respectability no
other course of action does' (148).
88 See Marks, 'Ladies, Loafers,' chap. 3.
89 *Thorold Post*, 24 March 1882.
90 Westfall, *Two Worlds*, 138.
91 Semple, 'The Impact of Urbanization,' 52; Clark, *Church and Sect in Canada*,
332–4; and Marks, 'Ladies, Loafers,' chap. 2.
92 Nicholson makes this point in relation to Irish-Catholic church attendance. See
Nicholson, 'Irish Tridentine Catholicism.'
93 St Catharines Baptist church minutes, 30 November 1844, CBA.
94 Session Minutes, Ingersoll Erskine Presbyterian Church, 1 July 1864, Regional
Room Special Collections, Weldon Library, University of Western Ontario.
95 See, for example, Thorold Anglican Church vestry minutes 17 August 1891,
21 May 1888, 3 December 1891 (Anglican Diocesan Archives, Diocese of
Niagara), and Thorold Methodist Church Board of Trustees minutes, 10 September
1888, United Church Archives (hereafter UCA).
96 Others used both systems for some time. Grant, *A Profusion of Spires*, 178.
97 See Marks, 'Ladies, Loafers,' chap. 2.
98 Board of Trustees minutes, Thorold Methodist church, 20 March 1882, UCA.
99 Semple, 'The Impact of Urbanization,' 52.
100 See Susan Houston and Alison Prentice, *Schooling and Scholars in Nineteenth-
Century Ontario* (Toronto: University of Toronto Press 1988), and David Marshall,
*Secularizing the Faith: Canadian Protestant Clergy and the Crisis of Belief, 1850–
1940* (Toronto: University of Toronto Press 1992), 23.
101 Grant, *A Profusion of Spires*, 197.
102 See Marks, 'Ladies, Loafers,' and O'Dell, 'The Class Character of Church Participation.'
103 Marks, 'Ladies, Loafers,' chap. 2. In this context the working class is defined as all
skilled, semi-skilled and unskilled wage-earners and members of their families. The
middle class consists of merchants, professionals, employers, clerks, agents, and

other 'white-collar' workers. Since this study only examines church members who lived in towns, very few farmers are included. They are categorized as 'other,' rather than as middle class. For further information see Marks, 'Ladies, Loafers,' Appendices A and B.

104 O'Dell, 'The Class Character of Church Participation.'

105 For a discussion of the predominance of women in American Protestant churches see Barbara Welter, 'The Feminization of American Religion, 1800–1860,' in Welter, *Dimity Convictions* (Athens: Ohio University Press 1976); Ann Douglas, *The Feminization of American Culture* (New York: Knopf 1977); and Nancy Cott, *The Bonds of Womanhood 'Woman's Sphere' in New England, 1780–1835* (New Haven: Yale University Press 1977).

106 The vast majority of these single male non-churchgoers were under thirty. O'Dell also notes that young men were less likely to be church members than older men, although she says less about the distinction between single and married men. O'Dell, 'The Class Character of Church Participation,' 143.

107 See Morgan, 'Languages of Gender,' 252–4.

108 R.G. Moyles, *The Blood and Fire in Canada: A History of the Salvation Army in the Dominion, 1882–1976* (Toronto: Peter Martin Associates 1977), 5.

109 *Sentinel Review* (Woodstock), 6 June 1884.

110 The Salvation Army therefore attracted at least as many Ontarians as the major labour movement of late-nineteenth-century Ontario, the Knights of Labor. Kealey and Palmer have argued that the Knights organized at least 21,800 workers in Ontario. The Knights, however, appear to have attracted more skilled workers than the Army, whereas the Army attracted larger numbers of working-class women than the Knights. See Lynne Marks, 'The Knights of Labor and the Salvation Army: Religion and Working-Class Culture in Ontario, 1882–1890,' *Labour/Le Travail* 28 (Fall 1991).

111 It appears to have been common to be converted by the Army but to return to one's own denomination rather than be enrolled as a Salvation Army soldier.

112 *Toronto Mail*, 17 July 1882. In a few towns both middle- and working-class people appear to have been attracted to the Army; see, for example, Kingston's *Daily British Whig*, 17 July 1883.

113 See Marks, 'Ladies, Loafers,' chap. 7. Workers clearly predominated in the Army in Petrolia and Listowel. Both towns had populations under five thousand. The predominance of farmers in Feversham can be explained by the fact that this was a largely rural community.

114 Marks, 'Ladies, Loafers,' chap. 6

115 This impression is reinforced by the surviving Army records. For example, soldiers' rolls for Listowel and Petrolia for the 1886–1900 period show that women made up at least 58 per cent of all soldiers. Corps Records, Salvation Army Archives, Toronto.

116 *Fredericton Evening Capital*, 20 October 1885; *Northern Advance* (Barrie),

13 October 1883. More than half of all female converts were servants within each of the three Ontario corps for which converts' rolls have survived.

117 The other reason for women preachers in the Salvation Army was the influence of William Booth's wife, Catherine Booth, who was a strong advocate of women's right to preach. See Marks, 'Ladies, Loafers,' chap. 7.

118 *Daily British Whig* (Kingston), 1 October 1883.

119 *Belleville Daily Intelligencer*, 5 December 1883.

120 *Woodstock Sentinel Review*, 6 June 1884.

121 *London Advertiser*, 14 July 1883.

122 *Toronto World*, 17 and 20 December 1883.

123 As noted above, Semmel and Thompson make this argument for early Methodism: Thompson, *The Making of the English Working Class*, 399, and Semmel, *The Methodist Revolution*, 193.

124 For similar patterns in Britain see Roland Robertson, 'The Salvation Army: The Persistence of Sectarianism,' in Bryan Wilson, ed., *Patterns of Sectarianism* (London: Heinemann 1967), and Victor Bailey, '"In Darkest England and the Way Out": The Salvation Army, Social Reform and the Labour Movement, 1885–1910,' in *International Review of Social History* 29, Part 2 (1984).

125 For a more detailed discussion of the Salvation Army's appeal to working-class values see Marks, 'The Knights of Labor and the Salvation Army.'

126 For biographies of officers that give some idea of their religious background see, for example, *War Cry*, 4 December 1886; 19 February, 19 March, 18 June 1887.

127 See Lynne Marks, 'Working Class Femininity and the Salvation Army: "Hallelujah Lasses" in English Canada, 1882–1892,' in Veronica Strong-Boag and Anita Clair Fellman, eds, *Rethinking Canada: The Promise of Women's History*, 2d ed. (Toronto: Copp Clark Pitman 1991).

128 *Petrolia Advertiser*, 8 August 1884.

129 See Marks, 'Working-Class Femininity.'

130 *Daily British Whig* (Kingston), 31 August 1883.

131 Comments regarding the Army's levity and vulgarity can be seen, for example, in the *Daily British Whig* (Kingston), 30 April 1883, *London Advertiser*, 7 April 1884, and *Sarnia Observer*, 16 May 1884.

132 *St. Thomas Times*, 17 August 1883; *Toronto World*, 5 September 1884.

133 *Ingersoll Chronicle*, 1 November 1883, *Newmarket Era*, 13 June 1884; also see *The London Advertiser*, 7 April 1884.

134 For a petition to pass such a by-law see *Ingersoll Chronicle*, 27 March and 10 April 1884; also see *The London Advertiser*, 19 and 20 June 1884.

135 See, for example, *British Whig* (Kingston), 31 January and 3 October 1883; *Barrie Northern Advance*, 30 August 1883; *Renfrew Mercury*, 15 April 1887; *Woodstock Sentinel Review*, 14 December 1883; *Huron Signal* (Goderich), 13 February 1885; and *Thorold Post*, 14 March 1884.

136 *Ingersoll Chronicle*, 13 December 1883.

137 Victor Bailey argues that this was the main reason for working-class opposition to the Salvation Army in England. See Bailey, 'Salvation Army Riots, the "Skeleton Army" and Legal Authority in the Provincial Town,' in A.P. Donajgrodzki, *Social Control in Nineteenth Century Britain* (London: Croom Helm 1977), 241.

138 See Westfall, *Two Worlds*, 59–60.

139 See, for example, *Free Press* (London) 22 November 1876, 14 May 1877, 14 September 1880; *Citizen* (Ottawa) 12 November 1877, 30 September 1878. Also see *Campbellford Herald*, 26 October 1882 and 23 August 1883, for comments about the harassment of churchgoers by young men.

140 See Marks, 'Ladies, Loafers,' chap. 4.

141 This does not mean that women never drank. However, it was assumed that drinking was a male vice. Therefore most women who drank, drank in private. See Cheryl Krasnick Warsh, '"Oh Lord, Pour a Cordial in Her Wounded Heart": The Drinking Woman in Victorian and Edwardian Canada,' in Cheryl Krasnick Warsh, ed., *Drink in Canada: Historical Essays* (Montreal and Kingston: McGill-Queen's University Press 1993).

142 See Peter De Lottinville, 'Joe Beef of Montreal,' *Labour/Le Travailleur* 8, no. 9 (Autumn/Spring 1981/1982).

143 *Thorold Post,* 1 January 1892.

144 See, for example, Roy Rosenzweig, *Eight Hours for What We Will: Workers and Leisure in an Industrial City, 1870–1920* (Cambridge: Cambridge University Press 1983), and Matt Sendbuehler, 'Making Toronto the Good: Class, Territory, Public Drinking and a New Moral Order in Late Victorian Toronto' (unpublished paper, University of Toronto, Geography, 1990).

145 For concern that young men frequented hotels after work see, for example, *Thorold Post,* 10 February 1882, 21 January 1887, 20 March 1891; *Campbellford Herald,* 1 December 1881.

146 *War Cry,* 18 June 1887. A similar pattern can be seen in other male Salvationist 'confessions'; see *War Cry,* 1 October 1887 and 19 March 1887. 'Confessions' may have been coloured by later conversions, but they do seem to reveal common social drinking habits among young men.

147 W.H. Graham, *Greenbank: Country Matters in Nineteenth Century Ontario* (Peterborough: Broadview Press 1988), 83–4; *Ingersoll Chronicle,* 28 May 1885, 21 January and 22 July 1886.

148 *Ingersoll Chronicle,* 25 February 1886.

149 Ibid., 21 January 1886.

150 Ibid., 10 March 1887.

151 See Bryan D. Palmer, 'Discordant Music: Charivaris and Whitecapping in Nineteenth-Century North America,' *Labour/Le Travail* (1978).

152 Reported in *Bytown Gazette,* 5 November 1869.

153 See Palmer, 'Discordant Music.'

154 Ibid., 48.

155 Ibid., 46.

156 *Times* (Ottawa), 5 January 1867, 2.

157 Ibid., 4 February 1867, 2.

158 Palmer, 'Discordant Music,' 51–2.

159 For a discussion of this trend see, for example, Karen Dubinsky, *Improper Advances: Rape and Heterosexual Conflict in Ontario, 1880–1929* (Chicago and London: University of Chicago Press 1993).

160 Palmer, 'Discordant Music,' 52.

161 Ibid., 48.

162 Ibid., 37–8.

163 For a discussion of the masculine culture of these associations see Marks, 'Ladies, Loafers,' chap. 5. For a discussion of men's participation in late nineteenth-century sports see also Nancy Bouchier, '"For the Love of the Game and the Honour of the Town": Organized Sport, Local Culture, and Middle Class Hegemony in Two Ontario Towns, 1838–1895' (PhD thesis, History, University of Western Ontario, 1990), and Alan Metcalfe, *Canada Learns to Play: The Emergence of Organized Sport, 1807–1914* (Toronto: McClelland and Stewart 1987).

164 See Mary Ann Clawson, *Constructing Brotherhood: Class, Gender, and Fraternalism* (Princeton: Princeton University Press 1989), 162.

165 See, for example, Gregory Kealey, *Toronto Workers Respond to Industrial Capitalism, 1868–1892* (Toronto: University of Toronto Press 1980); Palmer, *A Culture in Conflict*; Clawson, *Constructing Brotherhood*; Brian Greenberg, 'Worker and Community: Fraternal Orders in Albany, New York, 1845–1885,' in Charles Stephenson and Robert Asher, eds, *Life and Labor: Dimensions of American Working Class History* (New York: State University of New York Press 1986); and Mark Carnes, *Secret Ritual and Manhood in Victorian America* (New Haven: Yale University Press 1989).

166 Kealey, *Toronto Workers*, 98–123; Palmer, *Culture in Conflict*, 39–46.

167 See, for example, Marks, 'Ladies, Loafers,' chap. 5, and Darryl Jean-Guy Newbury, '"No Atheist, Eunuch or Woman": Male Associational Culture and Working-Class Identity in Industrializing Ontario, 1840–1880' (MA thesis, Queen's University, 1992), chap. 3.

168 Clawson, *Constructing Brotherhood*, 256. She also argues that the legacy of the lodges encouraged even class-conscious working-class men to define the working class in male terms, with negative consequences for working-class women, and indeed for the entire working class (259).

   In another recent study of American fraternalism, *Secret Ritual and Manhood in Victorian America*, Mark Carnes goes farther than Clawson and asserts the centrality of masculinity to the social and psychological meaning of the lodges in nineteenth-century America.

169 Clawson, *Constructing Brotherhood*, 82–3 and Carnes, *Secret Ritual and Manhood*, 52–4, 76.

170 Cited in Newbury, '"No Atheist, Eunuch or Woman,"' 73.

171 Most lodges required members to be twenty-one before joining, but the majority of initiates appear to have been under thirty. Newbury, '"No Atheist, Eunuch or Woman,"' 81–2.

172 *Thorold Post*, 27 December 1889. For similar events see also 8 and 15 June 1888; 18 January 1888; 21 February 1890; *Ingersoll Chronicle*, 20 April, 7 December 1882; 14 February, 1884.

173 See *Thorold Post*, 15 June, 18 January 1888; 24 April 1891. For a discussion of efforts to make lodge activities temperate, see Carnes, *Secret Ritual and Manhood*, 26–7; Clawson, *Constructing Brotherhood*, 160–1 and Houston and Smyth, *The Sash Canada Wore*, 114–16. These authors note that liquor was often banned from lodge rooms. This does not mean that it was banned from all lodge events.
   In many cases it is unclear whether alcohol was drunk at lodge social events, but the fact that temperance suppers are explicitly mentioned suggests that they were more the exception than the norm. The very existence of the temperance lodges reinforces the probability that alcohol remained part of socializing at most lodges.

174 For the American context see Clawson, *Constructing Brotherhood*, 186–7. Carnes also identifies a significant hostility among women to the lodges (Carnes, *Secret Ritual and Manhood*, 77–81).

175 See, for example, *Thorold Post*, 16 November 1883, 22 March 1889; *Ingersoll Chronicle*, 6 September 1883; *Campbellford Herald*, 25 March 1886.

176 See Noel, 'Dry Millennium,' 176–8.

177 Ibid., 159.

178 See, for example, Noel, 'Dry Millennium,' and Malcolm Graeme Decarie, 'The Prohibition Movement in Ontario, 1894–1916' (PhD thesis, History, Queen's University 1972).

179 Noel, 'Dry Millennium,' 176–7.

180 Noel, 'Dry Millennium.'

181 Ibid., 234.

182 Sharon Anne Cook, '"Continued and Persevering Combat": The Ontario WCTU, Evangelicalism and Social Reform' (PhD thesis, History, Carleton University 1990), 77.

183 See Jack S. Blocker Jr, *American Temperance Movements: Cycles of Reform* (Boston: Twayne Publishers 1989), 50. See also Decarie, 'The Prohibition Movement in Ontario,' 8.

184 See Noel, 'Dry Millennium.'

185 Marks, 'Ladies, Loafers,' chap. 4.

186 See Blocker, *American Temperance Movements*, and Decarie, 'The Prohibition Movement in Ontario.'

187 Sendbuehler, 'Making Toronto the Good,' 32, 54.

188 W.H. Graham, *Greenbank*, 91–2, and Cook, '"Continued and Persevering Combat,"' 79.

189 See, for example, *Citizen* (Ottawa) 12 June, 5 January 1867; *Free Press* (London)
     4 March, 6 February 1874. Though the Catholic Church supported temperance,
     there was little support from the church for prohibition. Decarie, 'The Prohibition
     Movement,' 31–2 and Clarke, *Piety and Nationalism*, chap. 6.
190 *Citizen* (Ottawa), 12 June 1847, 20 March 1852.
191 *Thorold Post*, 5 December 1884.
192 Ibid., 7 March 1884.
193 *Times* (Ottawa), 28 September 1870.
194 See, for example, Kealey, *Toronto Workers*, and Donald Harman Akenson, *The
     Irish in Ontario: A Study in Rural History* (Kingston and Montreal: McGill-Queen's
     University Press 1984).
195 See Kealey, *Toronto Workers*, 115–16; *Citizen* (Ottawa), 12 August 1878, 4.
196 *Citizen* (Ottawa), 3 July 1852, 2.
197 See, for example, *Union* (Ottawa), 1 October 1864; *Times* (Ottawa) 14 March 1856,
     3 October 1857, 6 January 1858; *Free Press* (Ottawa) 2 January 1877.
198 Kealey, *Toronto Workers*, 119.
199 Ibid., 114.
200 *Campbellford Herald*, 16 July 1885. Also see *Thorold Post*, 13 July 1883; *Ingersoll
     Chronicle*, 26 July 1883.
201 See Marks, 'Ladies, Loafers,' chap. 5.
202 See Newbury, '"No Atheist, Eunuch,"' and Clawson, *Constructing Brotherhood*.
203 Newbury, '"No Atheist, Eunuch."'
204 Although taverns were one of the few meeting places open to working-class men,
     they were not the only possible place for meetings. The Knights of Labor, an orga-
     nization which sought to avoid taverns, was able to find other meeting places.
205 Some major sources of gender exclusivity and frequent hostility to women workers
     among male unionists were the fear of competition from women and the belief that
     a woman's place was in the home as wife and mother. See, for example, Ruth
     Frager, 'No Proper Deal: Women Workers and the Canadian Labour Movement,' in
     Linda Briskin and Lynda Yanz, eds, *Union Sisters: Women in the Labour Move-
     ment* (Toronto: Women's Press 1983).
         It is true that both unions and fraternal orders held 'family' social events, but
     these were separate from the serious business of the organizations.
206 See Greg Kealey and Bryan Palmer, *Dreaming of What Might Be: The Knights of
     Labor in Ontario, 1880–1900* (Toronto: New Hogtown Press 1982).
207 Ibid.
208 Leon Fink, *Workingmen's Democracy: The Knights of Labor and American Politics*
     (Urbana: University of Illinois Press 1983), 3–15.
209 Fink, *Workingmen's Democracy*.
210 See Kealey and Palmer, *Dreaming of What Might Be*, 291.
211 *Petrolia Advertiser*, 19 November 1886.
212 *Thorold Post*, 11 February 1887.

213 Ibid., 19 August 1887.
214 Ibid., 17 June 1887, 3 February 1888. Also see Susan Levine, *Labor's True Woman: Carpet Weavers, Industrialization, and Labor Reform in the Gilded Age* (Philadelphia: Temple University Press 1984), 117–18, for a discussion of similar cultural activities among American female Knights.
215 *Thorold Post*, 19 August 1887.
216 See, for example, *Ingersoll Chronicle*, 20 January 1887; *Thorold Post*, 28 January 1887, 3 February 1888.
217 See Kealey and Palmer, *Dreaming of What Might Be*, 293.
218 For a discussion of how contemporary American labour leaders used Christianity in their critique of capitalism see Herbert Gutman, 'Protestantism and the American Labor Movement: The Christian Spirit in the Gilded Age,' in *Work, Culture and Society in Industrializing America: Essays in American Working-Class and Social History* (New York: Random House 1966).
219 *Journal of United Labor*, 25 May 1884.
220 *Palladium of Labor* (Toronto), 13 February 1886.
221 *Palladium of Labor* (published in Hamilton unless otherwise indicated), 27 October 1883. See also *Palladium of Labor*, 22 May, 20 March 1886; 14 March 1885; 29 December, 8 September 1883.
222 *Thorold Post*, 13 July 1888.
223 *Petrolia Advertiser*, 24 September 1886.
224 For a discussion of the controversy about Sunday streetcars in Toronto in the 1890s – the labour movement at first opposed Sunday cars and later supported them – see Christopher Armstrong and H.V. Nelles, *The Revenge of the Methodist Bicycle Company* (Toronto: P. Martin Associates 1977). In *Trade Union Gospel: Christianity and Labor in Industrial Philadelphia, 1865–1915* (Philadelphia: Temple University Press 1989), 47–52, Kenneth Fones-Wolf demonstrates that Philadelphia workers sometimes used Sabbatarian arguments to protect workers from Sunday labour, but more often opposed Sabbatarianism as an interference in their leisure.
225 *Palladium of Labor*, 8 September 1883.
226 Ibid., 27 October 1883, 14 March 1885.
227 Ibid., 29 September 1883; also see 16 October and 31 July 1886.
228 See Marks, 'Ladies, Loafers,' chaps 2 and 6.
229 Economic depression largely explains the decline of the Knights. See Kealey and Palmer, *Dreaming of What Might Be*.
    By the early 1890s the Salvation Army had been transformed into a social welfare organization that served the 'submerged tenth.' It was no longer a religious option for more than a tiny fraction of Ontario's working class.
230 See J.R. Miller, 'Anti-Catholic Thought in Victorian Canada,' *Canadian Historical Review* 66, no. 4 (December 1985); and Marks, 'Ladies, Loafers,' chap. 2.
231 See Marks, 'Ladies, Loafers,' chap. 5. In *Secularizing the Faith: Canadian Protestant Clergy and the Crisis of Belief, 1850–1940* (Toronto: University of Toronto

Press 1992), David Marshall argues that the emergence of commercial entertainment, which provided an appealing alternative to church activities, was a major factor in the secularization of English-Canadian society.

232 For one of the few works on this topic, see Carolyn Strange, 'The Perils and Pleasures of the City: Single, Wage-Earning Women in Toronto, 1880–1930' (PhD thesis, History, Rutgers University 1991).

Lindsay, Orangemen's Parade, 12 July 1907

Brass bands for Jesus: the Salvation Army's Lisgar Street band, Toronto, 1890

Annual march of a local fraternal order: the International Order of Odd Fellows, Amherstburg, 1892

The Salvation Army in Toronto, 1884: working people with banners flying

Labour and Management on the Great Western Railway

PAUL CRAVEN

On a bright June morning in 1864, twenty-two of the Great Western Railway's proprietors, officers, and servants gathered in the Hamilton sunshine to have their picture made (see p. 337).[1] Photographer Milne marshalled them on and around GWR locomotive number 8, the *Dakin*, christened *Woodstock* when purchased from the Schenectady works in 1853 but recently rebuilt and renamed in the railway's own shops. 'The poses and clothing reflect the sense of pride felt by businessmen and railway operatives,' writes one Canadian historian.[2] But who were these men? What brought them together, and from where? Of what were they so proud? And what have they to tell us about working for the railway in nineteenth-century Ontario?[3]

This chapter draws on the life experience of the men around the *Dakin* to explore the history of labour-management relations on the Great Western Railway. Its central theme is the unexpected effect of changes in business strategy and heightened competition on the railway's employment practices and on railway workers' lives. Neither the business history nor the labour history of the Great Western has been adequately depicted elsewhere. From one perspective this chapter might be seen as a cautionary tale of industrial restructuring and corporate downsizing. From another it is the story of a working-class community betrayed by continentalism and absentee ownership. Seen from within, though, it is above all an exploration of that most elastic of nineteenth-century employment institutions, paternalism.

The term 'paternalism' is used loosely in the labour-history literature to describe practically any arrangement by which the employer professes to take an interest in the worker's life outside of work; sometimes it seems to describe any arrangement of which the author disapproves. Probably in reaction to these vagaries, paternalism has been dismissed by some as merely a matter of management style.[4] In the sense that I want to use the term here, however, paternalism was much more than a matter of management style, although it was undoubtedly that as well. It was a basic strategy for recruiting, organizing, and disciplining labour to get work done, just as slavery and collective bargaining are. At the core of paternalism was a shared problem of scarcity: from the worker's point of view, the scarcity of steady employment, and from the employer's, the scarcity of capable experienced workers when most needed. Paternalism addressed this shared problem by an exchange. The employer undertook to supply steady work, or at least a steady income, and the worker undertook to remain loyal to the employer even when short-term employment elsewhere offered higher wages. Paternalism is so called because this exchange, maintenance for loyalty, mirrored the idealized relation between the *pater familias*, the male head of the household, and his dependents. In small-scale employments, where paternalism was truly a personal labour relation, the master might take the worker apprentice or journeyman into his own household, so that the metaphor of family relations for employment relations was an obvious one. This sort of thing was not unknown in nineteenth-century Ontario: for example, a Toronto newspaper complained in 1848 about merchants who lodged their clerks in boarding houses, because the employees were thereby 'debarred the privileges of a home, and the advantages of social intercourse with their employers' families.'[5] But paternalism could exist as well in the very largest workplaces, as nineteenth-century railway operations demonstrated.

On the railways, paternalism was especially characteristic of labour relations in the mechanical departments, where there was a premium on specialized, often imported, skills like those of fitters and boiler-makers, or on the bred-in-the-bone experience of engine-drivers (the Great Western used English rather than American occupational terms) who had learned the peculiarities of their equipment and the particulars of every mile of track from years spent as cleaners in the engine sheds, helpers in the shops, and firemen on the road. These were also the first railway trades to organize unions, and their experience showed that trade unionism was not necessarily incompatible with paternalism. But railway paternalism was not limited to the shops and running sheds. More than in any other nineteenth-century industry, most branches of railway work were organized as careers, with clearly demarcated steps on the ladder of success. While there were fines and other punishments for misconduct, even the occasional dismissal for cause, the more pervasive discipline was the prospect of advancement for meritorious service or demotion for want of care.[6] The habit of paternalism led to its adoption even in relatively common and unskilled railway employments where prospects for

On engine, left to right: Robinson, Forsyth, McMillan, Sharp, Robertson, Hall (on step), Payne, unidentified conductor, Penny. On ground, left to right: Reid, Wallace, G.H. Howard, Faulconer, Dakin, J. Howard, Swinyard, Baker, unidentified man, Weatherston, Ward, Neilson, Wilson

advancement were few, and where there were already well-developed labour markets.

In analysing a form of work organization like paternalism (or slavery or collective bargaining), it is important not to assume that because a form existed it necessarily worked well, or that the exchange involved was necessarily equal. These were (and are) dynamic, adaptive systems that changed in response both to external conditions and to the shifting interests and social power of their principals. They were at the same time ideological and cultural systems that shaped, although to varying extents, the attitudes and interests of those who lived them.[7] Paternalism was limited on the one hand by its expense for employers and on the other by the calculations of typically mobile nineteenth-century workers who might well prefer higher short-term wages and a chance at independence to a lifelong career on the railway. This was especially true for workers without scarce or specialized skills and with few prospects for advancement through the ranks. Railway paternalism seems to have worked best, from both parties' points of view, when workers with recognized and valued skills could find common cultural ground with their supervisors, when loyalty did not mean unmanly subordination. But ultimately everything turned on the perceived mutuality of the underlying bargain. When one or the other party realized or imagined that it did not need it or could not afford it, paternalism was shaken to its core. In some places it simply dissolved away; elsewhere it was shattered by workers' militancy; more commonly, at least on the railways, it devolved into a particularly autocratic form of industrial welfarism. That, however, is beyond the period and scope of this study, as is the persistence or recrudescence of paternalism in various forms in our own day.[8]

On the Great Western, paternalism was coloured by several factors that were either peculiar to that railway or more pronounced there than elsewhere. A significant proportion of the road's managers and skilled shopcrafts, and many of its original complement of engine-drivers, had a shared background on a small handful of English railways. The Great Western was more of a financial success than the other Canadian railways of its day and for a time was even quite prosperous. From the outset there had been conflict between the company's promoters in Canada and its shareholders in England, both of whom were often manipulated by the railway's managers through intrigues that attracted or suborned the support of the workforce. It was also coloured by a factor common to the whole industry: the all but exclusive masculinity of railway employment.[9]

A PRIDE OF RAILWAYMEN

The men who gathered around the *Dakin* on that June morning in 1864 were not a randomly assembled group who merely chanced to be about the Hamilton yard in their formal best when Milne opened his lens. They had been selected to mark an occasion. There in the centre of the frame stands the president of the Great Western, the chairman of its English board of directors, London alderman Thomas Dakin, and alongside him is his fellow director Thomas Faulconer. On this, their first visit to Canada, they have inspected the line and opened a new station and the railway's own rolling mill. This very morning the mayor of Hamilton has hosted a public breakfast in their honour, not without some opposition from the local elite, and now they are about to begin their journey home.[10] What better occasion for a souvenir picture, posed before the president's locomotive namesake and surrounded by loyal officers and workmen?

It was a representative group that gathered around the *Dakin*, although what it represented was in some ways best defined by what it did not. The Great Western had, along with its London directorate, a Canadian board, but its members were conspicuously absent that June morning. Within days of Dakin's and Faulconer's departure the Canadians protested that 'these Gentlemen did not afford them an opportunity during their stay here of frankly and confidentially discussing the present position and management of the Company's business, especially on those points on which the committee have felt called upon to differ from the General Manager.'[11] Foremost amongst these points was a fundamental conflict over business strategy. The Canadian directors wanted to use the company's power to set rates and build branches to develop Hamilton as a regional metropolis. The London board and its general manager in Canada, Thomas Swinyard, opted instead to enhance the Great Western's position as an intermediate link in the rapidly expanding American railway system, a strategy that in time would bypass Hamilton entirely. Differences like this one had divided the road's directors and managers since the beginning. They had contributed to a falling out with the company's original American investors even before the line opened. They had driven a wedge between the powerful Hamilton merchant-politician Isaac Buchanan and the GWR's first managing director, C.J. Brydges, in the mid-fifties when local interests agitated unsuccessfully for expansion south of the Hamilton-Windsor main line. Now the same underlying dispute had arisen again, this time over a plan by the company's arch-competitor, the Montreal-based Grand Trunk, to enter Great Western territory by taking over the Buffalo and Lake Huron Railway.

The group around the *Dakin*, proprietors, officers and servants, were allies in a common cause. The particular cause is of some significance – it included not only opposition to the Grand Trunk threat, but also support for a rate structure that favoured long-distance freight over the local interests of what the London board's secretary called that 'little Piddleton,' Hamilton, and a general determination to strengthen the hand of general manager Swinyard against the Canadian directors, whose connivings went 'to the root of destruction of all discipline or organization.'[12] As significant as the issues at stake was the fact of the alliance. For the Great Western depended upon its workers for support in its factional infighting, in its rate policy, and in its competitive struggles with the Grand Trunk and other roads, almost as much as it depended upon them to carry on the ordinary business of the line.

The alliance's campaign against the Grand Trunk's plans to merge with the Buffalo and Lake Huron Railway, thereby moving into the Great Western's own backyard, had been waged on several fronts. Swinyard and the company's solicitor, Aemilius Irving, were assiduous in their parliamentary lobbying, but no more assiduous than the Great Western's agents were in lobbying among the Buffalo and Lake Huron workers, many of whom had begun their Canadian railway careers on the Great Western. One of them explained his method in a note to Swinyard:

I have talked to the different R.R. Officials, Station Masters, etc., in this way, supposing your Supt should dismiss you justly or not as matters now stand you could go to the GT or GW and probably get another situation but in the event of all the roads being under one management if they [were] dismissed from one they would be excluded from all the roads in Canada. They would then if they wished to follow Rail Roading have to leave the country. They all as a general thing see it in this way, every one has some influence and it is well to strengthen our friends as much as possible in this way.[13]

Similarly, in the campaign to uncouple the Great Western from the local boosterism of the Hamilton businessmen who had founded the road, Swinyard mobilized the railway's workers. Isaac Buchanan, along with his elder brother Peter as London agent and Sir Allan Napier Mac-Nab as parliamentary fixer extraordinaire, had practically brought the Great Western into being in the late forties and early fifties. Now he was seeking re-election for his Hamilton constituency, claiming, 'I ought to be supported by every man of the Great Western even as a matter of his own and the Railways direct interest.'[14] Some London directors apparently considered throwing the railway's support behind Buchanan: solicitor Irving told Dakin's predecessor, F.S. Head, that if Swinyard was left to himself he could do as he liked with the staff, 'but the idea of coercing them to vote, would produce disaffection.'[15] Swinyard had other plans. When the Canadian directors let it be known that they supported Buchanan, Swinyard countered with notices in the shops saying that employees were to be allowed to vote without interference – and then gave them a half-holiday to attend the polls. With their support Buchanan's opponent carried the first day of voting, although he lost the election. The Montreal *Gazette*, a Grand Trunk partisan, charged that the men had been taken from their work to vote against Buchanan,[16] just as they had by Swinyard's predecessor in 1857.[17] Even the Toronto *Globe*, which as a fierce antagonist of the Grand Trunk was perforce an ally of the Great Western, had to admit that 'the influence that the GTR has with the present Government and the appearance of certain employees of that company at the polls for Buchanan undoubtedly influenced many GWR employees.'[18]

Everyone agreed that the Hamilton election was really a contest between the GTR and the GWR over the Buffalo and Lake Huron – 'between those in favour of the Amalgamation of the two Companies and those against it' – and that C.J. Brydges, now general manager of the Grand Trunk, had pulled what strings he could to get Buchanan re-elected.[19] The proof of that pudding was to come in August, when at a Hamilton Board of Trade public luncheon chaired by Buchanan, Brydges promised – vainly, as it turned out – to compete with the Great Western in its own home town.[20] By the time Brydges arrived for lunch the Great Western had fired its troublesome Canadian directors, 'to obtain a more harmonious action with the Executive.'[21]

Swinyard relied on the workforce again in the controversy that erupted a few days after Dakin and Faulconer left town. Outraged partisans of Buchanan and the Canadian board protested the municipal breakfast for the Great Western president. Swinyard instructed Samuel Sharp, the company's mechanical superintendent, to organize a show of support for the Mayor:

Some insulting remarks passed by Mr Sheriff Thomas has 'raised' the whole of the Employees of the Workshops – and to a man they intend being present at the meeting. I have just seen Mr Sharp – he has taken prudent measures to prevent any untoward exhibition of feeling on their part – and he has also taken the precaution to send a competent man to consider the Resolutions intended to be submitted, so there will be little danger of anything offensive being proposed. The object simply is to show that the Mayor had the support of the citizens – and that the inhabitants object to the proceedings of these 'few' who want to enrich themselves at the expense of the GWR.[22]

A RAILWAY CAREER

'All my politics are railroads,' the Great Western's founding genius, sometime premier, Allan MacNab, is reputed to have said. Great Westerners might easily have replied, 'All our railroading is politics.' To work for the Great Western was to be immersed in the public politics of elections, lobbies, and protest meetings, and in the corporate politics of lions and foxes, career advancement and survival. Opened in 1853–4 from Niagara Falls to Windsor and in 1856 from Hamilton to Toronto, this was the largest Ontario-based railway and one of the province's biggest employers until it was absorbed into the Montreal-based Grand Trunk system in 1882. Though it was promoted by Hamilton businessmen-politicians hoping to make their city the commercial capital of the western province, the GWR received the bulk of its capital from British investors, assisted by provincial and municipal loans and guarantees.[23] Like other large railways, although unlike most other Canadian undertakings of its day, the Great Western's daily business was overseen by a corps of full-time managers, engineers, and accountants interested in developing their professional careers. Local boosterism, absentee ownership, and professional management made a volatile mixture and one that greatly influenced the railway's labour relations.

The group around the *Dakin*, manly and loyal, citizens and inhabitants, were active participants in, and conscious members of, a political community defined by occupational interest and ethnic origin. The majority had been born in England, and many had been recruited from a handful of British roads to serve the Great Western. A delegate from London, Ontario, recommending restraint to a GWR workers' protest meeting in 1856, pointed out that, 'The greater part of the operatives who proposed to strike were thousands of miles away from their native country, and had much, nay everything, to lose in such a contest as might ensue.'[24] His plea was not successful, but their strike was. Common origins cemented the solidarity of the railwaymen. Their British industrial roots were woven into a fabric of patronage and clienthood that set them off from the rest of colonial society and fostered the railway's distinctive artisanal paternalism.

Thomas Swinyard became GWR general manager in 1862 after fifteen years on England's London and North Western. He succeeded C.J. Brydges, the Great Western's first general manager, who had been recruited at twenty-six from his position as assistant secretary with the London and South Western Railway. Brydges brought several officers and skilled workers with him from the L&SW, including William Bowman, the Great Western's first mechanical engineer. Bowman, who claimed after the event to have opposed the early opening of the line, parted company with the GWR less than two years later in the wake of a series of accidents and mishaps that wrecked a good part of the equipment in his care.[25] The superintendence of the mechanical departments was then divided between another Englishman, prudent Samuel Sharp, who became head of the car department when the company took over the facilities it had formerly leased to contractors, and the locomotive superintendent Henry Yates.[26] When Yates left the Great Western for its regional competitor, the Buffalo and Lake Huron, the London directors sent out Alexander Braid to replace him. Braid was a disaster: in short order he alienated the workforce and precipitated a general strike in the shops. He was hastily dismissed,[27] to be succeeded by Richard Eaton, a

London and South Western alumnus and the Great Western's most illustrious engine-builder.

In 1862 Brydges accepted the general-managership of the Grand Trunk in preparation for the anticipated amalgamation of the GTR and GWR lines. When the legislature refused to sanction the merger, he remained with the larger railway, and both Eaton and Sharp resigned their Great Western positions. Eaton became mechanical superintendent of the Grand Trunk. The Great Western board first accepted Sharp's resignation as car superintendent, and then a few days later 'availed themselves of the opportunity of effecting a considerable economy, by placing the Locomotive and Car Departments under one management,' making Sharp the GWR's mechanical superintendent.[28] He was active in the local St George's Society during his stay at Hamilton, and returned to England when he retired for health reasons in 1866.[29]

Sharp, Eaton, and the mechanics brought from England – 'a different class of men to any previously in the country'[30] – soon established the Great Western on the leading edge of mechanical innovation. Under the direction of Eaton and such foremen as Joseph Marks, who could recite the history of mechanical invention since Nero's time,[31] the GWR locomotive shops developed and adapted numerous improvements and modifications in engine building and fuel economy. Under Sharp and his foremen, the GWR car shops built beautiful and innovative passenger cars, as well as numerous freight cars of various types, furniture for stations, and other equipment. Their collective masterpiece was undoubtedly the car prepared for the 1860 royal visit, subsequently converted for use as the railway's official car. The furniture and fittings, of curled maple and black walnut, were made in the GWR workshops; the suspension and ventilators were of Sharp's own improved design; and the whole was carefully designed to highlight Canada's place in the front ranks of empire:

The arm-chair intended for His Royal Highness is most elaborately carved; on the back is the Prince of Wales' feathers and coronet, surrounded by the rose, shamrock, and thistle, while a wreath of maple leaves is gracefully entwined amongst them ... In the carving of the sofas, the maple leaf and beaver are quite prominent ... In the centre is a table, in the top of which, in a small diamond shape and space, has been inlaid fourteen specimens of our finest Canadian woods, and very beautiful they are.[32]

Sharp was succeeded as mechanical superintendent by another Englishman, his assistant William Aspley Robinson.[33] In the Great Western tradition, Robinson was a practical mechanic with several patents to his name.[34]

Like Sharp, chief engineer George Lowe Reid returned to England when illness in his family caused him to retire to Brighton in 1872 after twenty-one years on the Great Western.[35] The Howards, purchasing agent James and general manager's assistant Harry, were sent out by the London board in 1862.[36] John Hall, who had been a fireman on England's North Western and North Eastern railways and an engineman in Spain, had come out in the early fifties as one of the Great Western's first engine-drivers. Promoted in about 1857, Hall remained locomotive running foreman at Hamilton for more than three decades.[37] (Another of the Great Western's original enginemen, Peter Temple, had driven the royal train which took Queen Victoria on her first railway journey, from Windsor to Paddington: he became first Chief Engineer of Hamilton Division 133, Brotherhood of Locomotive Engineers.)[38]

John Weatherston, who was born in Scotland in 1804, began his railway career under George Stephenson in 1835. After several years of engineering supervision on various English lines, he worked in the head office of the London and South Western until 1852, when Brydges recruited him to become the Great Western's track superintendent. After twenty-five years in that position he joined the Michigan Central Railroad. His railway career almost ended in 1884 when, as an eighty-year-old track superintendent on the Canadian Pacific, he was badly injured in a derailment. He recovered to become general factotum of the little Hamilton and Dundas Railway, finally retiring at eighty-seven after fifty-five years of railway work.[39]

When the GWR commenced operations in the fifties there was no pool of experienced railway workers in the province. The company had either to import a labour force or create one. It did both. Managers, superintendents, and foremen were recruited from British railways, as were such skilled mechanics as engine-drivers, fitters, boiler-makers, and other shop crafts. Central-office clerks were also recruited from Britain, as were several of the original stationmasters.[40] Jobs requiring commercial skills or local knowledge without technical expertise – conductors, baggagemen, freight clerks – were more often filled locally. Less-skilled manual workers and trainees for skilled jobs were also hired locally: brakesmen, yardsmen, locomotive cleaners, car repairers, switchmen, watchmen, porters, plate layers (trackmen), shop helpers, and apprentices. Although the Great Western drew increasingly on local labour markets as they developed in the sixties and seventies, it continued to look to British railways for some of its skilled mechanics. In 1873, for example, the London board sent out five locomotive fitters from the North Eastern Railway and recruited a new assistant mechanical superintendent, John Ortton, from the London and South Western.[41]

George Forsyth had been general foreman at the company's round-house since at least 1856, when he appeared in Hamilton police court to prosecute a former shopworker for assault. Forsyth distinguished himself in October 1863 by his conspicuous efforts to rescue the engines when the roundhouse was destroyed by fire.[42] William McMillan had been the Great Western's wood agent since the mid-fifties. He left, along with Forsyth and several others, in an October 1865 cost-cutting purge but returned to his old job in 1870.[43] Ricocheting in and out of the Great Western service, he resigned in 1871, then was rehired two years later on the strength of his own report condemning his replacement.[44]

Peter Neilson started in the GWR traffic department at Lobo in 1854. By 1859 he was stationmaster at Dundas, where his quick action in telegraphing Hamilton about a runaway train earned him promotion to St Catharines at the expense of the former stationmaster there, who was demoted to a non-telegraph station at a lower salary. Neilson's son Hugh worked alongside his father as the St Catharines telegraph operator. By 1864 Peter Neilson was stationmaster at Hamilton. He was still there in 1867, but his subsequent career is unknown.[45] Edwin Penny was in 1864 the white-coated keeper of the railway's official car, 'a magnificently furnished mansion on a small scale' with pantry, drawing-room, dining room, fully equipped kitchen, wine 'cellar,' and 'sleeping apartments, with coal fire in each.'[46] Penny worked sixteen years for the Great Western, starting as a messenger and ending up as a conductor on the Sarnia branch line. He quit to run a hotel, but returned to railway work as baggage master on the Hamilton and North Western, where he was killed in an accident in February 1878, at age forty.[47]

William Wallace is first heard of in 1855 as the Great Western's stationmaster at Paris. He was promoted to freight agent at the Windsor terminal in June 1861.[48] When its Windsor stationmaster resigned the following year, the Great Western followed its customary cost-saving practice of rolling two jobs into one and made Wallace stationmaster and freight agent.[49] In 1862 he was appointed eastern-division traffic superintendent, replacing W.J. Spicer, who, like Eaton and several other of the Great Western's staff, accompanied Brydges to the Grand Trunk.[50] He became traffic superintendent of the whole line a year later and remained in that position until 1870, when the company's management was reorganized under a working arrangement with the Michigan Central Railroad. Wallace again had to accept a double-barrelled job, this time as assistant superintendent and stationmaster at London.[51] In 1872, during yet another reorganization, he resigned to become general superintendent of the GWR's new regional competitor, the Hamilton and Lake Erie Railroad.[52]

An important ingredient in the political glue of Great Western paternalism was patronage – the relationship of personal sponsorship and loyalty between superiors and inferiors in the employment hierarchy. When
managers and superintendents moved between lines they typically
trailed a string of subordinates behind them. The 'large desertion' of
Great Westerners who followed Brydges to the Grand Trunk in 1862
might be seen as a special case attributable to the vetoing of the amalgamation scheme,[53] but it was paralleled on a lesser scale several times
in the railway's history, as for example when locomotive superintendent
Henry Yates went over to the Buffalo and Lake Huron in 1856. The
B&LH sought Yates because, among other reasons, 'he will, from his
connexion [with the GWR], be able to command the best men, both
as fitters and drivers.'[54] A year later, when GWR locomotive foreman
Thomas Horton resigned to open a hotel – a favourite field of endeavour
for entrepreneurial railwaymen – and two hundred men under his supervision presented him with a purse of $200, former GWR foreman Goth-
waite, who had accompanied Yates to the B&LH, handed him $40 from
his friends on the Buffalo road, thereby suggesting that at least forty
mechanics and drivers had gone over with Yates.[55]

Yates's own career is interesting for its embodiment of the rags-to-
riches mythos of the pioneering railwayman. Beginning as a working
blacksmith during the construction of the Great Western, he found his
way to fortune as an 'almost independent nabob'[56] occupying a 'palatial
residence and grounds'[57] at Brantford and keeping a carriage and liv-
eried servants.[58] It was not always an easy road. Brydges' decision to
make Yates head of the Great Western's locomotive department was
unpopular with other members of the staff. Professionals in management
could be uncomfortable working alongside men like Bowman and Yates,
who had been promoted from the ranks. Former division engineer William Scott complained that among the reasons Brydges fired him was
'my opposition to making a mechanic, master-builder.'[59] Yates's move
to the B&LH was occasioned in part by his strained relations with some
of his fellow officers.[60] That history seems to have repeated itself, for in
1858 a B&LH director instructed the road's general manager that 'the
bickerings between Messrs Yates and Watts would not arise in England,
as their duties would be defined and their powers limited.'[61]

In 1862 Yates rejoined Brydges as chief engineer of the Grand Trunk.
He retired in 1866, apparently to speculate in the southwestern Ontario
oil boom from which the GWR profited so handsomely, and began to
capitalize on his railway connections by tendering for major building
projects. He was contractor for the Grand Trunk's Stratford passenger
depot in 1870 and for its 'mammoth' car works at Brantford the follow-

ing year.[62] By 1875 he was so well established that he could offer to build Montreal's Bonaventure Station for lease to the GTR.[63] No wonder that he was held out as an example 'of what a poor man may rise to in Canada.'[64]

Yates's translation from humble blacksmith to gentleman of leisure depended in great part on having a powerful patron in C.J. Brydges. To see what could happen when a man who lacked the protection of a patron misused patronage, one need look no further than Yates's replacement as GWR locomotive superintendent, Alexander Braid, who triggered the most serious strike in the whole history of GWR operations when he fired a popular foreman to make room for one of his own favourites. Braid was fired in turn, and he seized the occasion of his parting for a bitter attack on his fellow officers and Brydges in particular: 'I early became impressed that I was the wrong person for the appointment, and that I could not stoop, as the head of an important department, to those acts of meanness and oppression which were, on more than one occasion, presented for my adoption.' He proposed three reasons for having been fired: he was Scottish (that is, not English); he came from the Lancashire and Yorkshire Railway (that is, not from one of the roads centring on London); and his appointment (by the London board) ousted Brydges from direct control of the locomotive department.[65] All three reasons might be summarized by saying that Braid lacked both a patron and effective powers of patronage. Only the last will stand close scrutiny however: his traffic department colleague, W.K. Muir, made a brilliant career on the Great Western and its American connecting lines despite his Ayrshire roots and a background on the Glasgow and South Western and the York, Newcastle and Berwick railways.[66] Unlike Braid, Muir enjoyed Brydges' sponsorship and protection from the start and won the confidence not only of other powers in the GWR establishment,[67] but of the workforce as well. When he left the Great Western proper to head its Detroit and Milwaukee subsidiary in 1875, Muir was presented with testimonials from both the London, Ontario, business community and Division Committee no. 133 of the Brotherhood of Locomotive Engineers.[68]

A REGULAR GRADATION

Though the details varied over time, the Great Western grouped its operating employees into three broad departments: mechanical, engineering, and traffic. The mechanical department was responsible for building and maintaining engines and cars and for running the locomotives.[69] The engineering department was responsible for the upkeep of track, bridges, station buildings, and other structures, including workers' housing, and for the Great Western's rolling mill. The traffic department was responsible for the conduct of trains, the handling of passengers and freight in transit, and the management of stations. Central office departments were responsible for the requisition and distribution of stores and fuel, for auditing receipts and station returns, and for the company's police force.

Unfortunately there is little direct evidence of the number of Great Western employees. The railway distinguished between salaried employees on the 'roll of staff' and other workers on the 'wages list.' Fairly complete staff rolls have survived in the company records, but there are no wage lists except a few scattered pay books for the locomotive and car departments liberated from the wreckage of the Hamilton shops when they were finally dismantled by Canadian National.[70] If we extrapolate from occasional informal comments and from payroll accounts in half-yearly reports (discussed below), the Great Western may be estimated to have had about 2,000 operating employees in the late 1850s and early sixties, about 3,500 by 1870, and as many as 5,000 when employment peaked in the mid-seventies.[71]

The Great Western's official half-yearly reports include departmental schedules showing wages paid to certain classes of employees. Though the company's accounting practices changed from time to time, these figures were reported reasonably consistently from the mid-fifties until amalgamation in 1882.[72] They provide at least a good general indication of the railway's annual expenditure on revenue account for the largest occupational groups. For purposes of comparison and analysis, they are presented here in current dollars by fiscal year.[73] The aggregate payrolls shown here necessarily underestimate the railway's actual wage bill (and by extension, its workforce). They exclude most payments to supervisors, wages paid on account of capital (for example, to shopworkers building new locomotives or to trackmen laying down new sidings or extensions), and less populated occupational groups (including some telegraph operators) whose pay was included in more comprehensive account lines. These figures are summarized by department in Figure 1.

The car department accounted for about 10 per cent of annual payrolls throughout the period. Traffic accounted for between 40 and 45 per cent except in 1869–72, when as a result of greatly increased expenditures for maintenance of way, the engineering department's share of the payroll doubled in relation to the traffic department's. Track maintenance accounted for roughly 15 to 20 per cent of annual payrolls before 1869, increasing to almost 30 per cent before dropping off steadily after the introduction of steel rails in the later seventies.[74] The locomotive department accounted for almost 35 per cent of total payroll in 1860, falling off slowly but fairly steadily thereafter; it averaged about 25 per cent in the 1870s.

FIGURE 1
Payroll Components by Department, GWR: Fiscal 1855–81

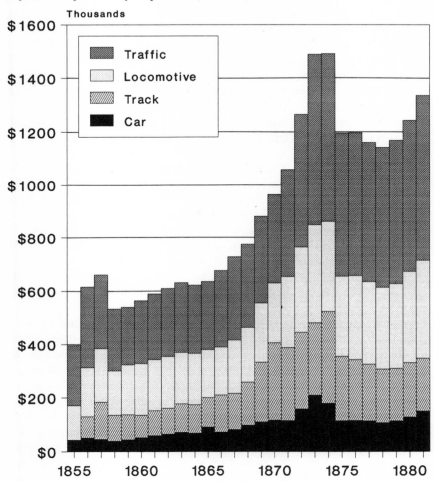

Each of the main departments was headed by a superintendent and had its own internal structure and lines of command. The mechanical department was divided into locomotive and car branches (until 1862 they were distinct departments), and the former was divided in turn between 'inside' workshops and 'outside' locomotive running. The outside department at each 'locomotive station' or division point – Windsor, London, Hamilton, and Suspension Bridge (Niagara Falls) on the main line – was supervised by a foreman, as was each of the inside workshops.

On the locomotives, firemen came under the immediate supervision of engine-drivers, while shop crafts worked under the direction of lead hands.[75] The shops also had a multitude of helpers, apprentices, and lads, some of whom were likely attached to particular tradesmen.

Apart from the rolling mill, which was headed by a supervisor responsible to the railway's chief engineer, the bulk of employment in the engineering department was in maintenance of way, where, as provincial railway inspector Samuel Keefer reported, there was 'a regularly organized system for every department of its service, from the highest to the lowest. For the care of the track there are competent and experienced Engineers and under them Inspectors, Road Masters and trackmen in regular gradation.'[76]

Responsibility for traffic was at first divided between passenger and freight departments, and later among geographical divisions. As their job title implied, stationmasters supervised a local staff which, depending on the size and importance of the station, might include freight, baggage, or ticket clerks, telegraph operators, freight porters, yardsmen, and switchmen. The stationmaster's equivalent on the trains was the conductor. He was encouraged to consider himself a line manager, the supervisor of a staff of brakesmen, and responsible for the conduct of the train.[77] His relation to the engine-driver was that of the ship's captain to its chief engineer.

Accompanying the detailed division of responsibility and chain of command within each department were rules and protocols governing interdepartmental relations, as for example between conductors and trackmen or station agents and policemen. The Great Western shared its telegraph lines with the Montreal Telegraph Company, which paid the wages of some of the telegraph operators at railway stations. General manager Swinyard complained in 1869 that the operators 'do not seem to consider themselves a part and parcel of the Railway Company,' and called upon telegraph superintendent T.I. Waugh to effect 'a decided change' so that 'every Telegraph Clerk employed on our line, whether jointly with the Telegraph Company or otherwise is held equally responsible with the Station Master and other employees for *protecting the interests of the Company*.'[78] The best example of interdepartmental protocols was the rule concerning conductors and engine-drivers:

Engine-drivers must not run a Train without a Conductor, from whom only they must take Signals relative to the movements of the Train, which, from the moment of starting to the time of arrival at its destination, is entirely under the orders of the Conductor, to whose instructions as to stopping and starting and time of moving the Engine, the Engine-driver is to pay implicit attention. But

Engine-drivers are held personally responsible if they obey orders from Conductors which are known to them to be contrary to the recognized Rules.[79]

These complicated supervisory structures were necessary because of the scale, diversity, and interdependence of the railway's operations, and of course because so many of its operations took place beyond the immediate reach or oversight of management. Although much operational decision making was centralized, at first in the general manager (especially during the Brydges regime) and later in the department heads, lesser authority and responsibility was much more widely diffused throughout the organization. There were comparatively few railwaymen who were not in charge of *something*, or who lacked the authority to order *someone* about. Moreover, the least powerful were encouraged by words, example, and shared experience to view their situation not as the bottom of the heap, but as the lowest rung of a ladder which they were expected to climb. A new general manager, Frederick Broughton, reminisced in 1876 that 'it was 35 years since he first saw railway service at 8 shillings per week' with nothing but his own industry to 'push him gradually along,' and instructed the railway's foremen accordingly: 'Their first duty was the exercise of great care in the selection of men employed by the Company ... They should do their utmost to encourage the men to properly discharge their duties, as it was only those who could hope for promotion ... He had received many letters recommending people for situations, but his answer was universal – he always promoted the men who had begun at the bottom of the Company's service.'[80]

The prospect of promotion – of railway work as a career – was an important ingredient of Great Western labour relations, along with patronage and community. Occupational mobility within the ranks of the railway could take the place of that spatial mobility which was so pronounced a characteristic of life in nineteenth-century Ontario. The province has been likened to a railway station, where although there were always crowds of people milling about, most had only just arrived or were already on their way elsewhere. What can be missed in this analogy is that even railway stations have permanent staffs. The Great Western's ability to retain skilled and experienced workers depended on its ability to persuade them that they could better themselves without going elsewhere. Railway paternalism involved not only maintaining workers over the long term, but offering them the chance to improve their lot as well.

The proper relation of supervisor and subordinate was a routine topic of comment at the frequent celebratory dinners, company picnics, and testimonial smokers that punctuated the railwaymen's communal existence. The complicated interrelation of subordination, mobility, and community was described by the chairman of the 1857 mechanics' festival shortly after the strike against superintendent Braid. It was not enough for the railway to hire only able and qualified employees: it must also 'create and preserve the disposition to exercise those talents. And nothing in his opinion was more effectual towards the attainment of these ends than occasional friendly and social meetings like the present, where from the heads of departments to the humblest servant of the company, all met on a footing of perfect equality.'[81]

When Swinyard invited the whole Great Western workforce to celebrate the Queen's birthday with sporting competitions and a picnic on the grounds of his Hamilton Mountain estate,[82] the London board approved of the occasion, noting that it 'established mutual confidence and good feelings without creating undue familiarity.'[83] But at less elaborate gatherings, where running foreman Hall might be prompted to exercise his celebrated light tenor or the Howards to show off their thespian talents, good feelings and familiarity went hand in hand.[84] While outsiders might wonder at the frivolity and expense of the Great Western's annual employee assemblies, 'the grand event of the excursion season,'[85] which drew three thousand people to the Waubuno picnic grounds and a similar number to Bush's picnic grounds at Niagara Falls,[86] or scoff at the propensity to make every career move the occasion for a party, most Great Westerners would have seconded the sentiments expressed by W.A. Robinson, Sharp's successor as mechanical superintendent, in responding to toasts at a fire brigade supper in 1867:

Although distinctions and different standings in every condition in life was necessary to the efficient carrying on of important establishments, yet after hours of duty, and on such occasions as these, he felt and regarded it as right to speak and act with employees as one man with another – man being after all what he made himself ... He strongly advocated the importance of unity of action and feeling, not only between master and man but between men themselves, without which no good or great work could be successful.[87]

Nor were such words unmatched by deeds. Robinson's mentor, Sam Sharp, had long championed such employee welfare schemes as a night school for child workers, a sick fund 'whence could be supported the widow, the orphans, or even the strong man, when he should be, unfortunately, struck by disease' or industrial accident,[88] and a reading room 'for the mental improvement and amusement of the men engaged at the Company's works.'[89] Robinson threw his support behind mechanical workers' mutual benefit schemes. The company furnished a reading room at St Thomas station, supplied with eight daily newspapers and chess and chequer boards for its Air Line employees' mutual improvement association,[90] and cooperated with the YMCA to establish a public reading room at Harrisburgh station.[91] By 1866, the Great Western's Hamilton reading room boasted 1,675 volumes, managed by a full-time librarian whose salary was paid by nominal membership fees and revenue from 'another source,' evidently disciplinary fines like those assessed in 1873 on two despatchers for mistakes in train orders.[92] Employees anywhere on the line could select books from the catalogue and have them sent to their nearest station. The library's collection had its origin in Prince Edward's donation for the use of GWR employees after he toured the line in 1860. Two car shop foremen were selected to buy a scientific library: one of them, upholsterers' foreman David McCulloch, became editor of the Hamilton *Spectator*; the other, paint-shop foreman Henry Buckingham Witton, became the first working man's candidate to be elected to the Canadian Parliament, in 1872.[93]

Witton was the very type of respectable, autodidact mid-Victorian artisan. Born in a Norfolk village in 1831, he was apprenticed to a coach-maker. He emigrated in 1853 and lived at Troy, New York, until coming to Hamilton and joining the Great Western in 1856:

On his first appointment the company profited largely by economies made by him – not the pitiable economies from which workmen suffer, but the wise ones of paying for the best article and the best man all that they are worth and making the most out of them. During all the years of his working life he has been gradually improving his original scanty education. After coming to Hamilton he acquired French and Latin, and applied himself with diligence to the study of practical geology, astronomy, and microscopy, to the latter of which he has devoted most of his leisure time.[94]

The Great Western supplied many of its employees with lodgings. Station agents, who were required to live at their stations, were routinely supplied with housing rent-free.[95] Boarding and bunk houses were established for train crews whose runs required them to spend some nights away from home. In 1873, when the GWR's divisional structure was reorganized so that some train crews were to be based at Suspension Bridge, the board was requested to 'provide in some way about 20 houses to be rented to Drivers and Firemen. At present there are no available Houses, and Employes will not erect them out of their Funds.'[96] Similar considerations probably accounted for the building of engineman's and conductor's houses at Petrolia in 1870 and a locomotive foreman's house at Clifton (Niagara Falls) in 1872.[97] In 1873 the Great Western assembled land for workers' housing near its new London car shops, where it built thirty 'small but neat' cottages to be rented to employees for five dollars monthly.[98] This supplemented the local housing market without supplanting it; 250 workers moved from Hamilton to London East to work in the new shops.[99]

Along the line of railway outside the towns and cities, the GWR found it increasingly necessary in the competitive labour market of the early 1870s to provide housing for its maintenance-of-way workers. Engineer Reid recommended spending $8,400 on trackmen's shanties in 1871, 'the object being to retain the Track Labourers on the Line, making it an object to them to settle permanently on the line.' Section men on the Sarnia branch struck to increase their wages from ninety cents to one dollar a day early in 1872.[100] Twenty-four wooden houses were built the same year because 'the best men in the Company's service were being drawn away by offers of higher wages, and they could only be retained by the Company providing for them dwelling-houses at the side of the railway track.'[101] The need persisted as the Great Western expanded through the decade: in 1876, for example, the company built twelve 'small houses or cottages for the Trackmen' on its Kincardine branch.[102] In 1874 it adopted the policy of renting to employees at a 10 per cent return on the cost of the housing, although station agents continued to occupy their houses rent-free. Employee tenants were to be responsible for repairs, and the rent was to be deducted from their pay.[103]

The Great Western aided public institutions that assisted its business by providing services to its workforce. The company's support for shopworkers' efforts to make over the Hamilton Mechanics' Institute in their own image in the mid-fifties has been described elsewhere.[104] The GWR made annual contributions to public hospitals at Hamilton and London, although the latter payment was suspended in 1870 because 'not a single case from the Railway was admitted in the past year.'[105] Some of the railway's charitable endeavours had no apparent business motive. In 1862, when general manager Swinyard appealed for contributions to aid the distressed Lancashire operatives, Great Western workers subscribed more than two thousand dollars.[106] Swinyard circularized the workforce again in 1868, this time for the relief of Nova Scotia fishing families.[107]

For the most part, however, GWR charity remained at home. In 1856, the railway company donated £13 10s to the Hamilton Orphan Asylum and Ladies' Benevolent Society to purchase firewood for the indigent; the gift was repeated in 1860 and may have been an annual subscription.[108] A few years later, shortages of supply led the Great Western to discontinue its former practice of permitting employees to buy cordwood at cost, despite a petition signed by twenty-two clerks.[109] By the winter of 1866 conditions had worsened, and Swinyard arranged to supply a thousand cords of firewood 'for distribution among the poorer of the Company's employees at Hamilton' at $4.25 a cord instead of the prevailing rate of $7.00. He offered the same terms to the Mayor for general charitable distribution; Hamilton Council first accepted the offer, then reduced its order when the wood proved to be of inferior quality.[110] Unlike the ingrates in municipal office, Great Western employees lavished praise on Swinyard for his 'liberal response' to their request for cordwood and his 'judicious and highly satisfactory arrangements' for supplying it.[111] During the financial panic of 1873 the Great Western decided to stop supplying firewood to most of its employees, offering to carry coal at cost instead. A month later it agreed to provide one thousand cords of wood at cost to destitute families in Hamilton and London, many of them laid-off railway workers.[112] Employee firewood privileges were abolished again in the spring of 1874, although at least one officer had his salary increased in compensation.[113]

The Fenian scare of 1866 gave the Great Western an opportunity to show its patriotic colours. While it avoided the Grand Trunk's military extravagances, the railway secured its shopworkers' assent to the establishment of a volunteer company at Hamilton, although the plan seems to have been stillborn.[114] At Suspension Bridge, stationmaster Price became Captain Price, commanding a company of Great Western volunteers with the aid of Lieutenant Butters and Ensign Stiff, better known in civilian life as freight agent and cashier respectively. The Great Western's part in the conflict seems to have gone no further than placing its cars at the disposal of the government. While the authorities came in for some criticism for failing to make use of the railway line during the Fort Erie invasion, it was conceded that the GWR dealt handsomely with its workers and the country generally by allowing its men time to drill at full pay, 'less, of course, the amount received by them from Government.'[115] The company's $1,000 was the largest single donation to the patriotic fund for relief of the Hamilton volunteers, and it was supplemented by an additional $560.95 subscribed by the railway's officers and men. At London the railway contributed a further $500 for the city volunteers.[116]

MECHANICAL LABOURS

John Robertson and William Payne were veterans of the Great Western's 'outside locomotive department' – the branch of the mechanical department concerned with running engines, as opposed to the 'inside' department which repaired, rebuilt, and constructed locomotives and other machinery – having joined the railway at its opening as fireman and engine cleaner respectively.[117] By the time of Dakin's 1864 visit, both had been promoted, Robertson to engine-driver and Payne to fireman.[118] Robertson later became a despatcher,[119] and Payne went into the locomotive shops as a fitter's assistant.[120]

Promotion from cleaner to fireman to engine-driver was a well-established career progression, one of the promises that mid-nineteenth-century railway companies held out to attract and retain skilled employees. Boys as young as eight or nine, many of them orphans lacking 'the first rudiments of a common education,' might enter the mechanical department as engine cleaners or other junior employees – a fact that led Samuel Sharp and general manager C.J. Brydges to establish a night school at the Hamilton works in 1858.[121] The need to retain skilled and experienced engine-drivers and shopworkers through slack times so that they would be available when business improved was at the core of Great Western paternalism. For locomotive superintendent Eaton in 1860, it justified an ambitious expansion of manufacturing in the railway's own shops, 'because we cannot possibly discharge our steady and experienced men at each recurrence of slackness in traffic.'[122] The practice persisted, so that W.F. Baines, who started on the Great Western in 1878, could find in his own experience a telling contrast with what he observed from his retirement in 1942:

The CN Ry around here is very busy and so is the CP Ry and TH&B and all are short of men. One reason for shortage is the different style of management. In my early days if it got slack the youngest firemen went into the round-house cleaning, but not now, they go on the street. The Co'y has permanent wipers, well these boys look for a job and when they get one they will not return to the railroad for they figure that if it gets slack again off they go and the manager of the plant that they deserted will of course not take them back so the railroad has to get green men if they can.[123]

Baines recalled cleaning some of the older GWR locomotives that were still in use in the eighties: 'I was the smallest cleaner and had to crawl in to clean that inside machinery.'[124] Thorough cleaning was necessary for the locomotive's mechanical efficiency, but that was not its only purpose. The GWR was justly famous for the beauty of its wood-burning engines, their wooden parts gleaming in dark green paint and their brass polished until it shone.[125] Engine-drivers and locomotive foremen took pride in their charges, and woe betide the cleaner who left a smudge on the paintwork or a dull spot on the brass. 'A good many engineers wore white overalls ... There was brass aplenty but no gas so once cleaned it was not much trouble. I fired for an engineer who told me that when he was firing or rather after he got through he used to sweep up the chips and lay a piece of carpet down on the deck.'[126]

When wood was replaced by coal, with its greasy smoke and dirty fallout, the art of locomotive decoration was discarded along with the engine-driver's white coveralls.[127] There is a note of nostalgic regret in the Great Western's 1879 rule that 'Engine-drivers and Firemen must appear on duty in as cleanly a state as circumstances will admit.'[128] Some of the wood-burners were converted to coal by the mechanical shops; others were scrapped. Percy Domville, son of the Great Western's last locomotive superintendent, began his railway career (along with his brother and brother-in-law) on the Grand Trunk's Great Western division at Hamilton in 1886: '[I] distinctly remember the old locomotives in what we called the "bone yard" in front of the erecting shop. There were all sorts and conditions in various stages of decrepitude, a number with the ancient wood burning smoke stacks, elaborate cabs (most of them made of walnut), huge cowcatchers and oversized bells.'[129]

The next step up from cleaning engines was firing them. 'You took wood from tender, piled some on deck, opened firebox door and threw it in. It had to be piled inside, to do that you had to give it a bit of a twist. You readily see if it went in higgledy-piggily there would be too much air and no steam. Put it in just as you would pile it up in a wood shed. Quite a knack but there is a trick to most everything.'[130]

Engine-drivers and firemen might have regretted the passing of the wood-burners, but even in the old days coal had had its uses. Baines again:

My own father fired about a year before he got married [in 1861] and I have heard him say that there was a big pile of coal and he used to walk in the steam from the cylinder cocks (they opened in the front and steam came through the pilot in clouds) and steal some blocks of coal and when going up the heavy grade from Hamilton to Copetown would put some coal in with the wood and it made a great fire.

Baines's recollections are testimony to two further points: that railway work tended to run in families and that like mechanically adept workers in many trades, engine crews developed their own techniques to supplement, improve upon, and sometimes to defeat the prescribed procedures: '[Locomotives 22 through 27] had very small fire-boxes and the 27 had a row of holes just above the deck leading into fire-box. These were put in to burn smoke but us fire-boys used to block them up. Reason was to help us get steam. Any air over the fire made us work harder.'[131]

The *Dakin*, like other Great Western locomotives of its vintage, had a bright brass handrail around its running board. While this undoubtedly enhanced the machine's appearance, it had a practical purpose as well. 'The Engineman must see that all parts of the Engine and Tender requiring oil, are properly oiled,' commanded the GWR's 1854 rulebook, 'as the value of any part of the machine which is damaged by heating will be deducted from the pay of the Engineman.'[132] When the locomotive was in motion, this duty was usually delegated to the fireman, 'who had to go out front with the tallow pot,' hanging on to the handrail as he lubricated the running gear.[133] This was one of the more dangerous aspects of the job. GWR fireman James Fitzgerald broke his shoulder and suffered internal injuries when he slipped and fell onto the cowcatcher while oiling a moving locomotive in 1862,[134] but he was more fortunate than the Welland Railway's 'poor young' Thomas Harrington, who died after being thrown twenty-five or thirty feet from the frame of the locomotive he was oiling when it collided with another engine,[135] or the Grand Trunk's Alfred Boase, who was killed by being struck in the head by a passing express train while oiling his engine at Port Union station.[136] In 1862 the *American Railway Review* advertised a Patent Steam Lubricator invented by the Great Western's thirty-year-old locomotive shop foreman Joseph Marks:[137] 'For oiling the CYLINDERS, VALVES, PISTON RODS, and other parts of an Engine working in steam ... It is put up and worked in the cab of Locomotives, thus avoiding the dangerous necessity of going outside to oil the cylinders.' By Baines's time, all the Great Western's engines had been fitted up with inside oiling apparatus and had had their brass handrails removed.[138]

After several years firing, a man might be allowed to try driving an engine – at first in yard work under close supervision, then perhaps to relieve regular engine-drivers. There was no formal proficiency test during the Great Western years; as late as 1889 the only formal requirement on the Grand Trunk was a test for colour blindness.[139] Practical experience was everything, not only in familiarity with the road and signals, but also in knowing the idiosyncrasies of particular engines and the mechanics of running repairs. When the GTR's antiquated *Lady Molson* was sold to the Hamilton and Lake Erie railway in 1879, 'Timothy Long came with her as engineer and was the only man who could handle her.'[140] Although later in the century some railway managers and most shop crafts unions would try to enforce a strict separation between driving and repairing locomotives,[141] there was no question during the Great Western years that every engineman was to be a practical mechanic, as familiar with the 'catechism of locomotives'[142] as with the road and signals. Especially in the early years, Great Western engine crews had not only to be prepared for, but actually to expect, breakdowns on the road.

The 1854 rulebook gave explicit instructions about what to do 'when any of the Cars of a train are on Fire,' and mandated a toolkit suitable for all sorts of running repairs, including lifting a derailed engine or car back onto the track:

Each Engineman shall have with him while on his journey, the following articles, viz: a Hand Signal Lamp, a complete set of Screw Keys, one large and one small Monkey Wrench, three Cold Chisels, a Handhammer, an Axe, one Crow Bar, two Screw Jacks, a large Chain, or Tail Rope, two short coupling Chains with hooks, links and pins, – a quantity of Flax, Gaskin, and string for packing, &c.; oil cans, large and small plugs for Tubes, an iron Man-drill for driving the same, two or more Fire Buckets, two Red Flags, and a pair of Tongs; for all of which the Engineman is responsible.[143]

The fire buckets and the instructions about burning cars were necessary because of the tendency of wood-burners especially to throw off sparks: Northern Railway locomotives were responsible for forest fires that destroyed much of the standing timber between Barrie and Collingwood in the late sixties.[144] Once again Joseph Marks came to the rescue with his Patent Spark-Arrester: 'This invention ... has been fully tested by several years' use on the "Great Western R.R." and has entirely superseded the common stack for both wood and coal engines ... [and] has resulted in a reduction of the fuel accounts about 50 per cent, and a very important reduction of losses from fire.'[145]

Before being allowed to take an engine on the road, a new driver would work engines in yard service. In the 1850s and 1860s the Great Western employed 'engine turners' (the English term: the later, American, usage is 'hostler') to run detached engines in the yards and to fuel and water them.[146] This job was eliminated in an 1870 cost-cutting drive: 'For the future, the engine-drivers are to take their engines in and out of the engine houses themselves, thus saving several hands.'[147]

A COLONIAL RAILWAY

To this point we have approached labour and management on the Great Western from several viewpoints: the lives and times of various individuals; certain of the events that threw them together; some of the institutions that structured and gave meaning to the workplace community; the character of railway work and something of its inward significance. If we are to understand what became of all this, how it was ultimately undone, we shall have to leave the engine sheds and station yards for a time, and look at the Great Western, not as an industry, a setting for work relations, but as a business, an opportunity for profit. We must step out of the boots of railway workers and supervisors and into the pockets of the company directors. Once we have grasped the essentials of their business strategy and understood how it was constrained, we can resume the story where we left it, among the working men of the mechanical departments.

The Great Western was built to connect two American lines – the New York Central and the Michigan Central – by a short route across the Niagara peninsula and southwestern Ontario. Businessmen and investors from the two states were prominent in the early promotion and direction of the line, committing $800,000 to its construction on behalf of the New York and Michigan railroads. The Great Western's chief engineer when construction began was Roswell Benedict, an American from New York State. When he was fired for cost overruns and too intimate a relationship with Samuel Zimmerman, the railway's piratical contractor, he was replaced at the American shareholders' insistence by another American, John T. Clark. Clark oversaw construction until 1854, when his reluctance to sanction the opening of the road in its then unfinished state coincided conveniently with his appointment as New York's state engineer and chief surveyor.[148] The Great Western was able to promote itself in the United States as the short route from New York to the west, and in Britain as the western link in the all-red main trunk line. Both themes were sounded by the company's president, Robert W. Harris, in an 1853 report to the shareholders on both sides of the Atlantic:

In brief it may be said that no line of railway on this continent is, perhaps, so favourably placed as the Great Western Railway, passing as it does through a rich and thriving province, forming a part of the great highway of travel through that country, and also forming the shortest possible connecting link between the great commercial and manufacturing districts of America, and those magnificent Western Territories into which Europe has for the last twenty years been pouring its redundant population, and which are now probably the most prosperous agricultural communities in the world.

But from the beginning, its business was beset by calamities both external and self-imposed. The Great Western's effectiveness as a bridge connecting New York and Michigan was compromised by the Canadian legislature's insistence, ostensibly for reasons of military security but also to appease the promoters of competing lines, that it be built on the broad 'provincial' gauge. The New York and Michigan lines were standard-gauge roads,[149] so the Great Western's through freight connections involved the expense and delay of unloading and reloading at both termini. The immediate effect was to alienate the American investors, who had made the standard gauge a condition of their participation. Largely for this reason, but also because of friction with British investors and managers over such issues as whether the road was to be built of British or American rails,[150] whether it was to employ British or American enginemen,[151] and whether the western terminus was to be located to suit the convenience of the Michigan Central Railway,[152] the American investors withdrew from the company in 1854. At the same time, the Great Western's alternative strategy as a crucial link in the Canadian main trunk line was compromised by its directors' and managers' propensity for ill-conceived quarrelling with their Grand Trunk counterparts at crucial intervals, beginning with MacNab's insistence in 1852 that the Great Western be permitted to build an extension from Hamilton to Toronto, thereby effectively though inadvertently cutting his road out of the Grand Trunk consortium.[153]

Despite the break of gauge and the desertion of its American investors, the Great Western remained dependent on its connections with the Michigan Central and New York Central for the bulk of its through traffic. The Great Western might be a British property run by British managers supervising British workmen, but its operations were constrained by and interdependent with those of the American roads. 'I fear Mr Brydges is very helpless in the matter,' replied the managing director of the Buffalo and Lake Huron to his British board's request that he arrange a better schedule of connections with the Great Western to avoid having to run trains at uneconomic speeds. The problem, Captain Barlow explained, was that the GWR timetable had to be arranged to meet the schedules of the Michigan and New York lines, 'and they will not alter their Trains or delay them.'[154] The need to reconcile timetables and allocate through passenger and freight receipts led to a regular pattern of conferences and correspondence among the managements of the three connecting lines.[155]

No amount of inter-company coordination could overcome the break of gauge at Niagara Falls and Detroit. At both places the Great Western employed huge forces of porters simply to transfer freight between broad-gauge and standard-gauge cars. It expended money and technical ingenuity in the attempt to develop a multi-gauge freight car, but without much success.[156] When Dakin and Faulconer met with MCR and NYC officials during their 1864 visit, they were urged to circumvent the Canadian broad-gauge legislation by installing a third rail along the main line, so that equipment of both gauges could share the track. The American railroads proposed to pay between them 60 per cent of the interest on new capital required to finance the third rail, provided the GWR laid it down immediately.[157] Friendly relations between the Great Western and its U.S. allies were further cemented in 1865, when W.K. Muir left his positions with the GWR and its subsidiary, the Detroit and Milwaukee, to become Assistant General Superintendent of the Michigan Central.[158]

The intricate rites of Dakin's visit in 1864 were not entirely propitious for the Great Western. The Dakin-Swinyard alliance succeeded in marshalling the Great Western workforce against Piddleton exceptionalism and so cleared the way for its continentalist strategy by putting the development of American through traffic above Hamilton's metropolitan ambitions. They were much less successful in warding off competition for that through traffic. The Grand Trunk consummated its marriage to the B&LH without benefit of legislation,[159] thereby gaining access to the Niagara Peninsula and a link to the American trunk lines. The Great Western's effective monopoly in the peninsula was broken, although for the time being the Grand Trunk lacked the capital to build the new track and bridges it required to tap the American through connection. Since it could only be a matter of time before the Montreal-based line exploited its new opportunities, the Great Western was pressed to stake its claim to the continental traffic without delay.

Construction of the third rail commenced in 1866, and later that year the GWR launched an enormous iron ferryboat to transport loaded freight cars across the Detroit River.[160] In January 1867 a 'great railway excursion party' celebrated the completion of an unbroken line of standard-gauge track from west of Chicago via Detroit, Hamilton, and Niagara Falls to the seaboard at New York. The festivities were marred only by a United States Customs ruling that through passengers' baggage must be detained for inspection, but the cheering crowd was assured by the Hon. J.V. Farewell of Chicago that the business interests of the country 'would sweep politicians out of the way, if the latter were too obstructive. Politicians were a graceless set of scamps anyway, and wanted looking after.' Before long, Toronto shippers were clamouring to have the benefit of the GWR's third rail extended to their city.[161] The New York, Great Western, and Michigan roads joined together to market the unbroken through route as the 'Blue Line' with its own distinctive equipment, including lavish sleeping cars turned out by the Great Western's Hamilton car works under licence from the Pullman company. These magnificent 'palace' cars were placed on public view in the Hamilton yards before being committed to service: 'Visitors are requested to be careful not to injure any of the fittings.'[162] One hundred and fifty Blue Line freight cars were among the first products of the new Ontario Car Company factory at London East, opened in 1871.[163] The Great Western began planning to move its own car shops to London during the same year: the contract was let in October 1873, and the new shops began operating a year later.[164]

The complete integration of the Great Western into the New York-Chicago traffic corridor was now realized. Swinyard and Dakin had played an ambiguous duet, declawing the Canadian board, fending off the Grand Trunk, and cementing the alliance with the Michigan Central, all the while parading the Great Western as a British railway. During these years, the road adopted some emphatically English trappings. In 1864, for example, the Great Western reorganized its freight delivery system along English lines.[165] The following year GWR officers and agents began to meet periodically to discuss the business of the road: 'These meetings are a new thing in this country, being adopted by Mr. Swinyard ... after having tried them successfully in England.' (In typical Great Western style, the inaugural meeting was followed by 'a pleasant, social time' at the general manager's home.)[166] Beginning with the half-yearly accounts for January 1869, the company's engineer and mechanical superintendent were required to certify the condition of the line 'in the forms prescribed by the [English] *Regulation of Railways Act, 1868*, although that Act does not extend to the Dominion of Canada.'[167] One of the first steps taken by a new slate of directors after the financial collapse of 1874 was to arrange for the company's accounts to be presented to the proprietors 'as near as circumstances will admit in the forms prescribed by Act of Parliament for the regulation of Railways in this country [England],' although that legislation was not in force in Canada.[168]

All this was no doubt reassuring to the British shareholders, who could take comfort in the impression that the Great Western of Canada was just another English road, managed by English officers, worked by English workmen, and directed by an English board, albeit at a remove of some three thousand miles. But it was mostly window dressing. With the onset of transcontinental railroad traffic in the late sixties and the emergence of Chicago as the transportation hub of the continent, the Great Western was becoming ever more tightly integrated into the American railway system.[169]

On Christmas Eve 1869, Thomas Swinyard sat down at his writing desk and drafted a letter of appreciation to his counterparts on other railways, announcing his retirement from the Great Western because the conclusion of a new arrangement with the Michigan Central 'renders unnecessary the continuance of the office of General Manager.'[170] In other letters written over the next few days he elaborated:

The present arrangement provides for the division of through traffic between the three Companies in agreed proportions – and for the working of the lines under a Joint Committee ... This arrangement is to be succeeded by another by which I understand the Lines will be actually amalgamated – if Legislative power can be obtained from the Dominion government.[171]

In England, the 'arrangement' was referred to delicately as 'the division in certain fixed proportions of the joint through traffic earnings on the one-purse system.'[172] The American railroad press gave a more robust account, saying that the scheme would 'virtually place the road under the control of the American connecting lines.'[173] Other accounts in the American press characterized the arrangement as a lease of the GWR and its Detroit subsidiary by the Michigan trunk line.[174] Dakin told the shareholders that he had entered the negotiations with authority to lease their line for up to twenty-one years, but declined to do so because of uncertainties about managing the transition when the lease expired. He had authority to 'fuse' the Great Western with the Michigan Central, but this would have required legislation. It was better to make a temporary arrangement for 'uniformity of management and consolidation of interests' and 'see how it worked.' By this account, Swinyard's job was eliminated on the advice of the Michigan Central board.[175]

However the arrangement is characterized, no sooner was it made than the Great Western applied to Parliament for permission to change over to the standard American gauge. The necessary legislation was passed expeditiously, and the railway began immediately to take up one hundred miles of outside rail. It ordered nine 'narrow' (that is, standard) gauge freight and seven passenger locomotives from the Rhode Island Locomotive Works and began construction of six more at its own Hamilton shops. By April 1871 it had arranged to sell eleven of its broad-gauge engines to the Grand Trunk.[176] When the Grand Trunk took it over a decade later, the GWR possessed more than 200 modern standard-gauge locomotives, of which 160 had been purchased from the Rhode Island works.[177] In its overnight transformation into an American standard-gauge line the Great Western incurred a staggering debt.

During the American Civil War, the Great Western had suffered enormous losses on its through traffic owing to the devaluation of United States currency. In the early 1870s, as the GWR became ever more tightly integrated into the American railway system, it continued to suffer from this cause. For example, the directors reported the cost of discounting and converting U.S. currency in the six months ending in January 1872 to be almost £28,000, and almost £35,000 in the next half-year; these were increases of £10,000 and £14,000 over the previous year. Although the American dollar had risen in value, the Great Western's U.S. currency earnings were rising more rapidly.[178]

In fact there was more American traffic than the existing line could handle. In the winter of 1872–3, the railway was severely embarrassed by a shortage of cars and by a two-month interruption of its Michigan connection caused by ice in the Detroit River. As many as fifteen hundred cars were tied up on each side of the river for two weeks at a time, waiting to be ferried across.[179] The GWR and MCR began exploratory drilling for a Windsor-Detroit tunnel, but abandoned the effort because of engineering difficulties.[180]

In the increasingly competitive environment of the early seventies the Great Western began a costly program of defensive expansion to safeguard its local traffic and its through connections. It leased and purchased several smaller southwestern Ontario lines, less for the traffic they would bring than to prevent their falling into the hands of its competitors. Pressured by the MCR, it began construction of a 'loop line' connecting Glencoe, eighty miles east of Windsor on the main line,[181] with Fort Erie, where it would use the International Bridge then being built by the Grand Trunk to cross to Buffalo. The new route, which bypassed Hamilton and London entirely, was shorter than the main line and avoided the latter's steep grades. It was intended to forestall construction of the recently promoted Canada Southern Railway south of the GWR main line, but the Canada Southern proceeded nevertheless. The costs of the loop line and its connections escalated out of control, and after it went into operation as the 'Canada Air Line' in 1874, the Great Western was committed to competing with itself for traffic. Although in its early years the Great Western had been among the most profitable of Canadian railways – indeed, the only one of the provincially guaranteed roads to repay its government loan[182] – the heightened competition and general economic collapse of the mid-1870s plunged it into profound difficulties.

In the summer of 1873 President Dakin made a second trip to Canada in an attempt to find out why net revenues were falling despite the increase in traffic. He reorganized the departmental structure and reinstituted the office of general manager, in which he placed Joseph Price, the company's treasurer. This was an implicit acknowledgment that the Great Western's interests were not well served by a collective management headquartered at Detroit. W.K. Muir continued as general superintendent responsible for the running of trains, with five divisional superintendents reporting to him, while Price took responsibility for all the other functions Swinyard had exercised as general manager.[183] No sooner had Dakin returned to England, however, than the financial panic of September 1873 swept across the United States. As business and trade

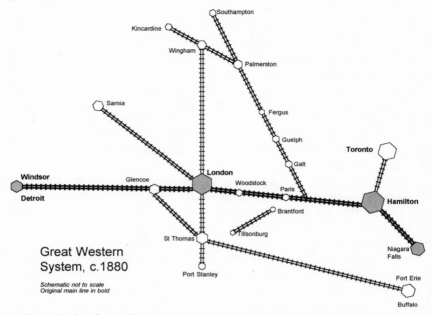

Great Western
System, c.1880

Schematic not to scale
Original main line in bold

collapsed, the Great Western was forced to cut its rates on through traffic to match its connecting and competing lines. The impact was so sudden and so great that the Dakin board was forced to renege on an announced dividend, and then to resign en masse when the shareholders protested.[184] A committee of investigation returned from Canada to announce that the company had been brought to the brink of ruin and should be completely reorganized.[185]

At the next half-yearly general meeting, a new president – the Right Hon. Hugh Childers, a former First Lord of the Admiralty, who had served on the boards of the London and North Western and the Great Indian Peninsula railways – delivered a cursory report, stating that his board had been in office only three weeks, and that he was about to leave for Canada to investigate matters for himself.[186] Childers acted energetically to reform the company's management in Canada. He finally abolished the Canada board, which had been limping along in a subordinate capacity since Dakin and Swinyard had stripped it of most authority a decade earlier. C.J. Brydges returned to the GWR as temporary Special Commissioner for six months. There was a thorough cabinet shuffle. GWR general superintendent W.K. Muir was to change places with his counterpart on the Detroit and Milwaukee (although Muir did not actually move from the GWR until 1875, when he became general manager of a competing line, the Canada Southern). The company's general manager (Joseph Price) and treasurer (Joseph Metcalf), both GWR employees of long experience, were replaced, and the head of the fuel department, William McMillan, was again dismissed, this time forever. Childers appointed as his new general manager Frederick Broughton, an experienced British railway official who had accompanied him on his tour of inspection,[187] and as treasurer another experienced British officer, Charles Percy of the Railway Clearing House. With these changes, along with chief engineer Reid's retirement in February 1873 after twenty-one years on the GWR and William Wallace's resignation in November 1872 to become general superintendent of the GWR's new competitor, the Hamilton and Lake Erie Railway, the old guard had largely passed from the Great Western general staff. This process was to be completed in 1875 when mechanical superintendent W.A. Robinson resigned. He turned down the New York Central's offer to head its engineering works in order to join his father-in-law's Hamilton stove company.[188]

Childers advised the proprietors that the Great Western had been suffering from three 'unfavourable influences' – the increased interest on debts incurred to build the loop line, replace iron rails with steel, and acquire the branches; the 'prostration' of trade generally; and increased competition.[189] 'It would be an act of cruelty to portray in its true colors the painful position of the Great Western Railway of Canada,' editorialized an American railroad journal in 1876, although it did not shrink from doing so:

Its net revenue is insufficient to pay the interest on its mortgage debt by over £100,000 a year. It has the Canada Southern on its south, controlled by Vanderbilt. It has an internal cancer of its own in the form of the loop line, and it has the Buffalo and Lake Huron section of the Grand Trunk running side by side, while the Grand Trunk proper has the shortest line to the seaboard, viz, from Chicago to Montreal. The Great Western of Canada has felt some of the plagues of Egypt, not the least of which are a president and general manager who know nothing of American railway administration.[190]

What had happened? As Figure 2 shows, the Great Western's traffic receipts had been growing steadily from the early sixties to 1873. For a few years beginning in 1868 they were enriched by the southwestern Ontario oil boom: the GWR completed a profitable extension to Petrolia in the fall of 1867. But working expenses had been growing even faster. In 1863 it had cost about 43 cents to earn a dollar's receipts; ten years later, it cost almost 67 cents. Traffic receipts fell off dramatically with the onset of the recession in 1874 and continued to fall for several years. Working expenses, however, continued to rise in the first years of the

FIGURE 2
Operating Statistics, GWR: Fiscal 1855–81

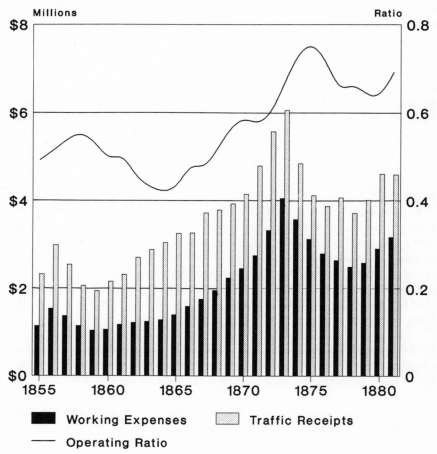

Expenses, receipts on left scale, operating ratio on right

recession and never returned to the levels of the mid-sixties. For the first three years of the recession, the operating ratio (calculated here as working expenses divided by traffic receipts) exceeded 70 cents in the dollar, peaking at 76 cents in 1875. From 1865 to 1873, traffic was expanding but at increasing cost. After 1873 traffic receipts nosedived, but expenses remained high. The Great Western's operating ratio remained above 60 cents in the dollar every year from 1874 on.

FIGURE 3

Fuel, Wages, and Receipts per Engine Mile, GWR: Fiscal 1855–81

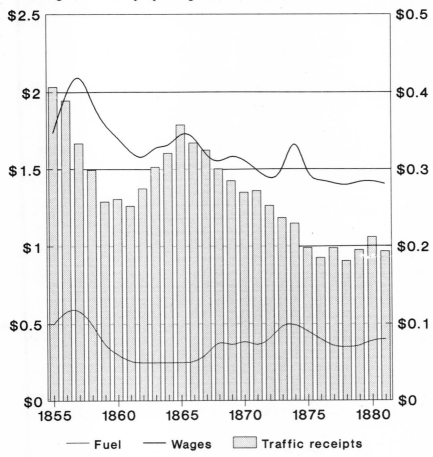

Traffic receipts on left scale; fuel and wages on right

The greatly increased operating ratio in the 1870s is not explained by increases in payroll or fuel costs, although both did rise in the first half of the decade. Figure 3 shows fuel and wage costs and traffic receipts per engine mile. Receipts were very high in the first few years of operations, when there was little or no competition and the lucrative passenger traffic benefited from the novelty of the railway. They fell precipitously in the recession of the late fifties. Traffic receipts per engine mile were

FIGURE 4

Car Mileage and Traffic Receipts, GWR: Fiscal 1855–81

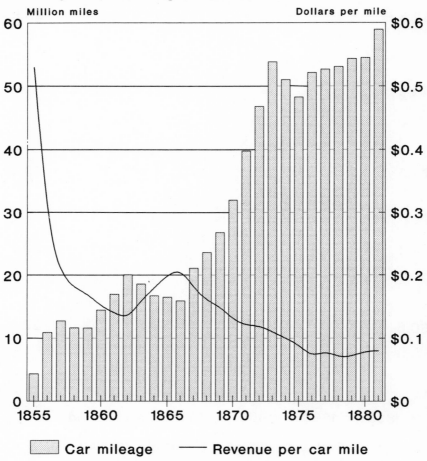

higher (at $1.79) in 1865 than in any subsequent year. They declined fairly steadily to 1875, and then levelled off at about one dollar. Aggregate wages were highest in 1857, at about 44 cents per engine mile. While they fluctuated through the 1860s and seventies with a significant 'blip' in the mid-seventies due to the suddenness of the drop in traffic, the clear trend was for total wage costs per engine mile to decline over the period, levelling off after 1874 at roughly 28 cents.

Early in the railway's history, the strenuous efforts of Eaton, Marks, and their locomotive department colleagues had cut the cost of fuel in

FIGURE 5
Train Size and Traffic Receipts, GWR: Fiscal 1855–81

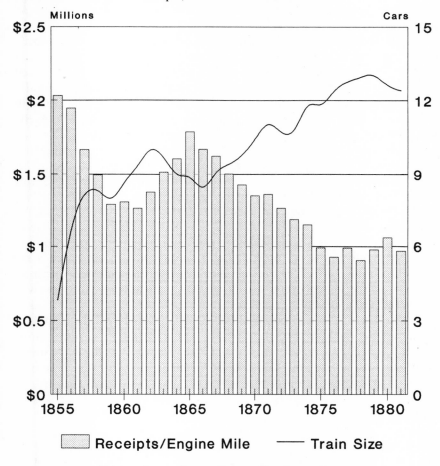

Train size • Car mileage/Engine mileage

half, from about 10 cents per mile in 1856 to 5 cents in 1861. It remained at that level until about 1867, when wood shortages began to push costs up. They had returned to 1856 levels by 1873, causing the reorganization of the fuel department's management and a decided shift to coal. One of the reasons for concentrating development in the 1870s at London rather than Hamilton was the availability of coal via the London and Port Stanley Railway, which the GWR leased from the municipality. Except during the 1874 financial collapse, fuel costs hovered between 7 and 8 cents per engine mile from 1868 to 1881. Declining wage costs and relatively steady fuel costs cannot explain the rapid increase in the GWR operating ratio after 1865.

It is attributable instead to a precipitous decline in the Great Western's traffic receipts relative to volume: the railway earned 27 cents per car mile in 1856, but only 7 cents in 1877–9 and 8 in 1880–1. Increased competition resulted in a decline in passenger fares and (especially through) freight rates so that the Great Western had to run four miles in the late seventies to earn as much as it had for running one mile in the mid-fifties. This relationship is shown in Figure 4. The decline, which began in 1866, reflected the growing importance of through American freight traffic to GWR revenues and corporate strategy. The decline in receipts per car mile was only partially offset by increases in the size of trains. Figure 5 shows the trend towards longer trains from 1866 to 1879, while receipts per engine mile (interpreted here as train mile) fell off.[191] Comparing Figures 4 and 5, it may be seen that earnings per car mile at the end of this period were less than half their original level, although trains were only about one and one half times as long. In other words, no more than about half of the decline in revenue per car mile was offset by technological or manpower changes related to longer trains. The rest was due to rate competition.

The collapse of the Great Western's rate structure and the crippling burden of debt acquired to fight off its competitors had serious consequences for labour relations in the 1870s. Paralleling these business developments, although not immediately caused by them, was the emergence of trade unionism in the railway's mechanical departments.

MUTUAL BENEFIT

Great Western workers acted collectively and self-consciously, sometimes to defend their employer and their jobs, and sometimes to obtain improved conditions or to protest poor ones. For the most part they used informal, ad hoc means of collective action. In 1856, workers in the wood department struck against a wage cut, possibly in response to the introduction of woodcutting machinery.[192] In November 1863 switchmen in the Hamilton yard petitioned unsuccessfully for a wage increase, about the same time that twenty-two clerks petitioned for cheap firewood.[193] Freight labourers (porters) at Queen's Wharf in Toronto struck the Great Western in 1873 and succeeded in having their wages raised from $1.15 to $1.25 a day.[194] In 1872–3 GWR brakesmen petitioned for $1.50 a day, but when after several months of agitation their committee called a strike, only a handful were willing.[195] Some shop crafts and engine-drivers joined trade unions, and some conductors joined an association that subsequently reorganized as a trade union. In all three cases, the immediate attraction was mutual insurance. For most of the railway's history, the unions did not play a prominent part in collective bargaining. When they did, the outcomes were shaped by the established patterns of Great Western labour relations.

The first trade union to organize Great Western workers was the Amalgamated Society of Engineers, Machinists, Millwrights, Smiths, and Pattern Makers, the ASE, which established a branch at Hamilton in October 1857. The ASE was formed in England in January 1851, when branches of the former Friendly Society of Mechanics (founded at Manchester in 1826) joined with other machine-building crafts organizations to resist the dilution of their trades.[196] The employers responded the following year with an industry-wide lockout, forcing the Society to consider emigration as an alternative for its many unemployed members. In 1852 the ASE sponsored passage for twenty-seven families to Australia, where they formed the nucleus of the union's first overseas branch at Sydney. There is no record of the Society assisting group emigration to Canada, but the rapid development of the country's railways in the mid-fifties, along with the extensive participation of English contractors and managers in that development, created a wealth of opportunities for British craftsmen. The ASE's first Canadian branch was established at Montreal in 1853, when hundreds of British workmen were imported to build the Grand Trunk and its Victoria Bridge. Hamilton was launched in 1857 and Toronto in 1858, and branches were established at Kingston, Brantford, and Stratford at about the same time as the establishment of major railway shops in those places. The London branch was formed in 1874, the year the Great Western moved its car shops there from Hamilton.

There is evidence that the organization of the Hamilton branch was inspired by the strike against GWR locomotive superintendent Braid. The 11 December 1856 number of the ASE journal contained a 'Caution to Members going to Canada':

We are requested by the Committee of Workmen, employed on the Great Western Railway of Canada, to state that there is a dispute with the workmen on that line, and a new Managing Superintendent [sic] (Mr Braid, late of the Lancashire and Yorkshire railway) lately employed over them, and to request that no engagements should be entered into by English workmen, which would tend to defeat the object of the workmen in Canada.

Figure 6 shows that the Hamilton membership grew steadily until 1866

FIGURE 6

Amalgamated Society of Engineers, Reported Membership at Year End, 1857–8

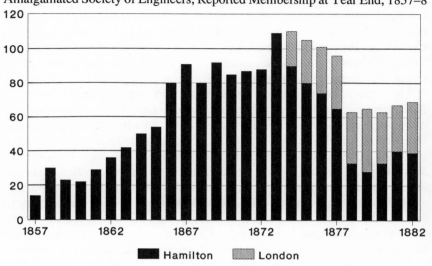

Hamilton   London

(when it surpassed the Montreal membership for the first time; the branch purchased '6 coloured emblems and 6 coloured keys' that year), and then remained fairly steady at about ninety members until it increased quite suddenly in 1873. The GWR board sent out five fitters to Canada that year; the Hamilton ASE branch recorded admitting seven fitters and a smith to membership. The falling off in Hamilton membership from 1874 on was compensated for at first by the growth of the London branch. Among the 250 Hamilton car shop workers who transferred to London in 1874 were a number in the ASE trades.[197] After 1877 the Hamilton branch fell on hard times; in 1880 it had to go to law to recover £3 4s from its defaulting treasurer.[198]

In spite of the close coincidence between the opening of railway shops and the founding of ASE branches, it is by no means self-evident that the union organized exclusively among railway workers, or even that the majority of its members worked in the railway industry. General membership records for the Canadian ASE branches, seem not to have survived. The branches' yearly returns, published in the central union's annual reports, supply few names and do not identify employers. They list the branches' auditors and the names of members who died, received benefits, or were 'excluded' (mostly for arrears, but in one Hamilton case for bigamy). The returns also list the members of other branches who were admitted on travelling cards, but while the branches in the

Grand Trunk centres filed several such reports before the early eighties, neither Hamilton nor London did.

The Hamilton branch reported 81 auditors between its founding and 1880. Since several members served more than once, these represent only 46 different people. Of these, 25 have been positively identified as Great Western shopworkers; only one of the remaining names appears in either the company's surviving pay lists or the Hamilton city directories.[199] The 25 ASE auditors who are known to have worked for the GWR filled among them a disproportionate 53 of the 81 positions. Occasionally one of these men would appear in the press as a workplace spokesman. Thus William Boustead, a Great Western machinist who served as ASE auditor 9 times between 1861 and 1877, was also vice-chairman of the 1860 mechanics' festival celebrating the first locomotive built at the Hamilton shops.[200]

There is scattered evidence linking some of the other members named in the branch returns to the railway. Several Great Western men received funeral benefits on the deaths of their wives. GWR workers in a variety of ASE trades – fitters, turners, boiler-makers, blacksmiths, pattern-makers, and bolt-makers – were 'excluded' for arrears in their 25 cents weekly dues.[201] Several died, of perils ranging from sunstroke to abscess to inflammation of the bowels, but none of obviously industrial causes. A few Hamilton members drew on the Society's benevolent fund, among them Samuel Holman, a fitter, who received £2 3s. in 1870 and succumbed to lung disease three years later.[202] W.A. Robinson encouraged the 'unity of action and feeling' by contributing to ASE benefit plates:

We have been requested by the Hamilton branch to announce that a member named James Stone arrived in that colony last June from Bristol and died in October of Typhoid fever. His wife arrived in Canada two days after his burial. The members of the branch made a collection for her, headed by a subscription from Mr. Robinson, locomotive superintendent. The total amount subscribed was upwards of £30.[203]

Daniel Black kept the Fountain Saloon on James Street, the site of many ASE and other trade union meetings. He also catered some of the Great Western picnics.[204] Upon Black's return to Hamilton from a visit to Scotland in 1865, the ASE presented him with a pipe and with a ring for his wife and proclaimed him 'the Landlord of our Club House.' The testimonial was signed on behalf of the Society by Great Western machinists William McDougall and James Flood.[205] In December 1866, fifty ASE members sat down to the Hamilton branch's annual dinner at the

Fountain Saloon. The platform party included GWR machinist William Thomson and GWR fitter John Greig, 'an old and esteemed member of the Society' who was to serve as auditor four times in the early seventies, including in 1873, when he himself was 'excluded' for arrears.[206]

In all, 232 names appear in the Hamilton branch reports to 1880. Just over half these names can be matched to the surviving GWR pay sheets or the Hamilton directories. Of the 123 references that can be matched, all but five can be definitely linked to employment in the GWR shops. They represent 70 individuals of whom 6 are known to have worked in the car department and 43 in the locomotive shop. About half were fitters; also represented were turners,[207] machinists, 'screwers' (in the car shop), smiths, boiler-makers, and pattern-makers. On the whole these were the higher-paid metalworking shop crafts. It is clear from the membership returns that even in these trades, only a small proportion of GWR employees were ASE members in the branch's early years. In 1857, when the newly formed Hamilton branch had about 30 members in a variety of trades, the railway's locomotive department employed more than 100 fitters. The mechanical departments employed about 130 men in ASE trades in the locomotive shop in 1863 and 30 in the car shop in 1862, when the branch had about 40 members.

Similar calculations are not possible for the period after 1863 because the detailed pay sheets on which they are based are unavailable. The much cruder aggregate payrolls tabulated in the Great Western's semi-annual reports show that expenditure on locomotive shopworkers' wages remained relatively constant at about $100,000 a year through most of the sixties, as shown in Figure 7. There is no evidence to suggest dramatic shifts in the craft composition of the shop workforce during this period. If we assume, as seems likely, that most Hamilton ASE members worked for the GWR and in the locomotive shop,[208] then the greatly increased membership in the decade after 1865 was not only an absolute but also a significant proportional gain for the union. In its best years, it may have included more than half of the eligible GWR shopworkers.

Little has been written about the ASE in Canada, and few records survive. Still less is known about the other British-based 'international' union of the period, the Amalgamated Society of Carpenters and Joiners. Forsey reports that its first Canadian branch was organized at London in 1871 with eighteen members, followed in 1872 by Hamilton (with nineteen members). Branches were organized at Toronto, St Catharines, and Kingston later in the decade.[209] Battye has suggested that its members, like the ASE's, were 'employed to a very large extent in the shops of the various railway companies.'[210] Although the Great Western's mechanical department had charge of constructing and repairing station buildings

FIGURE 7
Locomotive and Car Payrolls, GWR: Fiscal 1855–81

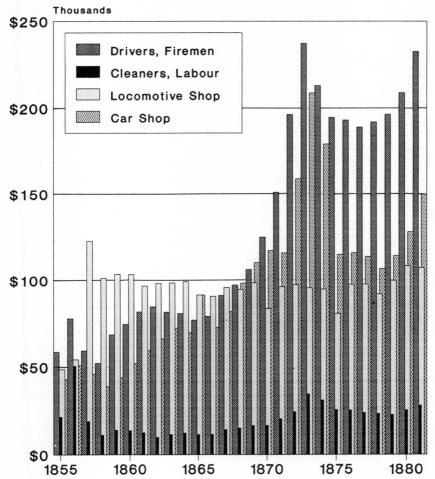

in the early years, members of the carpenters' society were more probably employed by Hamilton contractors than by the railway. It seems
unlikely that car builders and other woodworkers in the railway shops
would have belonged to a building trades union. Research to date has
revealed no direct evidence of any other union than the ASE in the GWR
shops.[211]

Outside the shops, the Great Western's only union was the American-
based Brotherhood of Locomotive Engineers. Whereas the ASE came to

the Great Western in the baggage of its English engine-fitters, the BLE arrived via the railway's American connections. The Brotherhood was born at Detroit in May 1863 out of a dispute on the Michigan Central and acquired its name the following year when Charles Wilson of the New York Central became its Grand Chief Engineer.[212] The Brotherhood entered Canada in 1865, when London Division no. 68 and Toronto Division no. 70 were chartered. The London Division organized the entire Great Western line until September 1871, when a distinct Hamilton local, Division 133, was established.[213] Thirteen Great Western drivers immediately transferred their membership from London to Hamilton.[214] A local at Point St Charles that organized Grand Trunk drivers out of Montreal was chartered in 1867. According to Tuck, the BLE's Canadian organization grew slowly in the sixties, so that between them the London, Toronto, and Point St Charles divisions had only 109 members by 1870.[215] Five years later its Canadian membership had tripled, and by 1876, said the Toronto *Globe*, the Brotherhood could speak for 90 per cent of the locomotive engineers in Ontario and Quebec.[216]

Under GCE Wilson the Brotherhood pursued a conservative policy. It had two objects: to act as a mutual benefit association for its members, and – as the *Globe* put it – 'to prevent strikes taking place except in such circumstances and for such reasons as would commend themselves to the judgment of any dispassionate and fair-dealing neutrals.'[217] These policies won it the patronage of such railway managers as the Great Western's locomotive superintendent Robinson and general superintendent Muir. Robinson encouraged GWR engine-drivers to join the Brotherhood, and from 1872 on the Great Western supplied and maintained the Division 68 meeting rooms at London. To mark their opening a grand ball was held at City Hall, under the patronage of Muir and the mayor of London, and with the music of the 7th Battalion band.[218] There were limits to the company's indulgence, however: it turned down a request for free passes for BLE members, saying that its connecting lines would not honour them.[219]

The Locomotive Brotherhood united the functions of fraternal order and mutual insurance society, providing both emotional and material support for the Great Western drivers. When a member died, it draped its hall in mourning for thirty days and voted the 'usual resolutions' of condolence and sympathy.[220] The divisions also sponsored smokers and other entertainments, like the 'Grand Concert & Ball' mounted by the Hamilton local in 1872 and attended by many of the railway's managers and superintendents.[221] The greatest incentive to membership was the mutual insurance scheme, which offered a semblance of financial security for engine-drivers' families.[222] Division 68 took an active role in reforming the BLE's benefit schemes in the early seventies.[223] Insurance payouts, which could be substantial, were publicized in the columns of the union's *Monthly Journal*. In 1871, for example, when William Ronald died of consumption, his estate received $3,000, and the same amount was paid to his fellow London Division engine-driver Thomas Brock, who was disabled by a 'lame elbow.'[224]

Conductors on the GWR, mindful perhaps of their supervisory status, sought the benefits of mutual insurance without the trappings of unionism. When a Great Western freight conductor, D. Underhill, died of 'quick consumption' in February 1870, his family received $2,758 from the United States and Canada Railroad Conductors' Life Insurance Company. The family of Hugh McEwan, another GWR freight conductor, received $2,909 from the same source when he died of 'inflammation of the lungs' a few months later.[225] The Railway Conductors' Life Insurance Association of the Dominion of Canada was organized in 1873; its relationship to the former company is uncertain.[226] While the association's first slate of officers was drawn exclusively from the Grand Trunk, other roads, including the Great Western, were represented on the executive committee. Its 1874 convention was held at Hamilton.[227] By 1878 the organization had expanded to include American conductors.[228] It was later to be assimilated into the Order of Railway Conductors.[229]

In their capacities as mutual benefit associations, the ASE, BLE, and Conductors' Insurance Association complemented, and in some degree competed with, the Great Western's employee benefits. The company had always provided compensation for the families of employees killed on duty. Thus when Joseph Kennedy, a fifteen-year veteran employed as policeman at Hamilton Station, was killed accidentally in 1870, the GWR accident insurance plan paid $300 for the benefit of his widow and large family, and the company contributed an additional $60 gratuity for the funeral and other expenses.[230] The following year, when engine-driver James Collinson died in a collision, GWR management was confronted with the fact that he held life insurance to the extent of $1,500, an amount far exceeding the traditional company benefit. Rather than be seen to pay inferior compensation, 'it was decided to aid the family by taking the sons into the service as they come of suitable age.'[231] A year later the officers reconsidered the matter and agreed to provide Collinson's widow with a $500 gratuity. The original resolution seems to have been taken up, for in 1878 a fireman named John Collinson was scalded in a collision at the Great Western's Winona station.[232] In November 1873 the management committee considered limiting the funeral and benefit claims of employees killed on duty, 'but on discussion it was thought the matter might safely be left to each Head of Department to see that only reasonable expenses were incurred.'[233]

Company welfarism sometimes influenced the nascent labour movement. At the founding of the Canadian Labour Protective & Mutual Improvement Association in 1872, GWR boiler-maker Robert Parker read out the statement of the Great Western mechanical department's sick and funeral society, founded under Sharp's aegis in 1859: 'The society had been twelve years in existence and had been found to work well. The number of members which had belonged to the society was 3,781. He proceeded to show how beneficial a society of this kind in connection with the league would prove to its members.'[234]

In 1877 the Great Western established a Provident Fund, perhaps to compete more directly with trade union benefits. Membership was to be compulsory for all new employees. Members in the train and yard service paid 60 cents a month, and others 50 cents. They were entitled to medical attendance, sick pay of $3 weekly for the first six months and $2 thereafter, a $100 flat payment for permanent disability, and a death benefit amounting to the proceeds of a general levy of the membership at rates ranging from 5 cents to 50 cents depending on the benefit class of the deceased and the members subject to levy, thereby institutionalizing the traditional 'whip-round.' The fund was governed by a committee consisting of the department heads and an equal or greater number of representatives elected generally by the members. Its original trustees were GWR solicitor Samuel Barker, locomotive superintendent C.K. Domville, and engine-driver P. Temple, who was also a BLE member.[235] One of the first beneficiaries was a Queen's Wharf yardsman, J. Herbert, who suffered a compound fracture of his left arm at work in January 1878: 'Dr Aikins removed several pieces of the broken bone, but it is feared the poor fellow will yet lose his arm. Fortunately Herbert had become a member of the GWR Company's Provident Society recently established, and thus provided for this emergency.'[236] By the end of 1878 the society had 2,418 members. It had paid benefits in twenty-one deaths, nine of them resulting from accidents on duty, and had forty-five members on sick relief at year end.[237] When section man Peter Jack fell to a horrible death from Wingham bridge in December 1878, his wife and three children expected to receive about $300 from the society.[238] In 1880 the Great Western secured legislation authorizing the establishment of provident, superannuation, and accident insurance funds. The company was to contribute not less than half, nor more than one and one-half times, the amount contributed by members.[239]

The ASE and BLE functioned for the most part as mutual benefit or insurance associations, but they were also trade unions with the object of representing their members in disputes with the employer. While there is no direct evidence that the Hamilton ASE branch engaged in its own name in collective bargaining with the Great Western, the leading figures of the Hamilton shopworkers' nine-hours movement identified themselves and their cause with the Amalgamated Society in 1872. The BLE first came to prominence in collective bargaining on the Great Western in 1876–7. In both instances, the GWR experience was distinctive. The Great Western shopcrafts were victorious in 1872, when all around them were falling in defeat. Five years later the railway company and its BLE divisions managed to avert a strike like those which developed on the Grand Trunk in 1876 and the Canada Southern and Midland railways in 1877. Although the old foundations of Great Western paternalism were beginning to crack under the stresses of increased competition and emergent trade unionism, they remained strong enough to sustain at least a semblance of the old order.

The nine-hours movement of 1872 was the first campaign to draw together Canadian workers and unions from different trades and places in a common cause. ASE members and railwaymen were prominent among its leaders, especially in Hamilton (James Ryan, Robert Parker and others), Toronto (Andrew Scott and James Gibson) and Montreal (James Black). The movement's story has been told elsewhere, although a comprehensive account is still lacking.[240] Here we focus on the Great Western's part in the Hamilton movement.

A fitter or machinist taking advantage of the GWR's Hamilton reading room one evening late in 1871 might have come upon this paragraph about the railway's English namesake as he leafed through the London *Times*:

It appears that in the locomotive and carriage department of this company at Swindon, the hours of labour have already been reduced, from 58½ hours to 57½ hours per week, and it is understood that Sir D. Gooch, M.P., chairman of the company, at the meeting of the directors to be held on the 15th inst., will recommend the Board to further reduce the hours of labour of the workmen in that department to 54 hours per week, to take effect from the 1st of January next.[241]

The British nine-hours movement of 1871 had been spearheaded by the ASE rank and file in the northeastern shipbuilding industry and spread quickly throughout the region. By October, when the leading employers had conceded the men's demands, the ASE executive assumed official leadership of a national campaign which was largely successful in achieving the fifty-four-hour week in the several branches of engineering in many parts of the country.[242] Though the contemporaneous struggle of some New York crafts for the eight-hour day undoubtedly contributed to the emergence of the movement among some Canadian workers, the British example, in particular its identification with the ASE, was by far the more important influence on the Great Western. The Canadian movement's most prominent spokesman, the recently arrived GWR machinist James Ryan, borrowed heavily from the rhetoric of the English movement in which he had probably taken part personally. Burgess[243] notes the English movement's propaganda about 'the increased opportunities "for mental and moral training" afforded by shorter working hours.' Ryan assured the Hamilton employers that the men would use their new-found leisure 'to study and learn' and to 'cultivate social and domestic virtues.' The English movement taught 'that a reduction in hours offered a disguised wage increase in the form of extra payment for overtime, while an outright wage increase would be more vulnerable to cuts during depressions.' Ryan argued that, unlike impermanent wage increases, the nine-hours system 'cannot retrograde. The hours of labour may become *less*, but never again *more*.'

Canada's nine-hours movement was publicly launched at a mass meeting at the Hamilton Mechanics' Institute on 27 January 1872. The site was significant, for one of the first organized expressions of labour-management cooperation on the Great Western had been C.J. Brydges' intervention in 1855–6 to open the Institute to railwaymen and reform its programs to meet their needs.[244] Of the five workers in the platform party, three – Ryan, Parker, and machinist Thomas Scarf – were Great Western employees.

The railway company first took official notice of the agitation on 15 March, when the Canada Board discussed the 'employees 9-hours movement and renewal of Fortnightly pays,' deciding to establish a petty cash account from which the mechanical superintendent could 'meet pressing cases where money on account of wages is required in advance of the usual pay days.'[245] Muir had apparently prepared a report on the movement by 9 March, although it was not presented to the Canada Board until 11 April. Earlier that month he met with C.J. Brydges of the Grand Trunk, F.W. Cumberland of the Northern Railway, and the managers of other roads to discuss common action:

From the different circumstances of the roads represented, it was found impossible to adopt a uniform rule for them all; but in view of the exhausting labour of many departments of the railway service, and the necessity for constant mental alertness, it was felt desirable by all present that every facility for relaxation, consistent with the efficiency of the service, should be extended to the men. Each company, it is understood, will make its own arrangements.[246]

Cumberland had already dismissed the Northern shopworkers' appeal for shorter hours.[247] Brydges played a more ambiguous part. The Montreal nine-hours league was organized in March at a meeting addressed at length by Grand Trunk machinist James Black.[248] A week later that city's employers met (in the mechanics' hall) under Brydges' chairmanship. They passed a moderate resolution opposing anything that would lessen their ability to compete, declaring at the same time 'that there is no immediate necessity for urgent or hasty action.' The meeting appointed Brydges to a committee 'to protect the interests of both masters and men,'[249] which promptly fulfilled the mandate of the resolution by doing nothing.

The Great Western's Canada Board considered Muir's report on 11 April, when there was a full discussion of the nine-hours movement in the company's Hamilton mechanical shops:

The extreme agitation in reference to this question was then considered. The General and Mechanical Superintendents attended and explained that numerous Deputations from the men had waited upon them and that a general strike was imminent, and recommended the Board to accede to the demand. In view of the fact that the Railroad Companies were situated differently from private manufacturers, it was considered best to accede to the request that 54 hours be considered a week's work, and that on and after May 1st all work be paid for by the hour.[250]

This decision was publicized immediately. Speaking at a demonstration on 14 April, E.K. Dodds announced that 'the railway company of Hamilton has granted the 9-hours principle. (Cheers) That was a happy omen of their success, and showed an appreciation of the wants of his fellowmen on the part of the Managing Director [sic] of that Railway.'[251] Within a few days the Toronto Leader announced that the Grand Trunk would outdo the generosity of the Great Western by giving its men the nine-hour day immediately rather than making them wait a week for it.[252] But the Leader story seems to have been inspired more by Tory fellowship than by fact, for although the Great Western shopmen at both Hamilton[253] and London[254] began working the nine-hour day on 1 May, 'the position of affairs between the Grand Trunk and their employees' remained foremost on the agenda of the Montreal nine-hours league a week later.[255] Brydges met with a delegation on 5 May, and offered a reduction in hours contingent on a reconsideration of pay rates. He apparently wanted to introduce a new grading system in the shops so that none but 'first class' men would receive an increase in pay.[256] It was only after a flying visit from James Ryan that the Grand Trunk dispute was resolved.[257]

Outside the railway industry, the nine–hours movement failed generally to achieve its goal of shorter hours, although it was a great spur to union organization and political action. Some writers have suggested that the railwaymen's victories were more apparent than real. Palmer argues that the nine-hour day on the Great Western 'cannot be seen as a major victory, for the men won relatively little. The workingmen's demand had been for a 54-hour week. In the winter they had been working a 53½-hour week already, while in summer months their week consisted of 56 hours. The company thus gave in to the men, losing, on an average, three-quarters of an hour a week throughout the year.'[258] This assessment echoes the contemporary argument of the Hamilton *Spectator*,[259] which was rebutted at the time by 'Humanitas' in the columns of the *Ontario Workman*:

You will allow me to correct a false impression that has been assiduously circulated respecting the concession the Great Western Railway Company have made for their workmen. I am sorry to say that two of our dailies wilfully misconstrued the purpose of that concession for party purposes ... The Great Western Railway workmen, when working full time, perform 58½ hours work per week (the 1½ hours being an old gift from the authorities to their men); and under the new system commencing the 1st of May they will for 54 hours' work receive the same pay as they obtained in the month of March for 58½ hours work.[260]

The real significance of the GWR concession was that under the new system the shopworkers were to be paid by the hour and at rates that would pay as much for 54 hours under the new regime as for 58½ or 56 under the old system of daily pay rates. As the railway's managers calculated it, 'This will mean an advance of wages equal to about 4½ per cent in the Mechanical Department, and about 8¾ per cent in the wages of the 'Inside' Men affected by the change.'[261] The Great Western shopworkers won this concession by the threat of a 'general' strike. In view of the experience of 1856 their employer had good reason to take them at their word. Moreover, their victory corresponded exactly to the principle James Ryan had set out at the first mass meeting: that a reduction in hours was a permanent advance, while a simple increase in wages could be lost with the first onset of recession. That lesson was to be brought home shortly.

RETRENCHMENT AND DECLINE

The early seventies had been years of expansion and apparent prosperity. The nine–hours movement had been a shopworkers' victory yielding significant wage increases. Other wages were also on the increase. Early in 1871, clerical salaries in the treasurer's and audit offices were raised by $50, $100, $200 a year.[262] In November 1872, the chief clerk in the general superintendent's office received a 50 per cent salary increase, from $1,200 to $1,800 a year, and his counterpart in the traffic superintendent's office got an even bigger raise, from $900 to $1,500.[263] Less dramatically but with a much greater effect on the company's costs, wages in the engineering department rose on average 10 per cent, an additional expenditure of almost £8,000 annually. Reid reported that wages in maintenance of way had risen 20 per cent since 1868.[264] A year later, engineering wages rose another 10 per cent above the 1872 levels.[265] As Figure 1 illustrates, the railway's aggregate payroll – compounded of employment levels, hours worked, and wage rates – reached nearly $1.5 million in 1873 and 1874, the highest level it was ever to achieve.

Speaking at St Catharines in 1872, James Ryan had called on political economy to justify the nine-hours movement: 'According to the laws regulating capital and labor, when work was plentiful they could legitimately ask for an advance; or if labor was scarce they could do so also. And in Canada, he was happy to say, work was very plentiful; it was not their fault if labor was scarce.'[266] Now, as the first shock waves of the New York financial crisis reached the Great Western yards, workers were about to experience the corollary of this proposition. In November 1873, department heads were ordered to make reductions in wages and workforce. Trackmen, who had recently been given raises to $1.12½ per day, had their wages cut to $1.00 and 400 men were discharged from the engineering department. Working time in the car and locomotive shops was reduced from nine to eight hours a day, and since the men were now paid by the hour there was a corresponding reduction in take-home pay. The mechanical department discharged 148 shopworkers. The indoor freight department discharged 33 men, and labourers' daily pay was reduced to $1.25 at Detroit and $1.12½ at Windsor.[267] By December the company was planning to make a thousand cords of firewood available at cost to destitute employees and former employees at Hamilton and London.[268] None of this was enough. In January 1874 the directors noted that wages and materials were still too costly: 'Renewed instructions have been given, that the most rigid economy shall be exercised in all departments, and that no further outlay of capital which can possibly be avoided, shall be made.'[269] Again in June and November the Hamilton and London shops were placed on short time. A local newspaper approved of the arrangement, saying that a reduction in time 'is by far the better alternative to a reduction of force': 'We doubt not this step has been taken by the management with as much reluctance, as the company has always endeavoured to insure to its employees full work and at the best wages.'[270]

In truth, however, that old bulwark of Great Western paternalism, the desire to retain its workers during economic downturns so that they would be available when times improved, was being shattered under the hammerblows of this recession. Moreover, its material foundation, the chronic scarcity of skilled or experienced labour, was also crumbling. The editorialist pointed to this, although apparently quite unwittingly:

With the large emigration streaming into the country it would have been unwise in the Great Western to add to the great numbers who will have to experience what it is to ask for work and wait to get it for although we are proud to say in this Canada of ours the industrious worker need not wait for long, undoubtedly some suffering and delay and disappointment must ensue in finding all who come work to do.

Nor was it the shopworkers alone who suffered from short time. In August a deputation of conductors waited upon Muir to ask for relief; they had been working less than half time for six months, mainly owing to the reduced number of trains. 'There is but one way to remedy the evil that we can see,' commented the London *Advertiser*, 'and that is to reduce the number of employees to what is actually required to do the business of the road, giving the preference to married men and those longest in the company's employ.'[271]

Other factors than the recession also contributed to these dislocations. The opening of the Air Line meant that still fewer trains were using the main line, so London began to feel the effects of the same railway outmigration that had benefited it when the car shop moved from Hamilton.[272] The new car shop was a mixed blessing. More highly mechanized and better laid out than its Hamilton precursor, it could turn out as many cars with a smaller workforce. Even so, a dozen men were discharged in January 1875 when the shops went on three-quarters time. The eight-hour day had become the rule in the London and Hamilton shops, and now a Saturday half-holiday further diminished hours and pay.[273] In the engineering department, the removal of the old third rail, the shift to more durable steel rails, and the simple fact that so much of the track was new meant significant decreases in maintenance-of-way payrolls, although for the time being there was no further reduction in the number of men employed.[274]

After his visit to Canada, President Childers complained that 'the staff, in almost all its branches, appeared to me greatly in excess of our wants. The number of superior officers might probably be reduced by one-half, and in every department large numbers might be discharged, without in the least diminishing the efficiency of the service.'[275] Later in 1875 he reported 'large reductions in the redundant staff of the various departments, the salaries and wages of the half-year being less than those of the corresponding period in 1874 by about 18 per cent. Since the close of the half-year these reductions have been carried out still further. But the staff may now be considered in a satisfactory and efficient condition.'[276]

That was the setting for the only serious confrontation between the Brotherhood of Locomotive Engineers and the Great Western. The circumstances were very different from those the ASE had found itself in when it joined the movement for shorter hours in 1872. Beginning on the Grand Trunk in December 1876,[277] engine-drivers in Canada and the United States participated in a wave of strikes whose common theme was resistance to wage cuts. In the summer of 1877 wage reductions by the Grand Trunk, Canada Southern, and Great Western prompted protests among the drivers and intervention by the Brotherhood. A compromise was quickly reached on the GTR, which was not anxious to replay the December conflict. On the Great Western, Broughton announced a 10 per cent wage reduction for all employees. While the conductors were said to be resigned to the cut, the engine-drivers threatened to stop work. A deputation met with Broughton on 21 July, and a few days later he responded with a modified circular. The wages of employees earning less than $30 a month were to remain unchanged; those earning between $30 and $40 were to be reduced by 2½ per cent, and there would be a 7½ per cent reduction for everybody else.[278] In the meantime, on 23 July, two hundred Canada Southern workers walked out to protest that road's 10 per cent reduction. The Canada Southern's engine shops were at St Thomas, which was also on the Air Line. The onset of the strike caused great excitement among Great Western employees in St Thomas, who formed the greater part of the crowd of three hundred that gathered at the CSR station to watch as the strikers attempted to disable the arriving Buffalo train. Rumours abounded that the Air Line, perhaps even the whole GWR system, would be struck that evening. A committee of officers rushed to London to meet a workers' delegation; they negotiated all night while crowds of off-duty railwaymen waited anxiously in the yards. At 4 a.m. an agreement was announced: the 2½ per cent reduction was to apply to men earning between $30 and $45, while those earning more would have their wages cut by 5 per cent. The cuts were to last for only three months.[279] To sweeten the arrangement, Broughton and his staff offered to submit to the 5 per cent reduction: 'This generalizing the reduction seems to have given very general satisfaction to the mechanics and workmen, and made everything work smoothly and harmoniously.'[280]

But this was not the end of retrenchment. The following summer another wave of cost cutting put the Hamilton and London shops on a thirty-eight-hour, four-day week for two months at two-thirds wages, closed the Hamilton engineering and carpentry shops, and resulted in layoffs of 300 or 400 men, including one trackman from every section gang.[281] Even a year later, outside locomotive payrolls were continuing to fall because of the decline in engine mileage, and though shop payrolls were up over the previous year, this meant only that the men were back on a five-day week. The first real signs of recovery came in the fall and winter of 1880, when inside and outside locomotive payrolls both began to rise with increases in working time and mileage. A year later a few more men were being taken on in the locomotive and car shops.

The financial crisis may have ended, but so had the patience of the proprietors with Childers' efforts to rescue the Swinyard-Dakin development strategy. They chose a new president, Lt.-Col. F.D. Grey, and sent him across the Atlantic to find an American lessee or purchaser. He failed.[282] Finally, in 1882, the Grand Trunk decided to pre-empt the risk that the Canadian Pacific Railway might take over the Great Western to break into the lucrative southwestern Ontario market.[283] At the GWR half-yearly meeting on 27 April 1882, Grey was deposed and the proprietors voted overwhelmingly to accept the Grand Trunk's offer of amalgamation. On 12 August the Great Western ceased to exist.

MANIFEST DESTINIES

The culture of Great Western labour-management relations changed significantly in the post-Swinyard years. With the Canada Board eclipsed and finally abolished, many of the day-to-day decisions that had once been the province of the general manager in consultation with that board were now delegated to the department heads.[284] Money from fines, uncollected wages, and other incidental receipts, which were once earmarked for such things as the reading room and the accident insurance fund, were now channelled into departmental revenues.[285] Formal incentive schemes were introduced to reward efficient employees with fixed bonuses.[286] The 'gratuities' paid in deserving cases of sickness, accident, or death, by which the board had once wielded powers of patronage, became institutionalized in the corporate welfarism of the compulsory Provident Society. The shift in public morality was mirrored in new concerns about employee temperance. In 1874 the railway banned the use of liquor on its premises by employees on duty: the lateness of the date and the qualifications on the ban are both interesting.[287] Public morality also explains why the GWR's Montreal agent had to leave town in a hurry after escorting two young women to a restaurant where, 'after treating them to wine, he conducted himself in an outrageous manner.'[288]

The old management prerogative of organizing GWR workers' votes fell into disuse in the 1870s, the victim of emergent labour politics, new forms of class consciousness, and ultimately the secret ballot. It did not disappear without a struggle. In 1867 an anonymous employee complained to the press that it was difficult for a man with a large family to be a free and independent elector when Swinyard had 'called the foremen of the different departments to him and told them to tell us that we were expected to vote for Mr Williams on Wednesday or lose our situations.'[289] In March 1871 general superintendent Muir found it necessary to publish the text of a letter he had sent W.A. Robinson:

Referring to what I told you the other day about the political candidates, you will, of course, be good enough to see that neither candidates nor their agents interfere in any way with the men in the works. We have no desire to influence them in any way, and all we propose to do is to allow them sufficient time, on polling day, to vote.[290]

It is tempting to read into this letter and its publication a disagreement between Muir and his mechanical superintendent, and to view the three-month leave of absence that Robinson began within two weeks as a result of it.[291] In the 1872 election Great Western workers certainly voted en bloc, returning H.B. Witton, the paint shop foreman. This election was the last bow for Isaac Buchanan, who had hand-picked Witton for the Tory slate.[292] Here, too, the company officially distanced itself from the contest. Muir issued a circular 'in answer to numerous enquiries from the railway employees' telling them they were to vote as they pleased, without fear or favour: 'The Directors of the Company have so decided.'[293] When Witton (who had presumably resigned his position to run) sought reinstatement after the election, the company left it to his department head to decide. Again in 1874 general manager Price issued a circular disclaiming any interest in influencing workers' votes and asking 'any employee of the Company who considers he has been moved from the ordinary course of his duty with the view of preventing him exercising his franchise, that he will individually report the circum-

FIGURE 8

Car and Traffic Wage/Mile Ratios, Fiscal 1857–81

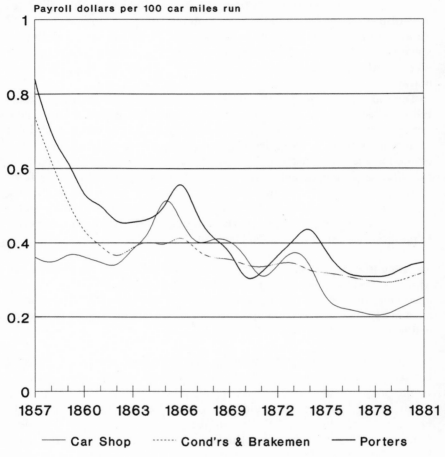

Payroll dollars per 100 car miles run

—— Car Shop   ······ Cond'rs & Brakemen   —— Porters

stances to me with full particulars.'[294] Even C.J. Brydges, who in the fifties had practically invented the fine art of GWR vote jobbing, felt
compelled upon his temporary return to the railway in 1874 to caution
department heads, foremen, and other officials against attempting to
influence workers' votes.[295] What had once been seen as the inspired
paternal guidance of the railway's leading personalities was now viewed
as the petty tyranny of 'meddlesome officials, dressed in a little "brief
authority." '[296]

FIGURE 9

Locomotive Wage/Mile Ratios, Fiscal 1857–81

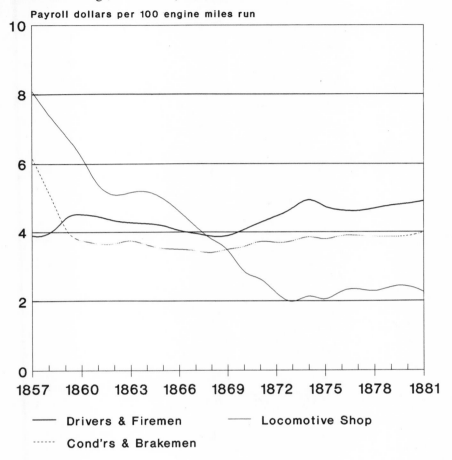

Payroll dollars per 100 engine miles run

Drivers & Firemen —— Locomotive Shop ——

Cond'rs & Brakemen ······

The greatest watershed dividing the history of Great Western labour relations in the early 1870s was not institutional or ideological but material. This was a fundamental change in the company's labour costs in relation to income. In every department of the railway service, the long-term trend was for payroll costs to decline in proportion to mileage but to increase in proportion to income. In other words, labour became increasingly productive but also increasingly expensive as the railway's receipts from increasing volumes of traffic plummeted. Though these were the

FIGURE 10

Car and Traffic Wage/Receipt Ratios, Fiscal 1857–81

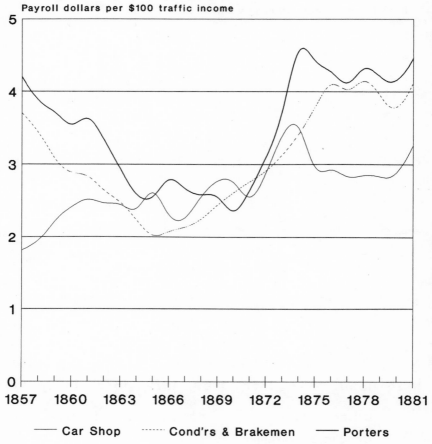

Payroll dollars per $100 traffic income

—— Car Shop   ······ Cond'rs & Brakemen   —— Porters

trends, there were significant fluctuations over the years, and among occupations.

If one (revenue-producing) car mile is taken as the unit of traffic, the Great Western's payroll costs may be seen to have declined quite steadily over the period. The railway paid out 9 cents in wages per car mile in 1855 (when passenger traffic accounted for a disproportionate share of receipts), 6 cents in 1856, 5 cents in 1857–9, 3 or 4 cents in 1860–6, 3 cents in 1867–74, and 2 cents thereafter. Figure 8 shows the declining trend in payroll costs per car mile for car shop workers, porters, and conductors and brakesmen. The apparent decline in conductors'

FIGURE 11

Locomotive Wage/Receipt Ratios, Fiscal 1857–81

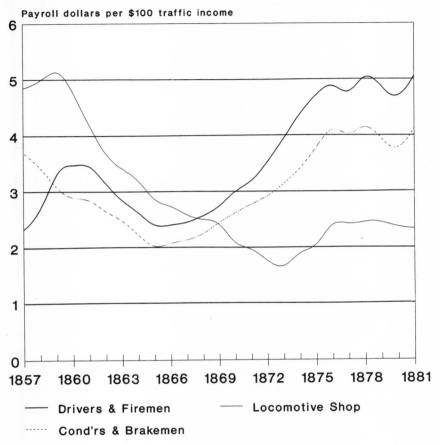

Payroll dollars per $100 traffic income

——— Drivers & Firemen   ——— Locomotive Shop

------ Cond'rs & Brakemen

and brakesmen's payrolls in relation to car mileage is partly explained by the increasing length of trains: train crews were not increased when engines drew more cars, although work unloading and repairing cars increased proportionately. Figure 9 shows the trend in payroll costs per locomotive mile for drivers and firemen, conductors and brakesmen, and engine shopworkers. Conductors' and brakesmen's payrolls fluctuated very little after 1860 by this measure, while drivers' and firemen's payrolls increased slightly after 1870, and locomotive shop payrolls plummeted until 1872, when they stabilied at about $2 per hundred engine miles run.

FIGURE 12

Maintenance of Way Payroll Ratios, Fiscal 1857–81

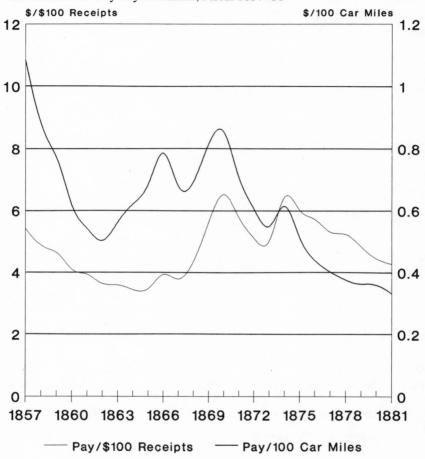

Compare these trends, calculated on a mileage basis, to the corresponding trends for income (see Figures 10, 11, and 12). While the dividing line shifts for different occupations, the general pattern is for payrolls to decline in relation to traffic income over the early years of operations, to level off somewhat in the mid-sixties, and then to climb rapidly in the seventies.

Too much stress ought not to be placed on this analysis. The aggregate payrolls, even for separate occupations, blend together information about the size of the workforce, hours worked, and pay levels that would be more meaningful if available severally. As we have already seen, the history of the railway and its labour relations was much more complex than numbers alone can portray. Nevertheless, there is a strong suggestion in these figures that the Great Western railway community of the 1850s and 1860s came to grief, not because labour costs got out of hand or industrial strife replaced artisanal paternalism, but because of the incredible pressures on corporate revenues that flowed from the company's strategy as an intermediate through carrier in an increasingly competitive continental industry. Viewed from the perspective of the late twentieth century, the Great Western collapsed under the weight of continental economic restructuring, despite continuous improvements in labour productivity and one of the most resilient and reciprocally accommodating labour relations systems of its day.

NOTES

Research for this chapter began under the auspices of the Canadian Railways Industrial Relations History Project, which I co-directed with T.D. Traves. The project had the generous financial support of the Social Sciences and Humanities Research Council of Canada. Data were collected with the assistance of Lynne Brenegan, Rose Hutchens, Robert Nahuet, and David Sobel. I am grateful to Tom Traves, who made helpful comments on an early draft of this chapter, and to Ralph Greenhill, who took the time from his own writing about Ontario's railways to hunt down several inaccuracies in a later draft. For those that remain I take sole responsibility.

1 In dating the photograph and attributing it to Hamilton photographer R. Milne I follow W.M. Spriggs, 'Great Western Railway of Canada: Some Particulars of the History of the Road and Its Locomotives from Its Commencement to Its Amalgamation with the Grand Trunk Railway in 1882,' *Bulletin of the Railway and Locomotive Historical Society*, no. 51 (1946), opp. 16. Spriggs's correspondence with several Great Western veterans (henceforth, Spriggs Collection) is preserved in the Regional History Collection, Weldon Library, University of Western Ontario. I have relied on Spriggs's publication and his correspondence for most of the identifications. The identification of the two central figures ('Englishmen, unknown' in the Spriggs correspondence) as Dakin and Faulconer is my own. I have spelled Payne's name to conform with extant GWR pay sheets. The careers of most of those pictured are summarized on pp. 342–5 and 355–6.

2 John C. Weaver, *Hamilton: An Illustrated History* (Toronto: Lorimer 1983), 40.

3 For studies of railway workers in Britain and the United States in this period, see, *inter alia*, Peter W. Kingsford, *Victorian Railwaymen: The Emergence and Growth of Railway Labour, 1830–1870* (London: Cass 1970); Kenneth Hudson, *Working to*

Rule: Railway Workshop Rules: A Study of Industrial Discipline (Bath: Adams and
Dart 1970); Frank McKenna, *The Railway Workers, 1840–1970* (London: Faber
1980); Walter Licht, *Working for the Railroad: The Organization of Work in the
Nineteenth Century* (Princeton, N.J.: Princeton University Press 1983); James H.
Ducker, *Men of the Steel Rails: Workers on the Atchison, Topeka & Santa Fe Rail-
road, 1869–1900* (Lincoln Nebr: University of Nebraska Press 1983); and Shelton
Stromquist, *A Generation of Boomers: The Pattern of Railroad Labor Conflict in
19th Century America* (Urbana, Ill: University of Illinois Press 1987).

4 Allan Greer, 'Wage Labour and the Transition to Capitalism: A Critique of Pentland,' *Labour/Le Travailleur* 15 (spring 1985), 7–22, at 12. My account of paternalism is obviously indebted to Pentland's 'personal labour relation,' although in a
different employment context and with differing emphasis. See generally H.C.
Pentland, 'The Development of a Capitalistic Labour Market in Canada,' *Canadian
Journal of Economics and Political Science* 25 (1959), 450–61; and idem, *Labour
and Capital in Canada, 1650–1860*, ed. P. Phillips (Toronto: Lorimer 1981).

5 Toronto *Artisan*, 12 Oct. 1848.

6 For a detailed discussion of these points as they apply to the Great Western and
Grand Trunk railways in the 1850s, see Paul Craven and Tom Traves, 'Dimensions
of Paternalism: Discipline and Culture in Canadian Railway Operations in the
1850s,' in Craig Heron and Robert Storey, eds, *On the Job: Confronting the Labour
Process in Canada* (Kingston: McGill-Queen's University Press 1986), 47–74.

7 Historians of nineteenth-century Britain have made important contributions to the
literature on these questions: see in particular David Roberts, *Paternalism in Early
Victorian England* (New Brunswick, N.J.: Rutgers University Press 1979); Patrick
Joyce, *Work, Society and Politics: the Culture of the Factory in Later Victorian
England* (Brighton: Harvester 1980), especially chap. 4; and more generally idem,
Visions of the People: Industrial England and the Question of Class 1848–1914
(Cambridge: Cambridge University Press, 1991).

8 For the experience of Ontario railway workers in the early twentieth century see
Mark Rosenfeld, ' "She Was a Hard Life": Work, Family, Community, Politics and
Ideology in the Railway Ward of a Central Ontario Town, 1900–1960' (PhD thesis
York University 1990).

9 There were no women in the shop crafts or the running trades. The Board of Railway
Commissioners instructed the GWR to remove one woman who kept a level crossing
in the 1850s because it felt that 'a man of active habits' was more suitable for the post.
Some station agents' daughters were paid to act in place of their sick fathers, and
there was the occasional woman telegraph operator. For the most part, though,
women played a background role. Thus Mrs Wynn, wife of the Windsor station master, was presented with a sewing machine by grateful employees 'in recognition of
the kindness she has always shown to them and their families in times of sickness and
trouble' (Hamilton *Times*, 9 Jan. 1867). The Great Western's Hamilton establishment
was enumerated in the 1871 census as consisting of 983 men and 1 woman.

10 Hamilton *Times*, 27 June 1864.

11 University of Western Ontario, Thomas Swinyard papers, v. 1429 (henceforth, Swinyard papers), 2 July 1864.

12 Swinyard papers, Baker to Swinyard, 30 Apr. 1864, 7 May 1864, 26 May 1864.

13 Swinyard papers, George Rumball to Swinyard, 3 June 1864.

14 Ibid., Isaac Buchanan to Swinyard, c. 30 Mar. 1864.

15 Swinyard papers, 6 Apr. 1864.

16 Montreal *Transcript*, 29 Apr. 1864.

17 Craven and Traves, 'Dimensions of Paternalism,' 64f.

18 Toronto *Globe*, 2 May 1864. Swinyard was advised to 'fix' *Globe* publisher George Brown to ensure passage of favourable legislation: Swinyard papers, Hon. G. Alexander to Swinyard, 22 Mar. 1863. Brown's rural property at Bothwell benefited from the location of the GWR station there (Hamilton *Spectator*, 3 Jan. 1856) and from the railway's heavy investments in southern Ontario petroleum development. Brown spoke in favour of the GWR's position and against the GTR–B&LH amalgamation during the legislative debate: Toronto *Globe*, 10 July 1866.

19 Montreal *Transcript*, and Toronto *Globe*, 2 May 1864.

20 Toronto *Globe*, 31 Aug. 1864.

21 Swinyard papers, Dakin to Swinyard, 27 Aug. 1864.

22 Ibid., H.C. Wynn to Swinyard, 2 July 1864.

23 For general histories of the Great Western, its origins, and its early years, see A.W. Currie, *The Grand Trunk Railway of Canada* (Toronto: University of Toronto Press 1957), especially chaps. 8–10; G.R. Stevens, *Canadian National Railways I: Sixty Years of Trial and Error* (Toronto: Clarke, Irwin 1960), especially chap. 4; Peter Baskerville, 'The Boardroom and Beyond: Aspects of the Upper Canadian Railroad Community' (PhD thesis, Queen's University 1973); Russell D. Smith, 'The Early Years of the Great Western Railway 1833–1857,' *Ontario History* 58 (Mar. 1966), 205–27; and Donald R. Beer, *Sir Allan Napier MacNab* (Hamilton: Dictionary of Hamilton Biography 1984).

24 Hamilton *Spectator*, 8 Nov. 1856.

25 Province of Canada, *Journal of the Legislative Assembly*, 1855, appendix Y.Y. (henceforth Coffin-Cameron commission). Bowman remained in Canada, joining the London and Port Stanley Railway.

26 The first references I have found to Sharp and Yates in the company records are notations of pay increases in what was still called the 'mechanical department' dated 7 Dec. 1854 but to take effect on 1 Jan. 1855: National Archives of Canada (henceforth, NAC), RG 30, v. 5, GWR Finance Committee Minute Book (henceforth, Finance Committee), 7 Dec. 1854.

27 Craven and Traves, 'Dimensions of Paternalism,' 66–7. Braid was killed in an 1859 accident while travelling as a passenger on the Great Western.

28 NAC, RG 30, v. 7, GWR Managing Committee Minute Book (henceforth, Managing Committee), 30 Aug. 1862; and Great Western Railway of Canada, *Report of*

the Directors for the Half-Year Ending ... (henceforth, Half-Yearly Report), 31 Jan.
1863.

29 Hamilton *Times*, 10 Apr. 1866.

30 Return of Staff, 9 Dec. 1854, supplied by Brydges to the Coffin-Cameron commission.

31 Toronto *Globe*, 11 Feb. 1860. Perhaps the reporter misheard 'Hero.'

32 Hamilton *Spectator*, 28 Aug. 1860, and 10 Sep. 1860; and *The Engineer* (London, England), 26 Oct. 1860, copying *American Railway Review*.

33 NAC, RG 30, v. 6, GWR Finance Committee Minute Book, #1595, 24 Dec. 1863.

34 Montreal *Herald*, 15 Feb. 1866; some of Robinson's other innovations and improvements are described in 'Locomotive Practice on the Great Western Canada Railway,' *American Railway Times* 22, no. 4 (22 Jan. 1870). He was later remembered for an apparently unsuccessful rear-view mirror for engine cabs: Spriggs collection, X1501, clipping from *CNR Magazine*, Aug. 1934. Some of Robinson's innovations are criticized from an engineering point of view in Peter Hanlon, 'William Aspley Robinson,' *Dictionary of Hamilton Biography*, vol. 2 (Hamilton: Dictionary of Hamilton Biography 1991), 132–3.

35 NAC, RG 30, v. 16, GWR English Board Minutes (henceforth, English Board), 26 Feb. 1873; and Myles Pennington, *Railways and Other Ways* (Toronto: Williamson 1894), 236.

36 Swinyard papers, Baker to Swinyard, 2 Oct. 1862.

37 Canada, *Royal Commission on the Relations of Labour and Capital*, Hamilton evidence, 768–79. For an annotated list of the Great Western's original engine-drivers, see Brydges' evidence to the Coffin-Cameron commission.

38 Brotherhood of Locomotive Engineers, *Monthly Journal*, Nov. 1872, 514; and Dec. 1872, 556.

39 Pennington, *Railways*, 233f.

40 Return of Staff, 9 Dec. 1854 (Coffin-Cameron commission). In December 1854 the company decided to advertise locally for additional clerks: Finance Committee, 7 Dec. 1854.

41 English Board, 19 Mar. 1873 and 30 July 1873.

42 Hamilton *Spectator*, 29 Nov. 1856 and 30 Oct. 1863.

43 Ibid., 9 Sept. 1857; Toronto *Globe*, 13 Jan. 1865; and NAC, RG 30, v. 4, Great Western Railway of Canada, Canada Board Minutes (henceforth, Canada Board), 22 Sept. 1870.

44 Canada Board, 14 Apr. 1871, 3 May 1872, 23 May 1873, and 5 Sept. 1873.

45 Finance Committee, 7 Dec. 1854; Managing Committee, 18 Nov. 1859; Archives of Ontario, MU 842, Hugh Neilson diary; and Managing Committee, 11 Mar. 1862.

46 Montreal *Transcript*, 6 Mar. 1860.

47 Toronto *Globe*, 12 Feb. 1878.

48 Finance Committee, no. 795 (Dec. 1857), 2 Feb. 1861; and Managing Committee, 6 June 1861.

49 Managing Committee, 2 Nov. 1861 and 11 Mar. 1862.
50 Montreal *Transcript*, 16 Sept. 1862; and Hamilton *Spectator*, 24 Oct. 1862.
51 Finance Committee, 4 Sept. 1863; Hamilton *Canadian Illustrated News* 2, no. 19, 26 Sept. 1863, 218; Toronto *Globe*, 21 Jan. 1870; and Montreal *Herald*, 22 Jan. 1870.
52 Canada Board, 23 Nov. 1872 and 3 Jan. 1873; and *Ontario Workman*, 24 Apr. 1873.
53 Swinyard papers, J. Braithwaite to Swinyard, 26 Feb. 1863.
54 University of Western Ontario, *Whitehead v. Buffalo*, II, 36, 5 July 1856.
55 Hamilton *Spectator*, 7 Jan. 1857, 21 Feb. 1857. The GWR apparently sold some mechanical stores to the B&LH in 1856–7: Hamilton *Spectator*, 11 Mar. 1857.
56 Brantford *Expositor*, 15 July 1870.
57 Ibid., 14 July 1871.
58 Hamilton *Times*, 15 Mar. 1866.
59 Buchanan Papers, v. 37, 30461–2, 22 Feb. 1854; and 'Statement of William Scott, late western division engineer of the Great Western Railway, to the Shareholders and the Public of North America, relative to the mode of his services being dispensed with by the board of that company' (Detroit 1854). For Scott's criticisms of Bowman, see his evidence to the Coffin-Cameron commission.
60 *Whitehead v. Buffalo*, II, 36, 5 July 1856.
61 Ibid., III, no page number, 24 Feb. 1858.
62 Brantford *Weekly Expositor*, 3 June 1870; Stratford *Beacon*, 10 June 1870; and Brantford *Expositor*, 14 July 1871.
63 NAC, RG 30, v. 1040, Grand Trunk Railway Executive Council Minutes, 3 July 1875.
64 Hamilton *Times*, 15 Mar. 1866.
65 Hamilton *Spectator*, 1 May 1858.
66 Hamilton, *Canadian Illustrated News*, 3, no. 1, 28 Nov. 1863; Hamilton *Spectator*, 1 Sept. 1865 (copying Ayrshire *Observer*); and Pennington, *Railways*, 125f. Baskerville ('Boardroom and Beyond,' 277) states that Muir had been at the London & South Western, citing NAC, RG 30, v. 874, Minutebook of the Detroit & Milwaukee Railway (henceforth, D&M Minutes), 22 Jan. and 7–8 Apr. 1858. These minutes merely record Muir's accession to the general superintendency of the D&M, however, and make no reference to his previous career. Brydges told the Coffin-Cameron commission in 1855 that Muir had been brought out 'from Scotland' and said he had worked for the Glasgow and South Western and the York, Newcastle and Berwick railways. The *Canadian Illustrated News* (28 Nov. 1863) reported that Muir's 'reputation ... had been wafted by fame to London. Mr Brydges when resident there had heard of him ... he darted on [Muir] at Glasgow and made him his own' for the GWR. There were three other Muirs on the GWR and D&M – Thomas, James H. and John H. – which may explain the confusion over antecedents. Thomas Muir was with the GWR from the beginning: he was employed in the audit office in 1855 (Canada Board, 2 Mar. 1855), becoming cash book keeper

in 1857 (Canada Board, #1135), and accountant by 1861 (Finance Committee, #1173, 2 Feb. 1861). The staff rolls show him receiving salary increases in 1855 (NAC, RG 30, v.2, Great Western Railway Minutes (henceforth, GWR Minutes), 2 Mar. 1855, and 1863 (Finance Committee, 14 Apr. 1863), and he was commended to Swinyard by the company's secretary-treasurer the same year (Swinyard papers, Bell to Swinyard, 28 June 1863) but I have found no reference to his employment with the railway after 1867, when he appeared in the Hamilton city directory as GWR accountant. There was a Thomas Muir connected with London's Ontario Car Company in the 1870s: London *Advertiser*, 9 Apr. 1874. James H. Muir's only appearance is in the Hamilton city directory for 1858 as an employee in the GWR freight office: he boarded with W.K. Muir. John H. Muir resigned as GWR ticket clerk, Suspension Bridge (Managing Committee, 20 May 1859) to become second clerk in the D&M's audit office when W.K. Muir moved from the Great Western to the Detroit line (D&M Minutes, 7 Apr. 1858). This suggests a connection between the two men, who may have been relatives. It is also possible that John H. and James H. were the same person, although I have found nothing in the staff rolls to explain why he should have been employed in the ticket office at Niagara and the freight office at Hamilton in the same year.

67 NAC, Buchanan papers, MG 24, D 16, v. 5, C.J. Brydges to I. Buchanan, 4 Mar. 1856; (henceforth, Buchanan papers); and Swinyard papers, T. Bell to Swinyard, 28 June 1863. Muir's daughter married William Cowing, the GWR's English-born St Catharines stationmaster. Cowing died, aged thirty-three, in 1866, and Muir's sixty-three-year-old Scottish-born wife died suddenly the same day: Hamilton *Times*, 26 May 1866.

68 London *Advertiser*, 5 Jan. 1875; and Buchanan papers, v. 49, 28 Dec. 1874.

69 For the mechanical department's locomotive- and car-building activities, see Paul Craven and Tom Traves, 'Canadian Railways as Manufacturers, 1850–1880,' *Historical Papers* (1983), 254–81.

70 For an analysis of the mechanical department pay sheets in the 1850s, see Craven and Traves, 'Dimensions of Paternalism,' 53–9. The January 1863 inside locomotive pay sheets are analysed in Michael B. Katz, Michael J. Doucet, and Mark J. Stern, *The Social Organization of Early Industrial Capitalism* (Cambridge, Mass.: Harvard University Press 1982), 36–7.

71 Railways did not include employment figures in their annual statistical returns to the government, except in 1860, when Samuel Keefer, the government inspector of railways, reported that the GWR had 2,049 employees. It is not clear whether this figure was an annual average or a count at a particular point in the year, but it may be taken as an upper bound. If we take the ratio of gross annual payroll to this employment figure and project it over the other years, we get peak employment figures of 3,505 in 1870, rising to an all-time peak of 5,430 in 1874, and falling to a trough of 4,154 in 1878. This calculation takes no account of changes in average wage rates or hours worked, however; at best, it supplies a rough estimate of the

upper bounds of employment, on the basis of some questionable assumptions (see below). Nevertheless, it is as close as we can come on the evidence currently available.

72 In compiling these data, it has been necessary to combine some small categories and exclude others that were not reported consistently and to convert the figures, which were reported at various periods in provincial currency, pounds sterling, and decimal currency, to dollar values at the exchange rates used by the railway.

73 The GWR reported its accounts half-yearly, ending January 31 and July 31. Throughout this chapter I have constructed fiscal years by summing the half-year results for July of one year and for January of the next year. Hence 'fiscal 1855' means the twelve months commencing February 1, 1855 and ending January 31, 1856.

74 Paul Craven, 'Maintaining the Way: Iron, Rolling Mills, and the Transition to Steel Rails in Canadian Railway Operations, 1850–80,' presented to the New History Society, Toronto, October 1986, and to the Symposium in Canadian Economic History, University of Ottawa, November 1986.

75 Spriggs collection, Baines to Spriggs, 13 July 1933.

76 NAC, RG 11, v. 134, Department of Public Works, Inspector of Railways letterbook, no. 42, 25 Mar. 1859.

77 During the period following the opening of the line when ballasting and other work were still being completed, conductors employed by the Great Western but assigned to gravel contractors' trains had the authority to hire the necessary crews: see Brydges' evidence to the Coffin-Cameron commission. There is a suggestion in this passage that conductors may have hired brakesmen in the ordinary course of their duties.

78 Swinyard papers, Swinyard to T.I. Waugh, 29 Apr. 1869.

79 Great Western Railway of Canada, *Rules & Regulations for the Conduct of the Traffic and for the Guidance of the Officers & Servants in the Employment of the Great Western Railway Co.* (London, Ont.: Advertiser Steam Press 1879), 33.

80 Toronto *Globe*, 13 Jan. 1876.

81 Hamilton *Spectator*, 25 Feb. 1857.

82 NAC, MG 29, A 29, v. 2, Joseph Hickson papers, Scrapbook of memorabilia, 1864–78, 25 May 1863; and Hamilton *Canadian Illustrated News*, 30 May 1863.

83 Swinyard papers, Baker to Swinyard, 26 June 1863.

84 Hamilton *Times*, 3 May and 7 Nov. 1866.

85 Ibid., 31 July 1867.

86 The Waubuno picnics were for employees west of Paris, and the Niagara ones for employees on the eastern portions of the line: Hamilton *Times*, 16 Aug. 1866; and Toronto *Globe*, 16 July 1870.

87 Hamilton *Times*, 31 July 1867.

88 Hamilton *Spectator*, 25 Feb. 1857.

89 Ibid., 24 Nov. 1864.

90 London *Advertiser*, 28 Mar. 1874.

91 NAC, RG 30, v. 8: Great Western Railway, Advises of Officers Minutes (henceforth, Officers Minutes), no. 347, 7 Mar. 1874; Canada Board, 19 Mar. 1874; and Montreal *Daily Witness*, 22 Oct. 1874.

92 Officers Minutes, no. 121, 5 Jan. 1874; Hamilton *Times*, 5 Feb. 1866, 27 Mar. 1867; and Officers Minutes, no. 148, 22 Dec. 1873. When the railway's officers met to discuss the disposition of fines in December 1873, however, they rejected proposals to place them in the library or accident insurance funds in favour of crediting them to departmental revenues: Officers Minutes, no. 163, 29 Dec. 1873.

93 *Ontario Workman*, 8 Apr. 1872.

94 Ibid., 5 Sept. 1872.

95 Finance Committee, 4 Nov. 1863; Canada Board, 19 Mar. 1874; London *Advertiser*, 6 May 1874; Half-Yearly Report (Engineer's report), 31 July 1874; and Officers Minutes, 5 Jan. 1874.

96 Officers Minutes, 4 Dec. 1873.

97 Half-Yearly Report (Engineer's report), 31 July 1870; Canada Board, 26 July 1872; and Half-Yearly Report (Engineer's report), 31 Jan. 1873.

98 Canada Board, 9 Oct. 1873; and London *Advertiser*, 19 Dec. 1874.

99 London *Advertiser*, 14 Nov. 1874.

100 London *Free Press*, 24 Jan. 1872.

101 Canada Board, 2 Dec. 1871; and Half-Yearly Report (Engineer's report), 31 Jan. 1872.

102 Half-Yearly Report (Engineer's report), 31 Jan. 1876.

103 Officers Minutes, 5 Jan. 1874.

104 Craven and Traves, 'Dimensions of Paternalism,' 65.

105 Canada Board, 28 Nov. 1870.

106 Hamilton *Spectator*, 4 Dec. 1862.

107 Toronto *Globe*, 30 Jan. 1868. For hard times in the fishery, see Phillip A. Buckner, 'The 1860s: An End and a Beginning,' in Phillip A. Buckner and John G. Reid, eds, *The Atlantic Region to Confederation: A History* (Toronto: University of Toronto Press 1994), 370.

108 Hamilton *Spectator*, 9 Jan. 1856; and Finance Committee, 7 Jan. 1860.

109 Finance Committee, 4 Sep. 1863 and 13 Nov. 1863. Myles Pennington told Swinyard that increased Grand Trunk firewood carriage rates had made Brydges unpopular among the Montreal working class: Swinyard papers, Pennington to Swinyard, 29 Sept. 1864.

110 Hamilton *Times* 14 Nov. 1866 and 16 Nov. 1866.

111 Officers Minutes, 5 Jan. 1874.

112 Officers Minutes, 5 Nov. 1873; and Canada Board, 5 Dec. 1873.

113 Officers Minutes, 26 Feb. 1874; and Canada Board, 6 Mar. 1874.

114 Hamilton *Times*, 24 Apr. 1866. There had been rumours of a GWR militia as early as 1862: New York *American Railway Review*, 16 Jan. 1862.

115 Hamilton *Times*, 23 June 1866 and 25 June 1866.

116 Ibid., 16 June 1866 and 27 June 1866.
117 NAC, RG 30, v. 6394, Great Western Railway mechanical department pay book (henceforth, Pay book), entries for pay period 1 June 1854.
118 Pay book, entries for January 1857.
119 Canada Board, 28 Oct. 1870.
120 Hamilton city directory, 1867.
121 Hamilton *Times*, 30 Jan. 1858; and Hamilton, *Canadian Illustrated News*, Feb. 1863.
122 NAC, RG 30, v. 1, Great Western Railway Board minute book (henceforth, Board Minutes), Locomotive Superintendent's report, 17 Aug. 1860; and see generally, Craven and Traves, 'Railways as Manufacturers.'
123 Spriggs collection, Baines to Spriggs, 15 May 1942.
124 Ibid., 24 Mar. 1934.
125 J.M. Cowan, 'The Great Western Railway,' *Wentworth Bygones* 5 (1964), 7.
126 Spriggs collection, Baines to Spriggs, 13 Feb. 1934.
127 A New York Central engineer contributed a poem on the subject to the *BLE Monthly Journal* (January 1872): 'For twenty years it's been my pride / To have my engines shine like gold, / But now they have painted all the brass, / And given us this confounded coal.'
128 *Rules & Regulations* ..., 1879, no. 128.
129 Spriggs collection, Domville to Spriggs, 9 Oct. 1940.
130 Ibid., Baines to Spriggs, 13 Feb. 1934.
131 Ibid., Baines to Spriggs, 13 Apr. 1934.
132 Reproduced in Coffin-Cameron commission, 213.
133 Spriggs collection, Baines to Spriggs, 27 Sept. 1933.
134 Hamilton *Spectator*, 18 Mar. 1862.
135 Toronto *Globe*, 22 May 1861.
136 Ibid., 24 Jan. 1877.
137 New York *American Railway Review*, 20 Mar. 1862. For Marks's age, see 1861 census manuscript, Hamilton, St Mary's Ward, #315.
138 Spriggs collection, Baines to Spriggs, 27 Sept. 1933.
139 See Hall's evidence to the 1888–9 Royal Commission, n. 37 above.
140 Spriggs collection, Cameron to Baines for Spriggs, n.d. (1934?).
141 Reed C. Richardson, *The Locomotive Engineer, 1863–1963: A Century of Railway Labor Relations and Work Rules* (Ann Arbor, Mich.: Bureau of Industrial Relations, University of Michigan 1963).
142 Matthias N. Forney, *Catechism of the Locomotive* (New York: Railroad Gazette 1874 and subsequent editions).
143 Reproduced in Coffin-Cameron commission, 215, 213.
144 Toronto *Globe*, 1 Sept. 1868.
145 New York *American Railway Review*, 2 Jan. 1862.
146 Hamilton *Spectator*, 3 May 1856.
147 Toronto *Globe*, 21 Jan. 1870.

148 NAC, MG 24, D 80, v. 3, John Young papers, Erastus Corning to Young, 3 Mar. 1852 (henceforth, Young papers); and Coffin-Cameron commission.

149 The 'provincial' gauge was 5 feet 6 inches between the rails. The Great Western referred to the American lines as 'narrow gauge' but I have used the term 'standard gauge' to distinguish their gauge of 4 feet 8½ inches, which was to become the North American standard, from the so-called 'light narrow gauge' of 3 feet 6 inches, which became popular for such colonization roads as the Toronto, Grey and Bruce and the Toronto and Nipissing railways constructed in the late 1860s and early 1870s.

150 On the compound rail dispute, see Craven, 'Maintaining the way.'

151 Buchanan papers, v. 37, 30461–2, 22 Feb. 1854; 'Statement of William Scott.'

152 Young papers, Forbes to Young, 7 May 1852.

153 Beer, *MacNab*, 289f.

154 *Whitehead v. Buffalo* II, 88, Barlow to Mackirdy, 1 May 1858. Brydges told the Coffin-Cameron commission that GWR trains waited for their NYC and MCR connections at Suspension Bridge and Windsor respectively, which sometimes meant they started their return trips an hour and a half later than the timetable specified.

155 Toronto *Globe*, 10 Apr. 1863.

156 Hamilton *Spectator*, 26 July 1864. Failures of change-gauge cars produced several accidents on the Grand Trunk: Toronto *Globe*, 12 June 1871, 28 Oct. 1871, and 21 Feb. 1872.

157 Half-Yearly Report, 31 July 1864.

158 Hamilton *Spectator*, 21 Dec. 1865.

159 The failed GWR-GTR-B&LH merger of 1862 required legislative consent because there was no power to amalgamate in the Great Western charter. The GTR and B&LH charters provided for union with other lines so no legislation was required.

160 Toronto *Globe*, 3 Apr. 1866 and 11 Sept. 1866; and Hamilton *Times*, 28 Jan. 1867.

161 Toronto *Globe*, 18 Mar. 1868; see also ibid., 30 Jan. 1871.

162 Hamilton *Times*, 10 May 1867; see also Hamilton *Times*, 2 May 1867, and Hamilton *Spectator*, 13 May 1867, and 28 Sept. 1867.

163 Montreal *Herald*, 20 Oct. 1871.

164 Canada Board, 29 June 1871, 17 July 1873, and 9 Oct. 1873; London *Advertiser*, 10 Nov. 1874. With the opening of the loop line and other branch construction, London was more centrally located than Hamilton, and the Great Western was outgrowing its Hamilton property.

165 Hamilton *Spectator*, 30 Aug. 1864.

166 Toronto *Globe*, 23 Dec. 1865.

167 Half-Yearly Report (Auditors' report), 31 Jan. 1869.

168 Half-Yearly Report, 31 July 1874, 27ff.; 31 Jan. 1875, 27; and 31 Jan. 1876, 35.

169 Half-Yearly Report, 31 July 1869, 18f.

170 Swinyard papers, Swinyard to Vanderbilt et al., 24 Dec. 1869. Swinyard's chief clerk, J.L. Taylor, went off to become assistant general superintendent of the Mis-

souri Valley Railway, under B&LH-GTR alumnus J.F. Barnard: Toronto *Globe*, 31 Dec. 1869, copying Hamilton *Times*.

171 Swinyard papers, Swinyard to John Livesey, 28 Dec. 1869; see also Swinyard to Robert Biggar, 27 Dec. 1869.

172 Half-Yearly Report, 31 Jan. 1870, 18.

173 *American Railway Times*, 8 Jan. 1870.

174 Ibid., 19 Feb. 1870.

175 London *Times*, 17 Feb. 1870. Dakin characterized the move as a cost-saving measure, but there may have been other motives as well. In 1886, when Swinyard applied for the general managership of an American railroad, the then President of the Michigan Central wrote to his counterpart on the New York Central to say, 'Mr Swinyard is not the man to succeed Mr Devereux ... I have but little knowledge of himself personally, but his record as Managing Director of the Great Western was not such as would commend itself to those controlling the Vanderbilt properties.' H. Bledyard to C. Depew, 26 Mar. 1886, quoted in T.C. Cochran, *Railroad Leaders, 1843–1899* (Cambridge, Mass.: Harvard University Press 1953) 74.

176 *Statutes of Canada, 1870*, 33 Vict., c. 50; Half-Yearly Report, 31 July 1870; and Canada Board, 14 Apr. 1871, 22 Sept. 1870, and 12 Oct. 1870.

177 I am indebted to Ralph Greenhill for this calculation.

178 Half-Yearly Report, 31 Jan. 1872, and 31 July 1872.

179 Ibid., 31 Jan. 1873.

180 The MCR finally built a Detroit-Windsor railroad tunnel in 1909: Dianne Newell and Ralph Greenhill, *Survivals: Aspects of Industrial Archaeology in Ontario* (Erin, Ont.: Boston Mills Press 1989), 185.

181 The main line was to be double-tracked from Windsor to Glencoe so that the main and loop lines could operate independently: Toronto *Globe*, 4 Jan. 1873.

182 This was pointed out by O.D. Skelton, *The Railway Builders* (Toronto: Glasgow, Brook 1916), 86.

183 This arrangement had actually been implemented in February 1873, although Price was not given the title until Dakin's visit in August: Canada Board, 28 Feb. 1873.

184 Half-Yearly Report, 31 Jan. 1874; and Toronto *Globe*, 9 Apr. 1874.

185 Toronto *Globe*, 7 July 1874 and 24 Sept. 1874.

186 Half-Yearly Report, 31 July 1874.

187 At the time of his appointment, Broughton was general manager of the Mid-Wales and the Neath and Brecon railways: Half-Yearly Report, 31 Jan. 1875. He later told an Ontario legislative committee that he had had 'the entire control of different railways since the first of January, 1850': Select Committee on Railway Accidents, *Report* (Toronto 1880).

188 Hanlon, 'Robinson,' 132.

189 Childers' letter describing his trip to Canada was annexed to Half-Yearly Report, 31 Jan. 1875.

190 Quoted in Brantford *Conservative Expositor*, 28 Mar. 1854.

191 The length of trains as represented in Figure 5 is a statistical abstraction, useful for present purposes, but to be treated with caution. It does not distinguish among classes of trains, nor does it correct for the use of pilot engines or engines in yard service (which may or may not have been counted in the published figures on traffic-related engine mileage).

192 Montreal *Gazette*, 26 June 1857. For the railway's plans to replace manual labour by machinery for pumping water and sawing wood, see Board Minutes, 24 Aug. 1854.

193 Finance Committee, 13 Nov. 1863.

194 *Ontario Workman*, 26 June 1873, 11.

195 London *Free Press*, 26 July 1872, 12 Feb. 1873.

196 For general histories of the ASE see James B. Jeffreys, *The Story of the Engineers* (London: Lawrence and Wishart 1945), and Keith Burgess, *The Origins of British Industrial Relations: The Nineteenth Century Experience* (London: Croom Helm 1975), chap. 1.

197 Calculated from branch returns in the ASE annual reports for these years: I should like to acknowledge the assistance of the Amalgamated Union of Engineering Workers in granting access to these records at its General Office and of Anne Forrest in retrieving them.

198 ASE, *30th Annual Report* (London 1881), Hamilton branch report income statement.

199 The manuscript census for Hamilton does not reliably identify Great Western workers. However, the city directories published in 1858 and 1867 often (although not always) identify residents' occupations and employers. Locomotive and car department pay sheets have survived for the mid-fifties and early sixties. These records were searched for the names of ASE auditors using stringent criteria: first and last names (or initials and last names) must match, allowing for variations in spelling; occupation must match one or more of the ASE trades; if the only match is with the city directory, employer must be given as GWR. This search identifies persons who worked at one time for the GWR and served at that or another time as ASE auditors. Owing to the unavailability of employer information after 1867, it cannot be stated with certainty that all such persons were working for the GWR during their term as ASE auditors.

200 Toronto *Globe*, 11 Feb. 1860.

201 For the dues figure, see letter of 'Amalgamated,' *Ontario Workman*, 11 Aug. 1873.

202 Alexander and James Holman were GWR pattern-makers; Samuel's employer was not identified.

203 ASE *Journal* (from card file of excerpts maintained by Amalgamated Union of Engineering Workers, as originals of this serial were inaccessible for the period of interest), 8 Dec. 1866.

204 Hamilton *Times*, 21 July 1866.

205 Hamilton *Spectator*, 4 Oct. 1865; employment identified from 1867 city directory.

206 Hamilton *Times*, 14 Dec. 1866 and 22 Dec. 1866; identifications from 1867 city directory; ASE *Annual Report* for years noted.

207 All locomotive shop turners were included as matches. Only those identified as 'iron turners' were included as matches in the car shop, since wood lathe operators were not among the ASE trades.

208 There is no evidence to suggest that the large, although temporary, increase in car shop employment in the early 1870s included an increase in the number of workers in the ASE trades.

209 Eugene Forsey, *Trade Unions in Canada, 1812–1902* (Toronto: University of Toronto Press 1982), 57f. The record is a bit confusing. Although Forsey states at p. 58 that the Toronto branch was formed in 1873, his account of the formation of the Toronto Trades Assembly (p. 92) has its organizing committee visiting the Amalgamated Society of Carpenters and Joiners in 1871.

210 John Battye, 'The Nine Hour Pioneers: The Genesis of the Canadian Labour Movement,' *Labour/Le Travailleur* 4 (1979), 38.

211 John Miller, 'President of the Moulders' Society,' attended the ASE's annual dinner in 1866 but he does not seem to have worked for the GWR, which employed only one or two moulders in its shops: Hamilton *Times, 22* Dec. 1866.

212 Joseph Hugh Tuck, 'Canadian Railways and the International Brotherhoods: Labour Organization in the Railway Running Trades in Canada, 1865–1914' (PhD thesis, University of Western Ontario 1976), 11.

213 *BLE Monthly Journal*, Aug. 1871, 358f.

214 Ibid., Sept. 1871, 420.

215 Tuck, 'Brotherhoods,' 15.

216 Ibid., 15; and Toronto *Globe,* 8 Jan. 1877.

217 Toronto *Globe*, 2 Apr. 1873.

218 Toronto *Leader*, 3 Apr. 1872; and Tuck, 'Brotherhoods,' 18, 37. Before the Great Western gift, Division 68 met at London's Moral Temperance Hall: *BLE Monthly Journal*, Nov. 1871, 526. The new hall was decorated with pictures of locomotives donated by some of the leading American engine builders: *BLE Monthly Journal*, Dec. 1872, 270.

219 Officers Minutes, 11 Dec. 1873.

220 See, for example, the obituary notices in the *BLE Monthly Journal* for London Division members Edward Tonkins (May 1872, 222) and William Pitt (July 1872, 318) and for Hamilton Division Chief Engineer Peter Temple (Nov. 1872, 514).

221 *BLE Monthly Journal*, Apr. 1872, 161ff. Division 133 repeated the event the following year: *Ontario Workman*, 24 Apr. 1873.

222 Tuck, 'Brotherhoods,' 3, suggests that engine-drivers turned to the Brotherhood because commercial insurance rates were too high for railwaymen and says that insurance was the chief reason men joined the organization.

223 *BLE Monthly Journal*, Jan. 1871, 19; Feb. 1871, 59; Apr. 1871, 158f, 176; June 1871, 246f, 251f; and Aug. 1871, 343.

224 Ibid., July 1872, 368.

225 Ibid., Oct. 1870, 463.

226 Toronto *Globe*, 6 Mar. 1873.

227 Montreal *Herald*, 5 Aug. 1873.

228 Toronto *Globe*, 10 Oct. 1878.

229 A Great Western representative was said to be among the 120 members of an 1881 ORC excursion over the principal railways of the United States and Canada: Montreal *Railway Journal* 1, no. 9 (21 Oct. 1881).

230 Canada Board, 2 Sept. 1870.

231 Canada Board, 14 Apr. 1871, 16 Feb. 1872.

232 Toronto *Globe*, 25 Nov. 1878.

233 Officers Minutes, 17 Nov. 1873.

234 *Ontario Workman*, 9 May 1872. The inference that this was the mutual benefit society promoted by Sharp in 1859 is my own. I have found no other reference to this 'statement.' Parker could not have been referring to the English Great Western's several friendly societies, however. The latter railway's provident society was founded in 1838 and had 4,202 members in 1871; its medical fund providing attendance to employees at the Swindon works was founded in 1847; its mechanical employees' sick and funeral benefit was established in 1843; and its enginemen's and firemen's mutual assurance society, which had 1,220 members in 1871, began in 1864: Kingsford, *Victorian Railwaymen*, appendix I.

235 Toronto *Globe*, 18 Aug. 1877; 'Rules of the Great Western Railway Provident Society' (Hamilton: The Society 1877).

236 Toronto *Globe*, 14 Jan. 1878.

237 Ibid., 2 Apr. 1879.

238 Ibid., 24 Dec. 1878.

239 *Statutes of Canada, 1880*, 43 Vict., c. 49.

240 See, *inter alia*, Bryan D. Palmer, *A Culture in Conflict: Skilled Workers and Industrial Capitalism in Hamilton, Ontario, 1860–1914* (Montreal: McGill–Queen's University Press 1979), chap. 5; Gregory S. Kealey, *Toronto Workers Respond to Industrial Capitalism, 1867–1892* (Toronto: University of Toronto Press 1980), chap. 8; and Battye, 'The Nine Hour Pioneers.' A short synthesis may be found in Bryan D. Palmer, *Working Class Experience: Rethinking the History of Canadian Labour, 1800–1991* (Toronto: McClelland and Stewart 1992), 106–8. See also the chapter by Craig Heron in this volume.

241 London *Times*, 8 Nov. 1871, 5.

242 Burgess, *Origins*, 41ff.

243 Ibid., 42.

244 Craven and Traves, 'Dimensions of Paternalism,' 65.

245 Canada Board, 15 Mar. 1872.

246 Toronto *Globe*, 15 Apr. 1872.

247 Toronto *Leader*, 19 Feb. 1872; and see Battye's account, 'The Nine Hour Pioneers,' 34f.
248 Montreal *Herald*, 6 Mar. 1872.
249 Ibid., 12 Mar. 1872.
250 Canada Board, 11 Apr. 1872. The General Superintendent's report referred to in this minute has not been found.
251 *Ontario Workman*, 18 Apr. 1872.
252 Ibid., 25 Apr. 1872.
253 Ibid., 9 May 1872, quoting Hamilton *Standard*, 1 May 1872.
254 London *Advertiser*, 6 May 1872.
255 Montreal *Herald*, 4 May 1872.
256 Ibid., 6 May 1872.
257 *Ontario Workman*, 9 May 1872.
258 Palmer, *Culture*, 297 n. 85.
259 Hamilton *Spectator*, 12 Apr. 1872.
260 *Ontario Workman,* 23 Apr. 1872.
261 Canada Board, 11 Apr. 1872.
262 Ibid.
263 Ibid., 23 Nov 1872.
264 Half-Yearly Report, 31 July 1872.
265 Ibid., 31 July 1873.
266 *Ontario Workman*, 2 May 1872.
267 Canada Board, 18 Nov. 1873.
268 Ibid., 5 Dec. 1873.
269 Half-Yearly Report, 31 Jan. 1874.
270 London *Advertiser*, 8 July 1874 and 30 Nov. 1874.
271 Ibid., 19 Aug. 1874.
272 Ibid., 13 Jan. 1875, 21 Jan. 1875, and 30 Jan. 1875. The Air Line had about five hundred employees in May 1874: ibid., 2 May 1874.
273 Ibid., 22 Jan. 1875, 30 Jan. 1875.
274 Half-Yearly Reports (Engineer's reports), 31 Jan. 1876, 31 July 1876, 31 Jan. 1877, 31 Jan. 1878, and 31 Jan. 1880.
275 Half-Yearly Report, 31 Jan. 1875.
276 Ibid., 31 July 1875.
277 Shirley A. Ayer, 'The Locomotive Engineers' Strike on the Grand Trunk Railway in 1876–1877' (MA thesis, McGill University 1961); and Desmond Morton, 'Taking on the Grand Trunk: The Locomotive Engineers' Strike of 1876–7,' *Labour/Le Travailleur* 2 (1977), 5–34.
278 Toronto *Globe*, 23 July 1877.
279 Ibid., 24 July 1877, and 26 July 1877.
280 Ibid., 11 Aug. 1877.

281 Ibid., 4 June 1878, 11 June 1878, and 15 June 1878.

282 See Currie, *Grand Trunk*, 239.

283 Grey understood the potential for an alliance with the CPR: Half-Yearly Report, 31 July 1881, 11f.

284 For example, in 1874 department heads were given authority to issue stores requisitions without the general manager's countersignature: Officers Minutes, 18 Mar. 1874.

285 Officers Minutes, 29 Dec. 1873, and 26 Feb. 1874.

286 Officers Minutes, 11 Dec. 1873; and Canada Board, 19 June 1874.

287 London *Advertiser*, 30 Mar. 1874. The notice quoted the *Railway Act* prohibition on employee use of alcohol.

288 Toronto *Globe*, 18 Mar. 1879. The fact that the father of one of the women threatened to shoot him may also explain his flight.

289 Hamilton *Spectator*, 5 Sep. 1867.

290 Montreal *Herald*, 24 Mar. 1871.

291 Muir undertook direct supervision of the mechanical department in the meantime: Canada Board, 14 Apr. 1871.

292 Palmer, *Culture*, 146–8. The secret ballot was the theme of one of Witton's few parliamentary speeches.

293 Toronto *Globe*, 18 Nov. 1872.

294 London *Advertiser*, 19 Jan. 1874.

295 Ibid., 6 Jan. 1875.

296 Ibid., 19 Jan. 1874.

Great Western Railway works, Hamilton, c. 1862

Great Western Railway erecting shop, Hamilton, c. 1862

The Home as Workplace

BETTINA BRADBURY

'Time passes rappidly [sic] with our varied employments,' wrote Anne Bellamy in her diary of 29 January 1856. Well it might. The tasks that this Upper Canadian miller and farmer's wife listed during one year of her diary included making various kinds of clothing, cooking a wide variety of foodstuffs, nursing sick and pregnant neighbours and relatives, performing domestic labour such as daily dish washing and spring cleaning, and working in the garden. Her work kept her busy throughout the day and across the seasons; indeed 'busy' was one of the words she used most frequently in her diary.[1]

Yet the work she did was less varied than that of many farming women and less physically demanding than that done by the wives of the emerging working classes of Upper Canadian villages, towns and cities. Anne was part of an emerging local elite that made money by combining farming with saw and grist milling. Their income allowed the men to employ growing numbers of workers in their mills. It permitted women like Anne to share or avoid domestic labour in the home by employing a servant. And it allowed others, like the Bellamys, to set up their sons as manufacturers. Opportunities for wage labour expanded as such small entrepreneurs and wealthy capitalists set up mills, workshops, and factories in towns and cities across Ontario, reshaping local economies and class and gender relations and fuelling the growth of a working class increasingly dependent on wages. The production of a wide array of basic commodities at lower prices, the growth in the amount of cash in the economy, and better transportation changed what the colony's men and women made and bought, what they wore and ate, and what kind of work they did.

This chapter is an attempt to look into the households of the families that became largely dependent on wages in Upper Canada and Ontario between the 1850s and the end of the century.[2] Such working-class families were a minority of the province's population throughout the nineteenth century. By the end of the century, however, as artisanal production diminished and as wage-earning opportunities increased in factories, in workshops, and on construction sites, a majority of the households in the growing cities and in many smaller towns and villages had become dependent on wages. While many of the tasks performed by wives and children in working-class homes were similar to those done in agricultural, artisanal, or even professional and bourgeois households, dependence on wages shaped their work in specific ways.

It is not easy to look inside the homes where women of the emerging working class worked to feed, clothe, and nurture their husbands, relatives and children.[3] The key lies in finding both an adequate theoretical approach and the sources that will allow us to see and understand what they were doing, how they did it, and the relationship between their daily tasks and the transformations occurring in the wider economy. Canadian historians have written more about the work performed in the homes of farm and pioneer women than about their counterparts in the newly emerging manufacturing towns and cities of Canada.[4] That is not surprising. Not only were rural families in the majority, but because many of the pioneers were more highly educated, more of them kept diaries detailing much about their families and their daily work. Furthermore, the publication of the works of Susanna Moodie, Catharine Parr Trail, and other such relatively well-off nineteenth-century writers drew attention to farm work for women.[5] From such sources we can learn about the tasks of farmers and their wives as well as their domestic servants.

Few working-class women, in contrast, appear to have kept diaries, and few letters or other writing by such women have been preserved in archives. It is easier to find out about the formal paid labour of women outside the home than about what was done inside. Nor did nineteenth-century Canadians show great interest in the work done in working-class homes – no Mayhew, Rowntree, Booth, or disciple of Le Play systematically studied urban Ontarians.[6] It was only in the last two decades of the century that the Bureau of Industries started to collect data on wages and the cost of living. That information was filtered through the perceptions of male reporters and statisticians with little interest in home-based ways of getting by. Indeed nineteenth-century statistics gatherers seldom showed much interest in any form of production that was not for sale or export, or in any kind of exchange at the local level. To see into the daily lives of working-class women, men, and children, to describe the tasks they performed at home and to hear their voices is a challenge. We have to learn about their work in different ways, piecing together fragments from censuses, contemporary investigations, newspapers, civic documents, and records kept by charities or the legal system. We have to listen carefully to what husbands and fathers said about their families, their wives, and their work. The evidence for this chapter is drawn largely from such sources. I also draw on secondary studies of particular towns and communities by historians whose main interest was not work done in the home, but whose findings tell us something about wage labour and some family strategies for survival. Only occasionally do these sources allow us to see things from the women's point of view. They do underline the importance of such labour. I hope that other researchers will undertake more systematic and detailed studies of similar questions either in particular communities, especially the small and medium-sized towns that have received so little attention from historians, or during a particular strike or economic depression when the public took a greater interest than usual in work performed in the home.[7]

In looking at the home as a workplace I start with five rather simple assumptions. First I assume that most people in nineteenth-century Ontario lived in households, and that this was the predominant social unit within which daily survival was organized. Most, but not all of these households were made up of families, usually nuclear, but sometimes extended by the presence of relatives, boarders, servants, domestics, or other residents. Their size and composition changed over the life cycles of the family and the life course of individuals. Because of the high death rates of the nineteenth century, many families were headed by one parent, sometimes permanently, sometimes until remarriage created a new, blended family.[8]

Second, I assume that there was a division of labour by sex and age within families and households. In working-class households it was increasingly likely to be the men and older sons and daughters who were employed in the formal wage-labour market. Mothers and younger children were the main workforce of the home.[9] Their daily work and activities were centred on the maintenance of life and were crucial to reproduction, to daily replenishment. It is not always possible, however, to determine just who was responsible for all of the work that went on in the home – raising pigs, chopping wood, and so on, because the sources tend to identify the product rather than the work process involved. Wages gave economic power to those earning them, but in a time when few could afford to pay for food, clothing, and shelter in the marketplace, most were dependent on those doing the housework. This relationship was characterized by an interdependence that usually made daily survival possible but which was no guarantee against violence or abuses of power.[10]

Third, I assume that the production, the managing, stretching, and generating of money, and the raising of children that went on in the home was indeed work whose importance we must recognize, even though it is difficult to measure.[11] Those performing this work possessed a set of skills that might be used only for the immediate needs of their families or exchanged for other goods and services or cash. To acknowledge these 'varied employments' as work suggests that the home was the most usual workplace for the majority of the nineteenth-century adult population.

Fourth, I assume that the emergence of wage labour involved a re-articulation of the links between households and the wider economy rather than a complete separation of home and work. It seems important to examine the various interactions between the two; it is not particularly useful, however, to identify home-based work as part of the informal economy, and other work as formal. This over-dichotomizes what I hope to show is a more complex and shifting situation.[12]

Finally, I assume that despite similarities in the domestic labour performed in homes across the province wage dependence was different from other ways of making a living. This makes it crucial to start an examination of the home as a workplace with the wage earning of those who left each day.

Wage-Earning and Working-Class Households

MALE FAMILY HEADS

Over the second half of the nineteenth century, women in cities, towns, and villages across Ontario were increasingly likely to need the wages of other household members to perform much of their daily labour. In two-parent families the principal earner was usually the husband. As the children grew up, boys were more likely to be secondary earners than girls, but both contributed wage and domestic labour to the family economy. Most wives and mothers worked for wages only in emergencies. Their money managing and stretching was a full-time occupation. The amount the family head could earn, the frequency he could find work, and how often he was paid, along with his willingness to hand it over to his wife for 'the necessaries of life' dictated the family's standard of living and determined what other kinds of work were done by his wife and children.

The spread of wage labour that accompanied the growth of construction and industry in Ontario's economy did not guarantee wages that would enable most men to feed, clothe and house their families as well as pay for medical care, fuel, basic furniture, schooling, and modest entertainment. We need to know much more about employment, wages, prices, and standards of living in this crucial period of Ontario's development.[13] The evidence suggests a working class within which skill, the availability of work, sex, and age made a great difference to earning power.[14] Rosemary and David Gagan have concluded, 'Working-class families, through their members' combined diligence, appear to have been able to accumulate modest savings, to have enjoyed an increase in the purchasing power of their collective wages relative to the basic cost of living and even to have acquired tangible wealth in the form of rateable real or personal property.'[15] This may have been the situation for relatively skilled workers in trades that were steadily in demand and whose families were small or of an age where the sons could also contribute their wages.[16] But it was not likely to be the case for the vast majority of the working class – those in families headed by the semi- and unskilled, men whom the Gagans suggest were increasingly marginalized.

A Kingston labourer, James Rushford, was adamant when he gave evidence to the Royal Commission on the Relations between Labour and Capital in 1888: 'A laborer who gets only $1.00 a day and has two or three small children cannot half support his children and clothe them the way he should, and he cannot pay school taxes and give them an education. There are hundreds of them that way.'[17] His claim is supported by evidence taken by reporters for the Bureau of Industries across Ontario in 1889. That year, the labourers who were surveyed averaged $302.60 in annual wages. Their expenses totalled an average of $343.07. Even with the additional $37.26 raised by other family members such budgets did not balance.

A difficulty in balancing budgets was not limited to labourers and their wives. Most blacksmiths and carpenters living in Toronto in 1888 and 1889 did not earn enough to allow their wives to balance their budgets.[18] 'Do you think a man who has $1.75 a day can support his family comfortably if he is sober, and industrious, and intelligent?' Mr. Carson asked R. Clements, a carpenter who was a witness at the same hearings in Ottawa in May 1888. 'It would depend upon the size of his family. If he had a small family, of course he could do it by being economical,' Clements replied. Only when asked by the chairman, 'Does it not depend a great deal upon the wife?' did he reply 'Exactly.'[19] Even at $2.00 a day, a moulder, Thomas Picket, suggested he could not bring up his family of six or seven in Toronto

respectably and live in a respectable way, and make both ends meet ... I know it for a fact. I have been here three years and I cannot rub one cent against another, and I conclude that I have not lost one day a month through my own neglect. I heard the question asked of a witness, how long it would take him to build a house. It would take me a thousand years to build a house in Toronto, if I continued to live in a respectable way such as a workingman is expected to live and bring up his family. [20]

He reported that wages in his trade had increased, but not enough to keep up with the rising cost of living, especially that of 'dry-goods, eatables' – bread and vegetables, and rent. In his trade the pay was relatively high at 22½ cents an hour. Men worked 10 hours a day and 5½ days in the summer for about twenty-two dollars a week. The three moulders whose testimony was reported that year by the Bureau of Industries averaged $14.40 for a sixty-hour work week.

A wife's ability to perform her main task – transforming the wages of others into food, meals, clothing, and comfortable shelter and raising the children – depended on her husband's earnings, the number of children she had, the size and age of the family, and how often her husband could find work. The irregularity of work was a constant difficulty. Employment possibilities varied greatly between trades, with the seasons, and with economic ups and downs. Toronto workers surveyed by the Bureau of Industries in 1888 averaged about 268 days of employment – forty-four weeks if they worked six full days a week.[21] The workers giving evidence at the Royal Commission hearings of the same year suggested that much shorter work periods were more common. Few men in construction worked more than eight months a year.[22] A Windsor carpenter, George Jenkins, said there was 'not a man in Windsor with whom I am acquainted who makes full time.' Some averaged eight or nine months, some seven. The likelihood of steady work depended on the nature of the work available and hence varied across the province.[23] In Ottawa the largest number of workers reported only 150 to 200 days a year, compared to Almonte, where the majority reported over 300. Different seasonal rhythms in men's work made important differences to the challenges facing housewives. Research is needed on how often such men found other work, what they did when they had no work, whether they did other things to earn money, and what this meant for their wives.

Seasonal unemployment was often predictable. Some men were used to finding alternative winter work in the shanties. Men and women could negotiate credit if they knew work would resume at some particular time. Cyclical unemployment was more devastating, especially in the Great Depression which started in the United States in 1873 and then spread out across Quebec and Ontario.[24] At first some women could stretch what money they had, borrow from friends, or negotiate credit. As men found fewer and fewer days work, family members sought other ways to get by, some eventually selling their furniture to pay the rent and then turning to charity. At Toronto's main institution offering relief to people living in their own homes, the House of Industry, the numbers shot up. In 1874 about 560 families living at home received help. By 1877 over 1,000 were being given some fuel or bread. Between 1874 and 1877 the number of four-pound loaves of bread distributed doubled from around 12,000 to over 28,000 and the amount of coal from 250 to 500 tons. The soup kitchen increased its output from 90 gallons a day in 1873 to 170 in 1876. The numbers receiving aid only began to fall after 1881.[25]

Lack of work and illness quickly ate into all wages, placing different burdens on the wage earner and those responsible for making ends meet at home. Illness was widespread. The poorest were usually the most vulnerable as the effects of inadequate diets were compounded by the unsanitary state of the parts of town where they so often lived, especially in the larger cities. When a *Globe* reporter interviewed an unemployed Toronto labourer, Mr Gloynes, in February 1883, he was coughing 'in an ugly fashion.' He explained that his two greatest fears were sickness and lack of work.[26] Some men belonged to benevolent societies and some unions provided for periods of sickness or for the death of the wage-earner. In 1888, the International Moulders' Union, for instance, paid four dollars a week when a member was sick. Unionized cigarmakers in Stratford reported receiving five dollars a week. While this might cover a family's rent it was not enough for food as well, even in the smallest family.[27]

WAGE-EARNING OFFSPRING

Working-class families were most vulnerable to poverty before their children reached working age. Once the children were old enough to earn, many of them were sent out to seek some form of paid labour. From the 1860s on, more children were able to find some kind of work, although the possibilities varied from town to town and year to year. The proportion of sixteen-year-old boys reporting a job in Hamilton, for example, rose from 51 per cent in 1851 to 66 per cent twenty years later. Girls' participation in the formal labour market was more erratic, falling in Hamilton for all age groups – among sixteen-year-olds from 34 per cent in 1851 to 26 per cent in 1871.[28] Some offspring undertook full-time work. Others found odd jobs or seasonal work. The particular local economies of parts of cities, or of small towns offered specific possibilities. In Chatham the pickling and canning works employed some fifty to seventy men, women, and children, black and white, between July and the end of October. In 1887 the men could earn $1.25 a day, and boys and girls about 60 cents. They worked for sixty hours a week. The local reporter felt it necessary to explain that this employment of children was 'not in any way due to the dissipation of parents here.' Rather the factory was a resort for people when regular work was slack during the summer. In Cornwall, in contrast, where wages were lower than in most other parts of the province, many children under fourteen, as well as those aged fourteen to eighteen were reported to work in the mills 'mainly because the wages paid to heads of families are insufficient to maintain all without the aid of the children.'[29]

In some trades boys in their late teens and early twenties could rival the earning power of their fathers. But daughters, wives, and young sons could not. The wages of older sons in particular offered the possibility of major improvements in a family's standard of living, often after years of scrimping on what the husband could earn alone. The need for older children's wages reshaped the relationships within working-class families, and the nature of childhood changed, as growing numbers of children remained with their parents longer than in the days of pre-industrial or even early industrial capitalism. Where earlier a craftsman might have apprenticed a son out to learn a trade, increasingly the sons stayed home, contributing some or all their wages to the family economy. Girls were as likely to help their mothers with domestic work in the home as to seek wage labour.[30]

In many families, income was so low that even the small wages a youngster under fourteen or so could earn made an important difference to the family budget. Contemporary reformers expressed horror at finding such children in factories, too often ascribing it to the greed or dissipation of parents. But the parents themselves could be acutely aware that they were sacrificing their children's education for the money they so badly needed. The moulder Thomas Picket expressed some of the anguish many men must have felt when they were obliged to make this choice:

I have four boys. I mean to give them a fair education, but the little one of my boys has been able to clothe himself. I merely mention these facts to show that there must be thousands of working men worse off than I am ... I do not believe five percent of our trade or of any mechanical trade can save a dollar in Toronto. When I say that I mean the building trade, the mechanical trades, and the iron trades. There may be some exception ... such as printers who have constant work the year round.[31]

As the century advanced, growing numbers of working-class youngsters did attend school, not only because reformers believed they should, but because parents like Thomas Picket believed education was important. They continued, however, to alternate between school and money-raising or money-saving tasks because so many working-class families could not earn enough to cover their basic costs. The small amounts such youngsters could earn underlines the need for extra cash. Boys under sixteen working as moulders making agricultural implements, for example, earned an average of only $3.18 a week during the last week of April in 1884, compared to the $11.00 male moulders earned. Boy woodworkers earned $3.63 compared to the $8.73 of adults, while girl bookbinders brought in only $2.47, and adult women a dollar more.[32] Nevertheless, family income increased more rapidly with a steadily earning teenage son than with a pay increase or extra day's work for the father.

When a woman's husband died, the earnings of her children were one of her principal ways of getting by. A working-class widow could seldom manage alone even if her husband had worked in one of the rare workplaces that gave some kind of pension to widows or had made provision for her through life insurance or in a will.[33] Take the case of one Toronto woman reported by the Bureau of Industries in 1888. She had two dependants, one of them under sixteen. In 1888 she had worked 56 hours a week for 265 days. Her total earnings were $242.83, less than half the average Toronto wage of $527.14 for those with dependants. Living had cost her $280, so she finished the year with a $61.50 deficit.[34] The children of widows were among the youngsters reported to be working in various kinds of factories across the province, like the glove works in Brockville. In Aylmer many of the women working in the canning factory were reported to be 'widows and the daughters of widows who must work at something for a living.'[35]

Female wages were generally so low that deserted wives and all widows but the wealthy lived in precarious states of dependence on others. Those unable to live by their own earnings or by those of their children and who found no other ways of making money turned to relief agencies and charities, often making up the majority of those helped.[36] Widows predominated among the clients of the Toronto House of Industry, and their ways of getting by starkly reveal the difficulties faced by women heading a family when few jobs were available to women, when wages could be as little as half those of men, and when support systems or day care were few or non-existent. Most widows with young children found work they could do from their homes, partly because the skills they possessed were ones that were done in the home – cooking, sewing, washing, and caring for children or the sick – and partly so they could earn and care for their children at the same time. Seldom did such earning prove sufficient. We will return shortly to such home-based tasks.

HOUSING

The size and quality of the houses in which most working-class families lived and the women worked and raised their children depended largely on the earning capacity of the head of the household, as did the likelihood of owning one's own house.[37] The families of labourers were most likely to live in small dwellings, built of wood rather than brick or stone. They were less likely than others to be connected to the city water mains. In Hamilton 'common labourers' households dwelt in the most miserable houses,' according to Michael Doucet and John Weaver.[38] One Toronto doctor believed that the average working man's dwelling was so small as to be 'a menace to the health of the occupants.' Mayor Howland agreed with him. 'I have heard of many cases,' he told the Royal Commission on the Relations between Labour and Capital in 1888, 'where decent people were in two small rooms.'[39] The families of skilled workers were generally housed somewhat better.

Rent, the least flexible item of family budgets, ate up a large part of most men's wages. It could be reduced if necessary by moving to lower-quality housing, or farther from the centre of town, although then more time was spent getting to work and home again. In budgets collected by Edward Young in 1873, apparently from Ontario workmen, rent accounted for between 12 and 20 per cent of expenses. Fuel for heating and light used up another 10 per cent or so of the money spent.[40] (See Table 1.)

Keeping the rent down was a constant struggle. Many families 'made extraordinary efforts' to save as much as possible when they could, hoping eventually to buy their own house.[41] While urban residents were consistently less likely than rural families to own their house, remarkably high numbers appear to have succeeded in buying some kind of home during the 1870s. Gordon Darroch and Lee Soltow have found that a quarter of labourers in urban areas of Ontario were homeowners in 1871, compared 'with about 30 per cent of all the other urban occupational groups.' They also argue that for household heads of all occupations, the likelihood of owning a house increased with age, so that 'owning one's own home would have been an expectation of virtually all heads of households' in mid-Victorian Ontario.[42] Research on Kingston suggests, however, that in that town labourers were less and less likely to own their own houses as the century advanced.[43]

Certainly, the possibility varied, with success likely being greater in small towns, where land prices were low, than in growing cities, where much land was in the hands of speculators.[44] In St Thomas, one observer suggested in 1888 that the majority did own their own homes, remarking

TABLE 1
Proportion of Annual Expenditures for Rent, Food, and Clothing, 1873

	Belleville 2 children		Cornwall 4 children		Hamilton 5 children		Ottawa 3 children	
Rent	16%	$ 52	12%	$104	20%	$176	12%	$ 52
Food	47	153	54	467	46	393	52	238
Fuel and light	10	31	7	62	12	107	11	52
Clothing	15	50	12	100	12	100	16	75
Other	13	41	16	135	10	86	9	42
Expenses		$328		$ 868		$862		$459
Income		$416		$1040		$780		$468

SOURCE: Based on Edward Young, *Labor in Europe and America: A Special Report on the Rates of Wages, the Costs of Subsistence, and the Condition of the Working Classes, in Great Britain, France, Belgium, Germany, and Other Countries of Europe, and Also in the United States and British America* (1875; repr., Westport, Conn.: Greenwood 1970), 840.

on the 'surprising economy' that could make that possible.[45] A Hamilton printer argued it would take a man 'about ten years to secure a home of his own, and perhaps longer,' if he tried to do it from his wages rather than by a loan.[46] Some managed to buy land in depressed times when prices were low. Others did so because their wives scrimped and saved consistently. 'I think a great deal depends on his own habits and the helpmate he has,' replied one Kingston engineer when asked how long it took to save for a home out of a man's wages.[47] Some ethnic groups seem to have placed great stress on owning their home. The Irish in particular were especially likely to buy houses, whether they lived in cities like Hamilton, in small towns, or in rural parts of the province.[48]

Home-owning was a way of controlling one part of one's life, of being independent of landlords, free from paying rent, and secure in old age. A house of their own also offered the working classes a place that was theirs to control and theirs to work in – a valuable base for home production and earning. However, this was only true when loans were paid off and taxes could be paid so there was no risk of being evicted for non-payment of a mortgage or city taxes. The 1889 Bureau of Industries report suggested that home-owners had a lower cost of living – $16.40 on the average that year – than renters. In some towns, however, there were large numbers of owners for whom 'the charge for instalments, interest and taxes' was 'in excess of the rent paid by tenants.'[49] While employers no doubt hoped that home-ownership would render workers less militant, it could also give families a secure base during strikes or economic downswings.[50]

Another way of saving on rent was to share a house, whether rented or

owned. In August 1871 the *Globe* reported that a rise in rents was causing 'mechanics to crowd some of the smaller houses, two or three families sharing the habitation of one.'[51] Doubling up with another family
may have·allowed some women to share domestic tasks and child care.
But for others it meant conflicts over cooking facilities and an over-
crowded living and work space. Such sharing is particularly difficult to
measure. The censuses do not always distinguish between families sharing housing and families taken in as boarders. Furthermore, sharing is
often hard to identify. One person might rent a house and take in another
family who paid board. Or a landlord might divide a house into separate
apartments. Such practices could result from need, entrepreneurial ambitions, or a mixture of both. Often, sharing was temporary, occurring in
an economic crisis when work was scarce or rents particularly high, or
when a family had just arrived in a new city. It was largely an urban phenomenon, predominating among families headed by labourers and the
semi-skilled. Recent research on Montreal suggests that many of those
sharing housing there were relatives.[52]

Not all sharing caused overcrowding, but it could. And disputes were
likely to erupt over lack of space and the use of the kitchen. Most conflicts probably went no further than the ears of the neighbours but a few
spilled out into the streets and the police courts. In 1870 an argument
between two Ottawa families over the use of the kitchen they shared
became so acrimonious that they ended up in court.[53] In another case the
Ottawa Citizen reported facetiously on a 'long rigmarole about two families, who, living in a house divided into two tenements by a thin parti-
tion, could hear all the good things said of the other, felt themselves at
times not overmuch flattered by the compliments each in turn dealt out
and received from the other.'[54]

MEN AND SHORTER HOURS

It was not only the amount of wages that men and children could earn
that influenced the nature of their housing and women's work in the
home. Wage-earning set up rhythms that permeated the lives of those at
home as well as those working elsewhere. Wage labour took most earners out of the house to factories, workshops, mines, forests, and construction sites. Industrial time had a direct effect on family time and
reshaped the workforce at home as well as in the formal labour market.
We need to think about the meaning of time spent at work not just for
those subjected directly to the time demands of industrial employers, but
also for those affected at second hand – their spouses, parents, or children. When workers organized for a shorter work week, they were in

part claiming the right to spend more time with their families or to work and relax at home. Changed hours also influenced those reproducing their labour power. Usually this was implicit in the workers' demands; at times it was explicit. The nine-hour movement of the early 1870s has received most attention in Canada as an example of early organizing that transcended the limited identities of town, trade, and region.[55] While most historians writing about it have acknowledged in passing the importance men placed on having time for their own intellectual and moral development, and the need for married men to spend time with their families, they have given only minimal attention and thought to these reasons for shorter hours.[56] Yet the nine-hour movement, like other claims for shorter hours, was about how much time might be spent at places other than work, including at home. And such demands were often made in conjunction with requests for or statements about the best timing of wage payment, a question of central importance to house-wives.[57] In this sense questions of time, hours, and wage payment were about reproduction as well as production; about leisure as well as work. And these two issues – hours and the timing of wage payment, were central to working-class demands throughout the century. They did not grow only 'from work-place experiences,'[58] but represented a renegotiation of the bridges between work and home, work and leisure, production and reproduction. Such issues deserve greater attention than they have received from Canadian historians.[59]

Though the nine-hour movement failed to win nine-hour days in most cities, over the following decades workers in many organized trades did succeed in shortening their working week. This was achieved more often by working a shorter day on Saturday than by working nine hours each day. At times shorter hours were, for the employers, simply an alternative to closing down for a while.[60] The issue was highlighted in the questions sent to local reporters by the Bureau of Industries in 1887, and in the evidence collected by the Royal Commission on the Relations of Labour and Capital in 1888. Both the reports and the testimony give us some idea of the extent to which family and home life constituted part of the rationale of workers for shorter hours during the last two decades of the century. When workers were asked to comment on the effects of shorter hours, they stressed four things: family time, home improvement, self-improvement, and the importance of spreading work around.[61] They generally also made a distinction between how shorter hours would be used by married men and by single men. What they might mean for women – either those who were earning wages, or those reproducing them at home – was seldom mentioned. Family time and home improvement deserve further attention here.

The Guelph working man reporting to the Bureau of Industries in 1887 tied shorter hours specifically to family issues, arguing that it would give men

time to get acquainted with their families and improve mind, body and estate. As it is they go to bed tired, and become subordinate to the machine they have to tend ... When the workers have Saturday afternoon in the summer they can do little jobs of work for the improvement of their homes or get an airing for themselves and families, do their marketing in time and get all necessary work done.[62]

The London reporter made similar comments:

Shorter hours of work are of advantage to the toiler, as they give the married man more time at home in summer to cultivate his garden and lawn, and otherwise improve his property, and to assist the mother in the development and culture of their children, that she, too may have more time for social enjoyment and recreation, and lead them to think that it is not all of life to grub for an existence, and that there is a drop of pleasure in the ocean of life. I am afraid that I cannot speak thus of many of our young men. Their tendency to gamble and drink and sport forbids that.[63]

These explanations require further examination. Mr A. Blue, Secretary of the Bureau of Industry detected 'a dash of sentimentality,' in such responses.[64] Yet a different analysis can be made of such claims. First they underline the centrality of time in the conflict between labour and capital. Secondly, the claims are made for men only, not for women, and are seen as different for married and single men. The movement for shorter hours is assumed to be male. Thirdly, the claim to more time is based on the need for family time as well as personal time. This family time is presented as both economic – time to garden and fix up homes, hence saving money – and social or familial – time to spend with wives and children.[65] The alienation from one's offspring that long hours away from home could produce is suggested in the idea of the Guelph man who talks of the importance of getting acquainted with one's family. The London man both asserts his right to some influence on the socialization of his children and acknowledges that wives too should have a chance for recreation.

What men did with their extra free time and how their wives felt about men being home for more of the day requires further investigation. When an article in the *Globe* contended that working men's wives did not want their husbands home an hour earlier in the evening, as they preferred to be alone or gossip with other wives, one printer's wife disagreed strenuously. She wrote to the *Ontario Workman* on 9 May 1872, strongly supporting shorter hours, urging other women to stick by their men in times of strike, and arguing that such time would be well used. 'The extra hour is spent at home, tis true,' she wrote, 'in the shape of gardening, fixing up things generally, or reading and writing, and – "miserable fellow" – playing with the children.'

The uses men appear to have made of shorter hours seem to confirm Gary Cross's suggestion that 'the short-hour movements may have been an adaptation to the separation of work and life (home) in order to fulfil family responsibilities.' He sees such demands as part of 'the obvious quest for a new definition of family built less around economic exchange than the morality of childrearing and reciprocal affection.'[66] Yet, justifying demands for shorter hours by the need to spend time on family and home was also a way of drawing harder lines between wage earning and the family. This crystallized the identification of wage earner with the family head, the person who ideally in the skilled working man's view should have been the only one working.[67] Stressing family time may also have been a claim to respectability that was seen as good tactics in gaining wider acceptance for both shorter hours and a family wage.

Working at Home

The diverse domestic tasks that women performed for their own families and at times for others were increasingly the major kind of work performed in Ontario homes. As live-in apprenticeships declined, as growing numbers of men and sons and daughters left their homes daily to work for wages or attend school, the home became feminized – a place where women worked with some help from their children. Clearly that work was not independent from the wage-earning of other family members. The tasks and rhythms were more varied than those of factory workers, but this did not make the home some kind of separate, pre-industrial enclave.

As long as there were some wage-earners in a family, some of the timing of that work was determined by the hours that wage earners were away. E.P. Thompson's suggestion that the rhythms of women's housework were closer to the conventions of 'pre-industrial' society passes too quickly over this point.[68] Furthermore, in the early years of industrial development, employers were able to keep wages relatively low precisely because women's domestic labour provided such a large proportion of family subsistence. Its benefits clearly accrued both to wage-earners and to the owners of mills and factories able to pay accordingly.[69]

Women's work in the home was crucial. Whether a family could muster one or several wage-earners, most wives had to work hard at making the money earned go as far as possible. They were the ones who had to 'study how long she must make the bag or barrel of flour last.' Among the 'more prosperous working-class families,' Jeanne Boydston has argued, 'household manufacturing, and gardening ... functioned as means of avoiding cash outlays,' while shopping carefully or in bulk might save money. In poorer families 'wives (as well as children) were responsible for finding ways to increase the household provisions without spending cash' – including scavenging and even at times stealing.[70]

At the core of the work in homes across the province were the production or purchase of food and the preparation of meals, sewing, and mending, and cleaning – what Marvin McInnis refers to as 'conventional household tasks' – that went into caring for families of all classes in cities, as on farms.[71] Most of this was women's work, whether it was performed by the mistress of the house, her children, or a servant. What distinguished working-class homes was the need to rely on a wage to pay for many of these goods and services, as well as for shelter, education, and other expenses.

The tasks and aptitudes that went into this work were ones that married women could use to raise the standard of living of their husbands, children, and themselves. Most entered married life having helped their mothers on farms or in cities, or spent time as a domestic in the homes of others. They drew on skills learned, often applying them in new and changing circumstances. Daughters, widows, and wives in need of extra cash could also trade their skills for fees or wages if necessary. They might use them separately – cooking and selling meals, taking in washing, sewing dresses, or knitting. Or they might wield them in combination by taking in boarders or working as a general servant. But work in the home included more than cooking, cleaning, sewing, and the production of goods. Women's domestic labour involved services too – feeding babies, looking after children, caring for sick and elderly relatives, providing sexual satisfaction for husbands, and dealing with the disagreements and worries of old and young alike.[72] Most of these services could also become the basis of raising cash if necessary.

What was produced, rather than purchased, scrounged, bartered or, in some cases, stolen, depended on the amount of cash or credit available, on the abilities and values of housewives, and on the possibilities of making and saving money in particular neighbourhoods and towns. In the majority of working-class homes survival depended on some blend of production, exchange, purchase, and sometimes scrounging or theft. The relative weight and significance of these is virtually impossible to measure. The ways of getting by ranged from the purchase of all household needs – the assumption behind most analyses of the cost of living – to relative self-sufficiency in food and clothing.[73] It is possible in theory to envisage five different kinds of relationships between the work done in the home and the wider economy and labour market. In reality, families seldom fitted neatly into one category.

In the first situation, an adequate income generated by the wage earners of the family would have allowed the wife to put most of her energy into making careful purchases of the goods and services the family needed. The wages could be earned by one person or several. If there was only one, this would approximate the concept of the family wage, favoured by skilled craftsmen. A second possibility might involve some members of the family working at home for wages, as in the sewing industry, where work was put out to women in their homes by clothing manufacturers. Thirdly, those at home might produce goods or provide services for cash. Or, fourthly, these goods and services might be exchanged for others in some kind of relationship we would see as barter. One woman might raise chickens, for example, while another took care of her children in return for eggs.[74] Finally, in the situation most approximating self-sufficiency, and most likely among the poorest urban families or in times of crisis or severe economic depressions, those at home, largely women helped by their children, produced, provided, or scrounged, largely avoiding purchases either to save money or because the state of transportation and markets meant that commodities were not available.[75]

Clearly these are hypothetical situations. In reality the same family could engage in all these different relationships at the same time with the balance varying over their life cycle and with their financial state. Which one predominated would depend on when in the nineteenth century they lived, what was available in the marketplace and at what price, whether they were in big cities or smaller towns, and on how much revenue or wages was brought into the household. More personal factors – the particular skills of the housewife or other family members, their health, and their place and reputation in the local neighbourhood could all come into play as well. Who did the work varied too, although increasingly most of the day-to-day housework and money stretching fell to the wives.

The advantage of looking at work performed in the home in this way is that it does not draw hard lines between formal and informal markets, and it suggests the many different ways that work at home could interact with the wider economy. We get away from the kind of oversimplified idea, which is criticized by Joy Parr, that industrialization led automatically to the separation of home and workplace and the elimination of production from the home. The expansion of industrial production did not generate one dominating mode of production in which productive activity became concentrated in industrial workplaces, she argues. Drawing on her research in late nineteenth- and early twentieth-century Hanover, in southwestern Ontario, she suggests that the 'nature and location of production and exchange continued to move, both away from and towards the money economy as the characteristics of those engaged in work and the technology of production change.'[76]

Working-class women's main source of help in their own daily work was their children. They taught their sons and daughters to perform domestic labour largely by demanding that they help with every kind of chore. Boys were expected to chop wood, carry coal, fetch water, and run errands. Girls learned cooking, sewing, cleaning, and nursing by doing them at their mothers' side. Children made work for mothers, and children worked for them. Historian John Bullen wrote, 'At any hour of the day, youngsters could be found sweeping steps, washing windows, and scrubbing floors.'[77] Truant officers investigating children's absences from school found girls cleaning, babysitting, sewing, and caring for sick members of the family. Children of either sex might carry laundry 'to and from their homes while older siblings assisted with washing and ironing'; or they might help change sheets, clean rooms, serve meals, and wash dishes, especially in homes with boarders. Mothers sent them out to find discarded coal, wood, fallen foodstuffs, and anything else that might be used in the home.[78]

Youngsters were particularly good at scrounging, that art of turning someone else's rubbish into usable items, although this particular skill was by no means limited to the young. The greater the discrimination that faced old and young alike for their sex, class or race, the greater likelihood they would have to turn to such means of getting by. Blacks living in St John's Ward in Toronto were referred to disparagingly by a local policeman as 'finders.' From his description, their methods sound particularly systematic. 'They sally out just at daybreak' and, dividing 'into squads slowly patrol Yonge, King and Queen streets on both sides.'[79]

Such activities shifted rather too easily into theft, as Christine Stansell has demonstrated. The thin line was not necessarily clear to children, nor did it always matter to desperate parents. Respectability was not a luxury that everyone could afford to uphold. The theft of just a few sticks of firewood earned a young Toronto girl fourteen days in prison in 1859 because the magistrate considered 'pilfering wood' to be so common that punishment was necessary despite the 'pinching distress in the city.'[80] When Thomas and Mary Pool convinced a local magistrate in

Barrie that their children had stolen clothes off a neighbour's clothes line only as a prank because they had quarrelled with the plaintiff's children, who knows what the truth was?[81] Street trades, prostitution, and theft offered children sources of economic independence that could strain their relations with their parents. But the money they helped earn or save could also enable a family to get by. As more and more were able to find jobs, the possibility of a better standard of living based partially on children's earnings increased for families with offspring of earning age.

Throughout the century the numerous attempts to get more and more children into school were intended in large part to prevent children from contributing to the family economy, especially in towns. Whereas rural children's contribution to farm work was generally accepted, 'working-class parents of absent children were periodically assailed by charges of criminal neglect and indifference ... The exigencies of working-class family life ran counter to nineteenth-century educators' instincts for punctuality, regularity, and permanence.'[82]

The compulsory education laws pitted the educators' desires against family needs. 'The compulsory education law is intended for the benefit of young children whose parents desire to obtain money for their services when they should be at school: who are willing to sacrifice the future advancement of their offspring for their own immediate gain,' wrote the Toronto inspector of schools in 1874.[83] Such laws could not eliminate such contributions to the family economy, as the truant officer quoted above discovered. Home responsibilities did not prevent children from enrolling in school; rather they 'precluded regular attendance at school,' setting up urban patterns of absenteeism different from the seasonal ones of agricultural areas. Children continued to stay home to cut wood, mind ill family members, and perform household tasks.[84] But from mid-century on, they also spent more time in school. Regulations regarding attendance were tightened, and growing numbers of parents sought better chances for their own children.

As keeping children home to help with the 'trivial' pursuits related to women's work at home came under growing public attack, women were more and more likely to perform their domestic tasks at home unaided by youngsters. At the same time their older sons in particular were more likely to find work. Yet the laws passed during the 1880s acknowledged the economic need of some families by allowing children 'employed in any manufactory' to attend school only half time.[85] Paid, formal labour was thus legitimated, while helping a mother with household tasks was less acceptable.[86] As schooling and wage labour drew their sons and daughters out of the home, mothers spent more time working in the home alone with their babies and pre-school children.

THE RHYTHMS OF WORK IN THE HOME

In wage-earning families housewives fitted their tasks into and around the rhythms of other people's labour and wages. Their workday usually started early, the exact hour determined by the kind of breakfast they made, the hour at which the family wage-earners had to start work, and the distance they had to travel. While some wives may have slept, leaving their husbands to organize their own departure for work, most would have risen early, to make breakfast and usually a lunch to take. In the homes of Ottawa bakers in the late 1880s this could mean waking up early enough to get the men to work by 5 o'clock.[87] In the cotton mills of Cornwall and Kingston, or the wool-working factories of Almonte work started at 6:30 a.m. In towns dominated by one or two large factories that hired children as well as adults, housewives throughout the town would have been up around 5:30 to prepare not only their husbands but their offspring for their day's work.[88] In St Thomas no one was likely to sleep in: at 6 o'clock every weekday morning, 'a 2 minute blast from the great whistle at the Canada Southern Car Shops' roused the townspeople from their slumbers and was said to be audible for fourteen miles.'[89] Shift-work, extended shifts, and overtime in rush season set up their own rhythms, creating different tasks for home-makers and disparate daily patterns in towns.

Not all wage-earners were gone for the whole day leaving the house-keeper free to organize her own work. Some wives made lunches and sent a child to the factory with a lunch pail; others had children or husbands who came home to eat at noon.[90] Most workers returned nine to twelve hours later, seldom leaving work before 6 or 6:30 p.m. Hungry, weary wage-earners walked in, doubtless expecting dinner on the table and some emotional support. For, as 'Vincent' wrote to the *Labor Union* in 1883, real working men had feelings, emotions, and nerves. 'After his day's work he is hungry and tired; sometimes he is discontented ... He has to work ten hours a day; sometimes he walks a mile or two before and after work, and saws wood when he comes home.'[91] For some husbands a disappointing meal justified physical violence. This was especially likely when they had stopped to drink on the way home.[92]

SHOPPING AND THE TIMING AND NATURE OF WAGE PAYMENT

Even when men had steady work, their wives could not always ensure there was food on the table. One of the revolutions of the nineteenth century was the likelihood that many foodstuffs would be purchased rather than made at home. Because their husbands were away for most of the day, women were the usual shoppers. It was when shopping that women confronted their dependence on the wages of others most blatantly, though they themselves may have seen the situation differently. To purchase food and other goods meant using either the wages earned by husbands and other wage-earners or credit acquired on the strength of their earning power. Much more research is needed into shopping and the workings of credit for ordinary people in nineteenth-century Canada. It is possible, however, to sketch how the ways men were paid would have influenced a housewife's ability to shop carefully, seek out bargains, and exercise some autonomy in the realm of consumption.

Payment in truck, in store bills, credit with the storekeeper, or in any other way than in hard cash tied a household to specific stores, removing any freedom of choice as to where to shop, and leaving them at the mercy of such shopkeepers, who might set whatever prices they wished. Examples of such kinds of payment can be found in the 1850s,[93] and occasionally even the 1880s.[94] From mid-century on workers requested payment in cash. By the late 1880s most urban Ontario workers did receive cash,[95] but payment in scrip continued in some of the shanties and some single-enterprise towns, most often where most of the workforce were single males or married men working away from home. The Bureau of Industries' report for 1887 suggested that the old system of taking 'truck' for labour, or paying in storebills seemed to be 'becoming extinct.' The London reporter suggested, 'The old barter business is about entombed without any prospect of resurrection.'[96]

Payment in cash was a great advantage for wives responsible for turning that wage into food, clothing, and shelter. Cash allowed housewives some liberty in the realm of consumption, making them, within the limits of the amount of the wage and the options in their town, free shoppers. This became more and more true as stores began to compete for customers, not by offering credit, but by reducing prices for goods that were only available if paid for with cash. Like the 'free labourers' unleashed by the decline of petty commodity production and the rise of wage labour, women with cash for shopping were 'free and unfree', but in different ways.[97] A woman with money in hand could shop where she chose. 'If you want to save money, buy for cash,' advised one 'cash store' in an 1880's Hamilton publication.[98] Yet most housewives remained largely dependent on the family's wage-earners, on their finding work, being paid, and handing over some or all of their wages.

Cash was important, but so too were how often it was paid and being able to predict when they would receive it. When payment was spread out over long periods, was irregular or unpredictable, or when work was short, women had a different shopping and housekeeping experience.

They had to negotiate with merchants and shopkeepers and seek out those willing to give credit. The evidence suggests that merchants may have treated fortnightly and even monthly accounts as equivalent to cash when they knew the pay was coming in at a specific time. An advertisement for a grocer in the *Palladium of Labor* in February 1884 promised that the shop would treat 'three months credit the same as cash,' suggesting that such a lengthy period was unusual enough to attract customers.[99]

Some storekeepers charged heavily for credit. When men working for shingle and lumber mills along Muskoka Bay called for weekly payment and complained about the costs of credit during the hard winter of 1887–8, a Knights of Labor investigation found that 'the monthly payment system was reducing the real value of the workers' earnings by as much as 35 percent, so exorbitant was the cost of credit.' In 1886 an operative at the cotton mills in Cornwall called for payment every two weeks instead of monthly, arguing that more frequent payment would allow workers to purchase their goods for 10 to 15 per cent less and avoid costly entanglements of credit.[100] An anonymous Toronto machinist advocated weekly rather than monthly payment to the 1888 Royal Commission, arguing, 'It would keep them out of the credit system, which is so injurious to workingmen. At the present time if a man is a little extravagant with his pay when he gets it, it is a long time before he gets relief.'[101]

There does seem to have been widespread reliance on personal credit extended over varying terms during this period. A woman might easily pledge her husband's name for basic necessities when the merchants knew the man was earning. But to negotiate 'trust' at times when payment was irregular or work short would have been a stressful experience requiring special skill.[102] Low wages, lengthy or irregular pay periods, and even a running monthly account could erase the benefits of payment in cash, tying families to specific suppliers in a web of obligation and debt. An Ottawa baker advocating membership in the Knights of Labor argued in 1888 that many labourers did not belong, 'and their wages are not sufficient to keep their families going. They buy at the butchers and at the grocers and then they cannot pay.'[103] At times non-payment of debts led to the seizure of part of a man's wages. Toronto labourer Joseph Bissel argued that weekly payment would be a great benefit to men with a family, limiting the garnisheeing of wages, and stopping the bosses from having 'such a pull on the men as they have now.'[104] The seizure of wages for non-payment of debt limited what families could live upon. At times it also led to dismissal. In 1873 management at the Great Western Railway was fed up with the increase in such orders and the trouble they caused the paymaster. They decided that any 'employee whose wages are garnisheed more than twice will be discharged.'[105]

Gradually, from mid-century on, growing numbers of workers persuaded their employers to pay them regularly on specific days. Unorganized workers, various unions, and the Knights of Labor all made demands to employers about how often they should be paid and on what day. Among the principles of the Knights of Labor was the 'enactment of laws to compel corporations to pay their employés weekly, in lawful money, for the labor of the preceding week.'[106] By the 1890s most wages were reported to be paid 'weekly, although in many cases still fortnightly or monthly. With some few exceptions, wages are paid in full ... Wages as a rule are paid in cash, and this together with the fact that they are paid weekly so much more than was formerly the case, is believed to be almost entirely owing to the more complete organization of labor.'[107]

A woman waiting for money for the necessaries of life was more and more likely to get it weekly as long as her husband had a job. What day she might have cash to shop with, however, varied across the province and between industries. And this, as husbands recognized, made a difference to how well she could shop. 'Each establishment appears to have its own favorite date and mode of paying ... Where the wages are handed over weekly, Friday and Saturday are the most popular, although Monday and sometimes Tuesday are used by some employers.'[108] Men seem to have been quite clear about which day they preferred to receive their pay. Most, like the Hamilton building trades workers who petitioned their employers during the spring of 1886, preferred to be paid on Fridays so their wives could take advantage of goods available at market on Saturday mornings. They claimed that the purchasing power of their money was greater earlier on Saturday than later in the day, when meats and produce 'were generally the culls of the market.'[109] The majority of men replying to questions at the Royal Commission hearings of 1887–8 preferred Friday night. 'Of course to a single man it does not make much difference,' a London printer, W.A. Clarke, explained, 'but it enables the wives of those who are married to go on the market if they choose on Saturday.'[110] Some employers recognized the advantages of market shopping. A St Thomas contractor argued that by paying on Friday he was offering 'an advantage of 10 per cent to the men's families to have the money to use on Saturday's market,' and that it was equally convenient for him.[111]

This nearly unanimous agreement on the advantages of Friday payment underlines the importance of farmers' markets across Ontario, as well as highlighting the importance of the timing of wage payment for wives. In small towns with one main employer, the question of when workers should be paid could pit the workers and their families against the local merchants. Rumour had it in Hespeler in 1888 that the local postmaster and storekeeper was trying to make arrangements with the owner of the woollen mill, the largest employer in town, to ensure that he received the local people's patronage. He was said to be trying to make sure the mills stayed open until 4 o'clock on Saturdays instead of noon, as was then usual. This would not have given the men or their wives time to travel to Galt, where they preferred to do their shopping.[112]

The phrasing of much of this discussion about shopping requires some attention. Employers seldom stated explicitly that it was the women who did the shopping; they were not alone in this. While the advantages of shopping at market on Saturday mornings were always the rationale for Friday payment, just who was doing the shopping was frequently hidden either in passive verbs or in a general reference to the family. A London moulder argued that Saturday payment was preferred 'so as to go on the market.' The Secretary of the Manufacturers' Association saw it as enabling men to 'devote earnings to their families.'[113] Some married men only acknowledged that this was their wives' work when pushed by one of the commissioners to be more explicit. The particular way some of them phrased their claim, writing women's role out of the shopping process, suggests that during the 1880s in Ontario we may be seeing one element of the 'denial of the economic worth of housework,' that Jeanne Boydston sees as an integral part of the development of industrial capitalism in the northeastern United States. Employers and some employees had begun to equate men's role as wage-earners with the whole family economy.[114] Most men, however, worked on Saturday mornings and were therefore not free to shop. Whatever they said about money going further or going 'on the market,' the usual shopper had become the housewife.

This was not true of all men giving testimony, and it seems to have been less common among the unskilled, where the challenges of stretching wages were greater than among the skilled. Some of the men who were explicit about their wife's role in household management presented budgeting as a joint decision, some as their wife's domain. A Burlington machinist, for example, stated in 1888 that he had been able to save up for his retirement partly because he had no children. The other reason was that he had been 'exceedingly fortunate in my matrimonial adventure, and it was our united purpose to purchase the best that, consistently with our circumstances, we could obtain, and to make use of that purchase economically.'[115] The Toronto moulder Thomas Picket, in contrast, made it clear that his wife did the shopping and that he did not necessarily think she shopped well.[116] When one Toronto labourer was asked in 1883 what sort of food his family ate, he told the reporter his wife was the one who knew about such things.[117]

In the towns of Ontario, employers' decisions about how often and when to pay their workers influenced the timetables of domestic labour, setting up rhythms of purchasing that varied from town to town. These would have been manifest to visitors in the numbers of women in the streets, at the general store, or at the market. For the families themselves, pay-day was probably more often marked by a better meal that launched a period of declining standards across the ensuing fortnight or month as the money ran out. While those that could do much of their shopping on Saturday mornings probably did so, others had to make their purchases or pay off their debts when they had cash in hand. If the evidence of workers at the Royal Commission is representative, women were most likely to be seen out shopping with cash in hand in London on a Tuesday (as Monday was the most frequently mentioned pay-day), and in Chatham on Saturday. In Ottawa, in contrast, there were so many different pay-days they might be seen almost any day. In Toronto, Saturday noon or night ran neck and neck with Friday.

Yet daily shopping was also part of most women's domestic labour. Whereas vegetables, fruit, and perhaps meat and dairy products were available more cheaply at markets, bread, flour, sugar, and other staples were likely to be bought at the corner stores and groceries that abounded in the cities, or at the general stores of smaller towns. It was probably in such stores that credit predominated. David Sobel reports that in the southern half of St John's Ward in Toronto in 1881 there were some thirty small grocers, many at street corners, and apparently worlds apart from the 'exclusive fancy goods, clothing stores and eating houses,' grocers, fruit dealers, and butcher shops that lined Yonge Street and Queen Street on the eastern and southern boundaries of the ward. Most women lived close enough to shops to leave their youngsters at home for a while alone or watched over by an older sibling. Those that had to stay at home for one reason or another could buy from the hawkers and foot pedlars, who were likely to live in this poorest part of the city.[118]

It is interesting that virtually all discussion of shopping in the testimony of workers at the Royal Commission in 1888 dealt with food shopping. This is not surprising since the major part of most wages was spent on food. But we need to know much more about working-class purchases of furniture, appliances, clothing, utensils, and other goods. For gradually, as the prices of those things dropped with factory production, more and more of the working class became part of the potential market for these products. More research is also required into the kinds and costs of credit, as well as into the use of pawnshops, second-hand shops, and other more formal ways of exchanging used goods. Advertisements in Toronto papers suggest that during the 1880s stoves, coal, clothes wringers, and sewing machines could all be purchased with small weekly instalments.[119]

HOME-BASED TASKS: FROM STRETCHING WAGES TO MAKING MONEY

Food and Meals

The largest part of most nineteenth-century working-class family budgets was food. In the budgets collected by Young in 1873, food purchases took up about half of family incomes. Here was an area where a wife's abilities could have a real influence on her family's standard of living. Saving money on food might involve careful shopping, learning how to use the cheapest cuts of meat, seeking out bargains at market or at specific shops, raising food, or scrounging for it. Wives could also minimize expenditures by eating the cheapest foodstuffs themselves, saving the better food for the wage-earning members of the family.[120] While few working-class families could achieve self-sufficiency in food, many could avoid being totally dependent on the market by keeping a garden or a few animals. Families of all classes had a better chance of ensuring that their milk was pure, their meat healthy, and their vegetables fresh in the summer if they kept animals or a garden. Although Canadian winters were long, Ontario had a good climate for summer produce. Vegetables, fruits, meat, and eggs could also be exchanged or sold, bolstering shaky wages and improving standards of living.

Small towns usually offered more space for gardens and animal keeping than a city like Toronto. The 1871 census reports that residents of Thornhill to the north of Toronto harvested apples in great quantities. About half the urban households there produced butter; a few kept pigs.[121] In Hespeler, whose wage-earning residents, male and female, were mostly employed in the local woollen mill, some 30 per cent of the 151 families had pigs, and about 40 per cent had killed swine or sold them for slaughter or export. A third of the families also had milk cows. Just over one in ten local families were making their own butter, half grew potatoes and about a quarter grew apples.[122] In Brantford, which had nearly four thousand residents in 1871 and was being promoted as a commercial hub, labourers' and carpenters' families in one of the poorer sections of town were supplementing their wages by raising cows and pigs, by growing apples and potatoes, and making butter. Like many other wives in smallish towns across the province, Sara Wells helped stretch her bricklayer husband's wages by keeping a cow, making 150 pounds of butter, and caring for her quarter acre garden, which produced 5 bushels of corn, twenty bushels of potatoes, and six bushels of apples.

This family with five children under eight would certainly have eaten better thanks to such produce. Some may also have been sold or exchanged for goods or services.[123] Even as late as 1890 cows owned by people living in Brantford were driven up Brant Avenue and down Church Street to pasture on Kerby Island.[124]

Women who moved into towns and cities from rural areas were used to being responsible for the kitchen garden. Many immigrants had traditions of keeping a garden. Joy Parr documents the importance of gardens, chickens, and cows among the woodworkers of Hanover well into the twentieth century. Among these German immigrants, gardening and the raising and butchering of animals appear to have been largely male employments.[125] Jane Synge also reports that Hamiltonians who had been youngsters at the beginning of the century recalled that it was their fathers who had grown the vegetables.[126] Certainly gardening was male work as paid labour.[127] But, as the men were generally away for ten or more hours a day, six days a week, garden care and the supervision of pigs, cows, or other food animals was often the task of the women and children. Jean Scott reported briefly in her 1892 investigation of female labour in Ontario that 'market gardening' was 'a means of subsistence' for some married women.[128] A Toronto truant officer, W.C. Wilkinson, found two ten-year-old truants in 1872 in a field near Palace Street, where they had gone seeking their runaway cow. Another time he found an eleven-year-old boy helping his father in the garden.[129]

Gardening, of course, required not only time and energy, but also a minimum of space and light. In Ottawa, gardens were reported to the census takers of 1871 more often by families with a skilled than an unskilled head, probably because their lots were larger. The produce grown there included carrots, potatoes, beets, and turnips.[130] Unskilled workers were well aware of the advantages a garden offered. One labourer who had worked for twenty years on the Ottawa locks of the Rideau Canal pointed out the unfairness of the situation where men working 'up along the line to Kingston Mills have houses from the Government and a garden, and they can grow potatoes and get a great deal of fuel free,' yet were paid the same wage as Ottawa men, who received none of these extra 'privileges.'[131]

It was not only among the working class of towns and small cities that animals and gardens were important ways of making or saving money. In 1861 there were over 1,300 pigs in Toronto and about 1,000 cows. Hamilton households reported 840 pigs and 608 cows.[132] As late as 1881 there were still over 1,000 pigs and a similar number of cows reported in Toronto, but only about 500 cows and fewer than 300 pigs in Hamilton. In St John's Ward Toronto, labourers predominated among those keeping only pigs. There, for example, some forty families reported keeping 159 pigs when the census was taken in mid-winter of 1861. There were about the same number of cows. Workers in the construction trades and those with no occupation were also disproportionately represented among pig owners. Most, like the black, American-born, bill poster Rich Chase and his wife Sophie, had only one pig. One family with six children and a husband with no occupation kept ducks, and a sixty-year-old widow kept twenty ducks and a rooster on her 35-by-75-foot lot on Emma Street. Another widow, with no other visible means of support, kept 16 cows and 8 pigs. As in Montreal, those with cows tended to be wealthier people, including lawyers and wealthy widows. Carters, who had to rent or buy houses with space for their horses, took advantage of the space to keep pigs and cows as well.[133]

Lorna McLean has uncovered relatively high rates of animal holding in Ottawa, where 'a wide variety of animals' were kept in 1871. Pigs were kept in back yards across the city, and in houses near to unoccupied 'grazing' space by the river or railway yards. There too, working-class families of Irish or French-Canadian background were especially likely to keep pigs. She estimates that a '150 pound pig sold with a dressed weight of approximately 100 pounds could pay the rent for two to three months, or provide enough cash to purchase part of the winter's fuel.' Or it could provide 'bacon, ham, pork, and lard for the family'. Whereas pigs could forage for food, cows were more expensive to feed, costing up to $128 a year for hay, unless they were left free to graze. Once this possibility was curtailed by the passing of by-laws forbidding them to roam, cows became a more solidly middle-class animal, limited to those with the space to house them and the money to feed them.

As cities became more densely populated, pigs, goats, and other animals were increasingly viewed as undesirable. By the 1860s large towns like Toronto and even Brantford had regulations prohibiting 'horses, cows, cattle, goats, sheep, swine or geese' from running at large, as well as a complex system of fines and maintenance costs for the owners of errant animals.[134] Similar by-laws were passed during the 1870s in Ottawa.

Yet pigs, cows and the occasional goat continued to 'run the streets' of Ontario towns. In Ottawa they were reported to 'disturb neighbours' gardens,' and 'run wild' well into the 1870s, resulting in fines of one dollar for a pig owner and two dollars for a goat owner. Whereas the pigs were probably tended during the day by the women, it was the men as legal owners of such property who appeared in court. Some found ingenious ways to avoid paying. Patrick Conway managed to escape a fine in 1865 by convincing the magistrate, to the great joy of the local reporters, that 'his hogs took the liberty complained of without his knowledge or sanction.'[135] Richard Ryan, a Toronto resident, escaped being sentenced in 1871 for letting his flock of thirty geese 'live and resort for the most part on the streets of the city' by denying they were his.[136]

The ability to milk a cow or make butter could be used by wives to improve their families' standards of living. It might also help their daughters find work as domestics or cooks, for even in cities working-class girls were often expected to be able to milk a cow or make butter. This seems to have been especially likely in Ottawa, which housed over eight hundred cows when the 1871 census was taken.[137] Advertisements in the *Ottawa Citizen* in that decade included ones for a 'cook who understands making butter,' and a 'cook who could bake and milk.'[138]

During the 1880s small towns across the province also placed curbs on the movement of animals. In 1882, the year it was incorporated as a village, Woodbridge passed a by-law to restrain 'horses, cows, calves, bulls, rams, sheep, oxen, pigs of every description, geese, turkeys, hens and all other poultry' from running at large. In 1888 Hespeler council legislated to 'restrain and regulate the running at large of stock.' By the 1880s by-laws outlawed the keeping of pigs in large Ontario cities – in Toronto in 1882 and Ottawa in 1883.[139] By-law number 1231 outlawed pigs throughout Toronto but allowed those wanting to keep cows to do so as long as they could keep the stable or byre a specified distance from adjoining dwelling houses. The distances varied in different sections of the city. All would have excluded families in the densely populated downtown areas, while still making it possible for wealthier families on large lots to keep several cows to ensure a supply of untainted milk. Anyone housing their cows correctly could continue to use vacant lots throughout the city as 'pasture land or as a paddock.'[140] In Toronto and Ottawa, as in Montreal somewhat earlier, it was pigs, which were most likely to be kept by working-class families, rather than cows that were made illegal.[141] Some of the ways poorer families could remain self-supporting were being curtailed.

Poultry was cheaper to keep and needed less room than either pigs or cows. As laws and lack of space curtailed the possibility of keeping larger animals, chickens remained a possibility. They had the added advantage of not wandering, and were often kept in basements. In Ottawa the local paper warned residents that this practice not only caused smells, but could spread disease. When poultry were first counted in the census in 1891, there were over 18,000 in Toronto, a significant number in a city with about 27,000 families.[142] Keeping hens could save the housekeeper the cost of eggs – some 12 to 20 cents a dozen in the early 1870s, 15 to 25 cents in the early eighties.[143]

Whether women bought or raised animals, vegetables or fruit, nineteenth-century cooking entailed considerably more preparation than it does today. Animals raised at home had to be butchered, skinned, and hung. Fowl had to be plucked and their innards removed. Home-grown and purchased vegetables alike had to be washed, and sugar, flour, barley, and other grains picked over carefully to remove impurities.[144] Only then could cooking begin. In poorer homes cooking was very simple, limited by the income of the family, the number of pots, and the space on the stove. An 'ordinary meal' consisted of meat and potatoes, bread, tea, sugar, and perhaps coffee. Bread was the basis of most working-class diets. Some wives made it; more bought it.[145] Increasingly bread was the one food most likely to be bought ready made. Alexander Cousineau, an Ottawa baker giving evidence in 1888, stated that his customers were 'almost wholly with the working class.' Because it was so central to survival, most men giving evidence knew the price of a loaf.[146] Most families receiving relief from the Toronto House of Industry in the 1860s and 1870s received only bread – two pounds per person per week. Only the sick were given vegetables and other foodstuffs, and occasionally an elderly couple were given tea or sugar as a treat.[147]

The technology of cooking and all other domestic labour remained rudimentary in working-class homes. While capitalism had introduced major changes to the machinery of production, the only significant changes in nineteenth-century homes were the replacement of fireplaces for cooking with cook stoves, the connection of growing numbers of households to the city water supply, and, for middle-class families, the growing use of gas and electricity. The American historian Susan Strasser has shown what a full-time, labour-intensive, physically demanding job housework was for most married women during the nineteenth century. She demonstrates how women's role as providers of food changed through the century both as more goods could be bought rather than produced and as stoves replaced fireplaces for cooking. She argues that the advent of new fuels – first lighting oils, then, at the end of the century, electricity – together with the spread of running water, lightened women's tasks, changed the rhythms of work in the home, and created new kinds of dependency.[148] Ruth Schwartz Cowan has examined similar changes but argues, in contrast, that most nineteenth-century changes lightened men's and children's rather than women's labour and that women's work intensified as higher expectations about cleanliness and cooking prevailed.[149]

No Canadian research has examined what expectations were in working-class homes, or what technology existed. Neither electricity nor gas appears to have been installed in most working-class homes till after the turn of the century. Men in cities might chop firewood after work or on their days off and carry it in to the stove, but the long hours of their work made it likely, as Cowan suggests, that wives and children would have had to do so at times.

Fuel for heating and light used up about 10 per cent of the working people's budgets recorded by Young in 1873. Cheap cordwood was an important employment benefit for Great Western Railway workers, as Paul Craven shows.[150] Some economies could be made if families could afford to buy their wood and coal in bulk at cheaper times of year. Many, however, could not. When money was short, children were sent to scrounge for wood on construction sites or wharves, for wood shavings in mills, or for discarded lumps of coal and scraps of wood in back alleys and in rail and factory yards.[151] When every cent counted, such small economies made a difference. In the most desperate cases, people burned anything they could to keep warm. When Bridget Clark, a thirty-year-old Toronto widow, applied for charity in the winter of 1867, she had burned an old bedstead for want of fuel.[152]

By the 1880s Toronto newspaper advertisements proclaimed the blessedness of oil and gas stoves by emphasizing the labour they would save wives as there was 'no coal to carry, no ashes to remove.'[153] Yet such stoves were beyond the reach of most working-class families who continued to rely on wood, coal, and sometimes coke.[154] Some poor families bought stoves second-hand, and in dwellings where several families lived together they might share the stove. A widow, Bridget Murphy, and a deserted wife, Johanna Canrahan, were using the same stove in their shared house at the rear of King Street when they applied for help from the House of Industry in 1867. That same year the wife of a policeman who had lost his job, probably for drinking, captured the pity of the visitor from the House of Industry by reporting how she had gone to her former mistress as she had no fuel to roast the piece of meat she had for their Christmas dinner.[155] Among St John's Ward residents seeking relief in the winter of 1881 was an elderly couple, Mary Bolan and her husband, who shared their stove with another family, the Jacksons. The investigators for the Toronto House of Industry were reluctant to give the Bolans the coal they requested, fearing that the Jacksons would profit from it. When the Richards of Albert Street had sought relief, deep in the middle of the previous winter, they had no stove at all, possibly having pawned it to pay for food.[156]

Carrying water was as physically demanding as carrying wood or coal. 'A 2-gallon (9-L) bucket of water weighs about 16 lb (7.3kg),' quite a weight for a sick or pregnant woman obliged to lug it upstairs or across a muddy backyard.[157] The water that working-class wives used for cooking, washing, laundry, and cleaning came from a variety of sources. Evidence taken at the Royal Commission on the relations of Labour and Capital gives us glimpses of the provision of water in different Ontario towns. In Windsor, most households were connected to the municipal water system, which pumped water from the Detroit River, but a few wells were still in use. The local health officer was busily persuading the locals to switch to river water, although a few stuck to the 'idea that water from the river is scarcely good because it has not the old well flavor attached to it.' Given that the community upstream was sending its sewage into the river, their resistance was perhaps more rational than he implied! In Cornwall some houses still had no water laid on in the late 1880s. Paul Dane, a weaver at the Stormont cotton mill, reported that his family got their drinking water from a well and their washing water out of the canal. By hauling their own water they could save paying a man to bring it from the waterworks every month.[158]

In Petrolia the water seems to have been tainted by gas from the oil wells along with salt deposits, hindering the development of a municipal water supply. There, water was 'taken around every morning and delivered at the houses' at '1 cent a pail.' In St Thomas there was no waterworks, 'except from the creek.' Household water all came from wells, many of which were believed to be contaminated.[159] In 1888 the collector of information for the Bureau of Industries reported that the sanitary condition of St Thomas was

anything but satisfactory. Diphtheria and typhoid fever have been prevalent, the former in most cases being attributable to poor ventilation in old dwelling houses with low ceilings, and kitchen garbage thrown out upon the ground undergoing decomposition for want of drains. Fully three-fourths of the well water is condemned by the public and the board of health.[160]

Little wonder the citizens greeted the installation of water-supply systems with 'civic celebrations and rhapsodic editorials.'[161]

As the century advanced, women in the larger cities were more and more likely to live in houses connected to the civic water system. In Toronto the number of houses with a connection increased from fewer than four out of ten in the mid-1870s to between eight and nine out of ten by the early 1880s.[162] In Hamilton the situation seems to have been similar. In 1876 'water lines served barely half of the block frontages, but by 1896 the proportion had climbed to seven out of ten.' Doucet and Weaver suggest that the families of labourers were the least likely to be served and acknowledge how difficult it could be for them to persuade their landlords to connect their dwellings to the main.[163]

Poor families were consistently those least likely to benefit from city water supplies.[164] The wives of poorly paid workers, of sick or unemployed men, and widows continued to rely on water from wells and cisterns, collecting it themselves or badgering their husbands and offspring to do so. David Sobel found that in 1878, the year that the installation charge for attachment to the water mains was abolished in Toronto, the vast majority of households on streets like Agnes, Elizabeth, and Centre streets, in the southern parts of St John's Ward, where poor families lived, relied on wells and cisterns, with all the dangers of contamination that entailed. Only 6 of the 122 households on Agnes Street and 9 of the 209 on Elizabeth Street were attached to the city water supply. These figures excluded those living in houses built at the rear of the lot, which were even less likely to be connected.[165] Seven years later the situation had improved, but still only about half of the homes were using the city water supply. Others were still relying on wells and cisterns, some of them deemed foul, or getting their water in other ways.[166] Even when the house was connected to the water mains, most wives had only one tap, not always conveniently located. They still had to carry water to the stove to heat and to wherever the washing was done.

Nor was the carrying of tubs, pails, and basins of water finished once the washing or cleaning was done. Not only did many houses not have a water connection, but sewers were often rudimentary. Women continued to heave water out windows and dispose of their slops in the easiest ways possible, to the great and justified concern of health reformers and passers-by alike. While this may not have caused health problems in small towns where lots were large, in growing cities like Toronto, it compounded sanitary problems. When inspectors from the Toronto Board of Health investigated conditions in Saint John's Ward, they found that over a third of those visited on Centre and Chestnut streets were throwing their slops into the street. This compared to about one in ten households in the city as a whole.[167] The vast majority did not have yards that the inspectors considered unhealthy. Most housewives probably struggled to keep such small, unhealthy houses as clean as possible, with little help from landlords who did not always ensure that the water from wells was pure or that the house was served by the city water supply. The rudimentary state of sewers, often little more than open gutters or ditches, compounded the sanitary problems, especially in the densely populated parts of the cities.

Washing, Cleaning, and Charring

The need to carry water, the weight of wet clothes, and the physical labour required to wring them out and hang them to dry made washing the most hated of nineteenth-century household tasks. In summer firing up the stove to boil water overheated the houses, while in winter fingers froze in the icy rinsing water. Susan Strasser describes the work involved:

Without running water, gas, or electricity, even the most simplified hand laundry process consumed staggering amounts of time and labor. One wash, one boiling, and one rinse used about fifty gallons of water – or four hundred pounds – which had to be moved from pump or well or faucet to stove and tub, in buckets and wash boilers that might weigh as much as forty or fifty pounds. Rubbing, wringing, and lifting water-laden clothes and linens ... wearied women's arms and wrists and exposed them to caustic substances.[168]

Rural women sometimes wrote nothing else than 'wash day' in their diary for Monday, as if that was explanation enough. Sara Louisa Bowlby, who lived near Port Dover wrote rather smugly on the 3 February 1862, 'Today is washday for it is Monday, but it does not trouble me much for I am here in school.' Five years later her sister remarked, 'Monday morning wash day and raining in the bargain. Oh how disagreeable but it generally does rain on Monday.'[169]

Hauling large containers of boiling water was heavy, and dangerous, as in the case of an Ottawa woman who scalded herself with boiling water while doing her housework.[170] If a woman had a backyard wash house, she could keep the dampness and heat out of the house and avoid so much water carrying. One Toronto housewife living on Centre Street in July 1882 advertised in the *News* for a washing yard to rent. An outside yard may have offered a well, washing space, and somewhere to dry the clothes. For, in small urban homes with little outside space, it was also a challenge to get the clothes dry. On wet winter days the washing was hung in front of fireplaces or around stoves, creating a fire hazard. Outside clothes-lines criss-crossed the backyards and alleys, draping parts of the city in washing that stands out clearly in nineteenth-century photographs.

For most working-class women the technology of washing was simple – a washing tub and a washboard powered by their own exertion, though domestic washing machines were manufactured from the 1860s. In 1863 the Barrie newspaper was advertising V.R. Powers' Patent Victoria Washing Machine as the 'cheapest and the best on the market' – at $6.50. Ladies were invited to try it out.[171] The Knights of Labor newspaper that was published in Hamilton, the *Palladium*, advertised washing machines for home use during the 1880s. Drawing on the nativism that was rampant in campaigns against the importation of Chinese labour, the

Eagle Steam Washing Machine Company suggested that women could combine a boycott of Chinese laundries with saving the 'back breaking, woman killing' work with a washboard by buying a washing machine. Their machine was so easy, they suggested, that a fourteen-year-old could wash fifty to a hundred pounds in one hour.[172] Clearly some fractions of the working class were seen as potential consumers of such household appliances. Just who bought them and how widespread they were requires investigation.[173] So too does their usefulness. Susan Strasser suggests that few nineteenth-century washing machines saved much labour – they eliminated only the rubbing stage of washing. Overnight soaking and initial boiling were still necessary, and the agitators had to be cranked by hand.[174]

Washing took so much time, water, and energy that women tried to avoid it if they could. When one of the Stephens family in Glencairn, Simcoe County, agreed to board a young girl attending school in town, it was explicitly agreed that 'she is to have her washing done at home.'[175] Those able to pay for their laundry to be done were only too happy not to have this messy, wet, and lengthy task performed in their own homes. For those working-class wives whose family income had reached this level, hiring a washerwoman must have been a major time and energy saver.[176]

The wealthier women who avoided doing their own washing created opportunities for others to augment their family incomes. Housewives seeking washerwomen often specified they wanted the laundry done somewhere else – a 'Laundress to take home laundry weekly' – advertised one Ottawa woman.[177] Some seeking to attract good domestics clearly thought their chances were better if they specified that no washing was required. 'Wanted, at a private residence where a washerwoman is employed every week, a good general house servant,' wrote a Mrs Miller, the proprietor of a fancy goods store in London. An Ottawa woman seeking a 'servant who could cook' added 'washing given out.'[178]

Occasionally women who took in washing advertised their services,[179] but few washerwomen could afford advertisements. Many were widows, wives of sick men, or deserted women often with several children too young to earn even a child's pittance. Their employment agencies were signs on their door, word of mouth, or even the washing hanging on their lines. The rewards were small and unpredictable, never furnishing even the most basic living unless combined with other income or ways of economizing. And the work was likely to disappear when economic recessions hit. Hard-pressed widows who scraped 'together a paltry existence by scrubbing floors and taking in washing' were among those most likely to have to turn to charities like the Toronto House of Industry for food and fuel. Some washed in their own homes; more, perhaps lacking even the basics for washing, went 'out to wash and scrub.'[180] They tended to cluster together, sharing housing, child care, and poverty in poorer parts of the cities, which, like lower St John's Ward, were not too far from wealthier homes where they might find work.

While women who washed to make money could do so in their own homes, charring, that other set of basic household cleaning skills had to be done in the homes of others when done for pay. The sweeping, dusting, and general cleaning this involved were part of the work of most live-in domestic servants. As towns and cities grew, and as the century advanced, charring was more and more likely to be day work; indeed 'go out by the day' came to mean being being a charwoman. The wife of Mr Gloynes, the unemployed labourer interviewed by the *Globe* in 1883, was making $8 to $10 a month as a charwoman. This seems a remarkable income from such work; yet it was well under half of what even an unskilled worker like her husband might have earned at $1.00 to $1.25 a day had he found steady work.[181] The work day of such a woman involved piecing together income from the different families that employed her, either steadily or intermittently. Catherine Cox, a twenty-seven-year-old Toronto mother of two young girls whose husband had disappeared to the United States, had no regular work in 1867 but obtained 'a day now and then.' Poorer women combined charring with other ways of raising money. Margaret Keating of Toronto, who had been separated from her husband for some five years in 1867, combined charwork 'when she [could] get it' with quilting.[182]

Sewing and Knitting for Family and Pay

Like cleaning and washing, the skills involved in fabric making and transformation – knitting, sewing, mending, and in some cases spinning or weaving, were among the ones that women drew on for their own families and to raise money when necessary. Most women could sew at least well enough to mend clothes and make dresses, one of the last kinds of clothing to be available ready-made. Since clothing was a flexible expense, a wife's abilities could make major savings. In the budgets of 1873 outlined in Table 1, shoes and clothing absorbed somewhere between 12 and 16 per cent of expenditures. Ready-made men's clothing dropped in price in the later decades of the century as more and more was produced in factories, but new clothes were a luxury, bought infrequently and in good times only. Most women's clothes were home-made well into the twentieth century, so the cost of much women's and children's clothing was in the cloth. Women mended and remade their own clothes and those of their children.

Among working-class families it appears to have been increasingly rare for women to spin or weave at home.[183] Cloth could be bought at reasonable prices, daughters working in textile mills might bring small amounts home, and neighbours could exchange scraps. Knitting, in contrast, for those who could get wool, provided cheap socks, sweaters, gloves, and other winter clothing, or could be done to raise money.[184] What happened when women knitted for others requires investigation. Widows, deserted wives, and other women seeking relief from the Toronto House of Industry in the 1860s reported 'knitting and sewing.' This may partially have been because in 1864 they began to require that women applying for relief knit 'stockings and woolens, which the house disposes of for their benefit' to discourage lazy and drunken applicants. Knitting may have been easier for some older women than sewing, for it did not require quite such good eyesight, although arthritic fingers would make it extremely painful. Eliza Holland, an elderly widow who lived with her widowed daughter on Duchess Street in Toronto, was reported to be 'pretty well past work except a little knitting' in 1867. Her daughter took in sewing. Their plight moved the investigator to recommend that they receive bread for six weeks as well as coal.[185] Ann Tunor, probably a widow, was earning three dollars a week by knitting in 1881. Although the rent for what was most likely a run-down, unhealthy house at the rear of 18 Albert Street St John's Ward only cost her four dollars a month, she could not feed, clothe, and keep herself and her three young children on the remaining two dollars a week. She too turned to the Toronto House of Industry for food and fuel.[186]

Sewing was the skill most likely to enable a woman to add to the family's revenues. Across the province, in villages, small towns, and big cities women found numerous different ways to use their sewing to complement the wages of others, to tide them over in bad times, or to support themselves and their children. Some women whose husbands were unemployed or sick or had deserted them or died set up independently in their own homes as dressmakers, sewing for neighbours in exchange for other goods or services, or for customers for cash. Others no doubt found work at small local enterprises, relying on word of mouth, personal contacts, or advertisements in the papers. Until after the turn of the century, women's clothing continued to be custom-made by skilled seamstresses working from their homes or small shops. This practice provided employment possibilities for many women.[187] As the century advanced, more women sewed at home for factory owners who put out men's clothing and paid by the piece.

Sewing for cash thus took place in many different ways, some organized by the women themselves, others by industrial capitalists. Some women were skilled workers who made complete garments; others only completed work begun elsewhere. In the 1860s in Glencairn, a small lumber-milling village in the midst of Simcoe County farming country, the local shoemaker's wife, for example, earned 30 cents for 'facing mitts' and a further $1.40 for making 'pants and a vest.'[188] In 1870 a Mrs Duffy in Barrie advertised that she would 'clean clothing, removing spots and stains, repair gentlemen's clothing, and make up garments on reasonable terms and short notice.'[189] An Ottawa woman, possibly short of money after Christmas or, more likely having trouble balancing the budget when costs were highest and income invariably low, advertised in the local paper for 'employment in sewing. Would either sew at residence of employer or take sewing home to do.'[190]

Sewing, like washing or knitting, could be done at home. That made it desirable for women who were sick or weak or had children to supervise. Thus Elizabeth Waters of Pine Street in Toronto started 'taking in sewing for a living' after her 'health became bad' and she could no longer go out to service. Mrs Clark's history was similar. This widow, who was looking after her two children and her seventy-six-year-old mother, 'used to go out to scrub and wash,' but she had hurt her leg and could 'only sew.' Elizabeth Porter was also looking after an elderly mother as well as three children. After her plasterer husband disappeared, she and her mother tried 'to make a living by pant making.'[191]

The transformations that accompanied the growth of factories created possibilities of paid work at home for women in some sectors – especially clothing, while reducing them in others. Before the 1860s some of the sewing involved in shoe production had been put out to men and women working at home. Gregory Kealey reports that this practice was pretty well eliminated by the 1860s and gone by the 1880s. Most women employed in that industry were in specific departments of the new factories.[192] The plight of women whose skills had been rendered obsolete is captured in the comment of a visitor from the Toronto House of Industry on investigating Julia Burlow. In 1863 this widow was living in an upstairs room on Drummond Street with three children to support. She 'used to stitch boots and shoes – now her occupation is gone.'[193]

In clothing, in contrast, the expansion in Toronto, Hamilton, and other cities of factories making ready-made men's garments increased the possibilities of homework. Growing numbers of women, helped often by their children, found employment sewing at home on work put out by clothiers. In 1868 the *Globe* described whole families in Toronto that worked at home making some of the coarser descriptions of men's garments for the ready-made clothing market:

Often, in such instances, the child of eight or nine summers is made a source of material help ... In the same way the female head of the house, a group of daughters, and perhaps, the male members of the family if no better occupation is available, turn in to assist the father in adding to their means of support.[194]

Nearly thirty years later A.W. Wright still found that the women he visited in their homes were helped by children 'of very tender years.' The women and children worked irregularly, but for many more hours than allowed by the factory acts, which did not cover such workplaces.[195]

Homework was widespread. In Hamilton at William Sanford's enterprise, only about 10 per cent of the workers were employed within the factory in 1874. Some two thousand women worked outside.[196] Alexander Whyte Wright's 1896 'Report upon the Sweating System in Canada' gives some idea of the conditions of this kind of home work at the close of the century. He set out to determine the extent to which manufacturers were giving 'out work directly to people who make them up in their own homes,' giving it out to subcontractors, or having work done within their factories.[197] He found a mixture of all three, with the proportions varying in different towns:

'In Hamilton ... the greater part of the work is done by contractors and the balance by people who work at home. In Toronto the same system prevails, though in that city the proportion of work done in private houses is greater. In Ottawa, Montreal and Quebec the contract system scarcely exists ... the greater part of the work is done by families in their homes.'[198]

When Mackenzie King investigated how uniforms for the military and postal workers were being made two years later, he found a similar situation.[199] In 1901 when a question about the number of homeworkers was first included in the census, some 7,500 women across Ontario were working in their homes manufacturing for the garment industry.[200]

It was cheaper for capitalists to pay women to work outside the factory stitching together parts of garments that had been cut out by the more highly paid male workers under the factory roof.[201] There were no rents to pay, and the huge pool of females seeking work in their homes guaranteed that wages could be kept down and that they were unlikely to organize. While women may well have discussed the prices different employers paid and been acutely aware of the better places to seek sewing, they usually had little negotiating power.

Women working at home for clothing manufacturers used whatever space was available for their sewing machines and bundles of clothing, frequently setting up in their bedrooms or living rooms. Most worked on pants and vests or shirts, whereas those in contractors' shops more often made men's coats. They never made a whole garment. They sewed together the parts and returned them to the contractor or the factory. From the 1860s on they were expected to do their sewing on a sewing machine, and these were vigorously promoted by manufacturing companies, which arranged credit financing as well as repossession in cases of non-payment.[202]

The money women received varied, but it was always very little. The clothing-trades employers had no compunction about exploiting them both as female workers and as women working at home. Their pay was by the piece, and only by sustained labour, by working 'their nails bare' could they make even minimal earnings. Production was seasonal, characterized by dull seasons when little work was available.[203] Women sewing for an Ottawa dry goods firm that put out all its work in the late 1880s received 65 cents for a coat and $1.50 for a dozen shirts without collars, $1.80 with. The employer, Mr Charles Bryson, like so many other employers in the garment industry, had no idea how long it took a woman to make a coat. And, like other clothing contractors, he rationalized their exploitation by maintaining that the women sewed in their spare time, sitting down to the work 'any time they ... got to themselves.'[204] They did not. In 1868 the *Globe* reporter estimated that the mothers and daughters he visited were working '16 to 18 hours steadily for six days a week.'[205] Mackenzie King found women working similar hours in 1898.[206]

Jean Scott placed the wages of tailoresses between $3 and $4 a week in 1892, but pointed out carefully that for homeworkers 'all depends on getting steady work.'[207] Under these conditions it seemed 'almost inevitable' to Wright that wages fell to the 'lowest point at which employees can afford to work,' lower he was convinced, than in the contractors' shops.[208] Mackenzie King found in 1898 that homeworkers earned as little as $1 or $2 a week. Those working fifteen- or sixteen-hour days grossed only $3.[209]

The great advantage of homework for these women was, of course, that they could combine it with child care and housework. Mothers called on children of all ages to help while also keeping an eye on younger ones. For, as Jean Thompson Scott remarked in her study *The Conditions of Female Labour in Ontario*, published in 1892,

Women whose husbands are dead or are not able to support them, will not go out as long as they have children at home to care for, but prefer if they can, to engage in some work which will keep them at home ... In many cases they take in sewing or dressmaking, and do tailoring for the wholesale trade at their homes.[210]

Youngsters helped with sewing. They also went to the factory to collect the bundles of clothing and to return the completed garments. Without this 'cheap or free labour of children,' argues John Bullen, 'families would have gained virtually nothing for their efforts.'[211]

Clothing was the main but not the only industry where homework occurred. In almost any trade that entailed sewing, some work seems to have been put out during the 1850s and sixties. The *Globe* reported in 1868 that women who had built up their skill in the millinery and fur trades before their marriage occupied 'an idle hour at the fireside in the winter time stitching [to] augment their husbands' salary ... to the extent of six or seven dollars a week.' Women working at home in this trade were reported to be mostly sewing buffalo robes.[212] In Ottawa and Hull during the early 1860s some '20 or 30 families' were employed at home making paper boxes for the Eddy Company, which was at that point producing a wide variety of home cleaning equipment, including pails, wash tubs, zinc wash boards, clothes pins, broom handles, and matches.[213]

Women who combined sewing at home, washing for others, or charring by the day with the cooking, washing, cleaning, and child care they performed for their own families did not work what we would recognize today as a double day. The labour for their own families and that performed for others were sometimes combined, sometimes separate. Some took place in their own homes, some in the houses of others. Their work for others seldom took up a specific part of the day and their own labour another. Rarely did their money-generating efforts fill up such a chunk of their day that it was reported to census takers or enumerators for city directories. Usually it was not wage-earning, but payment for services rendered – with no fixed rate and no guarantee that it would continue. It was so like their own housework that it has faded from most historical records.

TAKING IN BOARDERS

For many women attempting to add to the family income, it could be more profitable to draw on their skills in combination by taking in a boarder or two than attempt to sell them separately by sewing, cooking, cleaning or washing. Recently arrived male and female immigrants, unmarried labourers seeking work in single-enterprise towns, young people new to the city and seeking work often had neither a mother nor a wife to feed, clothe, and care for them. This need for room and board opened up possibilities to many women seeking extra cash.

From small sawmilling villages like Glencairn in Simcoe County to downtown Toronto, the expansion in the scale of local enterprises and the demand for labour along with the continued need for women's cooking, sewing, teaching, and nursing skills provided numerous ways of generating income. In Glencairn some local women were able to make money boarding workers during the months they were working in the mill. Mr and Mrs James McBain, for example, had three male labourers boarding with them when the census was taken in 1871. In the previous two years McBain's account at the general store had been credited with $253 for taking in boarders.[214] Over the following two years he received a further $809.94 from M.N. Stephens, who owned the mill and the general store, for boarding his workers – pretty well double a labourer's wage. With three daughters, aged 22, 19, and 16 in 1871, the domestic work involved would not have been too onerous for Mrs McBain. In the same community, a Mrs Gravelle rented a house from M.N. Stephens, paid him for pasturing one cow, and was paid $105.96 for 216 days' board of men, and 67 days' board of carpenters between 1877 and 1878.[215]

The expanding economies, combined sometimes with housing shortages in many small Ontario towns and growing cities, offered many other ways in which a little money could be earned by offering room and board. Teachers had to be housed; so did children coming in from farms to attend school. Small municipalities paid families to care for orphans and indigents. A Mrs Warren of Thornhill was paid a set amount of money each month in 1861 'for foundling.'[216] In Woodbridge, several residents were paid for the 'keep of indigent persons,' and for 'board.'[217] The Cotton family of St John's Ward in Toronto was paid $8 a month in 1881 to take in two babies.[218]

Clearly, the boarding of farm labourers, mill workers, apprentices, transient workers, students, indigents, or foundlings could offer the possibility of earning significant amounts of cash. At $2 a week for a female and a dollar more for a male, board in Ottawa in 1870 could add $100 to $150 to a family's coffers minus costs. This was comparable to what a child might earn working in the sewing trade, and was a considerable supplement to the $300 or so a labourer might earn at $1 a day working six days a week every week of the year – a level of employment few attained.[219]

Boarding arrangements varied. Some families took one or two extra people into their homes. Other women, sometimes widows or deserted wives, set up more formal boarding or lodging houses, ranging from cheap and often dirty lodging houses to clean, well-furnished rooms with baths and toilet facilities. Such institutions were distinguished by the clientele they aimed at and the comfort they could offer. According to C.S. Clark, lodgers were lucky to have a sheet on their bed in some. 'Double, triple and even quadruple beds' were stuffed into 'single rooms and closets.' Flimsy partitions between rooms hid neither snores nor conversations.[220] Historians dealing with boarding houses have written largely of those set up for immigrants, especially sojourning males, or of boarders in relation to family structures.[221] More research is needed into other types of boarding arrangements. This clearly was an area where women could run a successful business out of their home if they had enough money, or daughters to help with the large amount of washing and cooking.[222] Census studies give us a good idea of how widespread this phenomenon was, but more research is needed into the kinds of families that decided to take in boarders, why they did so, the nature of their housing and financial arrangements, the work involved, and especially on how those extra residents fitted into the household.[223]

While working-class families did take in boarders and other residents to earn cash, the cost and the space needed made this practice more common among white-collar workers and professional families, who might house a young clerk or bank worker, than among the unskilled. All studies suggest that the likelihood of any families taking in boarders dropped between the 1850s and 1880s as housing crises diminished and wealthier families sought more privacy and their wives less work.[224]

Boarders were a mixed blessing. Taking them in usually involved cooking their meals as well as providing sleeping space and bedding. Lodgers who simply rented a room, eating their meals elsewhere, seem to have become common only at the end of the century.[225] Providing bed and board meant extra cooking, cleaning, washing, and even sewing for the housewife and the children. 'Family run boarding houses daily called on children to change sheets, clean rooms, serve meals and wash dishes. Some homes took in extra customers, or 'mealers,' at the dinner hour, often resulting in several sittings a day.'[226] Many working-class houses simply didn't have the extra labour power, the space, or the money to pay for bed linen.

Furthermore, boarders could be demanding about what they were fed, occasionally creating such a disturbance that they ended up in court.[227] Two male boarders in Ottawa in 1866 experienced the full force of their landlady's wrath when they complained about the quality of the 'grub' she provided. They tried to take her to court, but the case was dismissed.[228] Nor could boarders always be relied on to pay their board, behave respectably, or leave without some of their landlord's posses-sions. When money paid by boarders was crucial to a family budget, fail-ure to pay could have dire consequences for the boarder. One Ottawa boarder was brutally beaten by his landlord when he tried to leave with-out settling his debt.[229]

PROVIDING, EXCHANGING, AND SELLING SERVICES

Work in the home involved much more than the production or purchase of food, its transformation into meals, and sewing, washing, and clean-ing. Most women who married had children who required care as infants, socialization, and some supervision. Husbands expected atten-tion and sexual satisfaction. All family members were liable to fall sick frequently, especially in the crowded, poor dwellings of the lower levels of the urban working class. Elderly parents, even lodgers, might have to be cared for because they were either sick or simply old and frail. These services were fitted into a woman's daily routine, sometimes upsetting it completely, at others involving little mental or physical energy.

Like sewing, washing, or taking in boarders, these services could also be a source of extra money if necessary. Daughters or mothers might sell their bodies – regularly to make ends meet or occasionally in desperation or to pay for special treats. Women sometimes combined prostitution with selling alcohol illegally from their homes – another way of raising money at home, but prostitutes were most often single girls. Younger girls worked and lived together, often under the control and shelter of a madam, in a brothel that was both workplace and home. They appear to have moved frequently, sometimes to other established brothels, some-times setting up more cooperative arrangements with other prostitutes. Older women were more likely to work the streets.[230]

Prostitution was not the only way women could use their bodies to earn needed cash. Women with an adequate supply of milk might make money feeding other people's children or deserted babies. Formal adver-tisements for wet-nurses seem pretty rare, but there are enough in news-papers of the 1850s and 1860s to make it clear that this was a fairly widespread practice.[231] In Toronto, the House of Industry placed deserted babies with wet-nurses during the 1860s, paying women $4 a month or $1 a week for the care and the milk. Most women fed the child for at least a month, but on occasion they returned them earlier for a variety of reasons. Mary Fairburn fed the baby she had been given for only ten days, returning it because she was going to the States. Jane Baillie was given a two-hour-old coloured child in late April 1862. She appears to have nursed it for one month, but at the end of May she returned it. Why she did so is not clear. Had she disliked breast-feeding a coloured baby, she would probably not have kept it a month. On its return, however, the child was sent out to a 'coloured' woman, Emily Grant, who lived at 117 Elizabeth Street – the same street as Jane Baillie.[232]

Who were such wet-nurses? Detailed and careful research might reveal more about women like Emily Grant and Jane Baillie. Mothers whose own offspring had died or been weaned might take on such work; so might young unmarried mothers who had given up their babies after initially breast-feeding them. Some women nursed both their own child and another one. This is what the 'young healthy woman with her first child' who was 'desirous to procure a situation as a wetnurse' seemed to be offering when she advertised in the *London Free Press* in 1861.[233] The same year another London family explicitly sought 'a woman having more milk than her own child requires, who will be willing to suckle a little baby 3 or 4 times a day.'[234] To produce a milk supply for two children generally required plenty of food and rest. Perhaps Jane Baillie's surrender of the coloured baby was related to her health. One week after receiving another little baby in July, she returned the boy 'on account of being sick,' and her name does not appear again on the House of Industry's list.[235] While some healthy fit women could keep their milk supply steady over a long period, many could not. Wet-nursing was likely to be a temporary occupation, governed by the capacity of women's bodies.

Married women, widows, and young girls alike, in contrast, could look after other people's offspring. Young girls seeking to help the family finances were in demand to look after children. Advertisements specified the qualities desired – 'clean and careful girl' wanted 'to take charge of baby,' 'nurse to take charge of children,' or '13–14 year old girl as nanny.'[236] Older sisters cared for younger siblings. Mothers kept an eye on the children of others going out to work.

WHAT WAS A WIFE WORTH?

Women's and children's work cleaning, cooking, sewing, and shopping as well as caring for sick family members and calming tensions and conflicts went together to fashion the 'comfortable home' that 'makes the workingman all the more ready to work.'[237] As we have seen, each of the skills that went into running a household might also be used to stretch the wages a family head and older children could earn, to fill in if the wage-earners fell ill, took to drinking, deserted, or died. Much of this work went on when wage-earners were absent from the home. Men were aware of only some of the tasks their wives and children performed.

When their wives fell sick, the men no doubt became acutely aware of the different domestic tasks that kept their households going and made their lives more comfortable. When a wife died, the reality of their contributions hit with full force, as did the importance of a man's earning power when it was the husband who died.

In order to recognize the value of work done in the home, one can calculate what a man saved by having a wife.[238] Perhaps the best way of thinking about this is to consider the services a man might have had to pay for had his wife died in childbirth, leaving him with a newborn baby and three children aged, perhaps three, five and nine. No wage-earner could afford to quit his job to look after his children. A widower had to find other ways of combining wage-earning with fathering and domestic labour. Not surprisingly many remarried quickly. Some moved in with their parents; others drew on the services of sisters or older daughters. In the absence of these possibilities, our hypothetical widower would have had to turn to the female labour market. Perhaps it was just such a man who advertised in the *London Free Press* for 'a careful, middle-aged woman, who is with experience and of a kind disposition, to take charge of 3 young children.'[239] The first task facing a widower whose wife had died in childbirth was to find a wet-nurse for the newborn baby. He also needed someone to look after the children while he was at work, although the nine-year-old and perhaps even the five-year-old could be sent to school. To replace all his wife's services in the marketplace he would also have had to find someone to cook meals, clean house, do the washing, and perhaps do a little sewing. The easiest solution was a live-in housekeeper who would perform most of these tasks.

What would these services have cost him in mid- to late-nineteenth-century Ontario? We know so little about these casual labour markets that all that can be offered are estimates, although a careful systematic study in one town might reveal more consistent data. The fragments of information from different parts of the province used in earlier sections of this paper can be pieced together simply to give some idea of what it might have cost to replace a wife. We have seen that a wet-nurse could be hired in Toronto during the 1860s for $4 a month. A young nurse to look after the children might be had for not much more – say $4.50 a month. Laundresses in London around the same time could make about $6 a month. A general housemaid, willing to do plain cooking, but not wash-ing, might earn between $5 and $8 a month and live in.[240] If we add up the lowest of these costs, remembering that these were rates of pay that seldom allowed a woman to support herself, the total is staggering. During the 1860s our widower would have had to pay out some $20 a month if he had paid individual women to wet-nurse, care for his children, wash, and do housework and cooking. At $240 a year this would have consumed a fair proportion of most skilled workers' earnings and virtually all of those of a labourer, who might earn as little as $1 a day.

Clearly most working men could not afford to pay for a separate washerwoman, wet-nurse, housekeeper, and nurse for their children despite the minimal pay such women received. Nor would he need a wet-nurse for more than several months. Yet even hiring one woman to perform most of these tasks – perhaps a general housekeeper willing to cook, clean, wash, and sew could cost about $8 a month in the 1860s, or nearly $100 a year – a total still out of reach of a general labourer and most other workers. During the 1880s pay rates were similar. In Hamilton in 1881 a general servant could command $6 to $8, a housemaid or laundrymaid $7 to $9. In Ottawa a servant might get from $6 to $10, a cook from $8 to $12. Later in the eighties the average rate listed for the province as a whole was slightly higher – about $2.88 a week, or some $150 a year for a general servant. This was clearly more than most workers could afford.[241]

A different calculation produces a similar amount. In 1873 skilled workers like carpenters and machinists were paid 50 cents less a day if they received board. Over the year, their board would have cost them $182.50. If we deduct the lowest annual reported cost of food, which averaged $51 a person in Belleville, the rest of the domestic labour provided as part of the board was worth about $130 annually.[242]

None of these estimates take into account all the other aspects of a wife's work that saved or generated money. We have seen that women saved and made money by raising animals, producing vegetables, taking in sewing or washing, or going out by the day to scrub and clean other women's houses. Others shopped particularly carefully. Nor have I added what it might have cost had the man bought sexual satisfaction in the marketplace. All of these saved amounts of money can only be estimated, and their importance would have varied dramatically. Nevertheless, the attempt to reckon their worth does, I hope, underline the crucial contribution this work in the home made both to working-class families and to employers able to profit from it by keeping wages down.

At the very minimum a wife's domestic labour saved some $150 annually in the 1860s, perhaps nearer to $200 two decades later. Most widowers, indeed any married men, deprived of women's work and savings would have felt a sudden and rapid fall in their standard of living. Nineteenth-century wage-earners could only live in any comfort when an unpaid member of the household transformed their wages into a reasonable standard of living and stretched them when necessary.

Clearly, married men and earning sons and daughters were dependent on women's work in the home. Wives, in turn, were largely dependent on the wages of others in performing much of that work. Even the cash they earned themselves belonged legally to their husbands until 1872. This was modified somewhat by the first married women's property act of 1859, but court rulings affirmed that a husband's consent was required if the wife wished to dispose of her personal property. In 1872 the 'Act extending the Rights of Property of Married Women' gave wives power over their 'wages and personal earnings ... free from the debts or dispositions of the husband,' and allowed them to dispose of them without their husband's consent.[243] But no legislation recognized the value of domestic labour that saved rather than made money, and few wives earned wages, because work in the home remained a full-time, demanding job. Even when they did, few could earn enough to support their families themselves, even when they needed to as widows, deserted wives or spouses of sick and unemployed men.

Conclusion

The growth of industry in nineteenth-century Ontario transformed, but did not eliminate, the importance of the home as a workplace. The household remained the principal workplace, although there were changes in who worked there and the work they did. In the first half of the century farmers, artisans, professionals, and early industrial capitalists worked essentially out of their homes. Apprentices, domestics, and some farm labourers worked and lived in the homes of others. Homes were the major base for the domestic production of foodstuffs and clothing – largely the work of women. They were also the base for the production of a wide variety of other commodities, ranging from coffins and candles to sausages and cheese, that might be the work of either men or women. Housework continued to be the main occupation of the majority of the adult female population as well as of a large number of girls working in their own homes as well as in those of others.

Between 1850 and 1900 the varied employments undertaken in the home remained crucial to working-class survival, to the functioning of the labour market, and to the wider economy. Dependence on wages was seldom total. Women, helped by their children, and sometimes by the wage-earners too, found ways to produce and exchange goods and services that mitigated the dangers of relying entirely on wages.

The particular balance between purchase and production varied with the amount of wages earned, the life-cycle stage of the family, the local cost of food and rent, and the nature of the community in which working-class families lived. Overall, however, there were at least four changes in the second half of the century. Work in the home became increasingly female as more men, older sons, and some daughters were drawn into wage labour. Wage dependency increased as the possibilities of keeping animals and even gardens diminished and as people grew accustomed to goods like store-bought bread and manufactured men's clothing and aspired to a higher standard of living measured in part by store-bought furniture and kitchen utensils. As a corollary, the home production of food, clothing, and other goods diminished and the relative importance of good shopping and money management in the arsenal of a housewife's skills increased. Finally, by the last two decades of the century, male workers, especially those in organized skilled trades increasingly pushed for a wage that would support a whole family and began to talk in a way that at once celebrated women's role in the home but rendered their domestic labour less visible.

Despite these changes, the work done in homes across the province continued to be crucial to the survival and reproduction of the working class. Cash was not good to eat; wages had to be transformed into food, clothing, and shelter.[244] And they had to be stretched when money was low, work was irregular, or wage-earners were sick. As a result of lengthy strikes and long periods of unemployment or illness, some of the time working-class men and women had to continue to survive without wages. This could be done by wives' and daughters' drawing on housekeeping skills like washing, sewing, and cooking to earn cash. Mothers and sons and daughters could seek paid wage labour themselves. Or families could try to survive as much outside the cash economy as possible by scrounging, begging, or stealing food and clothing or by turning to charity. Thus, while working-class households as a whole were increasingly likely to buy rather than produce some of their basic foodstuffs, clothing, and household linen, there were fluctuating proportions of the working class that relied on home production, exchange, and various other non-wage means of survival.

Nineteenth-century workers were not concerned only with the control of work processes, but also with other issues that touched more closely on their family lives. The struggles of wage earners over hours, wages, and frequency of payment derived from and influenced consumption and daily life in the home. Men equated shorter hours, which usually meant having Saturday afternoon off, explicitly with having time to spend with their families. Across the province unionized and non-unionized men and women persuaded their employers to pay them more often and on specific days, arguing that this would help them or their wives shop economically. To the extent that they were successful and that family wage-earners handed over what they earned, this simplified the wives' task of making ends meet. At the same time, however, the identification of those wages with the wage-earners, and especially the family head hardened. Being a worker, earning a family wage, and being a man became intimately intertwined and in starker opposition to that increasingly female space – the home.

When wives could save money or make money by producing foodstuffs or other household needs themselves, they raised their family's standard of living. They also gave themselves some autonomy, a measure of independence from their reliance on the wages of others. For much of the century, that autonomy was limited by the law. Even after the law was changed to give married women the right to keep their own property and wages separate from their husband's, the economy and wider society offered working-class wives little chance to accumulate much of either. The importance of their work sustaining and perpetuating their families and the working class kept most women close to home. They were increasingly dependent on the wages of others to perform their daily tasks, which society was less and less likely to view as work.

NOTES

Much of what I draw on here was uncovered by Jennifer Steel, Jennifer Lund, Lisa-Anne Chilton, Jeanie Tummon, Lynn Berry, and Leigh Valliere, students in my graduate class in women's history at York; and by Helen Harrison, who did some of the research for me. I thank them all for sharing their findings.

1 'Diary,' Mrs Anne B. Bellamy, 29 January 1856, 20 October 1854 to 23 October 1855, Archives of Ontario, MV 838.
2 My ways of looking at what was going on in nineteenth-century Ontario homes are influenced by my study of Montreal during the same period. See Bettina Bradbury, *Working Families: Age, Gender and Daily Survival in Industrializing Montreal* (Toronto: McClelland and Stewart 1993). For a careful analysis of some of the concepts used in that study see Cynthia Comacchio, 'Beneath the "Sentimental Veil": Families and Family History in Canada,' *Labour/Le Travail* 33 (Spring 1994), 279–302.
3 The writing to date has over-dichotomized the study of the family wage economy, ascribing wages largely to men and offspring, and domestic labour to wives. While work on women's labour has revealed the variety of means by which they stretched their husbands' wages, little attention in Canada, or elsewhere, has been paid to non-wage strategies that were more likely to be undertaken by men – hunting, fishing, producing a variety of goods for sale, etc. Even the question of men holding several occupations has received little attention.

4 On rural women see especially Marjorie Cohen, *Women's Work, Markets, and Economic Development in Nineteenth–Century Ontario* (Toronto: University of Toronto Press 1988); Eliane Leslau Silverman, *The Last Best West: Women on the Alberta Frontier, 1880–1930* (Montreal: Eden Press 1984); Rosemary Ball, '"A Perfect Farmer's Wife": Women in 19th Century Rural Ontario,' *Canada: An Historical Magazine* 3, no. 2 (December 1975).

5 Susanna Moodie, *Roughing It in the Bush* (1855, repr. Toronto: McClelland and Stewart 1962); Susanna Moodie, *Life in the Clearings versus the Bush* (New York 1855); and Catharine Parr Traill, *The Canadian Settler's Guide* (1855, repr. Toronto: McClelland and Stewart 1969).

6 Henry Mayhew, *London Labour and the London Poor: The Classical Study of the Culture of Poverty and the Criminal Classes in the 19th Century* (London: Griffin, Bohn and Co. 1861–2, repr. New York: Dover Publications 1968); Charles Booth, *Life and Labour of the People of London* (London: Macmillan 1904); B.S. Rowntree, *Poverty: A Study of Town Life* (London: Thos Nelson and Sons 1902); Frédéric LePlay, *Les ouvriers européens: Études sur les travaux, la vie domestique et la condition morale des populations ouvrières de l'Europe* (Paris: Imprimerie Impériale 1855). The studies of two disciples of LePlay can be found in Pierre Savard, ed., *Paysans et ouvriers d'autrefois* (Quebec: Les Presses de l'Université Laval 1968).

7 For a fascinating look at what can be teased out of newspapers, government documents, and charity records about the ways that both men and women got by during a lengthy strike, see Bruce Scates, 'Gender, Household and Community Politics: The 1890 Maritime Strike in Australia and New Zealand,' in Raelene Frances and Bruce Scates, eds, *Women, Work and the Labour Movement in Australia and Aotearoa/New Zealand* (Sydney: Australian Society for the Study of Labour History 1991).

8 A useful discussion of households and their place in the economy can be found in Joan Smith and Immanuel Wallerstein, *Creating and Transforming Households: The Constraints of the World Economy* (Paris and Cambridge: Cambridge University Press 1992), 7–10.

9 I do not study this question systematically here but draw on the census-based research of Michael Katz, *The People of Hamilton, Canada West: Family and Class in a Mid–Nineteenth Century City* (Cambridge, Mass.: Harvard University Press 1975); and Michael Katz et al., *The Social Organization of Early Industrial Capitalism* (Cambridge, Mass: Harvard University Press 1982); David Gagan, *Hopeful Travellers: Families, Land, and Social Change in Mid-Victorian Peel County, Canada West* (Toronto: University of Toronto Press 1981) and Bradbury, *Working Families*.

10 Barbara Laslett and Johanna Brenner, 'Gender and Social Reproduction: Historical Perspectives,' *Annual Review of Sociology* no. 15 (1989): 282. Ellen Ross, '"Fierce Questions and Taunts": Married Life in Working Class London, 1870–1914,' *Feminist Studies* 8, no. 3 (1982); Kathryn Harvey, '"To Love, Honour and Obey": Wife-

Battering in Working–Class Montreal, 1869–1879,' *Urban History Review* 10, no. 2 (October 1990); Carole Turbin, 'Beyond Dichotomies: Interdependence in Mid-Nineteenth Century Working Class Families,' *Gender and History* 1, no. 3 (Autumn, 1989).

11 Meg Luxton, *More than a Labour of Love: Three Generations of Women's Work in the Home* (Toronto: Women's Press 1980); Paula Bourne, ed., *Women's Paid and Unpaid Work: Historical and Contemporary Perspectives* (Toronto: New Hogtown Press 1985); Bonnie Fox, ed., *Hidden in the Household: Women's Domestic Labour Under Capitalism* (Toronto: Women's Press 1980).

12 Joy Parr, *The Gender of Breadwinners: Women, Men, and Change in Two Industrial Towns, 1880–1950* (Toronto: University of Toronto Press 1990), 242–3.

13 David and Rosemary Gagan begin to pursue this question in 'Working-Class Standards of Living in Late-Victorian Urban Ontario: A Review of the Miscellaneous Evidence on the Quality of Material Life,' *Journal of the Canadian Historical Association* 1 (Victoria 1990). See also Trevor O. Dick, 'Consumer Behavior in the Nineteenth Century and Ontario Workers, 1885–1889,' *Journal of Economic History* 46 (June 1986); Michael Piva, *The Condition of the Working Class in Toronto, 1900–1921* (Ottawa: University of Ottawa Press 1979); and Edward J. Chambers, 'Addendum on the Living Standards of Toronto Blue Collar Workers in the 1900–1914 Era,' *Histoire sociale/Social History* 20, no. 40 (November 1987).

14 Bureau of Industries, Reports, 1888–9; Royal Commission on the Relations of Labour and Capital, Ontario Evidence, 1889 (hereafter RCRLC); Edward Young, *Labor in Europe and America* (1874; repr. Westport, Conn.: Greenwood 1970). Peter Baskerville and Eric Sager, 'Unemployment and the Working-Class Family: Work, Family and Income in Urban Canada in 1901,' paper presented at the Carleton Family History Conference, May 1994, suggests that in 1901 wages dropped significantly as men aged and the amount of time they worked fell.

15 Gagan and Gagan, 'Working-Class Standards,' 192–3. The Bureau of Industries' reports on which they base their study need to be read critically. They seem to report only wages earned in employment. Any money raised in other ways is hidden. The contribution of adult children also seems to be ignored. Furthermore, assumptions such as the notion that being able to purchase an increasing amount of what one needs necessarily represents an improvement in standard of living should be reconsidered. Growing purchasing power may reflect an increasing dependence on purchased commodities more than anything else.

16 The findings of Baskerville and Sager based on the 1901 census suggest a much less rosy picture than that given by the Gagans. 'Unemployment and the Working-Class Family.'

17 RCRLC, 1045.

18 Bureau of Industries, 1888, 1889.

19 RCRLC, 1121.

20 RCRLC, 154.

21 Bureau of Industries, 1889, 28; Gagan and Gagan, 'Working Class Standards of Living'; Bureau of Industries, 1888, 42.

22 RCRLC, 1078, 1108, 679, 687, 866, 424.

23 See Bureau of Industries, 1887, 23, for an example which lists the number of workers employed by town in each range of days.

24 More research on how people managed during this great depression would be useful. See Debi Wells, '"The Hardest Lines of the Sternest School": Working-Class Ottawa and the Depression of the 1870's' (MA thesis, Canadian Studies, Carleton University 1982).

25 Toronto House of Industry, Annual Reports, 1873–82.

26 *Globe*, 3 February 1883, cited in David M. Sobel, 'Household Economies and Material Life: Family Survival in Southern Saint John's Ward, 1879–1885' (Major research paper, History, York University 1982), 48.

27 RCRLC, 147; Bureau of Industries, 1888, 132.

28 Katz, Doucet, and Stern, *The Social Organization*, 254. I look more explicitly at girls and domestic labour in Bettina Bradbury, 'Gender at Work at Home,' in Bettina Bradbury, ed., *Canadian Family History: Selected Readings* (Toronto: Copp Clark Pitman 1992).

29 Bureau of Industries, 1887 Report, 38.

30 Katz, *The People of Hamilton*, 273–6; Katz et al., *The Social Organization*, 254–6, 312–19; see also my *Working Families*, 144–50.

31 RCRLC, 154–6.

32 Bureau of Industries, 1884, 33–41; See also Craig Heron in this volume.

33 Lorna McLean, 'Single Again: Widow's Work in the Urban Family Economy, Ottawa, 1871.' *Ontario History* 83, no. 2 (June 1991). We need to know more about how working-class families used life insurance during the nineteenth century and about the prevalence of work-based pension and insurance schemes.

34 Bureau of Industries, 1888, 46–7.

35 Bureau of Industries, 1889, 10.

36 RCRLC, 159, 286, 591, 803, 618, 924, 969–70.

37 R. Harris, G. Levine, and B.S. Osborne, 'Housing Tenure and Social Classes in Kingston, Ontario, 1881–1901,' *Journal of Historical Geography* 7, no. 3 (1981), 281.

38 Doucet and Weaver, *Housing the North American City* (Montreal and Kingston: McGill-Queen's 1991), 434.

39 RCRLC, Evidence of Dr Oldright, 95; Mayor Howland, 166. Michael Doucet and John Weaver suggest that about half the households in the city were in houses of fewer than five rooms, and that they averaged about one person per room, perhaps less. They believe that the 500 to 700 square feet occupied on average was probably more than immigrants had known previously, though small by today's standards. *Housing*, 437–41.

40 Young, *Labor in Europe and America*, 840. Unfortunately there is no indication of

how these budgets were collected or of the occupation of the person reporting. Nor does the author explain whether there were one or more family earners. I have recalculated the totals, rounding the figures.

41 Gordon Darroch, 'Early Industrialization and Inequality in Toronto, 1861–1899,' *Labour/Le Travailleur* 11 (1983), 40; Richard Bushman, 'Family Security in the Transition from Farm to City, 1750–1850,' *Journal of Family History* 6 (1981); Harvey Graff, *The Literacy Myth: Literacy and Social Structure in the Nineteenth Century City* (New York: Academic Press 1979); Doucet and Weaver, *Housing.*

42 Gordon Darroch and Lee Soltow, *Property and Inequality in Victorian Ontario: Structural Patterns and Cultural Communities in the 1871 Census* (Toronto: University of Toronto Press 1994), 74, 67.

43 Harris, Levine, and Osborne, 'Housing Tenure,' 284.

44 Doucet and Weaver, *Housing,* 63, 235. They give no details of the actual size of Hamilton's working-class housing, but they argue that plans for inexpensive housing suggest it was generally between 600 and 1,700 square feet until the turn of the century, when it was slightly larger. Frame buildings, for example, still made up 47 per cent of Hamilton's housing stock by 1891, although it had decreased from 66 per cent three decades earlier. The following discussion also draws on Michael Doucet, 'Working Class Housing in a Small Nineteenth Century City: Hamilton, Ontario, 1852–1881,' in Gregory S. Kealey and Peter Warrian, eds, *Essays in Canadian Working Class History* (Toronto: McClelland and Stewart 1976), 89; Katz, *The Social Organization;* Darroch, 'Early Industrialization'; Harris, Levine, and Osborne, 'Housing Tenure'; and Darroch and Soltow, *Property,* 67–91.

45 RCRLC, 564.

46 RCRLC, 747. Research on home-ownership has focused more on the percentages of people who owned their houses as revealed by assessment rolls than on the process by which people saved or borrowed. We need to know more about building societies, other lending institutions, construction trades workers who built in their off times, and saving in general. A Chatham real estate agent reported charging 8 per cent on a thousand dollar loan to build a house, RCRLC, 723. Evidence about building societies can be found in RCRLC, 86, 149, 376, 736.

47 RCRLC, 944

48 Katz, *The People,* 83; Darroch and Soltow, *Property,* 72.

49 Bureau of Industries, 1889, 41.

50 John Battye, 'The Nine Hour Pioneers: The Genesis of the Canadian Labour Movement,' *Labour/Le Travailleur* 4 (1979), 35.

51 *Globe,* 18 August 1871, editorial.

52 See Gordon Darroch and Michael Ornstein, 'Family and Household in Nineteenth-Century Canada: Regional Patterns and Regional Economies,' *Journal of Family History* (Summer 1984). Problems in determining exactly how the enumerators determined household boundaries suggest these results should be treated with caution. Gilles Lauzon's critique of such work shows that in taking the enumerators'

boundaries between families and households at face value, they were likely to interpret Montreal families in duplexes and triplexes as two and three families respectively sharing housing. Gilles Lauzon, *Habitat ouvrier et révolution industrielle: Le
cas du village St-Augustin* (Montreal: RCHTQ 1989). Much of the debate on this
question has taken place in Montreal, where the duplexes and triplexes posed particular difficulties for census enumerators. See also Bradbury, *Working Families*,
76–8; Jason Gilliland and Sherry Olson, 'Claims on Housing Space in Nineteenth-
Century Montreal,' paper presented at the Conference on House and Home in
Canadian Cities, 1850–1950, McMaster University 1993.

53 *Ottawa Citizen*, 4 January 1870.

54 Ibid., 25 July 1868, 2.

55 Craig Heron presents the earners' arguments for a nine-hour day: their claim to a
reward for the new gains in productivity, their need for more time for moral and
intellectual development, with a brief reference to the potential of being better 'family men,' *The Canadian Labour Movement: A Short History* (Toronto: Lorimer
1989), 15. Bryan Palmer argues that time was the only capital workers had, but he
interprets the movement as 'an effort to secure fundamental social reform and a
shift in the nature of productive relations,' *Working Class Experience: Rethinking
the History of Canadian Labour, 1800–1991* (Toronto: McClelland and Stewart
1992), 89. Battye's main theme is the organization of the nine-hour movement. Yet
he does explain that T.C. Watkins, chair of the major Hamilton meeting that cam-
paigned for nine hours linked the reduction of hours from ten to nine with 'the paying of workmen on Friday evening instead of Saturday,' *Globe, Spectator*, 29
January, 1872, cited in John Battye, 'The Nine Hour Pioneers,' 27.

56 Elsewhere, too, historians have seen shorter hours as a way for workers to extract a
larger share of the economic gains of increased productivity or to reduce seasonal
unemployment more than as a way of gaining family time. See, for example, Gary
Cross, 'Worktime and Industrialization: An Introduction,' in his *Worktime and
Industrialization: An International History* (Philadelphia: Temple University Press
1988), 8–9. He describes the demand for a uniform workday spread out over the
year as 'the quest for a regular and predictable separation of work and 'life.'

57 See Paul Craven in this volume. The Canada Board of the Great Western discussed
these issues concurrently on 15 March 1872. See Bryan Palmer, *A Culture in Conflict: Skilled Workers and Industrial Capitalism in Hamilton, Ontario, 1860–1914*
(Montreal and Kingston: McGill-Queen's University Press 1979), 132.

58 Gregory S. Kealey, *Toronto Workers Respond to Industrial Capitalism, 1867–1892*
(Toronto: University of Toronto Press 1980), 63, makes this argument about the
coopers' interest in shorter hours directly after quoting their contention that shorter
hours would allow workers more enjoyment of 'the associations and endearments of
the enlightened and intelligent home circle.'

59 See Gary Cross, *Worktime and Industrialization* and *Quest for Time: The Reduction
of Work in Britain and France, 1840–1940* (Berkeley: Unversity of California Press

1989), and for a useful introduction to recent works on the subject, Steven J. Ross, 'Living for the Weekend: The Shorter Hours Movement in International Perspective,' *Labour/Le Travail* 27 (Spring 1991), 267–82.

60 Bureau of Industries, 1888, 41.

61 These are slightly different from the five reasons Ross highlights in his review 'Living for the Weekend,' 270. He includes escape from worsening work conditions.

62 Bureau of Industries, 1887, 41.

63 Bureau of Industries, 1887, 41.

64 Bureau of Industries, 1887, 40.

65 See also Karen Dubinsky's discussion of how the Knights of Labor referred to the family in '"The Modern Chivalry": Women and the Knights of Labor in Ontario, 1880–1891' (MA thesis, Queen's University Canadian Studies, 1985), 108.

66 Gary Cross, 'Worktime and Industrialization,' 10.

67 Bonnie Fox, 'The Rise and Fall of the Breadwinner-Homemaker Family,' in Bonnie Fox, ed., *Family Patterns, Gender Relations* (Toronto: Oxford University Press 1993), 147–50; Martha May, 'Bread before Roses: American Workingmen, Labor Unions and the Family Wage,' in Ruth Milkman, ed., *Women, Work and Protest* (London: Routledge and Kegan Paul 1985).

68 E.P. Thompson, 'Time, Work-Discipline, and Industrial Capitalism,' *Past and Present* 38 (December 1968), 79.

69 Jeanne Boydston, 'To Earn Her Daily Bread: Housework and Antebellum Working-Class Subsistence,' *Radical History Review* 35 (1986), 9.

70 *Ontario Workman*, 14 August 1873, 3; my thanks to Chris Burr for this reference; Boydston, 'To Earn Her Daily Bread,' 13–15. Her ideas are developed more subtly and at greater length in her *Home and Work: Housework, Wages and the Ideology of Labor in the Early Republic* (New York: Oxford University Press 1990).

71 R. Marvin McInnis, 'Women, Work and Childbearing: Ontario in the Second Half of the Nineteenth Century,' *Histoire sociale/Social History* 24, no. 48, 249.

72 My discussion here draws on Luxton, *More than a Labour of Love*, 18. See also Veronica Strong-Boag, 'Keeping House in God's Country: Canadian Women at Work in the Home,' in Craig Heron and Robert Storey, eds, *On the Job*, 125; Susan Strasser, *Never Done: A History of American Housework* (New York: Pantheon Books 1982), 6, 36–8; Ruth Schwartz Cowan, *More Work for Mother: The Ironies of Household Technology from the Open Hearth to the Microwave* (New York: Basic Books 1983).

73 The budgets produced by the Ontario Bureau of Industries, like Marx's theorization of the 'means of subsistence,' assume all household needs are purchased. Boydston, in 'To Earn Her Daily Bread,' 9, and *Home and Work*, xiii–xix, ably shows how the distinctive value of housewives' labour is largely unrecognized in traditional Marxist analyses.

74 This fourth possibility would include the kinds of accounting systems in general stores where little hard cash changed hands, but accounts were credited when women kept boarders or sewed clothing, etc.

75 Such relative self-sufficiency was quite different from that obtained by farming families wealthy enough to produce most of what they needed and with sons and daughters able to provide both farm and domestic labour.

76 Parr, *The Gender of Breadwinners*, 242–3.

77 John Bullen, 'Hidden Workers: Child Labour and the Family Economy in Late Nineteenth-Century Urban Ontario,' *Labour/Le Travail* 18 (1986), 166, reprinted in Bradbury, *Canadian Family History*.

78 Bullen, 'Hidden Workers,' 174.

79 Quoted in David M. Sobel, 'Household Economies and Material Life: Family Survival in Southern Saint John's Ward, 1879–1885' (Major Research Paper, History, York University 1982), 13.

80 *Globe*, 7 March 1859.

81 Christine Stansell, *City of Women: Sex and Class in New York, 1789–1860* (Chicago and Urbana: University of Illinois Press 1987), 203–7; *Barrie Northern Advance*, 22 June 1864.

82 Susan E. Houston and Alison Prentice, *Schooling and Scholars in Nineteenth-Century Ontario* (Toronto: University of Toronto Press 1988), 98, 217–8.

83 Ontario, *Annual Report of the Normal, Model, High and Public Schools for the Year 1874*, quoted in Bullen, 'Children of the Industrial Age: Children, Work and Welfare in Late Nineteenth Century Ontario' (PhD dissertation, History, University of Ottawa 1989), 340.

84 Houston and Prentice, *Schooling and Scholars*, 217–18; Bullen, 'Children of the Industrial Age,' 340, 326.

85 Ontario, *Statutes*, 1881, Chap. 30, quoted in Bullen, 'Children of the Industrial Age,' 342.

86 This discrepancy was partly remedied in 1891 when a new law allowed a child to be absent from school with permission from a justice of the peace or the principal if 'the services of such child are required in husbandry or urgent and necessary household duties, or for the necessary maintenance of such child or of some person dependent upon him.' Ontario, *Report of the Minister of Education for the Year 1891* (Toronto 1891), 155, quoted in John Bullen, 'Children of the Industrial Age,' 345.

87 RCRLC, Henry Barrell, baker, Ottawa, 1119; S. Slinn, baker and confectioner, Ottawa, 1113; R.E. Jamieson, baker and grocer, 1107.

88 Bureau of Industries, 1887, 40.

89 *Stratford Beacon*, 4 July 1873; my thanks to Paul Craven for the reference.

90 This practice depended on how far away their work was, whether they were allowed out, and how long they were given for lunch. See RCRLC, 271. The possibility of going home for lunch seemed important to the men taking evidence at the Royal Commission of 1888. They fairly consistently asked whether young women, in particular, ate their meals at home. Witnesses reported that girls from the Hamilton and Kingston cotton mills, a Kingston confectionery-making establishment, and the Ottawa parliamentary printing office did so unless there was too much work, in

which case they took food with them. See RCRLC, Evidence of John Mill, Ontario Cotton Mill, Hamilton, 879; Mark Limembeck, cotton spinner, Ontario Cotton Mill, 894; Samuel Rowcroft, mill overseer, Kingston, 977; Samuel Robinson, baker, Kingston, 1001; anonymous paper folder, Ottawa, 1163.

91 10 February 1883 , quoted in Palmer, *Culture in Conflict*, 69–70.

92 Kathryn Harvey, '"To Love Honour and Obey."'

93 Palmer, *Culture in Conflict*, 11; William T. Wylie, 'The Blacksmith in Upper Canada, 1784–1850: A Study of Technology, Culture and Power' *Canadian Papers in Rural History* (Gananoque: Langdale Press 1990), 50. Donald M. Wilson reports that from the 1850s the Rathbun Company, centred in Belleville, had paid its lumber workers in vouchers or coupons for goods at the company store, for rent, for fuel supplied by the company, and for various other items as the need arose, suggesting that virtually no cash transfers occurred. They appear to have been still doing so in the 1880s. *Lost Horizons: The Story of the Rathbun Company and the Bay of Quinte Railway* (Belleville: Mika Publishing Company 1983), 45; Leo Johnson, *History of the County of Ontario, 1615–1875* (Whitby: Corporation of the County of Ontario 1973), 214.

94 Bureau of Industries, 1884, lxviii; RCRLC, Hodgins, cigarmaker, 653; Wrigley, 569; Andrew Smith, carpenter, 699; Robert Mills, cigar maker, St Catharines, 919; Andre Carroll, printer, St Catharines, 926; Henry Barrell, 1119, 1125.

95 Cobourg mechanics were apparently divided on this question or did not want to link it to a call for shorter hours. An amendment to a resolution about hours adding that they would 'take no store pay, but cash' was defeated in July 1836. Quoted in Edwin C. Guillet, ed., *The Valley of the Trent* (Toronto: Champlain Society 1957), 279. Questions about payment in cash were asked regularly by the Bureau of Industries, and a question on the subject was in the schedule of questions asked by the RCRLC in 1888.

96 Bureau of Industries, 1887, 36.

97 Pat and Hugh Armstrong, *Theorizing Women's Work* (Toronto: Garamond Press, 1990), 73.

98 *A Book of Recipies containing Advertisements of Hamilton Businesses at the Time of Publication* (Hamilton Public Library Special Collections, n.d., circa 1880s).

99 *Hamilton Palladium of Labor*, 23 February 1884, quoted in Sarah Elvins, 'Mary Brown Went to Market: Women and Household Consumption in Late-Nineteenth-Century Hamilton, Ontario,' graduate paper, History, York Unversity 1994.

100 Gregory S. Kealey and Bryan D. Palmer, *Dreaming of What Might Be: The Knights of Labor in Ontario, 1880–1900* (Toronto: New Hogtown Press 1987), 360, 357.

101 RCRLC, 66.

102 RCRLC, 663, 697, 767–8, 875–6, 1065, 1091, 1134, 1166.

103 RCRLC, 1134.

104 RCRLC, 27.

105 GWR Advises of Officers Minutes, 5 November 1873, National Archives of Canada, RG 30, v. 8.

106   Read by Thomas Towers, to the RCRLC, 871.

107   Bureau of Industries, 1889, 5.

108   Bureau of Industries, 1887, 36.

109   Bureau of Industries, 1887, 36.

110   RCRLC, 97. For paydays and preferred paydays see pp. 6–7, 30, 41, 52, 66, 75, 104,
      124–5, 129, 176, 190, 247, 271, 357, 439, 452, 467, 541, 580, 597, 602, 610, 622,
      629, 671, 683, 696, 707, 746, 787, 797, 805, 809, 824, 857, 371, 886, 903, 942, 945,
      953, 1002, 1005, 1081, 1101, 1102, 1108, 1117, 1124, 1140, 1169, 1170, 1176,
      1185; quotations, 66.

111   RCRLC, 541.

112   *The Galt Reporter*, 7 December 1888.

113   RCRLC, 597, 190.

114   Boydston, 'To Earn Her Daily Bread,' 10, 13; Boydston, *Home and Work*, 50–5.

115   RCRLC, 825.

116   RCRLC, 149–50.

117   *Globe*, 3 February 1883, quoted in Sobel, 'Household Economies,' 46.

118   Sobel, 'Household Economies,' 16–17.

119   Sobel, 'Household Economies,' 44.

120   Laura Oren, 'The Welfare of Women in Labouring Families: England, 1860–1950,'
      in Mary S. Hartman and Lois Banner, eds, *Clio's Consciousness Raised: New Per-
      spectives on the History of Women* (New York: Harper Colophon Books 1974).

121   MS Census, Thornhill, 1871.

122   MS Census, Hespeler, 1871.

123   MS Census, Brantford, Division 2, 1871.

124   Jean Waldie, *Brant County: The Story of Its People*, vol. 2 (Paris: J.R. Hastings
      Printing and Lithographing Ltd 1984), 123, 189.

125   Parr, *The Gender of Breadwinners*, 190–3.

126   Jane Synge, 'Family and Community in Hamilton, 1900–1930,' 30, 59, manuscript,
      privately held, cited in Weaver and Doucet, 196–7.

127   See, for example, *Ottawa Citizen*, 29 September 1873, 1; 28 February 1876.

128   Jean Scott, *The Conditions of Female Labour in Ontario* (Toronto: Warwick and
      Sons 1892), 25.

129   Bullen, 'Children of the Industrial Age,' 122–3.

130   Lorna McLean, 'Home, Yard and Neighbourhood: Women's Work and the Urban
      Working-Class Family Economy, Ottawa, 1871' (MA thesis, History, University of
      Ottawa 1989), 71–2.

131   RCRLC, 1158–9.

132   The families in each of these cities numbered 8,479 and 3,332 respectively. *Census
      of Canada, 1861*, Appendix 11, and Table 1.

133   MS Census, 1861, Toronto, St John's Ward.

134   By-laws regarding pound keepers and roving animals were passed in 1868 and
      amended in 1869, 1874, and 1876. These early amendments are found in by-

law 474, *Consolidated By-Laws of the City of Toronto* (Toronto 1876), 196–205.

135 *Ottawa Citizen*, 17 August 1866, 11 March 1869, 24 February 1865, 10 October 1870, 11 August 1873.

136 *The Globe*, 14 July 1871; 17 July 1871.

137 McLean, 'Home, Yard and Neighbourhood,' 60–7.

138 *Ottawa Citizen*, 3 April 1877, 4 April 1877.

139 Laws restricting pigs to specific areas of Ottawa were passed throughout the 1870s. In 1883 pigs were banished from the whole city. McLean, 'Home, Yard and Neighbourhood,' 74–5. Research is required on other towns. See also Bettina Bradbury, 'Pigs, Cows and Boarders: Non-Wage Forms of Survival among Montreal Families, 1861–1881,' *Labour/Le Travail* 14 (Autumn 1984), 9–46.

140 By-law no. 1231, passed 7 August 1882, Appendix to Toronto Minutes, 1882, 564–6.

141 Bradbury, 'Pigs, Cows.'

142 Cohen, *Women's Work*, 166.

143 The families whose expenditures were surveyed in 1873 (Young, *Labor in Europe*) paid between 15 and 42 cents a week for eggs, with the exception of two reporting no expenditure. They may well have had their own chickens. For prices see Ontario, Department of Immigration Report, 1881, *Sessional Papers* (6), 1882, 41.

144 On cooking in the nineteenth century see Strasser, *Never Done*, 11–31; Cowan, *More Work for Mother*, 40–67; and Una Abrahamson, *God Bless Our Home: Domestic Life in Nineteenth Century Canada* (Canada: Burns and MacEachern 1966), 162–73. Purchased food was especially likely to be adulterated and contain impurities. Some discussion of this can be found in RCRLC, 96.

145 A Chatham labourer, William Partridge, pieced together a living digging out cellars, mixing mortar, carrying hods, or doing anything that came in handy. He reported that they sometimes bought bread and other times made it. He told the commissioners in 1888, 'We buy both [bread and flour]; sometimes we get two two-pound loaves for nine cents.' RCRLC, 461.

146 RCRLC, 351, 461, 1133. On diets among the poor of Toronto, see the interviews of workers in *Globe*, 3 February 1883.

147 Toronto House of Industry, 'Visitors' Recommendations,' 1867–1870.

148 Strasser, *Never Done*.

149 Cowan, *More Work for Mother*, 66–8.

150 Workers and other witnesses at the RCRLC stressed the price of fuel. See, for example, 701.

151 Bullen, 'Children of the Industrial Age,' 124.

152 Toronto House of Industry, 1867, case no. 5.

153 *World*, 27 July 1881, quoted in Sobel, 41.

154 The House of Industry gave families wood until the early 1860s, when a rise in the price led them to change to coal. In the 1880s they again gave out some wood and

began to distribute small amounts of coke as well. Toronto, House of Industry, Annual Reports, 1837 to 1892.

155 Toronto House of Industry, cases no. 687, 1881 and 418, 1880 quoted in Sobel, 63; cases no. 23 and 96–7, 1867.

156 Sobel, 'Household Economies.'

157 Letty Anderson, 'Water Supply,' in Norman R. Ball, ed., *Building Canada: A History of Public Works* (Toronto: University of Toronto Press 1991), 196.

158 RCRLC, 385, Evidence of Dr John Coventry, Medical Health Officer, Windsor; 1094–5, Evidence of Paul Dane, Cornwall, weaver.

159 RCRLC, Petrolia, 717, evidence of Dr John B. Tweedale, Physician to the Board of Health at St Thomas, 501.

160 Bureau of Industries, 11.

161 Anderson, 'Water Supply,' 196.

162 *Globe*, 24 May 1872, quoted in Elwood Jones and Douglas McCalla, 'Toronto Waterworks, 1840–77: Continuity and Change in Nineteenth-Century Toronto Politics,' *Canadian Historical Review* 60, no. 3 (September 1979), 316, 320. The number of households connected to the civic water supply was 4518 at the end of 1877 and some 16,000 by the end of 1883. There were 10,671 families reported in the 1871 census and 17,967 families in 1881; Toronto, Board of Health Survey, 1885, quoted in Sobel, 'Household Economies,' 30.

163 Doucet and Weaver, *Housing*, 442.

164 G.P. deT. Glazebrook, *The Story of Toronto* (Toronto: University of Toronto Press 1971), 129; Sobel, 'Household Economies,' 25–6.

165 Sobel, 'Household Economies,' 25–6.

166 Toronto, Board of Health Survey, 1885, quoted in Sobel, 'Household Economies,' 30. It is quite possible that the city water supply was equally dangerous since the sewer outlet for the city was much too close to the water-intake pipe. Typhoid broke out in 1891 and again in 1895, and citizens were again buying water from carts. See Glazebrook, *The Story of Toronto*, 175.

167 Toronto, Board of Health Survey, 1885, quoted in Sobel, 'Household Economies,' 30.

168 Strasser, *Never Done*, 105.

169 Sarah Louisa Bowlby, Diary, 3 February 1862; Helen Valdora Bowlby, Diary, 13 May, 1867; Margaret Bowlby Papers, Archives of Ontario, MU 282.

170 *Ottawa Citizen*, 24 July 1877.

171 *Barrie Northern Advance*, 6 January 1863.

172 *Hamilton Palladium of Labor*, 7 November 1885, quoted in Dubinsky, '"The Modern Chivalry,"' 46.

173 The 1891 census lists 22 factories producing washing machines. Before that they are not listed separately.

174 Strasser, *Never Done*, 117.

175 Diary of W.A. Stephens, Wednesday, 16 March 1856, privately held. She paid 7s 6d board weekly.

176 See Stanislas Lortie, 'Compositeur typographe,' in Pierre Savard, *Paysans et ouvri-ers québécois d'autrefois*, 90, 106, 111.

177 *Ottawa Citizen*, 23 February 1878.

178 *London Free Press*, 23 June 1871; *Ottawa Citizen*, 26 June 1876.

179 *Ottawa Citizen*, 17 November 1875.

180 James Pitsula, 'The Relief of Poverty in Toronto, 1880–1930' (PhD dissertation, History, York University 1970), 112; Toronto House of Industry, 1867, nos 28, 63, 102. When such women applying for help described what they did, going out 'washing and scrubbing' were invariably linked. Few of these really poor women appear to have taken in washing – perhaps because they lacked the facilities in their own houses to do large amounts of washing.

181 *Globe*, 2 April 1881 for wages; 3 February 1883 for interviews. Research in diaries or household accounts of wealthy urban women might reveal how much charwomen were normally paid. Newspaper advertisements, reports of immigrant agents, and other sources often list wages for domestics, but seldom if ever for charwomen.

182 Toronto House of Industry, 'Visitor's Recommendations,' 1867.

183 On the earlier nineteenth century around Montreal see David-Thiery Ruddel, 'Consumer Trends, Clothing, Textiles and Equipment,' and on rural families in eastern Ontario see Janine Roelens and Kris Inwood, '"Labouring at the Loom": A Case Study of Rural Manufacturing in Leeds County, Ontario, 1870,' *Canadian Papers in Rural History*, 7 (Gananoque, Ontario: Langdale Press 1990).

184 Traill underlined the importance of this skill for settlers in 1855: 'There is no country where there is so much knitting-work done as in Canada.' She gave the example of a settler's young daughter who had provided for her clothing before her marriage with the fruits of her knitting. *The Canadian Settler's Guide*, 184.

185 Toronto House of Industry, 1867, case nos 65, 108, and 156. Annual Report, 1864, 10. Of course it was in the interest of such women seeking relief to argue that they were trying to support themselves, so perhaps such mentions of occupations should be treated warily.

186 Toronto House of Industry, case no. 119, 1881, cited in Sobel, 'Household Economies,' 64.

187 See, for example, the reminiscences of M. Alberta Auger, reproduced in Beth Light and Joy Parr, eds, *Canadian Women on the Move, 1867–1920* (Toronto: New Hogtown Press and OISE 1983), who apprenticed in a woman's home in Salem, Ontario, early in the twentieth century.

188 M.N. Stephens, 'Journal no. 1,' 1869–70, Archives of Ontario, MU 6009. In such small local economies where formal exchange was largely organized through the account books of the general store, little cash actually changed hands. It is hard to know whether the women would ever have benefited individually from their efforts, for the money made was credited to their husbands' accounts, as was to be expected at a time when economically and legally a wife's identity disappeared into that of her husband.

189 *Barrie Northern Advance,* 13 January 1870, 3.

190 *Ottawa Citizen,* 28 December 1878.

191 Toronto, House of Industry, 1867, cases no. 26, 76, 1870, case no. 710.

192 Gregory S. Kealey, *Toronto Workers,* 21–3, 39–43.

193 Toronto House of Industry, 1863, case no. 28.

194 *The Globe,* 28 October 1868.

195 'Report upon the Sweating System in Canada,' Canada, *Sessional Papers* 61, 1896, 7–8, 11.

196 Canada, House of Commons, *Journals,* 1874, App. 3, 'Report of the Select Committee on the Manufacturing Interests of the Dominion', 22–4.

197 'Report upon the Sweating System,' 1896, 3.

198 'Report upon the Sweating System,' 1896, 5–6.

199 William Lyon Mackenzie King, *Report to the Honourable the Postmaster General on the Methods Adopted in Canada in the Carrying Out of Government Clothing Contracts* (Ottawa: 1900).

200 *Census of Canada, 1901.*

201 On the sweating system and the clothing trades in general in Canada see Michelle Payette-Daoust, 'The Montreal Garment Industry, 1871–1901' (MA thesis, History, McGill University 1986); Mercedes Steedman, 'Female Participation in the Canadian Clothing Industry, 1890–1940' (PhD dissertation, University of London 1990). Jenny Morris's comparison of the tailoring trades in two English towns is useful for showing the different forms sweating could take in different places, and the centrality of the sexual division of labour, and for defining terms: 'The Characteristics of Sweating: The Late Nineteenth-Century London and Leeds Tailoring Trade,' in Angela John, ed., *Unequal Opportunities: Women's Employment in England, 1800–1918* (Oxford: Basil Blackwell 1986).

202 Bradbury, *Working Families,* 139.

203 *The Globe,* 28 October 1868.

204 RCRLC, evidence of Charles Bryson, dry goods merchant, Ottawa, 1164. Similar quotations can be found in other evidence at the Royal Commission of 1888 as well as in all the investigations of industry undertaken during the nineteenth century.

205 *The Globe,* 28 October 1868.

206 William Lyon Mackenzie King, 'Report,' 12–14; *Globe,* 19 November 1898, 1.

207 Scott, *The Conditions,* 21.

208 'Report upon the Sweating System,' 1896, 7–8, 11.

209 William Lyon Mackenzie King, 'Report,' 12–14; *Globe,* 19 November 1898, 1.

210 Bullen, 'Children of the Industrial Age,' 25.

211 Bullen, 'Children of the Industrial Age,' 133.

212 *The Globe,* 28 October 1868, 1.

213 *Journal of the Board of Arts and Manufactures of Upper Canada,* May 1862, 137.

214 M.N. Stephens, 'Journal no. 1,' 1869–70.

215 M.N. Stephens, 'Cash Book,' Ontario Archives, MU 6022–23, 1875–79.

216 MS Census, Thornhill, Markham Township, 1861, township debits and credits.

217 Woodbridge Cash Book, 1898 to 1907, Vaughan Township Archives, Town of Woodbridge Municipal Records, G4–989.2–992.1.

218 Toronto House of Industry, case no. 805, 1881.

219 McLean, 'Home, Yard and Neighbourhood,' 39.

220 Boarding houses and brothels mixed at times – at least in the rhetoric of reformers. See Lori Rotenberg, 'The Wayward Worker: Toronto's Prostitute at the Turn of the Century,' in Acton et al., *Women at Work: Ontario, 1850–1930* (Toronto: Women's Educational Press 1974), 42–3. C.S. Clark describes the disgusting people one could meet and places one might find in Toronto at the end of the century in *Of Toronto the Good* (Montreal: The Toronto Publishing Company 1898; repr. Coles 1970).

221 Robert H. Harney, 'Boarding and Belonging,' *Urban History Review* 2 (October 1978); Katz, *The People of Hamilton.*

222 Jean Scott makes passing reference to running boarding houses and taking in boarders as employment for married women, *Female Labour*, 25.

223 Court cases often tell much about boarding, as boarders were frequently witnesses.

224 Overall the number of households with at least one boarder dropped from somewhat under one in three in 1851 to about one in five ten years later. Unfortunately Katz's figures do not allow us to see which of the families with boarders also had servants. *The People of Hamilton*, 36, 222; McLean, 'Home, Yard and Neighbourhood,' 34–7; Gagan, *Hopeful Travellers*, 138.

225 Richard Harris suggests that in 1900 three-quarters of Toronto lodgers in private homes were boarders rather than roomers, though by the First World War roomers predominated. 'The End Justified the Means: Boarding and Rooming in a City of Homes, 1890–1951,' *Journal of Social History* 26, 2 (Winter 1992), 335–9.

226 Bullen, 'Children of the Industrial Age,' 134.

227 *Ottawa Citizen*, 15 January 1877.

228 *Ottawa Citizen*, 6 January 1866, 2. Lorna McLean found that four of the forty-six widows living in Bytown in 1871 and listing a job reported keeping a boarding house; 'Home, Yard and Neighbourhood,' 86.

229 *Ottawa Citizen*, 8 November 1873.

230 Mariana Valverde, *The Age of Light, Soap, and Water: Moral Reform in English Canada, 1885–1925* (Toronto: McClelland and Stewart 1991), 82–3; Lori Rotenberg, 'The Wayward Worker,' 33–70; Constance Backhouse, 'Nineteenth Century Canadian Prostitution Law: Reflection of a Discriminatory Society,' *Histoire sociale/Social History*, 18, no. 36 (November 1985); Lorna McLean, 'Behind Bars: Women and the Criminal Justice System in Four Communities in Ontario, 1840–1881,' paper presented to the Canadian Historical Association, 1993; Clark, *Of Toronto the Good*, 86–136; Debra Clipperton, 'In Bad Company: Prostitution and Brothel Life in Toronto, 1871' (graduate paper, History, York University 1994).

231 *Ottawa Citizen*, 7 January 1854, 5 September 1873; *London Free Press*, 8 October, 19 December 1861; 28 June, 29 July 1862

232 Toronto City Archives, House of Industry, SC35–D, Box 2, File 4, 'Children out to Wet-Nurses,' 1862. This practice appears to have begun in the 1830s and stopped in the early 1870s, when the numbers of children listed as placed out in the annual reports dropped to 0. The list of children placed with wet-nurses exists for only part of 1862.

233 *London Free Press*, 8 October 1861.

234 Ibid., 19 December 1861.

235 There are too few cases to measure the death rates among the babies wet-nursed. On this in Montreal see Peter Gossage, 'Les enfants abandonnés à Montréal au 19e siècle: La crèche d'Youville des Soeurs Grises, 1829–1871,' *Revue d'histoire de l'Amérique française* 40, 4 (printemps 1987).

236 *Ottawa Citizen*, 26 May 1875; 12 January 1878, 4; 8 February 1878, 4.

237 *Ontario Workman*, 12 September 1872, 4.

238 Jeanne Boydston has shown that it is possible to place a dollar value on domestic labour. She does so by adding up the average wages of cooks, domestic servants, washerwomen, sewing women and those who cared for other people's children or the elderly. This approach has the advantage of highlighting the economic worth of women's labour, although by adding together the possible earnings from each task separately she inflates their worth. 'To Earn Her Daily Bread,' 9, 17–19; *Home and Work*, 130–4.

239 *London Free Press*, 3 March 1863.

240 Wet-nurse, Toronto House of Industry, 'Children out to Wet Nurses,' 1862; Laundress, *London Free Press*, 28 June 1869; Housemaids, *London Free Press*, 6 July 1865, 2; 23 June 1871.

241 Ontario, Annual Report of the Department of Immigration, 'Return of average wages paid to labourers etc., 1881,' in *Sessional Papers*, 1882, 42; ibid., 1883, 23; Ontario, Bureau of Industries Annual Report, 1885, 51; 1886, 280.

242 This exercise is as hypothetical as the previous one. Board no doubt covered some of the rental costs as well. I have not calculated rentals. For the annual cost of food per person I have taken the $153 reported by the Belleville family in Table 1, and divided by three, therefore allowing one half of an adult food portion for each child in the family. Food costs per person, again calculating children as half an adult, in the families in the other towns average $116 in Cornwall, $87 in Hamilton, and $68 in Ottawa.

243 Constance Backhouse, 'Married Women's Property Law in Nineteenth-Century Canada,' in Bettina Bradbury, ed., *Canadian Family History: Selected Readings* (Toronto: Copp Clark Pitman 1992), 331, 335, 355, 342.

244 Michael Merrill, 'Cash Is Good to Eat: Self-Sufficiency and Exchange in the Rural Economy of the United States,' *Radical History Review* 4 (Winter 1977).

Getting dinner ready

Toronto children cleaning doorstep, turn of the century

Family maid

Factory Workers

CRAIG HERON

The night sky had only begun to pale into grey as Ottawa's bakers shuf-
fled into the bake shops to begin work at five in the morning on 4 May
1888. In the next hour, the first light of a gloomy dawn fell over hundreds of men and boys trudging along the river under a light drizzle to
get to their jobs in the city's lumber mills and woodworking factories by
six o'clock. An hour later, men arrived at Thomas McKay's flour mill to
start milling, just as women turned up at Woodburn's print shop to begin
their bookbinding work. The numerous milliners and dressmakers heading for Crawford Ross's shop could wait somewhat longer for a break in
the weather before presenting themselves for work at 8:30. A half dozen
government commissioners got a more leisurely start on the day when,
at 2 p.m., they convened the first Ottawa hearings of the Dominion government's Royal Commission on the Relations of Labour and Capital,
popularly known as the 'labour commission.' Over the next two days the
commissioners none the less put in long hours listening to testimony
from industrialists, craftworkers, female wage-earners, and young boys
of twelve and thirteen from all these Ottawa workplaces and several
more. This was the end of their tour across urban industrial Ontario,
which in thirty-eight days of testimony had already revealed the remarkable industrial transformation the region had undergone. In their long
hearings the commissioners had heard many different versions of this
story. The wide range of experience revealed in Ottawa was typical of
the unevenness and diversity laid before them across the province.[1]
 Coming at the end of some five decades of industrial innovation and
on the eve of the great early twentieth-century leap into 'mass production,' the Labour Commission's deliberations are a particularly useful
benchmark of Ontario's First Industrial Revolution. Yet they do not
stand alone. The 1880s witnessed a remarkable proliferation of investigations into the work world of the province's industrial wage-earners –

two other federal Royal Commissions, detailed annual reports from the statistical staff of the provincial Bureau of Industries and from the new factory inspectors, reports in business journals, articles in daily newspapers, and increasingly voluminous writing by the leaders of wage-earners' organizations. The centre of attention in all this poking and prodding into the world of wage labour was the factory system, a mode of organizing industrial production that struck many people in Ontario as either impressively or disturbingly new. The discussion of workers and factories that follows here leans heavily on this great volume of writing that appeared in the 1880s but also moves back through the more opaque preceding half century, much of it explored by other scholars, to try to appreciate how much had changed since the 1840s and why.

Within the limitations of the research and the constraints of space, it is possible only to sketch a general outline of regional industrial change that may help to guide future research. Each of the main sections in this essay presents one piece of an argument about this period of Ontario working-class history. The first section suggests the limited scope of Ontario's industrial revolution and the diversity of experience within it, especially the striking regional differences throughout the province. The second points to the equally limited and uneven transformation of the work processes in the province's factories, which left in place a considerable amount of manual labour, both skilled and unskilled. The third outlines the complicated recruitment methods of industrial employers. The fourth section explores the emerging systems of factory management and the continuing importance of paternalism in the social relations of the Ontario factory regime. And the final section considers the rise of substantial organized resistance from Ontario factory workers in the 1880s, when the practice and promise of paternalism began to crumble.

ONTARIO'S INDUSTRIAL REVOLUTION

Debating the Concept

In 1871 a Hamilton journalist announced that the country had been passing through an 'industrial revolution.'[2] It was to be a full century before many scholars began to take notice of this great change in Canadian social and economic life. What exactly were these writers separated across time talking about? The phrase has always been more of an evocative metaphor than a term of precise analysis. In the broadest sense, it has been used to denote the emergence of a new phase of capitalist accumulation through more effective use of labour power. Within the work world itself, it appeared as a shift from independent commodity production to wage-earning in some kind of large-scale workplace. The form could vary between industrial sectors, but in manufacturing the long-term transition was from household or artisanal workshop to factory. Implicit in the term are new technology, power sources, and management practices, larger units of production, and in many cases a concentration in urban areas, all of which profoundly disrupted not only older forms of work, but also the whole societies in which they existed. In particular, the industrial revolution is credited with accelerating the formation of new social classes, especially the working class, and creating the conditions for serious social conflict. The distance between 'pre-industrial' and 'industrial' could be long, circuitous, and tortuous and was sometimes never finally bridged, but with time this transformation brought into being new ways of working and living in the shadow of urban factories.

Ironically, at roughly the same time that writers and researchers were first discovering an industrial revolution in Canada, the term was falling into disfavour among many scholars of British and European history. They were reacting against the limitations of both the critical anti-capitalist and the more celebratory neoclassical traditions in the writing about industrialization in the eighteenth and nineteenth centuries. In their divergent ways, both had emphasized a dramatic, cataclysmic breakthrough (or 'take-off') from a pre-industrial to an industrial society in a brief, concentrated period, during which large, centralized, highly mechanized, steam-powered factories came to dominate production and introduce shockingly new forms of work.[3] In the late 1970s, an alternative perspective began to take shape in much of the new social history of the working class and in the renewed theorizing about labour processes and labour markets. This new view involved three new analytical departures. First, the various 'big-bang' theories of industrialization fell apart under closer scrutiny. It became clear that even in Britain there had been a widespread expansion of industrial production, wage-earning, and capitalist social relations in the rural countryside before the putative great turning point at the end of the eighteenth century – a phase eventually known as 'proto-industrialization.'[4] Even by the mid-nineteenth century, moreover, the industrial transformation remained incomplete and uneven across the industrial landscape; as the new terminology would have it, it was a process of 'combined and uneven' development. This new appreciation of the industrialization process did not assume that 'traditional' sectors simply lagged behind the 'modern' sectors, but that apparently pre-industrial, labour-intensive forms of production would continue to coexist with newer production, albeit in a somewhat altered state. Such a new perspective drew into the analysis the often neglected (and poorly quantified) household production, frequently carried on by women and children outside the framework of formal wage-earning.[5] These new writers have emphasized the complexity and contingency of the industrializing process.[6]

As several of them now argue, however, it would not be helpful to jettison completely the idea that one period of industrial development was distinct in important ways from another. Certainly there was a constantly evolving process of industrial recomposition, rather than a single leap or 'take-off,' but closer examination has revealed a pattern of sharply demarcated phases in that evolution. These are much clearer when we move further away from the aggregate economic data that dominate the neoclassical economic histories and towards a wider appreciation of what have been called 'social structures of accumulation' – that is, when we think of a process that integrates the dominant forms of capitalist activity, systems of production, state intervention, and social relations among classes, sexes, and ethnic groups. Over the past two centuries we can see three major phases, each with both old and new elements – probably best understood as three successive and distinct 'industrial revolutions.'[7] In each we find plenty of continuity from the past, but also enough abruptly new developments to suggest that the social structure of accumulation has lurched decisively in a new direction and that a 'revolution' is once again under way in production. From this perspective, we would not expect to find a single moment of accelerated growth that created a new industrial capitalist economy in Canada at the end of the nineteenth century, but rather an initial phase stretching from the 1840s to the 1890s, to be followed by a fundamental restructuring of industrial production and of the working class in a 'Second Industrial Revolution' after the turn of the century and a third reconstitution after 1940. (It can be argued that we have been living through a fourth since about 1975.) This essay is concerned with the working-class experience in the first phase only.[8]

A second intellectual and political influence has altered our view of an industrial revolution. Feminist writers have reminded us that industrial capitalism was also patriarchal, that is, that male power was reconstituted on a new basis within the working-class family and the capitalist workplace. Working-class men found wage-earning jobs and became the chief breadwinners for their families, while the primarily domestic responsibilities of the females in these families limited their occupational and income-earning opportunities in the capitalist labour market and heightened their dependence on men's wages. Specifically, working-class women were much more likely than men to be working at home for no wages or to have only a brief, premarital spell as a wage-earner in a cheaply paid job ghetto designated as 'women's work.' Male factory owners built the patriarchal social relations of the family into their management systems, while skilled craft workers wove their gendered privileges into their sense of their own skill and 'manhood.' For workers, then, an Industrial Revolution was also an experience of gender as well as class.[9]

The third important new insight emerging from the new social history of industrialization was the variation in the process among nation states and among regions within them. An industrial revolution did not involve simply carrying the pioneering British model far and wide (in a process loosely dubbed 'modernization'). Factories and workshops appeared and evolved in different countries in response to particular resource endowments, state policies, and markets for products and labour.[10] In the same vein, the new research has stressed the regional diversity within countries.[11] In Canada there are now various local studies suggesting that, despite some striking parallels, the major regions of the country all followed different paths of industrialization.[12]

Gradually these insights have been incorporated into the writing on Ontario's First Industrial Revolution. Factories did not loom large in the economic landscape of the province charted by the two dominant schools of economic history in Canada before the 1970s. The 'staples' school of political economists concentrated exclusively on the export of primary resources and the economic relationships that resulted. In all his voluminous writings, the commanding figure among these political economists, Harold Innis, wrote nothing substantial about manufacturing in the Canadian economy. His brief 1934 essay on Ontario scarcely acknowledged the secondary manufacturing that sustained the southern part of the province.[13] The new generation of scholars who undertook to revive and build on the older school of Canadian political economy was often at pains to minimize the importance of manufacturing in Canadian economic development and indeed to suggest that it was deliberately stifled by commercial and financial interests in the Canadian bourgeoisie.[14] The second group of economic historians, those of the neoclassical persuasion, showed somewhat more interest in manufacturing, but usually only in the statistical evidence of its output and in the folly of Canadian tariff policies for protecting it.[15] Neither the factory itself nor the social relations that it embodied were ever in the foreground. So, as late as the early 1970s, the story of industrialization in Canada, particularly in Ontario, had to be pieced together from a variety of other sources – company histories, local community studies (both antiquarian and scholarly), the scattered observations of historical geographers, and the writings of two mavericks influenced by Marxism – Stanley Ryerson and H. Clare

Pentland (whose unpublished doctoral thesis was soon to become an underground classic).[16]

It was labour historians digging into the nineteenth-century experience of Canada's first working class who began to tackle the questions of industrialization more systematically. They were eventually joined by a few practitioners in economic, urban, and women's history, and a new general framework of Canada's industrial development began to take shape. The most influential voice at the outset of this new scholarship was Clare Pentland. He brought to light many pockets of pre-industrial wage-earning and the paternalistic social relations within them and also investigated the conditions that permitted the creation of a capitalist labour market in central Canada. Eventually he was criticized for seriously misunderstanding and distorting that transition from pre-industrial to industrial.[17] Steven Langdon undertook a more detailed exploration of the process of capitalist industrialization and workers' active role within it.[18] The historians who contributed most to this new history of the Ontario working class, however, were Gregory Kealey and Bryan Palmer, who used their separate, penetrating studies of Toronto and Hamilton and their jointly written work on the labour movement of the 1880s to open up the industrial transformation in late nineteenth-century Ontario, especially the fascinating contours of working-class resistance, to more sensitive, sophisticated analysis.[19] The extensive groundwork they laid was immeasurably useful for an understanding of working-class experience in this province.

All this preliminary scholarship had three related weaknesses, however. First, it presented the Ontario evidence within a universal paradigm of industrial capitalist development; in other words, the formation and struggles of the working class seemed to unfold in a pattern roughly similar to those in most other industrializing areas of the world in the period, especially Britain and the United States. By extension, readers might also easily assume that the wider experience in Ontario was simply Toronto and Hamilton writ large. Second, this work placed the male craft worker, his union, and his public life at the centre of the story, to the virtual exclusion of all others, most particularly female wage-earners. And third, these writers said little about the effects of gender within the process of class formation. Marjorie Griffin Cohen underlined this neglected element in her important study of the transition from rural independent commodity production to urban wage-earning in nineteenth-century Ontario. She emphasized the crucial ways in which women's unpaid domestic labour in patriarchal households shaped their experience in the capitalist labour market.[20]

In the end, all these debates have taught us that to assess the experience of workers in Ontario's First Industrial Revolution requires a sensitivity to structure as well as agency, to continuity as well as change, to diversity as well as shared experiences, to the differences, in particular, of occupation, region, and sex.

Ontario Industrializes

Before 1840, manufacturing in Upper Canada felt virtually none of the shock waves hitting industrial life in the imperial heartland. By the 1820s and 1830s Canadian merchants were finding markets in Britain for the small surpluses of grain and square timber produced in the colony, and shipbuilding in several small Great Lakes ports became a significant industrial spin-off of such trade. But the fluctuations in imperial demand made this an unstable basis for economic expansion. Local markets were active but small. The great majority of the population lived and worked in semi-isolated farms. Like European peasants, the farm families produced a great many of the goods they needed in and around their households. From the beginning they also relied on artisans sprinkled through the countryside. Local millers processed their wheat, wood, wool, and leather for family use, often on a barter basis or in return for up to half the product. Eventually skilled artisans such as blacksmiths, millwrights, weavers, shoemakers, and other well-rounded craft workers also supplied from their workshops a considerable range of articles not made at home or imported from Britain or the United States; these goods were sold by pedlars and shopkeepers. Local merchants often combined several of these industrial and marketing activities for the pioneering communities. In the handful of larger towns in the colony, some artisans produced bread and a few other essentials for urban and military populations that could not produce for themselves; others turned out such luxury goods as wigs, watches, or carriages for an upper-class clientele. All of this localized production benefited from the 'tariff of bad roads' – the poorly developed transportation system that limited the circulation of cheaper mass-produced goods from outside the colony – but it also suffered from the insecurities of consumer demand. This was not a ripe terrain for industrial capitalist investment, as the frustrating efforts to get a number of ironworks well established in the province made clear. Many artisans survived only by trying out or combining a variety of occupations, including farming.[21]

During the 1840s and 1850s, the shifting structures of the Upper Canadian economy and society opened up the first opportunities for significant industrial innovation. When the British mercantilist system that had partially protected Upper Canadian trade in natural resources was dismantled in the mid-1840s in favour of freer international trade, some wild fluctuations threw the export industries into temporary tailspins. Yet the demand for the principal Upper Canadian products grew steadily in Britain and increasingly in the United States, especially after the signing of the Reciprocity Treaty of 1854. Within the colony, a new class of merchant-capitalists and liberal politicians steadily assumed control of the state from the old aristocratic oligarchy and began to overhaul state apparatuses and policies to facilitate the development of a bourgeois capitalist society. In civil society various voluntary societies, from evangelical churches to mechanics' institutes, promoted the ideas, values, and morality of the new bourgeois culture. The colony's population began to grow more and more quickly as immigrants arrived in huge numbers after 1840, principally from the British Isles; at the same time cheap, easily accessible farm land was getting scarcer. A new social structure of accumulation was emerging based on larger, more secure markets, a new economic elite, a new bourgeois culture, state support, and, above all, wage labour.[22]

The main stimulus to industrialization in this period was the growth of trade in natural resources from Upper Canadian forests and farms, whether for export, for down-river sales in Lower Canada, or for the growing urban markets in the province. The first steps came in three sectors. One was the processing of agricultural and forest products. Early in the nineteenth century merchant-millers in the settled parts of the province had begun to expand beyond 'custom work' for the local population to wider trade, but after 1840 they sold much more. Operators of flour and woollen mills, tanneries, breweries, and distilleries still relied on farm families to supply them, and they benefited from the great expansion of commercial agriculture, mostly wheat production. The 1851 census takers found scores of flour and woollen mills across the province, a few of them among the largest employers in manufacturing. By 1871 Ontario had some 900 flour mills, and 210 woollen mills.[23] By the 1880s, however, these agriculturally based industries had peaked and were in many cases in decline. After 1860, other food-processing enterprises – first cheese, much later canning and meat packing factories – had begun to proliferate as urban populations expanded and farmers converted from wheat farming to commercial dairying and mixed farming.[24] In the forest-products industry, the growing shift by mid-century from squared timber to sawn lumber prompted numerous entrepreneurs to establish sawmills independent of farming populations and to process logs gathered by their own crews of wage-earners from the virgin forests well beyond the settlements, first along the lakefront and in the Ottawa Valley and then along the edge of the Canadian Shield through the centre of the province to Georgian Bay. Throughout the second half of the nineteenth century, sawmills provided more jobs than any other manufacturing industry in Ontario, with a total work force rising from 6,300 in 1861 to 17,000 in 1881 and 24,000 in 1891 (see Table 1).[25] The processing of minerals was much more limited and less important in Ontario's industrialization experience. The small primary iron industry collapsed completely after 1850, and most other mineral exploration projects were failures. There were two great exceptions: the oil boom in southwestern Ontario that began in 1861 and spawned forty-six oil refineries over the next decade, and the equally successful salt industry that grew up in the same period in the Goderich area.[26] In all, the processing of primary products employed roughly three factory workers out of ten in Ontario between 1871 and 1891 (see Table 1).

The second stimulus to industrialization came from the transportation sector, as the colony's leading mercantile interests undertook to improve the flow of products from Upper Canada and the American Midwest to distant markets (and the profits into their pockets). This was done initially with steamboats on the lakes and rivers, then with new canals, and finally, by the end of the 1840s with railways. Thus the artisans in the larger commercial towns found a growing demand for steam engines and other metal equipment, along with some orders for machinery for the many new mills.[27] The railways that started fanning out across southern Ontario after 1850 at first relied on these local workshops, but eventually they opened their own metalworking shops, which rapidly became the largest manufacturers of producer goods in the colony. By the early 1860s, railway companies were operating the province's only two rolling mills, in Toronto and Hamilton.[28] Late nineteenth-century census takers always found the various branches of metalworking to be the largest general category of manufacturing employment (see Table 1).

Third, after 1840, consumers on the more commercially successful farms and, eventually, in the growing towns and cities had somewhat more income to spend on household needs. And the railways made it much easier to reach many more of them. The major beneficiary of the new rural spending was undoubtedly the agricultural-implements industry, which began turning out mowers, reapers, and sundry farm machinery for the larger farm population interested in mechanizing. And with increasingly large, sophisticated factories, it was able to produce for international markets before the end of the century.[29] But farmers and city dwellers were also interested in buying boots and shoes, stoves, wagons, cloth, furniture, pianos, newspapers, and much more.[30] By the 1850s numerous artisans, often recent immigrants from the British Isles or the United States with capital and skill,[31] had responded to this

TABLE 1
Employment in Manufacturing in Ontario, 1871–91

	1871						1881						1891					
	Establish-ments	Employees	Percentage				Establish-ments	Employees	Percentage				Establish-ments	Employees	Percentage			
		N	Age 16+		Under 16			N	Age 16+		Under 16			N	Age 16+		Under 16	
			M	F	M	F			M	F	M	F			M	F	M	F
PRIMARY PRODUCTS[a]																		
Agricultural																		
Breweries	105	536	96	1	3	0	106	935	97	0	3	0	82	1,008	96	1	3	0
Butter/cream							23	94	74	12	12	2	45	132	91	7	2	1
Cheese	323	909	58	33	6	3	551	1,638	79	17	4	1	893	1,930	88	8	3	1
Cider/wine	48	106	88	0	12	0	126	256	90	2	7	1	179	396	80	15	5	0
Distilleries	18	421	99	0	1	0	11	260	99	0	1	0	8	404	97	2	1	0
Fish curing													71	352	96	1	3	0
Flour	951	2,759	96	0	4	0	2,407	6,472	96	1	3	0	1,078	3,653	97	1	2	0
Fruit/vegetables (canned/dried)													62	1,959	15	64	9	12
Meat curing	105	661	91	5	4	0	94	485	94	2	4	0	299	952	89	5	6	0
Rope and twine	12	128	56	6	38	9	11	164	61	16	15	7	12	242	58	27	12	2
Tanneries	426	1,584	96	1	3	0	316	1,528	97	2	1	0	233	1,632	97	1	2	0
Tobacco	42	707	53	13	23	12	59	1,164	63	16	16	5	11	576	54	28	8	10
Misc. agric.	47	485	22	62	8	9	48	420	38	45	8	10	79	283	54	41	5	1
TOTAL	2,077	8,296	83	9	6	2	3,752	13,416	88	6	4	1	3,052	13,558	79	14	4	2

Forest																		
Asheries	267	598	95	0	5	0	157	373	98	0	2	0	74	132	95	0	5	0
Paper	12	344	67	19	9	5	19	690	71	20	6	3	34	1,792	79	16	3	2
Saw mills[b]	1,837	13,851	94	–	5	–	1,761	16,846	94	0	6	–	1,895	23,851	94	0	6	–
Misc. forest	17	27	96	0	4	0	13	86	92	0	8	0	17	165	86	10	4	0
TOTAL	2,133	14,820	94	1	5	–	1,955	17,995	93	1	6	–	2,020	25,940	93	1	5	–
Minerals																		
Iron							3	110	99	0	1	0	10	1,188	96	0	4	0
Lime	559	1,099	96	0	4	0	515	1,133	93	–	6	–	508	1,005	95	0	5	0
Marble/stone	98	577	97	0	3	0	187	859	98	0	2	–	286	1,556	98	0	2	0
Oil	46	433	91	1	8	0	32	379	100	0	0	0	21	276	100	0	0	0
Salt	16	175	100	0	0	0	26	243	93	0	3	4	19	245	88	3	7	2
Misc. minerals	29	245	93	1	6	0	36	242	92	0	8	0	80	1,752	96	1	4	–
TOTAL	748	2,529	95	–	4	0	799	2,966	96	–	4	–	914	4,834	96	1	3	–
SECONDARY PRODUCTS																		
Beverages/food																		
Aerated water	25	80	76	0	24	0	51	174	83	5	10	2	82	233	92	4	4	0
Bakeries	385	1,239	79	9	10	1	541	2,029	75	14	6	2	789	2,334	77	17	5	1
Chocolate/coffee/spice							11	52	88	0	12	0	17	107	76	21	3	0
Confectionery													130	1,179	58	34	5	3
TOTAL	410	1,319	79	9	11	1	683	2,255	78	13	6	2	1,018	3,853	72	22	5	1
Chemical products																		
Chemicals (unspecified)	13	65	88	6	6	0	17	70	90	4	6	0	82	397	75	18	6	1
Dyeing/scouring	5	9	67	11	11	11	20	85	49	41	9	0	36	188	44	50	4	2
Paint/varnish	2	6	100	0	0	0	14	59	88	8	4	0	32	179	91	4	5	0
Patent medicines	12	60	57	30	13	0	15	101	56	35	8	1	69	194	69	27	3	1
Starch	3	63	75	2	24	0	3	86	77	2	21	0	4	163	72	7	21	0
Vinegar	9	34	92	0	9	0	12	37	84	5	3	8	17	178	79	18	3	0
Misc. chemical	9	53	70	2	26	2	8	53	81	0	19	0	43	325	71	21	6	3
TOTAL	53	290	75	8	16	1	89	491	72	17	10	1	283	1,624	72	20	6	1

TABLE 1 (*continued*)

	1871						1881						1891					
	Establish-ments	Employees					Establish-ments	Employees					Establish-ments	Employees				
		N	Percentage					N	Percentage					N	Percentage			
			Age 16+		Under 16				Age 16+		Under 16				Age 16+		Under 16	
			M	F	M	F			M	F	M	F			M	F	M	F
Clothing																		
Boots/shoes	1,965	6,354	84	10	5	2	2,042	5,827	86	9	4	1	2,328	4,410	89	9	2	–
Clothing/tailored goods	942	6,248	37	58	2	3	1,121	8,569	34	62	2	2	2,121	12,835	34	62	2	2
Corsets							2	263	7	88	2	3	20	620	11	84	1	4
Dresses/millinery	493	2,126	4	87	1	8	1,061	4,661	1	89	–	9	3,851	10,645	2	91	–	7
Furs/hats	53	550	30	56	5	8	55	661	34	63	2	1	84	1,050	33	65	1	2
Gloves/mitts							15	269	18	75	0	7	28	360	39	57	2	2
Shirts/collars/ties							19	230	6	93	–	–	53	1,201	11	88	1	–
Misc. clothing	8	24	42	50	4	4	19	40	28	65	5	3	78	514	32	65	3	0
TOTAL	3,461	15,302	52	42	3	3	4,334	20,520	40	54	2	3	8,563	23,404	40	53	2	5
Leather products																		
Harness/saddles	676	1,773	93	1	6	–	1,338	2,911	95	1	4	–	906	1,852	95	1	4	0
Misc. leather	5	33	70	30	0	0	8	72	67	32	1	0	14	96	55	42	2	1
TOTAL	681	1,806	93	1	5	–	1,346	2,983	95	2	3	–	920	1,948	93	3	4	–
Metal products																		
Agricultural implements	173	2,143	94	2	5	0	141	3,201	95	–	4	–	130	4,029	96	–	3	0
Blacksmithing	2,894	4,810	97	0	3	0	3,586	6,026	98	–	2	0	4,069	5,333	98	–	2	0
Boilers	11	179	93	0	7	0	17	260	88	0	12	0	13	171	96	0	4	0
Bolts/nuts/nails/tacks/screws	1	16	75	0	25	0	3	146	66	5	27	2	11	586	63	15	22	–
Bridges													1	125	100	0	0	0
Edge tools	22	223	98	0	2	0	13	337	98	0	2	0	18	452	99	1	0	0
Engines	6	508	96	0	4	0	8	560	99	0	1	0	15	1,232	99	0	–	0

Fittings (brass/iron/etc.)	32	191	82	1	18	0	75	1,084	93	–	7	–	32	679	91	2	7	–
Machines	253	4,686	93	–	6	–	342	5,021	96	–	4	0	337	6,198	97	1	2	0
Furnaces/stoves/heaters													17	385	96	1	4	0
Pumps/windmills	146	263	95	0	5	0	211	415	97	0	3	0	259	470	96	–	3	0
Railway cars/locomotives	2	60	100	0	0	0	2	1,622	98	0	2	0	10	1,681	98	–	2	0
Rolling mill products	2	425	87	0	13	0	1	225	89	0	11	0	1	200	100	0	0	0
Saws/files	4	63	97	0	3	0	10	165	99	0	1	0	13	282	94	1	5	0
Sewing machines	10	569	71	–	30	–	7	604	91	–	9	0	5	368	99	1	0	–
Tin/sheet iron products	440	1,251	92	1	8	–	670	2,049	89	2	8	1	34	232	88	–	12	0
Tinsmithing													792	2,278	92	2	5	–
Wire							2	19	68	0	32	0	35	433	81	6	12	2
Misc. metal	32	270	90	–	9	0	38	387	90	–	10	0	164	1,393	90	6	5	0
TOTAL	3,268	15,656	93	–	6	–	5,126	22,121	95	–	4	–	5,956	26,527	95	1	3	–
Printing/publishing																		
Bookbinding	21	365	36	50	5	9	35	651	35	47	7	11	41	795	48	47	4	1
Engraving/lithographing	6	98	54	35	7	4	17	170	81	4	15	0	25	464	79	15	6	–
Printing/publishing	191	1,784	73	7	20	0	248	3,242	74	6	18	2	359	4,694	77	13	10	–
TOTAL	218	2,247	66	15	17	2	300	4,063	68	12	16	3	425	5,953	73	18	9	–
Textiles																		
Carding/fulling	158	338	82	1	17	–	72	173	75	14	8	2	44	164	57	34	10	1
Carpets							9	13	54	38	8	0	344	689	45	49	4	2
Cotton	5	495	21	36	18	25	11	1,738	27	34	18	29	9	2,495	42	42	9	7
Flax													39	1,406	62	8	24	6
Hosiery	10	244	21	67	7	4	66	1,316	26	66	4	5	35	530	28	60	3	9
Knit goods													74	992	26	62	4	8
Scutching	24	480	62	12	19	7	29	978	61	11	20	8	5	89	89	2	7	2
Woven goods													604	781	33	61	3	2
Wool	233	3,696	46	34	12	8	993	5,221	46	41	8	6	304	5,191	44	43	8	5
Misc. textile							3	19	84	0	16	0	33	461	46	43	5	6
TOTAL	430	5,253	46	32	14	8	1,183	9,458	42	40	10	9	1,491	12,798	44	42	9	6
Wood/paper products																		
Bags/boxes, paper							11	179	26	51	8	16	23	434	28	65	2	5
Barrels	669	1,837	95	0	5	0	640	1,843	91	–	9	0	533	1,667	91	–	9	0

TABLE 1 (concluded)

	1871						1881						1891					
	Establish-ments	Employees	Percentage				Establish-ments	Employees	Percentage				Establish-ments	Employees	Percentage			
		N	Age 16+		Under 16			N	Age 16+		Under 16			N	Age 16+		Under 16	
			M	F	M	F			M	F	M	F			M	F	M	F
Baskets	15	48	56	17	23	4	22	99	58	6	35	1	139	380	53	27	16	4
Boxes, wooden	78	355	78	9	13	0	4	80	90	0	10	0	12	132	86	2	13	0
Brooms/brushs	2	34	21	41	8	30	58	552	81	9	8	2	54	514	78	16	5	0
Buttons							7	407	30	51	11	8	4	433	48	40	10	2
Cabinets/furniture	536	2,769	90	5	5	–	625	3,460	86	5	8	–	701	4,720	90	4	5	1
Carriages	1,421	4,780	96	–	3	0	1,690	5,391	97	–	2	–	1,561	5,096	96	–	3	–
Musical instruments	26	387	94	1	6	0	29	817	93	3	4	0	60	1,941	94	–	6	0
Planing/moulding							57	520	96	0	4	0	233	1,948	96	0	4	0
Sashes/doors/blinds	156	1,548	91	–	9	0	281	2,286	96	1	4	0	324	2,381	96	–	4	0
Shingles	414	1,541	72	0	26	1	204	910	82	1	16	1	295	1,492	89	–	11	–
Ships	19	460	95	0	5	0	15	367	99	0	1	0	15	597	95	0	5	0
Staves							27	253	86	0	14	0	43	1,012	86	14	0	0
Wood turning	52	120	90	0	10	0	38	133	94	0	6	0	65	251	95	1	4	0
Misc. paper													8	135	39	42	9	10
Misc. wood	61	295	66	5	22	6	131	611	69	5	26	1	185	893	89	6	4	2
TOTAL	3,449	14,154	90	2	8	–	3,839	17,908	89	3	7	1	4,255	24,026	90	5	5	–
Miscellaneous																		
Brick/tile	309	1,939	86	1	13	–	400	2,768	85	1	13	–	463	3,791	86	–	14	–
Electrical light													48	287	98	–	2	–
Electrical products													14	164	94	5	1	0
Gas	11	113	99	0	1	0	23	241	99	0	1	0	30	317	99	0	1	0
Glass	3	98	70	0	30	0	6	330	77	–	23	0	9	315	72	1	27	0
Indian wares							50	70	36	64	0	0	100	132	41	23	22	14
Jewellery/watches	93	235	86	3	11	0	188	422	89	2	9	0	362	947	91	5	3	–

Photographs	97	194	78	9	9	4		103	200	80	16	4	1		189	424	69	25	4	2
Pottery	58	207	93	1	6	1		72	265	87	7	5	0		60	179	92	2	6	0
Trunks/boxes/valises	27	165	50	17	21	12		13	191	62	18	15	6		25	541	74	13	11	2
Misc. specialized	122	530	74	15	8	2		235	1,625	62	21	11	6		225	1,690	74	20	5	–

SOURCE: *Census of Canada*, 1871, vol. 3; 1881, vol. 3; 1891, vol. 3. Construction trades and industries have not been included. Calculations of percentages are mine.

NOTES TO TABLE 1

[a] Too often Canadian political economists have overlooked the fact that these 'staples' had to be at least partially processed before being exported. The 1957 report of the Royal Commission on Canada's Economic Prospects first introduced the term 'primary' manufacturing to cover 'relatively minor processing' of natural resources and thus strengthened the often false impression of the degree and sophistication of manufacturing involved. It also forced some curious divisions, so that flour production was 'primary' but making woollen textiles was secondary, even though both used agricultural 'natural resources.' See Bertram, 'Historical Statistics.'

[b] There is a legitimate question to be raised about the statistics on sawmill employment. Since the numbers are vastly larger than those defining themselves as millmen in the 1891 occupational census, is it possible that the lumber companies included their woodsworkers in the totals listed under industrial establishments? The census takers were given two separate forms for industrial establishments and 'Products of the Forest' (Nos 6 and 7 respectively). The instructions to enumerators were explicit about the distinction between logging and sawing: 'This schedule relates to the products of the forest, in the state in which they are got out simply, and must not be confounded with returns of saw-mills, ship-building yards, or other industrial establishments' (Canada, Department of Agriculture, *Manual Containing 'The Census Act,' and Instructions to Officers Employed in the Taking of the Third Census of Canada (1891)* (Ottawa: Queen's Printer 1891), 24). Unfortunately Schedule 7 did not ask about the number of employees in the woods – hence the confusion. It is no doubt possible that there was sloppiness in the recording of the industrial statistics (and, since the manuscript industrial censuses after 1871 were destroyed, we have no way of checking). But it seems reasonable to conclude that the figures for sawmills are more or less accurate, that is, that they drew in large numbers of Ontario wage-earners each season that they were open. The wide gap between the industrial and the occupational data is probably explicable by the seasonality and occupational pluralism of so many workers who passed through these mill jobs, and who probably never thought of describing themselves as permanent 'millmen.'

· – Indicates less than .5 per cent.

demand by expanding their workshops, while many wealthy merchants who had been importing manufactured goods invested in new industrial enterprises.[32] In both cases, the goal was what has become known as 'import substitution.' The production of consumer goods, especially clothing, soon brought together some of the largest workforces in Ontario's industrial economy (see Table 1).

This industrialization process emerged in three spurts, each prompted by new market opportunities or difficulties. The first lasted to the economic collapse of 1857 and saw the rise of the first large saw, flour, and textile mills, railway shops, and expanded workshops in many industries. In the second phase – from 1860 to 1873 – in response to the expansion of railways and the stimulus of the American Civil War, 'manufactories' proliferated across the province and the first more specialized factories emerged in industries producing such consumer goods as shoes, agricultural implements, stoves, sewing machines, newspapers, clothing, and furniture. In the final phase – from the late 1870s to the early 1890s – the resource industries geared to export, especially lumber, remained important, but proportionally much more new investment was driven by production for the domestic consumer market.

This was by no means a smooth path of growth and prosperity. The province's new industrial-capitalist economy was a chronically insecure and unstable edifice. Wage-earners had to cope with annual cycles that still brought seasonal shut-downs. In 1871 the census takers found that only three out of five industrial enterprises in Ontario ran the year round (though they employed 70 per cent of male workers and 75 per cent of female workers).[33] The climate dictated some of the seasonal shutdowns, especially in the many workplaces powered by water (62 per cent of those reporting any power),[34] which could be disrupted by winter freeze-ups, spring floods, or summer drops in water levels.[35] Hot summers could also curtail work in such places as tobacco factories, glass works, and even an Ottawa dressmaking and millinery shop.[36] Climate, however, was most important in shaping the annual cycle of natural-resource production. The province's largest industrial sector, sawmilling, was organized entirely around the changing seasons, so that the mills were open only from about April to November. Oil too could be pumped only in the warmer months. Similarly the processing of farm products covered only a short spell on the calendar, especially flour milling and the canning industry, which took off in the 1880s. Predictably the numerous agricultural-implement plants had to organize their production in reverse – from fall to spring, with a lengthy summer shutdown – in order to have equipment ready to sell to farmers during the summer.[37] Many of the new factories, however, had to follow a different pattern of seasonal swings based, not on the climate, but on cycles of consumer demand. The Labour Commission heard reports of two-to-four-month shut-downs every year in boot and shoe, confectionery, and tobacco factories and stove foundries; there were even longer closures in clothing workshops. Few industries escaped a shut-down of at least three to six weeks a year.[38]

The economic insecurity had more to do with larger structural problems in the new economy. Ontario manufacturers had to weather some dramatic swings in the international business cycle, notably the severe depression of 1857–60 and the prolonged slump that set in after 1873, which was relieved only for brief periods in the 1880s. Although it did not stop all industrial growth, as economists once argued, this so-called Great Depression certainly made survival and adaptation a challenge for the province's industrialists.[39] Equally troubling, though, was the small size of the domestic market available to industrialists, which limited their ability to expand and specialize their production facilities. Compared to the United States, Ontario's population was small, and after 1850 it grew much more slowly as immigrants increasingly tended to bypass the region. Moreover, its farmers had only limited cash for purchasing manufactured goods.[40] Here is undoubtedly a large part of the explanation for both the frequency of business failures (an international phenomenon)[41] and the slowness of some consumer-goods industries to emerge. The characteristic industry of the British and American industrial revolutions, cotton mills, arrived relatively late in Ontario – in 1871 there were only two good-sized mills, at Merritton and Dundas, and by the end of the decade only two more, at Cornwall.[42] Not surprisingly, then, Ontario's industrial establishments remained comparatively small. In 1871 the census takers discovered that the province's two largest employers were railway shops – the Great Western with 984 workers in Hamilton and the Northern with 561 in Toronto. But only three other firms – a Toronto boot and shoe factory, a Hamilton clothing enterprise, and a Toronto furniture works – had more than 400. In all, only 21 firms had more than 200 employees and only 19 more had over 150. Only 71 industrial establishments had more than 100 workers; they employed 14,091 workers (an average of 198.5 each), a mere 15 per cent of the province's industrial workforce. The mean size of Ontario's industrial establishments that year was only 4.4 employees. Roughly two out of every five firms had only one worker, and nearly 85 per cent had under six. In only a few industries – railway shops, rolling mills, cotton factories, engine works, and distilleries – did any firms come close to dominating production. In contrast, the handful of impressively large firms in sawmilling (such as those at Hawkesbury, Ottawa, Trenton, and

Deseronto) and flour milling existed in a large sea of small-scale manufacturers and contributed only 12 and 18 per cent respectively of total
value added in the province's production. By 1891 some sectors had relatively more large establishments – agricultural implements and cotton,
in particular – but the average number of workers in all industrial establishments that year was still only five.[43]

To make matters worse, Ontario industrialists could not be certain
of controlling their own markets against outside competition, either
regional or international. Montreal had always loomed as the premier
manufacturing centre of the St Lawrence waterway system, especially
with its cheaply produced consumer goods. By the 1880s, Ontario boot
and shoe manufacturers, some of the earliest contributors to the province's industrial revolution, had more or less given up the battle with
Quebec producers, and textile and tobacco manufacturers were feeling
the same pressure. Far more threatening, however, was the steady flow
of cheap British and American goods into the province. The high American tariffs imposed in 1866 cut Ontario manufacturers out of the southern markets but did not prevent the dumping of cheaply produced
American products in Ontario, especially in the deep depression of the
1870s. In that decade, the convergence of two sources of uncertainty for
Ontario manufacturers – the business cycle and intense competition –
created a crisis that threatened the survival of many of them. Some producers quietly colluded to control price competition among themselves,
but the most widely discussed solution was tariff protection. From the
beginning of Ontario's industrialization process, industrialists had cam-
paigned for a state policy to limit competition in the domestic market by
raising tariffs. They got some help in the provincial tariffs of 1858-9,
watched that protection eroded in the new post-Confederation commercial policies, and then battled successfully for the elaborate package for
stimulating manufacturing development in the National Policy inaugurated by the Macdonald Tory government in 1879. In the next four years
there was a small flurry of new investment in manufacturing including a
considerable expansion of the province's cotton textile production.
Small-scale producers took a new lease on life, and overproduction was
soon a serious problem in many sectors. 'There is scarcely a little town
or village in Canada but has a cabinet factory with power going,' a Toronto cabinet manufacturer told the Labour Commission. 'Those men are
not making money ... the market is not sufficient to keep all those factories in a healthy state of operation.'[44]

For our purposes it is perhaps most important to note that, in the dark
moments of the 1870s, many manufacturers had come to realize that
tariffs were not a panacea and that, over the longer term, they needed to

cut their costs of production to compete in the larger, more crowded Canadian and North American markets. The Chatham agricultural-implement manufacturer who argued in 1887 that he had to produce a thousand fanning mills to make the same profit he had made producing seven hundred five years earlier voiced a common concern.[45] It was the industrialists' drive to modify and intensify the labour process in various ways, as much as the proliferation of new factories, that gave so many Ontario workers a sense of living through a profoundly disturbing industrial transformation.

For the working-class experience within this process of industrialization, it is also important to note that the new industrial enterprises were widely scattered across the province, principally in regions not far removed from commercial agriculture and logging.[46] Much of the initial industrial development took place outside large cities, in communities of well less than five thousand people. This pattern was encouraged by the profusion of farm families with some disposable income and the many good sites for water power across the province; and by the proliferation of railway lines in the 1860s and 1870s throughout the settled agricultural regions. The industrial centres where the new enterprises clustered had many similarities, but between the 1840s and the 1890s they tended to be of three types. First and by far the most common was the small, multi-factory town serving a nearby (and, it hoped, growing) agricultural hinterland. Each one was unique, but one could expect to find in these places some combination of agricultural-implement works, woollen mill, stove foundry, furniture or woodworking factory, wagon shop, brewery, tannery, and eventually perhaps a knitting mill. Throughout the period, these businesses ranged in size from a cluster of artisanal workshops to quite a large factory. The large-scale enterprises that had emerged by the 1870s could be found even in towns and villages as small as Oshawa, Galt, and Dundas. Even before the 1890s some towns developed a degree of industrial specialization, notably in metalworking and machine building, or in woodworking, especially in southwestern Ontario, where much of the province's furniture and musical-instrument production was concentrated.[47]

The second type of manufacturing town was a commercial and transportation hub, generally with metropolitan ambitions to dominate the trade of a much wider hinterland. Toronto and Hamilton were the most successful contenders in the 1840s and 1850s, but towns like Sarnia, Windsor, London, Oakville, Port Hope, Whitby, Belleville, and Kingston shared some of the same characteristics.[48] In many ways, these towns had a mixture of industries similar to those of the agricultural service towns, but here one was less likely to find milling operations and more likely to encounter two additional economic sectors – metalworking shops turning out heavy transportation equipment (such as the Hamilton and Toronto rolling mills and the Kingston locomotive and steam-engine factories),[49] and the first large-scale producers of light consumer goods, such as boots and shoes, ready-made clothing, tobacco, daily newspapers, and some processed food and drink (such as biscuits and liquor), made possible by larger pools of labour (steadily restocked with new immigrants) and the extensive trading networks into the hinterland of each metropolis. Some of these were also administrative towns where manufacturers could sell to governmental institutions and a better-paid white-collar workforce. The Toronto and Ottawa printing industries, for example, grew up under those circumstances. In 1871 Toronto had only 12 per cent of Ontario's industrial production, in striking contrast to Montreal, which had 43 per cent of Quebec's production.[50] But by the 1880s Toronto had won its commanding position over all other towns of the region – symbolized by the relocation of the Massey agricultural implement works from Newcastle to Toronto in 1879.

The third sort of industrial centre – the more specialized mill town – was considerably different. Some, like Ottawa, Belleville, Peterborough, Bracebridge, Collingwood, and many more, were the sites of extensive sawmilling. Others were specialized textile centres, first the larger woollen-mill towns that began in the 1860s (especially such eastern-Ontario centres as Almonte and other mill villages on the Mississippi in Lanark County and towns on the Grand River in Waterloo County) and then cotton-mill towns in the 1870s (notably Merritton, Dundas, and Cornwall, which by 1878 reputedly had the largest cotton factories in the Dominion). The sawmilling communities were often short-lived, as the nearest forests fell to the logger's axe, and they tended to have many fewer spin-off industries, beyond the production of such simple wood products as staves, shingles, and other construction materials. Western Ontario also had its own distinct resource towns – the oil-refining centres of Oil Springs, Petrolia, and Sarnia, which were also in decline by the end of the century when the resource was exhausted.

These three urban forms were not neatly divided into distinct regions, but by the 1880s a slight regional specialization had begun to emerge. The leading metropolitan centres were clustered on the west end of Lake Ontario. The most successful mixed-factory towns were spread through the south-central and southwestern part of the province, while such eastern-Ontario towns as Belleville, Kingston, and Brockville were clearly stagnating – only 30 per cent of Ontario's manufacturing employment was found in this region in 1881. The mill towns tended to be dispersed along the extremities of eastern, central, and western Ontario, though clearly the Grand River textile centres were exceptions. There was also a discernible west-central region of faster growth and partial concentration, especially of larger metalworking firms; this region started in Toronto and extended around the west end of Lake Ontario and westward up the Grand River Valley through Wentworth, Brant, and Waterloo counties, with a leap over to London in Middlesex County.[51]

So, to a considerable extent, the first phase of industrialization in Ontario was a decentralized process based on the proliferating opportunities in an expanding economy of farm, forest, and transportation. Compared to the British and European experience, or even that of Quebec and the Maritimes, Ontario's First Industrial Revolution was at first based much more heavily on the processing of natural resources produced in the countryside and on serving the needs of those rural producers. (In Britain much more of the countryside was filled with rural outworkers engaged in manufacturing.) The small factory town with its close hinterland figured much more prominently in Ontario than in the other Canadian provinces, where industrialization was much more concentrated in large cities. The output of Ontario factories also had its own special industrial mix. Forest products loomed extremely large. The textile industry concentrated predominantly on coarser woollen goods, and, in contrast to Britain and the United States, did not include cotton mills until relatively late. There was no munitions industry to compare with the extensive armament factories that were so important to the development of precision metalworking elsewhere.[52] Metalworking was concentrated, to a limited extent, in machinery production for the transportation industries, but far more in consumer goods, so that the iron moulder was more common than the machinist or boilermaker. Perhaps most important, in the absence of coal resources or high-quality iron deposits, there was no primary iron and steel industry. Even the rolling mills that had opened in the 1850s were closed in 1872, when foreign steel rails began to replace the iron rails previously rolled in Ontario's mills. (Hamilton's rolling mills reopened in 1879, but they simply rolled scrap for nails and other metal goods produced locally.[53]) The province's extensive metalworking industries had to rely on imported iron. Finally it is worth remembering that, despite all the remarkable growth of industrial enterprises, manufacturing in this predominantly agrarian province still drew in the same proportion of the gainfully employed in 1891 that it had in 1851 – roughly one-fifth. To point to all these limitations is not in any way to diminish the sense of a 'revolution' that people thought, quite correctly, they were living through. At the end of the period, Ontario may still have lacked the concentrations of large factories that had grown up in Manchester and Chicago, but workers in the province's factories found themselves confronting a system of production that had profoundly new elements.

REORGANIZING THE WORK

In pre-industrial Upper Canada manufacturing generally meant the exercise of manual skill and strength with simple tools and occasionally animal or water power to make a product from start to finish. The work was done by an individual or a small work team either in and around the family household or in a relatively primitive mill or artisanal workshop. Wage labour was not the predominant way to get this work done, but it was certainly not unknown. In the small workshops, especially in the towns, craft workers might take on a journeyman or, more likely (to avoid high journeymen's wages), an apprentice or two to work with them on the skilled work, and occasionally a day labourer to help with the heavy unskilled tasks. Mill owners often hired millers and sawyers. In the few large manufacturing enterprises that existed, such as the iron works and the shipyards, owners relied on a more regular wage-earning force. To curb footloose habits at a time when labour was scarce, these workers were sometimes legally bound to their 'masters' with contracts of indenture that stipulated the mutual obligations between the parties, but by the early nineteenth century that understanding was most often informal and unwritten. In a relationship of 'paternalism,' workers would be expected to serve faithfully and obediently, while the employers promised to pay both a wage and some part of their employees' room and board, often taking them into their own houses where their wives would be expected to provide for the workers' daily needs. Many more workers in all occupational groups probably had briefer, more casual relations with employers that took them away from farming or other independent production for only short spells. By the 1830s, in the larger lakefront towns, especially Toronto, the odd woodworker or metalworker was using a simple machine, such as a lathe powered by water or, in a few cases, by a small steam engine. Yet with only these few isolated exceptions, employers put these men and women to work on well-recognized skilled and unskilled manual tasks and, aside from trying to exercise strict discipline and to keep wages reasonably low, undertook no fundamental restructuring of work routines and practices.[54]

By the 1840s and 1850s, however, competition in the new industrial-capitalist economy stimulated would-be industrialists to organize production in new ways in the hopes of substantially increasing their profits. They had no set formula for how their new operations might run.[55] Some production problems had already been addressed elsewhere, notably in the texile industry, and the managerial and technological solutions could simply be imported. In others, such as metalworking, it made no sense to introduce technology and work routines that would not pay in the colonial economy. (Puddling furnaces and rolling mills were much slower to appear in British North America than in Britain, for example.)[56] In many industries, it was an age of considerable local experimentation. Over the second half of the nineteenth century, more and more Ontario employers had to find ways to extract the maximum effort and highest output from the wage labour they paid for. This eventually forced them to reorganize the labour process, recruit from new pools of labour, and develop new systems to instil the necessary discipline and morale. There were some clear continuities from the past, but some dramatically new departures.

Throughout the period, however, in many Ontario enterprises, the lack of a large, secure market for identical products put sharp limits on capitalists' ability to alter the labour process. From the early days of industrialization, most Ontario manufacturers trying to make more money had found that to reach more customers they had to expand their product lines rather than increase the number of identical products. Lumbermen and flour millers were almost unique in their ability to produce huge quantities of identical or similar products.[57] In 1871 census takers concluded that 'the division of labour is not carried on to the same extent as in the older societies of Europe, and in the same establishments there are often to be found grouped together several branches of industry.' Many manufacturers complained to parliamentary committees in the 1870s that their markets were too small to permit product specialization. 'They have factories on the other side where they can complete one hundred machines where we can complete ten,' a London machinery manufacturer told the Labour Commission a decade later. 'The only thing running against us is that we have not quite enough people in Canada to let us run into specialties.' These structural limitations were to have important consequences for what many Ontario employers expected from their workers.[58]

Towards Factory Production

At first, in most industries, the new capitalists probably tried to turn out more goods for the expanding markets simply by hiring more workers, especially skilled workers to carry on their customary craft production under the entrepreneur's roof but with their own tools.[59] For the many firms producing a wide range of goods for a small market, the flexibility and ingenuity of these workers were crucial. Their bosses relied heavily on their expertise and inventiveness and often gave them con-

siderable independence and supervisory responsibility in their work.[60]
The smaller number of industrialists able to increase specialized production of a narrow range of goods in larger workplaces, however, soon
discovered that craft workers were not an easy workforce to push
harder. As we will see, they had a strong spirit of independence and
carefully guarded the 'arts and mysteries' of their craft, which included
the technical details and rhythm and pace of their daily work. And
employers believed that there were seldom enough of them in the provincial labour market. So employers began altering workplace practices
to use this labour more effectively, or even to do without it altogether.
Many scholars have adopted the term 'manufactory' used by Marx and
many Canadian contemporaries for this kind of expanded workshop that
still functioned primarily on manual skill but was moving sharply away
from artisanal practices.[61] Across the industrial landscape, the ways in
which the capitalists reshaped the labour process in manufactories fall
into five categories, each of which eroded the artisanal practices still
further.

The first was an attempt to limit the range of products the craft worker
was expected to turn out, on the largely correct assumption that repetitive work on similar goods could encourage a speed-up. As a machinist
told the Labour Commission in 1888, 'a journeyman going into such a
shop will be at the same job all the time for he gets perfect at that kind of
work and it pays the employer better to have him kept at it.'[62] The
skilled wage-earner thus lost the artisan's contact with his customers and
control over the choice of products to manufacture, and some of the
crafts began to fragment internally between those workers making goods
to order and those producing for mass markets. By 1870 Ontario's moulders were becoming segmented into specialists working on either brass
or iron and, within the latter group, on stoves, agricultural implements,
or machinery. Printers had separated into newspaper, book-publishing,
and jobbing labour markets. Some furniture makers made only chairs.
Movement between the branches of these industries became less and less
common, and union solidarity between them was not even assured.[63]

Closely tied to this kind of narrowing of craft practice was a second
innovation – a narrowing of the range of tasks that the craft worker
would be expected to perform by using cheaper, less-skilled labour for
work that did not require his knowing hand. Craft skill remained at the
centre of production, but it was to be applied more intensively, with
fewer interruptions for lifting, hauling, and fetching. The cigarmaker
could stay at his bench while others prepared the tobacco and brought
it to him. The cabinet-maker would have his wood cut and planed by
other workers. The stove moulder did not assemble the parts of the

stove he had cast; that became the job of the new occupational group known as 'stovemounters' (one of whom, Alan Studholme, served as the only independent labour member in the Ontario legislature from 1906 to 1919).[64] Inside the larger foundries, patternmakers and coremakers became new occupations distinct from moulding, and 'bench' moulders (who worked on smaller parts) became distinct from those making the larger castings on the sandy floor. Likewise in large machine shops, such as at the Massey works, 'fitters' became a separate occupational category from machinists.[65]

In many industries, especially metalworking, this narrowing and specialization of skill was about as far as managerial innovation could go. The pressure then built up for the third step – simplifying or reducing as much as possible the training period for skilled work and recruiting workers who had not served full apprenticeships. These efforts produced some of the fiercest battles with printers, moulders, cigarmakers, and any other trades where craft skills remained important throughout the period.[66] In the midst of a major confrontation with the shoemakers' new union, for example, a frustrated boot and shoe manufacturer denounced the hundred men in his factory for refusing to allow a single boy to work with them: 'The consequence was that men had to do the boys' work; and what could be done by a boy for two dollars a week the firm had to pay a man ten dollars to do.'[67]

In many other industries, where the market was large enough to allow for high-volume output, industrialists moved toward a fourth form of industrial transformation – a much more extensive subdivision of skilled labour into simpler tasks that could each be carried out by narrowly specialized, minimally trained, and cheaply paid workers. In the 1840s and 1850s subdivided labour was most evident in the textile, sawmilling, and boot and shoe industries. Others soon followed. A visitor to an Oshawa agricultural-tool plant in 1862 was quite struck by this process: 'While in ordinary cases – such as axe making – the one person can do the various parts necessary, in this establishment they pass through the hands of eight persons before they are finished.' He also stopped at the province's largest factory, E.B. Eddy's woodworking operation near Ottawa, and found that making a pail involved 'a good many operations, and at each time by a separate individual.' Likewise, in the chair department of a Bowmanville furniture factory, 'each man has his part to do, a chair having to pass through six different hands before being completed.' A tour of the Joseph Hall agricultural implement works a few years later prompted a similar observation: 'Each man has his own specified work to perform, and by this system an agricultural machine was able to be finished, not only in much shorter time, but in a much better manner, than could be done by other means.' At the end of the decade a journalist found the division of labour in Wantzer's large sewing-machine factory in Hamilton 'carried to the last point of perfection.'[68] Between the 1860s and 1880s many other large factories incorporated this kind of advanced subdivision of labour. By 1888 the manager of Toronto's largest boot and shoe firm, J.D. King, could claim that a boot passed through the hands of fifty workers before it was completed.[69]

Some industrialists organized a division of labour between their central factory building and the households of workers or small workshops of subcontractors. This kind of 'putting out,' or outwork, was primarily an attempt to build on female domestic skills and to avoid the risks of full-time recruitment and management. From the 1860s onward, it was widespread in the emerging ready-made clothing industry, especially in Toronto and Hamilton, where women took home bundles of pre-cut cloth to stitch into garments, or worked in small subcontractors' workshops (known as 'sweat shops' by the end of the century).[70] Occasional references to putting-out have surfaced in other industries, such as paper-box-making for the E.B. Eddy works and weaving cane seats for chairs at the Bowmanville furniture factory in the 1860s,[71] but, overall, outwork played no significant part in Ontario's First Industrial Revolution, except in the garment industry.

The fifth possible workplace innovation was closely connected to the subdivision of labour, namely, mechanization, a process that seemed to accelerate in the 1870s and 1880s. By 1871 half the province's industrial employees (nine out of ten of those in the sixty largest firms) worked in establishments with the most powerful new machinery – improved water-powered engines and steam engines.[72] These could simply make available unprecedented strength – to grind wheat or to shape iron in huge forges and rolling mills or tobacco in plug moulds, for example.[73] But more often these power sources were linked to specialized machinery that was intended to replace some part of craft skill and thus cut labour costs. Looking back at a family business built up to a workforce of 150 by 1875, a Smiths Falls agricultural-implement manufacturer bragged to a parliamentary committee that productivity had increased with mechanization: 'There was a time several years ago when we could not produce over $1000 per man; but with improved machinery we can now turn out from 30 to 40 per cent more.'[74] Many industrialists must have expected the same results.

From the 1840s Ontario's textile mills offered some of the most prominent examples of relatively complex machinery for carding, spinning, weaving, and so on, all of it developed in Britain or the United States.[75] Equally striking were the lumber mills, where by the 1850s multiple-blade gang and circular saws powered by water or steam were rapidly replacing the manual routines of the hewer of squared timber and the hand sawyer with the simple, single-blade saws. The fact that these mills ran smoothly with considerable labour turnover suggests their considerable success in reducing skill requirements for the province's leading mass-production industry.[76] In the 1850s skilled tailors and shoemakers also first faced the disruptive effects of the sewing machine.[77] After 1850, in fact, dewy-eyed visitors to the province's new industrial workplaces began reporting regularly on the machinery used by metalworkers, woodworkers, and many others.[78] Invariably such commentators praised the speed of the new machinery. In a typical account, a tourist in 1850 reported his amazement at the woodworking machinery in the already large Jacques and Hays furniture works in Toronto: 'From the rough timber a neat bedstead can be made and put together in the short space of two minutes.' Fourteen years later, another visitor to the same factory marvelled at 'an admirable contrivance for doing perfectly in less than a minute that would require an hour to do imperfectly by hand labor.' The Labour Commission heard similar comments. 'Spokes were formerly made by hand, but it was an everlasting job,' a St Thomas manufacturer of carriage woodwork explained in a characteristic defence of technological change. 'The only successful way of conducting the trade is with the aid of machinery.' An Ottawa furniture manufacturer boasted that his output had increased by 50 per cent in ten years 'in consequence of improved machinery and the men being able to turn it out faster.'[79] Of course, a parallel series of newspaper stories made it clear that this fast-paced new technology often made the factories much more dangerous workplaces and the scenes of innumerable grisly accidents.[80]

The 'labour-saving' (that is, labour-displacing) qualities of the new machines also got plenty of attention. Towards the end of the period, a *Globe* reporter found the Massey factory in Toronto 'a marvellous study in labor-saving machinery; it really looks as if it was the machines that are human and the men that were machines. The steam-driven tools pick up bars and rods of iron, bend them, and shape them as if they were bits of tin.'[81] The Labour Commissioners heard much about labour displacement. 'I know they have one machine in the waggon shop here that takes the place of about twenty men,' a Chatham man reported. A Toronto carpenter was convinced that a particular woodworking machine would 'mortise as much as fifty men in a day, or probably a hundred men.' Some employers agreed. 'One machine may do the work of seven or eight hands, sometimes, and thereby might throw six hands out,' the manager of a Kingston hosiery company admitted. 'I think the tendency of machinery is to displace men,' a Toronto cabinet manufacturer declared. 'You turn out more work with the same number of men.' Most industrialists tried to dodge the issue of technological unemployment by arguing that the new technology had allowed them to expand their businesses and increase employment overall or that the job opportunities in the wider economy had grown. Few workers bought this argument.[82]

Perhaps most disturbing for Ontario's craft workers was the potential for de-skilling through mechanization. Of all the many voices the Labour Commission heard on this question, two will suffice to convey employers' satisfaction and workers' grief. A Chatham flour-mill owner explained:

With the introduction of roller mills and improved machinery, we do not need so many skilled men. An ordinary intelligent mechanic, or an intelligent man, is able to run a roller mill as well as a skilled miller could do. When there were stones to be dressed, under the old system of grinding, a man required to serve an apprenticeship to the business, and have a great deal of practice, but now machinery has changed all that.

With much more regret, an aged millwright described how new machinery had changed his craft:

When I first went to the trade we had a casting from the foundry. An ordinary mechanic like myself would take and lay the work out. Then he would chip it with the hammer and chisel, and after that chiselling process he would file it to make it true, square, and clear of twist. Since the introduction of the planer has become universal, an unskilled man starts a planing-machine, which moves back and forth, and does the work silently and cheaply, and to a certain extent only does it better, but it may be at one-fourth the cost, and in one third the time.[83]

At the same time, the popular fascination with the new technology in the Ontario factory system should not blind us to the relatively small extent of mechanization in Ontario's First Industrial Revolution (as in Britain's).[84] In most industries the organizational changes in the workplace were at least as important as the technological. In some, the subdividing of labour was adequate. In many cases, machinery did not yet exist to replace craft skill or, quite commonly, could only be introduced in part of the operation. A visitor to a large Cobourg woollen mill in 1864 extolled the virtues of the machinery used to process the wool into cloth, but also paused to describe the skilled manual tasks of the 'burler,' who spread out the woven wool and corrected the imperfections left by the machines – undoing knots, 'picking out gouty threads and mending the gaps thus made by running in even ones, and rendering it as perfect as possible.'[85] The large Jacques and Hay woodworking factory in New Lowell still relied heavily on hand lathes as late as the 1870s.[86] Hart Massey's agricultural–implement works included some impressive technology in the woodworking and machine shops, but nothing to speak of in the firm's large iron foundry, where, as in most of the province's foundries, moulders still made their castings by hand.[87] George Brown and many of his fellow newspaper publishers had installed steam presses run by specialized machine operators, but until the arrival of the linotype machine in the 1890s, they had to rely on skilled compositors to set the type by hand.[88] On one floor of Jacques and Hay's much admired furniture factory in Toronto, narrowly specialized workers mass-produced simple chairs on whirring machinery, while upstairs skilled cabinet-makers assembled fine furniture by hand. In a Kingston bakery, the bread was prepared by hand while the biscuits were machine-made.[89] In the province's few glass works, glass-blowers still used their own strength and dexterity.[90] There were also contrasts between sectors of particular crafts; for example, coopers worked by hand for breweries and flour mills but with new machinery for the distilleries and the burgeoning oil industry.[91] In general, the smallness of the product markets open to most Ontario manufacturers meant that the production runs in their factories were too small and varied to allow for the specialization of tasks either by hand or with machines that would make much of the new machinery pay. They needed workers and machines with the flexibility to shift to the constantly changing specifications of new orders.

Skill

There was clearly a trend here toward skill dilution as a solution to the high cost and inflexibility of labour in Ontario's first industrialization process. Yet even where machines were in place, we should not assume that they wiped out manual skill. The ability of textile machinery to completely replace hand spinning and weaving, and of the rolling-mill technology to displace traditional blacksmithing were exceptions. Just as often the new machinery was simply incorporated into the craft. The tailor's adaptation to the sewing machine without losing his craft status was perhaps the best example. Even more important, many new machines demanded new skills (though employers were seldom eager to admit this). Operating a machine in this period was generally far from mindless. The stationary engineers eventually convinced the public that their work tending the new steam engines demanded careful training.[92] The millers in the highly mechanized flour mills continued to be highly

valued for the considerable skill in their jobs, and even after the introduction of new rolling technology in the 1870s and 1880s, the Chatham
mill owner who praised its de-skilling qualitities was frustrated with the
improperly trained 'unskilled men ... not fitted for their duties' who presented themselves as millers. 'You have got to trust certain things to
them,' he complained, 'and they learn at your expense.' Likewise the
sawyer in even the most mechanized sawmills had to be 'a man of outstanding ability, intelligent, agile and well-trained.'[93] The new occupational category of machinist similarly denoted men who used more
sophisticated machinery to add more precision to their skills. In the rolling mills the puddlers who purified the iron and the rollers who passed it
back and forth through the mills also became extremely valuable skilled
workmen.[94] Amidst the whir of the de-skilling machinery in the province's largest furniture factory, an observer was still impressed that in
much of the wood turning 'the hand still guides the tool, and guides it to
admiration,' and that fine furniture production still required 'skill and
dexterity.'[95] The cutters inside the province's clothing factories quickly
won their employers' respect for their abilities. Even in the highly subdivided textile industry, mule spinners and weavers emerged as powerful
groups of skilled men (and, occasionally, women).[96] The most skilled
element in the new boot and shoe factories, the male lasters who put
together the uppers and soles, had a similar status. A Hamilton shoemaker who worked at trimming described how men who were able to
run one of the new machines could earn the high wage of $15 a week: 'It
is a new machine, and there are not many who understand its working.'[97]

Unlike old-time artisans, most of these workers had more narrowly
focused skills that had to be exercised in quite specific industrial situations, but they had to use considerable judgment and discretion to do
their job properly and were generally allowed considerable independence on the shop floor. Employers often made every effort to hold onto
such a workforce, especially by moving to 'short time' (a shorter work
week) rather than shutting down completely during economic crises.[98]
As we will see, several of these new skilled groups struggled hard to get
some recognition of their new skills and emulated the older trades in
creating craft unions.

In a few of the highly mechanized operations, we also hear the first
assertions of pride from those whom social scientists would eventually
call 'semi-skilled' – machine operators engaged in repetitive work. A
nail maker who had just described to the Labour Commission the routine
of his job as 'sitting down and turning a rod in the machine' bristled
when a commissioner suggested, 'There is not much skilled labor about
it, is there?' The indignant worker insisted, 'It is skilled labor making

these nails ... and I have been twenty-eight years in the business, and should know something about it.' A machinist with a seven-year apprenticeship and thirty-two years' experience behind him who was working on a planer in a Hamilton factory reported, 'Before I came here they had a man four years at it, but they could not run it satisfactorily till I came. He spoiled work which had to be done over again. There is no man who can run a machine properly after [only] three years' apprenticeship.' A Toronto machinery manufacturer similarly explained, 'We have laborers who we considered skilled, because they have worked so long at the trade.' These workers were not interchangeable parts in some huge industrial machine. Their pride in their competence would help to fuel working-class resistance to the new industrial practices by the 1880s.[99]

We must also recognize the gendered dimensions of skill. In this industrializing period (as later), technical skill was formally recognized and rewarded only if it was found in male hands. Craftsmen tied their manual competence closely to their masculine identity – their much-vaunted 'manhood' – as breadwinners, and, as we will see, employers incorporated these assumptions into their wage structures, despite clear evidence that not all women wage-earners were simply untrained and unskilled. A woman working in an Ottawa printing office claimed that it would take 'pretty near a year' for women like her to become competent folders. A foreman in the city bindery agreed. Similarly, as their employers readily admitted, female stitchers in Toronto and Chatham corset factories needed at least six to eight months to learn their skilled tasks properly.[100] A Paris knitting-mill owner might similarly contend that female labour naturally had 'a quickness and deftness not obtainable otherwise,' but like other employers, he never elevated these valued attributes to the level of well-rewarded skill. The chief employer in that town, John Penman, regularly had to reach outside the country to find female weavers and knitters for his knitting mill, but he still paid women less than men. So too did the Cornwall cotton manufacturers.[101] Skill, then, was socially constructed, and to be a woman was to be denied full recognition for technical competence.

Not all manual labour was skilled, of course. The new factory system was no less reliant on the brute muscle power of unskilled labourers. Occasionally steam or water-power could be used to replace their work. By far the most impressive examples were in the flour mills, where closely linked mechanical devices driven by water-power carried the wheat through its several stages of transformation into flour without contact with human hands, and in the saw mills, where a handful of workers used primitive conveyor belts to move the logs from the millpond, through the saws, and out to the lumber yard in a matter of minutes.[102]

But outside these industries, the mechanization of the lifting, hauling, loading, and unloading of raw materials and finished products was generally a feature of the Second Industrial Revolution, not the First. Indeed, a visitor to state-of-the-art rolling mills in Toronto in 1864 described men carrying iron rails by hand, and commented on how he was nearly knocked down by the many labourers scurrying to and fro with wheelbarrels full of material. A former executive of the Ontario Rolling Mills Company in Hamilton later recalled similar work in the 1880s: 'All the lifting was done directly by hand labor and so cheap was this labor that it was really more economical to employ direct human effort than machinery. Even cranes, derricks, tackle and all the various simple labor-saving devices were rarely used in any factories at that time.' Reports and statistics from other establishments in the same decade suggest the same continuing reliance on the brute strength of many unskilled labourers, rather than the twentieth-century world of conveyor belts, travelling cranes, and fork-lift trucks.[103]

Human mental and manual capacities were thus by no means eliminated in Ontario's First Industrial Revolution. Certainly few of the province's craft workers could claim to work in conditions identical to the self-employed artisan – the shift to wage-earning had deprived them of too many crucial elements of control over investment and marketing. But in many industries across the province, considerable numbers of skilled workers in both old and new occupations and in large and small factories were essential to the production process and thus retained varying degrees of job control. Indeed the importance of the 'manufactory' brought a large increase in craft workers rather than a decline. The persistence of skilled work inside the Ontario factory system down to the 1880s helps to explain how some wage-earners continued to be able to shift into self-employment or small-scale entrepreneurship,[104] but also how craft unions could remain such a potent force in several cities until the end of the century.

In the broadest sense, then, Ontario manufacturers put together what we can call a 'factory system.' As the workplaces got larger (fifty workers might be some kind of turning point), as specialization and the subdivision of labour expanded, and as more machinery was installed, a transition from 'manufactory' to full-fledged 'factory' eventually took place. By the 1880s this kind of new capitalist workplace included the larger saw and flour mills, agricultural implement works, woollen, cotton, and paper mills, distilleries, tobacco factories, boot and shoe factories, sewing-machine factories, and some furniture factories (see Table 1). But many workplaces had not evolved far in this direction. The outcome of the capitalist reorganization was extremely uneven within and between industrial sectors. The small size of markets and units of production and the workers' own insistence on defining and shaping their own work practices guaranteed that. Ontario's late nineteenth-century factory system remained a patchwork of varied approaches to organizing work and cheapening the costs of production in an increasingly competitive economy. As I continue to use the term 'factory' in this chapter, it will be intended to encompass all this diversity, rather than to mean a narrowly specific form of industrial-capitalist workplace.

FINDING THE LABOUR POWER

Where could Ontario manufacturers hope to find the workers for their new factories? In time, they might expect that a well-stocked, self-regulating capitalist labour market would supply their needs, but for much of the last half of the nineteenth century no such equilibrium of supply and demand was possible.[105] To mobilize and hold on to a suitable, reliable factory workforce was no easy task. There was no large reservoir of craft workers in the countryside comparable to that available to British industry. After 1850 the number of immigrants declined and many still found their way into farming or moved on to the United States. Indeed, the little research done so far suggests that many workers were highly mobile in this period, moving often between jobs and communities. Frequently they followed the custom of their trade in travelling extensively to broaden their experience or, more often, simply looked for steady, more satisfying employment. Indeed, all these perambulations eventually created a continental labour market in particular skills, a growing craft identity, and the basis for a continental labour movement.[106] Moreover, potential wage-earners had their own inclinations about how a capitalist labour market should work. Many craft workers tried to control the market for their skills by using their unions to restrict the number of practitioners. Employers also had to recognize (as modern economists seldom do) that workers were not isolated individuals in an impersonal labour market, but rather members of families rooted in a variety of household economies. Both rural and urban families determined who among them should be sent out to earn wages and under what conditions. The male head of household was the most likely to be the chief breadwinner, but children and young adults, especially the males, might also be sent out to increase the family income. The young females might also be withdrawn from the paid workforce from time to time to help out with the family's domestic labour. These family decisions could mesh with industrialists' needs, but they could also frustrate them if urban wage-earning became a less attractive option, or if prospects looked brighter elsewhere. A Cornwall cotton manufacturer highlighted this problem in his 1876 testimony to a parliamentary committee: 'If we had more working people among us their families would be a great help; we have to draw largely from well-to-do farmers. This kind of help has to go home during the harvest and Christmas holidays. All these things work against us.'[107] Under these complex and shifting circumstances, Ontario's first industrialists tried to find the labour power to run their factories, primarily through labour migration and on-the-job training.

Men

Skilled male workers inevitably posed the biggest headache for employers – a North-America-wide malady, in fact. Not only were there frequently not enough of them,[108] but they were highly mobile and liable to leave one employer or one community after only a short stay, especially if they were young or were recent immigrants.[109] A few manufacturers experimented with the labour of Ontario prisoners, but those projects generally proved too unpopular and unproductive for widespread adoption.[110] Most employers expected the pool of new immigrants to wash up willing workers on their doorsteps. By the time of the Labour Commission hearings in 1888, there seemed to have evolved two distinct sources for skilled migrant labour. One group came from outside the country, the most well-rounded generally from Britain, the most specialized from the United States.[111] In general, those skilled men who arrived from abroad to work in Ontario factories were more likely to have served a formal apprenticeship elsewhere and to have accumulated experience in several larger industrial cities. Often they were specifically recruited and imported during a strike,[112] or at the start-up of a new industry, especially those with technologically sophisticated workplaces such as railway shops or textile and lumber mills.[113] But gradually, cheap transatlantic steamship fares and railway tickets encouraged the migration of new recruits more or less regularly. Throughout the second half of the nineteenth century, the transportation companies and the Dominion and provincial governments spewed out glowing advertisements to entice British, western-European, and American immigrants. Emigration societies in Britain also sponsored the emigration of unemployed workers. To stimulate the recruitment of newcomers, the Canadian state paid bonuses to emigration agents and gave discounts on travel fares to bona fide immigrants, in the face of growing criticism from the labour movement that the local labour markets were being flooded. State and business none the less had difficulty holding new immigrants in the labour pool of such an uncertain regional economy.[114]

The second group of potential recruits into skilled jobs were workers migrating from the villages of the Ontario countryside. They had probably grown up in rural, even agrarian surroundings and had picked up what skills they had more informally among family, relatives, and neighbours on farms or in small country workshops, where strict apprenticeships might be rare. In his autobiography, John Woodside, a moulder, recalled how he left his family's farm to learn his trade in an Owen Sound foundry in the 1860s and ten years later got a job in the Joseph Hall agricultural-implement works in Oshawa with the help of a boyhood friend. The best-studied examples of this pattern of labour migration are blacksmiths, moulders, and the woodworkers of Waterloo, Grey, and Bruce counties, who were steeped in German rural craftsmanship. Employers and workers in several trades – printers, moulders, harnessmakers, carriage builders, and bakers – told the Labour Commissioners about the 'country boys' who arrived in their midst. Manufacturers in the smaller towns probably drew regularly on such a labour pool, but these workers also migrated to the larger cities. A Toronto moulder with thirty years of work experience told the Labour Commission, 'There are a great many moulders, or boys, who learn the trade outside in the country towns who come into the city and they do not even have to serve their time at all.' This resentment prompted urban craft workers to intensify their efforts to block the flow of these competitors with demands for strict apprenticeship training.[115]

Many industrialists hoped that the overall growth of their industry in a particular district would build up a sufficient pool of experienced labour. 'The Gartshore Works many years ago caused Dundas to abound in thoroughly trained and skilled workers in iron,' a newspaper reported in 1872, 'and the "graduates" of the old Establishment – if we may use the expression – have made Dundas an iron working town.' Hamilton had a similar opportunity thanks to its many foundries. By the 1880s the Toronto garment industry had benefited from the increasing concentration of skilled Jewish tailors. At that point, too, Toronto's largest boot and shoe manufacturer, J.D. King, explained that 'shoe factories have been going on so long in Toronto that we never take on inexperienced hands at all.' This was likewise a crucial factor in the success of the Lanark County woollen industry. Yet it could take time to reach that critical mass, and an Oshawa agricultural–implement maker and the Cornwall cotton manufacturers lamented in the mid-1870s that they still lacked such a pool of skilled workers.[116] Until the end of the century, neither the Ontario government nor the municipalities put any money into technical schools that might have helped to increase their labour pools.[117]

In the face of an uncertain labour market, industrialists could train their own labour, and many did, at least to some extent. Boys from their own employees' families or from the town beyond the factory walls were regularly presented to them to be trained.[118] There is also evidence that apprenticeship did not disappear quickly from all trades. In 1865 a London printing office was still announcing the availability of apprentice indenture forms,[119] and the newspapers sometimes published both advertisements for apprentices in printing, blacksmithing, moulding, baking, and other trades[120] (including only two for young women – dressmaking and millinery)[121] and reports of court cases about apprentices' conflicts with their masters.[122] The 1888 Labour Commission heard a great deal about the decay of apprenticeship in many industries, though probably some witnesses' points of comparison were outside the country rather than in Upper Canada,[123] but in several branches of metalworking and woodworking, it still survived on a small scale, generally for only three to five years rather than the seven that British craftsmen served.[124] By that time, few Ontario employers bound their apprentices with indentures because in their experience too many would leave before completing their term.[125] 'Boys, after they had served a year or two, thought they were full-fledged machinists,' a Hamilton machinery manufacturer said, 'and they could do better elsewhere, and they wanted to go away.' A Chatham flour-mill owner had a similar experience: 'Boys will come into the shop, and in a year or so they will pick up a sort of trade, and start out thinking they are skilled mechanics.' A foreman in a St Thomas woodworking factory (who twenty years earlier had been the last in his workplace to be indentured) voiced a common complaint about boys' cheekiness when he told the Labour Commission, 'If you take a young man in now, you do not know the minute he is going to get saucy and leave you, after you have shoved him along a bit'; in eight years only two or three workers had stayed long enough in this factory to accumulate much proficiency as woodworkers.[126] To encourage their long-term commitment, some employers introduced graduated annual wage increases instead.[127] In any case, unionized craft workers, especially printers, fought a steady battle to prevent the shops from being flooded with apprentices and to ensure proper training.[128] 'A boy comes into an office scarcely able to read or write, and is taken on to sweep the room and go on messages,' an Ottawa printer complained, 'and when he takes up with business he is not taught it, but picks it up the best way he can, and to a right-thinking man that is totally wrong.'[129] Many craft workers told the commissioners that they would prefer to have indentures restored to apprenticeship.

In less clearly defined crafts, a more informal on-the-job training often took place.[130] In industries with any degree of subdivision of labour, some employers began to develop internal labour markets, to recruit and promote the less skilled into the more skilled machine-operating jobs, thus benefiting from their informal on-the-job training. W.E. Sanford of Hamilton described a 'school of labour' connected with his clothing enterprise, 'where we help young girls by teaching them the business, and in that we have been able to keep up the supply of labour which we require.' The railway shopcraft workers had always risen through the ranks in this informal way. George Tuckett also described this as his preferred method of filling positions in his Hamilton tobacco factory in the 1880s, and Samuel Lennard said that, to get skilled workmen for his knitting mill in the same city, 'we have educated them since we commenced ... in the art of knitting.' Other testimony described the same on-the-job training for Windsor wire workers, St Thomas woodworkers, and Ottawa flour-mill workers, box makers, and biscuit makers.[131] This could be reliable but also cheaper labour, as an Oshawa agricultural-implements manufacturer explained: 'When we teach a man to make forks in our neighbourhood we can get him at a cheaper rate than by employing a man from the States.'[132] This was a slow, uncertain process of recruitment, however, and few firms had the stability to guarantee the long-term employment that these internal job ladders assumed. In any case, many workers moved on too frequently.

On the whole, apprenticeship, formal or informal, was not the way most employers of skilled labour expected to find their skilled help. More often they looked outside their own enterprises. Whatever the source, Ontario's first industrialists learned that the capitalist labour markets for various kinds of skilled labour functioned unpredictably, and to whatever extent possible it was important to hold onto the experienced skilled men they had attracted into their factories.[133]

In their fluctuating and uncertain needs for less skilled labour, Ontario's industrialists had more choice and flexibility. Manufacturers admitted to parliamentary investigators in the 1870s that they had little trouble finding their unskilled help and that it was consequently cheaper on the whole than for their competitors to the south.[134] Usually, it seems, they could find strong young men recently off the immigrant ships[135] or just in from the farm willing to do heavy labouring work for low wages and for the short spells that they were needed. A Brantford unionist complained in 1884 that, owing to mechanization, 'the shops are filled with young men from the country, leaving their regular avocations and working cheap.' A Woodstock unionist reported a similar development two years later: 'Some firms are in the habit of putting green hands from the country on machines they know nothing about.' Sawmills certainly drew on this kind of labour for their seasonal work.[136] They also encouraged another form of occupational pluralism by using some mill hands as lumberjacks in the woods in the winter.[137] Few manufacturers recruited from the new pools of immigrants from southern and eastern Europe that had found their way into American factories by the 1870s and 1880s.[138] But tobacco firms brought in American blacks, and Jacques and Hay imported some for the unpleasant work in their hair factory at New Lowell. The sawmills often used the muscle power of male French-Canadian migrants,[139] and the textile industry in eastern Ontario, and even in Dundas, reached out to the growing number of French-Canadian cotton workers with experience in the New England mills.[140]

Women

Employers could also hire female workers, especially those under thirty, who were available in Ontario cities in even larger numbers than men in this industrializing period.[141] And the census reports on manufacturing show that many more women found manufacturing jobs after 1870; the number rose rapidly from just under 10,000 in 1871 to nearly 25,000 in 1891, while their proportion of the manufacturing workforce climbed from 11.6 to 16.1 per cent (see Table 2). Yet their participation in the labour force was strictly limited by their families and by the industrialists themselves. In Ontario, in contrast to Britain, several European countries, and the New England textile communities,[142] married women seldom worked outside the household for wages, even in textile towns. With only rare exceptions, wage-earning females were young, single, and solidly attached to the patriarchal household economies of their working-class families. They found wage-earning jobs intermittently between the end of school and the beginning of their marriages, in response to their families' varying need for their wages or their domestic labour. That period usually lasted into their mid-twenties, as the age of marriage rose in Ontario in the last half of the nineteenth century.[143] The gender of the 'working girls,' as they were popularly known, was crucial in determining their factory experience both in their families' expectations and their employers' employment policies. Industrialists knew that women could not demand a breadwinner's 'family wage,' and therefore they could get away with paying them much less than men, as we will see below.

In the blunt words of a London cigar manufacturer, 'It is more profitable to us or we would not employ them.' He also claimed that 'women do not go on strike and do not get drunk.'[144] A London printer voiced the suspicions of many male workers in 1888: 'The proprietor says he likes to have girls because they never ask for a raise of wages, and he can get

TABLE 2
Sectors of Ontario Manufacturing Employing Most Female Labour, 1871–91

	1871			1881			1891		
	Age 16+	Under 16	Total	Age 16+	Under 16	Total	Age 16+	Under 16	Total
Dresses/millinery	1,856	167	2,023	4,138	436	4,574	9,649	789	10,438
Clothing/tailoring	3,628	175	3,803	5,332	144	5,478	4,463	263	8,160
Wool	1,258	277	1,535	2,385	304	2,689	2,230	255	2,485
Fruit/vegetables (canned/dried)							1,257	231	1,488
Cotton	179	124	303	596	366	962	1,053	177	1,230
Shirts/collars/ties				215	1	216	1,051	6	1,057
Furs/hats	308	48	356	416	5	421	678	16	694
Knit goods							613	77	690
Corsets				232	8	240	520	23	543
Woven goods							474	17	491
Confectionery	115	17	132	294	46	340	402	32	434
Baked goods	608	96	704	522	67	589	399	23	422
Boots/shoes	181	34	215	308	73	381	399	11	410
Book-binding	164	10	174	863	65	928	372	8	380
Hosiery				5	0	5	318	49	367
Carpets	64	16	80	138	21	159	341	13	354
Paper				91	28	119	294	31	325
Bags/boxes, paper							282	22	304
Total female	9,853	1,301	11,154	17,981	2,143	20,124	24,597	2,439	27,036
Percentage of workforce	11.6	1.5	13.1	14.9	1.8	16.7	16.1	1.6	17.6

SOURCE: Census of Canada, 1871, vol. 3; 1881, vol. 3; 1891, vol. 3. Calculations of percentages are mine.

rid of them some day when he does not need them. They get married.'[145] But industrialists also knew that bourgeois Victorian notions of fragile femininity and inevitable motherhood – the so-called cult of true womanhood – limited the kinds of jobs that they could ask women to do. The industrial workplaces into which wage-earning women were drawn were therefore predominantly extensions of their long-established spheres of labour in the family household – clothing, textiles, food processing, and the like – or involved light tasks that could be construed as needing special female attributes, notably 'nimble fingers.' It was the latter ideological rationale that allowed manufacturers to introduce women workers into several different industries where they had seldom been before in the days of pristine craftsmanship.

How, then, could a factory owner use female labour? Only in dressmaking and millinery shops did women apprentice to be the main craft workers of the trade, and they dominated this popular, more respectable work as they did no other industry (see Table 2).[146] In a few other crafts involving relatively little manual strength, especially tailoring, and, to a lesser extent, cigarmaking and typesetting, employers introduced women as cheap substitutes for male craft workers, sometimes in the midst of a strike[147] and usually in a restricted role in production. Generally, though, they did 'women's work' in female job ghettos and did not compete directly with men. In 1871 and 1881 more than four out of five adult female wage-earners could be found in clothing and textile production, and by 1891 the proportion was nearly nine out of ten. Other than in some food processing,[148] women formed an insignificant proportion of the workforce in primary industries, metalworking, and woodworking (see Table 1).

Wherever they worked, women factory operatives most often became a part of the overall process of the subdivision of labour and dilution of skill, usually filling the least skilled jobs in the new occupational hierarchies. The province's woollen and cotton industries had used them from the beginning as carders, weavers, and ring spinners (though never as mule spinners, loom fixers, or dyers).[149] Both custom tailors and the ready-made clothing industry relied heavily on their labour power, principally for the simpler work on pants and vests (though sometimes on more complicated garments too).[150] In shoemaking they did basting and tacking and plain stitching on sewing machines.[151] In cigarmaking they packed tobacco or rolled cheaper cigars.[152] In baking they worked with the machines to make biscuits, crackers, and candies, while men made the bread.[153] In the less conventional occupations that became 'women's work' in the new factory system, small handfuls of women were put to work on simple, repetitive tasks, often with light machinery. Visitors to

Eddy's huge woodworking factory at Ottawa found young women in the 'rather ominous' sulphuric haze of the match department, not by the saws.[154] Elsewhere, in printing they fed the presses, folded, stitched, and collated books in the bindery, but only occasionally set type.[155] Hardly any women showed up in the province's heavy metalworking factories, but small clusters appeared in shops producing screws or sheet-metal products and occasionally in a foundry fashioning small sand cores for the male moulders, or perhaps doing a little soldering.[156] They also found work in paper factories and worked on paper products, such as boxes and stationery.[157] In a few cases, as we have seen, industrialists got around the controversial issue of bringing women into factories by organizing the subdivision of labour so that women worked in their own households; many of these women were widows or married women who were the chief breadwinners. This may have been the largest single category of factory-related employment for women, though the statistical reporting of homework is unreliable (see Table 2).

The use of female labour in these ways to degrade established craft practices raised the hackles of adult male workers, especially the skilled workmen. Caught on the horns of a patriarchal dilemma, these men could readily recognize how important a woman's wages could be for her family, but they also worried about threats to their role as chief breadwinners if they had to compete with poorly paid women. Their masculinity was bound up in their pride as competent producers deserving of good wages and thus as good providers for their families.[158] Several groups of craftsmen in late nineteenth-century Ontario criticized the employment of women as degrading to their craft – notably tailors, printers, and cigarmakers. In 1856 the London tailors' society linked the arrival of women with all the degrading tendencies within their trade by demanding that 'all custom work ... be done on the premises at which it's offered for sale, a discharge of female tailors and an end to the use of sewing machines.' A decade later these men were still bemoaning the fact that 'so much is given out to women that the tailoring business is fast degenerating.' Not surprisingly, craft unions showed a general indifference to organizing the female practitioners of their trade.[159]

To some extent, the perspectives of male bosses and their male workers converged. In the 1888 Labour Commission hearings, they both often shared a discourse of disparagement and exclusion. Repeatedly men argued that women wage-earners were incompetent or unreliable, either because of biological or physiological limitations or because of their brief stint in the paid workforce. 'Almost invariably they do their work in a very inferior manner,' a Toronto printer insisted. 'They do not take the trouble.' Printing was 'a life occupation for the men' but 'only a temporary occupation' for the women. A Windsor publisher was similarly dismissive: 'They are not as good as men, and cannot make themselves as useful. If they had nothing to do but set type they would be all right, but they have not the endurance of men, and that is another drawback.' A London cigar manufacturer who had filled his factory with female labour was none the less similarly contemptuous of their abilities: 'As between a man and a woman, a woman can never make as good a cigar as a man, that is taking ten men and ten women ... A man will take a pride in getting up an article nicely where a woman will not.' Unfortunately, he explained, since cigars produced by men and women sold at the same price, his profits would be larger with cheaper female labour. One of this man's competitors in Kingston shared these sentiments: 'They don't work as hard as the men do: they are not so ambitious.' When asked if a tailoress could make as good a vest as a man, a London tailor replied, 'She might manage to make one that would pass as well, and a man not as experienced as a tailor would not know the difference ... [But] a practical tailor could tell the difference.' Again, she found work in some of the city's clothing shops only because her labour was cheaper.[160] There were nonetheless class differences in this wall of masculine scorn that relegated women to narrowly circumscribed occupational niches. Employers were more frustrated that the demands of the household economy made these women less reliable sojourners in the wage labour market, but the male workers more often feared the degradation of their crafts and the threats to their status as breadwinners. They also showed more sympathy with their bargaining power as wage-earners and thus became a leading voice in pushing for the Ontario Factory Act (enacted in 1886), which put special protections on the working hours of female labour.[161]

Women thus found themselves in a paradoxical position as wage-earners. More and more jobs were opening up for them in the new industrial workforce, but their family responsibilities, even before marriage, and the attitudes of male manufacturers and male wage-earners, and the larger patriarchal ideologies restricted their employment possibilities to only a few industries and only a few job ghettoes – the less skilled, more repetitive, less well-paid, dead-end work, often attached to specialized machinery.

Children

In similar ways, child labour in factories was rooted both in the new needs of industrialists for cheap, unskilled labour and in the customary place of children in the family economies of both rural producers and urban workers. Boys and girls had long been expected to contribute their paid or unpaid labour to the well-being of their families from an early age, and, as opportunities for young workers began to open up in the rapidly expanding industrial workplaces of the 1860s and 1870s, many youngsters from working-class families began to march through the factory doors to earn wages for their family coffers. Throughout the period many commentators saw parental greed behind child labour in Ontario.[162] In the same vein, the Labour Commission heard numerous employers of juvenile labour justify their profit-making employment practices virtually as charity. 'It would be a great grievance to some parents if we refused to employ their children,' a Dundas cotton manufacturer insisted. 'Their work is a great assistance to them.' According to Hamilton's leading tobacco manufacturer, George Tuckett, some parents saw a factory as a reform school: 'The mothers come to me and say that their children will not go to school, and in order to keep them off the streets, they send them to me.' (Ironically, when pressed, employers seldom knew anything about local working-class household economies.) The Cornwall correspondent of the Ontario Bureau of Industry was closer to the mark when he said in 1887, in tune with his fellow reporters across the province, 'The reason of their employment is mainly because the wages paid to heads of families are insufficient to maintain all without the aid of the children.'[163] School officials wanted these youngsters to spend more of their time in the classroom, but such schooling as they got had to be sandwiched between their work at home and in the factory. 'Sure she needs meat first,' the guardian of a thirteen-year-old mill girl told a factory inspector, James Brown, when he suggested schooling for the girl. Of course, many children themselves would often 'rather work than go to school,' as one told a government commissioner in 1882.[164]

Until the late 1880s, there was no popular consensus on a suitable age for starting full-time wage labour. In Hamilton in 1871, working-class boys tended to begin work at age twelve and girls a couple of years later; scattered evidence over the next twenty years suggests that this may have been the threshhold for much juvenile wage-earning.[165] Certainly some children, especially boys, started as young as nine or ten, but they were probably a small proportion. A letter to the *Almonte Gazette* in 1862 complained that there was a 'considerable number in Almonte working in the woollen mills who are under 12 years.'[166] Two decades later, a special federal Royal Commission on factory labour counted 173 children under age ten (and over 2,000 between ten and fourteen) in the 465 factories and mills in the five eastern provinces it visited.[167] The 1888 Labour Commission heard several reports of Ontario boys starting work at nine, ten, or eleven – in Ottawa sawmills, in a Toronto box factory, in cotton mills (where a boy of eight managed to earn ninety-two dollars in one year), and in southwestern-Ontario canning factories.[168] The first factory inspections in the late 1880s and early 1890s also turned up quite young workers, who were usually sent home immediately. But these were probably instances of dire family need and not typical cases.

Most employers claimed, probably truthfully, not to know the real ages of their young workers. Before the 1886 Factory Act required employers to get age certificates from the parents of young employees, they probably cared much more whether the child was physically fit for the job, and perhaps whether he or she was related to a highly valued adult worker. The 1882 commission on factory labour found employers had no record of their employees' ages.[169] Inevitably that looseness brought many children aged twelve to fourteen, especially boys, inside the Ontario factory system, as the nervous defensiveness of employers in the late 1880s suggests: 'I don't think there are more than six under fourteen years, and they have worked at the mill a long time,' the manager of a Kingston cotton company proclaimed. The first Ontario factory inspectors had an extremely difficult time determining precise ages. Under the Factory Act, the legal age for wage-earning – and thus the effective end of 'childhood' – was set at fourteen for girls and twelve for boys (the difference was eliminated in 1895; Ontario's compulsory school-attendance legislation of 1891 similarly set fourteen as the common cut-off point). Both before and after the new legislation, 'child labour' in this strictly defined sense seems to have had a relatively small place in Ontario's industrial economy – manufacturers did use such young workers but were simply not dependent on recruiting a huge proportion of their juvenile workforce from this age group. But if we extend the definition into early adolescence, as school reforms did in the 1920s, we find a large number of young workers under sixteen. Overall, between 1871 and 1891, they never made up much more than 8 per cent of the total manufacturing workforce, but in some industries their proportion ranged between a quarter and a half (see Table 3). In fact, by the early 1880s the Dominion government thought that child labour had become a serious enough problem to merit particular investigation.[170]

It would be misleading to lump boys and girls into one category of juvenile labour, since the patterns of their employment were, on the whole, quite different. Far more adolescent boys than girls worked for wages and in far more industries, and they seldom did the same jobs (see Tables 2 and 3).[171] Industrial capitalists put boys to work in three different ways. A few might be recognized apprentices, as we have seen. Many more did light labouring – carrying, fetching, sweeping, and

TABLE 3
Sectors of Ontario Manufacturing Employing Labour under Age 16, 1871–91

	1871			1881			1891		
	Male	Female	Total	Male	Female	Total	Male	Female	Total
Lumber	728	26	754	1,004	8	1,012	1,342	1	1,343
Dresses/millinery	17	167	184	18	436	454	43	789	832
Wool	459	277	736	495	304	799	424	255	679
Clothes/tailored goods	133	175	308	210	144	354	212	263	475
Printed/published products	360	0	360	585	66	651	456	15	471
Flax							336	90	426
Fruit/vegetables							185	231	416
Cotton	88	124	212	11	366	377	220	177	397
Cabinets/furniture	133	4	137	287	17	304	229	24	253
Shingles	402	13	415	150	7	157	169	1	170
Carriages	162	0	162	122	10	132	151	3	154
Barrels	92	0	92	172	0	172	142	0	142
Agricultural implements	105	0	105	122	10	132	140	0	140
Baked goods	126	17	143	120	46	166	108	23	131
Machines	292	4	296	200	0	200	130	0	130
Tinsmithing							121	8	129
Musical instruments	23	0	23	35	0	35	117	0	117
Blacksmithing	158	0	158	98	0	98	108	0	108
Boot/shoe	286	96	382	224	67	291	91	11	102
Sashes/doors/blinds	143	0	143	97	0	97	101	0	101
Total labour under 16 years	5,787	1,301	7,088	7,009	2,143	9,152	7,511	2,439	9,950
Percentage of workforce	6.8	1.5	8.3	5.8	1.8	7.6	4.9	1.6	6.5

SOURCE: *Census of Canada*, 1871, vol. 3; 1881, vol. 3; 1891, vol. 3. Calculations of percentages are mine.

generally helping (some were specifically named 'helpers'). In fact, few industrial operations were without a least a handful of young male teenagers on the premises. Saw operators used many such boys to cart away scrap and small pieces of wood – an extremely dangerous job.[172] But both boys and most wage-earning girls also got low-skilled jobs directly in production processes that had been extensively subdivided and, in many cases, mechanized. Their labour thus played a vital part in the transformation of the labour process in this period; as a Toronto shoemaker lamented in 1871, 'boys and girls were placed at work which the skilled mechanics ought to have done.'[173] They could not be used in all industries – the heavier metalworking factories, in particular, seldom took on young workers below age sixteen.[174] This young labour was most heavily concentrated in the textile, clothing, woodworking, food-processing, and tobacco industries.[175] Nor was juvenile labour evenly distributed across the province. Young workers appeared in some of the consumer-goods industries in the metropolitan centres and were certainly crucial to the mill towns that produced textiles and wood products. But, as the Bureau of Industry correspondents confirmed in the 1880s, they were far less common in the small, mixed factory towns, where the subdivision of labour and skill dilution might not have advanced as far, and where, presumably, there were enough adult workers willing to take on the lower-paid unskilled jobs.[176]

Generally the youngest workers could be found feeding or tending light machinery, in the spinning departments of cotton mills, on picking and carding machines in woollen mills, on knitting machines, cork-making machines, tin-can stamping machines, nail-making machines, wire-making machines, biscuit-making machines, folding machines in book-binding operations, printing presses, and on planers, rip-saws, cross-cut saws, sandpapering machines, and jointers in woodworking factories. In 1852 an Ottawa reporter found a thirteen-year-old boy running a steam engine, and thirty years later the 1881 commission on factory labour claimed to have discovered several boys of that age in charge of boilers and engines.[177] In some cases they became part of a largely non-mechanized labour process. Most young male and female tobacco workers were hired to stem the leaves. 'The older hands would not be so nimble,' George Tuckett of Hamilton argued in defence of employing 120 to 150 boys and girls, many as young as fourteen. Some worked directly on the cigars: 'We take a girl and teach her to make the inside of a cigar, what is called the bunch,' John Rose, the London cigar manufacturer, explained, 'and we teach another girl to roll them up.' Girls might be used for other simple manual tasks – cleaning fruit in a canning factory, pasting and tacking in a shoe factory, japanning tin cans, finishing blinds in window-shade factories, rolling chocolates in candy factories, or wrapping and packing the end product in biscuit, confectionery, soap, seed, or other factories.[178] Some employers continued to use the term 'apprentice' for this kind of wage-earner, and in a few cases, especially textile and clothing production, they paid the newcomers to the job nothing while they learned (for up to six months).[179] Yet generally the range of tasks they learned was far too narrow to be considered an apprenticeship for skilled adult work. 'They go around taking up what they can, but do not become thorough mechanics,' a Toronto journeyman gilder told the Labour Commission. A St Thomas manufacturer of carriage woodwork admitted that the work of his young male machine operators was 'no trade to them,' though they might graduate to heavier, better-paid men's work. A woodworker in a London agricultural-implement works explained that becoming a well-rounded workman was impossible as long as the boys were 'always kept on that saw or machine.' A tobacco manufacturer in the same city was even blunter: 'As soon as they are out of their time, they demand journeymen's wages, and I have no more use for them.'[180]

Throughout most of this period, boys and girls responded to the same factory bell and worked the same hours as their adult workmates, sat on oversized, uncomfortable benches and stools designed for adults,[181] and were otherwise treated like adults except for their much lower wages. So, to take a stark example, twelve-year-old boys worked in Ottawa lumber mills six days a week from 6 a.m. to 6:30 p.m., with fifty minutes at noon for lunch and frequent overtime, for forty cents or less a day. Small wonder, in the words of a factory inspector, that 'the employer seemed to consider that class of labor as very saving and economical.'[182]

Juvenile labour evidently posed problems for Ontario industrialists, however, and by 1891 some seem to have stopped relying so heavily on children under sixteen.[183] The decline was not precipitous but steady. Overall, the proportion of wage-earners under sixteen declined from 8.3 per cent of the manufacturing workforce in 1871 to 6.5 in 1891, but mostly it was boy labour that was slowly contracting: the percentage of girls (most of them in clothing and textiles) remained roughly the same (see Table 3). Perhaps the lower number was merely due to the economic slump in that year. Or perhaps employers had learned that boys caused so many accidents and disciplinary problems – by joyriding on overhead pulleys, for example[184] – that they were too severe a drain on productivity. A foreman in a large western-Ontario furniture factory told an inspector that as boys became familiar with the machinery they became 'correspondingly reckless.'[185] The central-district inspector similarly noted the 'tendency of young people to talk and "lark" with each other while operating dangerous machines or working near them.' His eastern-Ontario colleague noted 'in every instance where children are employed their extravagance and carelessness in the performing of their work.'[186] Girls were not exempt from this criticism: a Kingston cigar manufacturer complained to the Labour Commission that the young girls in his factory 'could make so much more than they do, but there is too much nonsense about them.'[187] Occasionally these workers might even strike, as they did at the Wanzer sewing machine works in 1886.[188] A few years later, a factory inspector suggested that canning companies were replacing their young workers with machines.[189] Certainly, as the Second Industrial Revolution unfolded after 1900, the mechanization of the work once done by young hands was to become common. But there is no evidence that this was a widespread trend across the industrial landscape in the 1890s. More likely young women were the immediate replacements; in the industries where boy labour was falling off, adult female employment was rising by 1891, notably in the production of food, chemical, printed and published, textile, and wooden products (see Table 1). Perhaps, too, by the 1890s, the public disapproval embodied in the new Factory Act had given some employers second thoughts about using particularly young workers. The much publicized debates about child labour that had preceded the legislation must have sensitized many industrialists to the issue and encouraged them to avoid the prodding of even the most polite inspectors.[190]

Of course, in the face of a weak system of inspection and enforcement, some child labour simply went underground. A factory inspector told the Labour Commission how one firm 'had two boys under packing cases while we were going up the stairs and they sent them down by the hoist.'[191] And both parents and bosses undoubtedly continued to misrepresent children's ages easily enough, as the inspectors regularly lamented. The same inspector reported:

Parents having in the majority of cases, neglected to register the births of their children, it is difficult to verify the certificates of age given by them. Out of nearly one hundred, considered doubtful and sent in to the Registrar-General's Department for verification, only twenty-five per cent. were found to have been registered. I have reason to believe that children have, in many cases, been instructed to state their age as greater than it really was.

A Cornwall doctor, hired to assist the eastern-Ontario inspector, was likewise convinced that the children he interviewed at the large cotton factories 'had been coached as to their ages, as they seemed to know how old they were required to be in order to obtain employment in the mill.' At the turn of the century, an inspector discovered that only eight of fifty-three age certificates provided by parents matched the government birth records.[192] Ultimately, it is impossible to know precisely how much young labour continued in Ontario manufacturing at the end of the century. Certainly few late nineteenth-century photographs taken on the back steps of the province's factories lack a fresh young face or two, testifying to the importance of juvenile labour markets in Ontario's First Industrial Revolution. And the objections to their employment continued into the early twentieth century.[193]

Wages

Finding the necessary labour power for Ontario factories in the late nineteenth-century, then, involved the creation of a number of distinct labour markets, each with its own difficulties and possibilities for employers and each offering quite different rewards for wage-earners. A complex structure of wage payment that corresponded to the new divisions of labour, dilution or continuities of skill, and gender differences had emerged by the 1880s. To some extent, the overall patterns are elusive, since the forms of wage payment still varied widely. Some employers, as we will see, continued to provide amenities beyond simple wages. Others paid their workers enough to hire their own helpers. Still others paid 'learners' nothing at all. Throughout the period, wages could still be earned by the month, by the day, by the hour, or, in a growing number of industries, by the piece. Moreover, the surviving data on wages are scattered and limited. No consistent statistics were collected before the 1880s. None the less, from the surviving data we can glean some idea of how the dramatic changes in industrial life affected the relationships among the various wages of Ontario workers. Table 4 is based on the information on workers' weekly wages gathered by the Ontario Bureau of Industries for the week ending 25 April 1885, a relatively good year in the Ontario industrial economy. The wage-earners in manufacturing have been clustered into a ranking by income to suggest something about their value on the Ontario labour market. Unfortunately there is no way to control for experience within a single craft or industry, which could obviously affect some rates of pay, but as a snapshot of industrial wages in the late nineteenth-century Ontario economy, the data are suggestive.

Several important patterns emerge. The most striking are clearly based on age and sex. Across all industries, workers under sixteen, whether male or female, earned less than $4 a week, and females less than $3 (with only one exception, an unspecified cotton worker).[194] Similarly, no women earned more than $6, and only two highly skilled groups – cotton weavers and milliners – took home more than $5. Those

TABLE 4
Earnings Ladder, 1885

Males
  Axe-maker, Blacksmith (axes, boilers/engines), Brewer, Carriage-trimmer, Collar-maker, Cutter (tailoring), Distiller, Filer (lumber), Furniture-carver, Furniture-ornamenter, Glass-blower/pot-maker, Grinder (farm hand tools, saws), Gunsmith, Hat-curler, Machinist (farm hand tools), Moulder (boilers/engines, farm hand tools, farm machinery, stoves), Nail-maker, Organ case-maker/finisher/tuner, Painter (foundry), Patternmaker, Piano action-maker/fly-finisher, Polisher (axes, farm hand tools), Saw-maker, Spring-fitter, Wheel-maker

_____ $11.00 a week _____

Males
  Blacksmith (carriages), Boilermaker, Boot-and-shoe finisher/machine-operator, Brass-moulder, Carpenter/turner (farm hand tools), Carpet-weaver, Cigar-packer, Cotton-dresser/slasher, Engraver, Knitting-mill carder, Machinist (axes, boilers/engines, foundry), Millwright, Paper-mill machine-tender, Piano-maker (various), Safe-maker, Sash-door-and-blind-maker, Saw-temperer, Sewing-machine-fitters/woodworker, Silver plater, Stove-polisher, Tailor, Upholsterer

_____ $10.00 a week _____

Males
  Baker, Blacksmith (farm hand tools, farm machinery, foundry, general), Bookbinder, Boot-and-shoe-bottomer, Brushmaker, Cabinet-maker, Carriage-painter/woodworker, Cooper, Coppersmith (railway), Furniture machine-hand/sawyer/turner, Hat-finisher/maker, Locksmith, Lumber-edger/sawyer, Machine-hand (general), Machinist (farm machinery, railway shop, sewing machine), Marble-cutter, Miller, Pressman (newspaper), Organ action-maker/trimmer/various, Piano case-maker, Railway-shop fitter, Shovel-maker, Spring-maker, Stove-fitter/woodworker, Tinsmith, Tobacco-maker, Woodworker (farm machinery)

_____ $9.00 a week _____

Males
  Blacksmith (railway, stoves), Boot-and-shoe cutter/laster, Brass Finisher, Butcher, Cellarman (beer/liquor), Chair-maker, Cigarmaker, Compositor (newspaper), Cotton-mill card-grinder/loom-fixer/section-hand/weaver, Fanning-mill-maker, Furniture-finisher/varnisher/polisher, Grinder (axes, stoves), Harness-maker, Hat-blocker, Knitting-mill dyer/various, Lumber-culler/jointer/measurer, Machinist (stoves), Maltster, Melter (farm machinery, stoves), Moulder (railway), Paper-mill finisher/rag-cutter/various, Piano-polisher, Railway-shop car-builder/car-repairer, Rivet-maker, Saw-packer, Sewing-machine maker (various), Stereotyper, Stove finisher/japanner/mounter/nickle-plater, Tannery beam-hand/currier, Tool-maker, Wheel-spoke-maker, Whip-maker, Woodworker (railway)

TABLE 4 (*continued*)

_____ $8.00 a week _____

Males
 Baker (biscuit/confectionery), Confectioner, Boilermaker's helper, Boot-and-shoe sole-cutter, Bottler (beer/liquor), Cigar bunch-breaker, Cotton-spinner, File-maker, Flour-packer, Gas-works employee, Glass-packer/various, Hame-maker, Knitter/scourer, Labourer (general); Lumber piler/slabber/various, Marble polisher, Painter (railway), Pump-maker, Railway-shop worker (various), Saddler, Saw-polisher/unspecified, Shoemaker, Stove assorter/various, Tanner/tannery-yardman, Watchman, Wheel-bender/various, Woollen-mill assorter/carder/dyer/finisher/fuller/spinner/warper/weaver

_____ $7.00 a week _____

Males
 Blacksmith's helper, Coremaker (farm machinery), Cotton carder/dyer/finisher/mule-spinner, Knitting-mill picker/spinner, Packer (general), Paper-mill bleacher, Saw-filer, Soap-maker, Wire-worker, Wool carder-cleaner/picker/scourer/various

_____ $6.00 a week _____

Males
 Cotton picker-tender, Railway-shop helper, Saw-etcher
Females
 Cotton weaver, milliner

_____ $5.00 a week _____

Males
 Coremaker (stoves), Cotton car-stripper/card-tender, Knitting mule-piecer, Press-feeder (newspaper)
Females
 Boot-and-shoe operator, Carpet-weaver, Corset-maker, Cotton carder/finisher/inter-mediate-tender/reeler/roving-hand/speeder/spinner/warper/web-drawer/various, Dressmaker, Mattress-maker, Hat binder/various, Knitting darner/finisher, Compositor (newspaper), Paper rag-picker/various, Tailoress, Whip-maker, Wool darner/drawing-frame-tender/dresser/reeler/sheers-tender/twister/warper/weaver

_____ $4.00 a week _____

Males under 16
 Apprentice (farm machinery), Confectioner, Boot-and-shoe worker (various), Bottler (beer/liquor), Cigarmaker, Glassworker, Knitting-mill worker (various), Wool card-helper/finisher/picker-tender/piecer
Females 16+
 Bookbinder, Boot-and-shoe fitter/paster, Paper-bag/box-maker/machine-tender, Cigar bunch-breaker, Cigarmaker, Packer, Cotton beamer/drawing-frame-tender/slubber/spooler/twister/waste-picker/winder, Furrier, Glove-maker, Knitter/mender/spinner, winder/various, Paper finisher, Seamstress, Shirt-maker, Wool burler/finisher/speeder/spinner/spooler/various
Females under 16
 Cotton worker (unspecified)

TABLE 4 (*concluded*)

_____ \$3.00 a week _____

Males under 16
   Apprentice (farm machinery), Cotton twister/various, Knitter, Tobacco stripper, Wool carder/spinner/twister/various
Females 16+
   Confectioner, Packer, Stove solderer, Tobacco stripper, Wool winder
Females under 16:
   Paper-bag maker, Cotton spinner, Knitting finisher/picker/various, Wool spinner/winder/various

_____ \$2.00 a week _____

Males under 16
   Cotton doffer

SOURCE: Ontario Bureau of Industries, *Report* (Toronto), 1886, 40–7. I have divided the Bureau's occupational groups into rough income clusters. The Bureau defined 'various' as 'such occupations for each of which not more than one return has been received.'

earning between \$4 and \$5 were found in only boot and shoe, carpet, corset, and cotton factories. All other women wage-earners were paid roughly the same as adolescent boys, and occasionally less. At the same time, no males over sixteen earned less than \$4 a week, and most of those under \$6 were probably teenagers. Equally significant, in the seventeen jobs where the bureau listed both men and women with the same job titles (admittedly with no indication of different responsibilities), females earned on average only half as much as their male counterparts, and ten of these female groups earned even less.[195]

Other patterns in these wage data are more subtle. The tiny elite that earned more than \$11 a week were clearly the most highly skilled men, either in a few old, still vibrant crafts (such as glass-blowing or iron moulding) or, more commonly, at the pinnacle of a new occupational ladder, where they applied their craftsmanship as low-level supervisors (such as brewers, distillers, or wheelmakers) or as highly valued contributors to a subdivided labour process (notably in metalworking and the production of carriages, furniture, and musical instruments). The ranks of those earning from \$9 to \$11 a week contain some of the same groups but also many craft workers (such as bakers, brushmakers, and coopers) who were holding on with somewhat more difficulty and larger numbers of men with narrowly specialized jobs, rather than crafts, in a new industry (agricultural implements, textiles, tobacco, and so on), each demanding considerable manual competence. Virtually no full-fledged craft workers appear below that line, but in several industries with a more advanced subdivision of labour in their workforce, the occupational hierarchy slopes gently downward through various semi-skilled workers in the $7- to $9-a-week range. Mixed in here too are the adult male labourers. In cotton and woollen mills the jobs have extremely narrow labels and are separated by only slight gradations in pay.

So the creation of a well-stocked, impersonal, self-regulating capitalist labour market was no less complicated than the reorganization of labour processes in the new factories. Industrialists had to work with the unpredictable flow of regional and international migration, deeply rooted conventions about men's and women's 'spheres,' and workers' own sensitivity about status and remuneration. In the face of these difficulties, Ontario's first industrial capitalists undoubtedly found the labour power to make their factories work, though sometimes not as profitably as they would have liked. The scarcity of labour none the less haunted them at many points and shaped a crucial element in their management practice – industrial paternalism.

THE ART OF HANDLING LABOUR

'There is a great art in handling labour so as to make the most of it,' Canada's leading business publication explained in an 1871 editorial entitled 'The Effectiveness of Labour.' 'Let it be taken for granted that the object of the employer is to get as much for his money as possible.'[196] Given the limited substitution of machines for humans in Ontario's new industrial workplaces, the knowledge and discretion still required of many workers, including machine operators, and the all-too-common scarcity of labour in the industrializing economy, industrialists had to work out appropriate management policies. In part this was a question of morale and of loyalty to the industrial enterprise and its owner, in part one of discipline to increase what in the twentieth century would be called productivity, that is, getting more work out of the worker. The solutions developed fell within a general framework of paternalism, which required deference to the authority of the capitalist owner, and of patriarchy, which meant that authority was male and modelled after the hierarchical power relations of the patriarchal family.

The Personal Touch

In the evolving system of capitalist ownership and control, the years between 1840 and 1890 were the age of the capitalist patriarch. Most new industrial enterprises were owned and operated by one capitalist and his male kin, occasionally in partnership with another male partner or two. A single capitalist could, of course, preside over a huge enterprise, as many of the lumber magnates did, for example, but the firm retained their personal stamp. Even when there was important investment from outside, as in the case of Montreal capitalists' interest in eastern-Ontario textile mills, the operating control generally stayed in the hands of the local entrepreneur – in contrast to the great railway corporations of the period.[197]

Not surprisingly, then, the workplace relations of the new factory age were in many ways a continuation of what has been called the 'personal' labour relations of the pre-industrial era in British North America, in which the male head of the household had directed artisanal or domestic production for the market. The 'master's' hold over his 'servant' had been a blend of material provision (room, board, and other necessities), stern punishment, and legal prerogative occasionally codified in a formal indenture and always backed by the common law notion of a contract of employment enforceable in the courts. In return he had expected loyal service and obedience.[198] The industrial-capitalist employer of the second half of the nineteenth century used many of the same paternalist tools of workplace control. Payment by 'truck' (that is, scrip redeemable for merchandise, usually at a company store) survived into the 1870s in several mill towns, though workers elsewhere seem to have succeeded in driving out this constraint on their independence.[199] More important, an industrialist's legal powers were enhanced by the new master and servant legislation of 1847, and newspapers carried regular reports of workers and apprentices being dragged before a magistrate to be punished for disobedience or for abandoning their employers without permission. 'From the frequent lessons taught at the Police Court,' the *Ottawa Citizen* warned in 1866, 'servants should have a care lest they, in foolishly leaving their situations, lose their hard earned wages in law costs.' Not until 1877 did a disobedient worker cease to be a criminal in Ontario.[200]

Paternalism worked not simply because of coercion, however, but also because of industrialists' efforts to cultivate respect and loyalty among their workers. Inside Ontario's many diminutive workshops, especially in the smaller towns, the bond between owner and skilled men doubtless remained close and reciprocal in day-to-day work routines, including some elements of masculine solidarity among skilled men, since the owner was so often an accomplished craft worker himself and it was often possible for his employees to become self-employed.[201] Yet among these and other less skilled, female, or juvenile workers, the success of this relationship in the individual enterprise probably hinged most often on guarantees of employment at a time when workers were almost completely reliant on wages for their survival. Their boss would look after them, it often seemed, especially if they were valuable to the firm. In a few cases, they continued to get some kind of board from small-scale or isolated employers as late as the early 1870s. In many more, they were no doubt grateful for the minimal job security they received, as their bosses attempted to maintain a seasoned workforce through difficult times without complete shut-downs. One of the 'old hands' at the Waterous engine works in Brantford recalled in 1887 that C.H. Waterous had been 'more like a father than an employer,' especially in the depression of the late 1850s when 'he said he could not bear to see the old hands in want and so kept open, when we knew it was a great loss to him'; in fact, 'short time,' rather than a full lay-off, was a common and sensible practice among capitalists anxious to hold on to valuable workers in an uncertain labour market. One employee at the Massey agricultural-implement plant later claimed that Hart Massey went one step further and guaranteed life employment to anyone injured on the job. Workers may have been similarly appreciative of the efforts to hire members of their families, which helped stabilize the household economy and allowed working-class parents to give their sons a start in life.[202] Some workers (we will never know how many) waited patiently and deferentially to be promoted within the factory to more skilled work or even to a foremanship. Eighteen-year-old William Holden, a three-and-a-half-year veteran of a Hamilton tobacco factory, confessed to the Labour Commission his aspirations in the internal labour market: 'I consider they will put me in another year at making lumps for plugs ... They never take them on unless they have worked there a long time.'[203]

The power of the paternalistic capitalist, however, often extended well beyond his factory walls. Outside the large cities, workers would have encountered visible reminders of the class structure of their society, most particularly the baronial mansions that the capitalists and their families were moving into by the 1870s and 1880s. Within the town's community life, they might take a leading role in town councils, churches, and voluntary societies. They might subsidize schools, churches, and various leisure activities. They probably tried to infuse their working-class fellow citizens with the small-town boosterism spearheaded by local capitalists to promote profit making in their municipalities, in competition with other Ontario communities. Their political opponents complained, probably with good reason, that they also led their workers to the polls in elections, and although many workers would have been unable to vote before 1885 (and even after), we now know that the manufacturers who were rallying to the Tory party in the 1870s made particular efforts to build an alliance of 'producers' in support of the National Policy.[204]

In towns where a single employer was dominant, especially the small, single-industry mill towns, paternalism was less personal and more all-encompassing. Many workers lived in company housing, shopped in a company store, and benefited from services arranged or supported by the company, such as a school, church, doctor, or even accident insurance. Textile towns like Hespeler, Paris, Almonte, and, to some extent, Cornwall ran this way, as did Walkerville, the company town of distiller Hiram Walker in southwestern Ontario.[205] In the dozens of isolated sawmill towns, employers had little choice but to provide basic shelter, provisioning, and community services if they wanted to hold onto a workforce. Of course, once established, these facilities allowed the companies to cast a blanket of paternalistic discipline over the workforce. The major sawmilling company on Georgian Bay, for example, imposed a ban on alcohol in its mill towns. Since the company owned virtually all the property in Waubaushene, the site of its headquarters, there was no municipal government, and the magistrate was a company official.[206]

This kind of paternalism was reconsecrated in regular ceremonies. Each year industrialists across the province hosted picnics, Christmas dinners, or summer afternoon excursions for their workers and their families to symbolize the 'harmony of interests' that newspaper editors liked to extol.[207] Some firms equipped baseball teams, marching bands, or floats for the ever popular industrial parades through the city streets.[208] Occasionally workers responded with collective tributes to their employer. During a New Year's oyster supper hosted by an Ottawa employer, an older worker rose to speak: 'Sometimes you appear rather rough, when matters don't go right,' he declared, 'but then it's over in a minute, and after all we rather like to hear you scold a bit, for then we know that work is on hand and must be put through.' In 1868 a workman from E.B. Eddy's factory dropped by his house on Christmas Day to give him a dollar to help replace the part of his operation destroyed in a fire. A few days later the workers at Eddy's match factory (arguably one of the least pleasant workplaces in the province) presented his daughter with a piano. In 1872 L.C. Northrup's woollen workers in Almonte presented him with a Family Bible, a Masonic ring, and a silver pencil on his retirement. In the same period, workers in that town and in Lanark Village organized Christmas or New Year's dinners for the woollen manufacturers who employed them. When all of Almonte's woollen-mill owners announced a reduction to ten hours a day in June 1872 (for which the employees had petitioned the previous fall), their workers were 'so much pleased ... that a band serenaded the residences of the employers.'[209] Similarly, cotton-mill workers paraded the streets of Paris and Cornwall to defend their employers and themselves against attacks published in the Toronto *Globe* in 1882 by labour reformer Phillips Thompson.[210] A Brantford foundry worker addressing the first employees' picnic of the William Buck Company in 1886 praised his boss: 'The ministers of the city have been trying to settle what is termed the vexed question of capital and labor by words. But our employer took the best way, the practical way, by giving his means to enhance the enjoyment of all.' A weaver in the same town explained his workmates' sense of bereavement when the owner of the town's small cotton mill died in 1890: 'Most of the help of the cotton mill was brought to this country by Mr. Slater, and they realize that they have lost a friend, and they naturally desired to see their beloved master for the last time and attend his funeral.'[211]

However much these forms of paternalism may have infused small-scale or small-town industry during Ontario's First Industrial Revolution, it was much more difficult to find equally strong social cement in the larger industries in the bigger metropolitan centres, where a single employer had less influence on the local labour market and was less likely to cut as big a swath in social life off the job, and where, as we will see, the alternative loyalties of the urban crafts had taken root. More elaborate means were needed to attempt to continue the ideal of paternalistic control. The railways were the pioneers, in the 1850s, in establishing recreation programs for their shop-craft workers in order to co-opt and shape working-class leisure activities.[212] Elsewhere employers funded reading rooms or local mechanics' institutes to promote 'rational' leisure.[213] Few other factory owners did much more before the 1880s. The McCormick biscuit and confectionery company in London provided dining rooms for men and women. Hamilton's tobacco magnate, George Tuckett, doled out small Christmas bonuses to loyal workers in proportion to their apparent merit; 'they notice that we are watching their interests and rewarding merit, and therefore they watch our interests,' the firm's owner explained. The large Rathbun lumber company based in Belleville published a company newspaper known as the *Tribune* in the 1880s.[214]

Undoubtedly the most elaborate program to appear in that decade was introduced in the Massey agricultural-implement works in Toronto. The firm sponsored a benefit society, medical care, a brass band, a string orchestra, a glee club, a library association (which ran a reading room and lectures and debates), outing clubs, sports teams, a seven-hundred-seat meeting room known as Memorial Hall, and a company magazine, the *Trip Hammer*.[215] As the railways had already discovered by that point, however, this form of paternalism did not cement enough loyalty to prevent workers from forming unions. Massey had already had weak support and attendance for most of its program, but the walk-out of Massey's workers in early 1886 was the most overt, massive rejection of the family's paternalism, symbolized by the immediate collapse of the *Trip Hammer*.[216] Tuckett's workers were similarly contemptuous of their employer's paternalism that year and struck for two weeks before winning a settlement.[217] Most Ontario employers showed no interest in this scale of company welfarism in any case. Their workers considered themselves lucky to have clean drinking water, and they ate their lunch outside or at their bench or in improvised eating areas, not in company lunchrooms. They washed up on the shop floor or in nearby streams or waited until they got home.[218] They tended to their own injuries without a plant nurse. And they organized their own recreation with workmates, family, and neighbours. Only by the 1920s did 'welfare capitalism' become a significant force in the province's factory management.[219]

Supervision

Ultimately strict application of the workers' labour power was more important to companies' profit margins than welfarism. Who, then, supervised the wage-earners of Ontario's First Industrial Revolution? Because so many manufacturing enterprises in Ontario in the second half of the nineteenth century were very small, most employers could oversee their workers directly. Indeed, with only rare exceptions (notably the railways,[220]) we find no large new class of professional factory managers in the province's industries before the end of the nineteenth century. Many of the managers who appear in the historical record were either the partner in charge of operations or a member of the owning family. The Labour Commission was presented with a striking example of limited management when a clerical worker at Ottawa's large lumber firm, Gilmour and Company, explained, 'They have no manager; my position is that of book-keeper. I am sort of manager.'[221] At the same time, however, old-fashioned paternalism and patriarchy required innovation and adaptation in the new factory system, especially as workplaces got larger.

Some industrialists tried to maintain a system of direct supervision by delegating authority to some kind of subcontractor who undertook to produce goods for a stated fixed price. He would be provided with raw materials, whatever machinery was needed, and, in most cases, space inside the factory, and would hire, pay, and supervise his own labour without any interference from the factory owner. Existing research has so far told us little about the importance of this figure in Ontario's nineteenth-century industrial life. Elsewhere, we have learned, subcontracting took varied forms and did not appear in all industries or all departments of a company's operations.[222] By the end of the 1880s, the system was common in Ontario in some parts of large saw mills, tobacco factories, and rolling mills, and occasionally it cropped up in woodworking, as in London and Chatham furniture factories.[223] In most of these settings, the man in question was a skilled worker who worked by the piece and hired one or more boys as helpers at the lowest possible wages. In some cases, however, subcontractors organized production teams of predominantly adult workers. Since the early 1860s, clothing manufacturers in the bigger cities had used this system most extensively, turning over batches of garments to be sewn either in households by women and members of their families or in small contract shops outside their premises with anywhere from three to twenty workers. The number of women and men employed this way by one clothing firm could vary from a few dozen to some two thousand in the industry's giant, W.E. Sanford and Company in Hamilton.[224] In the testimony to the Labour Commission, it is clear why, wherever it appeared, this system soon became known as 'sweating.' A Toronto harness maker described the system in one American-owned leather-working factory:

The firm employs a contractor who contracts to make so many dozen sets for a certain wage; then he hires a fitter and finisher who fits and finishes the work with the contractor and then they employ either a lot of boys or young fellows who can just stop the men who are out of work. They are obliged to do that or starve. They pay next to nothing and if they work very hard and manage to knock out a dollar a day they do very well.[225]

In Chatham, which seemed to be either an unusual hotbed of subcontracting or else an example of its popularity in small towns, the Labour Commission discovered in 1888 that the owners of a small agricultural–implement factory had recently reverted to subcontracting. A woodworker explained what had happened:

One of the contractors was the foreman last year, and he has two other men with him, and the foreman who worked here for a number of years is one of the sub-contractors. I say that same foreman has worked the men harder, less wages have been paid, a cheaper class of men have been employed, and he has made a large profit, the proprietor paying him the same rate per fanning mill as the mills cost him last year, when he did the work by day work. The foreman, who, I say, is one of the sub-contractors, has made better wages for himself, and a large profit besides, out of the men under him.[226]

In this case, the employer's version of the story was not much different: 'The profit that the sub-contractor made was by looking after matters, and working the men a little harder, and looking after his own interest sharper than he would look after mine.'[227] This arrangement of work was not some kind of residue of the past, but rather a revival of an older form of supervision in new circumstances that allowed the industrial capitalist to stabilize labour costs and intensify work without any direct involvement himself.[228]

However widespread it may once have been, subcontracting was not typical in industrial Ontario by the 1880s. Generally, it was more common in larger factories to hire salaried foremen empowered to hire, fire, and discipline the workers in specific branches of the company's operations within a loose general framework of company policy.[229] 'We expect and exact a fair day's work.' a Chatham agricultural-implement manufacturer explained. 'It is mostly left to the foreman.' According to the manager of a Kingston knitting mill, 'that part of the business is in his charge. If he gets the work out it suits us, and he can do as he likes.' A labourer in the same city's locomotive works discovered that 'the foreman was the man to judge what a man was worth.' The manager of a Cornwall cotton mill agreed that these front-line officials had 'full control over their department ... and I would not interfere with their work.'[230] Some of the industrialist's paternalism inevitably passed over to the foreman, whose rule was based to a great extent on his personal rapport with his subordinates. Scattered through the daily press are accounts of testimonials and gifts for these front-line supervisors from allegedly grateful employees.[231] The relationship could also involve sponsorship and patronage, as a London moulder made clear when he complained that an American foreman at the local car works was firing local workers in favour of his compatriots.[232]

Discipline

If the personal touch of direct supervision remained in the transition to factory production, there were also many new managerial policies that deliberately sought to disrupt older patterns of industrial work. These began to appear in the larger, more aggressively managed workplaces as early as the 1860s, but they seemed to have spread much further once the post-1873 depression had convinced industrialists of the need for more intense use of the labour power they were purchasing. Central to the new industrial discipline was imposing a new sense of industrial work time. New disciplinary controls were imposed on all workers to instil more punctuality and commitment to regular wage-earning than had often existed in pre-industrial British North America. Workplaces ran to the rhythms of clocks, not tasks to be completed each week or each season.

Such dissolute habits as the extended weekend known as 'Saint Monday' had to stop. The working day was sharply demarcated by bells and whistles. 'They are supposed to be in their places and prepared to commence work when the whistle blows,' the managing director of Kingston's locomotive works insisted.[233] Many workers found their wages reduced for arriving a few minutes late. 'If they cannot cure themselves of that habit,' the manager of a Kingston cotton mill said, 'we discharge them.' Several other employers agreed. Some factory owners had all the doors to their premises locked except the main entrance where tardy workers had to present themselves to timekeepers. At the other end of the working day, a Cornwall cotton factory restricted access to the washroom just before closing time.[234]

Once the workers were under a capitalist's factory roof, he most often demanded that they stay at their jobs for a good long stretch, since the labour-intensive production systems of the period allowed for only limited increases in productivity. Factory buildings were designed with large windows to make maximum use of daylight, and gas lighting was often installed to keep workers on the job after dark. Ten hours was the typical working day across the province. Highly mechanized processes did not bring any reduction – indeed some of the most technologically sophisticated factories with the most advanced division of labour, notably the lumber, textile, and flour mills, frequently ran for eleven or twelve hours a day. Few industries besides the lumber and flour mills, and distilleries incorporated a night shift,[235] but overtime was common in busy spells. Most Ontario factory workers also worked a six-day week. By the 1880s there was pressure from workers for a half-day on Saturday, but outside Toronto the few establishments that cut back on Saturday working hours usually expected the workers to make them up during the week. In the sawmills, which generally ran no more than five or six months a year, seven-day weeks were not uncommon.[236] Relief from the gruelling routine of the typical fifty- to sixty-hour week came during the seasonal shutdowns that hit so many industries, or during economic slumps, when 'short time' or full-scale lay-offs were invoked.

Employers most often justified the long working days as a means of curbing working-class dissipation after work. 'The more spare time men have the more they are likely to form intemperate habits,' a Belleville manufacturer insisted. 'Shortened hours of labor, we believe, in 75 per cent. of cases would only tend to mischief,' an Owen Sound foundryman claimed. According to a Toronto watch-case manufacturer, shorter hours 'would simply mean in most cases more time to loaf and spend money in dissipation, and in very few cases would it be employed for mental improvement.' A Huntsville lumberman waxed philosophical on the subject: 'Long hours and low wages love the working classes, short hours and high wages are their curse.' Workers predictably denied such charges and, as we will see, organized to get more time away from the job.[237]

During these long working days, factory owners expected industriousness but also self-discipline. Stern rules were posted on many factory walls and on pay envelopes to remind employees that their time on the job was not to be disrupted by socializing, joking, swearing, or even smoking.[238] The pre-industrial work routines that could involve conviviality with visitors, drinking at work, and other forms of integrating work and leisure were banished. A Toronto moulder may have believed that in the foundry where he worked every man, except himself and one other, was 'drunk every chance he could get,' but the Georgian Bay Lumber Company fired any worker found drinking alcohol on the company's extensive premises.[239] A Kingston cotton-mill worker found herself sent home for two days 'as a correction' when she and her workmates were discovered 'getting in the hallway and making a noise at noon-hour.' Similarly a group of Cornwall's female cotton workers were disciplined for 'talking and laughing and clapping hands' in the presence of their foreman in the lunchroom. 'They are supposed to conduct themselves quietly during working hours,' their overseer said.[240]

At the same time, to tie workers down to their jobs and discourage sudden departures, the first industrialists appear to have made good use of the master and servant legislation that allowed them to take employees to court for running off. Even before the decriminalization of this workplace discipline through legislation in 1877,[241] they tried other methods too. In the 1860s the newly formed province-wide employers' association among foundrymen kept a blacklist of moulders who left their employment without their boss's permission – a 'slave law,' in the workers' eyes. So too did London's cigar manufacturers twenty years later. In the aftermath of the agitation for shorter hours in 1872, some Ontario manufacturers compelled their workers to sign 'iron clad' documents that, among other provisions, attempted to tie the workers to their jobs for as long as a year. In addition, the owners of large factories regularly held back up to two weeks' wages to inhibit footloose behaviour. 'That has been the custom in mills ever since I knew anything about it,' the manager of Cornwall's Stormont Cotton Mills told the Labour Commission.[242]

Of course, the coercion could be indirect. One of the best ways to instil industrious habits, many employers concluded, was to tie the workers' wages to their output. In the 1860s there were reports of daily quotas in the larger factories. At E.B. Eddy's huge woodworking complex near

Ottawa, 'like most of the establishments where Americans are proprietors,' a respectful visitor reported in 1862, 'the articles are made by the dozen or the gross; each person is bound to turn out so much each day; if they fail in this they are discharged.' Workers in Wanzer's sewing-machine works had to produce five hundred a week in 1870 or 'return to work at night,' according to a posted sign. But far more important and eventually more widespread was the introduction of piece-work. In pre-industrial Ontario, workers were accustomed to being paid by the day or the month. As late as the 1880s, wage rates in some industries might still be quoted by the month, but after 1870 wages per day and, in a few cases, per hour became more typical across the industrial landscape. Wherever the product market could absorb enough of a firm's output, however, workers were put onto piece-work to encourage them to speed up. This incentive system had appeared in some larger Ontario enterprises by the early 1860s. In a Hamilton garment factory, employees were seen in 1862 'working in gangs and by the piece.' An Oshawa agricultural-implement manufacturer required his fifty employees to accept piece-work and 'to make so many dozen per day,' thus being able to 'tell exactly how much each piece will cost, and what the value of each man is to him.' Twenty years later, at the end of their hurried visit to factories across central and eastern Canada, two royal comissioners tallied up roughly equal numbers of workers paid by the day or week and by the piece. But the much fuller labour commission testimony revealed that this kind of incentive wage had taken root most commonly in specific industries with large outputs for large markets, and not where short product runs or careful craftmanship predominated. Piece-work thus became another part of the process of splitting a craft between those doing made-to-order work and those in mass production, such as machinery and stove moulders, and printers in jobbing and newspaper shops.[243]

In many industries piece-work took hold without much opposition from the workers. The divisiveness of the issue was evident when the 1882 commissioners could get 'no definite answer' from the Toronto Trades and Labor Council on whether 'your trades prefer time or piece-work.'[244] A few years later the Labour Commissioners heard that printers and iron workers seemed satisfied to work on piece rates.[245] But moulders were less certain. Some readily accepted it as a way to increase their earnings. A Toronto moulder lamented the 'selfishness of men' that made piece-work so successful: 'So long as they can get dollars and cents they do not care as the amount of work they do.' Another in Hamilton saw the same problem: 'A man will be covetous and work himself tight out to try to earn a few cents more than his day pay.' But others grew to hate the system. Craftsmanship could suffer: 'In doing piece-work a man never tries to remedy his mistakes,' a London moulder insisted; 'he just goes right along, and if the work will pass he thinks it is all right. He will not take time to use his judgment in trying different ways of making work properly and in adopting a proper way of making a piece. He gets a job and runs it for all he is worth.' Speed-up was the inevitable result. 'It is better of course for the bosses,' a Toronto stove moulder argued; 'they can get more work for less money' by creating 'a rushing tendency on the part of the men and consequently a cutting down of prices.' Small wonder that a factory inspector would warn that piece-workers, 'in order to earn a fair wage, must take great risks.' Some workers also believed that both seasonal and structural unemployment increased. As the moulder's journal had noted in 1873, a stove moulder was 'doing the work of eleven months in eight, for eight months pay; and then has the satisfaction of starving the balance of the year.' In a similar vein, a Toronto moulder argued that piece-work was directly responsible for the high unemployment in the trade for the previous fifteen years: 'Where there are two men at present employed on piece work three men would be required if they were working day work.'[246]

But piece-work did not guarantee limitless increases in productivity. Some unions began to impose limits on their members' daily production and led strikes against payment by results, though the outcomes were mixed. Whether or not they were unionized, many workers eventually learned to restrain their own effort and to impose limits on each other, rather than risk lower piece rates that would make them work harder for the same money. 'I have heard it said that the girls [in a paper-box factory] did not want to make more, for the employers might cut them down on their piece work,' a Toronto worker reported. By the turn of the century, a new school of North American management experts would be looking for new ways around this widespread restriction of output that they dubbed 'soldiering.'[247]

Patriarchy

The patriarchal quality of the disciplinary codes and sanctions in the new factory system shone through in the different treatment of women and children from that of men. In some industries, as we have seen, employers allowed their male workers to hire the children and youths they needed as helpers and to exercise a father's authority over them. More generally, women and children, unlike most men, were fined for tardiness, unacceptable work, insubordination, and sundry other minor misdemeanors (including spitting on the floor or fixing their hair). 'Men will not put up with deductions from wages which they have toiled to obtain,' the pro-labour group of Labour Commissioners reported in 1889, 'and therefore the system is not applied to them.'[248] Sometimes the fines were clearly stated in posted notices, but more often foremen seem to have had the discretion to deal with the 'childlike' behaviour of women and children as they pleased. 'I happened to be out about an hour,' an Ottawa print-shop foreman related. 'When I returned I found them pulling each other's hair, and running about the floor; and as I came in I saw all this, I said: 'You will lose an hour' ... [;] something has to be done to keep order in establishments of this kind.'[249] In Ontario the Labour Commission did not hear any evidence of physical abuse to compare with the harsh disciplinary regime in Montreal's infamous tobacco factories. But there were strong hints that male foremen (there appear to have been relatively few women overseers)[250] were not above browbeating their female and juvenile labour with gruff or abusive language. 'I am no angel,' a foreman in an Ottawa printing office admitted; 'occasionally I might swear.'[251] There were also occasional hints of sexual harassment, such as the charges laid by some women in Elora's carpet factory in 1882, resulting in a criminal prosecution.[252] Almost all female wage-earners also felt the indirect prod of piece-work to make them work faster.[253]

As the Labour Commission often discovered, most male wage-earners were not subjected to quite the same rigid authoritarianism. They tended to fill more skilled, more responsible jobs, and, far more often, it seems, they demanded and got respect for their 'manhood' – in this case, independent control over the labour process exercised individually and together with their male workmates. They knew their work and, in many manufactories and factories, were left to do it. Yet deference to the overall paternalistic authority was expected, and when the independence and solidarity of the shop floor stood in the way of profit making, industrialists were not shy about attempting to bring the men to heel. The various tactics of diluting craftsmanship with poorly trained workers or dissolving it with the subdivision of labour, the use of children and women, and mechanization showed that the capitalist was willing to abandon his respect for his workmen and often to precipitate a confrontation with the men. Even more important, the disloyalty of joining a union of other craft workers outside the factory could not be tolerated. Union requests for negotiation were regularly brushed aside, strikes were fought and broken, ringleaders were dismissed and blacklisted, and occasionally ironclad contracts against union membership were forced on workers. In the colourful metaphor of a Hamilton rolling-mill official, when the owners could not tolerate the union among their workers, 'they just sat upon it and squelched it.'[254] In a few industries or towns, employers formed their own organizations to defeat the unions, though these 'bosses' unions' were never typical of industrial relations in the period.[255] Nowhere in Ontario did industrialists show any serious interest in stabilizing industrial relations with the kind of formal collective bargaining that was emerging in several British industries in this period.[256]

We can see then that managerial authority in the new factory regime of late nineteenth-century Ontario rested on the continuing power of paternalism and patriarchy but with a few new variations. A single male figure still tended to preside over each unit of production, and he still exercised his authority by the double-sided process of paternalism – the promise to care for his industrial flock and the coercion to keep them in line. But a primary goal of the emerging system was to concentrate and intensify their labour through long hours and strict discipline in the workplace. There was no fixed managerial formula, however, and the new factory regime across the province varied considerably according to the skill and strength demanded of the workers, the volume of identical products turned out, the age and sex of the workforce, and occasionally the whim of the capitalist himself. The contrast between Tuckett's Christmas gifts to his tobacco workers in Hamilton and Rose's draconian authoritarianism in his London tobacco factory points to different possibilities. More often, however, each industry developed its own practices. The most rigid management appeared in the mill towns and in the 'mass-production' industries in the larger cities, while somewhat more flexible paternalism tended to continue in the hundreds of smaller-scale workplaces sprinkled through the mixed factory towns of the region. Yet, as industrialists across the province struggled to find their feet in the harsh economic climate that settled in after 1873, the efforts to intensify labour spread through much more of industry. The Labour Commission heard numerous voices of working-class outrage at many quite recent changes in industrial management – the new subcontracting schemes in a Chatham wagon works or a London furniture factory were striking examples. Perhaps the most bitterly resented practice, which revealed the shallowness of paternalism, was the bluntest method of reducing labour costs – slashing wages in times of economic depression, as many industrial enterprises did in the mid-1870s and again a decade later. The breakdown of paternalistic authority in so many Ontario industrial workplaces in the 1880s suggests how fragile and unstable this form of factory management could be once the workers discovered a common sense of injustice at the ways the factory system was working against their interests. 'Under the factory system, many employers fail to recognize an essential difference between machines and the human labor by which they are operated,' an editorial writer observed in 1896; 'kindly interest and consistent devotion have been replaced by indifference and distrust.' Ironically, this was not the voice of outraged labour, but of perceptive business opinion, the venerable *Monetary Times*.[257]

RESISTANCE AND STRUGGLE

Paternalism is a system of unequal social relations, but also one of reciprocity. It works to the extent that both sides are able to find some balance of separate and distinct interests through a complex process of negotiation and accommodation. We have already seen that within industry the dominant figure in the relationship might feel called upon to wield an authoritarian whip over the subordinate element to bring them into line. Yet the reverse could also be true. Occasionally the normally deferential workers might strike a defiant posture to remind the paternalist of their needs and interests. The outcome of that confrontation would probably be a new equilibrium within industrial paternalism. Many workers probably moved around between jobs and communities too often to settle comfortably into such a relationship, but before 1880 in Ontario, outside a handful of industries and trades in the larger cities, it was the struggles to ensure the mutuality between workers and bosses that seemed to form the main pattern of what would later be called 'industrial relations.' As we have seen, however, many Ontario industrialists began to shuck off the yoke of real, reciprocally based paternalism during the later 1870s and the 1880s, and to treat the labour power they purchased much more as an expendable commodity that could be intensified or dispensed with without the older sense of obligation. Bitter confrontations with their workers then erupted over the threat to their living standards from irregular employment and wage cuts or to their pride and self-esteem as producers, and many more workers put their faith in labour organizations to promote and defend their particular interests as wage-earners. The 1880s thus became a decade of widespread working-class organization and intense industrial conflict never before seen in the province.

The Revolt of the Urban Craft Workers

As the First Industrial Revolution unfolded in Ontario, working-class defiance percolated through many workshops, manufactories, and factories. Occasionally we can catch a glimpse of the work-group solidarity that must have flourished (as it certainly did later) as a source of resistance to unbridled managerial control. In Berlin (now Kitchener) unknown pranksters hid the factory bell down a well. In New Hamburg, carpet-mill workers let tardy workers in a window to avoid the foreman's wrath. A group of high-spirited women in a Kingston cotton mill derided and ridiculed their foreman when he tried to supervise their behaviour during their lunch break (we have already met him and his methods above). Rolling-mill men in Hamilton smuggled beer onto the shop floor. Boys and girls regularly turned some parts of their factory workplace into illicit playgrounds.[258] This kind of informal trench warfare against the elements of the new factory regime they disliked relied on conspiracies of silence and cooperation within a workforce. There were also more open collective efforts to change the terms of employment. In 1872, for example, sawmill workers in Ottawa and woollen-mill workers in Almonte petitioned their respective employers for shorter hours, apparently with some success.[259] Workers sometimes also refused to work until the terms of their employment had been modified, though often their bosses refused to deal with them and broke the strike as quickly as possible.[260] The ironies were evident in 1872, when the workers of Wanzer's sewing-machine factory in Hamilton presented the firm's manager with a glowing tribute on the occasion of his retirement only a few short months after their bitter dispute with him over the nine-hour day.[261]

A turning point was first seen in the late 1860s and early 1870s, when both strikes and union organizing increased in the province. Yet before 1880 this working-class resistance never extended much beyond a handful of crafts and the largest cities (see Tables 5 and 6). Many efforts have doubtless been lost to the historical record (Ontario had no official labour statistics before the 1880s), but it is hard to escape the conclusion that strikes and unions were the exception rather than the rule in this early period. In the 1860s and 1870s more than three-quarters of the strikes uncovered in the most thorough study to date involved craft workers in only six trades, and three-quarters took place in Toronto, Hamilton, Ottawa, and London. The rest were spread thinly through small-town Ontario. Similarly, the most encyclopaedic research on unions turned up only 17 local organizations in Ontario manufacturing in the 1850s, 36 in the 1860s, and 77 in the 1870s. In each decade more than half of these were in Hamilton, Toronto, and London; most other towns had only one or two. The explanation for this limited level of organization lies in the constraints of the general economic situation and in the unevenness and diversity of workers' experience across the province.

Before the 1880s, the structures of the employment relationship in most late nineteenth-century Ontario manufactories and factories did not

TABLE 5
Strikes of Ontario Manufacturing Workers, 1815–90

1815–59	Total	Toronto	Hamilton	London	Kingston	St Catharines	Oshawa
Tailors	7	4	1				1
Shoemakers	6	3	2			1	
Printers	4	3		1			
Bakers	3	2			1		
Rwy shop workers	2		1	1			
TOTALS	23	13	4	2	2	1	1

1860–79	Total	Toronto	Hamilton	Ottawa	London	Brockville	Oshawa	Brantford
Moulders	25	8	5		2	3	3	1
Shoemakers	9	3	1		1			
Cigarmakers	9	5	2					
Printers	7	3	1	3				
Bakers	4		2	1				
Tailors	3	2	2	1				
Sewing-machine workers	3					1		
Misc. metalworkers	3	3						
Coopers	2				2			
Bookbinders	2	2						
Leather workers	2		1	1				
Sawmill workers	2		1	1				
Agric. impl. makers	1		1					
Rwy shop workers	1		1					
Furniture makers	1	1						
TOTALS	74	27	16	7	5	4	3	1

TABLE 5 (concluded)

1860–79

	Galt	Aurora	Georgetown	Kingston	Prescott	Orillia	Perth	Smiths Falls	St Catharines
Moulders	2								
Shoemakers								1	
Cigarmakers					1	1	1		1
Bakers			1	1					
Sawmill workers		1							
TOTALS	2	1	1	1	1	1	1	1	1

1880–90

	Total	Toronto	Hamilton	London	Kingston	Brantford	Oshawa	Brockville
Moulders	24	6	2	3	1	2	4	4
Cigarmakers	10	1	3	4		2		
Shoemakers	10	6	4					
Printers	9	5		1				
Cotton workers	9		1		1			
Tailors	6	5	2		2			
Bakers	5	3						
Sawmill workers	4							
Agric. impl. workers	3	1						
Furniture workers	3	3						
Musical instrument makers	3	3						
Rolling-mill workers	3		3					
Corsetmakers	2	2						
Flour-mill workers	2							
Bookbinders	1	1						
Box-makers	1	1						
Pressmen	1	1						
Sewing-machine makers	1		1					
Woollen-mill workers	1							
Misc. mill workers	2	1				1		
Misc. metal workers[a]	7	1	3		2		1	
Misc. craft-workers[b]	7	6	1					
TOTALS	115	46	20	8	7	5	5	4

1880–90	Cornwall	Ottawa	Gananoque	Chatham	Merritton	Galt	Gravenhurst	Lindsay	St Catharines	Woodstock
Moulders						1		1		
Printers		1							1	
Cotton workers	4				2					
Tailors										1
Sawmill workers		3					1			
Agric. impl. workers			2							
Flour-mill workers				2						
Woollen-mill workers			1							
TOTALS	4	4	3	2	2	1	1	1	1	1

SOURCE: Unpublished data prepared by Bryan Palmer for 'Labour Protest and Organization in Nineteenth-Century Canada,' *Labour/Le Travail* 20 (Fall 1987), 61–84, which he generously made available to me. Tabulations of strike totals are mine.

a One each of blacksmiths, boilermakers, nailers, railway-shop workers, and stovemounters, and two of unspecified metalworkers.

b One each of brushmakers, framers, gilders, hatters, jewellers, trunkmakers, and varnishers.

TABLE 6
Unions of Workers in Ontario Manufacturing, 1850–80

By City	1850s	1860s	1870s
Hamilton	5	9	14
Toronto	4	6	11
London	2	4	9
St Catharines	1	2	6
Brantford	2	4	5
Kingston	1	3	3
Guelph	1	2	2
Oshawa	1	1	2
Ottawa		2	2
Peterborough			2
Stratford		1	2
Thorold			2
Woodstock		1	1
Barrie, Belleville, Bowmanville, Brampton, Brockville, Chatham, Cobourg, Galt, Georgetown, Ingersoll, Orillia, Perth, Prescott, Preston, Seaforth, Smiths Falls			1 each
TOTAL			77

By Occupation			
Shoemakers	21		
Moulders	12		
Machinists	7		
Printers	6		
Cigarmakers	5		
Coopers	5		
Tailors	5		
Cabinet-makers	3		
Miscellaneous	13		
TOTAL	77		

SOURCE: Eugene Forsey, *Trade Unions in Canada, 1812–1902* (Toronto: University of Toronto Press 1982), 9–89. Calculations are mine.

promote a militant class consciousness among the wage-earners within them. A stable working-class community was certainly less likely to emerge amid the insecurities and irregularities of Ontario's industrial economy. So many industries had prolonged seasonal shut-downs that many workers would doubtless have returned to farming or other occupations. During the deep economic slumps, especially after 1873, as businesses closed or went into bankuptcy, many wage-earners and their families must have moved on.

At the same time, we have seen that Ontario's First Industrial Revolution was an extremely uneven process, moving through particular industries and towns in very different ways. Three different kinds of manufacturing centres appeared – mill town, mixed factory town, and metropolitan centre. In each of these, industrialists brought together the raw materials for distinctive working-class communities with their decisions to invest in certain kinds of production to compete in particular markets, to organize specific work processes, and to recruit the necessary kinds of labour. The workers who gathered in each of these industrial centres proceeded to shape their own patterns of association, organization, and resistance or accommodation according to the structural constraints and opportunities they found. We still know little about how these local working-class communities took shape in Ontario, but it is clear that the result was three different patterns of working-class experience in the province's factory towns. In only a few of the larger cities did workers produce a self-conscious, independent, and aggressive form of resistance to the new industrial capitalism before 1880. After that date, a more generalized spirit of class-conscious protest began to percolate throughout industrialized Ontario, though the differences persisted.[262]

Two of the three kinds of working-class community were weak recruiting ground for independent working-class organization and action. Compared to workers in the average Ontario factory, mill-town workers – especially sawmill and textile hands – tended to work for large, impersonal firms with more advanced subdivision of labour, mechanization, and, in the case of textiles, female labour. Because their jobs were tied closely to one industry and had little independent status as crafts, these workers would have fallen more easily into the deference expected by the industrial patriarchs who effectively controlled the local labour market and most social institutions. In contrast, workers in the many small, multi-industry towns were more likely to find themselves in much smaller establishments, often with only a handful of employees, many of whom were probably versatile, skilled men. There it would not be easy for an occupational identity to develop among the sprinkling of workers in any trade, and there was not likely a yawning social gulf between them and the owner, who was often a skilled manual worker himself. Even in the growing numbers of somewhat larger factories in these towns, this respect for, and masculine solidarity with, a former-artisan-turned-capitalist could be potent cement between master and men. Craft workers were a prominent part of this small-town world, but in many cases their occupational trajectory and general craft experience were considerably different from those of their counterparts in the larger cities. As we have seen, Ontario had two different sets of craft traditions – one rural, the other urban. The rural craft worker was rooted in the agrarian experience, where skills were learned more informally and sometimes practised together with agriculture. These men had none of the corporate organizations of their urban counterparts.[263]

It is the workers in the few big cities, especially Toronto and Hamilton, who have become best known for determined self-organization in the late nineteenth century. These cities contained a remarkable range of factory wage-earning experience, including substantial clusters of women, children, and other unskilled recruits to the large consumer-goods factories that served the cities' extensive hinterlands with boots and shoes, clothing, tobacco, and so on. Yet, far better studied are the large numbers of urban craft workers, both specialized men in manufactories that produced such mass-market goods as stoves and ironware, newspapers, and the like; and the more all-round men in generally smaller workshops that turned out machinery, fine furniture, and a host of other consumer and producer goods. It was among these urban craft workers that the first elements of a labour movement emerged. Their experience with managerial innovation in the rapidly expanding manufactories sharply challenged the longstanding craft traditions with which so many craft workers in the larger towns and cities identified and the newer craft practices that these skilled wage-earners were evolving. By mid-century, they had a tradition of mutual support in times of economic distress. They also gathered in growing numbers in taverns and banquet halls to toast their patron saints. They marched proudly in parades beneath banners celebrating the glories of their trade and the virtues of manly independence and popular democracy. They reinforced their occupational solidarity in baseball games, balls, and family picnics.[264] And they dug in their heels against any effort to erode their crafts in the new manufactories where they were employed in growing numbers. Indeed these journeymen came to assume that only they could defend the integrity of their craft, as master artisans became more interested in profit than craftsmanship. Starting in the 1850s, they formed craft unions to control the daily labour process and to maintain their relatively high wages and occupational status. They tried to regulate the labour supply with formal apprenticeship training and unemployment programs that helped the jobless in their trade to set off 'tramping' in search of work. In fact, these craft workers were highly mobile, carrying their principles of organization, fellowship, and independence around the continent. The links between Ontario unions and American national craft organizations that began in the 1850s and 1860s – the origins of so-called 'international unionism' – were due to this mobility and the desire to control the continental labour market in their skills. The biggest industrial conflicts in southern Ontario took place whenever this kind of craft unionism collided with the new capitalist authoritarianism. These battles were often framed dramatically as a struggle for control of the workplace.[265]

Before 1880, then, unions in manufacturing industries were primarily a metropolitan phenomenon. Perhaps even more striking was the small number of occupations covered (see Table 6). Four-fifths were found in seven crafts – shoemakers, moulders, machinists, printers, cigarmakers, coopers, and tailors. More detailed studies have revealed why these were the wage-earners who unionized. In each case these industries were reaching out to a mass market, and the capitalist employers were consequently pushing hard to intensify the labour process and where possible to transform it. In each case, they had to confront large numbers of well-entrenched male craft workers whose skill was still vital to production. In the 1860s shoemakers were the first to encounter skill dilution, subdivision of labour, and mechanization on a large scale, and they launched a substantial resistance movement in the early 1870s. They set up branches of their new organization, the Knights of St Crispin, in twenty-one towns across the province.[266] Coopers made a similar stand against employers who adopted new methods for barrel production in response to the demands of the distillers, oil refiners, and salt producers.[267] Tailors met the challenge of the sewing machine in the 1850s by incorporating it into their craft, but they felt the new pressures of subdivision of craft skill as the ready-made clothing industry emerged in the larger cities.[268] Cigarmakers too had to confront such changes inside the big new tobacco factories.[269] Two large groups of craft workers – the iron moulders in the province's many foundries (especially the stove foundries)[270] and the compositors who set type in the offices of the new daily newspapers[271] – retained crucial manual skills and maintained persistent, determined organizations in the face of their employers' attempts to flood the respective labour markets with poorly trained, cheaply paid workers and to break their unions. At the same time, one group of craft workers who had emerged within the First Industrial Revolution rather than out of pre-industrial experience, the machinists, stood their ground in the railway shops, the province's largest industrial employers in the 1870s. They organized mostly within branches of the British-based Amalgamated Society of Engineers.[272] The common experience of all these unionists was the confrontation between capitalist market principles and their craft identity and practices.

Occupational solidarity was strong among these workers, but the exclusiveness evident in their desire to restrict access to craft training did not encourage much organizational initiative among the unskilled. (The moulders, for example, never tried to rally their less skilled workmates in stove factories or agricultural-implement works.) It even created divisions within crafts, between compositors and pressmen, and between stove and machinery moulders, for example.[273] But workers who regularly extolled the value of craftsmanship had little difficulty striking up bonds of solidarity with craft workers in other manufacturing trades and those in construction and transportation. By the early 1870s craft unionists had created the first 'trades assemblies' of craft union locals in Hamilton, Toronto, Ottawa, and St Catharines. The growing consciousness of a generalized craft worker identity was evident in the appearance of several additional unions of manufacturing craft workers in the larger cities in the late 1860s and early 1870s. Among them were bakers, butchers, carriage makers, broommakers, hatters, boilermakers, varnishers, and polishers. It was this expanding craft-union movement that fuelled the spectacular nine-hours movement in the spring of 1872 and launched the Canadian Labor Union (which was never more than an annual meeting of southern-Ontario craft-union locals) the next year. Most of this labour movement died in the depression of the mid-1870s.[274]

We should never forget, however, that this well-studied movement made few inroads into the Ontario manufacturing workforce. Before the 1880s, unions touched only a small minority of Ontario factory workers, namely, the adult male craft workers in the manufactories of the rapidly expanding industries, principally in five of the largest industrial towns – Hamilton, Toronto, London, St Catharines, and Brantford. Aside from the odd local of moulders or shoemakers, small-town Ontario never saw unions in their manufactories and factories in these early years, and there is no record of organization in such major resource-processing industries as sawmilling, flour milling, or textiles. At least for factory workers, then, it is not helpful to imagine that before 1880 Ontario wage-earners had 'a long history of resistance, challenge, and organization.'[275]

The Great Upheaval

After 1880, however, workers across the province organized in unprecedented numbers. Part of this expansion was the resurgence and reinvigoration of craft unionism.[276] But much more remarkable was the broadening of working-class organization, principally through a new movement known as the Noble and Holy Order of the Knights of Labor, which drew in thousands of workers who had never before belonged to unions and which touched towns that had never seen a union. The Knights' story has been well told elsewhere and need not be repeated here in detail.[277] In all, the order's 'missionaries' to the working class, as one of their Toronto leaders dubbed them,[278] probably recruited some

22,000 wage-earners in Ontario. The predominance of Toronto, Hamilton, Ottawa, London, and Kingston, which together had four-fifths of the Knights' 'local assemblies,' is not surprising. Yet the Knights' organizational flexibility, which permitted both occupationally based assemblies and 'mixed' assemblies of diverse crafts and occupations, made possible the appearance of labour organizations in some eighty-three municipalities, including all those with a population over 5,000 and four-fifths of those over 3,000. Craft workers took the lead and probably predominated numerically. But the less skilled and more narrowly specialized factory workers also joined in substantial numbers. Local assemblies of workers in boot and shoe, textile, lumber, agricultural–implement, and other large establishments dotted urban Ontario in the second half of the 1880s. For the first time in the province's history, women were included, either as members of mixed assemblies or in their own female locals.[279] Debates over the statistics on membership[280] cannot undermine the remarkable change that was evident among factory workers (and other wage-earners) after 1880. Far more of them were expressing a sense of collective working-class identity than ever before in the province's history.

Any explanation for such a change must begin with the larger industrial context. As we have seen, industrialists had done some serious soul-searching in the severe depression of the 1870s and saw the need for some major new departures. The most celebrated, the National Policy tariff, restricted foreign competition but stimulated a lot of new internal competition, as new factories opened, older firms expanded, and most industrialists simply jostled desperately for space in the limited domestic markets. By the mid-1880s overproduction was a serious problem. Survival required a cutting of production costs wherever possible. Some factory owners resorted to the familiar nineteenth-century solution by slashing wages. Still others looked for changes in the labour process that could help them. The increase in immigration also provided some relief.[281]

For most workers, then, the 1880s became not a decade of prosperity,[282] but of economic and occupational insecurity and uncertainty. Percolating through the language of the Knights' activity in Ontario were a sense of outrage and injustice and a palpable loss of faith in the industrial-capitalist economy in which they worked. Often it was the overstocked labour market and the consequent unemployment and economic insecurity that they attacked.[283] Pressures on the job were troubling as well, and, not surprisingly, strikes proliferated (see Table 5). Craft workers in the most dynamic industries once again rose in vigorous opposition to the continuing degradation of their crafts and struggled to establish the formal job-control mechanisms devised by their unions.

Workers in a wide variety of occupations – including some tough-minded, determined women[284] – also struck to protest wage cuts[285] and other threatening managerial innovations aimed at intensifying their labour, frequently through some complicated adjustment of piece-work.[286] These defensive struggles suggested that many of these workers without strong craft identities had developed a clear sense of what was customary and fair in their workplace routines and their living standards and what should not be tolerated. They expressed the evidently wide-spread commitment among many factory workers to maintaining the dignity of labour – the Knights' central message – and often fuelled the growth of the Order's local assemblies. In many factory towns and villages, the demand that seemed to encapsulate their resistance to the new capitalist labour market and employment conditions was a shorter working day. With only eight or nine hours on the job, male workers could both spread employment to the unemployed and limit the encroachment of the waged workplace on their domestic, social, and civic lives. In town after town, Knights' assemblies discussed the shorter working day and in some cases tried to get their employers to adopt it, generally without success. The town of Chatham saw one of the most concerted campaigns, as the local Knights of Labor asked all the town's manufacturers for an extra hour off on Saturday afternoon, only to be confronted with a lockout by a new employers' association.[287]

The 'Great Upheaval,' then, encapsulated the anger and concern of a great many Ontario factory workers about the transformation that had taken place in the province's First Industrial Revolution. It showed that the earlier willingness among both employers and workers to allow some version of paternalism to govern their relations had broken down, and that workers were now more likely than ever before to look to their own collective power to pursue their interests. Ultimately, though, what can we conclude about the effects of this wave of working-class resistance, spearheaded by the Knights of Labor, on Ontario's industrial life? The pinnacle of labour strength in the 1880s was undoubtedly Toronto, where by 1886 organized workers totalled five thousand and concessions on wages and hours were apparently extracted from some reluctant employers – probably most dramatically from the city's largest employer, the Masseys, in 1886. 'As labour organizations exist in greater numbers in Toronto than any other city in Ontario, or in the Dominion in fact, the consequence is seen in its generally higher average wages in all callings,' the Bureau of Industry's labour statistician reported in 1884.[288] Hamilton was close behind with some three thousand organized wage-earners. These metropolitan centres nourished the provincial leadership of the Knights, the most articulate intellectuals of the movement (like Phillips Thompson), and the most vibrant labour press.[289] In these cities the daily press also expressed fascination with and support for the cause,[290] and federal and provincial politicians scrambled to make legislative concessions. (The most notable were the collecting of labour statistics by the Bureau of Industries and the Factory and Workmen's Compensation acts in Ontario and the federal government's appointment of the Labour Commission.)[291]

But in the smaller factory towns and mill towns, a different story unfolded. Certainly several employers across the province felt pressured enough by the apparent strength of this labour organizing to try to shore up their workers' loyalty. Some took their first steps into paternalistic welfarism with new company picnics and the like, which may have reassured some workers.[292] Some reduced working hours slightly in 1886–87,[293] and there was a flurry of debate in at least three towns about ringing the towns' bells at seven o'clock to signal the end of all work.[294] Few of these changes seem to have lasted, however, and far more often the industrialists refused to make any concessions. Although there have been no careful statistical studies, impressionistic evidence suggests that far more strikes in small-town Ontario resulted in defeat in the face of the relentless hostility of the employers, and that workers' resistance in general made few dents in local employment practices. Outside the metropolitan centres, the influence of the Knights seems to have been fleeting: two-thirds of the local assemblies across the province appeared in the five years between 1885 and 1889, and outside Toronto they were in decline in most places, including Hamilton, by 1888. In the seven district assemblies organized after 1885, 87 of the 137 local assemblies whose dates are known – that is, nearly two-thirds – lasted only three years or less. A significant minority died after only one or two years.[295] It is hard to see how this brief 'upheaval' could have blunted the effect of industrial capitalism on the Ontario working class to any significant extent.[296] The reasons for this lack of success are not hard to find. Ontario's factory workers had to take their stand on the shaky ground of renewed large-scale unemployment[297] and in the face of dogged capitalist hostility. In these circumstances, they seemed to be quickly disillusioned with the Knights over their half-hearted strike leadership, partisan political squabbles, and insensitivity to craft-union prerogatives. The aggressive working-class consciousness and militancy soon ebbed away.

WEIGHING THE EVIDENCE

More than a century after the Labour Commission undertook its work, the efforts of the commissioners and so many of their contemporaries have helped us see the broad contours of labouring lives inside the new factory regime that had emerged in late nineteenth-century Ontario. A great deal more research in company records, local newspapers, unpublished census data, and so on will be necessary before the picture comes into sharper focus. But in the commissioners' work we can find some guideposts for understanding the process.

The transformation involved in this First Industrial Revolution disrupted much of the province's early nineteenth-century manufacturing practices. A large proportion of production was moved out of the household and artisanal workshop into new workplaces staffed by wage-earners. Wherever possible, aggressive industrial capitalists expanded their workforces and attempted to apply their workers' labour power more intensively. Their efforts included some combination of dilution of skill, subdivision of labour, mechanization, recruitment of poorly paid, unskilled workers, including women and children, and new supervisory techniques, from fines to piece-work. The large new factories where these innovations were pushed furthest gave contemporaries the unmistakable sense of living through an industrial revolution (and historians the grounds for agreeing with them). Yet the transition to this new phase of industrial capitalism was more uneven among manufacturing industries and towns and less throughgoing than popular and academic notions of such a revolution might suggest. In fact, despite the many technological and managerial changes, the new factory regime continued to rely to a considerable extent on manual labour, both skilled and unskilled, especially in the many 'manufactories' that proliferated across the province. In only a small number of industrial situations could Ontario industrialists escape their need for manual skill by dissolving crafts into narrowly subdivided, mechanized jobs for unskilled operatives. They were hampered not only by the smallness of the markets, which made 'mass-production' difficult in so many sectors in Ontario, but also by the deepening ideological (and legal) constraints on their use of female and juvenile labour. They most often also had trouble finding the skilled labour they needed. Consequently Ontario industrialists tended to retain and adapt some form of industrial paternalism to hold onto and motivate their valuable workers.

Of course, the same conditions laid the groundwork for industrial conflict, first, between the most capitalistic owners of manufactories in the larger towns and the growing numbers of their increasingly well-organized craft workers, and, then, as the promise of paternalism began to falter by the 1880s, between many more industrialists and all kinds of factory workers in towns and cities across the province, who were dismayed by the accelerated pace of change in their workplaces and in the capitalist labour market generally. By the 1880s workers were organizing in unprecedented numbers to try to impose some of the ethical constraints on the new industrial system that had begun to disappear with the decline of paternalism. Their resistance brought some concessions – higher wages and shorter hours in some cases, the first, quite limited labour-standards legislation – but it was floundering by the early 1890s. The industrial system was stabilized with a reinvigoration of paternalism where possible, but more often now with the more coercive power of an overstocked labour market to ensure compliance.

The Labour Commissioners developed a strong sense of this transformation from their trips through Ontario and the industrial towns of Quebec and the Maritimes. When they sat down to deliberate on the evidence they had gathered, they split roughly along class lines and issued separate majority and minority reports. The tone of these documents varied, but both saw the need for several government measures to make wage-earning in this new industrial economy slightly safer and more just. Unfortunately for the Ottawa millmen, bookbinders, and young labourers who took time off their jobs on 4 and 5 May 1888 to tell their stories to the commission, the Dominion government did not share this belief in state action to protect working people. It is perhaps fitting that this book should be appearing exactly one century after the government's only legislative response to the commissioners' recommendations – the adoption of Labour Day.[298]

NOTES

1 *Ottawa Citizen*, 3, 5 May 1888. On the Labour Commission see Greg Kealey, 'Introduction,' *Canada Investigates Industrialism: The Royal Commission on the Relations of Labor and Capital, 1889 (Abridged)* (Toronto: University of Toronto Press 1973), ix–xxvii.

2 Quoted in Steven Langdon, 'The Political Economy of Capitalist Transformation: Central Canada from the 1840s to the 1870s' (MA thesis, Carleton University 1972), 107.

3 For a review of the evolving conceptualization, see David Cannadine, 'The Present and the Past in the English Industrial Revolution, 1880–1980,' *Past and Present* 103 (May 1984), 131–72.

4 Maxine Berg et al., eds, *Manufacture in Town and Country before the Factory* (Cambridge: Cambridge University Press 1983); L.A. Clarkson, *Proto-Industrialization: The First Phase of Industrialization* (London: Macmillan 1985).

5 See, in particular, Raphael Samuel, 'The Workshop of the World: Steam Power and Hand Technology in Mid-Victorian Britain,' *History Workshop* 3 (Spring 1977),

6–72; Pat Hudson, 'The Regional Perspective,' in Hudson, ed., *Regions and Industries: A Perspective on the Industrial Revolution in Britain* (Cambridge: Cambridge University Press 1989), 5–38.

6 For strong statements on the validity of the concept of an Industrial Revolution, see Pat Hudson, *The Industrial Revolution* (London: Edward Arnold 1992); and Peter Stearns, *The Industrial Revolution in World History* (Boulder: Westview Press 1993).

7 David M. Gordon, Richard Edwards, and Michael Reich, *Segmented Work, Divided Workers: The Historical Transformation of Labor in the United States* (New York: Cambridge University Press 1982); Gregory S. Kealey, 'The Structure of Canadian Working Class History,' in W.J.C. Cherwinski and Gregory S. Kealey, eds., *Lectures in Canadian Labour and Working Class History* (St John's: Committee on Canadian Labour History 1985), 23–36; Craig Heron and Robert Storey, 'On the Job in Canada,' in Heron and Storey, eds, *On the Job: Confronting the Labour Process in Canada* (Kingston and Montreal: McGill-Queen's University Press 1986), 3–46.

8 I have written about the Second Industrial Revolution elsewhere; see 'The Second Industrial Revolution in Canada, 1890–1930,' in Deian Hopkin and Gregory S. Kealey, eds, *Class, Community, and the Labour Movement: Wales and Canada, 1850–1930* (Aberystwyth: Llafur and Committee on Canadian Labour History 1989), 48–66; 'The Crisis of the Craftsman: Hamilton's Metal Workers in the Early Twentieth Century,' *Labour/Le Travailleur* 6 (Autumn 1980), 7–48; and *Working in Steel: The Early Years in Canada, 1883–1935* (Toronto: McClelland and Stewart 1988).

9 See, in particular, Judy Lown, *Women and Industrialization: Gender at Work in Nineteenth-Century England* (Cambridge: Polity Press 1990); Harold Benenson, 'Victorian Sexual Ideology and Marx's Theory of the Working Class,' *International Labor and Working-Class History* 25 (Spring 1984), 1–23; Sally Alexander, 'Women, Class, and Sexual Differences in the 1830s and 1840s: Some Reflections on the Writing of a Feminist History,' *History Workshop Journal*, no. 17 (Spring 1984), 125–49; Sonya O. Rose, '"Gender at Work": Sex, Class, and Industrial Capitalism,' ibid., no. 21 (Spring 1986), 113–31.

10 See E.J. Hobsbawm, *Industry and Empire* (Harmondsworth: Penguin 1968); Ronald Aminzade, 'Reinterpreting Capitalist Industrialization: A Study of Nineteenth-Century France,' *Social History* 9 (October 1984), 329–50; William Sewell, 'Artisans, Factory Workers, and the Formation of the French Working Class, 1789–1848,' in Ira Katznelson and Aristide R. Zolbereg, eds, *Working-Class Formation: Nineteenth-Century Patterns in Western Europe and the United States* (Princeton: Princeton University Press 1986), 45–70. For stimulating efforts to place Canada within a comparative framework, see Philip Ehrensaft and Warwick Armstrong, 'The Formation of Dominion Capitalism: Economic Truncation and Class Structure,' in Allen Moscovitch, ed., *Inequality: Essays on the Political Economy of Social Welfare* (Toronto: University of Toronto Press 1981); and Gordon Laxer,

Open for Business: The Roots of Foreign Ownership in Canada (Toronto: Oxford University Press 1989).

11 Sidney Pollard, *Peaceful Conquest: The Industrialization of Europe, 1760–1970* (Oxford: Oxford University Press 1981); Hudson, 'Regional Perspective' and *Industrial Revolution.*

12 See John McCallum, *Unequal Beginnings: Agriculture and Economic Development in Quebec and Ontario until 1870* (Toronto: University of Toronto Press 1980); Gerald J.J. Tulchinsky, *The River Barons: Montreal Businessmen and the Growth of Industry and Transportation, 1837–53* (Toronto: University of Toronto Press 1977); Brian Young and John Dickinson, *A Short History of Quebec: A Socio-Economic Perspective* (Toronto: Copp Clark Pitman 1988); T.W. Acheson, 'The National Policy and the Industrialization of the Maritimes, 1880–1910,' in P.A. Buckner and David Frank, eds, *Atlantic Canada after Confederation: The Acadiensis Reader, Volume Two* (Fredericton: Acadiensis Press 1985), 176–201; Ian McKay, 'Capital and Labour in the Halifax Baking and Confectionery Industry during the Last Half of the Nineteenth Century,' *Labour/Le Travailleur* 3 (1978), 63–108; L.D. McCann, 'Staples and the New Industrialism in the Growth of Post-Confederation Halifax,' *Acadiensis* 8 (Spring 1979), 47–79; and 'The Mercantile-Industrial Transition in the Metal Towns of Pictou County, 1857–1931,' ibid., 10 (Spring 1981), 29–64; Robert Babcock, 'Economic Development in Portland (Me.) and Saint John (N.B.) during the Age of Iron and Steam, 1860–1914,' *American Review of Canadian Studies* 9 (Spring 1979), 1–37; Kris E. Inwood, 'Maritime Industrialization from 1870 to 1910: A Review of the Evidence and Its Interpretation,' *Acadiensis* 21 (Autumn 1991), 132–55; Phillip Wood, 'Barriers to Capitalist Development in Maritime Canada, 1870–1930: A Comparative Perspective,' Peter Baskerville, ed., *Canadian Papers in Business History* (Victoria: Public History Group 1989), 33–58; and 'Marxism and the Maritimes: On the Determinants of Regional Capitalist Development,' *Studies in Political Economy* 29 (Summer 1989), 123–53; John Lutz, 'Losing Steam: The Boiler and Engine Industry as an Index of British Columbia's Deindustrialization, 1880–1915,' Canadian Historical Association, *Historical Papers*, 1988, 168–208.

13 Harold A. Innis, 'An Introduction to the Economic History of Ontario from Outpost to Empire,' in Mary Q. Innis, ed., *Essays in Canadian Economic History* (Toronto: University of Toronto Press 1956), 108–22. Similarly a textbook of primary documents in Canadian economic history prepared by Innis and A.R.M. Lower contains only the flimsiest scraps of evidence of industrialization, most of which involved resource processing; see *Select Documents in Canadian Economic History, 1783–1885* (Toronto 1933).

14 The leading voice of this new school of economic historians was Tom Naylor, whose first essay on the subject ('The Third Commercial Empire of the St. Lawrence,' in Gary Teeple, ed., *Capitalism and the National Question in Canada* [Toronto: University of Toronto Press 1972], 1–42) became extremely influential in

the Canadian social sciences and grew into a factually unreliable two-volume study, *The History of Canadian Business* (Toronto: James Lorimer 1975). A much more respectable study of Ontario's resource industries by H.V. Nelles, *The Politics of Development: Forests, Mines, and Hydro-Electric Power in Ontario, 1849–1941* (Toronto: Macmillan 1974), inadvertently reinforced this overemphasis on 'staples' at the expense of a fuller understanding of Ontario's industrialization. For critiques of this perspective, see L.R. Macdonald, 'Merchants against Industry: An Idea and Its Origins,' *Canadian Historical Review* 66 (September 1975), 263–81; Robin Neill, 'The Politics and Economics of Development in Ontario,' *Ontario History* 70 (December 1978), 281–90.

15 Several Canadian neoclassical economists produced a flood of statistics in the 1960s on the timing of industrialization in Canada. The most important contributions were O.J. Firestone, *Canada's Economic Development* (London: Bowes and Bowes 1958), and 'Development of Canada's Economy, 1850–1900,' in *Trends in the American Economy in the Nineteenth Century* (Princeton: Princeton University Press 1960); G.W. Bertram, 'Economic Growth in Canadian Industry, 1870–1915: The Staple Model and the Take-Off Hypothesis,' *Canadian Journal of Economics and Political Science* 29 (May 1963), 159–84; and 'Historical Statistics on Growth and Structure of Manufacturing in Canada, 1870–1957,' in J. Henripin and A. Asimakopolas, eds, *Canadian Political Science Association Conference on Statistics, 1962 and 1963: Papers* (Toronto 1964), 93–146; J.H. Dales, 'Estimates of Canadian Manufacturing Output by Markets, 1870–1915,' in ibid., 61–91; Edward J. Chambers and Gordon W. Bertram, 'Urbanization and Manufacturing in Canada, 1870–1957,' in Sylvia Ostry and T.K. Rhymes, eds, *Canadian Political Science Association, Conference on Statistics, 1964* (Toronto 1966), 225–57; and Robert E. Ankli, 'Reciprocity Treaty of 1854,' *Canadian Journal of Economics* 4 (February 1971), 21–33. The outcome of that debate was a recognition that decennial census statistics revealed steady, if erratic growth in Canadian manufacturing in the late nineteenth century. This consensus frames the more detailed work of Ian Drummond on the Ontario economy in *Progress without Planning: The Economic History of Ontario from Confederation to the Second World War* (Toronto: University of Toronto Press 1987). For a slightly less blinkered neoclassical perspective, see Douglas McCalla and Peter George, 'Measurement, Myth, and Reality: Reflections on the Economic History of Nineteenth-Century Ontario,' *Journal of Canadian Studies* 21 (Fall 1986), 71–86.

16 Stanley B. Ryerson, *Unequal Union: Confederation and the Roots of Conflict in the Canadas, 1815–1873* (Toronto: Progress Books 1968); H. Clare Pentland, 'Labour and the Development of Industrial Capitalism in Canada' (PhD thesis, University of Toronto 1961), later published in revised form as *Labour and Capital in Canada, 1650–1860* (Toronto: James Lorimer 1981).

17 Allan Greer, 'Wage Labour and the Transition to Capitalism: A Critique of Pentland,' *Labour/Le Travail*, 15 (Spring 1985), 7–24.

18 Stephen Langdon, 'The Emergence of the Canadian Working Class Movement, 1845–75,' *Journal of Canadian Studies* 8 (May 1973), 3–13, and (August 1973), 8–24; see also Robert H. Storey, 'Industrialization in Canada: The Emergence of the Hamilton Working Class, 1850–1870s' (MA thesis, Dalhousie University 1975).

19 Bryan D. Palmer, *A Culture in Conflict: Skilled Workers and Industrial Capitalism in Hamilton, Ontario, 1860–1914* (Montreal: McGill-Queen's University Press 1979); Gregory S. Kealey, *Toronto Workers Respond to Industrial Capitalism, 1867–1892* (Toronto: University of Toronto Press 1980); and Gregory S. Kealey and Bryan D. Palmer, *Dreaming of What Might Be: The Knights of Labor in Ontario, 1880–1900* (New York: Cambridge University Press 1982).

20 Marjorie Griffin Cohen, *Women's Work, Markets, and Economic Development in Nineteenth-Century Ontario* (Toronto: University of Toronto Press 1988); see also Janice Acton et al., eds, *Women at Work: Ontario, 1850–1930* (Toronto: Canadian Women's Educational Press 1974).

21 Robert Gourlay, *Statistical Account of Upper Canada* (London 1822; abridged edition Toronto: McClelland and Stewart 1974); Edwin C. Guillet, *Pioneer Arts and Crafts* (Toronto: University of Toronto Press 1968); Felicity L. Leung, *Grist and Flour Mills in Ontario: From Millstones to Rollers, 1780s–1880s* (Ottawa: Parks Canada 1981); Elizabeth Price, 'The Changing Geography of the Woollen Industry in Lanark, Renfrew and Carleton Counties, 1830–1911' (Master's research paper, University of Toronto 1979); Mary Quayle Innis, 'The Industrial Development of Ontario, 1783–1820,' in J.K. Johnson, ed., *Historical Essays on Upper Canada* (Toronto: McClelland and Stewart 1975), 140–52; Douglas McCalla, *Planting the Province: The Economic History of Upper Canada, 1784–1870* (Toronto: University of Toronto Press 1993); Sidney Thomson Fisher, *The Merchant Millers of the Humber Valley: A Study in the Early Economy of Canada* (Toronto 1985); Leo Johnson, *History of the County of Ontario, 1615–1875* (Whitby: The Corporation of the County of Ontario 1973), 38–81; W. John McIntyre, 'From Workshop to Factory: The Furnituremaker,' *Material History Bulletin* 19 (Spring 1984), 25–28; Thomas McIlwraith, 'The Adequacy of Rural Roads in the Era Before Railways: An Illustration from Upper Canada,' *Canadian Geographer* 14 (1970), 344–60; and 'Transportation in the Landscape of Early Upper Canada,' in J. David Wood, ed., *Perspectives on Landscape and Settlement in Nineteenth-Century Ontario* (Toronto: McClelland and Stewart 1975), 51–63; James Herbert Bartlett, *The Manufacture, Consumption and Production of Iron, Steel and Coal in the Dominion of Canada, with Some Notes on the Manufacture of Iron and on the Iron Trade, in Other Countries* (Montreal 1885); T. Ritchie, 'Joseph Van Norman, Ironmaster of Upper Canada,'*Canadian Geographical Journal* 78 (August 1968), 46–51.

22 Pentland, *Labour and Capital*; McCalla, *Planting the Province*; Johnson, *Ontario County*, 128–71; Allan Greer and Ian Radforth, eds, *Colonial Leviathan: State Formation in Nineteenth-Century Canada* (Toronto: University of Toronto Press 1991); Bruce Curtis, *True Government by Choice Men? Inspection, Education, and State*

Formation in Canada West (Toronto: University of Toronto Press 1992); Leo Johnson, 'Land Policy, Population Growth, and Social Structure in the Home District, 1793–1851,' in J.K. Johnson, ed., *Historical Essays*, 32–57; Gary Teeple, 'Land, Labour, and Capital in Pre-Confederation Canada,' in Teeple, *Capitalism and the National Question*, 43–46; Graeme Wynn, 'Notes on Society and Environment in Old Ontario,' *Journal of Social History* 13 (Fall 1979), 49–65.

23 Leung, *Flour and Grist Mills*; W.P.J. Millar, 'George P.M. Ball: A Rural Businessman in Upper Canada,' *Ontario History* 66 (June 1974), 65–78; Fisher, *Merchant-Millers*; Price, 'Changing Geography'; North Lanark Historical Society, *The Development of the Woollen Industry in Lanark, Renfrew and Carleton Counties* (Erin: Porcupine's Quill 1978); McCalla, *Planting the Province*, 94–104.

24 McCalla, *Planting the Province*; Robert Leslie Jones, *History of Agriculture in Ontario, 1613–1880* (Toronto: University of Toronto Press 1946); J.A. Ruddick, 'The Development of the Dairy Industry in Canada,' in H.A. Innis, ed., *The Dairy Industry in Canada* (Toronto 1937), 15–123; D.A. Lawr, 'The Development of Ontario Farming, 1870–1919,' *Ontario History* 64 (December 1972), 239–51; Robert Ankli and Wendy Millar, 'Ontario Agriculture in Transition: The Switch from Wheat to Cheese,' *Journal of Economic History* 42 (1982), 207–15; Marvin McInnis, 'The Changing Structure of Canadian Agriculture, 1867–1897,' ibid., 191–8; Michael Bliss, *A Canadian Millionaire: The Life and Business Times of Sir Joseph Flavelle, Bart., 1858–1939* (Toronto: Macmillan 1978), 27–52. Kris Inwood and Tim Sullivan raise questions about the link between agricultural 'improvement' and industrialization; see 'Comparative Perspectives on Nineteenth-Century Growth: Ontario in the Great Lakes Region,' in Peter Baskerville, ed., *Canadian Papers in Business History*, vol. 2 (Victoria: University of Victoria, Public History Group 1993), 71–101.

25 For a discussion of the possible problems with these figures, see Table 1, footnote *b*.

26 W.H. Smith, *Canada: Past, Present and Future, Being a Historical, Geographical, Geological and Statistical Account of Canada West* (Toronto: Thomas MacLear 1851); Jacob Spelt, *Urban Development in South-Central Ontario* (Toronto: McClelland and Stewart, 1972), 55–100; A.R.M. Lower, *Settlement and the Forest Frontier in Eastern Canada* (Toronto: Ryerson 1936); and *The North American Assault on the Canadian Forest: A History of the Lumber Trade between Canada and the United States* (Toronto: Ryerson 1938), 27–52; Michael S. Cross, 'The Lumber Community of Upper Canada, 1815–1867,' *Ontario History* 52 (November 1960), 213–32; Richard M. Reid, 'Introduction,' *The Upper Ottawa Valley to 1855* (Ottawa: Carleton University Press 1990), xlvii–lxxiii; James T. Angus, *A Deo Victoria: The Story of the Georgian Bay Lumber Company, 1871–1942* (Thunder Bay: Severn Publications 1990); McCallum, *Unequal Beginnings*, 9–74; Leung, *Grist and Flour Mills*; Fisher, *Merchant-Millers*; Drummond, *Progress without Planning*, 93–7; Elizabeth Bloomfield and Gerald Bloomfield, *Industrial Leaders: The Largest Manufacturing Firms of Ontario in 1871* (Guelph: University of Guelph, Department of Geography,

Canadian Industry in 1871 Project 1989), 45; Dianne Newell, *Technology on the Frontier: Mining in Old Ontario* (Vancouver: University of British Columbia Press 1986); Edward Phelps, 'Foundations of the Canadian Oil Industry, 1850–1866,' in Edith Firth, ed., *Profiles of a Province: Studies in the History of Ontario* (Toronto: Ontario Historical Society 1967), 156–65; W.E. Brett Code, 'The Salt Men of Goderich in Ontario's Court of Chancery: *Ontario Salt Co. v. Merchants Salt Co.* and the Judicial Enforcement of Combinations,' *McGill Law Journal* 38 (1993).

27 See, for example, *Ottawa Citizen*, 12 March 1852.

28 Peter Baskerville, 'Donald Bethune's Steamboat Business: A Study of Upper Canadian Commercial and Financial Practice,' *Ontario History* 67 (1975), 135–49; George Richardson, 'The Canadian Locomotive Company,' in Gerald Tulchinsky, ed., *To Preserve and Defend: Essays on Kingston in the Nineteenth Century* (Montreal: McGill-Queen's University Press 1976), 157–67; William Kilbourn, *The Elements Combined: A History of the Steel Company of Canada* (Toronto: Clarke Irwin 1960), 33–62; Paul Craven and Tom Traves, 'Canadian Railways as Manufacturers, 1850–1880,' Canadian Historical Association, *Historical Papers*, 1983, 254–81.

29 W.G. Phillips, *The Agricultural Implement Industry in Canada: A Study of Competition* (Toronto: University of Toronto Press 1956); Merrill Denison, *Harvest Triumphant: The Story of Massey-Harris* (Toronto: Collins 1949).

30 Gerald Tulchinsky, 'Aspects of the Clothing Industry in Canada, 1850s to 1914' (paper presented to the Business History Conference, Trent University, 1984); and 'Hidden among the Smokestacks: Toronto's Clothing Industry, 1871–1901,' in David Keane and Colin Read, eds, *Old Ontario: Essays in Honour of J.M.S. Careless* (Toronto: Dundurn 1990), 257–84; Peter Bischoff, 'Tensions et solidarité: la formation des traditions syndicales chez les mouleurs de Montréal, Hamilton et Toronto, 1851 à 1893' (PhD thesis, Université de Montréal 1992), 35–77; McIntyre, 'From Workshop to Factory'; Joan MacKinnon, *A Checklist of Toronto Cabinet and Chair Makers, 1800–1865* (Ottawa: Parks Canada 1975); John Hall, 'One Hundred Years of Piano Making in Kingston,' *Historic Kingston* 39 (1991), 36–51; Wayne Kelly, *Downright Upright: A History of the Canadian Piano Industry* (Toronto: Natural Heritage/Natural History 1991); Martha Eckmann Brent, 'A Stitch in Time: The Sewing Machine Industry of Ontario, 1860–1897,' *Material History Bulletin* 10 (Spring 1980), 1–30; Thomas L. Walkom, 'The Daily Newspaper in Ontario's Developing Capitalist Economy: Toronto and Ottawa, 1871–1911' (PhD thesis, University of Toronto 1983).

31 T.W. Acheson, 'The Social Origins of the Canadian Industrial Elite, 1880–1885,' in David S. Macmillan, ed., *Canadian Business History: Selected Studies, 1497–1971* (Toronto: McClelland and Stewart 1972), 143–74.

32 There is no space here for an extensive digression on the question of the alleged conflict between industrial and commercial capital in this period, first argued by Tom Naylor and subsequently repeated by many other social scientists. There is now plenty of evidence to establish that no such split took place, that indeed mer-

chants in many communities invested heavily in the new factories, and that the alleged American domination of manufacturing was still many decades in the future. For examples in specific industries and industrial centres, see Macdonald, 'Merchants against Industry'; Kealey, *Toronto Workers*; Kris Inwood, 'Inter-Sectoral Linkages: The Case of Secondary Iron and Steel' (paper presented to the Canadian Business History Conference, May 1984); David G. Burley, 'The Businessmen of Brantford, Ontario: Self-Employment in a Mid-Nineteenth Century Town' (PhD thesis, McMaster University 1983).

33 Elizabeth Bloomfield and G.T. Bloomfield, *Patterns of Canadian Industry in 1871: An Overview Based on the First Census of Canada* (Guelph: University of Guelph, Department of Geography, Canadian Industry in 1871 Project, Research Report 12 1990), 28–30.

34 Elizabeth Bloomfield, *Water Wheels and Steam Engines*, 8.

35 Canada, Royal Commission on the Relations of Labour and Capital, *Report – Evidence, Ontario* (hereafter RCRLC), 1062; Ontario, Bureau of Industries, *Report* (hereafter OBIR), 1887, 39; 1889, 16; Knowles, 'Beyond Domesticity,' 104.

36 RCRLC, 743, 1185; *Canadian Manufacturer*, 30 June 1882, 258.

37 *Canadian Manufacturer*, 21 July 1882, 355; 1 September 1882, 546; Angus, *A Deo Victoria*; RCRLC, 261, 707, 882, 891, 1137, 1176; OIFR, 1888, 10, 1891, 7; Canada, House of Commons, *Journals* (Ottawa), vol. 10 (1876), App. 3 ('Select Committee on the Causes of the Present Depression of the Manufacturing, Mining, Commercial, Shipping, Lumber and Fishing Interests, Report') (hereafter Select Committee on the Causes of the Present Depression), 115.

38 RCRLC, 666, 685, 743, 784, 794, 842, 885, 936, 953, 1130, 1185; see also OBIR, 1889, 16; Ontario, Inspectors of Factories, *Report* (hereafter OIFR), 1889, 7, 40.

39 The pessimistic view of the period and the optimistic revisionism are set out in, respectively, O.D. Skelton, *General Economic History of the Dominion, 1867–1912* (Toronto: Publishers' Associates 1913); and Drummond, *Progress without Planning*, 103–33. For a statistical outline of business cycles based on the extremely limited data available from the late nineteenth century, see Edward J. Chambers, 'Late Nineteenth Century Business Cycles in Canada,' *Canadian Journal of Economics and Political Science* 30 (August 1964), 391–412; for more qualitative discussions of unemployment in the period, see OBIR, 1884–90; OIFR, 1888–90; Debi Wells, '"The Hardest Lines of the Sternest School": Working Class Ottawa in the Depression of the 1870s' (MA thesis, Carleton University 1982); James M. Pitsula, 'The Treatment of Tramps in Late Nineteenth Century Toronto,' Canadian Historical Association, *Historical Papers*, 1980, 111–32; Richard Anderson, '"The Irrepressible Stampede": Tramps in Ontario, 1870–1880,' *Ontario History* 84 (March 1992), 33–56.

40 Marvin McInnis, 'Marketable Surpluses in Ontario Farming, 1860,' in Douglas McCalla, ed., *Perspectives on Canadian Economic History* (Toronto: Copp Clark Pitman 1987), 37–57.

41 Of the province's sixty leading industrial firms in 1871, thirty-seven had ceased operation by the end of the century. Bloomfield and Bloomfield, *Industrial Leaders*, 53.

42 Ibid., 46; Elinor Kyte Senior, *From Royal Township to Industrial City: Cornwall, 1784–1984* (Belleville: Mika Publishing 1983).

43 Bloomfield and Bloomfield, *Industrial Leaders*, 13, 62–3; *Census of Canada*, 1891, vol. 3. Some calculations are mine.

44 A.H. Blackeby, *Report on the State of the Manufacturing Interests of Ontario and Quebec* (Ottawa: Queen's Printer 1885); RCRLC, 354; Kealey, *Toronto Workers*; Ben Forster, *A Conjunction of Interests: Business, Politics, and Tariffs, 1825–1879* (Toronto: University of Toronto Press 1986); and 'Finding the Right Size: Markets and Competition in Mid- and Late Nineteenth-Century Ontario,' in Roger Hall, William Westfall, and Laurel Sefton MacDowell, eds, *Patterns of the Past: Interpreting Ontario's History* (Toronto: Dundurn Press 1988), 150–73.

45 RCRLC, 494

46 James M. Gilmour, *Spatial Evolution of Manufacturing: Southern Ontario, 1851–1891* (Toronto: University of Toronto Press 1972).

47 Elizabeth and Gerald Bloomfield, *The Ontario Urban System at the Onset of the Industrial Era* (Guelph: University of Guelph, Department of Geography, Canadian Industry in 1871 Project, Research Report 3, 1989), 26; and *The Hum of Industry: Millers, Manufacturers and Artisans of Wellington County* (Guelph: University of Guelph, Department of Geography, Canadian Industry in 1871 Project, Research Report 9, 1989); Joy Parr, *Gender of Breadwinners: Women, Men, and Change in Two Industrial Towns, 1880–1950* (Toronto: University of Toronto Press 1990); Kelly, *Downright Upright*; Spelt, *Urban Development*; Johnson, *County of Ontario*; and *The History of Guelph, 1827–1927* (Guelph: Guelph Historical Society 1977); John English and Kenneth McLaughlin, *Kitchener: an Illustrated History* (Waterloo: Wilfrid Laurier University Press 1983). By 1871 the province's leading producers of agricultural implements were spread through such towns as Oshawa, Mitchell, Smith's Falls, Ingersoll, Brampton, Newcastle, Aurora, Gananoque, Bradford, Dundas, St Mary's, Belleville, Napanee, Strathroy, New Hamburg, Waterloo, Brockville, Seaforth, Milton, Galt, Clinton, Caledonia, Chatham, Lindsay, London, and St Catharines. Elizabeth Bloomfield and Gerald Bloomfield, 'Mills, Factories, and Craftshops of Ontario, 1870: A Machine-Readable Source for Material Historians,' *Material History Bulletin* 25 (1987), 44. By no means all small towns made this leap into the industrial age; Bloomfield and Bloomfield found that in 1871 only 67 of 148 urban and 'proto-urban' places in Ontario had at least one factory and only 23 had at least one manufactory; see *Ontario Urban System*, 34; also Stephen Edward Thorning, 'T.E. Bissell of Elora, Ontario: A Small Town Manufacturer and His Milieu' (MA thesis, McMaster University 1986), 15; OBIR, 1884, lxix. On the continuity of small-scale producers, see Gordon Darroch, 'Class in Nineteenth-Century Ontario: A Reassessment of the Crisis and Demise of Small Producers during Early Industrialization, 1861–1871,' in Gregory S. Kealey, ed., *Class, Gender,*

and Region: Essays in Canadian Historical Sociology (St John's: Committee on Canadian Labour History 1988), 49–72.

48 J.M.S. Careless, 'Some Aspects of Urbanization in Nineteenth-Century Ontario,' in F.H. Armstrong et al., eds, *Aspects of Nineteenth-Century Ontario: Essays Presented to James J. Talman* (Toronto: University of Toronto Press 1974), 65–79; Frederick H. Armstrong and Daniel J. Brock, 'The Rise of London: A Study of Urban Evolution in Nineteenth-Century Southwestern Ontario,' in ibid., 80–100; Langdon, 'Political Economy,' 88–94; Kealey, *Toronto Workers*, 18–34; Douglas McCalla, *The Upper Canada Trade, 1834–1872: A Study of the Buchanans' Business* (Toronto: University of Toronto Press 1979); and 'The Decline of Hamilton as a Wholesale Centre,' *Ontario History* 65 (1973); John C. Weaver, *Hamilton: An Illustrated History* (Toronto: James Lorimer 1982), 41–77.

49 Craven and Traves, 'Canadian Railways as Manufacturers'; Richardson, 'Canadian Locomotive Company.'

50 Bloomfield and Bloomfield, *Industrial Leaders*, 30–3.

51 Bloomfield and Bloomfield, *Ontario Urban System*, 26; Gilmour, *Spatial Evolution*, 121–52; Warren R. Bland, 'The Location of Manufacturing in Southern Ontario in 1881,' *Ontario Geography* 8 (1974), 8–39; Edward J. Chambers and Gordon W. Bertram, 'Urbanization and Manufacturing in Central Canada, 1870–1890,' in Sylvia Ostry and T.K. Rymes, eds, *Canadian Political Science Association, Conference on Statistics, 1964* (Toronto 1966), 225–57; John C. Weaver, 'The Location of Manufacturing Enterprises: The Case of Hamilton's Attraction of Foundries, 1830–1890,' in Richard A. Jarrell and Arnold E. Ross, eds, *Critical Issues in the History of Canadian Science, Technology, and Medicine* (Thornhill: HSTC 1983); Bischoff, 'Tensions et solidarité,' 44–60; Randy William Widdis, 'Belleville and Environs: Continuity, Change, and the Integration of Town and Country during the 19th Century,' *Urban History Review* 19 (February 1991), 181–208.

52 Gordon Laxer pursues the implications of this gap in the industrial structure in *Open for Business*.

53 Kilbourn, *Elements Combined*, 41.

54 There has not been much careful research of pre-industrial wage-earning in Upper Canada before 1840. This sketch is based on Pentland, *Labour and Capital*; Peter A. Russell, 'Wage Labour Rates in Upper Canada, 1818–1840,' *Histoire sociale/Social History* 16 (May 1983), 61–80; McCalla, *Planting the Province*, 92–115; William N.T. Wylie, 'The Blacksmith in Upper Canada, 1784–1850: A Study of Technology, Culture, and Power,' *Canadian Papers in Rural History* 7 (1990), 50–3; Elijah Leonard, *A Memoir* (London: Advertiser Printing n.d.); Innis and Lower, *Select Documents*, 296–7; Sally Zerker, *The Rise and Fall of the Toronto Typographical Union, 1832–1972: A Case Study of Foreign Domination* (Toronto: University of Toronto Press 1982), 3–49; McIntyre, 'From Workshop to Factory'; Upper Canada, House of Assembly, *Journal*, 1836, vol. 3, App. 102 (thanks to Paul

Craven for this reference); Bryan Palmer, 'Kingston Mechanics and the Rise of the Penitentiary, 1833–1836,' *Histoire sociale/Social History* 13 (May 1980), 7–82; Jeremy Webber in this volume. Rusty Bitterman's stimulating new work on pre-industrial wage-earning in Nova Scotia is suggestive of new directions that research on Ontario could fruitfully take; see Bitterman, 'Farm Households and Wage Labour in the Northeastern Maritimes in the Early 19th Century,' *Labour/Le Travail* 31 (Spring 1993), 13–45. The Lower Canadian artisanal experience has been covered more fully in Pierre H. Audet, 'Apprentices in Early Nineteenth Century Montreal, 1790–1812' (MA thesis, Concordia University 1976); Jean-Pierre Hardy and David-Thiery Ruddell, *Les apprentis artisans à Québec: 1660–1815* (Montreal 1977); Joanne Burgess, 'Work, Family, and Community: Montreal Leather Craftsmen, 1790–1831' (PhD thesis, Université du Québec à Montréal 1986); Grace Laing Hogg, 'The Legal Rights of Masters, Mistresses, and Domestic Servants in Montreal, 1816–1829' (MA thesis, McGill University 1989).

55 A considerable variety of 'factories' appeared in Ontario, as elsewhere. The term itself was certainly not used precisely. In the 1860s 'manufactory' was more common to describe the new larger units of manufacturing, while 'factory' seemed to have a more specialized meaning alongside 'mill' – cheese factories and so on, none of which were necessarily large or highly mechanized. By the 1880s, factory seems to have become the standard term for the industrial capitalist workplace, while 'workshop' had come to mean something much smaller and run on distinctly different lines. For the contrast, see, for example, the *Journal* of the Board of Arts and Manufactures in the 1860s and the reports of the Ontario factory inspectors in the 1880s.

56 Bartlett, *Manufacture*.

57 In the 1850s and 1860s, for example, Toronto's largest foundries each manufactured a considerable variety of iron goods – stoves, hollowware, engines, and sundry milling machinery. Only in the 1860s, at the time of railway expansion and the boost given to the economy by the American Civil War, was there a marked increase in specialization of production, and then only in some sectors – notably boots and shoes, woollen textiles, agricultural implements, and sewing machines. Nonetheless, even the province's largest agricultural–implement plant, the Joseph Hall works in Oshawa, which employed over three hundred men in 1872, was also producing an extensive line of other industrial machinery, including printing presses. *Globe*, 13 December 1856; *Mail* (Toronto), 8 April 1872; Bischoff, 'Tensions et solidarité,' 46.

58 *Census of Canada* (Ottawa), 1871, vol. 3, x; Canada, House of Commons, *Journals* (Ottawa), vol. 8 (1874), App. 3 ('Select Committee Appointed to Enquire into and Report to the House on the Extent and Condition of the Manufacturing Interests of the Dominion') (hereafter Select Committee on Manufacturing Interests); and Select Committee on the Causes of the Present Depression; RCRLC, 674. It was not usual for companies to specialize in only one part of their operation; for example, the huge Jacques and Hay factory in Toronto in the 1860s mass-produced chairs but

made much smaller runs of other furniture; Board of Art and Manufactures of Upper Canada, *Journal* (Toronto) (hereafter BAMUCJ), July 1864, 194–5.

59 *London Free Press*, 17 January 1864, 12 September 1870; Kealey, *Toronto Workers*, 46–7.

60 Pollin, 'Jacques and Hay,' 9–10, 24–5, 29–30; Kealey, *Toronto Workers*; Parr, *Gender of Breadwinnners*.

61 Elizabeth and Gerald Bloomfield have attempted to refine the concept of manufactory by separating out those that, according to the 1871 census, had water or steam power and those with more than twenty-five workers (see *Hum of Industry*, 39–40). Their elegant schema of factories, manufactories, mills, powered craftshops, and so on, however, does not seem helpful for understanding the evolving factory system in the period. In the first place, the presence of inanimate power tells us nothing about how it was being used in the labour process – often much of the production process remained manual, or the machinery simply allowed for more precision in skilled work (especially among machinists). And equally important, in 1871 few enterprises were so specialized that their whole operations could be easily slotted into one category – as we will see, powered machinery in one department might have no counterpart in another. For these reasons, I will continue to use the term 'manufactory' as a broad, relatively loose term to indicate workplaces where skilled workers still exercised significant amounts of manual control over the labour process.

62 RCRLC, 67.

63 Bischoff, 'Tensions et solidarité'; Gregory S. Kealey, 'Work Control, the Labour Process, and Nineteenth-Century Canadian Printers,' in Heron and Storey, eds, *On the Job*, 75–101; RCRLC, 608–9, 1118.

64 W. Craig Heron, 'Working-Class Hamilton, 1895–1930' (PhD thesis, Dalhousie University 1981).

65 Bischoff, 'Tensions et solidarité,' 51; RCRLC, 608. For drawings of a fitter in the Massey plant, see *Massey's Illustrated* 1 (May 1889), inside front cover, and Massey-Harris Co., *Visitors' Souvenir* ([Toronto] n.d.), in Ontario Agricultural Museum (hereafter OAM), Massey-Ferguson Collection, MH 154.

66 Kealey, 'Work Control'; Bischoff, 'Tensions et solidarité'; Palmer, *Culture in Conflict*.

67 *Globe*, 10 April 1871, quoted in Langdon, 'Emergence,' 16.

68 BAMUCJ, May 1862, 137; December 1865, 310; *Canadian Illustrated News*, 17 January 1863, 112; *Hamilton Spectator*, 22 December 1870 (quoted in Palmer, *Culture in Conflict*, 16).

69 RCRLC, 336.

70 *Globe*, 28 October 1868; Select Committee on Manufacturing Interests, 17; RCRLC, 629, 829; A.W. Wright, *Report upon the Sweating System in Canada* (Ottawa: Queen's Printer 1896); W.L. Mackenzie King, *Report to the Honourable Postmaster General on the Methods Adopted in Canada in the Carrying Out of Government Clothing Contracts* (Ottawa: Queen's Printer 1898); Tulchinsky, 'Hidden among the

Smokestacks,' 272–6; Robert McIntosh, 'Sweated Labour: Female Needleworkers in Industrializing Canada,' *Labour/Le Travail* 32 (Fall 1993), 105–38.

71 BAMUCJ, May 1862, 137; *Canadian Illustrated News*, 17 January 1863, 112. Penman's knitting mill in Paris may also have had 'inside' and 'outside' employees; see Knowles, 'Beyond Domesticity,' 170–1.

72 Bloomfield and Bloomfield, *Industrial Leaders*, 33–4. Water-power was by no means a declining technology across Ontario. The abundance of streams cascading down to the lakefront made it an abundant source, and several communities developed water-power canals in order to attract factories. Moreover, all but eight of the forty-three largest consumers of power in the province in 1871, the overwhelming majority of them saw and flour mills, used water-power (one used both water and steam). Steam engines tended to have smaller capacity (typically 20 h.p.) but to be more flexible. More industrial workers would have encountered them in 1871: of the 48 per cent of the Ontario industrial workforce that worked in establishments with either form of power, twice as many (32 per cent) found steam rather than water-power on the premises. The larger the town, the more likely was steam to be the motive power, reaching 95 per cent in Toronto and 98 per cent in Hamilton.

73 BAMUCJ, March 1863, 84; January 1864, 1.

74 Select Committee on the Causes of the Present Depression, 115–6.

75 For descriptions of the technology and division of labour in Ontario's textile mills, see BAMUCJ, September 1864, 255–7; July 1866, 198–9; RCRLC, 892–3; A.B. McCullough, *The Primary Textile Industry in Canada: History and Heritage* (Ottawa: Environment Canada, Parks Service, National Historic Sites 1992), 13–23.

76 John W. Hughson and Courtney C.J. Bond, *Hurling Down the Pine: The Story of the Wright, Gilmour and Hughson Families, Timber and Lumber Manufacturers in the Hull and Ottawa Region and on the Gatineau River, 1800–1920* (Old Chelsea, Quebec: Historical Society of the Gatineau 1965), 68–78; McIntyre, 'From Workshop to Factory,' 32; Angus, *A Deo Victoria*, 87–8; Charlotte Whitton, *A Hundred Years A-Fellin': Some Passages from the Timber Saga of the Ottawa in the Century in Which the Gillies Have Been Cutting in the Valley, 1842–1942* (Ottawa: Runge Press [1943]), 141–2; Jack Brown, *The Sawmills of Lanark and Renfrew* (Mallorytown: Author 1976); Donald M. Wilson, *Lost Horizons: The Story of the Rathbun Company and the Bay of Quinte Railway* (Belleville: Mika Publishing 1983), 18; Barbara R. Robertson, *Sawpower: Making Lumber in the Sawmills of Nova Scotia* (Halifax: Nimbus Publishing and the Nova Scotia Museum 1986).

77 Kealey, *Toronto Workers*, 39–40; Storey, 'Industrialization'; Palmer, *Culture in Conflict*, 12. Technological change in the clothing industry would continue in the late nineteenth-century with special adaptations for pocket stitching and buttonholing, steam-powered cutting, gas-heated pressing, and other minor modifications. Tulchinsky, 'Aspects of Clothing Manufacturing,' 13–14.

78 See, for example, *Ottawa Citizen*, 27 November 1852 (Ottawa woodworking factory); *Canadian Illustrated News*, 3 January 1863, 95 (Taylor safe works, Toronto);

Hamilton Spectator 1 May 1871 (Wanzer's sewing machine factory, Hamilton); *Mail* (Toronto), 15 April 1872 (Canada Tool Works, Dundas); *Globe*, 3 September 1888 (Massey works, Toronto).

79 William Chambers, *Things As They Are in America* (London and Edinburgh 1854), 115 (quoted in McIntyre, 'From Workshop to Factory'); BAMUCJ, July 1864, 194–5; RCRLC, 508, 1117. Similar woodworking machinery was reported frequently in testimony to the Labour Commission; see pp. 403, 422–3, 442, 462, 467, 509, 530–1, 607–10, 623–6, 647, 939, 947.

80 See, for example, *Almonte Gazette*, 16 July 1870, 26 July 1872, 27 June, 4 July 1873, 20 March 1874 (courtesy of Elizabeth Price); Eric Tucker, *Administering Danger in the Workplace: The Law and Politics of Occupational Health and Safety Regulation in Ontario, 1850–1914* (Toronto: University of Toronto Press 1990), 15–37.

81 *Globe*, 3 September 1888.

82 Amidst the voluminous commission testimony on technological change, see in particular RCRLC, 9–10, 38, 55, 61, 114–5, 124, 130, 141, 354–5, 443, 461–3, 472, 490, 509, 566, 596, 663, 669, 671, 677, 826, 884, 925, 929, 930, 980–2, 1034, 1117.

83 RCRLC, 490, 826.

84 Samuel, 'Workshop of the World.' Stephen Langdon's preliminary discussion of the First Industrial Revolution put too much emphasis on mechanization; see 'Political Economy,' 102–6, and 'Emergence.'

85 BAMUCJ, September 1864, 257.

86 Pollin, 'Jacques and Hay,' 28.

87 The main exception was the sewing-machine industry, where the tiny parts required encouraged the introduction of some mechanization in the 1870s and 1880s. The giant Massey agricultural-implement works did not have any moulding machines until 1889. Bischoff, 'Tensions et solidarité,' 95–98; Kealey, *Toronto Workers*, 75.

88 Kealey, 'Work Control.'

89 Massey-Ferguson Coll.; Bischoff, 'Tensions et solidarité'; Kealey, 'Work Control'; *Northern Advance*, 8 December 1863, 19 September 1866; BAMUCJ, July 1864, 194; RCRLC, 997.

90 Palmer, *Culture in Conflict*, 75–6.

91 RCRLC, 261, 400, 489; Kealey, *Toronto Workers*, 53–63.

92 They presented plenty of evidence to the Labour Commission that too many incompetent men ran steam engines and boilers and that public safety was consequently in danger. RCRLC, 207, 257–8

93 Leung, *Grist and Flour Mills*; Hughson and Bond, *Hurling Down the Pine*, 75–6; *Northern Advance*, 27 August 1857, 15 August 1860; *London Free Press*, 8 July 1865, 15 October, 4 November, 2 December 1868. RCRLC, 377, 490.

94 RCRLC, 786.

95 BAMUCJ, July 1864, 195. On the continuing skill requirements in furniture manufacture, see Parr, *Gender of Breadwinners*; Forster, 'Finding the Right Size'; Ruth

Cathcart, *Jacques and Hay: 19th Century Toronto Furniture Makers* (Erin: Boston Mills Press 1986), 31.

96 RCRLC, 893.

97 Ibid., 884.

98 OBIR, 1886, 205. Similarly, the Dominion Starch Works took its experienced workforce with it when it moved from Edwardsburg to Walkerville. RCRLC, 379.

99 RCRLC, 327, 762, 880–1.

100 Ibid., 287, 536, 1171, 1173.

101 Knowles, 'Beyond Domesticity,' 39, 96–8; Parr, *Gender of Breadwinners*, 15–17; Committee on the Causes of the Present Depression, 146.

102 The flour mills were mechanized quite early in the ninetenth century, the sawmills from the 1850s onward. Leung, *Grist and Flour Mills*; Angus, *A Deo Victoria*, 88–9; Whitton, *A Hundred Years A-Fellin'*, 141–2; Wilson, *Lost Horizons*, 18; Clyde C. Kennedy, *The Upper Ottawa Valley: A Glimpse of History* (Pembroke: Renfrew County Council 1970), 125–9.

103 BAMUCJ, January 1864, 1; W.A. Child, 'Iron Trade Built By Determined Men,' *Hamilton Spectator*, 15 July 1926. The Joseph Hall works reported only one six-ton steam hoist in its large agricultural-implement factory in Oshawa in 1872 in the midst of over three hundred workers (*Mail*, 8 April 1872). A detailed drawing of the huge Massey machine shop in Toronto in the 1880s showed manual lifting and carrying (OAM, Massey-Ferguson Collection, MM 127).

104 Bischoff, 'Tensions et solidarité,' 19–20; Price, 'Changing Geography,' 62 and App. A; North Lanark Historical Society, *Development of the Woollen Industry*, 13; Burley, 'Businessmen of Brantford.' In 1870 a British stonemason, Thomas Connolly, wrote to the Ontario minister of agriculture and public works to express his favourable impressions of industrial prospects in Ontario after a tour through the province earlier that year; among his observations, he noted that a mechanic's 'chance to become an employer or the owner of property is much greater' than in Britain; Ontario, Commissioner of Agriculture and Public Works, *Annual Report on Immigration* (Toronto), 1870, 28. Bryan Palmer has shown how these artisanal businesses could be perilous, however, and David Burley has revealed that they were much harder to start up by the 1870s; Palmer, *Culture in Conflict*, 13–14; Burley, 'Businessmen of Brantford,' 133–71.

105 H.C. Pentland has probably overstated the ease with which a capitalist labour market came into being in this period; see *Labour and Capital*.

106 RCRLC, 478, 535, 623; Zerker, *Rise and Fall*; Bischoff, 'Tensions et solidarité,' 134–43, 171–207; Michael B. Katz, *The People of Hamilton, Canada West: Family and Class in a Mid-Nineteenth-Century City* (Cambridge: Harvard University Press 1975); Michael B. Katz et al., *The Social Organization of Early Industrial Capitalism*; A. Gordon Darroch, 'Migrants in the Nineteenth Century: Fugitives or Families in Motion?' *Journal of Family History* 6 (Fall 1981), 257–77; Palmer, *Culture*

in Conflict, 3–4; Alan Wilson, *John Northway: A Blue Serge Canadian* (Toronto: Burns and MacEachern 1965), 14–27.

107 Committee on the Causes of the Present Depression, 146. See also Bettina Bradbury in this volume; John Bullen, 'Hidden Workers: Child Labour and the Family Economy in Late Nineteenth-Century Urban Ontario,' *Labour/Le Travail* 18 (Fall 1986), 163–87; and 'Children of the Industrial Age: Children, Work, and Welfare in Late Nineteenth-Century Ontario' (PhD thesis, University of Ottawa 1989); Chad Gaffield, 'Children, Schooling, and Family Reproduction in Nineteenth-Century Ontario,' *Canadian Historical Review* 72 (June 1991), 157–91; Gordon Darroch and Michael Ornstein, 'Family Coresidence in Canada in 1871: Family Life-Cycles, Occupations and Networks of Mutual Aid,' in Canadian Historical Association, *Historical Papers* 1983, 30–55.

108 In 1870, after surveying the province, a British workman concluded that 'a mechanic when in employment here is better paid than in England or Ireland, and has less competition in the labour market.' A few years later, parliamentary committees heard regular complaints from manufacturers of clothing, agricultural implements, and cotton about the difficulty of finding enough skilled labour and its consequent high cost; see Ontario, Commissioner of Agriculture and Public Works, *Annual Report on Immigration*, 1870, 28; Select Committee on the Manufacturing Interests, 8, 41–4, 142–8; see also Pollin, 'Jacques and Hay,' 15; BAMUCJ, 1865, 305; *Monetary Times*, 17 November 1871, 387; *Canadian Manufacturer*, 1 September 1882, 543; RCRLC, 710.

109 RCRLC, 37, 65, 66, 110, 146, 248–9, 251, 260, 372, 389, 398–9, 483, 630, 707, 749, 856, 1069, 1097,

110 *Monetary Times*, 11 December 1874, 656; 1 June 1877, 1383; *Ontario Workman* 3, 24 October, 21, 28 November 1872; Osborne and Swainson, *Kingston*, 192; Kealey, *Toronto Workers*, 140.

111 A London moulder explained to the Labour Commission, for example, that among his workmates those from Britain were the well-rounded moulders who worked on machinery, while those from the United States were narrower specialists in stove and hollowware work. RCRLC, 601–2. Years earlier a lumberman had warned the furniture manufacturer Robert Hay that British and American skills were not interchangeable: 'Canadian and old country people don't know how to saw or pile lumber properly for the American market.' Pollin, 'Jacques and Hay,' 30. On the general importance of immigrant labour for Ontario factories, see RCRLC, 65, 66, 117, 152, 372, 389, 391, 601–2, 625, 628, 630, 635, 797, 813, 958, 1007, 1027.

112 RCRLC, 842.

113 The new railways of the 1850s generally brought their skilled labour with them from Britain, Cobourg's Ontario Woollen Mill imported a skilled dyer first from France and then from Scotland, and the huge Georgian Bay Lumber Company brought the skilled labour for its many sawmills from the United States, especially Pennsylvania. A correspondent for the *Journal* of the Upper Canada Board of Arts

and Manufactures reported numerous examples of this kind on his tour through the emerging industrial centres in 1862. A new carpet factory in Elora similarly imported skilled workers, mostly from Philadelphia. Paul Craven and Tom Traves, 'Dimensions of Paternalism: Discipline and Culture on the Canadian Railways of the 1850s,' in Heron and Storey, *On the Job*, 47–74; BAMUCJ, September 1864, 255; Angus, *A Deo Victoria*, 64; BAMUCJ, January 1862, 9–10; February 1862, 47; Thorning, 'T.E. Bissell,' 10; see also *Canadian Manufacturer* 22 March 1883, 219. Direct importation continued when the local supply was insufficient, notably in the textile industries; see Ontario, Department of Immigration, *Report*, 1878, 21; 1881, 34; 1882, 37; 1885, 18; 1886, 18–19; *Canadian Manufacturer*, 20 January 1882, 25; 17 March 1882, 99; 6 October 1882, 722; RCRLC, 265, 1069. Federal and provincial immigration agents seem to have done little to supply specific needs for industrial labour. For a few years in the late 1860s and early 1870s, the provincial immigration department sent a circular to local mayors, wardens, and reeves, soliciting specific information on local labour needs, but the replies were spotty and the practice was discontinued. Ontario, Commissioner of Agriculture and Public Works, *Annual Report on Immigration* (Toronto), 1869–72.

114 Ontario, Department of Immigration, *Report* (Toronto), 1869–90; Macdonald, *Canada: Immigration and Colonization*. The peaks of immigration into the province in this period were in 1873 and 1883 at around 40,000 per year; except in the deep depression of the late 1870s, annual figures were usually well above 20,000. OBIR, 1886, 236.

115 Woodside's autobiography appeared in instalments in the *Canadian Foundryman* 8 (November 1917), 195–6; 10 (August 1919), 221; (September 1919), 270–1; (December 1919), 360; 11 (January 1920), 15; (February 1920), 48; (April 1920), 117; 13 (May 1922), 47; (July 1922), 36–7. Wylie, 'Blacksmith'; Bischoff, 'Tensions et solidarité'; Parr, *Gender of Breadwinners*; RCRLC, 37, 105, 146, 152, 213, 214, 362, 1155. Similarly a Toronto horseshoer told the Labour Commission that apprenticeship was almost unknown; 'they generally come from the country shops'; RCRLC, 105.

116 *Mail* 15 April 1872; Weaver, 'Foundries'; Tulchinsky, 'Hidden among the Smokestacks,' 261; RCRLC, 336; Price, 'Changing Geography,' 51; Select Committee on Manufacturing Interests, 40–4, 142–7.

117 Robert M. Stamp, *The Schools of Ontario, 1876–1976* (Toronto: University of Toronto Press 1982), 43–4. Toronto took the first step in 1891.

118 Peter Bischoff has painstakingly traced the transmission of the craft from father to son among moulders in central Canada in 'Tensions et solidarité,' 150–3.

119 *London Free Press*, 13 November 1865.

120 Ibid., 7 April 1857, 14 March 1866, 5 November 1869, 14 February, 12 March 1870; *Ottawa Citizen*, 31 July 1847, 5, 19 May 1849, 29 November 1851, 10 July 1852, 24 June, 19 August, 7 October 1854, 5 January, 9 March 1855, 5 December 1856, 11 May 1859, 20 November 1865, 29 November 1872.

121 *London Free Press*, 9 April 1856, 4 August 1862, 17 April 1864, 29 September, 6 October 1865, 24, 26 August 1869, 13, 19 November 1880; RCRLC, 347, 358; Burley, 'Businessmen of Brantford,' 109–10; Madeleine Muntz, 'An Early Parry Sound Millinery and Fancy Goods Shop,' *East Georgian Bay Historical Journal* 5 (1989), 80–95.

122 *London Free Press*, 8, 14 January, 4 March 1856, 10 April 1861, 9 May, 31 October 1864, 27 July 1865, 10 March, 11 July 1866, 17, 19 November 1868, 21 July, 28 August 1869, 19 April 1870, 9 February 1871, 17 April 1872, 20 April 1875, 24 January 1876, 13 September 1877, 16 March, 8 August, 28 December 1878, 10 March 1879; *Ottawa Citizen*, 19 March, 23 July 1853, 24 March, 11 July, 22 August, 29 September, 8 November, 21 December 1866, 11 February, 18 November 1868, 16 May 1870, 1 February 1872.

123 RCRLC, 177, 623, 1181; Jeremy Webber in this volume. The commission heard that apprenticeship no longer prevailed in brass finishing (RCRLC, 427), for example.

124 See, for example, RCRLC, 1116. The 1891 occupational census listed only 157 apprentices across the whole province. *Census of Canada, 1891*, vol.2, 164. For a comparative perspective, see W.J. Rorabaugh, *The Craft Apprentice* (New York: Oxford University Press 1985).

125 A major exception was the Bertram tool and machine works in Dundas, where apprentice machinists were still indentured in 1888 under a two-hundred-dollar bond posted by the boy's parents (RCRLC, 956). This system was still in effect in the plant in the mid-1920s. A similarly large London machine shop also used indentures (ibid., 672).

126 Ibid., 490, 532, 902; see also 1097.

127 Ibid., 565, 1116.

128 Ibid., 38, 40, 41–42, 44 (Toronto), 1157 (Ottawa), on printers; 65, 67 (Toronto), on machinists.

129 Ibid., 1181.

130 Ibid., 509 (St Thomas carriage works); 431 (St Thomas woodworking factory); 565 (St Thomas car shop); 1117 (Ottawa furniture factory).

131 Select Committee on Manufacturing Interests, 28; Craven and Traves, 'Dimensions of Paternalism'; Paul Craven in this volume; RCRLC, 427, 431, 743–44, 808, 859, 1095, 1102.

132 Select Committee on the Causes of the Present Depression, 75.

133 The managing director of Kingston's locomotive works told the Labour Commission that this concentration of skilled labour accounted for the new owners' decision to keep the operation in that city. RCRLC, 1027, 1029.

134 Select Committee on Manufacturing Interests, 40; Select Committee on the Causes of the Present Depression, 143.

135 The supply of immigrants was not always steady, however, especially in the smaller inland towns. In 1869, for example, Jacques and Hay made a visit to the 'Emigra-

tion office' to try to get more hands for their lumber mill at New Lowell. McIntyre, 'From Workshop to Factory,' 32.

136 OBIR, 1884, lxviii; 1886. We need far more research to determine the flow of men and women between the factory labour markets and their own families' household economies, especially those on Ontario farms. For some important insights, see Chad Gaffield, *Language, Schooling, and Cultural Conflict: The Origins of the French-Language Controversy in Ontario* (Kingston and Montreal: McGill-Queen's University Press 1987), 78–9.

137 Workers in the mills of the Georgian Bay Lumber Company got free housing if they agreed to work in the lumber camps in the winter. In 1883 the company's new president announced a preference for married men and built many more houses to accommodate a more settled workforce. Angus, *A Deo Victoria*, 89–90, 188–9; see also RCRLC, 1175.

138 A few workers gave the Labour Commission information on highly atypical use of such workers – Italians in Toronto clothing shops and a London cabinet works and German strikebreakers in a London cigar factory. RCRLC, 628, 653, 690.

139 Angus, *A Deo Victoria*, 67, 205; C. Grant Head, 'An Introduction to Forest Exploitation in Nineteenth Century Ontario,' in Wood, *Perspectives* (Toronto: McClelland and Stewart 1975), 104–5; Pollin, 'Jacques and Hay,' 12.

140 OBIR, 1884, lxix; 1886, 210.

141 Cohen, *Women's Work*, 120–1.

142 Louise A. Tilly and Joan W. Scott, *Women, Work and the Family* (New York: Holt, Rinehart and Winston 1978), 123–36; Tamara K. Hareven, *Family Time and Industrial Time: The Relationship Between the Family and Work in a New England Industrial Community* (New York: Cambridge University Press 1982), 190–217.

143 Cohen, *Women's Work*, 118–51; Jean Thompson Scott, *The Conditions of Female Labour in Ontario* (Toronto: University of Toronto 1892); Karen Dubinsky, '"The Modern Chivalry": Women and the Knights of Labor in Ontario, 1880–1891' (MA thesis, Carleton University 1985), 14–29; Knowles, 'Beyond Domesticity.'

144 RCRLC, 617, 620.

145 Ibid., 598; see also Langdon, 'Emergence,' 8.

146 *Globe*, 28 October 1868; Beth Light and Joy Parr, eds, *Canadian Women on the Move, 1867–1920* (Toronto: OISE Press and New Hogtown Press 1983), 90–1.

147 *London Free Press*, 12 February 1856; Kealey, 'Work Control,' 84.

148 Marjorie Cohen has clarified how women could be excluded from some important food-processing industries that had been previously part of their work in rural households, especially in dairy production. The same constraints did not hold for the canning industry, however, where females made up more than three-quarters of the workforce by 1891. My Table 1; Cohen, *Women's Work*, 93–117.

149 *Ottawa Citizen*, 26 July 1851; *Almonte Express*, 30 May 1862 (courtesy of Elizabeth Price); BAMUCJ, May 1862, 137; RCRLC, 859–61, 875, 877, 892, 893, 894, 1058, 1061, 1063, 1068, 1074–5, 1086, 1087, 1144; *Illustrated Historical Atlas of*

the County of Carleton, Ontario (Toronto: H. Beldon and Company 1879), xxix. Females typically made up a larger proportion of the workforce in a cotton mill than in a woollen mill; see Table 1.

150 BAMUCJ, January 1862, 9; *Globe*, 28 October 1868; RCRLC, 406–7, 627, 629, 829–33, 1164; Wright, *Sweating System*; King, *Clothing Contracts*; Tulchinsky, 'Hidden among the Smokestacks.'

151 RCRLC, 307, 309, 336–7, 885.

152 BAMUCJ, March 1863, 84. *Globe*, 28 October 1868; RCRLC, 617–21, 810, 962–3.

153 RCRLC, 1001, 1102; McKay, 'Baking and Confectionery Industry'; Margaret E. McCallum, 'Separate Spheres: The Organization of Work in a Confectionery Factory: Ganong Bros., St. Stephen, New Brunswick,' *Labour/Le Travail* 24 (Fall 1989), 69–90.

154 BAMUCJ, May 1862, 137; *Illustrated Historical Atlas of the County of Carleton*, xxvii.

155 RCRLC, 40–1, 44, 47, 108, 110, 113, 596, 1141–3, 1146, 1161–3, 1171–3. By the end of the 1880s virtually all the 35 women working as compositors in Toronto (alongside 595 men) were unapprenticed 'learners' who worked in non-union printing shops. In London there were apparently 10 female compositors, but none in St Catharines or Hamilton. Christina Burr, ' "That Coming Curse – The Incompetent Compositress": Class and Gender Relations in the Toronto Typographical Union during the Nineteenth Century,' *Canadian Historical Review* 74, no. 3 (September 1993); RCRLC, 635, 748, 925.

156 RCRLC, 326, 613.

157 Ibid., 110.

158 On the general question of working-class masculinity in this period, see Christina Burr, 'Class and Gender in the Toronto Printing Trades, 1870–1914' (PhD thesis, Memorial University of Newfoundland 1992); 'That Coming Curse'; and 'Defending "The Art Preservative": Class and Gender Relations in the Printing Trades Unions, 1850–1914,' *Labour/Le Travail* 31 (Spring 1993), 47–74; Ava Baron, 'Questions of Gender: Deskilling and Demasculinization in the U.S. Printing Industry, 1830–1915,' *Gender and History* 1 (Summer 1989), 178–99; Keith McClelland, 'Some Thoughts on Masculinity and the "Representative Artisan' in Britain, 1850–1880," *Gender and History* 1 (Summer 1989), 164–77.

159 *London Free Press*, 29 May 1855, 25 September 1865; RCRLC, 40–7, 108, 113; Burr, 'That Coming Curse.'

160 RCRLC, 41, 47–8, 392, 618, 627, 962. The Labour Commission did hear occasional admissions that women were just as competent as men; see the testimony of a Hamilton cotton weaver (893) and a St Catharines cigarmaker (919). But these voices were generally drowned in the flood of disparagement.

161 Tucker, *Administering Danger*, 76–136.

162 See, for example, *Globe*, 28 October 1868; CMFR, 2. The first factory inspectors

tended to share this view of parental responsibility for child labour; 'in nine-tenths of the cases,' eastern-district inspector O.A. Rocque argued in 1891, 'they are forced upon the employer through the influence of leading workmen or their parents employed themselves in the factory, under the pretence that they refuse to go to school and if not employed would remain on the streets and be out of their surveillance; whilst the true reason is a selfish desire to increase the revenue of the parents to enable them to live more in luxury and extravagance. In other cases children are sent to work to allow parents to remain idle and live in laziness and in all the evils which follow.' OIFR, 1891, 18.

163 RCRLC, 743, 879, 893, 895, 973; OBIR, 1887, 38–9. See also OBIR, 1890, 17; 1891, 8, 15, 18.

164 OIFR, 1890, 17; CMFR, 2.

165 Ian E. Davey, 'Educational Reform and the Working Class: School Attendance in Hamilton, Ontario, 1851–1891' (PhD thesis, University of Toronto 1975); Knowles, 'Beyond Domesticity,' 88–94.

166 *Almonte Gazette*, 15 March 1872. The woollen industry apparently used less child labour than the cotton industry: in 1871 census takers counted only 48 children under age 16 in Almonte's woollen mills, who made up only 13.6 per cent of the workforce; Canada, Manuscript Industrial Census, 1871 (calculations are mine). Both references courtesy of Elizabeth Price.

167 CMFR, 10–13.

168 RCRLC, 73, 141, 316, 651, 1136, 1152.

169 CMFR, 2.

170 Ibid., 2, 8, 10–13; RCRLC, 73, 141, 316, 651, 896, 972, 1136, 1152; OIFR, 1888, 10, 18, 30; 1889, 26, 28; 1890, 5, 20–1, 23; 1891, 14; Department of Labour, *The Employment of Children and Young Persons in Canada* (Ottawa: King's Printer 1930), 111–12.

171 In only a few industries were boys and girls at this young age used interchangeably for light, unskilled jobs, in contrast to their treatment at a slightly older age. In cotton mills, for example, children of both sexes under sixteen could be doffers and spinners, though only boys were packers, card tenders, and roving hands, and only girls were spoolers, weavers, and winders. OBIR, 1884, 35.

172 Pollin, 'Jacques and Hay,' 14–5; RCRLC, 141, 311 (Toronto), 649 (London), 689 (London), 1100, 1135–9, 1149–52 (Ottawa); OIFR, 1888, 30. For use of this kind of young labourer by other industries, see RCRLC, 613 (tin department of McClary's London foundry), 1075 (Canada Cotton Mill in Cornwall), 1117 (Ottawa furniture factory).

173 Quoted in Langdon, 'Emergence,' 16.

174 RCRLC, 427 (Windsor wire works); 565 (St Thomas car shops); 784 (Hamilton emery-wheel factory), 787 (Hamilton rolling mills); 820 (Hamilton forge works); 856 (Dundas machinery works); according to the Oshawa correspondent of the Ontario Bureau of Industry, the moulders did not allow apprentices to start at the

trade before age sixteen. OBIR, 1887, 38. It is significant that when the Ontario Manufacturers' Association first formally considered proposed new factory legislation, they passed no comment on the child-labour sections 'as so few members present were interested in child labor.' CMFR, 15.

175 Table 3; RCRLC, 305, 890–1; OBIR, 1887, 38–9; 1889, 10; Scott, *Conditions of Female Labour*, 20; Hughson and Bond, *Hurling Down the Pine*, 76. They accounted, for example, for 120–50 out of 425 workers in a Hamilton tobacco plant, 82 of the 208 in a Kingston cotton mill, 98 of 670 in a Cornwall cotton mill, and about a third of 80 in an Ottawa box factory. RCRLC, 743, 971, 1063.

176 RCRLC, 931, 933; OBIR, 1887, 38–9; 1888, 10–12; 1889, 10–14. The Perth correspondent noted that children under fourteen were unnecessary since 'there is an abundance of adult help at low wages.'

177 RCRLC, 308, 311, 424, 475, 623, 663, 840, 895–6, 933, 1102, 1144; CMFR, 6, 16; OIFR, 1889, 5; 1891, 23, 25; *London Free Press*, 3 January 1877, 15 November 1880; *Ottawa Citizen*, 13 March 1852, 16 February, 25 July 1870, 16 January 1872, 12, 20 August 1873.

178 *Globe*, 28 October 1868; RCRLC, 305, 309, 435, 473, 617, 666–7, 807–8, 962, 1104; Scott, *Conditions of Female Labour*, 20, 22–3.

179 *Globe*, 28 October 1868; RCRLC, 347, 893, 1074; Scott, *Conditions of Female Labour*, 20.

180 RCRLC, 178, 509, 618, 623.

181 Factory inspectors claimed this inadequate seating contributed to 'crooked spines, round shoulders and contracted chests.' OIFR, 1888, 5.

182 Ibid., 1891, 18.

183 The Bureau of Industry correspondents and factory inspectors had already noted a decline in the employment of children under fourteen after the introduction of the Factory Act. OBIR, 1887, 38; OIFR, 1889, 7, 8, 14, 19; 1891, 7.

184 Their exploits usually surfaced when one of them had a serious accident; see OIFR, 1888, 23; 1889, 26; 1891, 22, 23.

185 OIFR, 1888, 8.

186 Ibid., 1890, 20; 1891, 16.

187 RCRLC, 962.

188 Palmer, *A Culture in Conflict*, 25.

189 'The corn is hulled, the peas podded, the cherries pitted and the apples prepared by machinery nowadays, dispensing almost entirely with child labor,' the inspector wrote; 'even where light manual labor is required the canners prefer older hands to do it.' OIFR, 1891, 7. See also Lorna Hurl, 'Overcoming the Inevitable: Restricting Child Factory Labour in Late Nineteenth Century Ontario,' *Labour/Le Travail*, 21 (Spring 1988), 87–122.

190 The inspectors were mostly confident that the new legislation had a deterrent effect. OIFR, 1888, 6; Tucker, *Administering Danger*.

191 RCRLC, 316. He also later reported that one female employer 'of a masculine turn'

had threatened to tar and feather him if he returned, after he had launched a prosecution against her for employing three girls aged nine, ten, and twelve. OIFR, 1890, 14

192 OIFR, 1889, 28; 1900, 12.

193 Craig Heron, 'The High School and the Family Economy in a Factory City: Hamilton, 1890–1940' (paper presented to the Canadian Historical Association Meeting, 1990).

194 Evidence presented to the Labour Commission also indicated juvenile wages ranging from $1.50 to $4.00 a week (with girls on the lower end), or roughly a fifth to a third of that of a skilled man. RCRLC, 305, 308, 309, 424, 427, 475, 617, 665, 666, 667, 807, 837, 840, 879, 883, 962, 972, 973, 1100. In one Cornwall cotton mill, boys got 15 cents an day, according to a carder working there, and a boy in an Ottawa box factory said he got 25 cents a day. Ibid., 1075, 1151. See also Scott, *Condition of Female Labour*, 22.

195 This ratio was determined by a separate calculation with the same statistics. Other sources confirm this ratio. In 1862 a reporter for the *Journal* of the Board of Arts and Manufactures of Upper Canada, found women in textile and clothing enterprises paid approximately half what the men got (45 and 75 cents a day respectively, in contrast with $1 and $1.50) (BAMUCJ, January 1862, 9; May 1862, 137). Roughly the same proportions held through the 1880s; the Labour Commission learned that most women were paid in the range of $3 to $6 per week, again up to half the average male wages (RCRLC, 110, 287, 307, 336, 347, 365, 478, 596, 635, 810, 877, 885, 894, 1009, 1068, 1141, 1162, 1171, 1173).

196 *Monetary Times*, 8 December 1871, 446. A writer in the *Ontario Workman* on 13 June 1872 agreed: 'Employers generally strive to get as much labor and as many hours as possible from the workingmen for the lowest possible remuneration.'

197 R.C.B. Risk, 'The Nineteeth-Century Foundations of the Business Corporation in Ontario,' *University of Toronto Law Journal* 33 (1973), 270–306; Douglas McCalla, 'An Introduction to the Nineteenth-Century Business World,' in Tom Traves, ed., *Essays in Canadian Business History* (Toronto 1984), 13–23; T.W. Acheson, 'The Changing Social Origins of the Canadian Industrial Elite, 1880–1910,' in Glenn Porter and Robert Cuff, eds, *Enterprise and National Development: Essays in Canadian Business and Economic History* (Toronto: Hakkert 1973), 51–79. In 1871 there were only six incorporated firms among the sixty industrial leaders – three railway companies, two textile firms, and one locomotive manufacturer. Only eleven more of this group had incorporated by 1891. Bloomfield and Bloomfield, *Industrial Leaders*, 36–9.

198 Pentland, *Labour and Capital*, 24–60; Cohen, *Women's Work*, 29–117. See also Jeremy Webber's essay in this volume.

199 Akenson, *Irish*, 310; Wylie, 'Blacksmith,' 50; Johnson, *Ontario County*, 214; Gaffield, *Language*, 84; Wilson, *Lost Horizons*, 45. In 1852–3 workers in Brantford, Hamilton, and London unsuccessfully petitioned the provincial government to

'prohibit the payment to mechanics ... of wages in goods or way of truck' (quoted in Langdon, 'Emergence,' 8; see also Palmer, *Culture in Conflict*, 11–12), and the *Ontario Workman* railed against it twenty years later (9 May 1872). The Labour Commissioners asked many witnesses about the system, but found almost no trace of it.

200 *Ottawa Citizen*, 29 September 1866; Craven, 'Law of Master and Servant,' 200–4; Kealey, *Toronto Workers*, 148–52; Palmer, *Culture in Conflict*, 25.

201 Bischoff, 'Tensions et solidarité,' 60; Parr, *Gender of Breadwinners*; Margaret Watson, 'The Transformation of Paternalism: Workers and Capitalists in Brantford, 1880 to 1900' (MA research paper, York University 1985), 13–14. David Burley has established that the opportunities for self-employment were definitely narrowing by the 1870s in the important manufacturing town of Brantford; see Burley, 'Businessmen of Brantford,' 133–71.

202 *Expositor* (Brantford), 28 October 1887, quoted in Watson, 'Transformation of Paternalism,' 14; Pollin, 'Jacques and Hay,' 15–18; Select Committee on Manufacturing Interests, 57; RCRLC, 880, 1099, 1173; OBIR, 1887, 40; Mollie Gillen, *The Masseys: Founding Family* (Toronto: Ryerson Press 1965), 61–2. Little systematic research has yet been done on family and kinship links inside nineteenth-century Ontario factories. In Almonte, family groupings are evident in the woollen-mill workforce found in the 1861 manuscript census (courtesy of Elizabeth Price).

203 The Masseys, like other employers, liked to brag about long-service employees who had risen through the ranks; see the story on W.F. Clarke, moulding-shop foreman in the 1880s, who had started work for Daniel Massey forty years earlier. *Trip Hammer*, June 1885, 55. See also Wilson, *Lost Horizons*, 44–5; Craven and Traves, 'Dimensions of Paternalism'; RCRLC, 427, 431, 533, 743–4, 808, 859, 898, 1095, 1102.

204 Thorning, 'Bissell,' 10; Palmer, *Culture in Conflict*, 97–122; Kealey, *Toronto Workers*, 154–71; Peter Warrian, '"Sons of Toil": The Impact of Industrialization on Craft Workers in Late 19th Century Ontario,' in David F. Walker and James H. Bater, eds, *Industrial Development in Southern Ontario: Selected Essays* (Waterloo: Dept. of Geography Publication Series no. 3, University of Waterloo 1974), 69–99. On boosterism in late nineteenth-century Ontario, see Robert J. Morris, 'The Reproduction of Labour and Capital: British and Canadian Cities during Industrialization,' *Urban History Review* 18 (June 1989), 55; Thomas William Acheson, 'The Social Origins of Canadian Industrialism: A Study in the Structure of Entrepreneurship' (PhD thesis, University of Toronto 1971), 188–260; Johnson, *Ontario County*, 247–52, 282–316; and 'Ideology and Political Economy in Urban Growth: Guelph, 1827–1927,' in G.A. Stelter and A.F.J. Artibise, eds, *Shaping the Urban Landscape: Aspects of the Canadian City-Building Process* (Ottawa: Carleton University Press 1982), 30–64; Elizabeth Bloomfield, 'Building the City on a Foundation of Factories: The "Industrial Policy" in Berlin, Ontario, 1870–1914,' *Ontario History* 75 (September 1983), 207–43; 'Municipal Bonusing of Industry: The Legislative Framework in Ontario to 1930,' *Urban History Review* 9 (February 1981), 59–76;

and 'Community Leadership and Decion-Making: Entrepreneurial Elites in Two Ontario Towns, 1870–1930,' in G.A. Stelter and A.F.J. Artibise, eds, *Power and Place: Canadian Urban Development in the North American Context* (Vancouver: University of British Columbia Press 1986), 82–104; E.J. Noble, 'Men and Circumstances: Entrepreneurs and Community Growth: A Case Study of Orillia, Ontario, 1867–1898' (PhD thesis, University of Guelph 1980); Tom Naylor, *History of Canadian Business; Northern Advance* 4 January, 1, 8 February 1860.

205 Reid, 'Rosamond Woolen Company,' 279–80; Knowles, 'Beyond Domesticity,' 44–5; *Ontario Workman*, 27 June 1872; *Canadian Illustrated News*, 26 January 1878, 55; *Globe*, 27 May 1882; R.G. Hoskins, 'Hiram Walker and the Origins and Development of Walkerville, Ontario,' *Ontario History* 65 (1973), 122–31.

206 Angus, *A Deo Victoria*, 27–46, 55–71, 151–4, 175–9, 185–8; see also Radforth, 'Confronting Distance,' 82–4; Pollin, 'Jacques and Hay,' 8, 11; Wilson, *Lost Horizons*, 22, 45, 47, 53; OA, F209, MU 1957, vol. 11, ii.

207 *Almonte Gazette*, 3 January, 24 July 1868, 11 August 1871 (courtesy of Elizabeth Price); *Ottawa Citizen*, 4 January 1866, 11, 15 January 1867, 26 August 1869, 24 November 1869, 7 April 1879; *London Free Press*, 25 July 1865, 7, 19 July, 26 November 1869, 13 July 1870, 24 January, 16 February 1871, 7 February 1874; *Barrie Advance*, 13 July, 10 August 1864, 29 August 1866; Bischoff, 'Tensions et solidarité,' 21–2; Burley, 'Businessmen of Brantford,' 110–11; Watson, 'Transformation of Paternalism,' 18–19, 34–7; Knowles, 'Beyond Domesticity,' 43, 46.

208 Lisa Bowes, 'George Sleeman and the Brewing of Baseball in Guelph, 1872–1886,' *Historic Guelph* 27 (1987–8), 45–57; Kelly, *Downright Upright*, 55.

209 *Ottawa Citizen*, 11 January 1867, 28 December 1868, 4 January 1869; *Almonte Gazette*, 13 October 1871, 9 February, 21 June 1872, 2, 17 January 1873, 2 January 1874 (courtesy of Elizabeth Price). See also *Ontario Workman*, 30 May 1872, for a similar expression of gratitude in Toronto.

210 Kealey, *Toronto Workers*, 221–2.

211 *Expositor* (Brantford), 11 June 1886, 5 December 1890, quoted in Watson, 'Transformation of Paternalism,' 33–4, 36.

212 Craven and Traves, 'Dimensions of Paternalism,' 63–70.

213 Archives of Ontario (hereafer AO), F209, MU 1957 (McLauchlin Brothers' Lumber Company), vol. 9, ii (Arnprior 1858); Burley, 'Businessmen of Brantford,' 111; *London Free Press*, 19–20 November 1872; *Ontario Workman*, 28 November 1872 (East London oil refiners).

214 RCRLC, 666, 745, 808, 810, 816; Wilson, *Lost Horizons*, 32.

215 *Trip Hammer*, February 1885–February 1886; Denison, *Harvest Triumphant*. None of these employers tried profit-sharing, however. RCRLC; Michael Bliss, *A Living Profit: Studies in the Social History of Canadian Business, 1883–1911* (Toronto: McClelland and Stewart 1974), 89–91.

216 *Trip Hammer*, February 1885, 4–5; April 1885, 26; November 1885, 137; January 1886, 180; February 1886, 183–4, 193; Kealey, *Toronto Workers*.

217 OBIR, 1886, 206–7.

218 When the Gurneys installed washing facilities in their Toronto foundry, the moulders spurned the paternalism and refused to use the new sinks. Another Hamilton foundryman was convinced that moulders would never use company washrooms. RCRLC, 834–5.

219 James Naylor, *The New Democracy: Challenging the Social Order in Industrial Ontario, 1914–25* (Toronto: University of Toronto Press 1991), 159–88; Heron, *Working in Steel*, 98–111.

220 Paul Craven and Tom Traves, 'Labour and Management in Canadian Railway Operations: The First Decade' (paper presented to the Commonwealth Labour History Conference, Coventry, England 1981); idem, 'Dimensions of Paternalism'; and Paul Craven in this volume.

221 RCRLC, 1176.

222 Sidney Pollard, *The Genesis of Modern Management: A Study of the Industrial Revolution in Great Britain* (London: Penguin 1965), 51–63; John Buttrick, 'The Inside Contract System,' *Journal of Economic History* 12 (Summer 1952), 205–21; Dan Clawson, *Bureaucracy and the Labor Process: The Transformation of U.S. Industry, 1860–1920* (New York: Monthly Review Press 1980), 71–125; David Montgomery, *Workers' Control in America*, 11–12; David A. McCabe, *The Standard Rate in American Trade Unions* (Baltimore: Johns Hopkins University Press 1912), 62–5. In the United States, the system was most elaborately developed in the munitions industry, for which Ontario had no counterpart in this period.

223 Jacques and Hay ran the woodturning and hair-making branches of their operations in New Lowell on a contract basis; Radforth, 'Confronting Distance,' 94. See also RCRLC, 442, 602, 691, 743, 760, 810–11, 1105, 1134–5, 1137; OBIR, 1888, 11; OIFR, 1889, 5, 26; CMFR, 4; Palmer, *Culture in Conflict*, 255. Moulders had long been accustomed to hiring their own helpers, often known as 'berkshires,' though their union fought the system vigorously (Kealey, *Toronto Workers*, 67–8). The large Georgian Bay Lumber Company used subcontractors for piling lumber and for running lath mills at Waubaushene and Port Severn (Angus, *A Deo Victoria*, 88–9), and in 1886 Hamilton Brothers similarly contracted for saw filing in their mills for the following season (AO, F 131, MU 1221, Box 9, Contract, 8 September 1886); the Gillies Brothers received an enquiry about similar work (AO, F 150–4–2–7, 18 March 1872). In an interesting variant, William Doherty, a merchant-turned-organ-manufacturer in Clinton in 1876, was given access to equipment inside a local planing mill to build the cabinets. Kelly, *Downright Upright*, 46.

224 BAMUCJ 1862; E.P. Morgan and F.L. Harvey, *Hamilton and Its Industries: Being a Historical and Descriptive Sketch of the City of Hamilton and Its Public and Private Institutions, Manufacturing and Industrial Interests, Public Citizens, etc.* (Hamilton 1884), 21–4; RCRLC, 359, 628–9, 829–30, 931; OIFR, 1889, 7; 1891, 13; McIntosh, 'Sweated Labour.'

225 RCRLC, 213.

226 Ibid., 474; see also 469–71. In addition to the furniture fininishing already mentioned, a local flour mill also subcontracted its coopering; ibid., 489.

227 Ibid., 494.

228 In 1892 a Hamilton foundryman introduced the system in the midst of a strike. Palmer, *Culture in Conflict*, 90.

229 It is interesting that the Masseys' first proposal for a kind of centralized cost accounting in their Toronto operations, distributed to foremen in October 1888, used the subcontracting model. 'Each department shall be considered and treated as a separate business establishment independent of the Massey M'f'g. Co.; its foreman considered as the proprietor, who shall jealously look after its interests, curtail expenses as far as possible, and do all in his power to make a creditable showing,' the memorandum read, but there was no indication that the salaried foreman would get to keep any profits made this way, as the inside contractor would have. OAM, Massey-Ferguson Collection, MM 69 ('Prospectus of a System of Records to Show the Relative Standing of Individual Departments,' October 1888). In this large factory, moreover, foremen were not supposed to make a final decision about hiring or setting wages without consulting the superintendent; ibid., MM 32 ('General Rules and Regulations Regarding Foremen,' 1890).

230 RCRLC, 441, 982, 999, 1067; see also ibid., 1018, 1023–4, 1037, 1088.

231 *Almonte Gazette*, 10 April 1868, 24 December 1870, 4 April 1873 (courtesy of ELizabeth Price); *Ottawa Citizen*, 18 May 1867, 4 January 1868, 3 November 1869; *Ontario Workman*, 21 May, 27 June 1872. One of E.B. Eddy's foremen revealed how this relationship could involve collusion to defraud the owner, when he was caught in a scam of regularly 'giving in more time than was due and sharing with the men the proceeds of this nefarious practice.' *Ottawa Citizen*, 17 February 1867.

232 *London Free Press*, 11 January 1877. There was also some ambiguity about the ultimate loyalty of foremen, who had almost invariably emerged off the shop floor as skilled workers. In the 1872 shorter-hours strike in Hamilton, three foremen joined striking machinists at a sewing-machine works and publicly denounced their boss (Palmer, *Culture in Conflict*, 135). The printers were the only craft to succeed in keeping their foremen inside their union. Kealey, 'Work Control.'

233 RCRLC, 1024.

234 Palmer, *Culture in Conflict*, 21; Kealey, *Toronto Workers*, 54, 68; RCRLC, 376, 886, 978, 1024, 1067, 1174; OAM, Massey-Ferguson Collection, MM 33 (Massey Manufacturing Company, *Agreement Between Employers and Employed: Rules and Regulations, General Instructions* (Toronto [c. 1888–90]), 4. The practice of locking doors was frequently mentioned but was evidently far from universal since several of the Ontario Bureau of Industries correspondents reported in 1888 that it was actually not common in their towns. OBIR, 1886, 204; 1888, 10–12.

235 The Gooderham and Worts distillery in Toronto ran day and night, as did flour mills in busy periods. Many lumber mills also ran two shifts, one from 6 a.m. to 6 p.m. and another from 7 p.m. to 5 a.m. BAMUCJ, May 1862, 135; *Northern Advance*,

29 August 1866; *Mail*, 23 April 1872; *Canadian Manufacturer*, 21 July 1882, 355; 20 April 1883, 296; RCRLC, 489, 882, 1125–26, 1152. One of the first items of business of the newly organized Lumberman's Association of Ontario in 1888 was to urge the Georgian Bay Lumber Company to lengthen its work day from ten and a half hours to eleven to conform with other mills on the bay (AO, F 248, MU 1745, vol. 1, 8 February 1888, 132). The Waterous Engine Works began round-the-clock operations to cope with increased business in 1880 (Burley, 'Businessmen of Brantford,' 121). Bakeries, of course, and publishers of morning newspapers also expected night work from their operatives (Palmer, *Culture in Conflict*, 129; Kealey, 'Work Control,' 84; RCRLC, 1118).

236 Angus, *A Deo Victoria*, 89.

237 OBIR, 1886, 204–6; see also Palmer, *Culture in Conflict*, 26.

238 Massey Manufacturing Company, *Agreement between Employers and Employed*; RCRLC, 1102, 1058, 1116; Palmer, *Culture in Conflict*, 20–1.

239 RCRLC, 171; Angus, *A Deo Victoria*, 73; Peter Bischoff found a high incidence of drunkenness among moulders in the Hamilton police records; see 'Tensions et solidarité,' 110.

240 RCRLC, 976, 1074–5.

241 Some employers might still have recourse to the courts when an apprentice broke his indenture; RCRLC, 750.

242 Ibid., 654, 1061, 1068; Palmer, *Culture in Conflict*, 78–9, 81, 85; see also *Ontario Workman*, 23 May 1872; OBIR, 1885, cxxx; 1886, 202–3; 1888, 7–9; 1889, 2–4.

243 Russell, 'Wage Rates'; AO, F 150 (Gillies Brothers Lumber Company), 13–6–1, No. 29 (March 1872); 3–0–2, 19 April 1875; 3–0–3, 10 March 1876; 3–0–7, 5 March, 28 June, 2 July 1879; 3–0–8, 27 January, 29 March, 19, 25, 28 April, 1 September, 11 October 1880 (on the emergence of hourly wages, see Paul Craven in this volume); BAMUCJ, January 1862, 9; April 1862, 112–3, 137; Palmer, *Culture in Conflict*, 26. See also Pollin, 'Jacques and Hay,' 14; Select Committee on Manufacturing Interests, 44, 47, 58; Select Committee on the Causes of the Present Depression, 180; CMFR, 15; Karl Marx, *Capital*, vol. 1 (Harmondsworth: Penguin 1976), 692–700. The Labour Commission heard evidence on piece-work in barrels (RCRLC, 261, 398–9, 489); cigars (305, 962), clothing (287–8, 359–60, 406, 627, 829, 1187); confectionery (666–7); cotton (879, 893, 973, 1058, 1068, 1082, 1086, 1087, 1094); furniture (441, 443, 609, 691); harness (213); knit goods (859, 980–2); paper boxes (110, 364–5); pianos (947); rolling-mill products (760, 763, 786, 790); shoes (431, 884–5, 1049); stoves (144, 158, 173, 295, 373, 601, 612, 658, 784, 802, 821, 903, 949); tobacco (809); wool (665); see also Bischoff, 'Tensions et solidarité,' 104–7.

244 CMFR, 17.

245 RCRLC, 45, 763.

246 Ibid., 152, 158, 178, 822; see also 144, 431, 763, 802, 884; Bischoff, 'Tensions et solidarité,' 105. A gilder in the same city recalled that in 1885, when put on piece-

work, his fellow workers had 'worked so hard as to work themselves out of work.'
OIFR, 1888, 20.

247 RCRLC, 110; Kealey, *Toronto Workers*, 66–7; Kealey and Palmer, *Dreaming*, 113;
Craig Heron and Bryan D. Palmer, 'Through the Prism of the Strike: Industrial Conflict in Southern Ontario, 1901–14,' *Canadian Historical Review* 58 (December
1977), 423–58.

248 Their report also indicated that fining was a recent innovation, 'only in its infancy.'
Kealey, *Canada Investigates Industrialism*, 46–7.

249 RCRLC, 1175; see also 287, 337, 861, 879, 892, 1058, 1069–70, 1074, 1076, 1079,
1144, 1162–3. A moulder remembered that once it had been common to fine
workers for breaking a mould, but that system had been abandoned long ago; ibid.,
798. The Masseys' detailed system of fines for infractions of company rules seems
to have been an exception; see Massey Manufacturing Company, *Agreement
between Employers and Employed*, 11–12.

250 The Labour Commission heard of them in a St Thomas 'featherbone' factory and an
Ottawa print shop (RCRLC, 536, 1171).

251 Ibid., 1074–5, 1085, 1163, 1174–5.

252 Thorning, 'Bissell,' 17. It must be said that the Labour Commissioners pursued this
issue relentlessly, but accumulated little evidence, probably because of the little testimony they heard directly from women; see Susan Mann Trofimenkoff, 'One Hundred and Two Muffled Voices: Canada's Industrial Women in the 1880s,' in
Michael S. Cross and Gregory S. Kealey, eds, *Readings in Canadian Social History*, vol. 3, Canada's Age of Industry, 1849–1896 (Toronto: McClelland and Stewart 1982), 210–29.

253 RCRLC, 47, 110, 287, 359, 364–5, 406–7, 627, 665, 667, 829, 885, 893.

254 Ibid., 601, 614–15, 625, 650–1, 790, 1083, 1085, 1088; OBIR, 1884, lxix; 1985,
cxxxiv.

255 Examples included the province's largest stove foundrymen from 1866 on, known
as the Canadian Iron Founders' Association (*London Free Press*, 2 May 1866;
Ontario Workman, 30 May 1872; Select Committee on the Causes of the Present
Depression, 180; Canada, House of Commons, *Journals* [Ottawa], vol. 22 [1888],
App. 3 ('Report of the Select Committee Appointed to Examine into Combinations
Said to Exist with Reference to the Purchase and Sale or Manufacture and Sale in
Canada of Any Foreign or Canadian Products'), 8–9, 391–407, 699, 791–5, Bis-
choff, 'Tensions et solidarité'); newspaper publishers in Toronto in 1872 and in
Ottawa in 1873 (Zerker, *Rise and Fall*, 78–91; *Ottawa Citizen*, 4 August 1873);
London's cigar manufacturers in 1883 and Hamilton's in 1885 (RCRLC, 620–1,
650; Kealey and Palmer, *Dreaming*, 159); all manufacturers in Chatham in the mid-
1880s (RCRLC, 438–9, 443; Kealey and Palmer, *Dreaming*, 355–6); and the Lumberman's Association of Ontario, founded 1887 (AO, F 248, MU 1745).

256 See C.J. Wrigley, ed., *A History of British Industrial Relations, 1875–1914* (London: Harvester Press 1982).

257 Quoted in Bliss, *Living Profit*, 75.

258 Hamilton Group Archives (Burlington), New Hamburg Curtain and Rug Company, Letterbook, 1898; RCRLC, 790, 1074–5; OFIR, 1888, 23; 1889, 26; 1891, 23.

259 *Almonte Gazette*, 13 October 1871, 21 June 1872; *Ottawa Citizen*, 26 September, 1 June 1872; North Lanark Historical Society, *Development of the Woollen Industry*, 22. Jonathan Prude's discussion of this kind of informal protest in small New England textile towns offers some fascinating insights that could be pursued in Ontario mill towns; see *The Coming of Industrial Order: Town and Factory Life in Rural Massachusetts, 1810–1860* (New York: Cambridge University Press 1983).

260 For example, strikes at Ottawa sawmills in 1874, 1875, and 1877, all of them over wage cuts; see *Ottawa Citizen*, 29 May 1874, 13 July 1877, 10 July 1877.

261 Palmer, *Culture in Conflict*, 150.

262 The recent emphasis on community studies of the nineteenth-century working-class history in North America thus has considerable validity, though the less organized working-class communities have had far less attention than the centres of active working-class resistance.

263 Wylie, 'Blacksmith'; Bischoff, 'Tensions et solidarité'; Parr, *Gender of Breadwinners*.

264 Palmer, *Culture in Conflict*; Kealey, *Toronto Workers*; Forsey, *Trade Unions*; *London Free Press*, 13 September 1869, 18 January 1870, 21 January 1871, 11 August 1873, 7 April 1874; *Ottawa Citizen*, 15 April 1867.

265 Langdon, 'Emergence'; Forsey, *Trade Unions*; Zerker, *Rise and Fall*, 53–156; Kealey, *Toronto Workers*, 37–97; and 'Work Control'; Palmer, *Culture in Conflict*, 71–95; Bischoff, 'Tensions et solidarité'; Bliss, *Living Profit*, 86–9.

266 Langdon, 'Emergence,' 7; Kealey, *Toronto Workers*; Storey, 'Industrialization'; *London Free Press*, 2 December 1852, 15 May 1873

267 Kealey, *Toronto Workers*; Code, 'Salt Men of Goderich'; *London Free Press*, 2, 3, 8, 9 November 1869, 27 April, 20 May, 6 June, 10 September 1870, 12 June 1873, 29 August 1876, 5 February 1877, 5, 7, 21 October 1880. Even in the village of Elora, a newspaper editor could complain that the coopers, the only unionized workers in town, were 'striking too much lately for their own good'; quoted in Thorning, 'Bissell,' 10.

268 *London Free Press*, 2 December 1852, 10 January, 29 May 1856, 25 September 1865.

269 *London Free Press*, 30 October 1878, 12, 13 November 1880.

270 *London Free Press*, 2 May 1866, 17 March 1873, 11 August 1873, 13 January, 7 April 1874, 14 January 1879; Bischoff, 'Tensions et solidarité'; Kealey, *Toronto Workers*; Palmer, *Culture in Conflict*.

271 *London Free Press*, 14 January, 12, 25 February 1856, 13 September, 20 November 1869, 8 November, 6 December 1870, 6 June 1871, 25 January, 5 June 1872, 6 March 1873; Kealey, 'Work Control'; Zerker, *Rise and Fall*.

272 Kealey, *Toronto Workers*; Craven in this volume.

273 Kealey, 'Work Control'; Bischoff, 'Tensions et solidarité'.
274 Langdon, 'Emergence,' 12–23; Forsey, *Trade Unions*, 3–127; John Battye, 'The Nine Hour Pioneers: The Genesis of the Canadian Labour Movement,' *Labour/Le Travailleur* 4 (1979), 25–56; Kealey, *Toronto Workers*, 124–53; Palmer, *Culture in Conflict*, 125–52.
275 Kealey and Palmer, *Dreaming*, 45.
276 See Forsey, *Trade Unions*, 201–87, 320–38.
277 Kealey and Palmer, *Dreaming*. For local studies of the Knights, see George De Zwaan, 'The Little Birmingham on the St. Lawrence: An Industrial and Labour History of Gananoque, Ontario, 1871–1921' (PhD thesis, Queen's University 1987); Edward McKenna, 'Unorganized Labour versus Management: The Strike at the Chaudière Lumber Mills, 1891,' *Histoire sociale/Social History* 5 (November 1972), 186–211; Senior, *Royal Township to Industrial City*, 236–45; Dale Chisamore et al., *Brockville: A Social History, 1890–1930* (Brockville: Waterway Press 1975), 85–91.
278 Kealey and Palmer, *Dreaming*, 71.
279 Dubinsky, 'Modern Chivalry.'
280 Michael Piva, 'The Bonds of Unity: A Comment,' *Histoire sociale/Social History* 16 (May 1983), 169–74; Gregory Kealey and Bryan Palmer, 'The Bonds of Unity: Some Further Reflections,' ibid., 175–89.
281 Acheson, 'Social Origins,' 194–226.
282 Drummond, *Progress without Planning*.
283 See, for example, the reports of the Ontario Bureau of Industry correspondents in 1883–4; OBIR, 1883, 37; 1884, lxix.
284 See, for example, RCRLC, 288, 338, 1074–5; OBIR, 1884, lxx.
285 The great majority of the strikes reported to the Bureau of Industries after its labour statistics began appearing in 1883 were against wage cuts of some sort; OBIR, 1883, 39; 1884, lxix;, lxx, lxxii, lxxiii; 1885, cxxxi; 1888, 15, 16; 1889, 22, 23.
286 See, for example, the confrontation with Hamilton cotton weavers over 'an increased length in cuts or pieces woven,' and the extended conflicts in the Cornwall cotton mills in 1888 and 1889 over piece-rates; OBIR, 1884, lxix; RCRLC, 1059, 1062, 1066, 1068, 1070, Senior, *Royal Township to Industrial City*, 240–2; Kealey and Palmer, *Dreaming*, 358–9.
287 The outcome of this confrontation was fragmentation and at best partial success for some workers. RCRLC, 437–9, 441–3, 462, 468, 476; OBIR, 1886, 207; Kealey and Palmer, *Dreaming*, 355–6.
288 OBIR, 1884, lxxiii. Two years later the bureau reported that only in Toronto had 'the nine hour movement made great strides' (ibid., 1886, 205); in fact, from 1884 to the end of the decade, provincial averages for hours of work per week hovered around 58–9, while in Toronto the average dropped to 53–4 (ibid., 1887, 4; 1888, 24; 1889, 32, 34–5.
289 Kealey and Palmer, *Dreaming*.

290 Russell Hann, 'Brainworkers and the Knights of Labor: E.E. Sheppard, Phillips Thompson, and the *Toronto News*, 1883–1887,' in Gregory S. Kealey and Peter Warrian, eds, *Essays in Canadian Working Class History* (Toronto: McClelland and Stewart 1976), 35–57; Desmond Morton, 'The *Globe* and the Labour Question: Ontario Liberalism in the 'Great Upheaval,' May, 1886,' *Ontario History* 73, no. 1 (March 1981), 19–39.

291 Margaret Evans, *Sir Oliver Mowat* (Toronto: University of Toronto Press 1992), 191–7; Tucker, *Administering Danger*; Kealey, 'Introduction,' *Canada Investigates Industrialism*.

292 Belleville's Rathbun Company began publishing a company magazine for its mill-men. Brantford foundryman William Buck held his first company picnic in 1886. Wilson, *Lost Horizons*, 32; Watson, 'Transformation of Paternalism,' 33.

293 John Penman of Paris took this step in April 1886, as did the Gravenhurst lumber-men a year later. George Tuckett of Hamilton also proudly explained the new nine-hour regime in his tobacco factory to the Labour Commission, Knowles, 'Beyond Domesticity,' 41; Kealey and Palmer, *Dreaming*, 359; RCRLC, 745.

294 The towns were London, Galt, and Paris. Kealey and Palmer, *Dreaming*, 354–5; Knowles, 'Beyond Domesticity,' 173.

295 Calculated from the lists provided in Kealey and Palmer, *Dreaming*.

296 Gregory Kealey and Bryan Palmer made this questionable claim in their otherwise superb study; see ibid., 32–3.

297 OBIR, 1884–90.

298 Kealey, 'Introduction,' *Canada Investigates Industrialism*.

Before 1850 most Ontario residents wore boots and shoes hand-made by artisanal shoemakers. By the end of the century, factory production had pushed these men to the margins of the industry, where they did only repairs and expensive custom work.

Like these moulders at the Mowry and Sons Foundry in Gravenhurst, the skilled workers of Ontario's First Industrial Revolution liked to present themselves and their tools proudly to the photographers who called them out the back doors of their workplaces.

On 9 July 1884, Hart Massey took off his jacket and sat down with his machinists for one in a series of group portraits. Surrounded by the tools of their trade and the products of their labour, he visibly identified with the world of skilled men.

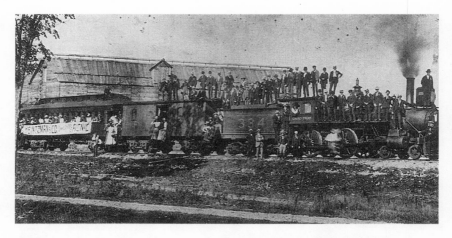

The Heintzman Piano Company was one of many firms to inaugurate company picnics in the 1880s, largely in response to increased industrial conflict and union organization.

The Massey Company band was one of many efforts undertaken in the 1880s to build workers' loyalty during their leisure hours.

Picture Credits

ONTARIO MINISTRY OF AGRICULTURE AND FOOD: p. 202 (wagon works, neg. Hof A2489); R.R. SALLOWS COLLECTION: pp. 103 (native workers, neg. Hof A93; back-breaking labour, neg. Hof A50), 104 (sharpening the cradle, neg. Hof A105)

HAROLD TURNER COLLECTION, ARCHIVAL COLLECTIONS, UNIVERSITY OF GUELPH LIBRARY: pp. 104 (Sangster and sons), 202 (threshing machine)

ARCHIVES OF ONTARIO: pp. 203 (ACC 13917-8), 275 (axemen notching pine, ACC 2271 55159; squaring timber, ACC 11778-4 S16944), 276 (river drivers, ACC 2203 S3625; camboose shanty, ACC 10010-44), 277 (ACC 6693 S11476), 333 (Orangemen's Parade, ACC, 13390-55), 334 (annual march, ACC 2537 512006), 477 (ACC 6355 S9103), 478 (Toronto children, ACC 6355 S8973; family maid, ACC 6355 S9572), 591 (ACC 9339 S15032), 592 (ACC 2203 S3613), 594 (Heintzman Piano Company, ACC 13917-11)

SALVATION ARMY HERITAGE CENTRE: pp. 333 (brass bands, 13944), 334 (Salvation Army, C143)

NATIONAL ARCHIVES OF CANADA: p. 337 (C28860)

STRATFORD-PERTH ARCHIVES: p. 411

ONTARIO AGRICULTURAL MUSEUM, MASSEY FERGUSON ARCHIVES: pp. 593, 594 (Massey Company band)

Index

THE ONTARIO HISTORICAL STUDIES SERIES

Peter Oliver, G. *Howard Ferguson: Ontario Tory* (1977)

J.M.S. Careless, ed., *The Pre-Confederation Premiers: Ontario Government Leaders, 1841–1867* (1980)

Charles W. Humphries, *'Honest Enough to be Bold': The Life and Times of Sir James Pliny Whitney* (1985)

Charles M. Johnston, *E.C. Drury: Agrarian Idealist* (1986)

A.K. McDougall, *John P. Robarts: His Life and Government* (1986)

Roger Graham, *Old Man Ontario: Leslie M. Frost* (1990)

John T. Saywell, *'Just call me Mitch': The Life of Mitchell F. Hepburn* (1991)

A. Margaret Evans, *Sir Oliver Mowat* (1992)

Joseph Schull, *Ontario since 1867* (McClelland and Stewart 1978)

Joseph Schull, *L'Ontario depuis 1867* (McClelland and Stewart 1987)

Olga B. Bishop, Barbara I. Irwin, Clara G. Miller, eds., *Bibliography of Ontario History, 1867–1976: Cultural, Economic, Political, Social*, 2 volumes (1980)

Christopher Armstrong, *The Politics of Federalism: Ontario's Relations with the Federal Government, 1867–1942* (1981)

David Gagan, *Hopeful Travellers: Families, Land and Social Change in Mid-Victorian Peel County, Canada West* (1981)

Robert M. Stamp, *The Schools of Ontario, 1876–1976* (1982)

R. Louis Gentilcore and C. Grant Head, *Ontario's History in Maps* (1984)

K.J. Rea, *The Prosperous Years: The Economic History of Ontario, 1939–1975* (1985)

Ian M. Drummond, *Progress without Planning: The Economic History of Ontario from Confederation to the Second World War* (1987)

John Webster Grant, *A Profusion of Spires: Religion in Nineteenth-Century Ontario* (1988)

Susan E. Houston and Alison Prentice, *Schooling and Scholars in Nineteenth-Century Ontario* (1988)

Ann Saddlemyer, ed., *Early Stages: Theatre in Ontario, 1800–1914* (1990)

W.J. Keith, *Literary Images of Ontario* (1992)

Douglas McCalla, *Planting the Province: The Economic History of Upper Canada, 1784–1870* (1993)

A.B. McKillop, *Matters of Mind: The University in Ontario, 1791–1951* (1994)

R.D. Gidney and W.P.J. Millar, *Professional Gentlemen: The Professions in Nineteenth-Century Ontario* (1994)

Edward S. Rogers and Donald B. Smith, eds., *Aboriginal Ontario: Historical Perspectives on the First Nations* (1994)

James Struthers, *The Limits of Affluence: Welfare in Ontario, 1920–1970* (1994)

J.E. Hodgetts, *From Arm's Length to Hands-On: The Formative Years of Ontario's Public Service, 1867–1940* (1995)

Paul Craven, ed., *Labouring Lives: Work and Workers in Nineteenth-Century Ontario* (1995)